000769   £15

DAYS IN THE LIFE

Also by Jonathon Green

The Dictionary of Jargon (1987)
The Slang Thesaurus (1986)
The Cynic's Lexicon (1984)
The Dictionary of Contemporary Slang (1984)
The Dictionary of Contemporary Quotations (1982)

DAYS IN THE LIFE

Voices from the English Underground
1961-1971

Jonathon Green

HEINEMANN: LONDON

William Heinemann Ltd
Michelin House, 81 Fulham Road, London SW3 6RB
LONDON   MELBOURNE   AUCKLAND

First published in 1988
Copyright © Jonathon Green 1988

British Library Cataloguing in Publication Data

Green, Jonathon, 1948-
   Days in the life: voices from the
   English underground, 1961-1971.
   1. British popular culture
   306'.1
ISBN 0 434 30420 4

Printed and bound in Great Britain
by Richard Clay Ltd, Bungay, Suffolk

For Lucien and Gabriel

INTRODUCTION

Thinking in decades is a spurious activity, beloved of and possibly invented by the media, and scarcely credible once subjected to even the most basic of factual, historical analyses. Events, even short-term developments, simply don't fit that conveniently into ten-year packages, starting on schedule and terminating just so. Yet such thinking is remarkably pervasive, nurtured no doubt by those same media, and now rendered quite acceptable at apparently every level of consumption. Nostalgia buffs, popular historians, merchandisers of every type . . . all subscribe quite happily to this sliced-bread view of the past. The population at large are more than happy to go along with the new chronology, defining themselves unselfconsciously as '60s people', '80s people' and the like.

Quite when the habit originated remains obscure: nineteenth-century commentators did not, if one can trust the dictionaries, talk of 'the 20s', 'the 30s' or whatever. Yet today the procession, ready-packed for colour-supplement recycling, troops uncomplainingly by: the 90s (naughty), the 20s (roaring), the 30s (depressed and red), the 50s (depressing and blue), and none more exalted and excoriated than the 60s. Years of revolt, years of carefree, sinless excess, of drugs, music, revolution and fucking in the streets, of Swinging London, of the ever-exciting tomorrow, that very first day of the rest of your life; when to be young was not only very heaven, but mandatory too.

Today, as those who were young then, or just becoming adults, are passing into middle age, the 60s seem the most inescapable of all those nostalgia-girt decades. Whether hymned by ageing hippies, still wreathed in rosy fantasies, or vilified by contemporary politicians, desperately hunting an easy scapegoat for over-complex ills, the image remains: something happened.

There is no need to detail here just what it was that did happen. I trust that the memories that make up this book will do that. What matters to me, and to many others, and which in the end justifies the gathering of all this material (itself only a fraction of the interviews I transcribed), is that the 60s have an importance over and above the mere provision of more nostalgia fodder. The simple fact that they annoy so many of today's politicians and other supposed opinion-makers surely lends the period a naggingly persistent relevance that cannot easily be ignored. The social and cultural advances of the period acknowledged radical changes in society. Such changes had been bubbling under since World War II, but the 60s gave them a form which all the population, rather than simply the avant-garde, could understand. There was no need to don bells or beads to sense the upheavals and advances in society. That those advances are now under such concerted threat from a government desperate to return to some prelapsarian moral Eden only proves their potency. 'Victorian values', after all, are as much a myth as the most zany hippie fantasy.

Repression inevitably follows liberality, especially in Britain's 'nanny state'. The irony of the 60s is that while the young generation of that era are indeed gradually coming to power, just as the hippies once hoped, their representatives are not the broad-minded and creative, but the dull and the philistine, who for a while were pushed into well-deserved obscurity. For those who believed to any extent in the 60s philosophy, the 80s, for all their glossy 'lifestyle niching', represent the revenge of the grey men. Britain's periodical fits of morality may indeed be incomparably ridiculous, but they are frenetic while they last.

To paraphrase a description first allotted to New York's Greenwich Village, 'the 60s', as apostrophised here, are not so much a chronological era as a state of mind. For who can state absolutely just when they began and when they ended? Some claim 1956 as the launching pad, the *annus mirabilis* of Suez, Hungary and *Look Back in Anger*. Others opt for 1957, the publication of *On the Road* (and Kerouac was writing of events already ten years old), or 1958, the first Aldermaston march. Then there's 1961, the Committee of 100; 1963, the Profumo Affair, Beatlemania and the Kennedy assassination; 1964, when there was elected a relatively liberal Labour government which tacitly accepted, even if it did not actually promote, the new freedoms; even 1965, when every beatnik aspiration seemed to climax, listening to poetry at the Albert Hall. As for closure: that same Albert Hall poetry reading; 1967, the first mass-marketing of the alternative society; 1971, the *OZ* trial; 1974, the oil embargo and the latest onset of economic decline. And there are more. The sole truth is that there are no cut and dried lines. This book opens in 1954, it could have started earlier; it ends around 1972, but there was much more to say.

The myth endures, whatever its dates, and there is substance to that myth. The phenomenon was not a hiccup in history, nor some quaint sideshow, pragmatically dumped into theme-park oblivion by a harder edged world. So many factors commingled to produce the cultural earthquakes which echoed on seemingly every front – political, socio-

viii

logical, intellectual, religious, creative – triggering storms that deluged traditional society, not just in Britain but around the world, with wave after wave of the new. Everything, we were told, was new. And novelty wasn't just the media's flavour of the decade: in many ways the hype came true. Some of the inventions – whether material or philosophical – took root and developed: they remain with us, tangible and intangible legacies of the period. Though all too often the 'novelty' was just that, glittering meretriciously in the lights, wilfully discarded when the carnival moved on. It was all too simple to confuse the one with the other, over-looking what might last and feting the ephemeral. Some does remain, much is the preserve of faded, embarrassing clips.

Everything seemed to come together at once. Apparent economic stability, the accelerating decline of Britain's traditional, pre-1939 society, a growing disenchantment with Establishment politics (left or right), the emergence of the baby-boom generation and, more important, of the marketing of whatever those young consumers wanted. This was the background, intensifying general social changes as the 50s progressed and the war years receded from view. To the fore were young artists and intellectuals, dealing with specifics – notably in politics and the arts. Looking for their popular culture to America and for their philosophical and political stimuli to France. Often the two coalesced, as at the Beat Hotel in Paris, where the twin inspirations met to cross-fertilise. One could not deny the essential elitism of such groupuscules, and they were swiftly corralled as 'Angry Young Men', 'Beatniks' and the like, but the culture they propounded did have one essentially fresh characteristic: for all that its proponents formed a contemporary avant-garde, their texts came from below. The new culture was not, as had been traditional, imposed from on high. By the turn of the decade, more and more of the discerning young, products not just of the baby boom but (in England) of the Education Act of 1944, were choosing to eschew the centre and move to the fringes of society and of art.

What followed, through the bulk of the chronological 60s, was the coming to fruition, on many levels, of the fantasies that the new society had been nurturing. For a while, as many of those involved attest, there were no limits. Cultural barriers tumbled, and with them emotional ones. As the hippies, quoting Plato, had it: 'When the mode of the music changes, the walls of the city shake', and even those whose vision had not been enhanced by LSD could feel the tremors.

The concern of this book is not the complete 60s, in all their gaudy glory, but a cultural subset of the era: a movement that, springing from an eclectic fusion of beats, mods, the New Left, black music and white teenagers, became known as the 'alternative society', 'the counterculture' or (most inappropriately) 'the underground'. It flourished, in its most visible manifestation, from the Albert Hall poetry reading of June 1965 to the *OZ* trial of July 1971, achieving its most fruitful period between 1966 and 1969. It was not simply that, as Jeff Nuttall put it, young people 'made war' on their elders, but that for a brief but influential period some of them attempted with varying degrees of success to step outside the bounds of established society and exist within a world whose only limits were of their own definition.

Of course the degree of success did vary, and it is hard to deny the nay-sayers' refusal to accept as 'alternative' any movement that was still forced to depend on the state for heat, light and medicine; judged by those terms there was, other than in the odd commune, no success at all. The alternative society was largely a middle-class phenomenon, and it clung to certain middle-class creature-comforts, claim what it may. A further problem comes in defining a real political base. The hippies allied themselves only uneasily with the ideologues of the New Left, who in turn took on certain hippie trappings, but from a cautiously mandarin perspective. There was something called 'the Revolution', but quite what that meant was debatable. It existed more in terms of what it did *not* mean: it was not Marxist, indeed it was 'political' only in the widest sense, and in the end the 'Revolution' was no more a genuine one than (compared with the dissident struggles of the Soviet Union or Latin America) the 'underground' was a true underground.

Yet for that short period there were still identifiable institutions that could fairly be seen as alternative, no matter what authority powered their light-shows or printing presses. A middle-class movement, it produced, in parallel to the 'straight' world, the standard features of middle-class culture. There were newspapers, art centres, restaurants, record businesses, bookshops, art galleries, poster designers, illustrators, nightclubs, music venues, clothes shops and more. That many such establishments either moved, for survival's sake, into the harsher world of the real market-place, or collapsed alongside the wider hippie dream, is of course true. Yet today, two decades later, their influence can be seen as far outlasting their heyday. It would be as much a mistake to attribute all of today's design-conscious culture to the pop artists and graphic designers of the 60s, or the health-food boom to a single macrobiotic restaurant, as it would be to link AIDS to the 'permissive society' or route heroin in Glasgow via marijuana in Notting Hill. But the effect of those 'alternative' institutions has lingered, even if the current Establishment seems hell-bent on turning back the sociological clock.

To create this book I interviewed just over 100 former '60s people' (although none would wish to be thought of as trapped two decades or more in the past). Given the sheer numbers of those who were identified with the 'alternative world', even if one restricts the list to the higher profile personalities, this is of course a ludicrously tiny sample. Ideally one would have talked to everyone, but the age of hippie fantasies is over. In the event, the combined transcripts of even the 100-plus interviews ran to half a million words, and the 'rough cut' that represented my original manuscript ran to over 400,000. Inevitably, this massive declaration of past principle has had to be cut substantially. Had I interviewed, say, a further 100 the word-count would have been even more absurd, and the final book still no larger than it is. I concentrated, therefore, on talking to as many prime movers as I could reach. Even so, there are obviously certain absentees. Some of these simply preferred not to subject themselves to my questions, while others, proof of my inadequacy, I failed to track down. In the same way, certain topics have had to be sacrificed wholesale: the hippie trail (of which I collected many wonderful reminiscences), the burgeoning squatting movement, the early days of macrobiotic eating and other events the absence of which their participants will undoubtedly regret.

In the end I can only apologise for all my failings as regards content and stress how enormously grateful I am to everyone who gave me their time and their memories. Even if some of their *bons mots* have ended, as it were, on the cutting-room floor, I sincerely hope that the finished product will represent at least to some extent what they, and all those others who took part in the era but whom I was unable to meet, felt and experienced.

If it is of any consolation to those thus gelded, my own experiences have been largely discarded too. I would not wish to take unfair advantage and reintroduce them here. Nevertheless, if only to justify my editorial role, I shall set out briefly such part as I played in the counterculture. I was twelve in 1960, old enough to start cruising Better Books a few years later and Indica after that. I missed the poetry reading but managed Dylan's 'Judas!' extravaganza a year later. Oxford from '66 to '69 was a hermetic little world, with its own variations on hippie London. We read *IT*, and even more so *OZ*, took our drugs, wore the clothes, went wide-eyed to the Technicolor Dream and wandered the streets when in mid-'67 Hoppy brought a happening (complete with Suzy Creamcheese) to town. Steve Abrams was still in residence, our parochial Tim Leary. Down to London in '69 I tried to join Fleet Street but instead met Alan Marcuson who offered me a joint and the job of News Editor on *Rolling Stone*. This temporary glamour soon mutated into *Friends* and by the end of 1971 I had worked successively on *Time Out*, *INK*, and *OZ*, which with David Widgery and Pearce Marchbank I edited for a couple of post-trial issues. I lived for a while with Rosie Boycott and was thus privy to the founding of *Spare Rib*. These, then, are the bare bones. I'm not sure how much I believed the myths (my philosophies came from Lenny Bruce rather than Baba Ram Dass); certainly I enjoyed the lifestyle. In the eighteen months it took to amass this book, I never for one moment yearned to return, but understood, in present-day context, just how golden the age could appear.

In conclusion, my thanks, ritual but none the less heartfelt for that, to everyone who helped me assemble this book. Apart from the interviewees, who gave time, information and in many cases immeasurably valuable further contacts, I must mention Rupert Morris, who interviewed Jim Anderson and Jon Goodchild in California; Pip Hills for his hospitality in Edinburgh; Heather Laughton who transcribed a number of tapes. Jane Carr, copy-editing at Heinemann, has produced order from a much-cut and very bulky manuscript. I am grateful for her literate fine-tuning. My family, as ever, have been tolerant beyond the call even of affection.

To my editor Dan Franklin I owe inestimable thanks. Perhaps the best testimony of my admiration is that we have remained on speaking terms for all that forty per cent of the original manuscript has long since been consigned to the shredder. As the cliché has it, this book is as much his as it is mine; I hope only that he has derived as much satisfaction from its creation as have I.

Jonathon Green
April 1988

PETER ROBERTS: The underground happened as it happened when it happened as a development in society, as an outpouring into the world, however you choose to express it or explain it. There's a dozen ways. They all derive from the need to explain: this has happened, therefore we must explain it. Human beings have this need to explain, it's a habit, and it's very difficult to get rid of this need to explain, and to explain in terms of bipolar logic – cause and effect. But in the 60s we abandoned the need to explain. Why do we explain? So we can justify it, so that somebody else will think you're right. So what? We dispensed with the category of right or wrong. And what happens then? The world suddenly appears very, very different. It's not expediency, it's that there are many different structures, many different patterns, and you adopt the one you need at a certain time to try to fulfil some purpose.

'The Bohemian Element'

MICHAEL HOROVITZ: I went up to Oxford in 1954 to read English. We lived in little bohemian pockets, in semi-communal houses. There was a hut or studio in a back garden in Plantation Road. In this studio/hut were two basic residents who had a very early beat commune there through which would pass whores, poet-philosophers, artists and musicians and there would be a lot of music, mainly jazz. One of them was called Ray Cortenz, who was a Canadian expatriate with a beard, constantly rolling and smoking joints. His great friend was a very black, passionate Bermudan called Teddy Gordon, who never wore shoes and went everywhere in bare feet. He had an Afro long before Afros were Afros, and was quite a wild manic character. He'd been in Harlem briefly, at the time of the Boppers, which wasn't all that long before, and was always chanting bebop themes. My friendship with these blokes grew and I would go there quite often as a refuge from what we then called 'square Oxford scenes'. Life there really began at twilight and would come to its fullness with the moon as more bohemians and party-goers would fall in and the whores would be looking in between their night's trade, and there'd be jiving to these records which ranged from early, traditional jazz through to bop and post-bop. And part of the appeal of this place and this community was its secretness. And smoking dope was a wild new thing, and the utter difference of how everything looked and felt on those first early joints . . .

MICK FARREN: The root of the underground were hopheads and that really cut across a lot of class stuff. A lot of the older people – like Hoppy [John Hopkins], who was a renegade nuclear physicist – had graduated out of university with all kinds of bizarre skills and they didn't really know what to do with them. It took longer to wake up and say, 'What am I doing here at the nuclear weapons establishment at Harwell?' And you went up the Ronnie Scott Club and started smoking reefer and then you were even more confused about what you were doing working at Harwell.

JOHN HOPKINS: I went to Cambridge on a scholarship in 1955, from a public school. At school I was a wild card for some reason, and they tried to expel me for running a jazz society: I learnt to play boogie-woogie piano. Then off to Cambridge, reading physics and maths. I didn't have any particular career in mind but I'd always been good at maths so that felt right. When I was at public school I was what is now called gay, because that was the style and that was great, and when I was at Cambridge it took me a while to get into women, but by the time I'd been there a couple of years I'd managed and had my first real lover. Meanwhile I played piano in a traditional jazz band. A little bit of trumpet and a little bit of guitar. So I learnt about women and I learnt about music. And I just got a third-class degree. I left university at the age of twenty and I didn't want to go into the Army, do National Service. So I got a job with the Atomic Energy Authority. I became a reactor physicist.

MICHAEL HOROVITZ: Hoppy became a major presence around this emergent scene in Oxford, around 1959, when I think he had some sort of job at Harwell Atomic Research Centre, after finishing his degree at Cambridge. He got into outraging the bourgeoisie, smoking dope, and an overall sense of anarchism a few of us shared.

JOHNNY BYRNE: I was born in the Sean O'Casey slums of Dublin, the youngest of thirteen children. I was apprenticed when I was twelve and at the age of twenty the boss stepped forward and said, 'We're entering a slack period – will some of the single men take an unpaid indefinite holiday.' And I stepped forward and went to England. I got on the boat and ended up in Birmingham and four days later I met this Dubliner who was an electrician and he took me travelling. And I never went back. The long and the short of it was that I ultimately ended up working for a company which was absolutely in thrall to the Electricians' Union, which was full of reds in those days. This was about 1958. And Seamus Behan, who was Brendan Behan's brother, was running the ETU on this hype. If I came in at eight and worked until twelve I got time; if I stayed until two I got time and a half; if I stayed until four I got double time; and if I did a normal day's work I got triple time. And if I worked through until twelve o'clock at night it became astronomic. The upshot was that within a year I had more money than a working-class Irish guy could ever conceive of, so I asked myself the very sensible question, should I retire? I was 21. And I decided that I would retire and start writing.

MILES: I had left home in '59 and went to art college from '59 to '63, the Gloucestershire College of Art. My sort of mentor was a fully paid-up member of the CP, deeply radical and connected to the bohemian element at college. I was going to be an artist: I had a few shows and sold paintings even, but on a very amateur kind of basis. It was clearly not something I was going to live on. I went to art college at sixteen so my first introduction to anything political or adult in any sense was there. Art college then was really totally different than it is now. It was really happening, where all the good rock bands came from. The local band, whom in my capacity as secretary of the Students' Union I always hired for our dances, was the Ramrods which had Brian Jones on saxophone. When he moved to London he still owed me £2 which he never paid back.

GRAHAM KEEN: I was at art college with Miles. He was three years younger than I. I was born in '36 and I was at Cheltenham Art College from '54 to '58 – that was the time of the bohemians and existentialists in Paris. That was what really got us, and the kitchen-sink school as far as art went. I played in a jazz band, moving up from New Orleans to mainstream. That was our revolution.

MICHELENE WANDOR: A lot of those people like Miles are art school people from the late 50s; the university generation didn't hit until five years later. People who went to art college when I was at school were very wicked: they wore jeans and the girls wore black tights and had great black eye make-up and long straight hair and fringes and they were secular beatniks, not the intellectual beatniks. They were the rock generation, the Bill Haley generation; they'd caught on very quickly and they were very sophisticated.

JEFF NUTTALL: I did have concerns when I was doing my National Service. I was always worried about the fact that how was it that I knew that the world was almost certainly heading for nuclear war, and yet I never mentioned it to anybody and nobody ever mentioned it to me? I taught current affairs as an educational sergeant and you said that 'the nuclear bomb is inevitably part of our present-day defence strategy.' I would stand in the sergeants' mess and think, everybody here knows perfectly well that the kind of warfare we're practising, messing around with rifles on the square, is completely useless. But talk like that would just get you into trouble and I didn't have sufficiently clarified thoughts about it. Then there was the cold shock of the Suez invasion which occurred just as I was demobbed and a lot of my intake were recalled. Not me, thank God. And you began to take very seriously what was happening. That was followed immediately by the Hungarian uprising and the quelling of it, which destroyed any kind of flirtation people had at that time with Marxism and indeed caused huge Marxist groups, known as Trotskyites, to break away. My own politics were indecisive. I suppose they were apocalyptic, Nietzschean. But at the same time they were revolutionary: something had to change. I suppose I joined the movement with the Aldermaston march.

CHRISTOPHER LOGUE: In 1956 I'd just come back from Paris and my first contact in this country was Lindsay Anderson, whose films I much admired. We met. I'd written some poems that Paul Johnson, who was then the Editor of the *New Statesman*, published. One called 'To My Fellow Artists'. And in '57 or '58, I'm not quite sure, at a meeting called by the Free Cinema Movement people at the old National Film Theatre Lindsay put me on stage and I read this and a couple of other poems. It was the first large-scale poetry reading I'd ever done. I don't know where the involvement with the Aldermaston marches, CND, actually began. It was just in the air, and a lot of people thought that this was the right thing to do.

CND: 'There were thousands of us'

MILES: On the political side most people were galvanised by CND back in '59-'61. I certainly was. I went on the second Aldermaston march. Almost everyone I knew took their politics from CND; the people they met on the march. It was very similar to the US anti-Vietnam movement – more of a moral thing than a political thing. It certainly wasn't party-oriented.

MICHAEL HOROVITZ: The CND movement began for us partly through a dream a friend of mine had. There was an H-Bomb issue of *Isis*, which we all wrote for, and instead of the usual editorial at the beginning we simply printed his dream. It was of a very bare landscape, the sort of landscape and mindscape that's become a cliché now. Just an unpeopled, polluted landscape. When that issue of *Isis* was published it was quickly banned, because it contained a piece on the British emergency policies should there be a nuclear attack, revealing that only a few VIPs would get the slightest protection, and how vast the devastation would be. A couple of months after that there was a big meeting in Oxford Town Hall which was, if not *the* beginning, certainly a beginning of a nuclear disarmament movement. [Bertrand] Russell couldn't come, although he was advertised; there was J. B. Priestley, John Berger, Victor Gollancz, Philip Toynbee and a few other elder statesmen of radicalism and plain-speaking. Oxford Town Hall was packed out and they gave very good speeches and it was very inspiring. Soon after that the marches began. I wrote some anti-Bomb poems and when they asked me to read something at the climax of one march at Hyde Park I felt very privileged to be asked. I read an early version of a poem I had been working on for some years: 'For Modern Man' – against bombs and nuclear war. The final version was included in *Wholly Communion*, the book of Peter Whitehead's film of the Albert Hall reading. It was quite inspiring and rewarding to hear the support and applause and comeback, and to realise that I was not alone and that I'd said something that articulated what the other people there felt.

CHRISTOPHER LOGUE: I don't know who suggested the Aldermaston march, but it was that kind of time. You could speak freely to people; it was the beginning of a free association between people. If you thought that you had something to offer, you'd ring up somebody and you'd suggest it to them and you'd see what happened. And if nothing happened, then you did something else. I found myself on the first day of the first Aldermaston march in 1958. It was pouring with rain and there were about 150 of us marching along by London airport in the most dreadful weather. And then of course the sun came out and the weather improved greatly and by the end of the afternoon there must have been 50,000 people. And by the middle of the next day there were 100,000. Of course, it's *not* a political movement, and those that try to criticise it from a political point of view are just opposed to it for some reason or other. Usually they're playing politics, they're trying to call attention to themselves and get power. But the people on the Aldermaston march weren't doing any such thing and there was no intention that this should be an on-going strong political movement which would form a political party and then would return so-and-so and so-and-so . . . I suppose we did think of coming back next year – 'See you next year' – and then it ran for four years and then it was over. Then everybody in this country knew exactly, or had the opportunity to find out exactly, what this weapons deal was.

Now I don't think that CND is of any importance. Not really. It had a much greater social importance than it ever had politically. A lot of people suddenly realised that there were a lot of other people who thought along the same lines as they did and that they were humanists in politics and agnostics in religion and that they did want to create a better society. And they struggled hard to do it, and they took on the whole world, as young people are prepared to do. And the result of it was ten good years.

PETER ROBERTS: I'd always been a kind of outsider at school. It was the first Aldermaston march when loads of people like myself came together and realised that, contrary to our headmasters' propaganda, we weren't the only freak around, there were actually *thousands* of us. And that was wonderful. A seminal, seminal point.

JEFF NUTTALL: On the march you got pacifists, you got Quakers in large numbers, conscientious objectors, mostly from the middle class. You got contingents from trade unions. And you had the beatniks who suddenly emerged – and nobody had known about them outside their own favourite haunts – Soho coffee bars and jazz clubs. And they appeared in the standard uniform at the time which was tattered jeans and dirty old donkey jackets. Everyone wore black. Really filthy: the tidemark around the neck was a badge of authenticity. Long black filthy hair, always looking dead miserable as though they hadn't had a night's sleep for at least a week. Acoustic guitar on your back, and a bed-roll. People like Spike Hawkins – although they were privileged beatniks, because they were literate. Particularly Mike Horovitz who was at Oxford.

New Departures

MICHAEL HOROVITZ: I was going to do a B Litt. (first on Blake and then on Beckett) but various things happened and having given up on both theses I came round to a kind of reaffirmation of first things and felt that criticism was the enemy. So I became an anti–intellectual intellectual and tried to stop being an intellectual at all. And I thought that the real work was to make poetry and to realise visions, in the way Blake realised his Jerusalem by putting his work together. I had a bit of humility and thought that my own work isn't that great shakes yet but perhaps since I've got to know some of these writers and artists, many of whom had also just finished university, I could collect them together and publish them. Which turned into *New Departures*. There wasn't much money for it. There was a man called David Sladen who put up some of the money and I got a few ads. I think we printed about 3000 and they went pretty quickly. We were very new to printing and were not at all businesslike, but we had a bit of backing and a certain amount of goodwill. I think we helped to sow seeds that a lot of the underground press and communications then inherited and developed. And as soon as *New Departures 1* was published I thought, 'Let's not just have it lying dead on a page, let's bring it to life.' Most of the authors were alive anyway so we started 'Live *New Departures*' too. There was music directed by Cornelius Cardew who had been working with Stockhausen; various kinds of performers, all individuals with their own diverse interests.

7

GENE MAHON: In 1959 I had left Ireland where I was brought up and was living in Oxford, doing various jobs, and that was a very good place to come to. I was sort of a beatnik, on the edge. I started reading stuff like *Evergreen Review* and extracts from Kerouac and trying to understand Allen Ginsberg and had read Samuel Beckett because he was Irish but hadn't understood it. A bunch of people put on this Beckett play in one of the colleges. It was the early *New Departures* gang: John McGrath was involved, Mike Horovitz. Maybe Pete Brown was there, Spike Hawkins I think. And Johnny Byrne was around, he and Spike were like Mutt and Jeff, solid mates. I actually took them in hand a bit, saying, 'You know you're letting too many people in for free if you want to make money.' And I took over the door and charged everybody and made money for them.

MICHAEL HOROVITZ: I didn't yet see myself as a beat. Something of that came a bit later. There were beats in America, but our awareness of them and communications with them only began in 1958/1959. *New Departures 1* did include the first excerpts from Burroughs's *Naked Lunch* to appear in Britain – indeed, I inadvertently did his first cut-ups in the process. We'd only become aware of *Howl* and *On the Road* in the later 50s. Ginsberg and Corso visited Oxford in '57 or '58 for the first time. I didn't meet them that time but I was very aware of them. John Howe, who was at Brasenose later than me, formed a sort of early British beat pocket in Oxford. They met those poets and were very immediately taken with them and recorded readings they gave. Although the Americans only encountered a few people, that brief visit caused a lot of semi-revolutions amongst the individuals that were there. When I read the early beat writing in *Evergreen Review 2* in 1958 I didn't really like so much of it at the first reading. I recognised their involvement with and adaptation of jazz and admired that, but I disliked most of the poetry and I rather attacked the beat movement in an editorial in the first *New Departures*. There was also a bit of a spirit of rivalry: I was beginning to write my own poetry and I thought that my friends and I were just as good writers, and here were these guys only a bit older than us with world fame, shooting all these lines and hitting the headlines of *Time* and *Life* and so on. All the usual late teenage/young man's competitiveness. But gradually, through reading much more of their work and hearing records and tapes, between *New Departures 1* and the double issue *2&3* a year later I had been more or less converted.

JOHN HOPKINS: When I left Cambridge, before I went to Harwell, I went to Oxford to live and that was lovely. There were lots of really far-

8

out people, among whom was Mike Horovitz, who really contributed an enormous amount to my education. I went on CND marches, taking pictures. That appealed to another side of me. There was one year when we got as far as somewhere near Reading and the march turned sideways to find a Regional Seat of Government. I was taking pictures for the *Sunday Times* but they never used them cos it was security classified and they couldn't show anything. I didn't call myself a beatnik but I guess that was the word. Jack Kerouac's *On the Road* had an enormous influence on me. Whatever it was, I responded to that. And I developed a penchant for American culture that lasted for the next ten or fifteen years. It was like kids today, you join a band, and so did I, but it was a jazz band then.

Jazz

ROBERT WYATT: It all started for me in the 50s when I was a jazz fan. I still am. That was *my* underground. That was the life I discovered outside the prescribed life. I was born in 1945, left school in 1960. I hadn't got enough exam results to get any particular job so I worked in lots of things. The place where culture and politics seemed to meet for me was always centred around black music. Jazz in the 50s. That's the romantic period for me. To me protest music was Max Roach, Sonny Rollins and Charlie Mingus. I didn't understand folk music, I didn't even like the songs at the Aldermaston march. I knew about jazz, I wasn't particularly well read, but I knew the sleevenotes of about twenty LPs backwards and could spot a new bass player on the New York scene as quick as anybody.

JEFF NUTTALL: I was interested in jazz from a very early time, since the mid-40s. We were first of all ignited by jazz, which is American, but there were also elements of surrealism, which is French and German and Swiss. And maybe it was when those European elements were forgotten that it began to be enfeebled. It was America that brought in drugs and religion. There were these stages: the interest in jazz, the involvement in arts, the concern about the Bomb, attendance on the march, and the sense in the early 60s that the Aldermaston march had failed. In the mid-50s one would have thought that if thousands and thousands of people get up and demand an answer of Parliament, of NATO, that they would be forced to come out and give them an answer – but of course it wasn't fucking well true. All they did was completely ignore it. So one had what was later called 'creative alienation': you didn't want to know left or right, you didn't want to have any truck with established society. So what one did was to enter into a whole new philosophy of subverting the culture: 'When the mode of the music changes, the walls of the city shake.' And when the colour of clothing changes and, above all, when the practice of sexuality changes, the practice of living changes.

Notting Hill: 'The white nigger syndrome'

GRAHAM KEEN: In 1959 I deserted from National Service and hitchhiked to London to see a friend of mine from art college. I got up to town, we got on the Northern Line to go up to Highgate in the rush hour and he said, 'Read this,' and gave me a copy of *Howl*. Then I read *On the Road* and it was those two books for ever after. That brought in the beats and from then on we were looking for dope. What we wanted to do was get our hands on some 'tea'. By 1960 we'd found it. I got some through West Indians in Notting Hill. I used to go into basements at night. It was a very odd scene in relation to what came five or ten years later. We were all nervous as hell, shuddering. Also it was our first contact with black men. They were not the hip black guys of later on, they all looked like middle-aged men. There was a vague Rasta connection – a lot of them belonged to the Rastafarians but had none of the outward signs, none of the dreadlocks, none of that. They were ordinary guys: some out of work, some in.

MILES: The hip society in Notting Hill in those days was basically very involved with the West Indians. They were the only people around who had good music, they knew all about jazz and ska and bluebeat. They also smoked rather good dope. That was the classic excuse in court if anyone got busted: 'Where did you get it from?' 'I bought it from a black man in Notting Hill.' And the magistrate agreed: how can you possibly ever recognise them again, they all look the same. We knew a lot of black guys like Michael de Freitas and Asiento Fox, known as Priest, who was the head of the Rastafarians. A whole bunch of really nice guys who used to hang out in the apartment and sometimes stay for three or four days, sitting around smoking enormous spliffs. Lucky Gordon used to come by. John Michell owned property in Notting Hill and one of his buildings had a record shop in it that Alex Trocchi was involved in ... all these people go a long way back. I met Colin MacInnes a few times, in the French (as opposed to the French Pub) which was a teashop on Old Compton Street in Soho where you could get a cup of tea for 3d and Quentin Crisp used to hang out.

COURTNEY TULLOCH: The underground didn't draw everything from America. People like Hoppy came into contact with Rastafarians before they came into contact with white beats. The Rastafarians were the first group in the Western world to actually drop out of white society, saying, 'This is Babylon, we don't want anything to do with it.' There was a grouping of Rastafarians in Ladbroke Grove and people like Hoppy met them in their early days around Notting Hill. He'd have seen black people with long, long hair before any single white person had long hair. That's not to say that the influences from America or wherever didn't influence white youth – their long hair may have been copied from somewhere else – but the truth is that the Rastafarians were the first to drop out of Western society. And this was the flavour that was represented in the contacts between blacks and the young whites; these were the type of blacks in the Notting Hill area who were also thinking, 'This society isn't right for me.' It's the white nigger syndrome. Norman Mailer's white nigger. Whites who declared dissatisfaction with their emotions, their personality, and their cultural identity. They stated it themselves: 'We are sick: we have to burn this thing out of ourselves, to make ourselves human beings.' That's basically what the whole hippie thing was about: rediscovering yourself, killing the machine man, the machine society, cleaning it out of your mind, looking at yourself. But that was for them. I'm not saying there were no black people who took acid, but there were always Rastas like Priest saying, 'That's for *them*. Freaking out, you've got to freak out another way, you've got to rediscover your African-ness, not get like them.'

'A better quality of life'

LAURA MULVEY: It seems significant now that my generation, which I see as a pre-60s generation, turned against the values of British culture, also against British political traditions, British socialism – the values of Leavis, to put it in a nutshell. One can see two branches coming out of this: one was a movement towards a popular culture, which was epitomised by Hollywood cinema, preferably B movies, also of course American popular music – jazz and particularly rock'n'roll. This always seemed to have some kind of political significance which I could never put my finger on and can't to this day. But it seemed no accident that Suez and Bill Haley's first tour of Britain happened at the same time. I wasn't consciously listening to rock'n'roll as a political statement, but it was the pleasure side of this pre-60s revolution, and I see it as the first big shift which then allowed the 60s to take off with a big bang. The groundwork had been done in the mid-50s. The other branch was a turning towards Europe, French theory, French Marxist theory, as opposed to British Labour Party tradition, and then eventually to a French psychoanalytic theory. So there was a mixture of the high French intellectual culture and the low American popular culture.

11

SUE MILES: My conception of it was – and I had a comfortable upper-middle-class upbringing – that you weren't saying, 'We want more money,' you were saying, 'We want a better quality of life.' (What none of us understood was that was absolutely the best it was ever going to be.) It was saying, 'We don't want jobs, fuck you! We don't want to go and do that – that's the last thing we want . . .' I think it was probably the first time the children went to college without any idea of getting a job at the end of it. It had never occurred to me what I was going to do, never. I didn't know what I was going to do when school finished. I didn't think I was going to get married, but I think my entire family did, because I was completely ill-equipped to do anything else. I had had a very good liberal education, I knew all about Japanese basketwork and Martha Graham's dancing, art cinema and all that – but actually going out to work . . . please!

Notting Hill: 'That type of togetherness'

JOHN HOPKINS: I arrived in London on the 1st of January 1960 with a black-and-white camera in my hand and I got a job as an assistant to a commercial photographer. It was heaven. I was doing something I really wanted to do for the first time in my life. So eventually I became a photographer and a bit of a journalist. Armstrong-Jones was living down the road, photographers got to be very important. I lived in Camberwell and Pimlico and eventually landed up in Westbourne Terrace and Queensway. John Howe handed me my first spliff and I did a little buying and selling of what might now be called illegal substances, but I'm sure they weren't then . . .

GRAHAM KEEN: We all went round to Hoppy's flat to score. Immediately he got to London he was collecting grass down in the East End somewhere and you'd go to his flat and there'd always be a bowl of it there. You could help yourself. These Rastas used to come around . . .

MILES: Hoppy and I used to work with people who did *Teamwork* magazine, the magazine of the Standing Conference of West Indian Affairs. I did a cover which had to be taken to the Mangrove to be approved by the editorial committee. First of all there was a lot of rustling and 'What is this white boy doing in here?' sort of thing. Then they all had a lot of design theories, gave it a lot of criticism. The Mangrove used to be insane: the smell of dope coming out of the kitchen was enough to wipe you out just sitting at a table.

At one of the Aldermaston marches there was a West Indian contingent which included Priest and Pinto and a whole bunch of Rastas; when they took off their woolly hats it was the first time dreadlocks had ever been seen in Britain. We had this friend called Larry Lewis, and he'd lived in Hoppy's apartment and when Pinto and Priest wanted a banner painted for the Rastas it had to have a certain number of symbols. One was the Lion of Judah. Larry, being an American, was intrigued to find the lion on our eggs. So he used it for the banner, the Egg Marketing Board lion on the Rasta banner. Hoppy took the official photograph of these four very serious Rastas, all dreadlocks with the banner behind them with the fucking Egg Marketing Board lion on it and all these important things in front of them: a huge pile of dope, the sacred alarm clock with two big bells on it to symbolise when the white man would be thrown out of Jamaica, and maybe a big machete. It was all very secret and Hoppy had to give up the negatives.

SUE MILES: Blacks were a different world. We all learnt the ritual of dope smoking from them. Twenty-two paper joints, if you smoke a joint with your hat on you have to do this, you have to pass it to the right and so on.

HORACE OVE: I came here in 1960, just after the Notting Hill Gate riots. Coming off the train, being in England for the first time, this little paradise that you've been brought up to believe existed and the streets were painted with gold and the great empire . . . I arrive in Victoria and the first thing was I couldn't see a thing – the fog was a mess. I had to get to Brixton so I took a taxi and I couldn't understand what the taxi driver was saying, I'd never heard Cockney before in my life. I spent some time in Brixton where I stayed with a friend for a few weeks. Then I went to West Hampstead which was where most Trinidadians and Guyanese lived. I came to study interior design. I was a painter at home and I did photography. I was interested in film. I had this letter of introduction to a firm here. I got to the firm with the letter and the bloke read the letter and said, 'I don't know this person, I've never heard of him, I don't know what he's talking about and we don't have any sort of job for you.' And that was the beginning of discovering the mother country.

I was bumming around, living on the dole, doing odd jobs, and in those days you supported each other. If you were hanging out with the right crowd you didn't really have to worry about money or whatever. Your needs would be taken care of. That was what was incredible about that period, right through the 60s, people did that for each other. On the West Indian side of it, we also did it. People were coming over here and you had a flat, a room, and the next thing you knew you had six blokes living in it. And every lunchtime you had twelve, fifteen people for lunch, because nobody was working, nobody had money. But that was one of the important things: money didn't matter, making money, becoming rich, becoming successful, these things didn't matter. There was that kind of unity, that kind of togetherness; which lasted the decade, which spilled over into the middle-60s and went on.

MICHAEL HOROVITZ: I moved into Ladbroke Grove after I'd met Frances in 1960. There were a number of people living around the area. Hoppy at Westbourne Terrace, a lot of artists from the Royal College of Art, Hockney was up the road, David Oxtoby, another painter called Peter Lloyd Jones, Harry and Ruth Fainlight, Michael Hastings, John Michell, Alan Sillitoe, John Arden, Heathcote Williams, Logue, Trocchi . . . there was a loose-knit community. We didn't always love each other but we were aware of each other and met. There were lots of communal houses where you could always drop in and get a joint or a cup of tea, or companionship, conversation and music.

JOHN HOPKINS: I did my dope-dealing when it was grass, not hash, and I got out of that in a couple of years simply because by that time I was being a successful news photographer and I was trying to work for the *Sunday Times* and the *Observer*. I had a ball. I found that by doing two or three jobs a week for the *Sunday Times* I could earn what was really a good wage for that time, and I could still have time for the other stuff. So I got up to a lot of mischief. I did my first freelance feature, about dope, for *Queen* magazine. I worked a lot for *Melody Maker*, and also for *Peace News*. *Melody Maker* because I was into jazz, *Peace News* because . . . well, one does.

GRAHAM KEEN: *Peace News* was another big catalyst in the alternative business. The then Editor was Tom McGrath. He took me down to Kingsley Hall one night to see somebody he said was interesting. So there I was at Ronnie Laing's supper table with all the assembled loonies. *Peace News* had pieces on Laing and so on long before they were known outside the psychiatric world. McGrath was a wonderful guy – I recommended him as Editor of *IT*. But he had a habit, that was his problem.

The Beats: 'Why *should* we wash?'

JIM HAYNES: After the Second World War everybody was tired and the beat movement in America began examining why are we alive, why are we on Planet Earth? They started asking these questions and one of the

14

answers was: to have fun. I think that was the seed that was planted and it sprouted with an incredible aesthetic: do your own thing, and if you like what you're doing that's fine and don't be critical of others.

DAVID MAY: I was on holiday in Wales in 1960, standing in W. H. Smith in Barmouth, and these couple of real freaks came in and I first became aware of the fact that there were people who were seriously different. They had hair down their backs and wore sandals and jeans and so on. This woman turned to me – I was nine or ten years old – and said, 'There you are: that's what you could grow up like.' And I did. I grew up just like that.

JEFF NUTTALL: Dadaists, absurdists, surrealists had always believed that by striking an alternative aesthetic, by taking alternative pleasures, or by undermining the classical mode of representational painting, or established harmonic structures in music, by this you could change the face of society. What happened with the beats was that by merging this transformation of standards and aesthetic pleasure with an actual attack on political structures you effect a sort of non-specific revolution, which was not programmed, which was not dictated and didn't have an alternative set of rules. You'd scrapped the old rules and now, hopefully, a new set of rules would evolve from a way of life that had been established according to human pleasure and generosity. It erupted, I would say, with Allen Ginsberg's *Howl*.

JOHN WILCOCK: Artists are always picking stuff out of the ether and the first time that many new ideas get expressed is by an artist. Poets and writers are symbiotic, and poets are usually writing the kinds of stuff that artists are doing pictorially, this Sibylline garble of totally ambiguous stuff that you can't figure out, like you can't figure out the art. So the first time that the word on new things got out was when an artist – not a 'pretty' artist but an artist who was *per se* a revolutionary – starts to express something pictorially, then a poet starts to express it with words. Now historically, the first people after those two have always been coffee-shop pamphleteers, *samizdat* publishers, underground magazines. It just so happened that the 60s provided a lot of people who badly needed that new word, because they'd lost all belief and trust in the Establishment word. It found a very ready audience and it caught this wave of revolution.

SUE MILES: Good times in London were to do with art colleges and to do with words: it was to do with Kerouac, it was to do with beat poets

15

and being cool. You wore black, white lipstick and long hair that you could sit on and couldn't see behind; long hair was a ridiculously important, emotive subject. You were shouted at in the street, women too. The *News of the World* did this piece on 'Beatniks at Oxford' and my friend John Howe's quote was 'Why *should* we wash?' During that time it was all *New Departures*: Pete Brown, modern jazz and poetry. The great fantasy figures that one was really taken with were Alfred Jarry and André Breton and Marcel Duchamp – that modern avant-garde stuff – merged in with CND, with politics, with the idea that you should ban nuclear weapons. That then brought everyone who had surfaced by that time into contact with the law. Because of my involvement with Miles, I got involved with American beat poetry. Because he, when he was sixteen, had written to them all from Cirencester saying, 'I'm going to start a poetry magazine, will you send me a manuscript?' and they all did cos they were so astonished at this kid.

MILES: In 1960 I edited a little magazine called *Tree*. Mimeographed stuff, but it did actually have Ginsberg and Ferlinghetti in the first issue, which I think is the first time Ginsberg was published in this country. Somebody showed me a copy of *Bomb* by Gregory Corso which was first published as a long broadside, shaped like an H-bomb cloud. I was very knocked out, I thought it was a terrific poem and on the back it said, 'Write to City Lights for a catalogue,' so I wrote for a catalogue. And they sent back this postcard, cos they had only published about eight books in those days, and I thought *Howl* sounded a real interesting name for a book, so I got a copy of that . . . *Howl* totally blew me away, I just thought it was terrific. So when I started my little magazine I wanted to publish these guys. So I wrote to Ferlinghetti and he actually replied, saying he didn't actually want to send anything but reprint anything you want, not just his, but from City Lights books. So I just reprinted stuff. I think we were almost unique: in London the only people in touch with the beats were the *New Departures* crowd – Pete Brown, Michael Horovitz – who were the main moving force for modern poetry in Britain at that time. Mike had brought out *New Departures* in 1959, in Oxford. It had Burroughs, not Ginsberg, and he had got the material from Burroughs in Paris.

SPIKE HAWKINS: A lot of people, I found, had very little knowledge of what was happening in America. Especially with people like Corso, Ferlinghetti, Ginsberg. I had picked it up from my English teacher who was my guru. He opened up a lot of alleyways. Through these the way led to a delightful house, and within this house I found books and I

16

found bookshops such as Better Books and tiny volumes which were marked 'City Lights' and I started to read these. And prior to that, about a year previous, I had read a book called *Protest*, which was a collection of English and American writers in which was this poem called *Howl* by Allen Ginsberg and I thought, 'My God . . .'

MILES: On the literary side an awful lot of it came from the Beat Hotel in Paris at 9 rue Gît-le-Coeur and the people who came to London from the Beat Hotel. Americans who visited here, or Peter Wollen, Ian Somerville, people like that. They lived in the Beat Hotel and had all these connections back with the people they went to college with. The hotel was where Burroughs, Ginsberg and Corso lived for years and between them they generated a tremendous force, incredible amounts of correspondence, in touch with everybody, they were also great promoters of drug culture, and modern literature. They were pretty important. To people from London who visited Paris that was the hip scene to be involved with. Also they spoke English, which helped. Somerville had a long-running affair with Burroughs. Then in 1961 he and Burroughs and Mikey Portman were living in Tangier and Mikey Portman had a lot of connections back here. He was the godson of Lord Goodman and here you have an aristocratic connection.

PETER ROBERTS: My involvement with the underground began really at Oxford, about 1960. I was reading history. I was one of Oxford's leading beatniks. It was there that I was given the name 'Pete the Rat'. I was in lodgings at 99 Woodstock Road. It was a very free and easy house with many other seminal figures there. Then the landlord moved in his mother, old Mrs Rose, to look after it. Apart from myself there was a guy called Ron the Con, who was a kind of make-out artist: he had a little switch-board by his bed so he could turn the lights off, switch the gramophone on and all this kind of nonsense. One day Mrs Rose said to me, 'Where's your candlewick bedspread?' I had never noticed it had gone – I'd got better things to worry about. 'I dunno,' I said, 'I'd better have a look for it.' I couldn't find it and someone else in the house lent me their bedspread. I said, 'Look, Mrs Rose, here's my candlewick bedspread.' 'That's nice, Peter,' says she. Then she finds out it had been lent to me. There's a whole kerfuffle and she's threatening to throw me out. So I'm sitting there thinking, 'This is a real drag,' when in sneaks Ron the Con with a parcel wrapped up in newspaper: 'Here's your bedspread, I borrowed it to hang on the wall as a kind of hanging . . .' to make his seduction boudoir. So I showed it to Mrs Rose who said, 'That Peter – he's a nice boy, but he's a rat!' Whereupon Stuart Birtwhistle, another lunatic, started saying, 'Yeah, Pete the Rat, Pete the Rat!' and the name stuck.

JOHNNY BYRNE: In 1961 I started going to Liverpool. And I noticed the great energy and the activity around the scene. I fell in with a group of people who like me were absolutely crazy about books by the beats. In a very short time we were turning out our own little magazines. This was me, and a guy called Pete the Beat, and another one called Eddie Mooney, there was a group of them around, but there was no sort of cohesive thing. We were into jazz, poetry – straight out of the beatniks – and all around us were the incredible beginnings of the Liverpool scene. We met in a place called the Jacaranda where the Beatles, who could play four chords on their guitars, were just starting. And I started to live then in a basement with Sam Walsh, who was a Liverpool painter. It was in Gambia Terrace, a condemned area. Upstairs we had the Beatles doing their four chords and we didn't like the rock'n'rollers at all. Mal Dean, who's now dead, was a very important part of this whole thing; he was in the same art school year, doing illustration, as Lennon. We went off, hitch-hiking, 'on the road' during one summer. You could go all the way down to Cornwall. We were all keen on hitch-hiking, but this was the first time we'd actually set out in any serious beatnik way. We walked more than we hitched. Dean carried an enormous trombone, which he played at every opportunity, mostly to the cows. From St Ives, where we stayed for some of the summer, we then went down to the Beaulieu Jazz Festival, which was in its later phases; it was almost finished and there was an amazing meeting between Pete Brown and Mike Horovitz – almost like Stanley and Livingstone meeting. We all recognised kindred spirits and had long sort of jazzy, druggy conversations, all-night rapping, just as in the books. Even though we were all falling to pieces we thought this was the way it should be.

MICHAEL HOROVITZ: Soon after *New Departures 1* came out I went to Beaulieu Jazz Festival and coming out of another tent one morning I was greeted by a small wiry bearded figure with the words, 'Horovitz, ecch! Horovitz, ecch!' [from *Mad* magazine] and this was Brown who'd shared the tent with Vic Schonfield, Johnny Byrne and Mal Dean. They were all friends. (Although Schonfield soon developed an allergy to Spike Hawkins, and for a few months that autumn paid Spike a pound a day to stay away from the communal pad they were all sharing in Linden Gardens, Notting Hill – God knows where he got the money from.) There were a number of people like that who knew each other. Brown had been at journalism school and was passionately involved in jazz.

Adrian Mitchell meanwhile was just finishing his stint as a journalist, on the *Evening Standard* Diary. Mitchell's poetry was very exciting and very political. One of his poems, 'Veteran with a Head Wound', was about a victim of Hiroshima, and another was an attack on world leaders for countenancing the continuation of Bomb tests. It affected me more than the American beats. I thought this was better poetry. At the Albert Hall, in 1965, his two short poems, about racism in Alabama and about the Vietnam War, got probably the most concerted audience response. Pete Brown and Mitchell formed the nucleus of my basic poets' team in 'Live *New Departures*' from 1961 to '63.

JOHN DUNBAR: The Jazz Festival at Beaulieu, that was my first riot, that was good. All the teds suddenly wanted Acker. Poor old Lord Thing [Montagu] had flown in Little Fingers Montgomery 5000 miles to play and these fucking teds are going 'We want Acker! We want Acker!' and it just got crazier and crazier. I remember him standing out on stage saying, 'I say, could we have a bit of quiet?' 'Get down, you fairy!' and bottles were coming down and finally a lighting tower collapsed. It was complete, mad devastation over absolutely nothing, over fucking Acker Bilk. Crazy.

MICHAEL HOROVITZ: After meeting at Beaulieu Brown and I hitch-hiked to Edinburgh and wrote a poem on the way. Between lifts in lorries we'd scribble things and when we got to Edinburgh we sat down at a typewriter and typed up all these notes of spontaneous exchange and called it 'Blues for the Hitch-Hiking Dead' which became an endless English jazz poem of the road. It's never been fully published in print but was performed in many incarnations with many musicians.

JOHNNY BYRNE: When I was down in Cornwall this girl we took up with told us about this poet living in a hedge outside Aylesbury, and she gave us precise directions how to find him. And on the way up to London we went to Aylesbury, followed the directions, found the hedge, found signs of habitation, went to the local pub and discovered Hawkins.

SPIKE HAWKINS: Rumour had it that I lived in a hedge and of course the people of the area, Buckinghamshire, liked, as the English did at the time, to have their local village idiot; likewise, to be expedient, their local writer, their eccentric. This was acceptable. That was what I worked at. And one day this scruffy figure emerged, beard, with a very neatly wrapped Italian suit in brown paper, which I presumed to be some sign or omen – perhaps he'd been released from jail . . . It was Byrne.

19

Byrne said, 'I want you to meet Pete Brown, Horovitz and Victor Schonfield,' and I thought, 'My God,' and I gathered a few scattered poems, tied a string around them and we hitched up to London. We arrived at this room in Notting Hill, where I found five men sleeping. They were all wrapped up in odd blankets and one turned out to be Horovitz and another was Brown . . . It was Victor's room. We all had beards. We all lived in this room and there were five Germans opposite who were always saying, 'Zey haff fife beards . . . one, two, three, four, five . . .'

Victor did this beautiful thing: he would be making love to his girlfriend – he carried on his life quite normally while his five friends slept around him – and pulling off these condoms and throwing them. So about three o'clock in the morning there would suddenly be this flop by your side and this would be another ejaculation. I used to look upon them like exclamation marks in the night.

JOHNNY BYRNE: At the Beaulieu Jazz Festival, Hawkins, Dean and I and Horovitz and Brown decided to split the country, rather like the Popes decided to split Europe between Avignon and Rome. Hawkins and Byrne would have everything north of Stafford, and Horovitz and Brown would have everything south. And we would set up these readings. So Hawkins and I went straight back to Liverpool to set up the first of the readings at a place called Streate's Coffee Bar. The first poetry readings we had were a couple of local jazz musicians, and us mainly reading from poems in the *Evergreen Review*. We made trips to Better Books in London to get it. The following year, which was about '62, it was decided that we would extend our activities further because Brown and Horovitz had come up to Liverpool and there was the beginning of a community . . .

MICHAEL HOROVITZ: Around 1960 there evolved certain residencies and so on – the Café des Artistes, the Partisan Cafe in Soho (where Hawkins and Bernard Kops and a whole lot of musicians and folk singers converged). Then more and more jazz became involved. And other people started putting on poetry and jazz. And gradually we moved out of London, to Cambridge, to the north-east, and a bit later still to Liverpool where Byrne and Hawkins were resident. Brown and I took a troupe of musicians to Liverpool and did the first jazz-poetry in the north at the Crane Theatre in Liverpool and at the Manchester ICA. At the party afterwards Adrian Henri, who was the host, said, 'Oh this poetry stuff is all right, I think I'm gonna start doing it.' [Roger] McGough had read with us in Edinburgh. And [Brian] Patten, who'd sat in the front row of the Crane gig trying to hide his school cap, was this marvellous boy who came up and read rather different, passionate romantic poems. So the Liverpool Scene evolved around '62-'63, much the same time as the Beatles. But that was more pop poetry, whereas we were more bop poetry. Our analogy was with bop and to some extent we related to the beat poets, plus American and international protest and jazz poetry.

SPIKE HAWKINS: Johnny said, 'We'll go up to Liverpool,' and I said, 'OK.' There was a dance at Liverpool School of Art every quarter, and I was asked to do a reading. It was after this that Eddie [Mooney], who ran Streate's, asked me to start reading there and I got together a lot of jazz musicians who were eager for somewhere to play. And gradually it brought in others, from the States, from parts of England, and it was a wonderful joining together of talent: people from Liverpool, from the States, ourselves, a lot of first-timers. I had not been published. My reputation was pure word of mouth. This went on and on and on. There was this wonderful connection, a complete network of people, virtually penniless, travelling to and fro as they spread the word, bringing out new literature, new poems, prose, books . . .

JOHNNY BYRNE: We lived in Gambia Terrace about the time when the Beatles first went to Germany for the first time, I knew Stuart Sutcliffe very well, and John [Lennon] was living up there and a guy called Rod Murray and a guy called Daffy and someone else, maybe one of the other Beatles, I don't know. But when they went off the first time, having learnt to play their four chords, Hawkins and I were living down in the basement. It was a cruel and bitter winter and the water used to come up through the flagstones when it rained, and we were living on a loaf in which we made a hole and filled with a packet of chips and which you carved up like a meatloaf. Outside were all these paintings of Lennon's: the landlord had come and the Beatles hadn't paid their rent and the paintings were thrown out into the backyard where they were rotting. And I went out and I got all these paintings and I burnt I don't know how many to keep us warm.

SPIKE HAWKINS: The burning of Lennon's paintings took place one Christmastime. We had been given a turkey by two scrubbers, which we cooked with great care, and the next day we were about to eat it, when from its guts leapt a cat, who had eaten it from the inside.

JOHNNY BYRNE: I hated Lennon. Oh yes. Lennon's no hero of mine. I cannot separate people and what they do from what they are. Lennon was unmitigatedly evil as far as I was concerned. Perhaps evil is too strong a word, and I want to believe that people change, but he treated his wife Cynthia and his kid abysmally. And I have no time for that kind of activity. Even with all the pain of his background and all that there was a type of total brutality in his attitude to people. His one saving grace was that someone like Stuart Sutcliffe, whom I respected enormously and liked very much, did like Lennon. And he knew him in a way that perhaps no one else did at that time.

SPIKE HAWKINS: Sam Walsh let us have the basement rent free, but he wasn't paying rent either. George Melly would arrive, with whatever girl he'd picked up, and would borrow one of our beds. He did this wonderful thing: he'd always leave a pound underneath the pillow for us. One of the fathers of these girls, a dreadful docker figure, said, 'You don't want to lie around here all the time reading that rubbish. Why don't you get up off your arses and do some work? And I'll pay you.' The job involved a pile of railway sleepers, very heavy and large, which were parked over there, and we had to park them over there, a distance of twenty yards. It was like a pointless exercise in the Army. The gentleman made a rather silly mistake of paying us before twelve: of course we left and went off to another job, digging up Christmas trees in the Lake District. We went with Sam Walsh who didn't want to hitch with us but we kept on getting lifts and passing him and saying, 'Would you stop for our friend?' and he'd get in saying, 'Fucking hell, you bastards, you bastards,' and the driver would get frightened, thinking we were obviously three internees of a very long-stay mental wing in some distant mist-clouded hospital with chains on the gates . . .

JOHNNY BYRNE: Within the context of the people I knew there were about fifty beats. And there were many more who didn't move around. And within that fifty was a very small hardcore of people who did move around and the stories of being on the road in those four or five years are absolutely legion. For example, we worked out a system whereby I knew exactly on which part of the A5 to get off and look at a lamp-post in the middle of winter and get a message – I could find out where Mal Dean was, or where Hawkins was, and we had these little signs which would direct us . . .

SPIKE HAWKINS: There was a point, coming down from Liverpool, where one had to stop by a roundabout, and that was where we would leave signs saying where we had gone to or where we were going and Mal Dean would say, 'Have gone to Oxford to see Libby. See you at . . .' wherever we were staying in London. It went on like that, a bit of an

English *On the Road*. There was this circle around which one wandered. We would be invited to various towns. Tom Pickard did a lot of work. The communication between the cities was very great. You would go up to Newcastle and you'd say, 'Right, we're doing a thing down in London, you must come along . . . We'll put you up. I don't know if there's any money involved . . .' There was this wonderful, virtually pre-pubic excitement over it. London was no more the centre than anywhere else. There was constant movement. We were meeting people, communicating, establishing centres. There was a cohesion, as if we had rubber bands stretched all over England and we could just pull one . . .

JOHNNY BYRNE: Every year I would go into the Army, emergency reserve, to do two weeks' training. I used the money from this to pay for the readings up in Edinburgh, to get the money to hire the room and so on. I would get £100 for doing two weeks in the Army and the moment that finished, which was around July, I would go up to Edinburgh, find the place, alert everybody and up they would come – into this grotty cellar. I gave up my reservist fortnights as soon as we stopped going up to Edinburgh. It was only ever useful for funding those readings, although it was interesting because it widened my circle of input, as it were, and I had a lot of fun doing it. The first year I went there I had something like 100 black bombers, you could pick them up by the gross, and I was assigned to making tea for the 28 officers. And every morning I put about seven of them in the big dixie of tea I had to make. Half an hour later you'd see these young guys striding up and down – phew! – whipping the tops off plants with their swagger-sticks. At the end of the two weeks they said, 'Byrne, you are the best tea-maker we've ever had.' And they made a collection and they gave me 28 shillings.

SPIKE HAWKINS: Edinburgh was a brief respite where one would meet one's friends, swap ideas, very very exciting, highly powered, highly charged, new work, new faces, new women. I never sold out, my integrity to my work remained.

CND: 'It all seemed very urgent'
SUE MILES: I came to live in England in the summer of 1961 and a more grey and dreary place you'd never seen. Everyone in cavalry twills, tweeds, and wearing beige socks with sandals. I got involved with CND, as everybody did. If you look at the clips, it's very across the board. It's plastic mac people, it's not extreme, it's not beatniks, it's not weird-looking people . . . it's the Quakers, those kind of people. I think that CND and the Aldermaston marches were incredibly important, because

it was the first time that young people in this country had any reason to go anywhere else, and met people completely out of their class and their ordinary background. And it was vaguely left-wing and brown rice and lentils, hand-made pottery mugs. As David Widgery said, it was real coffee in mugs not Nescaff in cups. It was a certain kind of Hampstead liberalism where girls were allowed to have their boyfriends stay over-night in the same room with them. So I got involved with that, and with coffee bars . . . it was the very end of the ones in Soho: the Partisan and the 2i's, which I first went to in '58 when it was rock 'n' roll and sailors picking you up.

JEFF NUTTALL: Going off to Aldermaston did not fit in very well with my job, which was teaching. The first time I was arrested, with the Committee of 100, it was the most extraordinary comic occasion. I was charged and had to appear in the magistrates' court on Monday. Which meant that I had to take a morning off school. So I took my heart in my hand and rang up the headmaster and said, 'I have to tell you, Mr Roberts, that I have protested against the H-bomb by sitting down in Whitehall. I've been arrested, and I'm summoned to appear at the magis-trates' court on Monday. This means that I cannot attend school. This will no doubt meet with your approval: it is something which I deeply believe and something which I think everybody should do urgently. It is to do with mankind and my concern with the future of mankind.' And the voice from the other end said, 'I'm very sorry for you, but I think you have the wrong number.' I didn't go through it all again. I just rang up and said I had a cold.

DAVID WIDGERY: The march was a great quilt of different tendencies, marching briskly and terribly carefully marshalled by the CND people; and there were the anarchists, who had red and black flags, and the anarchist women were very beautiful. There were the SLL [Socialist Labour League]: very stern Trotskyists. Then there was the YCL [Young Communist League] from the North, often Glaswegian, involved with Holy Loch and so on, they were much more working class and they were much better singers than anybody else and they looked like they were having more fun, and whenever there was trouble they were very pro-minent. It all seemed very urgent then; it was very important that we did something about the Bomb and passive tactics weren't really working. Sitting down waiting to be carried away wasn't enough, we needed to be more forward. There was a good feeling about: you felt that things had to be done and things were quaking a bit.

JO CRUIKSHANK: When I was about sixteen I was very much tied into the Committee of 100. My father, who was definitely political, used to drive me to Aldermaston and just leave me to walk back. I had no choice. He'd put me in the loving hands of Pat Arrowsmith. My father was never more thrilled than when I was arrested at Ruislip one year, trying to climb this fence into a camp. There were all these soldiers with their rifles pointing at me and behind was Pat Arrowsmith going, 'Get up there, get up there!' and I didn't know where to go. Then this policeman appeared and said, 'Come on, love,' and I slid down to the ground singing, 'We shall not, we shall *not* be moved . . .' and I was carried into a bus. What really annoyed me was that as I was being carried past the police, and trying to look heavy and annoyed, all these policemen were winking at me and saying things like, 'Does your mother know you're out?'

SUE MILES: I think the politics that did exist, while no Old Left ideology, was slightly more than just vague pacifism. When you had the split between the Committee of 100 and CND, what it was actually about was whether you rang up the police and were all terribly fair about it and said, 'We're going to have a little demonstration in the Strand on such and such . . .' or whether you went, 'Right!' Spies for Peace printed a list of where all the RSGs [Regional Seats of Government] were in England and diverted the march there, which gave the authorities a really big fright. Suddenly thousands of hairy people show up outside this little suburban house that actually turns out to be an enormous bunker. That turned you on to politics, that and the drugs laws.

The Beats: 'The full fury hit us in '61'

JOHNNY BYRNE: The full fury of the beatnik thing hit us in '61 and in that year alone I logged up about a thousand miles, travelling around, meeting up with Brown here, meeting up with Horovitz there, meeting up with Miles somewhere else. We met Miles at the Edinburgh Festival, but we may have met him briefly in London at a reading there. We kept sort of meeting each other fleetingly and then gradually we got to know each other.

MILES: I became Miles in '61. There were three Barrys in my painting class, and one was my best friend, Barry Lowen, and friends in the end started calling him Lowen and me Miles and it was purely accidental, no big deal at all. I met Sue at a CND party in Cadogan Square. I was kind of fooled cos she still had this strong American accent, having only just arrived from the States. We all got together and there was a sort of endless party that went on. I was taken along to CND by a guy called

25

Mike Cooper who was a sort of pot-smoking/CND/artistic guy, part of the Graham Keen group of Cheltenham people. To a lot of us the great thing about CND was that it was the force that actually got us out of our small towns and introduced us to people who we could stay with when we went to London or, in my case, Oxford. In Oxford I hung out with a group who included Fred Young, head of youth CND, Robin Blackburn, Laura Mulvey and Peter Wollen. Mike Horovitz was there. When they moved to Oxford I followed them. Wherever there was a mattress on the floor I went.

'Oxford was where the whole thing got started'

ROBIN BLACKBURN: Most of the people on the editorial committee of the *New Left Review* were born in the decade from 1939. I was interested in poetry and I went to the Albert Hall poetry reading in '65. People like Horovitz were friends. I'd been at Oxford in '59–'60 before I got bumped out. I didn't feel any great contradiction between the poetry world and the political world. A number of other people who wrote for the *Review* felt the same: Peter Wollen, Kingsley Shorter, Alan Beckett. Often a third or even a half of the magazine would be about writing or cinema or rock, alongside the politics. So we felt part of the movement. I don't think we specifically identified with the American beats: our interests were more in continental Marxist theory, and avant-garde theory: Russian formalism, linguistics, Chomsky . . . But there was a personal overlap. Miles was a great personal friend of Peter Wollen and Laura Mulvey.

MICHAEL HOROVITZ: I knew the *New Left Review* people but always felt distanced from their politics. I always felt more like Mayakovsky among the intellectuals. Until the later 60s, when Robin Blackburn and Tariq Ali started all the provo activities, they seemed such literal-minded disciples of Sartre and purveyors of long words. Talking a lot but not getting that much done, beyond all their publishing.

PETER ROBERTS: Oxford was where the whole thing got started. It was at that time that I met Steve Abrams, who came the year after I went down. Nick Schoumatoff, an amazing man who's now living in New York. He's now a Tibetan Buddhist and runs a nature reserve in Westchester County.

STEVE ABRAMS: I came to Oxford from America in 1960, to St Catherine's. In the course of seven years I dined there twice. I was unknown in the college. They got furious when in 1963 I appeared for the first time in the Junior Common Room when they were raffling off a punt for May morning, and since it was known that I was writing a thesis about telepathy it was considered grotesquely unfair that I won the raffle. Before I came over here I had met three people who came to America, three little public schoolboys from Westminster School: two of them were the sons of preachers, I think. They were Andrew King, Jonathan Fenby and Peter Jenner. And the first time I found dope being smoked in Oxford was at a party one of them gave. In 1961. I think that year an American was busted with some dope, but nobody else was busted for the next five years. So all of the time I was in Oxford, up to 1967, it was cool. Oxford was turned on in the spring of '63. There was some poet who had gone to Morocco and come back with 40 kilos of kif in a sleeping bag. He was selling this at £4 an ounce and ten bob a matchbox.

JOHNNY BYRNE: Steve was interested in fairly phenomenological subjects; he was interested in ESP and all of those paranormal activities. Essentially all the poetry people were bookish in their basic instincts, they were people who loved reading and who loved books. To find a kind of focus, to live your life out of a book was an amazing thing. I was aware of the current of change and the pattern and what made it. Others, such as Steve, had stumbled upon this feeling, this current, and it was a one-time conversion or illumination on the road to whatever, and because it was concentrated into a single moment rather than a gradual expansion, it had such a profound effect, it hit them so hard that they never really looked out beyond this. I wouldn't say that they were casualties, but I would say that it had a fundamental effect. Abrams has dedicated his life to it, in the way that a Jesuit would dedicate his life, or any other committed person. Steve is an idealistic person and his idealism is much more profound than many.

PETER JENNER: I think the reason why Oxford and Cambridge people had such an influence in the early underground was because we'd been given the works: we'd scored somehow, through a combination of our parents and our abilities. In a sense one had got the best that traditional Britain had to offer, and it wasn't terribly impressive. We had it all, and we were looking for new answers. We were all fairly well off, we'd all got good degrees and we could go off and do whatever was required, in terms of running the Empire or becoming civil servants. So we were able to question what was going on. That's why it was so important in the underground. We were all very successful in conventional terms – and found them lacking. We'd won in the lottery and it was terribly unsatisfactory.

Mods: 'Something very sharp'

ROBERT WYATT: The big difference between the trad jazz people and the modern jazz people, which is where the word 'mod' really comes from – the modernists who went to modern jazz gigs – was that the mod thing tended to be more working class or East End Jewish, whereas the trad thing tended to be public school dropouts – much more English, people leaping up and down to trad jazz, already the thing of being ostentatious in dress, whereas the modernist thing was very much not ostentatious. Somebody else might notice how you had your tie, someone who knew about things like that, but it wasn't ostentatious. But we did want to function as a parallel world.

JEFF DEXTER: The first day I went to the Lyceum was in 1961. I was a fourteen-year-old schoolboy, just returned from summer camp. I went for the Sunday record show. I was about 4′ 8½″ tall, I had to pretend I was sixteen to get in, although I probably looked nine. But I managed to blag my way in. Ian Samwell, Sammy, was the DJ. He used to be one of the Drifters, with Cliff Richard. Over the next few months I heard music I'd never heard before. One of the records that year was 'The Twist'. In with the record was a picture of the foot movements and how you were supposed to do it. So I followed the instructions, did the Twist and got barred from the Lyceum for being obscene. Everybody was still jiving at the time. To dance apart, bend over backwards, twist your bum around – that was just an outrage in a Mecca ballroom. Anyway, I turned up the next week, tried to sneak in. These 6′ bouncers stopped me: 'The manager wants to see you.' He came out and said, 'You're barred, you're not supposed to be here.' I was a very cheeky young boy and though I was only 4′ 8½″ and he was 6′ 4″ I steamed fearlessly into him, told him he was wrong, this was the new dance, and it was really good for his ballroom. He said because I was so cheeky he'd let me back in, but never to do that dance in his place again. So I didn't do it, all evening, until very late on. Then I did and as I did it there was someone there with a film camera and it went out on *Pathé News*. I was thrown out of the ballroom again, of course. But the following week the film was round the cinemas – what's happening today in London, the first publicity on the mods – and I was the first person to be noticed doing the Twist, probably because I was so small and I was dancing with two girls a foot taller than me.

So the following week when I tried to sneak in again: 'The manager wants a very heavy word with you.' I tried to duck out but he came running after me, picked me up, carried me up the stairs into his office. I was petrified. But that was the place I had to be at the time, it was where all the other faces were. You *had* to be at the Lyceum for record night. He said, 'How would you like a job?' Word had got around about the *Pathé* film, the editor of *Dance News* had called the manager – 'Who's that guy?' – and Cyril Stapleton, whose band was about to start as resident band at the Lyceum, had seen *Pathé News* and said, 'I want that kid. Get him.' I was on the front of *Dance News* the following week, then on *Come Dancing* for a few weeks, in there with all these funny old straight dancers. I'd wear a mohair suit or a tux, something very sharp. Some people felt I was no longer a cool face, part of the young scene: I was in the mainstream now. But I thought it was wonderful, really fantastic.

I was still at school and they asked me to leave to go and work full-time. I'd just turned fifteen, which was the leaving age then, so I left. I started doing all those crazy 60s dances, and there was a new dance every week in those days. I was resident at the Lyceum and we did one-nighters round the country. If the steps weren't clear I'd make them up. It was a dance-crazy era. We were all trying to outdance each other, us young kids. This went on for about eighteen months. I was also working on the record show with Ian Samwell by then; we started the first mobile disco, called ourselves The Record Hop and opened at Greenwich Town Hall. And at the Lyceum I learned to sing with the orchestra all the dodgy hit records of the day and do comedy sketches too. Then we moved out to the Orchid Ballroom, Purley, which had just been refurbished. And I did the same things there, now with the Ray McVay Band. Sammy still on records, me working five or six nights a week, the records, singing, dancing.

Drugs: 'It takes you out of the box'

JOHN WILCOCK: David Solomon was running *Metronome* magazine which was the druggy musicians' magazine, as opposed to *Downbeat* which was the straight musicians' magazine. He called me into his office and said, 'We want you to try these pills that these professors at Harvard are experimenting with. We'll keep an eye on you. We promise you'll be safe, you'll enjoy it. We want you to take it and see how you feel and if you're interested – write about it.' I said, 'I don't know.' Mailer had offered me marijuana in 1955 and I'd turned it down. I thought drugs were real junkie stuff. But professors at Harvard . . . that sounded all right. So I took this pill, which was psilocybin, and that was the start of altering my consciousness. Then I read Huxley's *Doors of Perception* and got into mescalin. I met Leary – I'd actually met him in Mexico when *he* was down there doing his first experiments with drugs; a friend introduced me to him but I knew nothing about all that – and I asked him to explain the whole thing. He said, 'Well, it takes you out of the box,' and that was his whole explanation for drugs: 'It takes you out of the box.' And that still seems a very profound evaluation of drugs.

For most people getting stoned is the first time in their life that they've not been in control of anything and they've been able to step outside and maybe even look at themselves. Psychoanalysis may do it, over ten years, or ten minutes of group therapy, but nothing else will do it – except drugs. I never really liked acid, a typically American thing, scare headlines; it was flashy, fast, stupid. What I remember was the early mescalin. You could write to L. Light and Company in England and order grams of mescalin. It came in little brown bottles, cost $7.00 and we'd sit and put it on a piece of paper and halve it with a knife and put half in a capsule and take 500mg. It was a long trip. The first hour you wanted to throw up, then you'd gone over this path in the mountains and there you were in Shangri-La. You got these tremendous moments of lucidity, like looking through an incredibly clear lens that made things even brighter and clearer than they were. The drug experience, not drugs as such, was an incredibly important and valuable thing in a lot of people's lives. We used to have discussions about the ethics of whether it really was a good idea to put LSD in people's drinks, people who needed turning on, like politicians and so forth. We discussed the ethics of it so strongly, and it wasn't until years later we found out that the fucking US Army had been doing it without worrying about any ethics at all.

STEVE ABRAMS: I took my first acid trip in 1961. And three things happened: I got a letter from some guy in Czechoslovakia about secret experiments behind the Iron Curtain into ESP. I wrote back and out of the blue a letter arrived from Washington inviting me to apply for a grant from the Human Ecology Fund which later turned out to be the dirty tricks division of the CIA, the part of the CIA which launched acid on the world. It started in 1953 when they ordered ten kilos of acid from Sandoz and from 1953 onwards the HEF and the CIA got to approve anyone who got acid from Sandoz. They took over total control of acid. And a little group of lunatics in the CIA started taking it themselves. They started spiking each other, they lived together like karate masters. Their thing was spiking people. On one occasion they invited the Army chemical warfare scientists to a mountain lodge in Vermont and spiked the lot. One of them had a bad trip and they took him to New York, to one of their tame psychiatrists, and the night before his appointment he jumped out of a hotel window. They would go around bars in New York putting acid in people's beer then following them home. They'd have prostitutes pick them up and take them to safe-houses and do experiments with them, developing assassination techniques and so on. So to all intents and purposes LSD is a CIA invention, put about by CIA agents.

SUE MILES: We were all smoking grass – at this stage we didn't know hash existed. We then discovered that you didn't have to have 35 pounds of these leaves under your floorboards, you could have a little pound block, so convenient, 48 quid each. People I knew knew absolutely that you didn't mess around with hard drugs, which was heroin – I don't think we'd ever heard of anything else. I mean, a friend of ours discovered mescalin because he found a small ad in the back of *Exchange and Mart* in America and he didn't know what it was but he knew that it turned black-and-white films into colour after half an hour. He used to buy it by mail order from New Mexico. And drugs really did bring you up against the law. I was a proper, reasonable middle-class late-teenager and I'd never had any reason to have any contact with the police at all and suddenly there was this real criminal world. West Indians who had guns. If we'd been able to buy our ten-bob deal at the tobacconist we'd have never known any of that stuff.

SAM HUTT: In the early 60s if you smoked dope you were in a definite minority and you were definitely alienated. The alienation process had already started. You went to places round Notting Hill, like the Rio or the Number 9 in Westbourne Park Road, which were serious black caffs and you'd go and you'd get ten-bob deals, in newspaper – Jamaican grass. About a third of an ounce.

DAVID MAY: My brother had come to London in 1962 and I would come up and stay with him. He had a flat in Bayswater, a phenomenally good location. Notting Hill was the pits. It really was a sleazebag. My brother was into dope at a very early age. He used to go to the El Rio on Westbourne Park Road. It was *the* centre for scoring hash. It was a very dodgy scene: white boy goes down there into black man's territory. Here was my brother, a trainee surveyor at the LCC, very respectable. He used to tell me, 'You have to go down the stairs and out round the back and all these dodgy little basement rooms and eventually some guy would come out . . .' So he'd send it down to me in the post and when my mum would say, 'What's that funny smell?' I'd say it was French cigarettes.

HORACE OVE: The Rio was run by Frank Critchlow. The Rio was the first black restaurant in the Grove. Everybody used to hang out there and a lot of people used to go there to score and to hang out. The Rio

31

was the place owned by Frank before the Mangrove. And it was at the Rio that they got together to fight back against the race riots in the late 50s.

DAVID MAY: What Notting Hill was about was the 1958 race riots. I'm still amazed that it's become so rich and gentrified because when you get down to it it's still got fundamentally the same characters as ever. Black/white relations were much better then. All Saints Road wasn't the front line that it is now. Notting Hill had PC Pulley. He emerged as a superstar. He was the guy who picked on the Mangrove people. His line was, 'I am in no way racist, but these blacks are breaking the law with marijuana.' Dope was always at the centre. There were two cultures emerging: the straight culture and the underground culture and to the underground dope was fine.

SUE MILES: There was also that solidarity. Not many people smoked and you knew most of them. One of the great evening entertainments was to go up to the local constable and ask for a light. And he'd get out his box of matches and say, 'Here you are . . .' The drugs squad in Cheltenham had consisted of one person. But there was a lot of animosity to long hair and beatniks and so on. That was certainly visible in the country. We always used to get the shit beaten out of us at every end-of-term party because the rockers from the town, who actually spent their lives being employed by Walls sausage factory butchering pigs, used to come in with razorblades between their fingers and chains and knock the fuck out of all these poncy art-college students. And then they used to send in this enormous butch policewoman who'd stick a head under each arm and drag them out. And the principal of the college was terrified that he was going to get into the papers about 'drug-taking lefties'. It was also a time when no one admitted to sex. I got married because you couldn't get a flat if you said you lived with somebody. No real contraception, no abortion, all those kind of things. There was an overall atmosphere of oneself against society. That was also the first time that anybody in the middle classes was saying that the authorities were fallible, that they weren't all terribly nice people doing a great job on our behalf and that the politicians and the police didn't always tell the truth.

Art Schools: 'The real universities of the 60s'

PEARCE MARCHBANK: If you want to try to find somewhere from which you could say the whole 60s culture comes from, it was the art schools. Art schools in the 60s really were the laboratories that were making rock musicians and designers and painters, they were the real universities of

32

the 60s. Hundreds of rock stars started off as art students: Lennon, Townshend, Clapton . . . loads. The thing was that you were bombarded with a lot more than just a set syllabus. You had this thing called 'Liberal Studies' and the people who taught it were often very interesting. A. S. Byatt used to teach me literature. Art students had very open minds – we were interested in everything that was going on. The fact that we were technically being trained to design ceramic pots or books or theatre sets was irrelevant. You'd go to the canteen and you'd have a painter, a typographer, a film-maker, a graphic designer all at the same table, all talking, and you wouldn't get that anywhere else.

DAVID MAY: The art-school scene was the key to young bohemia. All my mates were there and they all played in the blues bands. All the stylish people went to art school. The Royal College of Art was very important. Universities, forget it, but the RCA was very hip, largely because of Hockney. Their dances were something else. People there were seriously into American style. And out of that art-school culture certain things were important: any of the creative arts counted far more than any technological development.

MICK FARREN: Art school – that's where it all comes from. First of all I'd been in Brighton, then I went to St Martin's. When I went to art school I thought it would lead to being a rock star. Art school is a good place to rehearse a band, as many of us discovered in that generation. As well as the London art schools there were those in the mill towns – Leeds, Manchester. Basically, we knew at St Martin's what was going on up in Hornsey, which had just lost Ray Davies, and we knew there was a hotbed of vice down in Ealing, with Pete Townshend and Michael English and people coming out of there . . . there were about four or five main schools and we all went to each other's dances and a lot of the early psychedelic effects turned up there.

'It was a very creative time'

SPIKE HAWKINS: We moved to 64 Abbey Road. There was a lot of writing going on, a lot of nights staying up. Dear Miss Linsley: we would all four of us fall down the stairs and she would say, 'Oh, having another party tonight, boys? It's so nice to see the young people enjoying themselves.' There was me, Roger Jones, Thom Keyes and Byrne. Keyes was writing *All Night Stand*. I was involved in so many things, but I think the high point was living at Abbey Road, with Johnny and I just writing. It was a very creative time.

33

JOHNNY BYRNE: It was about this time that we all decided that we would move. We – Hawkins and I – had had an appalling effect on Liverpool because we were totally unmanageable. In London we set up a series of magazines. The first one Roger Jones and I did. It was called *Beat Train* and it was really just a programme [for a reading]; I think that Miles was marginally involved in it. I took a flat in West End Lane that had Pete the Rat, who was a friend of Roger Jones', Thommy Keyes, and Dave Berry – who together with me had set up the Crane Theatre Poetry and Jazz Festival in 1962 when Adrian Henri was nothing more than a bellow in the audience. We had six people living there. Keyes was the first of us to hit it in an ambitious way: he wrote *All Night Stand*. We were living in West End Lane for a year or two, then Roger and Thom and I moved to this extraordinary house at 64 Abbey Road, run by this amazing woman called Miss Linsley who had about seven or eight or nine writers living in her house. She was a sort of hunchbacked old lady who lived in a kind of Victorian twilight and from the day I moved in in 1961 to the day she died in 1980 she only ever charged me two quid a week. On the ground floor and the first floor there were writers, always; on the top floor and in the basement there were trainee doctors, always. Steve [Abrams] sometimes stayed, and Pete the Rat, but Hawkins and I were always there, writing our stuff, doing our magazines.

STEVE ABRAMS: Nick Schoumatoff was around in London now, though he was mad at the time and living in his parents' flat and I was his only visitor. Schoumatoff for me was the most impressive figure who had been at Oxford at that time. He was blindingly brilliant for a year or two. I used to come once a week and play checkers with him as the sun was going down. He didn't allow any electricity to be turned on so by the time we were halfway through the game I couldn't see the board, so he'd always win. Schoumatoff got his sanity back from hearing the beginning of a Lord Buckley record, a version of 'The Nazz' that starts, 'Get those lions out of the front of the camels, they're in heat and the wind is blowing this way . . .' And he laughed for 20 minutes after he heard that then we went off to Harrods and he bought 93 packets of muesli and went off to the country.

JOHNNY BYRNE: When we first came to London Hawkins kept getting married; worse than that, every time he used to hang his trousers on the end of the bed, some bird would become pregnant. So he had about fifteen kids. Every time I said goodbye to a girl, Hawkins, who'd behaved himself impeccably during the time I'd been involved with her, would

34

move in. I'd meet her nine months later and she'd be out here, or worse than that I'd meet her two years later and she'd be holding twins. Hawkins crept up behind me, inseminating everything in my wake. While we were in Liverpool there was a lovely girl called Lee, a beautiful Marilyn Monroe type. Her brothers were local dockers, told Hawkins, 'You marry her or we'll break your arms.' So he married her. And then they said, 'You better go out and get a job or we'll kick your teeth in.' And the only way Hawkins could think of getting a job was to take 40 black bombers, start walking to Aylesbury and join the Army. He was discharged as psychologically unsuitable within two weeks.

A couple of years back Hawkins went up to Liverpool, walking around his old haunts, obviously feeling very paranoid, and there was a sort of tap on his shoulder and he turned round and there was this enormous constable. 'Are you Spike Hawkins?' 'Yeah.' 'John Frederick Hawkins?' 'Yeah.' 'Hello Dad! I'm Lee's son and I claim you as my father.'

Mods: 'Amphetamine, Sartre and John Lee Hooker'

DAVID MAY: What sent you to London from the provinces was the whole mod culture, which swept aside the early-60s beatniks. Mods were always intellectual. There was always a large gay element in it. On Saturday afternoon we'd go to get our hair done in the women's hairdressers. Then we'd go out in the evening, dancing. Saturday afternoon we'd go down the town, buying some new piece of clothing. We didn't fight rockers, we were far more interested in some guy's incredible shoes, or his leather coat. But underneath this, one did read Camus. *The Outsider*, there it was, it explained an awful lot. A sort of Jean Genet criminal lowlife was also important. These were the outlaw figures. People who went out and stole and so on. And until the drug squad appeared in 1967 there was this period, for me from the age of fourteen to eighteen, when the police didn't impinge at all. We lived in this whole other world: getting stoned and hoping to get laid. And soul music. And what had to happen, for everyone, was that you had to move away.

STEVE SPARKS: I was a mod. I was one of the original mods, one of the real Wardour Street mods. Not the post-commercialised mods, but back then when it was all existentialism and rhythm and blues. There were like 120 mods, period. Everyone else were the commercialised Carnaby Street mods. They came from Ilford, East London and North London; Tottenham; the Noreik Club axis, a Tottenham club; and a coffee bar in Ilford called the Mocha. Those were the centres around which mod grew. The Who, of course, were Shepherd's Bush, but that came later. I ran a folk club and I used to run a club in the back room of this pub in Barking and we used to have the High Numbers, as they were then, and all those Rik Gunnell Flamingo people . . . Georgie Fame, Geno Washington and the Ram-Jam band, that whole R&B/Flamingo sort of music. Pete Townshend used to punch holes in the ceiling of the club with his guitar. Amphetamine, Jean-Paul Sartre and John Lee Hooker. That was being a mod. And the clothes. Church's brogues . . . I still wear Church's brogues, the only thing left from those days. Silk and mohair suits.

PETER SHERTSER: The Firm started in the days of going to the Flamingo, where we used to get taken by guys of seventeen and eighteen in their cars. We'd all go out and have a laugh, one thing and another, get carted about, and we were only fourteen or fifteen. Very wide-eyed. By the time we were seventeen we all managed to somehow connive a car. I smashed the old man's car up, so that was it. He said, 'Right – I'm getting you a car.' I hadn't even passed my test. I was with Adrian Gurvitz and Bruce the Spiralhead. He had a high hairline and he used to put his hair up and hop about and he looked like one of the things out of Tod Browning's *Freaks*. I don't know who named the Firm – it might have been Mick Farren or Boss [David Goodman]. We'd team up with another mob – the Schnauzer (Malcolm Chiswick, he looked like Schnauzer out of *Car 54*) and Lawrence Silver. The Schnauzer had a mouth and a half – he could talk his way in and out of Buckingham Palace. The working-class Lenny Bruce. And his mate Lawrence Silver who was the poser. A swimming instructor . . . but he was a tough guy. So we'd all go out on Saturday night to a club and we'd all meet up in the Gondola in Wigmore Street. They had tables and chairs outside. Lawrence had an old Black Maria. We'd all meet up, have a drink, whatever, then we'd put all the tables and chairs in the van and piss off. The whole front of the restaurant disappeared. It was creative villainy, not really for profit. We used to go in the Golden Egg in Marble Arch – in those days that was the only 24-hour gaff – go downstairs to the storeroom, take out all those tomato ketchup things shaped like tomatoes and cover everybody. We used to take the waiters' bill pads, sit down and have the works and then write our own bill out. We never got busted, but what they did was hire a karate expert. So Lawrence Silver outed him. The next time we came back the karate expert had hired a dog.

MILES: There was this so-called street gang called The Firm: Peter Shertser and people. His stories were hilarious: 'I got in late last night, went up to my room and I was playing some blues record. My father came in and he objected so I was forced to knock him over . . .'

36

PETER SHERTSER: We used to enjoy a bit of wrecking. That started from fourteen or fifteen onwards. It was clever wrecking, not just vandalism. We'd cement a Hoover to a bath. Very Magritte influenced, Man Ray, all that kind of thing, thinking about Buñuel films. You had it all in and that's how it came out. We were mental. We used to meet up at like a Jewish nightclub on a Sunday evening when they had charity dos. It was like the old Zoot Money number: 'I took the front door in and took the back door out.' We were different: we took the back door in and took the front door out. We used to go in *everywhere* free. We'd all meet up – 20 or 30 of us – and some were pretty hairy characters. Real tough guys. If there was a problem they'd break the door down; or if there was a real problem – no fire exit, no toilet or no other way of entrance – we'd go to the front door and one of us would have a whistle. When he blew the whistle we'd push. And the tables and chairs and everything would go over, with the people, and we'd all rush in. It was terrible, but there was a sense of the absurd: they were all so locked into a fixed pattern and none of us were.

DAVID GOODMAN: The first time I noticed the Firm was in a spray painting in Barking or somewhere, on this wall: 'The Firm'. Liked it, didn't know what it was until years later when I met John Cox, who was in my gang and was also one of their gofers for a while. His initiation was, he told me, to go to this shop in Gants Hill and pull the shelves off the walls. Which he duly did. Then Peter Shertser and the late Ian Sippen marched in and said, 'Hello son, got our payment . . .'

PETER SHERTSER: We met Boss around '66. I was still in college, Barking Polytechnic, doing pharmacology. That's where I met a lot of the Firm. When I met him he wasn't involved in music or anything: he was just a guy who was a good guy and we got on. We all met originally through music and drugs.

DAVID GOODMAN: At school me and my friend Phil de Newman were the mods. His brother Colin was the real head mod, the stylist, and when he was still at the school we were just third-class tickets. It was basically very difficult to be a mod at boarding school. All the pair of us wanted to do was get out there and get a scooter and get some money to get some really nice snappy duds and stuff. We used to spend hours drawing shirts with button-down collars and design them in different shapes and draw paisley patterns and they wouldn't let me take art because I drew mods on scooters instead of drawing landscapes. 'Draw a landscape,' and I'd draw a seaside resort with mods with parkas on.

37

They brought in half-term holidays and we would head straight for Soho. Before we went we'd spend hours mapping out where we wanted to go – the Palladium, Drury Lane, Anello and Davide where I'd buy my Beatle boots, the 2i's coffee bar. It wasn't a rock and roll haunt any more but it was the first time I'd ever heard Prince Buster singing 'Madness', and another classic ska record called 'Carolina' by the Folk Brothers.

JOHN MARSH: What appealed to me about the mods was the physical, material style. I was totally sold on the look. Among certain mods a real dedication to pleasure existed. The kinds of pleasures were fairly basic, and rather alien to the hippie idea of pleasure, but above all there was the music. R&B, Motown, some of the jazz. There were some mods who liked it only because it was fashionable, but there was a hardcore of old mod types who were dedicated to it.

I was also in sympathy with the ideas of the beats, but loathed their physical appearance. Whereas it was vice versa with the mods, whose grubbier, more down-market excesses I loathed. Any attempt by me to get the two to co-exist, even in my own mind, was doomed to failure because the two were basically antipathetic. The mod thing was the first time in which I realised that there was somehow something wrong somewhere.

I never could come to terms with hippies and I never really was a hippie or part of that counterculture other than in the most peripheral sense. As a mod, what was happening, and where it was happening, and where it was going and all the rest of it was all kind of understandable. You were part of a certain sort of culture and group because of the possession of so many suits, how much chrome there was on your scooter, how many girls you'd had knee-tremblers with against the back wall of various West End clubs. It was understandable: where you stood, who you were, what you were was all fairly clearly defined.

STEVE SPARKS: Mod has been much misunderstood. Mod is always seen as this working-class, scooter-riding precursor of skinheads, and that's a false point of view. Mod before it was commercialised was essentially an extension of the beatniks. It comes from 'modernist', it was to do with modern jazz and to do with Sartre. It was to do with existentialism, the working-class reaction to existentialism. Marc Feld (who became Marc Bolan) was an early example of what was the downfall of mod, which was the attraction of people who didn't understand what it was about to the clothes. Marc Feld was only interested in the clothes, he was not involved in thinking. Mind you, it's quite hard to think on twenty Smith Kline and French Drinamyl.

38

MALDWYN THOMAS: I came across Marc several times, in his Marc Feld era, as one of the faces at the Scene. I kept bumping into him. I was going down the tailors and getting mohair suits. All sorts of wild suits: three-piece suits that weren't three-piece: the trousers and the vest were all in one, like a catsuit. Zoot suits, pork-pie hats. This was serious business – very serious being a face. Those sort of drugs, amphetamines, make things very serious anyway. I started going to the Scene when I was about fourteen. Off Wardour Street, it was a mod club. You spent all night at the Scene, you took blues, you went home in the morning.

PEARCE MARCHBANK: There were pills at the Scene. There used to be straight Coke and expensive Coke. Expensive Coke had something in it, probably amphetamine. I was there during a police raid once. Suddenly when you walked across the room there were pills all over the floor and your feet crunched when you walked.

RUSSELL HUNTER: You walked through a car park round the back of Piccadilly and there was a really seedy little club. And if you wanted to go in the club you gave them five shillings and if you wanted drugs you gave them a ten-shilling note. It was well accepted that if you gave them a ten-shilling note then they'd give you four blues and you didn't go into the club. It was a desolate, bomb-site car park and there was the remains of an old building the cellar of which had been propped up and turned into a club.

JO CRUIKSHANK: I lived in Richmond which was the hub of the mods and rockers world. That particular era in Richmond was amazing musically. The Stones at the Station Hotel, the Yardbirds at the Crawdaddy. Eel Pie Island with Long John Baldry and Rod Stewart.

There was a coffee bar there called L'Auberge which was the real meeting place. It was the mod café. There was someone called Johnny Vanstone who was the dealer of Richmond. Donovan on one of his LPs said, 'Thanks to Johnny Vanstone for every little blade of grass . . .' I realise now that he was one of the first junkies. He had this great gaping thing on his face that I imagine he'd picked at. It was the very beginning of heroin in England. The time when all you had to do was buy a jack on the black market – they were very cheap because no one wanted them – take it, then go to your GP, say you were a heroin addict. He would immediately take a blood test, say, 'Yes you are,' and register you, no problem. It was a sort of fun thing to do. I was terrified, but I had friends who did it.

39

EMILY YOUNG: I was at Putney High School. We used to go to these places in Richmond like the Crawdaddy Club where we saw the Rolling Stones. There was also a café called L'Auberge, which was a bit of a beatnik coffee bar. We used to go and see the Pretty Things and John Mayall, Long John Baldry. I was a beat, as we called ourselves. A beat meant you put lots of panstick on your face, lots of black eye make-up, white lipstick, then you'd wear black. Lacy stockings, short skirt, little high-heeled boots, black plastic mac with CND badges. There was a lot of dancing – all these different particular kinds of dances that you'd do. Because we weren't mods we had to not do those dances right, cos the mods would all be there in lines doing their dances, so we had to do these other things and people would come up and say, 'How d'you do that?' and we'd have to show them how we did these bastardised versions of mod dances. My elder sister *was* a mod and she had mod boyfriends and wore little tight sweaters and short neat skirts and patterned stockings and little chunky heels. Her boyfriends had the most fantastic record collection of original R&B.

'There was only one music, and that was rhythm and blues'

PETER SHERTSER: Rhythm and blues and blues music was the start of it all. There has only been in the last 30 years two types of music: rhythm and blues – which incorporates soul, gospel and blues – and rock'n'roll – which incorporates country music and blues and bits and pieces. Those two musics comprise everything that has come since. And that's why at that time it was so important. In the 60s there was only one music really – and that was blues music, and everything derived from it. The whole of psychedelic music came from blues: Grateful Dead, Doors, 13th Floor Elevators, Zappa. There was blues and country and everything else was a fusion.

STEVE SPARKS: I was always interested in sound. I was one of those horrible geezers who could tell what make the guitar was just by listening to the record: 'Oh no, John, that's a Gretch Tennessee, not a Gibson,' all that stuff. That world that the Rolling Stones came from. Import R&B fans. You had these people all over London who thought they were the only people in the world who knew about John Lee Hooker. Then you'd meet up and find there were more of you . . . That whole R&B explosion was a precursor of the underground.

DAVID WIDGERY: I lived in Slough which was on the confluence of the Aldermaston marches to London and the Thames Valley R&B scene

40

which centred on Windsor where John Mayall lived in a tree and the Rolling Stones made their debut. These were the influences I grew up with: this carnival of subversion of the CND that came through my town, which I was very keen on, it swept you up and that was great, and trad jazz and those sort of things. I learnt to play the trumpet in imitation of these people. Also there was the R&B thing which was the other thing you did after school: go to the Rikki-Tik club in Windsor. It was very exciting: Cyril Davies was the great attraction. People like Jagger were very much junior and trying to get an intermission spot with their devout imitation of what they imagined Southside Chicago blues would sound like. It was sort of like trad in a way, very much an imitation thing too.

PETER JENNER: Eric Clapton would never have seen Muddy Waters playing live; the Stones would never have heard Bo Diddley live. You'd have heard a couple of records and just tried to get the spirit. In fact they'd have been rather brought down if they'd seen them. I saw Muddy Waters live in America in 1960 and he played sitting down. That would have really upset the Stones.

ANDREW BAILEY: I was always a musician, always in a band. We'd change our name virtually every other gig in order to get more gigs. We'd play somewhere and people would say, 'I'm sure I've booked you before,' and you'd say, 'No, I don't think so.' We were a trad jazz band based on the Kenny Ball boom. There was that mini-scene after R&B and before the Beatles – trad jazz was very cool. That's what you listened to in Soho coffee bars. You sat there, nodded your head and drank your coffee.

PETER SHERTSER: We're into the music and we start listening to Luxembourg and so on and hearing R&B on the radio. Suddenly Georgie Fame, Zoot Money, the Animals, this and that are playing London clubs like the Flamingo and we all went down there, even though at our age – thirteen, fourteen – it was ridiculous. We all go down the Flamingo Club, to the all-nighters. We couldn't understand these spades, they're taking funny things, pills – what are they, ill? What's the matter with them? They're smoking this stuff that smells weird. What are they, herbalists? Never had a clue. But the music was great and it was an all-nighter and we were up all night, just adrenalin, and the love of the music, seeing Georgie Fame or American acts like Johnny 'Guitar' Watson or Larry Williams: it was fantastic music, it had depth to it, it grabbed you by the balls, it wasn't just someone going out there and performing – they were giving something to the audience.

The Flamingo had a mainly black audience but it was a white club. The owners were Rik and John Gunnell – very heavy guys. They used to come on stage, you'd see this guy, still had the clothes hanger in the jacket, and he'd get on stage with the scar: 'Hello, ladies and gentlemen, we got an act for you tonight . . .' You'd think, you don't mess with this man. The complete untouchables. Amazing characters. From then on in that's when the parents lost control. You were a free agent. We were looking for action: the Flamingo, the Marquee, Studio 51. That was a very unique club, owned by Ken Collyer, it was in Newport Street. That was Sunday afternoons. It would be people like the Downliners' Sect. That was all right, a kosher time to be able to go out, Sunday afternoon. Going to the all-nighters wasn't – they used to cause a lot of rows at home.

SAM HUTT: The resident bands at the Flamingo were Herbie Goins and the Night-timers, Chris Farlowe and the Thunderbirds, Georgie Fame and the Blue Flames, John Mayall and the Bluesbreakers, and then guests like Solomon Burke, a brilliant night. Enormous fat black guy: 'the king of rock and soul'. The crown, the cape with the ermine lining and the salmon-pink three-piece suit with the emerald lurex lapels. *This man is not joking.* And he comes on and he sweats and he sings and I'm standing on seats right at the back and there was this thirteen-year-old black girl screaming 'Fuck me! Fuck me!' to this great 21-stone geezer. That was very formative.

DAVID GOODMAN: The Flamingo was the most fantastic place. The atmosphere was just so beautiful. Little stage down in a basement in Wardour Street just opposite Gerrard Street, just below what is now the Wag Club. I saw some of the most incredible shows of my life there – Wilson Pickett, who was just unbelievable; I even saw Barry McGuire singing with Zoot Money's Big Roll Band, doing 'Hang On Sloopy' for something like 45 minutes; Eric Burdon and the Animals, Cream, John Mayall's Bluesbreakers with Eric Clapton, and the all-nighters, which were so much part of what was the mod scene.

CHRIS ROWLEY: I was at a sort of mix of public and grammar school. It was heavily football- and religion-oriented and I wasn't. We used to go off to the park and just not come back. Stay out all night. We'd go off to London and turn up to the Flamingo Club, an all-nighter. My second time there, down the front, surrounded by enormous black people, feeling rather intimidated but high on the experience, lo and behold out comes Screaming' Jay Hawkins, borne out in a coffin by four even bigger black

42

persons who set down the coffin while this music roars and rumbles and the band gets going. The coffin top flies open. Before anything else appears two hands come out with these rubber snakes quivering and shaking and they're only about three feet from my face. Then he comes out and does 'I Put A Spell On You'. It took me a few hours to recuperate. The rest of the set I was just, like, 'dadada!!!' This old guy did the magic. He was tremendous.

Happenings: 'It started at the Edinburgh Festival'

MARK BOYLE: For me it started at the Edinburgh Festival in '63 when we – in collaboration with a couple of other guys, one of them Ken Dewey, an American who's now dead – put on a happening. But we weren't underground, we didn't think of ourselves as underground: we were an official part of the goddam festival. That was John Calder's one. Charles Marowitz, who was working with Peter Brook, took part. And after that Brook went back to London and started the Theatre of Cruelty. The happening had this nude actress crossing on a lighting trolley because she wasn't allowed to move by the same laws that governed strip shows.

DAVID WIDGERY: Me and my mate would go up to London, when we got bored with R&B, and go to Ronnie Scott's Club in Frith Street and part of the tour would be going to Better Books. And in the basement there would be Jeff Nuttall creating an igloo out of bus tickets.

JEFF NUTTALL: Tony Godwin invited us to do a happening at Better Books. Everyone was wondering what the happening at Edinburgh had been about. It said I'd do one in Better Books. I'd met Herb Balu, who was an American theatre director who told me what was happening on the West Coast; I had access to American underground literature and I thought, 'Jesus Christ! These guys are still doing it.' I was very excited about happenings and very excited about assemblages: I was making junk sculptures. So I did the happening in the Better Books basement with Bruce Lacey and various other people.

MARK BOYLE: After the Edinburgh happening we did a series of events in London. The one that matters is a piece called 'Oh What a Lovely Whore' at the ICA in '64. People got very excited, there was a big crowd and suddenly we put out all the lights and I shouted over the microphone, 'We're not doing any events now, so if you want an event you're going to have to do it for yourselves!' and then spotlights came up all over the place and there were activities for everyone. I think this was the key

43

moment for me in the whole thing. To everybody's astonishment, including my own, everybody got stuck in. We all assumed beforehand that they'd all just say 'Oh yeah . . . mmm' and be blasé. It was outrageously successful. I don't think anyone who was there has ever forgotten it. I was amazed. They did smash the place to pieces, but they did it in a kind of ritual way that was astonishing.

'The Clark Kent of the underground'

JOHNNY BYRNE: There was a coalescing, we all pretty much fetched up together around about '64 and around this time people were beginning to talk about the Beatles; things were happening and people were beginning to feel that maybe there was something a bit more to them. After *Beat Train* we did something called *Night Train*, which Miles was involved in. Brian Patten was doing small magazines, a very important one in Liverpool called *Underdog*. And then we did another one called *Horde* and I started doing little literary bits of science fiction because I wanted to bring that in and leaven the magazines and get that going. As a principle we never produced more than one [issue] of them. I don't know how many they sold because Miles took care of all that.

PETER ROBERTS: Miles was around. He was slightly mocked for writing fan letters to Ginsberg and that kind of thing. He was very earnest. It wasn't really my personality: it's very pleasant for you to be earnest, mate, and we love you for it, but don't expect us to get earnest with you. Why don't you have a joint and relax? He never struck me as a terribly relaxed person.

MICHAEL HOROVITZ: Miles became very closely allied to Ginsberg, who, at first, as was often the case, had, I think, fancied him, and also, as is his way, had appointed him to some extent his St Paul and archivist and secretary, or English agent. Miles was very effective and became a sort of acolyte and representative of Ginsberg and Burroughs. He's a very clever chap and was very good at the commerce and the communications and so on. So he was gradually evolving as the little Wizard of Oz of it all, holding that system together.

JOHN SHEPPARD: Miles was terribly important, you just knew he was terribly important. He was providing a sort of organisational strength.

PETER SHERTSER: Miles has been a very great influence on my life. Miles knew that we weren't just ordinary lunatics and maniacs – because our behaviour could get out of hand, and often did. After he'd known us

44

a little while he wanted to write a sitcom round us; it would have been hilarious. But he used to make apologies for us to other people. He used to go, 'They're quite intelligent, you know.' But he was happy to have us around. He was very mild-mannered – the Clark Kent of the underground.

'Things started happening'

HORACE OVE: In 1964 London had changed a lot. The whole feel of that kind of freedom had started to take place. England before that was very conservative. When I arrived in '60 it still felt like after the war: it was very grey and people wore black and they wore grey and they were very formal and even the guy digging up the street would be wearing a suit, everybody . . . There was a heavy cloud over it. When I came back in '64 something had started to happen in everything – in the arts, in music – there was more money, the working class had more money, there were more working-class heroes, things started to take place and the politics started to change: things started happening.

MICK FARREN: I think the idea of changing the world had started almost immediately after the assassination of John F. Kennedy. The protest movement had become weird by then. The Times They Are a-Changing had come and gone. We were now Inside the Gates of Eden. My thoughts were always more of running amok. I never really believed in the ideologies. I think I actually believed in constant revolution and still do. Fuck all this shit. It didn't bother me none. It was all sorts of self-sustaining things. The CND geezers had become Marxists and they were so fucking incompetent they wouldn't be able to run a bunfight. Chairman Mao was not amongst them. I think the British revolutionary gene pool was probably wiped out somewhere outside of Barcelona. That was how we ended up with Harold [Wilson] basically – he was one of the ones who didn't go to Spain and felt ashamed about it. I don't know who the politicos were but they weren't at the Albert Hall watching Bob Dylan. I didn't see Tariq Ali up there.

MARK BOYLE: The fact of Wilson having won the election in '64, however much we all felt let down later, meant that everyone felt there was a kind of freedom around which hadn't been there before. The Arts Council was just starting to think in terms of funding individual artists. Jennie Lee put through the first budget for the arts. Jim Haynes said to us, 'You must go to Jennie. She wants to know artists to whom she can give money, not just artists who are already making a lot of money out of commercial galleries.' We wrote to her immediately, with a long list of proposals of what she should spend the money on rather than just frittering it away on £50 to this guy, £50 to that woman. Encouraging artists to work together, to get equipment, setting up a fund which would guarantee the mortgages of groups of artists who could get industrial premises, stuff like that . . .

PAUL MCCARTNEY: Coming in from the provinces to the centre – isn't that what cities are all about? Aren't cities made up of ants, the outside ants attracted to the Queen's lair? It seems to me that's what it is. There isn't such a thing as many people born in London at all. Peter Asher's a Londoner, [John] Dunbar was from Pinner, as was Gordon Waller. But you didn't bother with too much of that – somehow it wasn't to do with which area you were from, it was more just a level of thinking. The nearest you could come to it was student thought.

NIGEL WAYMOUTH: We were all friends – Miles, John Dunbar, all those people. It was a small circle and obviously everybody had word of each other and people would approach each other. You met through the jazz life, the beatnik life. John Dunbar I'd known for a long time, he and I grew up in the same patch together. I'm a boy from the suburbs of north London too. We'd wind up on Saturday evenings at the Cruel Sea in Hampstead waiting to get news of the latest party. He went to Churchill College in Cambridge with my best friend at the time. He married Marianne [Faithfull] so we knew all those people. The whole thing is so incestuous. Another of my best friends was at college in Reading and he was very very keen on blues and jazz and he used to go down to the clubs and he was a friend of Marianne Faithfull's and then Marianne and John got together and the whole thing is like a circle. People know each other through people and that's just how it went on.

PAUL MCCARTNEY: We were all reading Ginsberg and that stuff, everyone was. It's a point that people often miss. They say, for instance, that the Beatles' haircuts were invented by the Beatles, but actually we got this German guy Jürgen Vollmer to try and cut our hair like his. And the point I'm making is that he had a version of the Beatle haircut and this is German, Hamburg students. You'd come down to London and you'd see kids in London, students with the similar type thing, or in Liverpool at John's art college or all this kind of stuff. Students the world over were aware of that. So when we came down here to London all we did really was plug out of the Liverpool student scene and plug into the London student scene. So when we did come to plug into the student scene it would be people like Miles, John Dunbar, who was a student and Mari-

46

anne's husband at the time, Peter Asher, who like us had recently been a student, a bass player down a jazz cellar, although his was Westminster School and a much more privileged upbringing than ours had been, but good, it seemed to be good, they didn't seem to be a snotty crowd. So this was it: like, up north you'd be reading *On the Road*, and they would be reading *On the Road*. We'd be looking at the same kind of things.

JOHN DUNBAR: Through Jane [Asher], Paul [McCartney] moved in and lived in Jane's house which was round the corner from me. And the interest in jazz moved over into rock'n'roll, certainly the glamour and the loot was much more in evidence there. I was just hanging out. We had this weird Saturday night and Friday night ritual, meeting up in these pubs and exchanging lists of parties. You'd literally go to ten parties, to totally unknown houses. I knew all those kind of people like Andrew Loog [Oldham]. Aged eighteen and he was a good hustler, he was this guy around Hampstead. Andrew started off by seeing some terrible band on the telly and turning up and saying, 'I'm going to be your manager.' Peter Meaden, who was a good pal of Andrew's, was an unsung hero of that era: he discovered the Who and then totally fucked up, because he was so hyper that he then talked everybody out of things, he was so fast that he totally deconvinced everybody.

The Who: 'I went straight out and smashed a window'

PEARCE MARCHBANK: I went down one night to the Marquee to see some band and they were off and the Who had replaced them. There were about 50 people there and there were some very smart posters outside and all over Wardour Street. Black and white posters which looked extremely smart and unlike all rock'n'roll posters. They were much more like art posters or film posters. And there was this group called the Who, who had a rather smart logo. There were hardly any people in the Marquee and this guy, who I later discovered was either Chris Stamp or Kit Lambert, was walking round giving people whisky. This was to gee up the audience, since they were all there from the Railway Hotel or wherever. What they did on stage then was completely different to their records. Their show-stopper was 'Heatwave'; they never played their singles on stage. They had zip-up boots from Toppers in Carnaby Street and it was the very beginning of their pop art clothes; Roger Daltrey used to customise his terrible bri-nylon roll-neck sweaters by putting two bands of insulating tape down one side which would peel off as he got sweaty. Townshend was always getting very cross with them all. Moon looking *incredibly* young, younger than me. They had black polo-necked

47

sweaters like the Beatles at the very beginning. I gathered they were an art-school band by the look of them.

DAVID GOODMAN: I was still a bit shy, but grooving inwardly and the first time I came out of my shell was when I saw the Who at the Marquee. I'd never seen anything like it. I couldn't imagine that people could do such things. I went straight out and broke a window, I was that impressed. It broke down so many barriers for me, just that one evening of seeing the Who. The set was so fucking violent and the music so heady, it hit you in the head as well as the guts, it did things to you. You'd never heard anything like it: 'Maximum R&B' said the poster . . . and fuck me, was it! They used to do 'Smokestack Lightning', thirty minutes of it, and Townshend would go potty. This particular time I was in the second row of seats in front of the stage and there was this girl and he was beckoning her: 'Come up here and dance!' and she was going 'No, I can't', and he went bam! smack! on the mike and you're going 'Whaaatt?' and then you watch Keith Moon and you can't believe your eyes . . . That all really brought it home to me what I'd been missing.

'It didn't matter if you were competent or not'

PETER JENNER: I spent four years at Cambridge, doing economics, and shocked everybody by getting a first, including myself. I spent a year doing research after I graduated. I hadn't worked out what I was going to do. In those days the best thing you could do was become an academic. It was circular: the ultimate achievement of an education was to become an educator. Then you got tenure and you could become a gentleman and drink port. During my year's research I had a flat in Covent Garden above Marsh & Austin and I met Eric Clapton, who at the time was just leaving the Bluesbreakers, and this brought me into my first contact with British rock music. I'd always been very sniffy about it before, I was always a jazz snob. But I got bored with jazz. Eric lived in my flat for a while, so did Ted Milton, and through this lot I got to know Mick Milligan, who was a jeweller, and through him I knew June Bolan who later moved into my house in Edbrooke Road and came to work for Blackhill. I don't know when I got to know Hoppy but it was probably through Oxford, where I had a girlfriend and where my brother had married into the *New Left Review* circle and where I went quite a lot. When I met him he'd been at Harwell and was now a photographer living at Westbourne Terrace. I did score the odd ounce of grass from him, because he did have a very good line at one stage in £4-an-ounce grass.

PETER ROBERTS: The economic situation, whether you'd been to university or not, was this: you could bum around without doing any work and then you'd think, 'Shit! I'd like to go to Morocco so I'd better get a job for a few weeks' – and the job was there to be had. Whenever you wanted to work, there was a job there. You could give a job up just like that – because there was another one round the corner. You didn't want to hold onto a job. Pension rights? Jesus God! That's 30, 50 years away, you must be joking. You'd say, 'Oh God, I don't feel like working any more, I don't like the guy, I want to go off, I've got too much heavy enjoying to do, I haven't got time for work . . .' Then after a while you'd find yourself broke and you'd go and get another one. Like you can buy potatoes in a supermarket. You don't hoard them because you know there's *always* going to be a bag of potatoes there.

It wasn't a class thing: people took whatever they needed, whatever was the least hassle and the least bullshit. You had a good time, you rejected the whole philosophy you were brought up on. A lot of the creativity, the relaxed creativity, came out of this feeling that anyone who wanted to do anything could do it. A lot of the activities – it didn't really matter if you were competent or not. Take poetry: if you just wanted to write poetry, you did it. The stuff you wrote might be awful but it didn't matter a damn. And if you wanted to paint, you painted. Music was a bit different, because badly played music is painful for the listeners. The question, are you a better artist than anybody else, or do your pictures fetch a better price? – nobody even thought about. You just did things because you wanted to do them. Some people did worry, but not in our world.

MICHAEL HOROVITZ: We'd always try to mix business with pleasure, although business then was anathema. There was an awkwardness about being paid: on the one hand we wanted the money and liked being paid, but on the other we were anti what Brown called 'the television way of life': one's parents always watched television. There was an ambivalence about the so-called affluent society; there was this Ken Colyer-ish rugged clinging rather sentimentally and possibly self-destructively to an ideal of purity: that if you did get a lot of money it would be corrupt. I did slightly feel this about the Liverpool poets, that they'd kissed the leper of Mammon and were putting out these rather synthetic, inferior, superficial works to order for the consumer society, barely distinguishable from television and advertising jingles. Though this may also have been sour grapes . . .

Notting Hill: 'Colin MacInnes was an angry white man'

MICK FARREN: I was living in a Chinaman's house in Westbourne Gardens, off Powis Square. It was an Irish rooming-house and I roomed there. There was a Chinaman downstairs who, legend had it, was trying to raise enough money to ship his dad's body back to China and it was still in there. I don't know why, but the Irishmen weren't allowed to bring women in, but I was. It was a bit like living in a vertical bothy. Anyway, there we were and there were these degenerates that I knew: Alex Stoll, who later did the lights for the Deviants, a woman called Hilary, a couple of people we knew in the pub, a handful of proto-Rastas. Then there was the other end of the sort of Notting Hill Gate/Ladbroke Grove underground of that time which was Alexander Trocchi and Michael Abdul Malik – Michael de Freitas as he was then. Trocchi and de Freitas had a jazz record store on Ledbury Road, which was importing all the new stuff that was coming out, the Impulse stuff, Gil Evans and so on, and we were listening to that shit and playing round with slide projections and listening to an awful lot of Raahsan Roland Kirk and Charles Mingus and stuff and flashing lights at ourselves. And thinking, 'There's something in all this shit,' but we couldn't figure out what. We were smoking dope, which was a big deal in those days, because you went to jail for a joint back then, so it was highly clandestine and you kept the reefer under the floorboards. You bought it in pound deals. There was the Rio, before the Mangrove opened, on Westbourne Park Road and Ledbury Road.

COURTNEY TULLOCH: The Rio was a place where you could find black people, where you could go and sit down, where you could talk, where people had ideas and people expressed their dissatisfaction. People used to drop in: if there was a community centre for black people, it was the Rio, on Westbourne Park Road opposite the Great Western Road. I came there from Nottingham, where I'd been living with my parents, after it had been a centre that made the headlines during the Profumo Affair. They all used to come to the late-night sessions down in the Grove to meet these eccentric 'newcomers' as Colin MacInnes called them. *Absolute Beginners* and all that type of flavour was coming in. Night-time people: these lovely blacks amongst us who will liven up the night-time and make our city a little bit more full of flavour ... Which was what the Rio meant to people like Stephen Ward and so on. All kinds of people in high places used to go for their quaint cup of coffee down in the ghetto. Slumming.

The Rio represents a lot of different things to different people. There were people who would buy a bottle of whisky, go to the Rio, take it out of their coat pocket, sit down, pour it in a cup and drink it; there were people who sat down, smoked a cigarette, had a coffee and reminisced about when they were growing up in Trinidad; there were people who looked through the window to see which white is coming down the road and wonder what do they want and how could they con them. And for certain white kids it might have been a place where you scored drugs. People who were in that line of business may well have used the Rio, and people knew they could contact them there. I don't think the café was responsible for dealing; it was a café and people used it for all kinds of different things. It was a late-night place and people used it.

MICK FARREN: Across the street from Trocchi and de Freitas' record store was a corner store called the Safari Tent which was run by some old gay black geezer and you got odd people in there, really odd people, geezers in pork-pie hats who looked like Mingus. I used to buy reefers off motherfuckers like that. There was a couple of white dudes who sold reefer, but I think they just bought more off the same guys. This was all left over from Colin MacInnes' time. That was where I went, with all these bopsters. We went to see the Rolling Stones, whatever, all that sort of shit, but this whole kind of post-bop stuff was . . . interesting. The blacks in London were highly involved until we got our own shit together. When I got to the Grove there weren't any white joints, apart from the pubs, and that was only really Henekey's and Finch's. There was a cusp between Colin MacInnes and the hippies, between the old-time academic beatniks and the younger hipsters.

COURTNEY TULLOCH: Colin MacInnes fed off what was happening in the Grove. It was something for him to write about. Colin was around, he was a very regular person around. He knew most people, he learnt the accents and he tried to understand. And in his own peculiar way he tried to represent some things in a way which perhaps appealed to the sympathies of like-minded white liberals like himself.

HORACE OVE: Colin MacInnes was an angry white man. Angry with his world, his own class; angry about the way the white working class were treated in this country; angry about the way blacks were treated in this country, and he wanted to do something, and expose himself to it. He was one of the only writers that wanted to write about black people and live among black people, and he got beaten up by black people, slept with them, ate with them, and wrote about them, and he understood them because he exposed himself in the most dangerous situations to find out.

51

His only fault was that he was pushing too hard, he was angrier than them. So although black people got involved with Colin and understood him and he helped a lot, they were still a bit scared of him in a way, because he would get very upset if he didn't understand what was going on, and what you should do with it. He was the only person who wrote an interesting article about Michael [de Freitas] after everybody had condemned him. I found him very interesting because I got very friendly with Colin. The first time I met him we had a big argument and he said, 'I like that. I like someone who fights back.' I got to know him and he took me into McGibbon & Kee and demanded that I did some of his book covers. So I did *Absolute Beginners* and others. They didn't want to employ me: I was a West Indian and what did any West Indian know about photography? And Colin said, 'If you don't do it you can't publish my books.' He was like that.

Drugs: 'You couldn't give grass away'

PETER BROWN: In those days it was a little like *Absolute Beginners*. We always smoked hash, nobody smoked grass. All the blacks smoked grass. All the white, middle-class, so-called hippies dealt and smoked hash. So the hash business was in white hands and the grass business was in black hands. Hash was £7 an ounce, grass was £5 and, believe you me, you couldn't give grass away, hash was so cheap.

PETER SHERTSER: There was a great division between black and white. If you went to a black club you felt very much on your own. Most of the dealings you had with blacks, in Notting Hill, was to go and get some smoke. But the black guys always dealt in weed, which was not always of good quality, and the white guys always dealt in hash – and never the twain really met.

RICHARD TRENCH: There were a few dealers who were black and they were funky. You wanted to meet the black women but somehow you didn't, you only met the black men. There was the Flamingo where you could hear soul, but the real reason you'd go there was because you'd be the escort: some girl would want to go there but they didn't want to go with you, they wanted to get picked up by some black guy. Not that you realised it at the time. The dealers would often be older, in their 30s, and cooler, and you'd be on your best behaviour. But blacks were much more a concept than a reality. A highly approved concept.

GENE MAHON: The first time I smoked grass was when I was living in

Hampstead and a friend of mine said, 'I was at a party last night with some Jamaicans and I've got some marijuana, would you like to try some?' and I said, 'Certainly.' I'd always read about it in *Evergreen Review*, funny stories about people being stoned. I was going down to the French in Old Compton Street and scoring ten-bob deals, then going down into the john in Cambridge Circus, which was in the middle of the island at that point, and rolling up big spliffs and smoking them in the street. All the dope came from Cyprus, and a ten-bob deal was a big handful in a wodge of newspaper.

I spent some time in a black household. Our amusement was to get seriously stoned, drink cider and eat foo-foo. Our great delight was to listen to a record of *Waiting for Godot*, the American cast recording with Bert Lahr. Wonderful! It was a favourite thing to put on when one was stoned.

JEFF DEXTER: I didn't smoke dope until 1965. There was always grass around the Flamingo but I didn't smoke it for a long time. I wasn't paranoid about drugs. I'd taken Purple Hearts, they were part of the new culture. Just to keep your head so you could work, then go out all night and move on without sleeping or eating, not worrying about going home for dinner. It was hard to stay in the straight world, but I carried on with Mecca right up until 1966 when one night I had to come on after Ike and Tina Turner at the Hammersmith Palais. They'd just done an hour and we had to close the show. I had dropped acid, which I'd been taking for a while, so I could watch the Turners and then I came on stage and looked around at the band. They looked really horrible. It was so absurd to follow Ike and Tina Turner with Ray McVay, who were just doing their job, playing the hits of the day. I looked at the band and thought, 'That's it. That's the past. We have to move on.'

MILES: Early in '65 Hoppy had got together with Kate Heliczer. At this point Sue and I had moved into a room in Westbourne Terrace. There was Hoppy and a woman called Gala Mitchell, a guy called Alan Beckett, John Howe upstairs. Peter Wollen had had the room we moved into. An important person who had lived there was a woman called Alexandra who was a junkie. I nursed her through her first cold turkey in '64 and I've never felt romantic about junk ever since. There were also bloodstains all over the bathroom ceiling where some friend of Burroughs had been shooting up. There was definitely a drug interest in the apartment. There was a great deal of pot. Drugs in 1965 were almost entirely pot and hashish, hashish normally arriving in half-kilo blocks. Hoppy was a main

53

dealer. People went to the West Indians but where did the West Indians get it? Where did Lucky Gordon come to score? Westbourne Terrace. People like Nick Schoumatoff from Oxford used to come up to score. Johnny Byrne and I co-edited a literary magazine, called *Night Train*. Thom Keyes was another key person. All those people were responsible for the forerunner of UFO. They became very involved with something called the Happenings Club.

The Goings-On: 'A very anarchic stage act'

SUE MILES: The very first thing was the Goings-On, which was Sunday afternoons. That was all the old poet people like Johnny Byrne and Hawkins and the Pink Floyd – the first time I ever heard the Pink Floyd. Squeak, squeak – I told Miles, 'They'll never catch on ...' Anybody could get up and do anything they wanted. It was actually very good in a funny sort of way. There was all sorts of poets, bits of magic – Spike Hawkins dropping bits of broken egg down Johnny Byrne's back. Then there was something that Mal Dean did, also on Sunday afternoons.

JOHNNY BYRNE: Hawkins and I used to do things down at the Marquee. We called ourselves the Poison Bellows. We'd do a very anarchic stage act where we used to burn up things and set them alight and throw buckets of water over them and it was very crazy. We had this thing about people who used to go around saying 'Yeah, yeah' to everything and we really wanted to shock people out of that and really get their critical faculties working. One of the things that happens in any movement is that people accept anything, and we simply wanted to shake them out of that and so Hawkins and I would do anti-magical tricks and anti-conjuring tricks and fairly shocking things. It didn't last very long because part of the act was an enormously heavy pianola and we couldn't cart it around.

Westbourne Terrace: 'I had to teach myself offset printing'

JOHN HOPKINS: I met Miles a long way back, and Sue Miles, because like many people they came to stay in my place in Westbourne Terrace. Miles was really interesting: he didn't hold with any of this hierarchical who you can speak to and who you can't. I think he was the first person to publish Burroughs or Ginsberg in the UK.

Miles and I published a thing called *Longhair Times*. I had to teach myself offset printing. I bought a printing press and set it up in my room in Queensway. So I taught myself offset litho printing in order to print this thing, because we couldn't afford a printer. There was one

54

edition: mainly Ginsberg, with a scattering of luminaries like Ferlinghetti and so on; Archie Shepp – I went to New York and got him to give me a poem.

MILES: Hoppy and I were very close at that time. When I was at Cheltenham, I usually stayed at his place on Westbourne Terrace when I hitch-hiked up. We worked pretty well together. The first thing we did was to release an album of a poetry reading by Ginsberg, Ferlinghetti, Voznesensky and Corso that was held at the Architectural Association in the summer of '65. Just after the Albert Hall, but nobody knew about it. We were just going to bring out little magazines, but in fact what first happened was we brought out this spoken word album. Hoppy and I had started this company called Lovebooks Ltd with Michael Henshaw, who was our accountant. Mike was also Centre 42's accountant, and for Pauline Beoty and Clive Goodwin and all kinds of theatrical people, everyone involved in the 'kitchen sink' school of drama: the hip accountant.

SUE MILES: There was this group, living in Hoppy's flat at 108 Westbourne Terrace. Miles and I, Hoppy, Peter Wollen, John Howe, Adam Ritchie, Alan Beckett, Gala Mitchell, who was in *Blow-Up* – quite a lot of us. And there was a split there. There were the theoreticals, the *New Left Review* mob. They didn't have anything to do with things like the Albert Hall poetry reading. Much too messy, much too nasty, much too like real life. A lot of things like, 'Shall we take the lid off Bhutan this month?' and I remember someone saying, 'But I hate the workers, really . . .' So there was a division: those who were getting involved in this messy, *On the Road*, Dylan world, and the others. And that coincided with the Beatles, and with Donovan. 'Sunny Goodge Street'! He used to sing at poetry readings at Better Books – while Miles fixed the projector or whatever.

The New Left: 'An intellectual fashion really'

ROBIN BLACKBURN: We were smoking dope too. Though I don't think we necessarily believed that this was making a huge political statement. It was much as one might also be drinking wine of an evening. By itself I don't think it added up to a very hefty political statement. But among the things that defined a new Left, as against a traditional, rather stuffy old Left, was that one was not upset by and even saw a role for hash or LSD. One would say that it assisted a little bit in knowing oneself, but really it was just having fun. It was an element of hedonism. And that's also why we would write about rock. Certainly people would never turn on at office meetings. We wouldn't imagine that our political senses would be improved; still less would we have pints of beer or wine. If you're having a political discussion you're having that. But afterwards . . .

DICK POUNTAIN: I was a Communist from my first year at college. In my first year I started reading Marx and Engels, I read the *Dialectics of Nature*. A bunch of guys in my year were in the CP and they signed me up. I wasn't really very political at school at all except I had one friend who was a mathematical genius who became an anarchist and he had a bit of an effect on me, but you couldn't be political at school. When you were at school in those days you were a schoolboy, there was no real question of anything else. I stayed in the CP for about three years. It entailed mainly student politicking, which at that time was largely connected with Greece, cos there were heavy things connected with Greece and there were a lot of Greek students at Imperial [College]. We used to do things like helping them take over the London Hellenic Association for the Left. It was just before the coup.

NINA FISHMAN: I started at the University of Sussex in the autumn of 1965. I was nineteen. I'd come from America where I'd done two years at the University of Colorado in Boulder. My orientation with the Left was via Cambridge where I had a boyfriend. In 1962 when I was a schoolgirl of sixteen, my father had had a fellowship in economics at Cambridge and I had been a groupie of the Cambridge University Left. What had been happening between 1962 and 1965 was the last red dawn of CND. It was that period when what was gestating was the alternative society but what it looked like was very much what student left-wing politics had always looked like since the war. The people I knew were luminaries of the Cambridge University Labour Club: Alan Green, Ben Brewster, Regan Scott, Anthony Barnett, James Hinton, although he was in the Communist Party. That is another feature of the time: you were either in the Labour Party or the Communist Party. People would come to my flat and have discussions about, 'Could Bukharin be resurrected? Could Bukharin be made the hero?' The focus was still very post-war in that one was looking back to the Russian Revolution. Tony Cliff's book about Russia was a seminal tract which had to be read. This was the time when the New Left actually became fashionable. Suddenly Ben Brewster and Anthony Barnett began to have discussions with Perry Anderson and Robin Blackburn and translate Lukács, etc. It was an intellectual fashion really. What was interesting, as it always is when anything changes as seminally as it did in that period, was that intellectually the Old Left was

56

no longer defensible to these kids at Cambridge. One of the reasons for this has to be the coincidence of 60s prosperity. I don't think CND had any influence on this. CND was very much an expression of the old left-wing moralism.

DAVID WIDGERY: I'd been a pacifist and encountered CND. Then I got involved in CND and the people who seemed to be pushing things in CND turned out to be the Young Communist League (YCL) which in those days were quite a culturally tough group, they were always at the front of the Aldermaston march and they'd play guitars and so on. And I thought they seemed to be good and they were the ones making the running. The ideology didn't matter, I just drifted into the people who looked like they were having a good social scene where you might meet a girlfriend and that type of thing. I joined them in Slough. And the main leader of the Communist Party in Slough was a park attendant called Sid Rawle. He was a NUPE shop steward and eventually he was given an island by John Lennon. However, I had joined the wrong Communist Party branch. It had actually been heavily infiltrated by Trotskyists and I was expelled almost immediately in a mass purge: 'You, you and you – out!' They included me by mistake but I became an honorary Trotskyist simply by being expelled, and I went through this rapid Trotskyfication in the SLL [Socialist Labour League] which was a very tough, quite proletarian, doctrinaire group. I had about a year of that: lots of meetings – you had to learn off by heart the five reasons why James Buchanan betrayed the 4th International – lots of paper-selling, things like that. Quite educational and it inoculated me against that sort of fanaticism ever since. You had to learn what Marx said and what Lenin said and what dialectical materialism is and so on. Something that everyone should go through, but only once, and not for very long.

Happenings: 'A quality of regression'

JOHN HOPKINS: 'Happening' was the name for a generalised event, thought to be run by an artist. This was an excuse for not following the script. There were some really great happenings at Better Books. A room full of smoke and people sitting around and all falling over each other and it was terribly erotic, something you weren't expecting at all.

JEFF NUTTALL: Bob Cobbing, who was for a while the manager of the Better Books paperback department, is a very pivotal figure at this time. He was in on everything. I met him through Art Together, which was something he was running in Finchley. The writers' wing was called Writers' Forum, the visual artists were called Group H and the music

57

wing was called Music Now or something like that. We made things, we had exhibitions, we had poetry readings. We were both teaching and for a while we both taught at the Alder School, a big and terrible secondary modern school in East Finchley, right in the middle of the most hideous estate. We put out *My Own Mag* and various other publications from the Alder School. And we also involved the pupils in what we were doing. We had this thing called the Rhubarb Club. We did these wild paintings, the kids wrote poetry and the headmaster was absolutely terrified. Cobbing and I did these disastrous exhibitions, extremely scandalous. I did one with sculptures made of condoms. We had a lot of trouble with the chairman of the Finchley Art Society at that time, who was an extremely reactionary person and who would throw a lot of flak at some of our exhibits. Her name was Margaret Thatcher. We had a wonderful time shadow-boxing Margaret Thatcher. She came along to a Group H exhibition and said, 'That must be removed.' It was one of the most innocuous works in the show – a splash of white paint on a piece of white board. An action painting. We tried to get her to say why it was obscene and we discovered that she thought it was an ejaculation. There was real filth all over the bloody walls and she picks the one thing that isn't.

DAVID ROBINS: If I could have some of these people erased from my mind by hypnosis Bob Cobbing would be the one I'd start with. He was an elderly geezer. He was certainly in his fifties back then. Those people came into their own then. What they were all about was people like Ezra Pound and so on and they wanted to do something like that in England. But they didn't have what it took. It was all an attempt by the Brits to get some kind of native avant-garde going. Jeff Nuttall and so on. Inflatables, happenings, and so on.

JEFF NUTTALL: I was going to do this happening and Mike Kustow said that he could line up the cast of the *Marat/Sade* to do it for me. All I would have to do would be to write the scenario, design it and direct them. But they were just back from their American tour and Mike said they didn't want to do it – they were too tired. Actually I think he probably forgot to tell them. I was living at the time at a place called the Abbey Arts Centre in Barnet, a Victorian place with four strange art nouveau cabins inhabited by artists. So I knocked on various doors and simply asked people if they wanted to do it. And they did. We did the happening and we liked doing it and I said, 'If we want to stick together we can do a happening every two weeks – and I know where: in the Better Books basement.' And so we did. The first one we did was an exhibition of ourselves. We fitted ourselves out as sculptures and

58

prepared ourselves in various ways, wrapping stuff round ourselves, and I hid myself behind a screen and just had my belly and my prick and one finger coming through holes. People were sent invitations to a private view. So they came round and looked at the sculptures. They were served sherry, which was what you got at private views, and they wandered round and said, 'They're real . . .' and a girl touching my belly said, 'Well, it's warm.' And that was called the People Show – and that was the first People Show.

JONATHAN PARK: In the mid-60s there were many Hampstead bottle parties where the most rank Beaujolais was drunk and fake poetry was talked about. I went to many of those, but in the late 60s, under the influence of the Americans who had come over, rather more diverse parties would take place, with strange events which were in the nature of happenings. Scottie and Hermine and Graham Stevens and Modelle Jardine were happening artists who worked in that milieu. They concentrated on inflatable creations.

Scottie was a mystery: a real jingle-jangle Mr Tambourine Man; he wore that sort of clothes. He concentrated on inflatable pricks which could be anything from 20 to 40 feet and in some cases 200 feet long. He was one of the first English people to be inspired by American happening artists and he understood that the Americans, despite their radicalism, did manage to obtain money for their various activities. He understood this equation and determined to fleece whoever he could for whatever he could get. He would promise untold joys, crowd interaction, artistic endeavours, amazing manifestations and con them for as much money as he could get – which was probably 10 shillings. He called himself Swizpricks, because all he used to do was manipulate a large inflated phallus. Sometimes he'd get inside and sit in the balls, shooting Verey lights out of the top. He'd blow up these cocks any time and anywhere and completely destroy anything that was going on. We did this event at St Katherine's Dock, before it had been gentrified, and he sat in the balls setting off explosives and lights and so on and he burnt himself. Thereafter he always wore an asbestos waistcoat, asbestos armband and asbestos chaps. Dr Who crossed with a cowboy.

DAVID ROBINS: A lot of people got involved in putting out little magazines and writing poems for three other people to read and that was their life and some of them are still doing it. Mike Horovitz is still doing it. *New Departures* is like New College, Oxford. New College, Oxford, which is 500 years old, is still called New College, it's the same about Horovitz and *New Departures*. There's nothing new about Michael: he's a terrible poet and always will be a terrible poet. The Liverpool poets are the same: their work eerily remains untouched, there's no inner changes in them. But in the 60s Brian Patten was being talked about by the glitterati as the new Shakespearian wonder. Looked at now, there was a quality of regression in the whole scene. The Beatles' music was kind of regressive, nursery rhymes, and it sounds like it now. What you've got here, in this avant-garde, is the liggers.

Better Books: 'A labyrinth which was supposed to be an indictment of society'

MILES: After college I went down Charing Cross Road to try to get a job and things in those days were so different. I got a job just like that, within a few hours. In a bookshop. I'd always wanted to work in Better Books because Better Books was the hot place, you could get all these imported Grove Press books and stuff and City Lights books. There were no jobs going there but I got a job next door at Joseph Poole's. But I hung out at Better Books a lot. It had started around '58, an offshoot of Bumpus, and they were both owned by Tony Godwin. When a job came up in Better Books' paperback section, round the corner in New Compton Street, he employed me to be the manager of the section.

SUE MILES: So I was at art college, and Miles was running Better Books and publishing *Longhair* magazine. Basically what happened was that there was a switch-over to rock'n'roll and the Beatles. It was the summer. And we were all terribly poo-pooey about pop music. It was all serious, grim jazz. The North Lancashire Jazz Appreciation Society used to meet in a flat we lived in. All with little goatees and their berets and you never went to a party without somebody appearing with their bongos. Everyone was 'man' and 'cats' and completely sexist. We were all 'chicks'.

MILES: For the whole of 1965 I was the manager. It was the time that Jeff Nuttall did his event in the basement, when you had to crawl through a tunnel and got covered in feathers; William Burroughs' voice was played on a tape recorder.

JEFF NUTTALL: The sTigma was a sort of labyrinth which was supposed to be an indictment of society. It would look very tatty and very comic now. We did consider turning live snakes and live rats loose in it. It was supposed to be a shocker, to drive people out of their minds.

MICHELENE WANDOR: There was Jeff Nuttall, but I didn't like his scatology. He was very much at the centre and very important, though I

60

thought he was off the wall. I went to a couple of events in Better Books, but not some of the more esoteric happenings in which you had to crawl through things. I thought that was disgusting, condoms hanging from wires and so on.

MILES: I was very involved with auto-destructive art, and Gustav Metzger and all those guys came in. The two prevailing movements were happening art on the one side and pop art on the other. I had been to the Young Contemporaries show in 1960, the star pupils from the Royal College of Art, and been very moved by Hockney. Had I had £40 I would have bought one, but my entire grant was £50 ... The people we were really knocked out by were Warhol and Claus Oldenberg, Rauschenberg ... the pop artists.

America: 'Almost no one actually *went*'

PETER JENNER: There was this spirit, this idea that there should be some sort of linkage with America. I'd gone to America and seen all the jazz and blues. America was much more exciting than it is now – because you couldn't get there easily. You couldn't get records unless they were issued in England: there were no imports. The same with books. There wasn't easy communication with America. People didn't flip from one to the other in the way they do now. There was an awareness of what was happening in America, but an enormous ignorance about it. A lot of rumours. I don't think that makes the English underground an *ersatz* culture, though. It was inspired by the West Coast but it was very, very English. While we read our Ferlinghetti and read our *Naked Lunch* and Jack Kerouac and we read about what was happening in San Francisco, almost no one actually *went*. So it was all our own manifestation and we took on that spirit. We took on the PR of it, rather than the reality of it, so it wasn't absolutely imitative, and that was what was so important and that's why it was interesting and that's why it was creative.

MARK BOYLE: In my mind one of the problems was that all this PR about what was coming from the States began to affect what was happening naturally here. People had been following what seemed to us to be a natural course and suddenly there were all these intrusions from over the Atlantic. People began to think they ought to be more American and people really believed that they were actually following that idea. Which was wrong, because we weren't.

JOE BOYD: The Englishness of groups like the Beatles, Rolling Stones, Pink Floyd was easily as marked a characteristic as their Americanness.

61

In a way, the best groups, the most influential, the most powerful and the ones that did best in America were the ones that were quite unafraid to be English. In a way, Americans, if they sang blues, were obsessed with sounding like black men, whereas Mick Jagger, the Englishman, showed them all how to sing blues and be unashamed of being white and being a kind of tarty little English schoolboy. There wasn't the same awkwardness, it was a much more relaxed position towards shopping in different cultures among the English.

SUE MILES: Miles and I were younger but we were still actually the tail end of the 50s, aping the Americana: Chuck Berry, Big Bopper, lager, dope, *On the Road* (in *England*?) – all copying American culture, and we were very old-fashioned. We were not pushed by any major issues. There was no draft, you could piss around in England quite a lot. Whereas in America when it got to Vietnam it became serious – if you went against society they came after you and they put you away for thirty years.

ROBIN BLACKBURN: The American underground seemed to be the real thing, the original expression. I was quite entertained by them. They had a spark for which we were very grateful. The thing that we were deeply relating to was American culture. We did make our own contribution to it, which was basically English rock music. And that was quite impressive, it was something of real world class. But as far as much of the counter-culture was concerned, the leading edge of what was happening was in the United States. In the first place the Vietnam War, however much one might demonstrate against it here, was theirs. You also had things like experimental cinema groups, writing, the sheer numbers of alternative newspapers. There was a tremendous sense of vitality.

JONATHAN MEADES: The English underground seemed to be almost totally preoccupied with the American avant-garde, which was very formless and unrigorous compared with the French avant-garde of that time. People in the English underground were very much taken with 'anything goes'. The European avant-garde was extremely alien to the Anglo-Saxon mind. I always felt that there was a terrific, not exactly antipathy towards mainland Europe among my contemporaries, but a kind of studied indifference. Those were the years when people would go off to Morocco. They didn't go to France particularly, they didn't go to Italy. They looked towards Morocco or India or the States. Yet up to about '65 or '66 there were still a lot of French movies being shown and something like John Calder's list had various titles – Beckett, Robbe-Grillet – that were part of that culture. American culture up to that time

62

had been a tributary culture but by the late 60s it had taken over and become the mainstream. People like Miles didn't really know about European culture, none of them knew anything at all from a literary or theatrical point of view. Part of it was that they despised writers. They revered social prophets, but writers as such . . .

Pop Art: 'Targets, chevrons, crisp hard edges'

PEARCE MARCHBANK: What I liked about the Who and the Beatles and Stones was that they took what they liked from previous generations but there was this whole new thing going on. It was primary colours, it was hard-edged, it was crisp. *Ready Steady Go!* sums it up. If there'd been a rock 'n' roll *Monitor*, that would have been a beat generation programme. But *Ready Steady Go!* was targets, chevrons, bright colours, crisp hard edges.

There were fantastic art exhibitions in London. In 1964 there was this great big show called the Gulbenkian and there was *54-64* at the Tate, which had a whole room full of American pop art: Rauschenberg, Jasper Johns, targets and flags and what have you. Then you'd drift off to see the Who and you'd put two and two together. There seemed to be a direct line between what was on at the Tate Gallery and what was on at the Marquee. The hard-edge school of painting was going on in New York, the cool school, people like Larry Poons and Ad Reinhardt were painting in New York. Their stuff was being shown in Britain. Peter Blake, David Hockney had just come out of the Royal College and were starting to work on their own and being exhibited all over the place. The Robert Fraser Gallery, which got terribly trendy later, had opened. All those people were being influenced by something that was to do with fun, to do with 400-foot-long popsicles, painted by a man who used to actually paint real billboards. That was Rosenquist. The thing was that it was bright and clean and new, and to me Ginsberg, Ferlinghetti and Burroughs were to do with something that was messy and dusty and old, even though I appreciated a lot of the content of their work, when I actually sat down and bothered with it. But Hockney wore a gold lamé jacket, and they were wearing seamen's sweaters, duffel coats, wellington boots and baggy trousers and sandals.

The thing that first attracted me to CND was the logo, it's brilliant. But when you went into the marches, they weren't sharp enough. Pathologically I was a mod. Listen to the first chords of 'I Can't Explain' by the Who. One of the best openings of any pop song written and it's absolutely clean and concise, just like what they wore on stage, before they got into the 'Magic Bus' era. Tight and clean, just like the look of the catalogues at the Robert Fraser Gallery.

NIGEL WAYMOUTH: Pop art was very much in vogue. There were certain trends in painting at the time that influenced design, very much so; but they also came together with this rather softer vision, slightly more art nouveau-ish, cult, the druggy side, the softer edges. I suppose there was a psychedelic school: Michael [English] and I who were a team, Martin Sharp, Mike McInnerney. We were quite jealous of each other, but we were all great mates and I suppose we did rub off on each other what we were doing. We wanted to project the same ideas.

Wholly Communion: 'What's the biggest hall in town?'

MICK FARREN: In 1965 basically two things happened: we found that up the other end of the Grove there were some other people who looked like us. And down in Chelsea there were people who looked like us, but we didn't know how to get in touch with them. The first thing that I recall was the Wholly Communion poets' conference, which I didn't actually go to . . . because if I'd gone I'd have had to be painted blue, because my friend Alex was involved with something that Jeff Nuttall was doing.

SUE MILES: Allen Ginsberg came to England in May and he stayed with Miles and me in Hanson Street. He came as a result of being invited to Cuba and the Cuban police not liking his sexual carryings on, and they found his notebooks and they deported him and the only place they could send him was Prague. And the Czechs had much the same response to him. He was then sent to Moscow and then he went back to Prague where he was voted King of May by the students and he was deported to London after this, having not paid a single penny for this world tour. He stayed with us and he had Barbara Rubin with him. She was an experimental film-maker whose great technique was to run the film through the camera twice. And swing it round her head. He was 38 and into taking his clothes off. All the time.

MILES: I met the Beatles by default. I met them through Ginsy. He didn't know them but he wanted to know them and he was introduced to them by Dylan. It wasn't a very successful meeting. Then in '65 on his birthday, June 3, he wanted to have the Beatles to his birthday, he thought that would be nice. So since I already knew how to contact them we invited them all. George and John came to the birthday party, which was held in Chester Square. The trouble was that by the time John and George arrived, with their wives, Allen had taken all his clothes off and had his underpants on his head and a No Waiting sign hanging round his

64

dick. John was very upset at finding Allen completely naked. First of all he and George instinctively looked around to check that there were no photographers, then John told me, 'You don't do that in front of the birds.'

MICHAEL HOROVITZ: The Beatles came to Ginsberg's birthday party at David Larcher's pad in Kensington and were embarrassed because he stripped naked. He thought this was appropriate – be in your birthday suit for your birthday party. Although Lennon and McCartney quite liked him, they also kept this piss-taking distance from it all, from Ginsberg in particular, and from the rest of the poets. Miles was a useful shield who kept them apart from the heavy paranoia of some of the people such as Harry Fainlight who some of the time very much wanted to be promoted on the pop level. So the pop world and poetry world were feeding each other, but they still kept apart.

DAVID WIDGERY: I went to interview Allen Ginsberg for *Sixth Form Opinion*. When he was in London for the poetry reading I attached myself to him, not knowing anything about sex in general and homo-sexuality in particular, and Ginsberg took a tremendous fancy to me and seduced me. I eventually managed to escape on my Lambretta and got home with a sore bum and a bit of apprehension.

So I hooked up with Ginsberg and was rather taken over by that and thought it was all rather good. At that time he was going through a very intense mystical thing, but we were all moving rather more politically because of the influence of Vietnam. He was very much 'Everyone must make love tonight, everyone must meditate, the Viet Cong must join with the Americans and suck each other's cocks,' and that really wasn't what we were saying. We were saying the Vietnamese must beat the Americans, so there was this discrepancy.

MILES: 1965, June. I was managing the paperback section of Better Books. En route to New York from Prague, Ginsberg stopped off in London. Having got to London he came in to Better Books. He had nowhere to stay. We immediately suggested that he did a reading there. So Ginsy came in and I offered to put him up and he moved in with us in Hanson Street. He gave a reading at Better Books which, even though we didn't advertise it, was totally packed. Half the audience were Ameri-can. Gerard Malanga, Warhol, Edie Sedgwick, even Baby Jane Holzer – the whole lot were over here: Andy was swinging through Europe on a big promotional trip. And Barbara Rubin came over, and all the people from *Fuck You* magazine, and Kate Heliczer who was the star of the most famous Warhol movie of all where Gerard Malanga gives her a blow-job – the first time that had ever been put on film. She brought tapes of the Velvet Underground who at that time hadn't made any records.

SUE MILES: There was an afternoon when Allen realised that Gregory Corso was in Paris, Ferlinghetti was coming to London, Pablo Neruda and Pablo Fernandez were here, and Andrei Voznesensky. Major international poets, nearly all in London and this should be celebrated: there should be a poetry reading.

MILES: There was a gathering in Better Books down where the poetry readings took place. There was Dan Richter, the editor of a magazine called *Residue*, an American who had moved to London because his wife was English. He had been one of the apes at the beginning of *2001*. Sue Miles, Barbara Rubin, Kate Heliczer, and there was a Dutch girl. We were discussing how crowded Ginsberg's reading had been and how one should do some more readings and where could we have them. We discussed a number of places and they were all turned down on the basis that they really weren't big enough.

SUE MILES: Barbara Rubin turned round and said, 'What's the biggest hall in town?' and we all went 'The Albert Hall.' And she got the phone, dialled the number and said, 'Hi. How much is it to book the Albert Hall?' '£450.' 'When's the next free date?' 'Ten days' time.' 'We'll have it.' Down with the phone and that was it. Dan Richter's wife Jill put the money up. There were ten days in which to publicise it.

MILES: We were all saying, 'Gee, that's a bit ambitious . . .' and so on. Then we thought, 'Well, American know-how and everything. These people know things that we don't know . . .' Barbara was very very good at promotion: she called up every newspaper in town and we had daily press conferences, photo sessions on the Albert Memorial, daily bulletins, and boosted it as a big international poetry reading. Everybody was going to be there: Voznesensky, Ferlinghetti and Corso who were in Paris, Simon Vinkenoog from Amsterdam, Pablo Fernandez, the Cultural Attaché for the Cuban Embassy and a poet, and all kinds of people. They all promised, though they didn't all necessarily read in the end. We caught the press's attention and we got lots of articles.

It was all very hectic: I was using Better Books as the headquarters for ticket sales but that fairly rapidly moved off elsewhere. The impetus switched to an apartment on Cromwell Road, which was where Paolo

Leonni was living. He was a buddy of Gregory Corso from Rome. A guy called John Esam, who lived there, got involved and people do suggest that that was where the money went. Ferlinghetti arrived from Paris and he moved in with Julie Felix the folk singer, who had a TV show and was hanging out with these strange people who were followers of Bart Hugues, a Dutch madman who believed that the only way to really get ahead was to get a hole: trepanation, which he had indeed performed upon himself. Everyone you talked to about it instantly had lots of friends who'd get involved and there was this endlessly growing constituency. One realised that there really were a lot of people interested, but the catalysts were all American, I'm afraid.

MICHAEL HOROVITZ: In the years 1960–63 there was a lot of poetry performance going on, a lot of it with jazz musicians or things like [John] McGrath's plays or Cardew's music, and the Goings-On (although that was later). We had big concerts in St Pancras Town Hall, some with jazz, some with CND. So this sort of performance was gradually multiplying in different parts of the country, gradually opening up with more people taking part. Then in 1965 I met with Ginsberg and Trocchi in Better Books and we hatched this plot to hire the Albert Hall and have a big poetry reading.

I was very much involved in the setting up of the Albert Hall gig. John Esam and Dan Richter did the business. Richter's wife put up the money. There was this woman called Barbara Rubin who was tagging along, quite a powerful Jewish New York entrepreneur. She was going to film it, but in the end it was Peter Whitehead. They conceived the idea with Ginsberg and me. I had arranged Ginsberg's first reading at the ICA, in May 1965, and that was very successful. He'd just been in India and was playing his bells and chanting, and I joined in the chanting. This Tibetan chanting I remember as being the background sound to that summer. We decided to have a bigger reading, and Ginsberg said, 'Yes, let's bring together you English assholes.' There was a lot of conflict and Ginsberg somewhat resented the fact that we'd made our own scene and worked differently and he was rather competitive. But essentially he wanted to bring everything together and we planned this big thing in the Albert Hall. We decided to do it, then about ten poets had a meeting at Trocchi's house in St Stephen's Gardens [W11] and improvised this Invocation which was published as part of the programme. Esam, Trocchi, Pablo Fernandez (who didn't turn up at the gig, we assumed that the Cuban Embassy, where he'd been Cultural Attaché, stopped him mixing with decadent bourgeois degenerates), Ginsberg, Paolo Leonni, Fainlight, Ferlinghetti, Richter, Simon Vinkenoog and I. So Esam and

Richter dealt with the administration and Ginsberg and Trocchi and I dealt with the artistic side. We did a lot of work, put Ginsberg on television, sprayed all the press, and quickly got masses of helpers. It was a glorious summer and people were in the mood of going to the next party and that was the big summer party: poetry at the Albert Hall.

MARK BOYLE: It was the technique that was the key thing, the absolutely brilliant technique. They announced to everyone who they were getting. They named three people who were coming from America – Corso, Ferlinghetti and Ginsberg – and none of them were booked when they announced it. But because they announced these three, everyone wanted to be in on it.

CHRISTOPHER LOGUE: American beat culture may well lie at the root of the underground, but I was ten years older and I really wasn't much involved with it. In fact the only time I became involved with it was at that poetry reading at the Albert Hall, which wasn't organised by the beats at all. It was organised by Alex Trocchi. He put it together with the boy who did the mime inside the ape-skin for *2001*, Dan Richter, and John Esam. Esam, Richter and Trocchi did the organising. It was much more Trocchi's thing, much more to do with his kind of proselytising for something called *Sigma* that he had going at the time with Jeff Nuttall.

Really the thing that made the Albert Hall reading in terms of the number of people who knew about it, and went to it, was the BBC news. It was marvellous weather, there was a continual atmosphere of goodwill and the opportunity to do things in the air and that lasted for a long time. Trocchi called me up and said, 'Why don't you come down to the Albert Memorial. There's a lot of really interesting people just hanging about.' This was on the Saturday. So I went down there and there were a lot of people there, quite interesting-looking people, and it was fun and it was sunny and the girls were very pretty and what more could you ask for . . . It was a very quiet time in society. There were no troubles, no serious troubles, no great dispute or feeling of anger or hatred. And the BBC had nothing to report on their Nine O'Clock News. Somebody had told them about this so they came down and they did a long ten-minute item which they put out at nine pm. It was a marvellous item. Clearly the news editors were delighted. And it announced the show and the whole of the South of England saw it, that this poetry reading was going to take place at the Albert Hall from six o'clock onwards the following day – you could not have asked for better publicity. So the next day the Albert Hall was full.

MILES: By the time we actually reached the Albert Hall the programme was enormous. Everybody wanted to do something: Bruce Lacey wanted to do something with his robots. He was a mad anarchist, been in the Beatles' first film. Jeff Nuttall was working with him. Their particular event never happened because somehow or other Jeff got welded to a bath in Sir John Barbirolli's dressing-room backstage. Lacey had filled the bath with some kind of green goo which Jeff got stuck to.

JEFF NUTTALL: I was going to perform a happening with John Latham, and he covered himself with blue paint and this blocked his pores and he passed out. And he had to be put in a bath. I had funny paint on as well and I got in the bath with him. The caretaker, who was outraged by whoever these people were who had taken over the Albert Hall, came into the dressing-room, suspecting that drugs were being smoked. 'What's going on 'ere?' and people just giggled cos they were stoned out of their heads. Then he burst into the bathroom and said, 'Oh my Gawd, oh my Gawd!' and went. I didn't read myself, but I heard the readings. It was superb. Ginsberg was wonderful, Ferlinghetti too – all the professional rhetorical readers were very good indeed. [Harry] Fainlight was the star by default. He got pilloried. He was going to read his poem 'Spider' and he started to talk about 'Spider' and it was clear that he couldn't stop talking about it. He was delaying reading it by talking about it – which was something he frequently did. He was out of his bonce on amphetamines.

MILES: There were a lot of fuck-ups at that reading which no one really knew much about. Alex Trocchi was the compere; he insisted he had a major role being the older statesman, etc, etc. Out of his brain on heroin. I think we had about 7000 people, it was virtually full.

MICHAEL HOROVITZ: We all threw different things into the Invocation and Ginsberg insisted on this phrase 'You are not alone.' It did touch a lot of people, and it was in that poem 'Be Kind' Ginsberg wrote specially: 'Tonite let's all make love in London . . .' which Whitehead used as the epigraph for his book. The sort of society that the Albert Hall brought together was largely comprised of people who had read the beat poetry and come to our gigs or generally evolved their own different consciousnesses more or less privately, I think a lot of people came from out of London and hadn't been in cities where there had been much coming together, much communalism. To these people that line, and Mitchell's 'Tell me Lies about Vietnam', did offer a kind of catharsis and revolution and liberation. The Albert Hall event had a different kind of structure, unlike most other demonstrations at the time: people sitting and standing and chanting, dancing and smoking pot; it was mainly very ecstatic and very relaxed. Nuttall and John Latham brought strange papier mâché creatures that walked through the audience; there was this extended party feeling. It was a different kind of public meeting that, as far as I know, has never quite been emulated. Among those 7-8,000 people there must have been a few thousand who probably hadn't been to anything like that, hadn't heard the sort of things they'd been thinking or dreaming or confiding to a lover or onto paper, articulated in this explicit, bold, celebratory way.

CHRISTOPHER LOGUE: The idea of a gathering of the tribes – what rubbish! A lot of people who went to that poetry reading had never been to another poetry reading in their lives. Either before or since. It was an event. Normally you'd expect to get 25 people to a reading; if you were very lucky, 100. If you get a lot of publicity and there's maybe three or four good people or the Poet Laureate, 600. When at the Isle of Wight Festival I read to 150,000 people, it was not because of me – it was because of Bob Dylan. But at the Albert Hall it was the other way round – it was the poets that did it. They drew it. It was like all of those poetry readings – it had its moments. It was a very nice event. It was incredibly long-winded. You'd get some people on the stand and they had no idea about the audience, they just want to go on and on and on and you've literally got to tear them off the stand. It was quite funny: you had to send two other poets up to drag them down.

MICHAEL HOROVITZ: Some of the planning of the Albert Hall reading was at 101 Cromwell Road where John Esam and Nigel Gordon lived. At one time Logue came and asked to make a phonecall. And he was overheard saying in his loud, rasping voice, I'm sure quite deliberately, 'I'm in this bloody *pad* full of beatnik poets plotting to take over the world at the Albert Hall. They're all nuts. For God's sake come and bail me out . . .' I remember Esam saying, 'We've got to have Logue, because he said he'll come and throw bad eggs otherwise.' So on the one hand he was mocking us, but on the other he clearly wanted to be on the bill.

JIM HAYNES: Everybody said the same thing: 'God, I didn't know we were so many.' It was a realisation that 'God, I thought it was just me and a few friends, but *this* many . . .' That was the revelation of the evening. There were lots of people out there like us.

SUE MILES: I remember saying to Miles, 'What are you going to do if

450 people don't come?' That was the break-even point. 'Is Jill rich enough not to be paid back?' 7500 people rolled up! It was extraordinary, like suddenly discovering that there were more of you around than you thought. It was that kind of beginning. Ghastly poetry, unbelievably bad. A lot of English poets who really shouldn't have been allowed and a lot of people like Allen getting very drunk – because he had to wait seven hours. Burroughs didn't read but there was this tape played over the PA: 'You give me a garbage can and I'll sit and look at it for ever . . .'

MILES: The reading itself, despite all the publicity, was a dreadful reading. It was one of the worst poetry readings ever. Ginsberg was very upset by it. It was bad because he got drunk and gave a very poor reading. The audience was restless, they couldn't hear what was happening properly. Voznesensky refused to read. Things were so chaotic and he didn't want to be associated with it. Gregory [Corso] hadn't done a reading in two years, and he chose to read a pretty obscure, long autobiographical poem that was completely ill-suited to this situation. The main thing that was wrong with it was that forty poor English poets, poor quality that is, got up and read their awful bullshit and made the whole thing so boring. They had insinuated themselves and Trocchi could never say no to anyone. He just wasn't a good compere, he didn't know how to organise the thing or keep control of the mike. People used to rush off with the mike. Simon Vinkenoog, who was on an acid trip at the time, grabbed the mike and went rushing around shouting in Dutch.

MICHAEL HOROVITZ: At the Albert Hall Ginsberg and Simon Vinkenoog were saying, 'These drugs are wonderful,' and although I had originally followed that more or less mystical orthodoxy, I had found that the higher up I went with any drugs the harder were the bumps coming down. I didn't share the optimism that if all the governments dropped acid all the time everything would be OK. When Fainlight read a rather nightmare poem, 'The Spider', about his acid vision of horror in New York, Vinkenoog suddenly interrupts him, jumping up and down and waving his arms like a bird and crying, 'Oh come, man, come!' implying that he should be enjoying the drug and why doesn't he relax and open up and stop being such a fuddy-duddy intellectual. And Fainlight is going on about 'My heart is an oven baking spiritual bread / Come and eat of your fellow children,' rather attacking Ginsberg, as if he were making concentration camps for consciousness. Fainlight stared at him, and Vinkenoog is going, 'Come, man, come!' and Fainlight said, 'You naive idiot,' or something like that. 'This is all to say that these drugs aren't all sweetness and light.' And this introduced a real conflict into the

71

poetics of the evening. Some people didn't want to get into this heavy stuff, just wanted another poem, and were shouting 'Get him off!' and Fainlight, who was a very sensitive and uptight character, started agitating, and Trocchi got up with his pipe and tried to behave nicely and said, 'Come on, just read your poem, it's a good poem . . .' and Ginsberg was shouting, 'Read poem! Read poem!' and it all got very strident. But for Fainlight himself it was not only dramatic but traumatic and it haunted him for the rest of his short life.

SPIKE HAWKINS: The Albert Hall was a surging thing. I read, a few small things. It was very exciting being led along by Pete Brown and Horovitz and I said, 'Where do we go?' and they took me down to this tunnel and it was very badly lit, and suddenly this lid went up and I found myself with the light of the world upon me, and thousands of people, just coming out of this little hole in the ground onto the stage. I felt this must be some sort of metaphor. I was totally astounded by it.

SUE MILES: Ronnie Laing decanted Kingsley Hall patients for the night, thought they'd have a good evening out. Real schizophrenics running around the flat bit in the middle. How it was done was that there was a central stage that was just a floor, with seats all the way round it. All the nutcases ran jibbering round.

MILES: The interesting thing was that it did show that there was a constituency, that there was this enormous group of people. In hindsight you can see the poetry reading as a transition between the two parts of the 60s. It did occur exactly in the middle of the 60s, summer of '65. It presupposed the flower power era of '67 by the fact that Kate Heliczer and her girlfriends all went down to Covent Garden the night before and picked up all of the flowers that hadn't been sold and they were handing out great armloads of flowers to everyone coming in and their faces were painted in psychedelic markings. It was a pre-indication of what was to come. A lot of the audience was still composed of very straight people. One guy yelled out to Trocchi: 'Sir, when will we hear some real poetry?' I don't know what people like that were expecting. Maybe it was all projection, maybe we didn't have a constituency and everyone was straight.

JOHNNY BYRNE: The thing that struck me most about the Albert Hall reading was the sense of . . . almost the unbelief of those who were most closely involved with it. It was like a fantasy that they'd had of how things should be and how things should go and suddenly they'd woken up and it was really happening. And that sense of unreality carried all the way through the entire proceedings. There were always those at the heart of it who saw it as the great opening up and believed that it would lead on to bigger and better poetry recitals and the coming together of people. I sensed immediately that, ironically, it was actually the last of the poetry recitals. It was a sense of total now, everything was locked into a total, frozen moment of time. It had to be savoured then, because it was not going to be around tomorrow.

PETER BROWN: I found the poetry reading ... kind of foreign. Put it this way, you couldn't dance to it. There was a poet there who read a poem which consisted entirely of sneezes, I think he was German. Well, that may have been very avant-garde but it was a throwback to the old bohemian artistic crowd of the 50s and early 60s. It was marvellous to see people like Ginsberg, as it would be marvellous to see Elvis Presley: you might not like his music any more, but you'd still want to see the man live.

CHRISTOPHER LOGUE: Peter Whitehead made a film of it – *Wholly Communion*. And the big disadvantage of the film is that the audience is missing. The audience were just as interesting, in fact more interesting than the performers. Undoubtedly the best thing of the evening was a performance organised by Michael Horovitz of the Schwitters 'Sneezing Poem' with six poets who got up on the stage and they performed this poem. And it brought the house down. It's so funny. It's the only international poem in the world. They made it last for about ten minutes. It was so good, it was the best poem of the evening. It was certainly the best evening for anything to do with poetry readings and it was definitely an extraordinary moment, but it wasn't a high or low point – it had nothing to do with what went before and what went after – it was a one-off. Part of a mood.

MICHAEL HOROVITZ: To some extent the Albert Hall brought a lot of the things that were happening together and reduced the uptightness and competitiveness and intellectual distancings and refinements and narcissism and vanity, although in another way it almost intensified them and for certain personalities like the late Harry Fainlight it clouded them for ever. All these little local feuds were put into perspective, because all over the world there were other people in similar situations; that changed things and it became more international.

JOHNNY BYRNE: I would say that the Albert Hall was the end of the

73

genuine feeling of an alternative culture. Everything as far as I was concerned went downhill after that, even if some saw it as the seed of such things as *IT*.

SUE MILES: Esam was the man with the money. I don't know where Esam came from . . . from the vapour? He was a New Zealander, one of those people who just appeared.

'DEAN CASS': Towards the end of the evening Allen Ginsberg said to me, 'Have you been paid?' and I said, 'No, as a matter of fact I haven't,' and he said, 'Well, I haven't either. I think we'd better go and see about some money.' So he and I went to the box office and there was Esam and Richter with hundreds of pounds, going into a sack! So we actually went into the box office and said, 'Are we going to be paid for this?' and they said, 'Help yourself!' and we just took some money. Nobody else was paid, except Ginsberg and I! We didn't get much, I suppose it was about a hundred quid each and they got the rest. But a hundred quid in 1965 was serious money. So I took everyone out to supper afterwards on it, spending the whole lot in one go on a very, very good supper in a hotel just down Kensington Gore. Champagne and everything.

SUE MILES: None of us who had even the remotest connection with that event have ever been able to hire the Albert Hall again. Ever, ever, ever, ever, ever. They check. All those one-armed British Legion commissionaires had never in their lives seen anything like it. And hoped never to see it again.

Indica : 'A lot of people used to drop in'

MILES: After the poetry reading Paolo Leonni, who came over with Gregory, introduced me to Marianne Faithfull and John Dunbar at a dinner in Bianchi's. Better Books was going to be sold to Collins and we figured that it would no longer be as it was. I really wanted to maintain what I was doing, running a bookshop, promoting American avant-garde literature. It seemed to me that under Collins this would no longer be the case. Better Books was doomed and there would be no outlet for avant-garde publications in Britain. I wanted to start my own bookshop, which was a stupid idea really cos I had no money at all. So Paolo said, 'You should meet these friends of mine,' and there were John Dunbar, who wanted to open an art gallery, and Marianne, who wasn't yet his wife, and who didn't know what she wanted to do, other than look cute. Which she did. Enormously.

JOHN DUNBAR: There was this American guy, Paolo Leonni, involved in the poetry reading, who introduced me to Miles. He said, 'You should get together, you two, because you're both interested in doing something . . .' And that's how Indica started.

MILES: Indica was named after *cannabis indica*, obviously, but we always said it was named after our first show, which was called 'Indications' . . . of what was to come, etc. Indica was owned by a company called MAD – Miles, Asher and Dunbar. Myself, Peter Asher and John. I met Peter through John. I had no understanding of business; I just thought it would be a really good idea to get together with John. And we'll do this bookshop-cum-art gallery and change the world. And John had this old friend of his who was Peter Asher who would lend us money. Indeed he did.

SUE MILES: Miles did Indica because he got to know John Dunbar. John was the art critic of the *Scotsman*. John had a schoolfriend, who was Peter Asher, who reputedly had a couple of thousand pounds. He was Peter and Gordon. One of the few upper-class rock'n'rollers. We all went out to supper upstairs at Bianchi's and there was a brief conversation of why don't we do a bookshop and art gallery? Yes, why not. How much money have we got? Peter had either £2000 or £6000 and he split the money three ways: he lent a third to Miles and a third to John and charged them both interest.

MILES: Indica started January 1966. John and I borrowed £700 from Peter Asher. He had it after being Peter and Gordon – they had number one hits in America. They were enormous in America. Huge. I never paid him back but I don't think he really needs it now, even with the interest. Paul McCartney helped build Indica, put up the shelves and all the rest of it. He was very intimately involved with the whole beginnings of Indica. The original Indica was in Mason's Yard right next door to the Scotch of St James's. And indeed visible from William Burroughs' window, which was on Duke Street, St James's. So we had Bill and his various young boys hanging around quite a bit. There were workmen building the new Cavendish Hotel at the time and there was one of Bill's boyfriends who used always to strut through Mason's Yard and he used to wear a pair of trousers that were literally a pair of legs and a belt. And he'd wave at these workmen who were playing football: 'Score a goal for me, boys!'

JOHN DUNBAR: It was all done on a shoestring. We found this place off

St James's – Mason's Yard – for about twenty quid a week, and just did it. We started off with books upstairs and the art was downstairs. I went round from person to person collecting unusual art; as long as it wasn't straight pictures.

MARK BOYLE: We had this dealer come on to us and say that he'd heard about us and could he come and see our work. So we said sure. We were living in a flat in Ladbroke Grove. Then just minutes before he was due to arrive a couple of art students turned up. I stood there thinking, 'Oh God, this is actually one of the more important moments of my life and I get two art students who want to look at the work.' Then I thought, 'Come on. You can't actually change your whole way of life just because a dealer's interested in your work.' So I started to show them round the work and after I'd got them halfway round I suddenly realised that it was the dealer and his wife. And they were supposed to be coming to dinner. I was very impressed: I thought that any dealer that looked like an art student is really someone. So we sat down to eat and our eldest boy was watching *Top of the Pops* at the time and he came in and whispered in Joan's ear: it was Marianne Faithfull and John Dunbar, her husband, who had opened the Indica Gallery in conjunction with Miles and Peter Asher. And from Indica came *IT* and UFO.

JOHN DUNBAR: We never had a painting as such in the place. We had Takis, and Yoko Ono. All our exhibitions were very successful in terms of publicity, an amazing amount straight away, because there wasn't anything else going on in London, so the papers couldn't leave it alone, plus there were pop stars and stuff around and our openings were kind of wild ... Pretty soon afterwards we got another premises in Southampton Row for the bookshop and the gallery was left to art. They were still connected but I stayed with the gallery. It lasted about two or three years.

SUE MILES: Peter's sister was Jane Asher and her boyfriend was Paul McCartney. Because of this completely coincidental connection, we then got to know the rock'n'roll world. McCartney designed the first Indica wrapping paper, he lettered it all up, all by hand, and had it printed in some art shop. Miles, particularly, was the first person for those guys – the Beatles – to meet after they had been terrifically successful, but strictly pop successful, who talked about books. We used to send books over to them. It was just freaky – it all just mushroomed. There were all those Chelsea people, and they suddenly appeared. Beautiful clothes, and fleets of taxis would be sent to collect one and take one to parties and then you'd all go round to somebody else's house and somebody else's house and so on. And it was all such fun!

PAUL MCCARTNEY: I hung out with Miles a lot, because I was interested in that kind of thing and I'd really only got a bit at school or as a student in the pubs. He was a literature buff and he had his Indica shop and things. What was nice now that I was, quotes, a professional musician, and, more importantly, an adult, was that I could now spend a little bit more time on it, and get into a little bit more depth with someone like Miles. So we sat round at his flat many an evening; we'd ring each other: 'Are you doing anything?' 'No.' 'Great, come on over,' and we'd just hang out and he'd show me stuff, stuff from *Evergreen Review* and stuff. Then there were people like Robert Fraser and I'd get into the art world, because he was a good friend of mine. Miles was a great catalyst. He had the books. We had a great interest, but we didn't have the books. He had the books and the interest and once he saw that we were interested in these kind of things, particularly me cos I used to hang out with him cos I was near him, he showed us new things. And I'd had a great period of being avant-garde, going off to France, in disguise, taking a lot of movies, which I later showed to Antonioni. Very bizarre, but it really seemed exciting at the time.

MILES: Sue and I spent a lot of time with the Beatles. When we worked in Indica we saw a lot of Paul. He was almost mobbed one day walking down Duke Street, St James's. He came beating on the door and we had to let him in and there was this great horde of people following him. He'd been out looking for some kind of thread for Jane who wanted it for a dress she was making.

I knew nothing about rock'n'roll: when I first met McCartney I didn't even know which one he was. The first time I really had a long talk was after Indica had just moved to Southampton Row in March '66. I went back home and found McCartney sitting in my kitchen in Hanson Street, eating hashish cookies with Sue, and Sue being clearly quite pissed off that I'd arrived. I guess we'd told him the recipe when we first met and he'd just dropped by one day to see if we had any.

It was a small scene in those days. Now the Beatles have this legendary reputation, but it wasn't really like that. A best-selling record would sell 100,000 in this country. We saw an enormous amount of them, we went to movies with them, went to concerts with them, lectures, all kinds of shit. Of course you couldn't avoid feeling a certain amount of reflected glory, inasmuch as they were extremely famous and this was the height of Beatlemania. The press were usually there.

77

I must have been terribly pompous. I thought it would be very good for the Beatles to know about avant-garde music so I persuaded Paul to come along to a lecture by Luciano Berio at the Italian Institute. We got there and sat down and almost immediately the fucking press came bursting in with big flashlights and so on. That was the kind of thing that happened all the time.

JOHN DUNBAR: Paul helped the bookshop out with some loot occasionally, he made us some wrapping paper, a nice pattern – he just produced a great big pile of it one day. He bought a few things from the shows – so did John. Ringo made his own.

MILES: There was something of a cross-over from Swinging London. In the evenings quite a lot of people used to drop in and if any of the three of us were at the Scotch we'd take people back and show them the current show. Not that there was any money in it. I had no idea about money, absolutely zero. I hadn't the faintest idea about how capitalism worked. A good illustration of that is that at the end of our first fiscal year we sent the till roll to our accountant. What we used as the till was this Victorian till, a wooden box with a handle, which had been in the Asher household for some time. And the financial statement we got back from the accountants and the one that came out of our books was entirely different and it turned out that earlier, when Jane was seven or eight, she used to play shops using this till. So it was all there on the till roll and this stupid accountant had added it all in.

We had no idea what was going on. We sold some paintings but a lot more stuff was stolen. Though we were very lucky: the first show we had at Indica was the Groupe de Recherche d'Art Visuel, the leader of whom was Julio le Parc. As the show opened he won the Grand Prize for painting at the Venice Biennale so he was like the most famous painter on earth and we had a show of his on! One guy rushes in – 'I'm a big Texas art dealer!' and John Dunbar, who's completely stoned, says, 'I'm a little English art dealer.' It was pathetic really. Julio had left this insane price list – one thing would be a thousand, the next thing ten. A complete fucking joke.

SUE MILES: People were coming in saying, 'I'm a big art dealer from Milwaukee. I'll have eight of them.' We were going 'Eight? very good,' and we'd take them down and pack them up. And that's where Lennon met Yoko. Though Ian Somerville's theory was that she was a witch and she waited for him to cut his fingernail clippings off and she picked them up and put this kind of curse on him.

GENE MAHON: I knew Yoko before John did. When she was Yoko Cox and lived with Tony Cox in Park View Mansions looking onto the side of Regent's Park, just where the Mosque is now. With Kyoko. A sad little kid: I went there one evening and she was clinging to my hand because I made conversation with her and not wanting me to leave. There was this tiny little girl and I didn't know how to deal with this. I think the connection was through Cape Goliard. Yoko wanted to be in a black bag in Trafalgar Square but she needed bodyguards and called on a guy called Ed Klein and myself to be bodyguards. I always liked Yoko, she was interesting, nice.

PAUL MCCARTNEY: I introduced Yoko to John through my own interest in the avant-garde. John wasn't avant-garde till later. Then John became wildly avant-garde because he was so fucking constricted living out in Weybridge. He'd come into London and say, 'What've you been doing, man, what have you been doing?' and I'd say, 'What've you been doing?' 'Well, watching telly, smoking pot.' 'I went out last night and saw Luciano Berio at the Italian Embassy, that was quite cool. I've got this new Stockhausen record, check this out. We went down Robert's, got this sculpture, it was great, dig this. Wow, Paolozzi, great . . .' I think John actually said, 'I'm fucking jealous of you, man' – he just needed to get out of Weybridge. It wasn't his wife's fault, she just didn't understand how free he needed to be.

   Yoko showed up at my house and said, 'Have you got any original manuscripts?' She was doing a thing for John Cage in New York. So I was interested, I knew of him through Miles and various other people like Dunbar. I didn't want to give her one, because I keep them, and in the end I wasn't really too forthcoming – I just didn't want to give her one, quite simple. So I said, 'I've got this friend, who might be able to interest you . . .' Maybe if I hadn't done that there might not have been this sort of huge period for them . . . who knows? So then she went round to John. I think that was before the meeting in Indica which is the great story. I'm not sure, it might have been there she said, 'You're the guy Paul told me to come and see . . .' I'm not sure. I certainly do know that I met her before John as part of my interests.

MILES: The gallery side of things collapsed very rapidly. It didn't last long. Partly cos John wasn't hardly ever there. And we didn't have enough capital. We knew what to do but we were constantly running out of money. And when we ran out of money we went to Paul McCartney and Paul would say, 'Well, here's two thousand pounds,' or whatever. To him it was nothing. I remember one day he showed me a letter from his accountant, Harry Pinsker: 'Thought you might like to know that you're a millionaire.'

SUE MILES: That was Sergeant Pepper time. Indica came to an end, it went into liquidation owing £500 at the end of '68. Graft and no returns. It was exhausting to run things that were under-capitalised, under-financed, and where you were being ripped off. Miles was ripped off unbelievably at Indica. At one point we discovered that half the signed poetry books which we owned in our own house had gone.

JOHN DUNBAR: In a sense '65-'66 was the heyday. And things are always spoiled in a sense when it becomes everybody's, when it's always in the papers and blah blah. It's good fun for some, who are making loot, but at the same time it kind of dilutes the clubby atmosphere. I don't particularly think that it was better in '65 than in '85 except that I was twenty then and I'm 40 now. It was a very matey period. There were a lot of good people doing crazy things, there was no harassment from the police, no paranoia. You could wander around with dope, on planes even: you'd always take dope to Paris because there was never any dope in Paris. I lived in a flat with Marianne for a while, while that lasted, then I lived in the gallery for a while, then I got a flat in Bentinck Street. I was doing the gallery and Marianne was doing her thing and there were hundreds of people around all the time and that was a pretty hectic, crazy sort of existence.

Bob Dylan at the Albert Hall: 'He was obviously exceedingly stoned'

SAM HUTT: I didn't like Dylan until he went electric. I was very anti-folkie, I'd hated the folkie lot since the 50s because of people like Ewan McColl who said if you come from Yorkshire you've got to sing songs from Yorkshire; you can't sing a song from Cornwall, let alone a Country and Western song. Purists – the Stalinist intellect.

STEVE SPARKS: I saw Dylan in a play that he was in on BBC [*Madhouse on Castle Street*] and he sang a song about three white swans which he's never sung anywhere else and the tape has been destroyed. Later I saw him in the Gray's Inn Road above a pub, getting up out of the audience and singing in a folk club. And thinking he was Christ, the Second Coming.

VIRGINIA CLIVE-SMITH: He came and did a play on television and it was about the Deep South. It must have been about 1962 or slightly later. I remember him sitting on the stairs in this play, singing a song called 'The Swan on the River Went Gliding By'. When *Freewheelin'* came out I recognised the voice and I'd carried a flame for this person who'd sat on the stairs. Then I went to every Dylan concert. I made a vow that if I ever got to lay him I'd have myself sewn up.

STEVE MANN: I was running a folk club before I came to London. I was a folkie, having given up electric music for a couple of years after being a mod, and I was one of the people who was horrified about the idea of Dylan going electric – until I actually got there, and until I saw him. Folkies were incredibly factionalised. There were the traditional folkies, with their huge Fair Isle sweaters, their finger in one ear, which apparently helped you get the pitch better, preferably with a beard, a pint in the other hand, singing unaccompanied sea shanties. There was a huge link between CND, Aldermaston and folkies. I was a bit of an entrepreneur for Dylan. I arranged to get a whole load of tickets and sold them to everyone I could think of at an inflated price so I could go up for nothing. A whole load of us went up and it was just coincidental that my parents were away for the next two weeks and I had a two-week-long party. The house got totally trashed, somebody swallowed all the dog's Bob Martin tablets cos they thought they were drugs. And I thought, fuck it, I just don't care any more. The aged parents came back to a great shock, and I moved out very soon afterwards.

SUE MILES: Dylan in 1966 at the Albert Hall was the most extraordinary event. In the first half he was just earnestly twanging away, groaning away with the old harmonica and the guitar. Out for the intermission and the Band appeared and I remember thinking, 'This is great, this is wonderful. This is proper stuff!' Dylan had frizzy, slightly blue hair. He and Robbie Robertson rubbed up against each other all the time. It was great. Half the audience pissed off – all the ones that had rucksacks.

DICK POUNTAIN: I saw Dylan at the Albert Hall the first time he came, in '65, when I was still a student. When he did an all-acoustic set. And I was there the second time when he did an acoustic first half and then brought the Band on for the second half. I thought the second half was brilliant, it was the first time I'd ever heard heavy rock. It was probably the first time it had been played in this country, cos they just had all these amps that we didn't have. We were still using 25 watt amplifiers and they came on with a wall of amps. Before that, especially when you

81

saw people live, it was very weedy. Then Dylan appeared and did 'Like a Rolling Stone' and shook the roof of the Albert Hall.

STEVE SPARKS: I met Dylan around the time of the '66 concert and he was a real little shit and it was a real disappointment to me, because prior to that I thought he was the Second Coming, I thought Christ has returned and he's playing the guitar and blowing the harmonica and it wasn't until I met him that I realised that he was a little shit. Very pleased with himself and using smack, and I've never really liked anybody using smack. But Dylan at the Albert Hall was wonderful. At the concert I got stood up and went on my own and there's an empty seat beside me cos this girl never turned up – and there's a stupid girl.

MICK FARREN: Bob Dylan and the Band played the Albert Hall. There was this sort of phalanx of old fogies out to cause trouble, because they knew their days were numbered. Of the 3000 that the Albert Hall holds there were about 700 fogies and everybody else was like these strange-looking people that we'd only sort of glimpsed from the hilltops. And nobody had any particular focus and also no particular product to obtain . . . there'd be geezers marching in there with their wellies sprayed silver and looking a trifle ridiculous, like psychedelic landgirls . . . a lot of people basically dressed up like Bob Dylan, me included. When he got here he'd had quite a choice velvet suit, which was cool, but when he'd got to Carnaby Street he went and bought this hideous sort of giant houndstooth check thing, the one in the photograph. And all the ex-mods, who'd freaked their hair out by that point, decided that Dylan just had no fucking taste at all. So the only thing really left to the world was the long leather sports jacket (still a favourite of mine). Me, I had this high tab collar shirt, made of some kind of William Morris material, cos I got this girl to make it for me, I thought that was the coming thing. I had this theory . . . We all had these theories about what might be next. There were various examples of these, both good and bad . . . there was lots of people wearing stupid badges: 'I am an enemy of the State' and 'Kill a commie for Christ' were the very very first ones. First of all there was this sort of cultural burial, when Dylan comes out . . . [mimics Dylan 'folkie' whine]. Folkies go, 'Yeah, hooray!!' But everybody knows the fucking Band are coming on after the interval. Then the Band comes on and they all go crazy. Everybody's heard the recording: 'Judas' . . . 'Fuck you . . .!!'

STEVE ABRAMS: 'Judas', 'You're a liar' was not at the Albert Hall. That concert was in Manchester; the bootleg of *Live at the Albert Hall* was

82

actually made in Manchester. The most interesting part came in the first half of the concert when Dylan was about to sing 'Visions of Johanna'. He said, 'Now this next song is what your English newspapers would call a drug song, but I don't write drug songs, and anybody who says I do is talking rubbish.'

MICK FARREN: He was obviously exceedingly stoned and probably taking a lot of pills, that's what we all figured . . . 'Hey, he's taking pills . . . he's stoned.' Little did we know – amphetamine and heroin . . . So the Band came out, the folkies all cut loose, Dylan baits them, most of them walk out and then we all sort of closed in and there it was, the start of 'something entirely different'. 'Motherfucker!' we cried. All these fuckers who looked like us.

JOHNNY BYRNE: Not only did I go to Dylan at the Albert Hall, but I happened to be staying in the flat where he came back later and I don't know who was in the most electric state, Spike Hawkins or Dylan. Dylan was visibly vibrating. I should imagine it was the exhaustion and a good deal of substances. He was totally away, there was a yawning chasm between him and any kind of human activity.

SPIKE HAWKINS: Dylan was not a great guru. I've never found a guru, though I've always wished for one and I used to talk with my colleagues of the time, who always seemed to have one – Wittgenstein, Hume or somebody like this – but I never found anybody who really worked for me. Bits and pieces only. Finding a guru is rather like finding bits of oneself. Flashes while you're reading a poem or a novel and something strikes you and *that is you*. Dylan was not this, far from it. Dylan was important but only in terms of saying, 'We are building something. You're building that section, I'm building this section,' but there wasn't this awe that you'd get from the wet-knicker scrubber brigade.

'You've got to make me hip'

MICK FARREN: So that was the beginning of the summer. Then not much happened. It seemed that everybody was poised for something to happen, but we didn't know what it is, did we. The Rolling Stones had their photograph took in Hyde Park looking like Regency dandies. All them hard bad-trip records came out – '19th Nervous Breakdown', *Revolver* – everyone was sort of looking around wondering what the fuck was going on. Something was going on, but the storm hadn't broken yet. And then it did. By the end of the summer there'd been sufficient sort of encounters that people were starting to get to know each other. People

83

were going round to different pubs, outside their own neighbourhoods, because they'd heard a bunch of freaks hung out there . . . people from Chelsea would stop by Henekey's on the Portobello Road . . . they'd chat: 'Did you go and see Dylan?' 'Fucking great, wasn't it' and so on. It was all going on.

MICHAEL STOREY: Sixty-six: leaving school, the World Cup . . . I was supposed to go to university and didn't. The Cream came and did their second gig up in Newcastle where I was supposed to go and had actually started. That destroyed the whole idea of doing three years at university. I was also in love with a girl who went off with another bloke and I couldn't stay there. It was still like being at school. I wasn't really aware yet of what was going on in London. I was still an eighteen-year-old sixth former, out in the country, and I was catching up. My mother lived in Gloucester and I went home from Newcastle and met these people I knew who were all smoking dope and going up and down to London which meant that I started to get contacts in London. So we'd go up to London to see what was going on. That was what sped it all up. I went to Central School of Drama in order just to get to London somehow. I did a year there. I stayed in Horace Ove's pad and above us lived Michael X. Bush smoking, incredible dialogues, Black Power.

HORACE OVE: Michael Storey arrived at my house and knocked at my door. He looked pink with this country complexion, nice upper-class boy, clean, his little tweed jacket and so on. He rang my doorbell and I see this kid standing outside my door and he says, 'Tony sent me' – this was another friend of mine who knew him – 'and he said that you've got to make me hip,' and I said, 'What?!' and he said, 'You've got to make me hip so I know what's happening.' That's how our relationship started. So he came into my house and he stayed a long time.

STEVE MANN: I was a mod in Aldershot, where we lived, which wasn't much fun because you used to get beaten up by squaddies every night. I had an endless succession of scooters: LD125, LI150, SX200, TV175 – all Lambrettas. All very clapped out and highly unroadworthy. I went on a couple of runs to Brighton, I threw a deckchair through various people's windows, ganged up on rockers, if I could ever find one or two of them when there were at least 100 of us. I didn't really earn enough to be that into clothes, it was more mirrors for the scooter, extra bits of chrome.

I left school at the end of '66. I'd started an A-level course and then decided to jack it in cos I got a job on the local paper. So I was working on the local paper, taking a lot of pills, staying up all weekend and falling

84

asleep in Aldershot court on Monday morning, when I was supposed to be sitting there reporting. Came up to London quite a lot – mainly to the Flamingo, the Marquee. I went to the lunchtime sessions at Tiles. You could disappear down there at 1 o'clock, bright sunshine outside and suddenly you're in pitch darkness with Jeff Dexter being a mod.

Tiles: 'It wasn't just a dirty cellar'

RUSSELL HUNTER: Tiles was a great big place. It was the forerunner of the smart club. It tried to give the impression of being a bit classy – it wasn't just a dirty cellar. They had proper bars and a good dance floor and a fancy stage and it was well decorated and all the rest of it. It was *the* place to go for a while. Then, of course, as time went on, after UFO, Tiles started to have Jeff Dexter and they tried to hip themselves up a bit. They started the all-nighters on Friday nights. And we used to go to those, which were a hotbed of amphetamines, and every so often they'd have the big raid and the police rushed in and put up screens and body-searched everybody.

JEFF DEXTER: I was DJ at Tiles. Still doing soul shows. Tiles was a club in Oxford Street, set up as a replacement club for the Marquee, which had obviously had its day between 1964 and '65, in the mainstream of the new beat music scene. The Sellers brothers set up Tiles. It had Carnaby Street shops inside, a couple of coffee bars, a little hangout playroom – the first mixed-up club – and it had an incredible sound system for those days: something like 32 Marshall columns hung from the ceiling, so wherever you were you were blasted by it. It was the first place that developed a whole club around the new sound and the new generation.

After I'd been at Tiles for a while I began to see things different. The acid had burnt out a few brain cells and I became a bit more warped. I started introducing Dylan then, even Donovan, though I never liked him ever since his first appearance on *Ready Steady Go!* – another woolly-jumper wimp, not worth a listen – but he was singing about things that were beginning to interest me and he was always out on the scene, at the clubs, and he became quite an interesting character after a while. So I had some terrible fights, trying to introduce Dylan and Donovan into the heavy soul scene. Sometimes people would leap up on stage and knock me to the ground, threaten me with knives . . . it got a bit rough. It didn't really work on the regular shows so I started the Jeff Dexter Light and Sound Show once a week and I played newer music in between the soul stuff. A lot of people who were getting into the underground still liked soul, so it still had its place. I put the Pink Floyd on at Tiles after seeing them at UFO.

85

Swinging London: 'For us it was where it was at'

ANDREA ADAM: As I remember it, the expression 'Swinging London' just came out of the blue. One of the editors on *Time* used it jokingly. Somebody said 'Oh hey . . . what about that?' Then it became a working title. We never tried to push it as a concept, but it became the working title for the cover. And it caught on within the office and then it was used for the cover. Creating a *Time* cover was an enormous team effort. In this case the reporting was done by the London bureau and then it was filed to New York and it was written there. We were all totally riveted by London. London was special, it had a kind of mystique. But what prompted the bloody cover story was not a fascination with a socio-cultural phenomenon, it was the fascination among the senior editors for mini-skirts. There was no more depth of emotion than that. They were a bunch of the randiest pseudo-intellectuals you could ever have the misfortune to meet. Any opportunity to put legs, tits or bums in the magazine and they would do it. This was just another excuse for doing it. That's what made that cover a reality. We knew that there actually was a phenomenon going on in London which kind of differed from what was going on in the States. I don't think we understood it. We felt that the way in which England had adopted these new mores was based on some kind of cultural maturity, England after all being an older culture, where-as in the States it was yet another crazy fling. We felt that it had a legitimacy in London that we were uncertain about in the States. We perceived a kind of classlessness coming from the aristocracy, who were very heavily involved too, that we found very attractive. People seemed easy-going about their titles. At that time in New York everything English had a cachet. Nothing American did. Those who could afford it would go to London to get their hair cut at Leonard's. And stay at Brown's Hotel. We were fascinated. People would come back from London talking about shops called Granny Takes a Trip and stuff like that. Amazing, utterly exotic. For us it was where it was at.

The Speakeasy: 'There was a good deal of excess'

JEFF DEXTER: The Speakeasy arrived on the trail of all the great late-night clubs: the Scotch, the Crazy Elephant, the Revolution, the Cromwellian. It took over from the Bag O'Nails in Kingley Street. It was where I first saw Jimi Hendrix. The Speakeasy had a band every night, so a lot of the new bands would play there as a matter of course and all the stars would get up and jam. It was a great melting pot for the old and the new styles. Then they had these nights where they'd have new acts. Tony Howard was the booker. They had the Floyd, the Soft Machine, who had a residency there. It was open till 4am and often I'd

86

go there after work at Tiles. You'd have dinner, meet your friends and talk. A great melting pot for everyone in the rock business and the media.

ANDREW BAILEY: The Speakeasy, a dreadful place! It was this cellar off Margaret Street, a roadies' heaven.

JOHNNY BYRNE: It was a very good place by the standards of clubs, the one place which had any kind of real integrity and where the artificial hierarchical behaviour in the pop world simply fell apart. If you were down at the Speak you were one with whoever was there. There was no bullshit. There was a good deal of excess. There were usually all the groups. Behaviour was totally out to lunch; I always enjoyed my time there, it was very attractive.

JO CRUIKSHANK: I was going to the Speakeasy. I'd given up Blaise's and the Cromwellian where everything was pink and you wore dinky shoes and things. Little sparkly dresses. The Speakeasy was *bliss*. When you're young and vivacious and you don't get pissed, clubs absolutely adore to have you. You're just a sparkly young thing, you're not a tart – so they give you free memberships. The Speakeasy gave me a free membership. I used to go three or four times a week. I'd sit and drink and not drink very much but I'd want another, which I couldn't afford, and they'd say, 'It's all right, darling, we'll put it on Brian's bill.' So Brian [Jones] would come in, holding hands with Anita Pallenberg, and didn't know that in fact he was standing drinks for half the Speakeasy. There was always someone footing the bill without knowing it. Keith Richard was another. Jimi Hendrix used to come. I was sitting at a table one night, I'd been off to have a little dance and I came back and Jimi Hendrix was sitting there and I walked up and said, 'Sorry, this is my table,' and he was so polite and apologetic – 'Have I taken your seat, here have it back' – and I thought 'My goodness!' and I became a complete Hendrix fan after that. The Speak certainly wasn't a hippie club, it was a medallion man club – record producers and things. All the people you'd see parading on the King's Road on a Saturday you'd quite likely see at the Speak on a weekday night. No one ever went on a Saturday, of course – that was strictly for the plebs. Tuesday or Wednesday was when you went, showing how you didn't have to get up next morning.

MELISSA CHASSAY: At one time a girl was murdered after a night out in the Speakeasy. The CID were in every night for a while. And this was at the Speakeasy where everyone was taking drugs, had taken drugs or was trying to buy drugs. You'd go in: 'The CID are here again.' She'd been a Swedish au pair girl who was slightly on the game and spent her nights off at the Speakeasy. There was this marvellous evening when I was there with Jimi and H [Howard Parker] and various silent Guinevere-type girls and a CID officer approached the table and said, 'Could I sit down for a moment, I'd like to ask you some questions.' There's Jimi, there's the CID, there we all are. It was then typical of Jimi to say, 'How absolutely marvellous. Please sit down and tell me all about what it's like to be a detective.' We sat there and the whole thing completely changed as this CID man, having been rather terrifying, then explained the whole process of investigating a murder. All because of Jimi's natural charm and actual intelligence. By the end of the evening he said, 'I would never have said this earlier, but my daughter really loves you, will you sign her an autograph?'

SAM HUTT: I was a big Who fan. I got to know the Who well, they were quite a big part of the 60s for me. Keith Moon came into St George's [Hospital] and I was then working for two surgeons and he came in to have his hernia repaired. He bashed the drums so hard that he'd given himself a hernia. I assisted at his hernia repair. Got very pally with him. A lovely bloke – a lunatic and a bit dangerous and all that, but a lovely bloke at heart. And I'd go down the Speakeasy from time to time and visit with Keith and watch him spill champagne everywhere and get arseholed. I wasn't a great Speakeasy goer. I tended to go with Moony and the typical thing was [imitates Moon's harsh Cockney]: 'A bottle of champagne!' and it comes along and, 'Fuck me, I've fucking knocked it over! Let's have another bottle, all right, hey! Fucking champagne, eh. Fucking cunt! All right!' High-class drunken lunatic.

PETER SHERTSER: The Firm burnt the Speakeasy down. That was great, sitting outside watching the posers coming out – tears streaming, watching the fire engines, the police, the posers. We got a whole load of petrol, added calcium carbide, which when you throw water on it forms acetylene, put it over the toilet, the foyer and tossed burning rags in. We thought the prices were bad.

ROBERT WYATT: The Speakeasy was exactly the kind of place that I saw as really unpleasant. There was a sense in me that while I was flourishing as a member of the late-60s culture, this very thing that was flourishing was squashing something that I felt was really more oppressed. Rock groups meeting in expensive clubs that are difficult to get into . . . what's

88

all that crap? It was exciting and it was interesting, there were lots of new scenes, but it's very very hard to think of it as underground.

'Suddenly being front-page news'

PETER ROBERTS: 1966 was a wild year. Everyone was doing acid. There were parties all over the place. There was this enormous party at Christopher Gibbs' place in Cheyne Walk. Gibbs was away. Everybody turned up. Steve Abrams was there. It started at three o'clock in the afternoon. The BBC were there to film it. Everyone was out of it on acid . . . And there were these BBC characters wandering around holding themselves in, on their official duty, with microphones, cameras, staying away from all these mad freaks. The BBC were really a cabaret for us. There was this guy with a stick, curved, and this hand holding a microphone came round the door and he just very elegantly, very gently just pinned it to the ground with the stick. There was a scream and the hand vanished behind the door, leaving the microphone behind it. The next morning the radio had this 'What the Papers Say' type of programme. 'Shock! Horror! The *People* reveals BBC in drug party scandal' and on the front page of the *People* there appeared pictures of the party, oneself and all one's friends, with faces blacked out. Suddenly being front-page news in the *People* was a bit much.

Blow-Up: 'Tell Michelangelo my taxi crash . . .'

KIERAN FOGARTY: My friend George Galitzine rang me up at the end of the Oxford summer term of 1966 and said did I want to be in this film called *Blow-Up?* That was glorious. We duly assembled. I had at this time a girlfriend called Didi Verschoyle. Didi was stunningly beautiful – so stunning that Carlo Ponti wrote in an extra scene just so that she could do it – all it consisted of was that she should just walk very slowly down these stairs and the camera could linger in close-up on this fabulous 60s vision. But it got cut by express command of her father, because she was still under 21 and his permission had not been given.

About a day into this film, after we'd been milling around swilling whisky, not believing our luck – you asked for a drink and they'd say, 'What would you like, sir?' and you say, 'A Scotch and dry,' and someone brings you a litre of dry and a bottle of Scotch – there came a day when Didi realised that other things were happening, that there were more glamorous men. Carlo's getting his paws round her shoulder and David Hemmings wanted to have a drink and so on. So she offed me. I was heartbroken: first love, the glamorous circumstances, all very crucial. As a result of which George begged Sarah Ponsonby – later immortalised in the famous commune with Roddy Llewellyn, Princess Margaret and so on – who was then Carlo's casting assistant, to find something that would involve me. 'Ah!' she said 'The drug scene.' So there I was: I'd had a taste of pot but no real involvement. I was flung into this bedroom in Cheyne Walk, hair parted, purple shirt with paisley motifs, black knitted Jaeger tie, square-ended, black jacket. Plonked on the front of this bed with about another nine people on it and Antonioni tossed a couple of kilo-bags of grass on the bed and said, 'Right, get on with it.' It took five days. It just went on and on. Nobody wanted to stop. Indeed they weren't to be stopped, no way. Meanwhile catering batted out more steaks, the wet bar off-loaded case after case of wine and Scotch and anything else we could think of and the cameras just kept rolling. And it all ended up as about 30 seconds. It was a great party. Verushka, the model, who was not actually being filmed, was at one point lying on the bed and getting very stoned. Because I was the nearest person to her and still thoroughly heartbroken at that point she got me to cover for her while she went off to Paris to fuck somebody. And she kept ringing up at four-hourly intervals and the phone would ring and I'd pick it up – I was still in the same place, on this bed, and it would be Verushka: 'Tell Michelangelo that my taxi crash . . .' This very surreal comment, and you'd say, 'Oh, it's Verushka, her taxi's crashed, she'll be here in five or six hours.' It was a glorious party for us but nobody outside the bedroom got any grass. So there are all these shots of wonderfully dressed people who look to be having a grand time but the people in the big room, theoretically the most beautiful and everything else, had a rotten time, because all the action was going on in the bedroom where these cameras just kept rolling. People would stumble out going 'Yeeeaahhh' and go gibbering back. There is actually a moment in the film where you see somebody doing this. They got very frustrated out there: 'No cameras in our room . . .' Most of swinging London was there, every deb that was halfway decent looking, and wild they were too. Outrageously dressed, superheavy make-up . . .

HORACE OVE: *Blow-Up* was an interesting movie, and people judge a certain part of the 60s by it, but when it came out real 60s people thought it was crap. *Blow-Up* made an attempt, but it didn't capture what was the mind of the 60s people. Antonioni didn't know much about it. I remember him turning up at a few happenings and trying to set the scene and make movies. He was at the *IT* launch. The story of *Blow-Up* is interesting in a sense but nobody really, really made a film through the 60s head and mind and body and what they were doing. Nobody dealt with that, with that psychedelic world. I tried to make a piece of film at the time about the period but I didn't have enough money to finish it and I went to the BFI and the BFI were straight at the time, they thought I was off my head, they weren't ready for it, they didn't know what I was on about. *Performance* is closer. *Performance* got pretty close, yet *Performance* sat on the shelves for two years. But it got that feeling, that feeling when you were stoned. There was a simple little thing there when Mick Jagger was talking and a fly was flying around in the room and the soundtrack came up, and I think it hit him in his face . . . that was so fucking psychedelic, that piece of observation. Yet a lot of film-makers could look at that and not even know what it fucking means, but what it means was that everything was exaggerated under LSD, right into the fly, the spider, the flower.

Networks: 'So many scenes going on'

GENE MAHON: I was working as an overseas telephone operator. I had started painting and that gave me the days free in which to paint. Through a friend at the Goliard Press I met an American, Al Vandenberg from New York, who was an art director in London. Through him I got back into the design business for which I'd been trained. I started working at a company called Gerald Green Associates. Vandenberg, like most Americans, had come over and immediately put himself into the right scenes. He became very tight with Michael Cooper, the photographer, who had his studio in Flood Street, Chelsea. Michael Cooper was working with Jim Dine and Jim Dine was associated with Robert Fraser and exhibited in his gallery. Robert Fraser knew Lennon, Yoko, Jagger – that connection. It was the beginning of 'Swinging London'. One just drifted about, one met people. Beatnikery had passed on and this was a new world. One was just part of all that and just drifted around in it. There were just so many scenes going on and you were part of one or another but they connected.

MALDWYN THOMAS: It's very hard to fit it all together, because there were such tenuous links between the various scenes. Everybody did know everybody. And there were two things that everybody had in common: music and drugs. People grew up, came into pop music through rhythm and blues and black music and you just took the drugs and that just sort of mingled everybody in and out of society. You got kids who used to live in the suburbs coming in and mixing with the Beatles and so on. Scoring was classless. It certainly was when acid was legal. And we used to sit on the top of buses and smoke a joint and nobody knew. Pre-hippies and publicity days. When we were just mods or faces or whatever. I used to smoke going to work, on the tube.

MILES: The music business was the main way in which the working classes became involved. The people who were involved with fashion or art tended to be much more upper class. Robert Fraser, people like that. At that time he was already working for Christopher Gibbs and through him one tended to meet all these sort of people: Mark Palmer, Ormsby-Gores and so on. As soon as there was something to advertise in, which was *IT*, all those shops like Dandie Fashions and Granny Takes a Trip began to happen. Also the Chelsea people gave very nice parties and it was always very nice to go to a party and sit around and smoke dope with Mick Jagger.

MELISSA CHASSAY: I opened a shop called Buttercup in Church Street, Lisson Grove, with a girl called Celia Brooks who was a perfect 6os object of desire, very beautiful, always wearing nightdresses with nothing underneath. She was the girlfriend of Clive Goodwin, which is how he entered our lives. She had been going to a pottery class where the teacher, Brian Rice, fell in love with her and he introduced her to Derek Boshier who she then had an affair with and he introduced her to Clive who she then had an affair with.

So we crossed over from our world of acid, dope and Blaise's and the Speakeasy, into that of Michael White, Christopher Logue and Clive Goodwin. They were the grown-ups, although they had the same interests as ourselves: smoking lots of dope, staying up late. They were very much involved with the Left, the new liberalism and the new freedom of ideas. These were the grandees, the powerful version of the underground which was doing it more at street level. So Clive's apartment was a big mix. There was a lot of cross-over.

JO CRUIKSHANK: I had a tutor at Central called Derek Boshier. We used to do it, which you weren't meant to do with tutors. It was all rather clandestine, he used to meet me at the station after Holborn, all that sort of stuff. But he introduced me to people like Clive Goodwin, Michael White, Christopher Logue, Ken Tynan, that circle. This was a much more sophisticated world than the underground, but these were the people that ran the underground, the ones that made the happenings. It was Clive's money that backed *Black Dwarf* for Tariq Ali, things like this. It was interesting to see that so much of the underground was being funded by businessmen who were doing it very much for business purposes. They were already in their thirties, too old to get really involved, but they were getting a buzz out of what they did, so it was a rather wanky involvement. The same people got involved with *Spare Rib* later.

'This not quite seedy but not exactly salubrious house'

JOHNNY BYRNE: Jenny Fabian had been the only girl at a public school up in Highgate. Her father was a housemaster and Jenny was in love with the captain of the first eleven. She wanted to be one of the boys until her tits became too big and she had to become a girl among the boys, and she was very much a tomboy. In through the mezzanine, down into the dormitory, and then she would be dispatched by the captain of the first eleven to negotiate terms for the loan of the record player from old Spotty down the road. She negotiated terms: if she let them feel her right tit for five minutes she could borrow it for an hour. And later on Jenny used to go down to Heaven and Hell which was on Wardour Street and full of Italian croupiers and she became pregnant and was kicked out of home and lived with this croupier and they had two children. And one day she threw a bowl of spaghetti over him and was taken away by Hawkins and that was how she came over into our lives.

JENNY FABIAN: My friend Sian, who was living with us, appeared back one night, absolutely out of her brain, with Spike Hawkins. That really changed things, though I'm sure it would have happened anyway, because I was looking for it. You could say I was rescued, because I was waiting for somebody. I'd heard Bob Dylan, I knew there was something waiting for me out there and it was only a question of time before a catalyst appeared, and it was Hawkins. Hawkins was absolutely insane and absolutely wonderful: I'd never met anyone so mad. And this was too wonderful to be true. And he was married too, living in Islington with this wife and various red-headed children. Somehow that made it easier to have an affair with him, because he knew I was married and I knew he was married and it was easier that way rather than pretending anything. He was a mercurial figure, difficult to pin down. He used to come and vomit in my front room from time to time.

SPIKE HAWKINS: I found Jenny Fabian. I rescued her from this dreadful croupier who actually slapped me on the back several times later because it brought him an enormous amount of publicity when her book [*Groupie*] came out. I thought Jenny had potential. She wanted to be one of the gang, one of the boys. I introduced her to Andrew King who was then running Blackhill Enterprises. I had an affair with Jenny. We were very very close and I would talk to her about literature and she said literally, 'How do I write a book?'

JENNY FABIAN: Spike introduced me to Johnny Byrne and Thom Keyes. I always thought of Hawkins, Byrne and Keyes as this trio who

93

lived in this not quite seedy but not exactly salubrious house in Maida Vale.

STEVE ABRAMS: Keyes was an American, born Yuma City, California, educated at Malvern, mother lives in Liverpool, typical American lady, family have a bit of money. Irish father, a heart surgeon in a Las Vegas hotel, doesn't like Thom, because Michael Hollingshead and Thom and somebody else went in a car to see him and he refused to see Thom. Thom ultimately is American. But he is British in the important sense of having been to school here.

JOHNNY BYRNE: I had met Thom Keyes when he was about seventeen before he went to Oxford. Thommy thought I was God because I seemed to command regiments of women who would do my bidding at the drop of a hat. So when I moved to Liverpool he stuck firmly with me. He had independently been interested in beatnik literature. Keyes was the only beatnik I knew who drove around in a sports car. He moved around in all kinds of circles; he'd come up through Christ Church, Oxford, and when he came to London he would go to the Casanova Club where he had a gambling account, so when I was hungry I'd go with him and we'd get these free steak sandwiches. Thommy was crucial in the sense that he straddled about five different worlds at the same time and you always had the feeling that he was playing at his lives. He was incredibly randy and there was always the feeling with Thommy that he was a dirty schoolboy who never quite got over getting his finger round the elastic of a little girl's knickers. After *All Night Stand* he brought the big outside world into our lives; we had all of these famous people coming to our place, largely at Thommy's instigation. Thommy is 'Theo' in *Groupie*: it gives a very good idea of his state of being at the time. By that time he had moved further and further away from his old-time Oxford image – the guy driving around in his little MG sportscar. He's too cynical to believe in anything, too lazy to actually apply his energies in any particular direction. Thommy has been compared to a bird sitting in a nest, its beak open waiting for things to be thrust in.

JENNY FABIAN: I did used to go round and visit Thom in Maida Vale when he was writing *All Night Stand* or when he was waiting for it to be published. The most sordid thing: all these empty Fanta bottles under the bed and filthy underwear everywhere. Really disgusting. Keyes was absolutely unbearable. You had to be able to deal with him and unless you were very very self-confident it was quite hard. He treated Johnny and Spike like shit. He treated everyone like shit. As the days went by at

94

Cranley Mansions he became so spaced out on methedrine who knows what was really speaking. I spent quite a lot of time there, especially when I was living in Lots Road. I did move in briefly, stayed there for a few weeks or months. Everybody did for a while. People were always being thrown out or moved in. He was a real little führer, that's exactly what he was playing at. But it was his place: you couldn't tell him to piss off, and it was comfortable there. Steve Abrams had turned up, but he didn't make any impression on me, cos I was busy screwing pop groups.

STEVE ABRAMS: Basically Cranley Mansions was Thom Keyes, Johnny Byrne, Spike Hawkins, and at one point Brian Patten. There was a guy called David Rook, he was in film and had lots of beautiful girls around him. With him went an otter which lived in one of the bath tubs. Cranley Mansions was a completely mad place. When Keyes was at his worst he had a sign up about who could be admitted to the house: there were seven people who could be admitted, nobody else. Me, Marlon Brando, Vadim . . . Neither Brando nor Vadim were likely to come round but they were the first two people that Regina fucked when Thom took her out to Hollywood.

The Notting Hill Free School: 'It was truly tramps and culture crossing'

GRAHAM KEEN: Around '63–'64 Hoppy had gone off to America and came back with a whole load of new ideas. One was the Free School and one was an underground newspaper. We tried the Free School first. That was Michael X on the fringes, John Michell, various people. We got this basement to hold our meetings in in Powis Terrace. It was opposite David Hockney's studio. Michell was the landlord and all the rest was prostitutes.

JOHN SHEPPARD: Hoppy was very charismatic, there's no question about it. I know such things were not permitted, but if ever I saw a bloody leader it was Hoppy. He was this very magical figure, and he had a way of dancing around, physically, an alighting butterfly.

STEVE ABRAMS: You could put the very beginning of the underground in '65 when Hoppy started the Free School with Michael X and a few other people. He started UFO, *IT*, the Free School and he had one or two other things going as well. He was really organising everything.

JOE BOYD: I had returned to London in November '65 to start working at Elektra records. I rang up Hoppy the week I got back. He told me there was going to be literally that night a meeting which I ought to attend. So I attended the first meeting of the London Free School. The people at that meeting were Hoppy, Andrew King and Peter Jenner, Alan Beckett, Ron Atkins, Kate Heliczer. John Michell was involved as the landlord. Someone at the meeting knew him and said that he had a derelict property in Powis Terrace. The main thrust of the meeting was that the people in the room and their associates were possessed of a number of skills and trained in certain things which would be of benefit to the community if offered in a constructive way. It was an idea to start a community based on the idea of further education for the under-privileged of Notting Hill Gate. We certainly felt that it ought to have a political consciousness. But it wasn't politics of a specific party nature: it was oblique, really – no left/right spectrum. We had a big meeting in the basement of the church, now torn down, on Elgin Avenue at Chippenham Road. We'd publicised it a lot on the streets, but very few people turned up. When it eventually got going in Powis Terrace I went there very infrequently. I went to some organisational meetings, I made some vague commitment to contribute something on the subject of music, but I don't think it ever really came to much. Originally we had some legitimate local people – some old Irish people, some West Indians – but the courses didn't really get going in any really organised way. The place turned into a rehearsal studio for some local musicians who eventually played at UFO. The main thing was that it ended up being a galvanisation of certain forces and energy.

JOHN HOPKINS: The Notting Hill Free School was a scam, it never really worked out. What happened was that Michael X owned this building, 22 Powis Terrace, Dave Tomlin lived in the basement and we tried to run this thing called the Free School. It was opposite where Michael had an office. It never really worked out but it was enough to get me busted: at my trial they brought up this thing that here was this guy smoking dope and trying to run a school – what's going on? Michael owned this building with John Michell. Pete Jenner was involved. Joe Berke, who in my view *was* a berk. I didn't get on with him very well. I guess I wasn't very experienced in the ways of the world. I thought that his Anti-University was a great idea but I didn't really get on too well with all those shrinks. So the Free School never really got off the ground and it's an idea that really shouldn't be inflated with too much content, cos there really wasn't too much content.

COURTNEY TULLOCH: The Free School was in this basement, painted all psychedelic. Dave Tomlin lived down there. Every time he stepped out of his house there was some policeman waiting for him. One day two policewomen were trying to arrest him. He's saying, 'Well, if you can carry me, take me, but I am not moving a single leg . . .' and there were these two women, one on each arm, trying to pull him. Dave is saying, 'If you want me, you can have me, but I'm not moving.' That was poetry. That was his political statement.

PETER JENNER: God knows where we dug up the idea of the Free School. Basically it was a realisation, as we'd all recently come out of school and college and university and were all bohemians and beatniks, that the education we'd been given was not really an awful lot of good. It wasn't really what it set out to be. It was a reflection of various forms of alienation within the education system. Felix de Mendelsohn was involved, Ron Atkins, who was a jazz writer. John Michell was the landlord. Michael X had got the building from his Rachman days. Then there was Mrs Laslett involved, she was some sort of social worker in the area. She helped start the Notting Hill Carnival with us and Michael X. The Free School started the Carnival with Mrs Laslett. I had the first cheque book for the Notting Hill Carnival, I was the initial treasurer. Never did much and then I passed it on.

COURTNEY TULLOCH: A lot of people claim to have started the Carnival and I don't know what the truth is. What happened was that when the Free School started it also combined various LSE-type people, Jenner was one. You're getting the sociologist mentality come in. The *Transatlantic Review* people. And people who were into trepanning: bore a hole in your skull and stay high for ever. So you're getting those kind of influences coming in. And you're starting to get people who've come from North Africa and Americans and so on. All kinds of people would turn up, spend a little time, then go about their business. There were all sorts of influences and you cannot define who started Carnival.

Rhaunie Laslett was a local person. Somebody knocked on her door – the Free School getting to know your community – and she opened the door and they said, 'This is what we are doing, blah-blah-blah,' and she said, 'Of course, me love, I will do anything you want me to.' And Rhaunie became a community person. She became acceptable to Westminster Council and people like that. 'All the poor children, the drug addicts dying in attics, oh dear, I have to go and drag them out in the mornings, I need some money . . .' Rhaunie used to have a list on the wall with all the things she was doing and she made sure that when the Council was coming she had a representative one of each problem. Carnival was kind of the same thing. But who it was was the musicians.

The people who actually know about Carnival were the Trinidadians. People like Michael, Horace Ove, Stefan Calipa (who's now an actor) were all steel pan musicians, from Trinidad. There was a tremendous wealth of serious musical ability based on the Trinidad Carnival. And Frank Critchlow, who ran the Rio and then the Mangrove, was a Trinidadian, and Russ Henderson, who had the first band that knocked up and down the street was a Trinidadian. They were the musicians and that was Carnival. We used to go on the street: Rhodan [Kentish], Darcus [Howe], Stefan, myself – that was the little group of people, about 50 people. We had one little lorry we'd put the musicians on, and we'd start from outside Rhaunie Laslett's place. But nobody can say *they* started Carnival. It came from a community effort, an attempt to bring a black perspective into the wider consciousness. The whites were saying, 'Make them feel at home,' and the blacks were saying, 'We've got our talents which are not going to be suppressed, but if they want to do a little organising, go to the Council and get the money, let them do it. Then when the day comes we'll get our thing together.' And you go back to the Rio and get yourself together.

MICHAEL HOROVITZ: At that time all the local squares (in W11) were surrounded by big wire fences, stopping anyone from getting into them. On the other hand there were a lot of (largely non-white) kids wanting to play and at risk of being run over in the streets. So we started a campaign called 'Open Up the Squares', aimed at these private landlords who kept them locked up. We had the kids going round the streets chanting, 'We want somewhere to play! Open up the squares!' Then, on some bank holiday, we planned with the local activists – Sebastian Clarke, Rhaunie Laslett – two things. One was the Notting Hill Fayre, out of which grew the Notting Hill Carnival, and the other was the opening up of the squares. There had used to be a goose fair or something, spelt F-a-y-r-e, before the last war, and Hoppy said, 'Hey, man, there used to be this fayre thing! Listen, man, you poets, we ought to get together and start "Live *New Departures*" in the local community and get things moving round here. There's all these unturned-on people who don't realise that in amongst them there's all these turned-on people. If we can get them together . . .' So on the appointed day we had the first Fayre, which was quickly renamed the Carnival, and overlapped with wall-paintings and various series of events including jazz poetry, and the first light-shows by Mark Boyle and Joan Hills and the birth of new-wave pop groups, including the Soft Machine and the Pink Floyd. At this first Notting Hill Fayre there were floats and musicians and so on and we had a guy in a gorilla costume and two people in a pantomime horse costume leading

98

this march of hundreds of local kids and all of us, some dressed up and some not, all with wire-clippers in our hands, and all advanced simultaneously on all these squares. Somehow the police had been alerted but they only put up a symbolic resistance. This turned out to be terribly funny because among those they tried to arrest were the gorilla and the pantomime horse. They of course were quite hard to get into the Black Maria. And by lunchtime all these squares had just had their locks smashed and the wire cut and were open. And they've stayed open ever since.

JOHN HOPKINS: I'd met Jenner when we took acid together. We used to hang around the Grove and get up to some mischief there. And there was Gustav Metzger, the most paranoid artist I've ever met in my life. He put on a thing called the Destruction in Art Symposium (DIAS). It was held on the site where the Westway is now. Cleared of houses and like a great bombsite. His idea of art was to build something and burn it down. Jenner got involved in that.

GRAHAM KEEN: Jim Haynes was doing the Destruction in Art Symposium at the Jeanetta Cochrane [Theatre], that's when I met him. One terrific night when he put on *Son et Lumière for Bodily Functions and Fluids* with Mark Boyle and Joan Hills. What they did basically was that he coughed up phlegm, he pissed into bowls, had throat mikes, penis mikes and so on to amplify the sound throughout the auditorium and the resulting fluids were placed under microscopic slides and then blown up and projected on a huge screen.

COURTNEY TULLOCH: One day Hoppy went around and collected a whole list of people's names and addresses and telephone numbers, and without asking their damn permission put it on a couple of sheets of foolscap – 'The 100 Prime Movers in London' or whatever – and circulated it all over London to each of the hundred. All of a sudden people were coming from all over the bloody place ringing my door bell because my name was there. 'You are the one hundred people who are producing the energy in London now, so here is your names and addresses cross-fertilised.' And Hoppy was an excellent talent in terms of that sort of activity. People would start ringing up: 'I'm doing this, can you assist with that . . .' and you found all kinds of people. Freaked-out hippies would come and stand outside my door and chant all day and night and I can't sleep. This guy Rolo used to worship me. I was his God, literally. He used to come right outside my flat in St Luke's Road and I was his God. So I used to say, 'Rolo: now you must go to Wales and sit down in

a tepee and stay there for two weeks because I want some peace.' Rolo
would go away for two weeks – but two weeks on the dot he would be
back again.

EMILY YOUNG: Hoppy, John Hopkins, turned up at Holland Park
Comprehensive saying, 'We have started a place called the London Free
School, just up the road a bit, and people can come there and you can do
what you want, do poetry, music, art and we're going to put on shows,
it's for everybody to come along and have a good time.' So me and my
friend Anjelica went along.

Hoppy was a bit like this cultural pusher hanging round the school
gates. There was a tremendous fuss about all this later, which ended up
with him going to prison because there were all these females going off
and taking drugs and going to bed with odd people and how exactly had
the school allowed this to happen, why had this man been allowed to
come in? And who was he? My parents said it was either run by the CIA
or it would die within two days.

The Free School was at 26 Powis Terrace. There was Hoppy, John
Michell, Mike McCavity, who was a true man of the road, not as culturally specific as later hippie tramps like Eric. He was Irish, he had
ginger whiskers and he really was McCavity the Mystery Cat: you
never knew where he came from or where he went. He was fairly mad,
but he had a beneficent air about him. It was truly tramps and culture
crossing. I was delighted by it. I just loved it. The incredible poverty
– mud floors, and we'd go out at night and steal railway sleepers, and
we'd carry them back. Hoppy was there in the daytime, being slightly
more cultural, but at night was the action. We made fires, because it
was so cold, and soup, vegetable soup from vegetables which you
picked up in the market.

So I was living this very curious double life. I'd go home at five or six
in the morning, get up and have breakfast, go to school, then go back to
the Free School and maybe go to sleep with the others. We were like a
bunch of wild animals really. People were very dirty. And they told
wonderful stories. I'd go home at home-time from school, then I'd go
out in the evening, then I'd go home again and then I'd crawl out after
about eleven when everyone had gone to bed. I walked everywhere; two
o'clock in the morning I'd be stopping people in the street and asking
them for cigarettes and for money for the cigarette machine – for these
fellows I was so enamoured of, these poets of the road. There was also
Dave Tomlin, who was my boyfriend; Neil Oram; Michael X would
come by. People would warn me about him and say, 'Be careful about
him, because he might try to take you off and exploit your youth and

sex.' He never did – I thought it might have been rather interesting. I was out for experience.

There were early concerts for the Pink Floyd at All Saints Hall – I was there, every Friday night. They were starting to build the motorway and they'd knocked down this run of houses. It was the dark side of the moon, the other side of wonderful Britain. It was the Martian wasteland, there were dead donkeys lying around, and dead people, a dead baby one time. A very weird place, desolation. And we'd have happenings: huge bonfires and musicians would come and Dave Tomlin played the saxophone and wrote poems and we'd take a lot of acid. These were wild creatures: you couldn't place them as bohemian or anything – they weren't middle class, they weren't literate. They were all appreciably older than me, but there was romance in these people, they were gypsies, they really were.

GRAHAM KEEN: The Free School was an alternative social work thing really, as opposed to a place for actual teaching. The initial idea was that anybody who had anything to teach would set up a class. It was fairly half-hearted. Nobody really wanted to do very much canvassing and the kind of people that came around weren't the indigenous population who naturally enough and quite rightly viewed us with a great deal of suspicion. At the Free School we came into contact with all sorts of people. We invited Muhammad Ali, who was over here to fight Henry Cooper, and he came around to Rhaunie Laslett's house, to meet the locals. That was through Michael X. A couple of days later Michael took me to the Mosque in Regent's Park and Ali was sitting there with Herbert Muhammad, who was next in line to Elijah Muhammad, and people were being taken up to him and introduced to him and Michael said, 'This is a young white boy that is doing a lot for our people,' and I shook hands with him. Then we all photographed him on the steps outside. We'd made efforts to encourage Michael to get involved, since he was doing things in the area and we were just starting. One night Michael X came round and walked up and down the basement of the Free School where we were having our first meeting. He came down and swaggered about with a silver-topped cane, obviously trying to put on an impression. I think he was more weak than anything else. Really he didn't have anything going either for the blacks of the area or for anybody else.

EMILY YOUNG: Nothing was really taught but it was great fun. Local people could come in and play their instruments and it was a place for them to rehearse. John Michell had an interesting influence. He was knowledgeable, he did have these odd books – and there were a lot of books, great enthusiasm for interesting old arcane knowledge books, and there was a lot of talk about flying saucers, the measurements of Jerusalem and all this stuff. A lot of discussion about the whole of one's life being encapsulated inside one cell of one's body. Talk about Ronnie Laing and anti-psychiatry, all those new ideas. I think we all knew that we were loopy, really. If you look at the personal psychologies of every single person there, I really believe that everybody had a problem and there was a sort of safety with your peers, that people couldn't handle the big world, that they weren't successful people in those terms but they were intelligent and sensitive and creative and however odd you were you were acceptable. I think all over the West there was this whole questioning of the status quo: that people were *wrong* and that the government was *wrong* and the institutions were *wrong*. I was a *classic* delinquent. I used to steal money from my parents, then take them all out to breakfast. They were all poor and undernourished and junkies and God knows what and I was doing my Lady Bountiful, endlessly. Wandering those dirty backstreets, the whole thing was like a film set. It epitomises London to me: late nights in North Kensington.

PETER JENNER: The Free School didn't do much, but we did all become distracted by it. Very little was actually taught. There were a few classes but it was all going to start properly in the autumn and this was still the summer. And we realised that we needed to produce a newspaper, a magazine, an information sheet. This was originally done at Hoppy's place, and it later became *IT*.

COURTNEY TULLOCH: Before *IT*, in the Free School era, Hoppy had a little magazine called *The Grove*. The Grove was a black name. The blacks renamed the area: the white hippies talked about Notting Hill Gate so it was 'The Gate' and the black people centred on Ladbroke Grove, so it was 'The Grove'. So Hoppy, who wanted to show how in touch with black people he was, knowing the black name, called his magazine *The Grove*.

MICHAEL HOROVITZ: There were a lot of graffiti in the Grove: 'The tigers of wrath are wiser than the horses of instruction', 'The road of excess leads to the palace of wisdom' and so on. Heathcote [Williams] wrote absurd ones: 'Enoch Powell is Vanessa Redgrave in drag'. On a wall in Moorhouse Road somebody had painted 'Hashish is the opium of the people' and after about two years someone finally painted it immaculate white. And the very next day, on this new temple of whiteness, someone had written in the night in huge red letters, 'Look, the wall is white again!'

All Saints Hall: 'A very significant place'

PETER JENNER: The other thing we realised was that we couldn't do much with the Free School without some money: to pay for the magazine, generally to get the word around. So how do you raise money? You have socials, as they used to be called. So there we were, the local community group, and we got the local church hall for a social. All Saints Hall. And I was now managing the Floyd so I thought: let's put on some gigs. And that's where they started and they instantly went off like a rocket. They started in September and by Christmas we'd had centre-page spreads in *Melody Maker* about the Pink Floyd. We none of us knew what had hit us. It was probably 7/6 at the door. It was a tiny church hall, it couldn't have held more than 300, it was heaving. You couldn't move. Originally it was all word of mouth – all our mates, the community. Suddenly it hit a responsive chord.

It wasn't too psychedelic. Smoking dope, but not much acid. We'd read about it, but there wasn't much around. And the only people who smoked, in any considerable sense, were me and Syd [Barrett]. Roger Waters was convinced at that time that I was a drug dealer and that Andrew [King] and me were actually dealing. I wish I had been.

There were these two guys, I don't know who they were, who turned up from America and did the blippy lights, the oil slide-show. They just turned up and said they were from San Francisco and they did lights, so we said, 'Great, come and do some lights.'

COURTNEY TULLOCH: All Saints Church Hall was a very significant place. That was *the* venue, that was *the* place. The local vicar was willing to allow the church hall to be used as a community resource. One part of it we used to use as the first playgroup. This is another area of the whole thing: the community comes together, defines its needs, and begins to work to establish something. We established the principle of under-five playgroups, and all sorts of ideas that are now replicated throughout the country actually come from there. Law centres, community councils, black theatre. It all comes from All Saints Hall. Keith West put on Langston Hughes' *Shakespeare in Harlem* there. These were some of the people who'd been extras in *Cleopatra*, like Horace Ove had been, who came back and thought, I am an actor, I am an artist . . . Hoppy was one of the first people to develop the sense of being an alternative impresario. He would get people who would do mime, he would put on some fantastic stuff in All Saints Hall. That's where all the ideas were germinated.

The Pink Floyd: 'What we wanted was an avant-garde pop group'

PETER JENNER: Hoppy, Felix de Mendelsohn, Ron Atkins and myself put together this label for a band called AMM which Joe Boyd put on Elektra. Their music was called 'Extracts from a Continuous Perform-ance' – because all noise is music. The idea of the label was that it should be avant-garde music, break down the barriers between classical music, folk music in its widest definition, and pop music. Modern, progressive, avant-garde music. We knew nothing. We signed an outrageous contract with Elektra in which we got 2%, out of which we had to pay for re-cording. So I worked out that we were never ever going to earn a penny, let alone pay the recording costs, and what we needed to make this label work – this was during the Beatle era – was a pop group, because we all knew that pop groups sell lots of records. Now I didn't know anything about pop music, but I did know that pop music sold lots of records. I probably had it very wrong about quite how many, but pop stars earned £100 a week and pop groups sell lots of records. What I hadn't realised was that an awful lot of them don't sell lots of records, but in a sense I was right: we needed huge volume and it was only going to be through a group that was in some way pop that we'd do this. So what we wanted was an avant-garde pop group.

GRAHAM KEEN: One afternoon at one of the happenings at the Marquee there was a group from Highgate who played a couple of numbers and Hoppy and Alan Beckett and Pete Jenner, who had already been involved in the Free School, went up and asked them if they had a manager.

PETER JENNER: While I was marking some exam papers at LSE I needed a break and I walked over to the Marquee and went to this gig, a private gig on a Sunday, at which there was 'The Pink Floyd Sound'. It was organised by Bernard Stollman. His brother Stephen ran a very avant-garde label in America which had the Fugs. So Bernard put on this show which he called a happening. There were various people sliming around in jelly and colour was being thrown all over them, that sort of thing. I saw the band and thought, 'Oh well, they'll do.' I did suggest they should drop the 'Sound'. The name came from a sleeve note which one of them had read, which referred to Pink somebody or other, and Floyd somebody or other, two old blues guys, and they just thought that 'The Pink Floyd' was a nice combination, and they called it the Pink Floyd Sound. So it referred back to blues. It was almost the first pop band I'd seen.

At that stage they were a blues band who played things like 'Louie-

Louie' – cos everybody was a blues band at that time – and then played wacky bits in the middle. So the solos were wacky, they just sort of went on. This was Syd Barrett and also Rick Wright. I wandered round the stage, trying to work out where the noise was coming from, just what was playing it. Normally you could hear something: that's the bass, that's the drums, that's the sax, that's the trumpet, you knew where everything was. But the Floyd, when they were doing their solo bits, I couldn't work out whether it was coming from the keyboards or from the guitar and that was what interested me.

JOE BOYD: I was living a very settled life, mainly concerned with running Elektra. But by the autumn of '66 things had begun to change in that I could see that things were moving in an interesting direction. The reaction to the release of the first album by the Incredible String Band, whom I was managing, was quite strong. People had predicted that nobody would like it because it was not traditional, but in fact there was a whole new audience that responded to it. They came out of folk, and they were definitely Scottish hippies. They took a lot of drugs, they meditated, they did all that kind of thing. At the same time signing the Doors and Love had changed the tack of Elektra and I viewed it as my brief to try to come up with equivalents in England.

Starting in August '66 I started going down every Thursday night to the Marquee to see the Move, who I thought were very very good. They were Brummies who were getting psychedelic-ed on beer and doing a very good job of it as well. What they were doing was in fact something that was never properly recorded but was very very much in the same line as the Pink Floyd, and in a way rather more advanced. It was cod-psychedelic, but very, very good. Long extended solos, feedback, all that stuff, and they were doing it right at the beginning of when people were doing it. I also went to see the Pink Floyd and I heard a tape of the Pink Floyd that Peter and Andrew gave me. So I tried to get Jac Holzman to sign both the Move and the Pink Floyd.

There was a tremendous feeling of a kind of an energy building up in a certain direction. I was being lured more away from the folk scene into the pop scene. It was my clear intention to take the Incredible String Band there with me. I said, 'The hell with the folk audience. I don't care about them as far as the Incredible String Band are concerned.' There was this new audience of hippies and you had, in my view, a phalanx of possibilities with the Move on the right wing, the Incredible String Band on the left wing and the Pink Floyd in the middle. That's what I wanted Elektra to do. Jac Holzman didn't see it that way and he got more and more alarmed at my spending my time promoting groups instead of promoting Tom Paxton. He didn't want them. So virtually a year after I arrived at Elektra in London Holzman and I had one of those 'You can't fire me. I quit' conversations. So there I was: out on the street with no visible means of support.

PETER JENNER: When we met them the band were breaking up. They were all going off for the summer vacation and they didn't know whether they'd get back together in the autumn. I said, 'You should stay together and sign to my label.' So they said, 'Come and see us after the vacation.' So I tracked them down and I did go and see them and they said, 'What we really need is a manager, cos otherwise we're going to break up, cos it's all too much schlep. We don't have enough equipment, we need someone to help . . .' and blah-di-blah-di-blah. I called Andrew [King], who'd just left British Airways, and he bought them some equipment, and we became their managers. The equipment instantly got lost.

JUNE BOLAN: I became their roadie; they had humpers but I drove. John Marsh did the lights. His wife Linda was eighteen and terribly pregnant and she used to go all over England with this huge lump and clean all the slides.

PETER JENNER: Sumi [Jenner] and I and Andrew built the first lights for the Floyd. Closed beam spotlights with gel which we sort of pinned on. We mounted them on boards, attached some wire and had a light switch which we just turned on and off. We had three lighting men after that: John Marsh, Joe Gannon and Peter Wynne-Wilson. Gannon was the first: about sixteen, a young bullshitting fresh-faced kid with an incredible amount of energy and loads of verbal who just whizzed in and whizzed out again. A very engaging chap. He emigrated to LA in '67, although he came back later. Peter was a friend of Syd's, he lived in the same flat. He was the handyman, he built their beds: he was the bloke in the communal flat who could actually do things, all the rest were hippy-dippy students.

JOHN MARSH: When I got to London I got a job in Dillons bookshop. There I fell in with the beginnings of the 'alternative' crowd. I shared a flat with some girls I'd known in Hoxton; one of their boyfriends knew Pete Jenner and Andrew King. And that was when the film began to speed up. It was then that I started hanging around the fringes of the early days of the Pink Floyd. I left the East End and moved into the top floor of a house that Pete Jenner owned in Paddington. That's where I met June Bolan, Linda [Marsh] and so on. I just literally drifted into working for the Floyd. I was working at Dillons, getting involved with Linda, moved to the top of the house in Edbrooke Road, spending more time hanging out with June, Micko, Pete and Andrew and to some extent the band. All this culminated in taking so much time off work that I got the sack through taking the day off to help the band set up the stage for the 'Games for May' Concert at the Queen Elizabeth Hall in early '67. I got taken on the Floyd payroll. I did a stint covering for Peter Wynne-Wilson as lights man, and when the Floyd found they could get my services cheaper than Peter's he got the elbow.

JUNE BOLAN: Peter Wynne-Wilson was the roadie for the Floyd. He'd never driven a car in his life, so I became the truck driver and secretary and wages payer and general factotum. In those days work and life were totally integrated, it wasn't that you stopped work at five and went home: you all lived together, you worked together, you went out together, you did everything together. I stood on doors at gigs with clickers to check the tickets of people coming in, humped huge speakers . . . that's what you did.

JOHN MARSH: Wynne-Wilson was one of the hippie aristocracy. His uncle was Bishop of Bath and Wells and so on. At this stage he was tied up with Susie Gorler-Wright, the psychedelic debutante. Both charming people, both very dedicated to the benefits of the acid culture. They were into areas I found incomprehensible. At one stage Alfred Jarry had written the description of a machine which would enable man to fly, to levitate under his own steam. Peter Wynne was totally caught up with this, and very keen to construct it. Fair enough, very jokey, lots of fun, except, as happened with so many people then, he began to believe his own bullshit. He became absolutely convinced that he'd constructed some device which enabled him to hover above Cambridge Circus. Not only did he believe that he had constructed the machine, but that the US Navy had done the same thing and had floating aircraft carriers off Vietnam.

JUNE BOLAN: I started working for the Floyd in 1966. I was living in the basement of Edbrooke Road off Elgin Avenue, on the dole, and Peter Jenner had the flat above, and Andrew King lived there as well. They were trying to get work for the Floyd. They had a telephone and the phone kept ringing all day, and because I was on the dole I answered the telephone. This went on for two or three months and I'd write down all the messages, then go up to Lisson Grove to sign on. One day I said, 'Look, this is a joke. You need a secretary. Pay me fifteen quid a week,' which in those days was all right and more than I was getting on the dole. So I became secretary. We all used to live there; it was wonderful – it was a whole commune. Because we lived so close to Portobello Road we had bicycles and we used to go down after the market closed and people would throw away the most wonderful fruit and veg. So we'd spend £2 on meat, which would be your basic in the pot, dried beans, lentils and things like that. And all your veg came from the market.

JOHN MARSH: The whole period after I went to London was desperately innocent. We were all so naive and inexperienced, although from the mid-60s we began to acquire some veneer of sophistication. Up until then life had been far more clear-cut. A state of genuine innocence, if you reckon that genuine innocence is the state of being unaware of being innocent. It was like diving into a whirlpool, really unprepared. Until I met Jenner and King I had felt that all of my friends were really much of a muchness. Then I realised that there was an awful lot, not just a little bit, that I didn't know about and it was a crash course in what was happening. Crash is the word.

JUNE BOLAN: You had one roadie, normally, who drove for you and loaded all your gear and the band all cleared up afterwards and put it all in the van. You'd do three gigs a night: a club called the Rikki-Tik in Windsor and another Rikki-Tik (I think in Hounslow) and then your third gig for the night, at two in the morning, would be UFO in Tottenham Court Road. I'd be driving and Peter Wynne-Wilson would off-load and everybody would roll in all the stuff. In those days they didn't even have castors on the speaker cabinets. And you carried them in and it was always down millions of stairs and you did the gig and then everybody hung around afterwards and you were all a bit stoned or somebody'd offer a joint or whatever. And you'd pack it all up and you'd go home and you'd have a wonderful evening and you'd get £25 a gig, all in. For everybody.

JOHN MARSH: Pete Watts, one of the Floyd roadies, would never stop at a garage unless it was giving quad Greens, so we were always running out of petrol cos the fucking roadie was so tight that he wouldn't buy petrol unless he could get quad Green Shield stamps. One time coming back from South Wales we ran out of petrol in the real wilds north of Swansea and Pete and Ron (the other roadie) were quite happy to sleep in the van and forage for petrol the next day. But my daughter had just been born and I was keen to get back to London. I ended up breaking into

108

three separate private garages and siphoning off petrol from nice house-holders' cars in order to get us far enough down the road to a garage.

JUNE BOLAN: You always went home after a gig because you couldn't afford to stay anywhere! You'd do Newcastle and back in a night. There were no motorways to speak of. They loved the Floyd out in the sticks. Northern audiences always seemed to feel they were deprived so anything that came from the South . . . It didn't mean you got any more money — they'd give you something for petrol but nothing else. The highlight of the evening if you'd been to Newcastle and were coming back was to go to the Blue Boar, the service station. You'd see people like the Small Faces, Spencer Davis, Soft Machine.

HORACE OVE: I remember Peter Jenner and his wife getting ready for a show at the Roundhouse and they were actually cleaning up the Pink Floyd and combing their hair, like kids. And that's when the whole psychedelic period started. The Floyd playing the All Saints Hall and so on. Light-shows. Arthur Brown coming out on fire.

JONATHAN PARK: My marriage having broken up and being footloose and fancy free, I went to the Roundhouse, which was where I first heard the Floyd play. There were probably two or three hundred, definitely a hippie gig. I remember that gig because I think it was the first time I ever actively rolled a joint for myself and turned on. I stood there watching, with this sort of reefer burning a hole in my pocket, looking around nervously and I thought, 'This must be the moment,' so I drew it out of my pocket, and popped it in my mouth, then of course I didn't have a match, cos I wasn't a smoker. I managed to get a match and I smoked the joint and watched the Floyd.

PETER JENNER: I'd met some of the Soft Machine at a party of Hoppy's, Daevid Allen I think, and Mike Ratledge lived upstairs in my house, endlessly playing 'Three Blind Mice'. The Floyd and the Soft Machine were not a team: professionally they were bitter rivals, although this was not articulated. I certainly thought that we were psychedelic and the Soft Machine weren't. They were just cashing in, somehow.

ROBERT WYATT: The Pink Floyd were with a lovely bunch of people, Blackhill, and they were very nice and I think they were an honourable exception to the shady rule about managers. I think they were nice people and really cared about the people they worked for. I think that most of us were less lucky than that.

MICHELENE WANDOR: We all knew him at Cambridge. Peter Jenner: the business beatnik.

PETER JENNER: The company name came from a little farmhouse called Blackhill Farm in the Brecon Beacons which Andrew and I had bought for £1000. So we called the partnership after that. It wasn't a company, it was a partnership between ourselves and the Floyd – very cosmic. Which made it very tricky when we broke up. We did buy the hippie thing. We were going to be alternative, all working together and everything was going to be democratic and groovy. We didn't know any better about resolving the problems that arose. We were incredibly inexperienced in things like cash flow and business management. By mid-'67 cash flow had taken on a meaning. There were a hell of a lot of people on the staff. One night there was a band meeting with 33 people, although that included the wives and girlfriends. There were maybe ten on the payroll. The salary bills were enormous and that just put us on a treadmill which we didn't really notice, because the money kept flowing in. Then the gigs started drying up. All the gigs we'd been getting were Top Ten gigs – when you had a Top Ten hit you got booked at £300 a night for two or three months, but unless you had another hit, you didn't get booked any more. I had no idea how successful we were being. No idea how to relate to it and work it out. Eventually our accountant did actually get over the point that there was no such thing as 'the company'. Somehow we all had this notion that 'the company' would pay for things, but he managed to get us to realise that we *were* the company, that there was no other pocket than our own. We didn't give any money to hippie causes. We might have done the odd benefit, given the odd fiver. We did UFO, for which we were paid very little money. Originally UFO was going to be our gigs. The Free School and the Floyd put on the All Saints Hall gigs but then we let Hoppy take it over because we wanted to do other things.

JOHN MARSH: Jenner and King I guess were skating on extremely thin ice and found it extremely difficult to know really where they were going. Along with most people who had a shot at the big time in those days, it all started out as art with a capital A, and the realisation that large sums of money could be earned out of that kind of thing proved as tempting to those guys as to anybody else. I believe that for a time there was a kind of phase [of thinking] that perhaps the big bucks could be used for some kind of wider purpose. I don't think this was outside the music business – they weren't into setting up alternative schools or what-

110

ever — but there was a belief for a while that the money earned by the bigger bands could act as food for smaller ones. The way Apple folded and the kind of rides Lennon and Harrison in particular were taken on was what was happening on a less intense level throughout that kind of counterculture society.

PETER JENNER: It may be hippie shit but it's really true. When there's no money changing hands, the spirit is *all*. Everybody's doing it because they want to do it, and it's fun. The more successful they became the more money became involved, and the more money became involved the worse they became. They became more of a hassle, they became more of a nightmare, you had to get record company support, you had to build stages, you had to pay for security, you had to pay for police. They couldn't believe that we were doing it just for love, that we didn't make money. But they couldn't accept the idea and they insisted that they should be put out to tender and that was it. That's when they started doing things with Richard Branson, loathsome people like that who started living off the underground, pretending to be hip.

ANDREW BAILEY: The underground was always incredibly entrepreneurial. When you think about what they managed to do with their limited resources — they didn't have merchant banks coming round and throwing money at them — it was pretty amazing that people could actually produce these things and I think they gave a lot of hope to other entrepreneurs. Branson was around, but he was only a tourist. He always was a Tory and an exploiter of the trends. He didn't bother with the hardcore underground, but he was very good at the fringes. He would have been found out, disparaged and vilified if he had tried to join in properly.

PETER JENNER: The Floyd were the *only* psychedelic band. Various bands came along later to copy, but at that time it was the Pink Floyd. They had this improvisation, this spirit of psychedelia, which I don't think any other band did. Even the Grateful Dead, they had improvisations but they seemed a perfectly ordinary group, playing with chords and things. The Floyd didn't play with chords. At their finest it was very extraordinary free improvisation, in the purest psychedelic sense. During the early UFO days, before Syd went crazy. We thought we were doing what was happening on the West Coast, which we'd never heard. And it was totally different. Attempting to imitate when you don't actually know what you're imitating leads to genuine creativity and I think that's what happened with the Floyd.

MELISSA CHASSAY: David Gilmour has always said that when the Floyd left Blackhill and went to Brian Morrison they discovered that Steve O'Rourke was the great deal-maker. They decided that they were a band who could make all their own artistic decisions; they were educated upper-middle-class boys and they didn't need a manager saying, 'Well boys, this is what you should do now,' but what they needed was a deal-maker. They didn't want to make deals, and they had this extraordinary thing which was based on Roger's communist upbringing: no interviews, no personality stuff; if you like the music that's what you're going to get. They did give masses of stuff to charity and they really did live up to a left-wing ideal, if that's possible, of a rock band. So Steve was perfect. He had no pretensions of telling them what to do.

PETER JENNER: The break-up was partly a combination of us getting involved in other things, and not being able to keep Syd in the band. It was all getting too much with Syd, just getting too spacey. The American trip, which Syd went on, was quite extraordinary. Round the beginning of 1968 Syd finally left the band and they came in and said, 'You don't believe in us any more without Syd, do you?' and we said, 'Well, frankly, no. I can't see how you're going to do it without Syd. Where are the songs going to come from?' So they said, 'We'd better go off and get someone else to manage us,' and they went off with Brian Morrison. And suddenly the work came in. Whether that was a seasonal thing, or whether it was a plot, I'll never know.

JOE BOYD: Just before UFO began I had set up Witchseason Productions when I thought I had signed the Pink Floyd to Polydor. That's why I had set up the company. The deal fell apart and ultimately I produced the record for the agency, Brian Morrison. The record was then sold to EMI, who didn't like outside producers and insisted that they use an in-house producer, so I ended up not continuing my association with the Floyd, much to my chagrin.

PETER JENNER: Gradually all sorts of dubious people began to get involved. The music business began to take over. The Gunnells started the Rikki-Tik clubs and so on. There were things like the Festival of the Flower Children. Joe Boyd got dumped as the Floyd's producer by EMI. They bullied us. Norman Smith, who was the A&R man at EMI, discovered us and in those days A&R men used to be producers and so he wanted to produce this band. So he got us to dump Joe and Joe got dumped, there's no question. I suspect that Norman was rather better for them. He had been the Beatles' engineer up to that time and had graduated to become a producer and he tapped them into that Beatles tradition. He helped them make good records. It's quite likely that Joe might have let them become more indulgent, because he didn't have the age and the experience at that time. There was enough madness flying around and the sanity and the boringness of Norman helped ensure that the Floyd made hits. Which was vital. If the Floyd hadn't had a hit they never would have got through the difficult times they went into – had they not had 'See Emily Play', had not the first album been successful. It went to Number Three. We were the first band to be signed by EMI with an album deal. We didn't have to have the hit singles first before we were allowed to make an album.

IT 'That was what beatniks wanted'

SUE MILES: After the Albert Hall Ferlinghetti came to stay with us and he proved that you don't have to be either intelligent or interesting to be a well-selling poet. He spent two weeks looking for the bathroom – he couldn't believe we didn't have a bath. Then Corso came. Then there was publishing. Then there was the whole thing: 'Why don't we do what they do in New York – a *Village Voice*?' 24-hour city, drugs and sex and rock'n'roll and all that. That was what beatniks wanted. That was the link: free sex, free drugs, being able to look weird and not being thrown out of your flat or perhaps not even given a flat because you had long hair. It was about challenging current attitudes about homosexuality, especially inspired by Ginsberg. He'd been asked, 'Are you married?' and had said, 'Yes,' and produced Peter Orlovsky on a network show in America. He'd also organised the first Legalise Marijuana demonstration, which was him, Peter, Julius, who's a catatonic, a three-legged dog and one friend standing on a corner in New York with a sort of soggy banner that says 'Dope Is Good' or 'Love Is Nice', standing in the rain. It was picking up and imitating American stuff really. They just had this folksy professionalism.

JOHN WILCOCK: The *Village Voice* began on October 26 1955. When I arrived in New York in 1954 I headed straight for Greenwich Village – because I'd always been in love with this idea of a community of poets and artists and writers, the centre of the artistic world. I was a journalist, so the first thing I wanted to do was start a newspaper. Four days after I arrived I was putting notices in bookstore windows – 'Do you want to meet to set up a Village paper?' – which was how I originally met Ed Fancher and Dan Wolf. But at that stage we had no money. A year later they got the money, met me in a bar and said, 'Let's do it.' And once I got into it I never got out. I went in as News Editor and as a columnist, although I had no idea of what I was going to write. I was working at an angle from the others. In 1954 there were no papers – nothing on the left, nothing even in the centre. Just straight papers. Dan and Ed wanted to address themselves to social and political issues in this context. I was not sophisticated enough to be into that: I just wanted to put out a paper in Greenwich Village. I just wanted to do wacko stuff. It was only when I went to Mexico in 1960, grew a moustache, smoked marijuana, that my life changed; I became politically conscious, a whole rebirth and after that I was a socially conscious activist.

MILES: After the Albert Hall poetry reading we did begin to believe that we could change the world. I wrote about this in an editorial for a magazine called *Longhair* which was published by Lovebooks Ltd at the end of 1965. In parenthesis it was called *NATO: North Atlantic Turn-On*. There was an enormous amount of Ginsberg in it, and the name came from Ginsberg. Because that had been the thing that struck him most about England, the long hair the men had. I was suggesting that it was time that there was some kind of cross-pollination of ideas between all the people then involved in the scene in London. There was a lot going on: in fashion, rock'n'roll, theatre, movies, poetry, literature. What we wanted to do was to put these people in touch with each other; there was actually a need, quite a strong need, for some sort of vehicle for their ideas. That was what we were preaching at the time. It seemed to us that a cross-over of ideas between all these different groups would be a very beneficial thing. The next issue we did appeared in a different format: it came out in a small number of copies and we handed it out at the Aldermaston march in 1966. And that was called *The Longhair Moon Edition of the International Times*. Or *Longhair Times*. *IT*, of course, grew out of this. It had in it an essay about LSD by Harry Fainlight; it had a competition paid for by Paul McCartney, who offered a hundred pounds or two hundred pounds for some film script for some weird thing he wanted to do with Jane [Asher]; a facsimile of a John Wilcock column in the *Village Voice* about the US underground.

JOHN WILCOCK: The *Voice* was still the only paper that took seriously all kinds of things that other people ignored. So I'd be getting letters from people who'd started funny little newsletters called *From the Bottom of the Birdcage* which came out on some college campus and I'd give it a plug in the column. There'd be letters saying, 'Gee, I thought I was the only person in America who thought the way I do, now I read you people and I understand there are other people out there . . .' We realised that we'd plugged into a community. Which Dan had always realised. He was

114

the first person to say that Greenwich Village was a state of mind, not a place.

PAUL MCCARTNEY: Putting money into the counterculture was doing things about changing the world, politically. Once it came to standing up, to being a political candidate and actually running for something, we ran for cover rather than running for anything. But when it was just Miles and I and he was pasting up *IT* and I'd be helping him with a photo or sifting an article or something and Sue his wife would be bringing in the tea – that really is what I like. I thought *IT* was good, interesting, some nice stuff in it.

MILES: The actual origins of *IT* are not that difficult: Sue and I went to Edinburgh in 1964 in order to get married, because our parents wouldn't allow it. So we went up there and got married with the help of a couple of beatniks who were so far outside society that they used quill pens and so on. One of them was the famous Rubber Man: he had this rubber hose that wrapped around him, on one end of which there was a mouthpiece and on the other was some kind of container with hashish in it. So you'd have this enormous sucking until he got red in the face and then he'd suddenly explode in a great burst of smoke and fall over. Pete the Rat had given me this connection in Scotland: Adam Parker-Rhodes. He was experimenting with the effects of LSD on monkeys. And he was unbelievably happy at being woken up in the middle of the night – we had hitch-hiked up, being completely broke. He was clearly a masochist and we immediately recognised the fact inasmuch as he said, 'I shall hide my good coffee. The last people who stayed here, they used it all up . . .'

Adam had to go off the very next day to London but his one introduction was to Jim Haynes and we met him and Jack Moore. Haynes had the Traverse Theatre and Europe's first paperback bookshop, which was based on City Lights in San Francisco. Jim showed us a good time. He was putting on *Ubu Roi* at the Traverse Theatre. Haynes' closest friend was Jack Moore and when we went back to town Jack came to stay with us. When we ultimately started *IT* these were the people we thought of when it came time to think of expanding the editorial board. Because it was clear that Hoppy and I didn't have enough connections. No one ever said, 'Right, let's do IT,' it was that Hoppy and I had always wanted to do some kind of mass communication paper, rather than the small press stuff we'd been doing.

SUE MILES: Haynes ran the Paperback Bookshop in Edinburgh, which was a very unusual type of bookshop for England – it was American, casual, drop in. He'd gone there because he'd been in the USAF and said to them, 'If you're going to send me overseas, will you send me near a university?' And he started the Traverse Theatre and there'd been all these power politics and he'd left it to them, come to London and was hanging around there. One of his friends was Sonia Orwell. He knew rich people. Jim is a really good hustler – not for himself, cos God knows he's a man with no taste and no interests – he'd eat Shredded Wheat packets with sugar on top – and he was a sort of catalyst: he knew Jennie Lee, all sorts of people. He'd come to London to be on the Arts Council and his friend was Jack Henry Moore.

CHRIS ROWLEY: Jack Henry Moore was an extraordinary individual, an intellectual Jew from Oklahoma who then migrated to New York and eventually to England in the early 60s. And without him a lot of these things – UFO and so on – would not have been possible. He was the only one who knew what he was doing: he was into tape recording, electronics, speakers, he really knew that stuff. He was one of the first people of the new order of putting on big presentations with electronics. He was also involved with *IT*.

JOHN LLOYD: Haynes was a kind of a cult figure for the anarcho-lefty-inclined students in Edinburgh, and acted very much as a proselytising force. The Traverse was certainly, in Scottish terms, and I think probably in UK terms, very innovative, more than anywhere else in the country at the time. He was bringing people from abroad, putting on the new plays – Beckett and Ionesco – and new plays from writers in this country; bringing over people like the Living Theater from America. Haynes began talking to people in Edinburgh about a new newspaper on the lines of the *Village Voice*, which he imported and sold in his bookshop. Myself and some other student journalists began thrashing out ideas about this paper in the anarchic way that Jim did. Jim was semi-officially encouraged: he gave a lecture during Freshers' Week when I went up to the university. He was a very charismatic figure.

DUNCAN CAMPBELL: Haynes had been very keen on starting a counter-culture paper in Edinburgh, which he wanted to call *Clype*, the Scottish word for someone who tells tales, a schoolyard word. He had various conversations with possible backers to try to get this kind of Edinburgh *Private Eye*, which had just started in London, off the ground. He was talking to student journalists at the time.

MARK BOYLE: We'd had an exhibition at the Traverse, which had just
116

started. Haynes was there and in trouble. The Traverse had run into debt and he was making the elementary mistake of putting his creditors onto the board of the Traverse Theatre and I kept thinking, 'That's a tragic error, my friend. You don't put creditors into a position of control.' So we said to him, 'You should come to London, you're needed in London.'

ANDREA ADAM: The Americans and Australians who came to London had so great an effect because we were unfettered, we weren't encumbered by the culture or by the place we lived. We could move about freely, say anything we wanted. We weren't going to offend family and friends. We felt free to offend everybody. That was the beauty of it, that we were mavericks. We weren't tied down to any tradition, we were uncluttered by tradition. We could see England from a different perspective, we weren't right in the middle – we were on the edge. And a lot of what we found was pretty hilarious. The class system was most peculiar, it made no sense, especially if you'd come from America where the attitude was that we were all brothers and sisters and we should love each other.

MILES: So Hoppy and I wanted to do this paper, but it was clear that we couldn't do it ourselves, for a start we both had other jobs. We decided to expand Lovebooks Ltd and take on new directors. We took on Jack Henry Moore, Jim Haynes and Mike Henshaw, who was the hip accountant who knew how to handle the eccentric artists. Haynes had an enormous number of contacts and he seemed like a good person to bring in the more cultural side of things that we knew nothing about. He came down here in '66 to do a season at the Jeanetta Cochrane, the theatre attached to the Central School of Art. And the producer of that season was Jack Moore, an American who'd been in the Fantasticks in New York, then come over here. Very gay. We had good contacts on the experimental music side, this guy Alan Beckett who Hoppy shared a flat with was very keen on avant-garde jazz and lots more. Through Peter Wollen we knew Cornelius Cardew, the John Cage influence. Another guy was Victor Schonfield who was involved in avant-garde music but who I'd known in Oxford around 1960 when he was the main pusher, hanging around in a dirty mac selling ten-bob deals. We had a good collection of people but we needed money. Jim was very good at getting money. He knew people like Sonia Orwell and Victor Herbert. A lot of people were approached for money but didn't give any, one of whom was Bobo Legendre, an American from the Deep South, who actually named the paper. She had 'big hair' as they say these days, and big everything else. She was this very rich woman on the New York theatre scene who was Senator Javits' wife's main rival for running the theatrical soirées. She knew that everyone wanted money out of her; she was very loud. Baby Jane Holzer was like her, va-voom!

SUE MILES: *IT* started because everybody said, 'Let's do something.' We had no concept of how difficult it was. It was letterpress. You couldn't get plates made. Censorship was really heavy: you had printers ringing up and saying – 'I'm not printing words like this – I've got women working here!' and all that kind of stuff. People going in the middle of the night and setting the type when the owners weren't there. The printers still had to lay it out – we didn't know what to do, there were no art directors. Jim [Haynes] had a friend here called Bobo Legendre who lived above a fish shop in Shepherd Market, an American. Southern American, rich. He got money out of her, and money out of Victor Herbert, the pyramid-selling guy tied in with Bernie Cornfeld. So Jim was this kind of go-between: on the one hand there were these hairy loonies, which was us, and on the other were these rather establishment, rich characters. Jim was pulling money out of them and for them it was all rather 'Let's be like the Sculls or Guggenheim in New York: patrons to the arts.' So the first typewriter *IT* had was George Orwell's, given by Sonia, which promptly was lost . . . or sold.

JOHN DUNBAR: Some guy who was doing the *East Village Other* came over, a refugee from the *Village Voice* who had started *EVO*, and he came over and he was talking one day in the gallery or the bookshop and it came out of this and the name came out and various other things. It was one afternoon, a lot of dope and joints, maybe even some acid. It all just came up. Including the name: *International Times*. I think it just evolved, I don't remember any one person coming up with it.

JIM HAYNES: I think Jack Moore thought up the name, but we all probably claim credit. You sit around in a room and everybody says about ten names out and everybody else says, 'No not that!' and in the end . . . somebody said it.

MILES: The name of *IT* came out of a meeting of various people to do with *IT* which was held above the fish shop in Shepherd Market which Bobo Legendre was renting. We were all sitting there saying, 'What are we going to call it?' and inevitably somebody said, 'Let's call it "it"' and I think Bobo was the one who said that and she was also the one who,

118

when we started to figure out all the different things *IT* could stand for, was the first one to suggest *International Times*.

SUE MILES: The origin of the name *IT*, I know, cos I was there: as the only woman there my job was to make the tea and the sandwiches and whenever they were going to actually make decisions I was asked to go out of the room. And I did. There were lots of conversations about what the name should be and we talked about the *IT* girl and being from a journalistic background I said, 'Well, call it *IT*. We've got *IT*!' And they said, 'What's *IT*? It's got to stand for something.' And I said, 'Well, *International Times*, I suppose,' and they said 'Fine!' We then made a mistake: the *IT* girl was Clara Bow, but we got a photograph of Theda Bara.

JIM HAYNES: I got the logo made. I knew the guy who did the graphics for the London Traverse and I asked him if he would design *IT*. He said, 'I won't design *IT* cos I've got far too much to do but I'll do the logo.' He did the logo, never got credit for it, never particularly wanted credit for it. It was the only thing he ever did for the underground, and of course he did the wrong girl.

I suggested that we launch *IT* at the Roundhouse and I got the Roundhouse from Arnold Wesker. I called up Arnold, who I knew through theatre connections, and said, 'We're having a little party to launch a paper, can we borrow the Roundhouse?' And he said, 'Well, I guess so. I'm going to be in Budapest giving a lecture.' I said, 'I promise we won't make a mess and it'll just be blah-blah-blah,' and he gave me the keys. And we did the party, which was the first big event ever at the Roundhouse. Centre 42, which he wanted to do, didn't happen. The difference between his approach and mine was that he had a big sign outside saying 'Centre 42 needs £540,000'; I wanted £5. 'You got a building? OK, let's use it. Let's start making it happen, let's do events in it . . .' The launch party did make money. Maybe £1000, and it launched the paper, and launched the Roundhouse as a space.

MILES: The *IT* launch was where Mike Henshaw, who was Centre 42's accountant as well as ours, came into play. Centre 42 had acquired the Roundhouse and had ambitious plans to turn it into a workers' paradise of some sort. Of course they weren't going to use it until then. So we said we'd very much like to and they charged us about forty quid. It was a complete fire trap. It hadn't been used since before the war. The balcony was completely unsafe – Gilbey's Gin used it as a store. It hadn't actually been used as a roundhouse since the turn of the century. In fact it was never used as a roundhouse for locomotives – it was for the winding gear to pull the trains up the hill from Euston Station, and once steam power was strong enough it became redundant.

It was grimy and very, very cold, cos it was October. We had the Pink Floyd and the Soft Machine. The Floyd got £15 because they had a light-show and the Soft Machine only got £12/10. It was the first big gig for both of them. The Soft Machine had an amplified motorcycle as part of their act. This guy called Dennis put contact mikes on the motorcycle and revved it up, wearing a long cape, a head-dress, something like that. They gave girls rides around the outside while the Floyd played. At the entrance there were big trays of sugar cubes that people were offered – although actually there was nothing in them at all. But an awful lot of people managed to trip out on them. Kenneth Rexroth covered it for the *San Francisco Chronicle* and said that the band didn't show up but the audience between them assembled a rough and ready pick-up band which made these awful squawking noises, which was what he felt about the Pink Floyd. He thought the whole place was going up in flames, a complete death trap.

Everyone we knew was there. McCartney dressed as an Arab . . . the most wonderful sight of all was Antonioni and Monica Vitti who was wearing this tiny little outfit . . . There was a giant jelly, about six foot long. Unfortunately the Pink Floyd's van ran into it so very few people saw it in its original glory. It was cast out of a bathtub.

CHRIS ROWLEY: A friend of mine took me along to something that turned out to be the *IT* opening bash, in early October at the Round-house. There was a giant jelly and Mike Lesser crawled through it. It was a cold, damp interior, very dark and musty. The Pink Floyd set up and had a little screen about the size of a painting on which the blob-show was projecting. All these little groups from all over London were massing together. First of all they'd done it at the poetry reading or the Dylan concert, where they'd seen each other. But at this *IT* thing they were actually rubbing up against each other, sharing joints, talking fran-tically about turning on the world. Everyone had made plans of various kinds and they all babbled away furiously about either electrifying the skies so that messages of love and peace could be beamed off the clouds, or turning European universities into a vast library of worthwhile in-formation and so on. It all seemed like jolly good fun and a good idea at the time. It was remarkably optimistic. When had there been such vast quantities of raw optimism among any group? Perhaps not since 1914 when the lads went off to die.

SUE MILES: It was another great event, like the poetry reading. Same thing, me saying, 'Do you think anybody's going to come?' I don't know how many did come, but there was only one lavatory.

PETER JENNER: It was very dark. The total power supply in the Roundhouse at that time was about as much as there was in the average kitchen, probably much less. So the Floyd frequently put all the lights out: we frequently blew the power. If you saw the place in daylight you would have been horrified. It was dank, really cold and wet and filthy and horrible but the excitement at that gig was enormous. It was like 'Wow! This is our place.' There was this great feeling; it was a classic gig, a terrific gig.

'The idea was to have an international cultural magazine'

MILES: We had all these people ready to write for *IT* but none of them could actually edit the damn thing or administer the paper. Sue did early advertising. The main problem then was who would edit it. Both Hoppy and I and Jim liked the idea of getting Tom McGrath, who was then editing *Peace News*. He had to be persuaded to leave and would only do it for £25 a week, which in those days was astronomical. We decided to give him that and everyone else £10. After the eighth issue he just disappeared one day, taking our only typewriter with him.

The idea was to have an international cultural magazine, to link London to New York and Paris and Amsterdam and so on. Also to unite the painters, the music people and dance people and the people involved in boutiques and the clothing scene. There wasn't much input from them but we did have various abortive attempts like 'The *IT* dress' and stuff like that. We had pin-ups too and they were based on the 'Slum Goddess of the Lower East Side' feature in the *East Village Other*. We had Jeff Nuttall doing cartoons, with one-offs from Mal Dean. It wasn't very visual, because of the nature of the printing method. We couldn't emulate the US papers, to our intense annoyance, because hot metal couldn't do it. It was only after we got busted that we found an offset printer.

JENNY FABIAN: I was an *IT* girl: a picture of me naked in a sink in Notting Hill Gate with a towel wrapped round my head. I don't know who took the photo. You couldn't see much of my body, you could see I was naked but I was all folded up. I had to fit into the sink.

JOHN HOPKINS: As we were putting the first *IT* to bed the phone rang and there was this woman on the phone and she said, 'Do you know where I can get hold of Donovan?' Nobody knew where to get hold of Donovan but later that night I found myself in bed with Suzy Cream-cheese. Suzy Zieger. She came from California. She'd been sent over to England because she'd been doing a lot of coke and fucking a lot of rock and roll stars: she was a groupie in the Hollywood Hills at the age of sixteen, seventeen. Her parents sent her to England to a shrink, to get her out of the way. They put her in the White House [hotel], where of course she had a telephone and to her that was freedom, not confinement. So I met her on the same day that we did the first *IT*. That of course threw my personal life into a state that it had never been in before.

JIM HAYNES: Jack and I knew Tom McGrath and we tracked him down and found out he was living in Wales in the middle of nowhere doing God knows what and we sent him a telegram that said, 'Come to London, you're editing a new paper.' He came to London and he was the editor for the first ten issues or something like that. My vision of *IT* was that it would be a European paper which would try to create a kind of underground consciousness throughout Europe. We'd get writing from Warsaw, Stockholm, Paris, Berlin, what have you. To a certain extent that happened. People reporting on what they were doing and trying to bring people together.

DAVID ROBINS: Tom McGrath was really one of the liggers. These guys were old, they'd had families which they'd left and been through a whole lot of stuff which I wouldn't know anything about. When you think about them now you've got to say that they were *meshugganehs*, they were mad and fucked up, very sexist, fantastically sexist, and obviously had a lot of hatred towards women.

MILES: *IT* was originally run on the classic sexist role divisions. That was the way Sue and I lived: I went to work and she stayed at home. Ridiculous. But we did try to change as soon as we found out about these new ideas. When we were in Endell Street we divided the editorship three ways: we had a hippie one issue, the next issue would be a woman and the next issue would be a black. Courtney Tulloch was the token black who edited every third issue.

SUE MILES: My job on *IT* was the advertising. I got four quid a week.
    Christopher Gibbs, whom I worked for later, bought out of solidarity a subscription for each of his five banker brothers and they all wrote saying, 'We'll sue you if you ever send this filthy rag to us again.' One of the things someone did was to grind up the mummified Egyptian shrew

mouse that Christopher had on his mantelpiece and pretend it was dope. Christopher said, 'I hope you got very high, because it was a very rare hit, man.'

JIM HAYNES: People were coming in and going out of the *IT* office all the time, it was like a continuous party. For a short period *IT* was actually edited in my house in Long Acre. This was in my kitchen and this was like a continuous party and it never stopped and we were coming and going at all hours of the day and night, bringing in news, typing in another room, telephone ringing . . .

MICK FARREN: After *IT* started to come out I ran into a few people who said, 'Go over to the Indica bookshop,' which at that stage had just moved into Southampton Row, and I went over there and I bought a load of stuff and there seemed to be all these people hanging out. Then I started going in there quite regularly. Miles was always bouncing about with the Beatles and stuff, though I didn't actually get to know him. I went on reading *IT* for a while and hanging out and then I got into a long conversation with Tom McGrath, who was the first editor, basically complaining that there was no rock'n'roll in it. It was very old-fashioned. There were all these old geezers: Jim Haynes, McGrath; the only one with any life in him was Jack Moore. Apart from Miles interviewing the Beatles in succession there was nothing in the paper on music. There was nothing about what was going on with all these people I'd seen wandering about. It was still talking about Jeff Nuttall. 'Fuck Jeff Nuttall,' we cried, 'there's all this strange shit. My friend Alex has this large sphere built out of plastic dispenser cups that is now seven foot across and he can't get it out of his room – this is more interesting than Jeff Nuttall.' And Tom thought this was a fine idea and he offered me some sort of non-specific job and at about the same time UFO opened.

JIM HAYNES: I was the first *IT* street-seller – I sold it in front of the Aldwych Theatre, I sold dozens and dozens of copies. I claim credit for the 'You can get *IT* here' signs, which I thought should be in every boutique, identifying that shop with the underground. And we'd publicise the shop in return.

JOHN HOPKINS: It was impossible! *IT* was impossible as a proposition and that's why it happened, because we didn't know that it was impossible and if we had known it was impossible we wouldn't have done it. The first edition we put together in metal – lead type – out in a printing works in what is now Hillingdon on a Thursday night and the printers had never seen people behaving like this. I didn't know I was going to run into metal type, nobody knew about that; I'd taught myself offset litho. It was an adventure. The printers were fine but they just weren't used to people coming in with this point of view: 'What's this . . . ? It doesn't fit . . . ? Allright, get rid of this . . . Can we have one of these . . . ? My God, we don't usually have headlines this size,' and so on. The people who ran *IT* were well defined, but the people who contributed weren't.

JIM HAYNES: In those days there were never contracts, there was never anything written, no owner, no shares – it was all done with an incredible sense of innocence. We'll do it . . . yes, let's do it. The payment for me was always joy. That was the number one payment. You got a sense of joy out of doing it, but that couldn't last for ever.

MILES: At the time *IT* started we knew we had a constituency – basically the people who'd gone to the Albert Hall poetry reading, six or seven thousand. We probably printed about 15,000 of the first issue and there weren't many returns. *IT*'s print curve began around 10,000 and went up to peak in May '68 around 44,000. There were a number of campaigns: one was the 24-hour city, to try to make London more lively, to change the licensing laws, have public transport running 24 hours a day – in other words, to return London to the state it was in before World War I. We had no clear idea of what we wanted to create, because there hadn't been that kind of mass youth culture before. Even in America the underground press had only been going for about five months. It was very much the Lower East Side drug scene that we were emulating – *EVO* was just a bunch of stoned freaks. It turned out that we did hit the right chord. We were fortnightly more or less: sometimes three-weekly and occasionally monthly. We addressed ourselves to the mythical community that we thought was there and it didn't take long for that community to begin feeding back. The What's Happening column filled right up and this cross-over really began to happen between the dress designers in the King's Road and the happening artists in the East End and so on. All kinds of connections were made. Quite amazing. How it really happened, I don't know. We were the forum; it wasn't directed by us in any sense, we didn't create the scene, but were used by it, and *IT* was very useful in that respect.

SUE MILES: The original print run on *IT* was 2500, and at least 1750 never left the cardboard box. The media grabbed it. You had Swinging London, then you had us. We were all on David Frost all the time. That was the one thing the underground press was brilliant at – we were fantastic self-publicists. Wonderful. Hoppy – who else would dress as Superman and try and run up Nelson's Column? And I suppose there wasn't very much real hard news going on. Reasonably affluent time, England wasn't fighting any wars, there were no big political issues, the whole thing about disarmament had gone pphhtt. The Labour Party were in power and for a while you had this period where the government were more progressive than the electorate. They'd brought in homosexual law reform, abortion law reform, and the end of capital punishment – issues that if you'd gone to the country on consensus you wouldn't have won on.

CHRIS ROWLEY: Issue One of *IT* had appeared in October 1966. I hung out at the office, did a bit of street-selling (they never paid me a penny for it, but I never did it for money, just went to the clubs, got free drugs ...). There was the office bookshop – Indica – where Miles had this marvellous mixture of Tibetan poetry, science fiction and William Burroughs. I spent a lot of time in there. Miles turned me on to various things, he'd point to various books and say, 'You ought to try this ...' I read a whole gamut of stuff: Burroughs, *Last Exit to Brooklyn*, all sorts of classics of the time. It was all getting very interesting. I became *IT*'s *ipso facto* office boy. I did various jobs, pushing things through mail boxes, that kind of thing. This was in Southampton Row, in the basement of Indica. One day I was in there and Alex Trocchi was there and he made this enormous show of shooting up, letting the blood run down the arm, trickling onto the floor, tying off, the whole thing. Everyone else left except me, and I just sat there chewing my sandwich, drinking my coffee and goggling: this is, like, the real thing at least! A real tourist sight.

SUE MILES: The editorial board of *IT* were taken along by Jim Haynes to meet Jennie Lee who would say, 'Why don't you join the Labour Party?' And we'd say, 'Why don't we *what*?' and we weren't joining any-thing. Least of all committees.

JOHN HOPKINS: As far as politics went, I wasn't a headless chicken, but I'm sure that at that age my balls were propelling me around. I was driven around by my balls from woman to woman and if I didn't have one I'd start to go 'Oh my God ... !' But I knew it was political, the underground, because I wrote half an editorial in *Longhair* magazine and Miles wrote the other half and the part that I wrote was political and that was in 1964 and I'd been on Aldermaston marches – it just wasn't necessarily conventional, party politics. I remember meeting Jennie Lee at the London Arts Lab. She sat down with us, the Minister of Culture, and she said, 'Nye and me worked all our lives to make a better society, and I think we did it. We've got the National Health, free education, so on and so forth . . . why do you say "Politics is pigshit"?' It was an unbelievable insult to her. I don't know what we replied; the older generation thought they'd made a better world and indeed they had, but the fact of the matter is politics is pigshit. You can't have pigs without pigshit, I'm afraid. I took photographs for the Labour Party in the '64 election – they ripped me off badly and I got annoyed. When I saw the way in which Harold Wilson just dumped disarmament as soon as he was elected I gave up politics. So when Jack Henry Moore coined that immortal phrase 'politics is pigshit', I could not help but agree. Frankly, nothing that happened since made me change my mind, the conviction has only got deeper. Politics is a profession that demands lying and cheating, despite the good intentions you have, because structurally it can't be any different. We sussed that then and we all felt we knew it. What we were doing was political, but it was not party politics. It was alternative politics.

DAVID WIDGERY: We always laughed at *IT* in our political wisdom – because they wanted to do such 'reformist' things as get the tubes to run late at night. That was such an American thing: New York has tubes that run all night, why don't we?

JIM HAYNES: The only politics in early *IT*s was extreme libertarianism and the bias towards an individual's right to do with his or her mind and body what he or she wanted to do. Sexually, drugs, reading, no censorship, smoke anything, inhale anything, inject anything: it's your life, baby – do it. And that really, really upset people: the drug part. The fact that we were not anti-drug made us implicitly pro-drug and to a certain extent that was right. The bizarre thing about it is that I never used drugs, never smoked, never injected, I am not a drinker and never was, didn't smoke cigarettes, my favourite drink was orange juice and here I'm writing this incredible libertarian defence of your right to do it.

DICK POUNTAIN: We terrorised the early *IT*. When they were still at the Indica bookshop one of the earliest *King Mob*/Situationist actions was going and breaking in there and scaring the wits out of them. Nothing violent, just language and posture and we stuck the Situationist poster up all over the place: a cartoon about the futility of politics and everyday life, a bit like the storyboard for a Godard movie. Our basic statement

126

was that they were agents of the spectacle and they were all going to be co-opted. This was also the time when the graffiti started going up around Notting Hill. 'The tigers of wrath are wiser than the horses of instruction,' all those.

MILES: Politically *IT* began with the best intentions. The first issue even has an analysis of the column inches devoted to China in the British press over the previous month, showing how insular England was when something like the Cultural Revolution was going on in China. Having no money and having no professional staff, *IT* tended to run what was current and what we ourselves were involved with. It didn't have political analysis. We believed what we printed, people believed anything . . . UFOs land in Hyde Park, fine, fine. We ran a double issue on CIA subversion in Sikkim. One put in what was around. A great number of the articles – people just wandered in with them. People read it because otherwise what choice did they have: *IT* or Fleet Street garbage. We figured, this is the readers' paper, if they want to bring in stuff, fine. We didn't feel too much responsibility in the sense of some kind of paternalistic attitude. The most active readers often became street-sellers. There were a lot of subscriptions, loads of copies went to Paris and Amsterdam. There was an amazing dedication by the people who worked on *IT*, staying up all night rolling up issues in brown paper wrappers and labelling them. It was almost like a religious thing, to get the stuff out. It's almost impossible to imagine any more. To have that kind of excitement and enthusiasm and belief in what you were doing.

'Real delusions of grandeur time'
JOE BOYD: There was no hippie philosophy as such in those days. You can look back and say, 'People believed in this, people believed in that,' but it was very diverse. It was impossible to be alive in the 60s, especially between '66 and '67, and not perceive that society was being affected by drugs, music and youth style. It wasn't a question of belief, it was a question of observation. Depending on your view, you either viewed this development with horror or with pleasure, and I was certainly one of those who viewed it with pleasure. Right up to the end of '67 there was a pretty universal agreement that there was a struggle going on between good guys and bad guys: the narcotics police were bad guys, most governments were bad guys, especially the American government, and people who were opposed to them were the good guys. There was a generational aspect but there were also a lot of older people. So it wasn't a matter of buying the hippie philosophy: if you were involved in the mainstream of events, it wasn't a question of agreeing or disagreeing, it

was plain that there were dramatic changes taking place in society and there were struggles going on. I didn't agree with every tactic or every approach that people had, but issues were very simple. Everybody was against the Vietnam War, everybody was in favour of legalising cannabis, everybody was in favour of a kind of liberation of repressiveness in mores, emotions, and there wasn't much that wasn't pretty unarguable.

RICHARD NEVILLE: The aim of the alternative culture was to shake up the existing situation, to break down barriers not only between sexes and races and God knows what else, and it was also to have a good time, it was to enlarge the element of fun that one had occasionally in one's own life and to make that more pervasive – not just for you but for everyone. I was quite keen to abolish this work/play distinction. There was something incredibly oppressed about the mass of grey people out there. I just thought that people on the whole looked unhappy: they seemed to be pinched and grey and silly and caught up with trivia and I felt that what was going on in London in the 60s would bring colour into those grey cheeks and into those grey bedrooms. With a bit of sexuality and exciting music and flowers if not in their hair at least in their living-rooms, somehow the direction of society could be altered.

I was never a great believer in materialism, and I'm still not. It seemed to me that one of the valuable things about the 60s was the elevation of non-material values. Going back to behavioural ideas, 'you are what you think', stuff like that which psychologically is still important. We thought we were going to change the world. Rock'n'roll was now global and penetrating even Russia, and therefore all the other paraphernalia was going to be global and penetrate; not just the drugs and the clothes. It was an attitude, a state of mind. And, after all, the world is made up of the state of mind of its inhabitants. So if you can alter the state of mind of people, this is fundamental, and I would say even now that it is a very important task to change the state of mind of human beings.

JOHNNY BYRNE: I didn't for a moment think we were going to change the world, because people don't change the world, it's people that change, not the world that changes. And people don't stay changed, they keep changing from A to B to C to D, and I always thought that 'changing the world' was a very simplistic thing.

JOHN PEEL: I believed absolutely, without question, initially. I really thought we were going to change the world. I believed almost anything. I'm very gullible. But then there was a huge excitement because you felt that you were in the vanguard of something, that things genuinely were

128

going to change. I remember reading at school that the Royal Society had seriously debated winding itself up, because they felt that everything there was to be discovered had been discovered, but since then there'd been this vast technological advance, but no corresponding moral advance, and I think that we felt, or certainly I felt, that what we were going to be responsible for would be the moral advance. It was terrible vanity, but I thought that we would be responsible for the moral advance that would match the technological advance of the previous hundred years. Quite clearly it came to absolutely bugger all. What morals these were I didn't of course know. I didn't think in terms of what the actual changes were, what the revolution would be. I assumed that it was going to happen . . . I thought that it would just spread by influence. Just by being super-nice to everybody . . .

JIM HAYNES: We really thought we could change the world. First and foremost it was going to be a world of mutual respect, mutual acceptance. No more prejudice: you could worship who you wanted to worship, how you wanted to worship, wear the clothes you wanted to wear, have the sexual attitudes you wanted, eat what you wanted to eat, drink, smoke . . . whatever you wanted to do – mutual acceptance. You were a human being and you had the right to do that. And I had the obligation to respect that, because that's what you wanted. We thought it made complete sense. Completely logical. There was no pointing a finger at anybody else and laughing at them, or criticising, or prejudging. We thought that everybody in the world would immediately recognise this home truth and it would happen. But they didn't.

RICHARD TRENCH: I wanted the world to change. I wanted it to be sort of left-wing socialist but I didn't want to work. It wasn't just dope, sex and rock'n'roll, it was far more well intentioned and far better. Everybody would work less, everybody would become middle class like us, everybody would read poetry like us.

NICOLA LANE: There was a spirit of the times which was very very strong: the feeling that the world could be changed. It's banal now but people did feel that at the time. It would be changed to a sort of Tolkienesque landscape where industry and nuclear weapons and nasty politicians would somehow fade away under the powerful vibes of the good people. Somehow they'd fade away and there would be all these very happy people getting their scenes together and doing their own thing. Somehow people felt that they would be literally magicked into the new world. There were conversations about how the force, the positive power of the hippies, their vibes, their wonderfulness, would overcome the forces of evil and corruption. And they actually felt that would be possible. The other kind of conversations dealt with a kind of undefined armageddon that would somehow leave the countryside pure and unsullied, but the towns would somehow fade away and great caravans of beautiful people would go forth into the countryside and lead beautiful lives on the land and be terribly happy. The motif was that all the bad things kind of vaporised.

MARK BOYLE: There was this very important hippie phrase: 'If you're not part of the solution, then you're part of the problem.' I *hated* that. And I used to scream at people, 'Don't you realise: we're *all* part of the problem, *and* we're all part of the solution!' I got very angry about some of the rhetoric. I was angry with them for not defining what they meant by 'peace' and 'love'. I said, 'Everyone through all time has been for peace and love, you've got to define what you mean.' But of course they couldn't define what they meant – because that would have split the whole thing apart. And the whole consensus among that group of people was entirely based on the fact that everyone was in favour of peace and love.

KEITH MORRIS: I had a studio in Gunter Grove; it was straight out of *Blow-Up*. It had the old minstrel gallery with the bars and the black beams, it was beautiful. I had a darkroom on part of the minstrel gallery, under which there was an area where people sat. I was doing a spot of printing one Sunday afternoon and underneath me was this meeting going on, chaired by Richard Neville, about how everything was going to work when they took over the world. It was real delusions of grandeur time. Richard, [Jon] Goodchild, Lyn Richards, who was going to be in charge of famine because she was good at cooking. She was Goodchild's girlfriend. Virginia Clive-Smith was there. Sharpie [Martin Sharp] was there, doodling. He just wrote out a hundred lines of 'I've got to get it together, man.' This hysterical meeting was going on and I couldn't help laughing, I was tittering away and I was repeatedly told to keep quiet. Richard's an intelligent guy and I don't actually believe that he thought he would ever rule the world, I'm not sure any of them did, but the gist of the conversation, of the meeting – this wasn't a casual occurrence, they'd all been summoned was changing the world. And what they were saying was, 'If we actually get left with sorting the world out . . . how can we do it?'

UFO: 'Suddenly there was somewhere to go on a Friday night'

SUE MILES: Hoppy started UFO to finance *IT*, because it couldn't make enough money out of advertising.

JOHN HOPKINS: There was a church hall off Westbourne Park Road – All Saints Hall. We started putting on weekly events, on Thursday nights, around October 1966. I started doing it as a desperate measure, not to make a profit, but just to pay the debts of the Free School, which must have been a few tens of pounds. Pete Jenner was around, a guy called Jack Braceland came along, and there was a light-show, some Americans from California. We'd never seen a light-show before. They started doing this light-show in the hall and it all got very popular. Joe Boyd was around. He was into music and he saw what we were doing and said, 'This is popular; if I find a place in the West End, what do you think about moving it all over there and seeing if we can make a go of it?'

JOE BOYD: Hoppy and I had this conversation about doing something on a regular basis and we formed a partnership to do a club and we had to find a place. Hoppy found the Blarney Club in Tottenham Court Road. We went down and met Mr Gannon. He was very amiable and he agreed to rent it to us for £15 every Friday night. He had the soft-drink concession. We didn't have a lease, it was an arrangement between us and him. Hoppy and I didn't sign anything, we just divided up the money every week. And some weeks I might take £50 or £75. We were debating between calling it 'Night Tripper' and 'UFO'. Like many things that happened with me and Hoppy, we each had ideas and rather than argue about them, we synthesised them. So we made up these hand-bills saying 'UFO – Night Tripper' and handed them out in Portobello Road.

JOHN HOPKINS: So he found this place called the Blarney Club and he came back and said, 'Look, I've found this place, how about it?' So we said, 'OK, we've got enough resources to put on two gigs: one on 23 December, and one on 30 December. Each side of Christmas: if we can't do it then, it ain't going to work.' Mike McInnerney had been doing some graphics for the London Free School and he helped with posters, so did Mike English and Nigel Waymouth, and it worked. Joe looked after the musicians, I looked after some of the other stuff and it was amazing. It went off like a forest fire. People got paid, and I don't think a lot of money got ripped off there. It cost ten shillings, maybe a pound to get in.

MILES: UFO was started almost immediately after *IT* began. We had enormous cash-flow problems of course, so we tried a number of different ways of making money. We had the Uncommon Market, which was a sort of jumble sale held in the Roundhouse, with various performances at the same time. To get some proper money turning over we started a night club. I had very little to do with it. Joe chose the music, Hoppy was in charge of everything else. It was held in an Irish dance hall on Tottenham Court Road called the Blarney Club. It had a wonderful polished dance floor.

JOE BOYD: We had these two dates at the Blarney Club, either side of Christmas '66. UFO – Night Tripper: Pink Floyd, whoever else, a lot of different people. They played the first four, they were the resident band, but we also had a lot of other things like theatre groups, avant-garde jazz, Kurosawa movies at four o'clock in the morning. It was great. It was packed from the first night. I wasn't surprised, but I was pleased. I thought there was an audience there. You could tell, you didn't have to be a genius to look around the streets and see there were a lot of people dressing in funny ways.

MILES: Because our 24-hour city programme hadn't quite worked out yet, we ran it from ten at night until eight in the morning, so that people could catch the morning tubes. By about five in the morning it got a bit funky, an awful lot of people curled up on the floor snoozing, meanwhile psychedelic music was blasting out. The Floyd and the Soft Machine were the main house bands, but we also had Procul Harum's second and third ever gigs, when they already had a Number One hit. The Crazy World of Arthur Brown. Enormous amounts of psychedelic drugs being consumed. Micky Farren had by then joined *IT* and he was on the door of UFO. He and Joy [Farren]. They used to stand on the door and trip out. Micky was in black leather, his James Dean/Elvis Presley phase.

MICK FARREN: Suddenly there was somewhere to go on a Friday night – this old Irish showband ballroom with a revolving mirror ball and stuff. I imagine if we were transported back there it would probably look like little more than an adventurous high-school dance, but at the time it was quite mind-blowing.

RUSSELL HUNTER: Micky was on the door with Joy. Before I knew him I used to go there. There was a guy called Manfred, who was very famous for dealing acid there. This terrible fat German. Jim Haynes was there, Miles . . . most people were there, only you didn't know their

132

names. David Medalla and the Exploding Galaxy, who lived at 99 Ball's Pond Road where the door was kicked in so often that they didn't bother to put it back. They were a free-form art group, but mostly they were a lot of speedfreaks dancing.

STEVE SPARKS: Then I discovered UFO. I sort of wandered down the stairs and there was Micky and Joy and I blagged my way in, I looked round and I thought, 'This'll do, this looks interesting.'

UFO was magic, I really liked UFO. Having come from running all sorts of clubs, dances and folk scenes in the East End, UFO was so wonderfully naïve. It was so innocent. You really didn't need heavy bouncers. This was a great shock to me, because you used to need bouncers in the folk clubs that I ran, cos they'd come in – seventeen pints and ready to kill. The gentleness and the naïveté of the whole thing . . .

JOE BOYD: We originally decided to do UFO as an experiment, two weeks, and two weeks only. It went very well, everybody enjoyed it, everybody said, 'You've got to do it again.' We needed a rest, we didn't have anything booked for the next two weeks, and we decided to do two-week bursts. We'd book everything in a two-week lump and we'd do one poster for two weeks. So we had a bit of money and we decided that now we wanted to make it even more successful and we wanted to have some fun with the promotion and not just hand out leaflets in Portobello Road. That's where we came to the posters. I said I have this friend named Nigel who would do a great poster and Hoppy said I have this friend called Michael who would do a great poster. So, following our usual policy, we said, 'Let's put them together.' They'd never met each other and we basically locked them in a room and said, 'Come out with a poster.' And they came up with the best thing they ever did. The gold candy-stripe UFO poster, for the second lot of two weeks, in January 1967.

MARK BOYLE: Mike English did the two great posters of the era, for UFO. I remember walking down the street and seeing one of them for the first time and thinking, 'God! what a poster,' not knowing what it was, then starting to think, 'What's it actually advertising?' and working it out and realising, 'That's us!'

CRAIG SAMS: My connection to the underground came through Michael English who I had known in Ealing and who now did the posters for UFO. UFO was every other weekend, so on a lot of the alternate weekends Michael, his girlfriend Angela, and Pete Townshend and Karen his girlfriend and me would get together at Karen's place in Eccleston Square and trip the night away. We had our own little UFO. That gave us something to do on the alternate Fridays. Once we were all walking down the street just past the Victoria Coach Station, it was really freezing cold but Townshend had stripped down to his shirt – 'Cold is just a state of mind, man' – and we were all barrelling along, just full of our own incredible strength, and some car pulls up. The classic scene: a head comes out and somebody says, 'Hi, Pete Townshend. I think your last album was fucking great!' and then the guy drunkenly heaves all down the side of the car. Suddenly you realised the huge distance between where we were going, into spiritual realms, and fifteen pints of lager, which was where a lot of the mods had gone. But we'd all come from the same roots – soul, dancing and mild pharmaceuticals.

JOE BOYD: It was during that period that I was informed that not only was I going to get rowed out as the producer of the Pink Floyd, but they were going to put their prices up. So we then brought in the Soft Machine. That actually began a kind of quest for a constant turnover of new groups being brought into the orbit of UFO. We had Arthur Brown, the Bonzo Dog Doo-Dah Band, Procul Harum, Tomorrow.

PETER BROWN: My hero, the best dancer I've ever seen: Arthur Brown. A fantastic dancer. And if you see any character in the entertainment business who dedicates their whole being to make every night's performance like an opening night, then you know they'll never last. Well, Arthur was like that. It was obvious that he was going to burn out, because every performance was a total performance, the man literally burnt himself out every night.

JOE BOYD: Arthur Brown was playing in a supper club in Mayfair, doing a novelty act in this weird little bar in Mayfair, which was rather posh, with the fire, the whole bit. He suddenly emerged on this tiny stage wearing this fiery crown, with Vincent Crane on the organ. Victor Schonfield told me about him. I just went down to see him and, 'Hey! Great. Let's have him at UFO,' and two months later he's swinging from the chandeliers at the Roundhouse and his record is Number One.

ROBERT WYATT: When you arrived at UFO, early on, they were usually playing Monteverdi or something. I was probably more awestruck by the place than most of the punters, who I felt took it for granted.
  It wasn't any easier playing UFO than the circuit, but the demands

were our own. We were able to develop our own idiosyncrasies. Our management had immediately put us on the road on a circuit where you had to play for dance audiences. We weren't very good at that. So the great thing for us about UFO was that the audiences weren't demanding in the same way. They were sitting about, most of them were asleep as far as I could see. The very things that were our faults on the regular circuit – that of all the bands playing 'Midnight Hour' or 'Knock on Wood' on any particular evening we would play it worst, if we played it at all – became bonuses at UFO. We couldn't play that stuff, or if we did people didn't realise that was what we were playing.

CHRIS ROWLEY: UFO, down in this cellar, was a disgusting-looking place in the daylight but transformed by the light works and Jack Henry Moore's little team of people putting up screens and shining the blob-shows around. Manfred, the German acid dealer, attended and distributed the product on a handsome level. At the third UFO he gave out 400 trips. A lot of Americans: Suzy Creamcheese, who was Hoppy's woman. I saw Suzy Creamcheese and two other girls love-bomb a bunch of rather uptight young mods who got into the club. The third or fourth UFO. These mods were standing there pilled up, chewing, looking around them, semi-freaked-out. And the girls noted that these mods were semi-hostile, almost lashing out at the hippies round them. So these girls descended on them semi-naked, clad in gauzy stuff with flowers and all the rest of it, and caressed them. These guys did not know what had hit them. But they calmed down and later on they were to be seen holding flowers and talking to Manfred.

PETER SHERTSER: We used to go down to UFO and we would cause so much trouble. We figured the best way to pull was the ladies' toilets. There's so many people around: to save milling around stand in the bog and you're going to see them all at some point in the evening. So that's where we used to go – very good. We used to disrupt everything at UFO, throw buckets of water over people, all kinds of silly, childish things, but because they were all so crazy, they never knew any different. This was before we got into acid and we were saying: 'What is it with these people?' Bit by bit we learned and we were there every weekend.

DICK POUNTAIN: Just about anyone could turn up and perform if they wanted. I saw [Mick] Farren there for the first time, before the Deviants even. I can't remember what the band was called but they were unspeakably awful. It was garage stuff, punk thrashing years before it was thought of, basically because they couldn't play. A bit Velvet Underground-ish; Farren was wearing black leather from head to foot.

MICK FARREN: We called ourselves the Social Deviants and that didn't do much good until basically we started playing UFO. And Jack Braceland who was one of the people doing lights there made us house resident band at this converted strip club he ran down on Gerrard Street. A psychedelic joint. And we laboured in that mine long and hard and met a lot of strippers who came down after work. Being a resident band in a converted strip club in the middle of Soho was quite an education for a young lad.

CHRIS ROWLEY: Happening 44 was a small psychedelic club that ran for about five or six months on Gerrard Street in Chinatown just round the corner from Ronnie Scott's. It was basically run by a couple of old ... beatniks isn't the right word, but they had connections with the film world: the Bracelands. They had a nudist colony out in Watford. One night I went out to a party there: grass, champagne, and slightly fleshy women in their late thirties who were very ready to take off all their clothing and drag anybody away into a series of nest bunks at the back.

JOE BOYD: We had Jack Braceland, fifty years old, doing a light-show at UFO. He came from Watford where he ran a nudist colony and had Happening 44 on Gerrard Street, the place I first saw the Fairport Convention. It was this strip club in the daytime, just a little hole in the wall. He did a promotion there one night a week. Hoppy knew him and we gave him a little corner of UFO. He didn't have the main light-show but he had a corner and people could go dance in his lights. Basically he was a nudist. And there were a lot of people like this, it wasn't just a generational thing.

PAUL MCCARTNEY: You'd go down UFO and see the early incarnation of the Floyd. They'd be down there, a lot of projections, lots of people sort of wandering about, that was nice. It was all like a trippy adventure playground really. Chaplin films going here, Marx Brothers here, Floyd up there, conjuror over here or something – just a nice circus-cum-adventure playground.

JOHNNY BYRNE: I found it curiously tacky, but in retrospect it contained all the best of the cultural movements because it was still young and naïve enough not to doubt what it was doing, there was no cynicism there, there genuinely was the coming together of the various strands.

136

JIM HAYNES: There was a lot going on in UFO but the main thing was people meeting and gossiping. The human, social side was almost more important than anything else.

CHRIS ROWLEY: You'd circulate: do UFO for two or three hours, then hang out at 44 for a little while, then back to UFO. The next night, when Middle Earth was open, you'd do the same thing between UFO and Middle Earth. Eventually 44 closed and Middle Earth became much bigger.

Light-shows: 'You had to have things going "Pow!"'

PHILIP HODGSON: John Massara and I were doing light-shows in our school holidays, that's where it all started. In 1966, after we'd both left school, we started doing lights at UFO in Tottenham Court Road. Then Middle Earth. John was working full-time on the lights but I spent a year in the civil service the first year out of school and doing light-shows at the weekends. There were a lot of people doing that – weekend freaks.

It was all very easy doing lights. You got some glass slides, got some ink, slapped them together and slapped them in front of the projector. Mark Boyle was one of the big originators over here. He'd still be classed as daddy of the UK light-shows. Joe Gannon was also involved. Loads of people did it. If you worked for any of the groups at UFO you'd tend to cross over. One group would finish and you'd just stay on for the next one until your ink ran out or whatever and then you'd push off and someone else would step in.

MARK BOYLE: We had already been doing what came to be known as light-shows in '63. It was a natural development from our work. We realised that our pieces were fixed and permanent presentations of chunks of the world, but we also realised that the world's not a fixed and permanent place. So we started to make a series of performances to show our awareness of that. The first light-show we did was in '63. We did some work with Horovitz's *New Departures*: there were a few gigs there with avant-garde musicians and composers and we would come and contribute a light-show element. We would make our light-show into another instrument. Then we did this piece 'Suddenly Last Supper' in '63 in our house and I suppose that was the first light-show that was done publicly in this country.

The problem for us was the spread of bad light-shows. According to *IT*, three weeks after we did our first show at UFO there were 120 groups in London doing it. The question was one of quality, and of having new things all the time. We prided ourselves on having a completely new effect each week. And there was always this row of guys sitting in front of us who'd turn round with a cheerful smile and say, 'We'll have that!' We saw it more in terms of explosions. There were bubbles and so on, but to get the real quality you had to have these things going 'Pow!!!' right across the screen in three colours, lightning effects, turbulence.

It was certainly the visual medium of the underground and from our prejudiced point of view it was one of the elements that made that particular cultural scene so different from any that had gone before. That there *was* a visual side to it. In none of the other 'music revolutions' had there been this visual side.

ROBERT WYATT: Mark Boyle was burning himself to pieces doing these experiments with different coloured acids. You just saw him with these goggles, looking all burnt and stuff, high up on some rigging. He used to play tricks, he used to make bubbles come out of people's flies and things. You couldn't see exactly what he was doing from on stage, but the atmosphere was good.

PETER JENNER: I don't think, with all due respect to Mark, that his lights were art. It was just that he called himself art, I don't think he was any different from Peter Wynne-Wilson or any of the others. He sussed that it was a good idea to call himself art; some of the others should have been a bit more hip and called themselves art – they might have done rather better.

ROBERT WYATT: The Floyd always had their own lights people, but no one else did and Mark used to do the place, not particularly the groups, but the walls, everything. The light-shows meant that what we shared with the Floyd was that as personalities you could hide and the overall group effect could be more important than the individuals. The normal thing would be that there would be a focus on one or two individual performers, even in the R&B bands, the lead guitarists would get that focus. Whereas we and the Floyd would hardly be recognised off stage, nobody knew what they looked like through the light-show. The anonymity of light-shows was nice – the fact that you were almost in the same swirly gloom that the audience were in was relaxing and you could get a nice atmosphere going.

JOHN MARSH: Light-shows in those days were desperately unsophisti-

138

cated. Pre-laser, even pre-video era. Everything very crudely mechanical, very crudely assembled, but for the time, pretty effective. The Floyd had two effects which no other band had, both built by Peter Wynne-Wilson – one called the Daleks, the other was flashes – and these put them, in light-show terms, streets ahead of everybody else. But this was still manually operated, switch-oriented kind of stuff. We had one marvellous effect: projecting the polarised stress patterns in condoms. That was wonderful. This was a time when jo-bags were still essentially thick, unlubricated rubber. What we did was cut them up into flat sheets of material, placing them between two sheets of polaroid film and stretching the things so that the stress patterns in the rubber, which was semi-transparent, were projected onto the stage: it was a beautiful effect. We were stopped one time for some minor traffic offence: I was sitting on the front seat of the van, a pile of Durex in front of me, a pair of scissors and a record sleeve, cutting up these johnnies. The police were absolutely aghast. 'That's just our roadie,' says Peter. 'He's cutting up johnnies, but he's crazy . . .'

SAM HUTT: I went to UFO quite a lot. Saw the bands, the very loud music, the oil lights and Joe Gannon, who used to run a light-show. I remember near the end with Syd [Barrett], him coming up and somebody had given him a bottle of mandies. Mandies were the big bouncing-around drug, very dodgy indeed, and probably a very good idea that they took them off the market. Syd appeared on stage with this jar of Brylcreem, having crushed the mandies into little pieces, mixing them up with the Brylcreem and putting this mixture of Brylcreem and broken mandy tablets all over his hair, so that when he went out on stage the heat of the lights melted the Brylcreem and it all started to drip down his face with these bits of Mandrax.

JOHN PEEL: Being a timorous chap, I found UFO slightly intimidating. In California we hadn't bothered much with the clothes and stuff. I'd gone along to things like the recording sessions that produced *Surrealistic Pillow* and done a lot of gigs, especially at Pandora's Box which produced the Sunset Strip riots when they closed it down, which was what [Buffalo Springfield's] 'Hey, Look, What's That Sound?' was all about, but people weren't that much into hippie clothing. I hadn't got any of the stuff. So I had to buy myself a pair of ghastly, vast trousers and a very, very expensive kaftan made out of a bedspread, and the obligatory bells and beads. I felt incredibly foolish in them, I must admit, and even in UFO I felt rather out of place.

SUE MILES: John Hoyland, the writer not the painter, lived above the opticians in Tottenham Court Road, on the corner of Percy Street. He said that every Saturday morning it used to sound like a herd of goats in an Alpine pasture were going by when all the hippies and their bells were finally decanted from UFO and trolled off up the road.

The Soft Machine: 'The only other bloke in Kent with long hair'

PEARCE MARCHBANK: I never really liked the hippie ethos. I could never, for example, understand why people regarded the Grateful Dead as the next best thing to Jesus Christ. The Velvet Underground were obviously *far better*. They were to do with *black leather*: who wanted all these smelly old caravans hanging around with wigwams and so on? They were clean, New York, hard-edged. The Soft Machine were the same: Mike Ratledge in his long leather coat.

ROBERT WYATT: In Canterbury I got into a local sort of beat group, the Wild Flowers. The name had nothing to do with flower power; we lived in the country and Hugh Hopper had a book called *Wild Flowers* and I think he thought it up. Wild Flowers was the beginning of what became the Soft Machine. Hugh Hopper's brother Brian, who played saxophone, was a friend of Mike Ratledge and when Mike Ratledge came back from university and wanted to play, we were the only people there to play with. So he joined the band, playing piano. But nobody in the band was trying to do the same thing at all, which is why it was quite original and why, after a couple of years, it fell apart. It was a constant process of disintegration really, getting in new people to fill the gaps. Which in the 60s was rare, because most bands were quite stable. I talked to Nick Mason of the Pink Floyd about that once. I said, 'How come you lot have stayed together so long?' and he said, 'We haven't finished with each other yet.' But it kept changing, we kept on tinkering with it and tinkering with it and throwing each other out of it and leaving it until eventually all the kinks were ironed out of it and in the end it became a standard British jazz-rock band. I don't know what happened in the end. I stopped listening after a while – I stopped listening before I even left.

When we came up to London there were two connections: Daevid Allen had the connection with people like Hoppy. The other connection was Kevin Ayers, who played bass guitar and wrote songs. He was the only other bloke in Kent with long hair.

The name Soft Machine came through Mike Ratledge. He had books like *V* and all that kind of thing. I knew the name was taken from Burroughs but I don't think it intrigued me enough to get a copy. Wild

Flowers more or less became the Soft Machine. We trickled up to London and then regrouped, one by one.

Kevin Ayers was important in that he knew the Animals office, where Hilton Valentine and Chas Chandler were already starting to manage, and they signed us up really on the basis of Kevin's songs. They were looking for something commercial. Chas was always looking for Slade, and eventually he found them, meanwhile he had to put up with people like us and Jimi Hendrix. Shortly after we joined Chandler Hendrix came to London and musically that was tremendously important for lots of people. For me too, if for nothing else than that what he let Mitch Mitchell do on drums gave me space for what I wanted to do on drums. We were using a lot of jazz ideas on drum kits that there hadn't been room for in the constricted time-keeping stuff I'd been doing before. Of course this was quite the opposite of what Nick Mason was doing with the Floyd: he was a kind of ticking clock there – which is just what they needed. For electronic rock his approach was more suitable – uncluttered. People like me and Mitch were probably too busy, but at the time it seemed exciting. So Kevin actually got us a deal and turned us into a group that had a manager and so on. He liked bossanova and calypso. Ray Davies and the Kinks, who started using stuff like that quite early on, were a big influence on him. One record company bloke told us, 'I don't know whether you're our worst-selling rock group or our best-selling jazz group.'

The Macrobiotic Restaurant: 'getting the message across'

CRAIG SAMS: On February 14 1967 I opened the Macrobiotic Restaurant in a place called the Centre House off Campden Hill Road. They had radionics and various other new-age activities going on. The guy who ran it was into health foods so he let us have the restaurant in the basement. It became an instant success and people just came flooding in. It was the only alternative restaurant-type venue anywhere in London. It went on for a couple of months and one night we had a party at which Graham Bond played and around 1 o'clock in the morning it got too much of a party and the next morning the writs started to arrive from our neighbours. So we got thrown out. They were upset with us upstairs as well; I remember Christopher Hills, who ran the Centre House, calling down one day, 'Can you *please* not smoke marijuana – we can smell it on the third floor.' After that we put in a guest book which said, 'I am not in possession of any kind of drugs,' and everybody signed it including Yoko Ono and various other customers. Brown rice and vegetables was 2/6, felafel were 1/3 each. Nothing ever came to over five bob. People wrote out their own chits for what they'd had, someone would watch the till and take their money. It was very trusting. But one night I did a check on the tickets and found out that we had moved 24 slices of apple crumble and only one had been paid for; so after that we went onto a slightly more structured basis. The restaurant generated about £70 a week in sales, of which ten or twelve was profit. At UFO they had this little tea and sandwiches bar and I would bring down rice rissoles and vine leaves stuffed with brown rice – portable macrobiotic food – and give it to the people in the catering area and they would sell it and I would charge them a price for that. And I'd collar people after they'd bought this macrobiotic food and bore them about macrobiotic food, and when they came into the restaurant we'd sit down and give them a two-minute speech – just getting the message across.

101 Cromwell Road: 'If you boiled instant orange juice you'd wind up with an orange'

STEVE ABRAMS: 101 Cromwell Road, which went on for years, was a critical place. George Andrews lived there, John Esam, a guy called Nigel whose flat it was and lots of others.

STASH DE ROLA: 101 Cromwell Road: the Pink Floyd living upstairs; Christopher Case on another floor, a Cambridge-educated American – now an antique dealer in Japan, and then Robert Fraser's gallery assistant; Also Nigel and Jenny Lesmore-Gordon, and John Esam whom I used to call 'the spider': he lived in a sort of warren, a windowless sort of gallery he'd made in a corridor.

JOHN HOPKINS: John Esam was a New Zealander, and he blew in from Greece around 1964 with Daniel Richter. Dan was a very experienced person. I think he was into smack in those days when very few people were. They were both very experienced and we were pretty wet behind the ears compared to them. He was really a bright guy.

VIRGINIA CLIVE-SMITH: John was like a spaceman: I'd only just arrived in London, I still had the moss on my elbows, and John Esam was just this incredible character who laid everything that moved and had the most extraordinary magic about him. He would take people over totally. He would create such energy around him that he was fascinating, almost the way a cobra fascinates a bird.

STEVE ABRAMS: John Esam was a great friend of mine; in fact he gave me my first acid trip in England. Then he became so miserable after

142

that. But every time you saw him he would sort of glow when you said hello to him; it was like you were back on your first acid trip. The first person to proselytise acid in England was Michael Hollingshead who had his World Psychedelic Centre in Chelsea somewhere, and the alternative was Esam.

VIRGINIA CLIVE-SMITH: Within a couple of weeks of meeting John he and a remarkable photographer/film-maker called David Larcher took this moss-covered creature which was me into a basement opposite the Park where David Larcher lived and handed me the proverbial joint. On meeting John and Larcher and various other people one had this extraordinary sensation that there was something, that life was not going to be as mundane, that there was something that perhaps one had never realised was there. It was rather like lifting up a boulder or opening a door and suddenly there was Aladdin's cave.

PETER ROBERTS: Somebody turned up at 101 Cromwell Road from the States who knew John and they brought several thousand trips with them. Everybody was having a fine old time and then the police walked in. Somebody threw a load into the garden and the police grabbed it. There were 4000 trips concealed in a doorknob in another flat in the neighbourhood. There was a bit of mass hysteria and the guy who was the ringleader came round to Redcliffe Square: 'I've got to get out of the country. The police have taken my passport.' I said, 'Here, have mine.' So he did, and he got out of the country with it. I reported the passport lost and that was fine.

VIRGINIA CLIVE-SMITH: The police came in through the door and John threw all these sugar cubes out of the window into the garden and a policeman caught the bag. They tried to get him on ergotamine, but they couldn't – acid was still legal. But it was pretty nightmarish: it went to the Old Bailey and it was extremely serious.

STEVE ABRAMS: They had a certain problem: having got the acid and having arrested him they discovered that acid was not illegal. They concluded that acid was ergot, and it is a semi-synthetic derivative of ergot. Ergot was controlled as a poison so Esam was charged with conspiring to manufacture poisons, which would have an unlimited sentence under the Poisons Act.

The case was exceedingly interesting: there were the police forensic scientists and there was a pharmacologist we knew called Collier. The police then brought in Albert Hofmann from Switzerland who had

143

discovered acid and was to testify as to whether LSD counted as ergot in connection with the Poisons Act. The question was whether you could get lysergic acid out of ergot. The government were essentially saying that if you boiled instant orange juice you'd wind up with an orange. Hofmann said he had extracted lysergic acid from ergot. We brought in Chain, a very eccentric man, greatly disliked by his colleagues and the co-discoverer of penicillin with Fleming. Chain stated that the material Hofmann had extracted the LSD from was not genuine ergot, but some kind of phoney ergot. At one stage the four expert witnesses stood up, got into a sort of football huddle, told the judge to piss off and stood there for ten minutes arguing among themselves. Then they all approached the bench together and told the judge that they had decided that Hofmann was wrong and Chain was right and they had to let Esam go.

After that Esam was a changed person; he wouldn't have anything to do with drugs. He didn't take another drug for at least ten years. He was so miserable that he'd have been much happier if he had taken them. One night at Ronnie Laing's house I got Laing to pass a joint to Esam and we managed to get Esam stoned for the first time in ten years. He was quite happy. I think after that he left England, returned to New Zealand, got himself a job and rejoined society.

'OZ 1 was not psychedelic'

RICHARD NEVILLE: I had founded *OZ* in Australia with Martin Sharp and it proved an enormous success and also eliminated the necessity of work because just doing the magazine seemed to give one a reason for hanging out. It blurred the division between work and play. It had proved successful, it was a very useful way to vent your own ideas. I used to want to be a writer but I couldn't actually write, so to be an editor is a wonderful little road. You're dealing with writers, you're selecting them, you're having an impact, but you're not actually sitting in rooms writing 10,000 word articles yourself. Being an editor was something that fitted my personality at that time.

So I got to London, I saw all these kids dressed up in generals' uniforms and Napoleonic hats, there was a colour and confidence, a new kind of music ... people were breaking barriers and boundaries but there was no really formalised expression of this. The first moment I arrived in London, September '66, there was nothing being published. I was taken to meet Miles in Indica Books, and we had a little talk. I sensed there was a sub-stratum of genuine irritation with the society. There was no access to rock'n'roll, pirate radio had gone, women couldn't get abortions, this again was something which seemed like another piece of repressive puritanical behaviour that one wanted to fight, and there was the marijuana issue. Just little things going on, over and above dressing up.

So I thought about starting *OZ* in London. Martin and I talked about it, I was living with Louise [Ferrier] who'd been a girlfriend in Australia. An article appeared in the *Observer* about Australian *OZ*, so Mary Kenny from the *London Evening Standard* phoned up, came over and I told her, 'Yes, well, maybe I'll start *OZ* in London.' I happened to sit next to Paul Johnson at dinner one night and he wrote a very generous paragraph in the *New Statesman*. And from there on it started to galvanise almost of its own accord. There was indirect financing: I was using Jill [Nevilles'] phone, working out how I'd get the money to pay the bills later. It was really a juggling act, there weren't a lot of funds.

MILES: Richard came round and they took a lot of stupid photographs in Indica which were in the first issue. For a sort of put-down thing about hippies. But we were both persecuted by the Establishment and we did develop mutual interests. It made a lot of sense for our street-sellers to sell both. When we really got into trouble we thought that maybe we could do joint issues which would be like the *Sunday Times*: *IT* would be the printed part and *OZ* would be the colour supplement. We were friendly enough. I used to write for *OZ*. There was no exclusivity. There was no competition between us, not really. *OZ* took off in the way *IT* did: there was a community responding to it. The first edition was a cynical pale attempt at *Private Eye* but that was only on the stands for a few issues before it completely changed its direction and from being deeply cynical of hippies, the next issue was super-hippie.

DUNCAN CAMPBELL: I remember *OZ* advertising itself as the one that was going to take on *Private Eye* and getting the first editions where they had a takeoff of *Private Eye* and thinking they were uppity Australian boys who would never make it.

RICHARD NEVILLE: *OZ 1* was not psychedelic, not at all. It was more satirical, out of the *Private Eye* mould, really a lineal descendant of what we'd done in Australia. In fact, in the gatefold of *OZ 1* there is almost a send-up of the freak scene, some of it shot in Miles' bookshop, because I was really quite ambivalent about that scene. And there were old-fashioned articles demolishing God and strange stuff, and a very good piss-take of *Private Eye*. Peter Cook publicly burnt that issue of *OZ* in a pub in Soho. Martin and I were taken to meet Richard Ingrams. He was not hostile but he was paranoid. He loathed the idea of us starting another magazine, a magazine that was even going to mention the word 'satire'. He asked whether we were pooves, because our hair was long.

Odd people turned up in my life through phonecalls. They'd heard about *OZ* and they wanted to write. Alex Cockburn, Stan Gebler Davis, Colin MacInnes – I just phoned him up and he said, 'Great, terrific.' Nik Cohn I phoned up but he just hung up on me: he was so shocked when I told him how much we were paying, or maybe that we didn't pay at all. Some people were very rude, some people were very supportive. David Widgery I certainly regard as one of the finer talents that we recruited. He was fantastic. I was sitting up in this attic room at the top of my sister's flat and he just came up and handed me this stuff about *Private Eye* – I hardly knew him – and he went away and I read it and thought it was *brilliant*. And ever since then I got him as involved as I possibly could. And I think he brought in Nigel Fountain and others. There was untapped talent: David was untapped, I think Germaine [Greer] was untapped. She was wearing a twinset, with pearls, she had her hair in a beehive, she was in Cambridge. She was making a lot of noise down in Cambridge but no one else was using her. She wrote 'In Bed with the English' for my second issue and then regularly after that. And there were quite a lot of people who wrote for those issues of *OZ* that have gone on to real success.

DAVID WIDGERY: I met the *OZ* people in '67. I was very angry about Swinging London. I said it was all a hoax and had nothing to do with reality and I was writing articles like that once every three months for *OZ*. I just changed the adverbs occasionally! I'd written something for the *New Statesman* on Swinging London, an angry young man type of thing, and somebody told me there was this guy from Australia and he was publishing some sort of student magazine and he wanted articles, why not go and see him. So I traipsed off somewhere and there was this strange man sitting with his girlfriend surrounded by the memorabilia of his recent trip to Nepal, and wearing a little Afghan vest – embroidery on the outside, fur on the inside, absolutely hilarious. So he asked what I'd like to write about and I said I'd like to write an attack on Swinging London, and Martin Sharp virtually resigned over the issue cos he thought Swinging London was so wonderful.

OZ in those days was not at all psychedelic. It was more satiric. I joined very early on and I collaborated on a parody of the *New Statesman* with people like Alex Cockburn and Angelo Quattrocchi from the *New Left Review*. It was just another magazine until about issue six, purporting to be satirical, mainly in competition with *Private Eye*, and hyped like mad by Richard Neville who, despite the hippie surface, was a bright

146

guy. A very good editor, but much less radical than many other people, more a longing to be invited to dinner parties with Alan Brien and Claire Tomalin sort of person: quite an adept social climber. Which in a magazine editor of the time was a very considerable attribute. And his success was keeping together a very disparate group of writers. And Jim [Anderson] and Marsha [Rowe] and Louise [Ferrier] used to run these wonderful parties, at which Richard would bring together all the different strands. Londoners would never dream of inviting Nicholas Tomalin together with Mad Max the hairy hippie or whatever. But Richard just did it and gave Tomalin gossip for months.

RICHARD NEVILLE: The anger in *OZ* and the alternative world was quite genuine, David [Widgery] once used the phrase 'gut radicalism'. There was a genuine anti-authoritarian streak, not only in myself, but in Martin [Sharp], in Marsha [Rowe] and so on. Revolution was in the air: the very first political meeting I went to in London was held in my basement: we formed something called the Free France Committee, which was to raise money for the French students who'd been hit over the head with truncheons. The police were after them and they'd left France and they were now refugees. Revolution began to come from the neighbourhoods, it came from things like Paris. We certainly went on Vietnam marches, I remember Germaine burning an Australian flag on one of them. The very first issue of *OZ* has an incredible caricature of Lyndon Johnson, lambasting his skulduggery. I went to America in '68 and went to Yippie meetings. I was really quite influenced by a lot of that early Yippie writing – *Revolution for the Hell of It* – beyond Marxism.

DAVID WIDGERY: My politics were firming up all the time by '67. I joined the International Socialists, as they then were, after quite a lot of listening at the LSE to various people such as Isaac Deutscher, Ralph Milliband, E. P. Thompson – those more seasoned Marxists who were now beginning to attract a new audience having been out of the picture for the last twenty years during the Cold War. And I started reading people like Trotsky and Rosa Luxemburg and they were very exciting. It was terrific. So I was becoming more political but with a difference. The 22 bus goes from Hackney to the World's End and intellectually I was going backwards and forwards in the same way: my soul was in Hackney but my heart was in the World's End. When I'd get fed up with the Left I'd go and be a bit psychedelic for a while then I'd very quickly get fed up with psychedelia and go back to the Left and so on.

147

JIM ANDERSON: I went to London in '63 intending to be a writer and an artist. I taught part-time in secondary modern schools, mostly deprived black kids who needed remedial reading and special treatment. And in between I went off travelling in North Africa and places like that so I could write my novel, which was called *Where Have All the Flowers Gone?* and never got published. In 1967 I met Richard Neville at the Legalise Pot rally in Hyde Park where he was selling the first of the psychedelic *OZ*s. It was not very good, still rather satirical, but by then it was being bracketed with flower power and hippies, and Richard, I think, had just smoked his first joint and been given his first acid and so had I. I didn't know Richard in Australia and I wasn't particularly interested in magazines – I saw myself as a serious writer, not a journalist. So I met Richard at the rally, talked to him briefly and then went off and later met Allen Ginsberg. Then I went to Tunisia where I wrote another unpublished novel and didn't really return to London until 1969.

RICHARD NEVILLE: I had also met Jon Goodchild. I was at a dinner very early on with Lyn Hodenfield [née Richards] and there was a guy called Jon Goodchild there. So I said, 'Hey, Jon, are you interested in doing some design?' and he designed the first issue of *OZ*. He was quite prepared to stay up for three or four days without sleep designing *OZ* for very little money. So Goodchild, a true-blue Englishman, worked on *OZ* as a designer until plucked by Jann Wenner of *Rolling Stone*.

JON GOODCHILD: I was working as a design consultant when I met Richard. He said he was looking for somebody to put this magazine together and I volunteered. He was putting together this underground journal that he used to do in Australia which had got him into trouble there and he wanted to do it here. He wanted to do something to compete with *Private Eye*. And we started to do it in his basement. I was politically aware, but I wasn't active. I was bored with being a designer and working with advertising agencies, I had got pissed off with the whole scene and I think this was an interesting respite.

TONY ELLIOTT: I knew Goodchild quite well. Despite being the absolutely seminal graphic designer that he was – those old *OZ*s are so incredible – you couldn't find a much more middle-class, straight down the line, you have to say, hustler. A very organised guy. I remember seeing him for the first time, coming into Pete Ledeboer's place, Big O posters in Kensington Market, I couldn't believe this guy with the frizzy hair and this incredibly long sheepskin coat. He looked like an extra out of *Quest for Fire*. Very stylish.

148

RICHARD NEVILLE: *OZ* went psychedelic in issue no. 3. I think Martin had started taking acid. Prior to that he was a satirical social commentator. I hadn't taken acid at that stage. The staff was me, a guy called Peter Ledeboer who broke away and started Big O posters, an Australian called Paul Lawson and several others who later broke away. Louise was no doubt an uncredited dogsbody.

MARSHA ROWE: Without Louise *OZ* would never have happened. I think without Louise Richard couldn't have done half the things he did. But it was always a very strange relationship. Richard was always with other women. She would be upset, but she also had other relationships. She was like the wife, the sister, the mother, and she was a very good friend to me. Louise helped create the social ambience of Palace Gardens Terrace which was very important: a lot of the work was done from there and a lot of people came to see Richard or Jim there. She was like a social secretary and she used to smooth things over. I can't see Richard operating without her at the time. She didn't ever want to be involved in the magazine more than the bits and pieces that she did. She'd do one article, or research for one thing and she went off quite happily and did that, but she didn't want to work full-time. That wasn't important to her identity.

RICHARD NEVILLE: It wasn't just taking acid that changed *OZ*. I also had begun reading the American underground press, particularly the *East Village Other*. John Wilcock, with whom I'd corresponded in Australia when he was on the *Village Voice*, turned up in London and I gave him *OZ 6* to edit. And John did shake us up a bit. He was no great acid freak, but he was really into the underground press. He was more uncritical than we were of all the different things going on, so he would accept all sorts of ideas that I normally would be a little bit dubious of . . . He was into saying, 'Now then: Michael X, he looks interesting, have you met him?' 'No.' 'Oh well, let's ring him up,' and we'd go off on a 31 bus to meet him. John taught me that if you're editing a newspaper not just to rely on who you meet at dinner or on friends of friends, but that you could actually phone somebody up and go and see them and get them involved.

DAVID WIDGERY: I was always a great admirer of John Wilcock. He was a great inspiration to Richard and tremendously underestimated as an original thinker and as a pioneer of that whole era of journalism. He published *Other Scenes*. One always assumed that the underground press was founded by Americans but this Yorkshireman Wilcock was there first.

149

JOHN WILCOCK: By the mid-60s the *Village Voice* was getting a bit tedious. The owners' natural conservatism was beginning to assert itself. They were making money now and they wanted to make more and the advertising manager was telling me I shouldn't write certain things in the column cos it offended the advertisers. I wasn't allowed to put 'fuck' into the column, as in mentioning Ed Sanders' magazine *Fuck You*. Writing about marijuana in the column was probably the first there'd been outside the medical press. The dope thing was brewing in the early 60s and it was considered to be dangerous to write about it: people would know you liked illegal drugs. But all I did was quote things carefully, like the BMA report that said it was harmless.

I had already said to people, 'You could almost run a paper on the ads the *Voice* turns down,' referring to what were then very innocent sex ads that the *Voice* wouldn't run. Lo and behold, papers started up: the *Berkeley Barb*, Art Kunkin's *LA Free Press*, *OZ* in Australia.

In 1965 I went off to Japan and when I came back the girl I'd been living with had left me and was now living with Walter Bowart, the guy who started the *East Village Other*. I met him, saw the first edition of *EVO*, which I loved so much that I immediately started writing a column for it. I called it 'Art and Other Scenes'. Walter knocked off the 'Art' and it became 'Other Scenes'. I was still writing for the *Voice* until they told me I couldn't write for both papers, I'd have to choose. So I chose *EVO* and I left the *Voice*. Walter made me editor. And we thought about all the papers coming out, there were more now, and we created the Underground Press Syndicate. We typed up a manifesto saying that everyone who became a member could use each other's stuff. The only obligation was to send a copy of each issue to all the other members.

I did nine issues of *EVO* and then had a big fight with Bowart about a negative and extremely stupid review of *Chelsea Girls*. *EVO* was supposed to be a hip paper and this was foolish, running this dud review by a movie-maker who was jealous of Warhol. So I decided that it shouldn't be run and Bowart and I had a fight and I walked out. I was on my way to Japan again and I went to see Kunkin in LA and he asked me to edit the *Free Press*. I said OK, as long as I had total autonomy. I spent three months there. It was exactly the right time, the beginning of '66, there was the first Human Be-in on January 16 in Golden Gate Park, there were riots on the Strip, everything was booming. We really caught a wave and we doubled the circulation of the *Free Press*. Then I had to go to Japan and while I was there I met two kids who were doing their underground paper. And we did a joint issue of their paper and my *Other Scenes*. We broke the story on marijuana use in Vietnam. Everyone knew but there was no evidence and we faked a letter. I stole a piece of paper from the USO and faked the second page of this letter home, admitting dope-smoking, throwing it in casually, then reproduced it on our front page. After that I went to London and this time I collaborated with Richard Neville on the sixth issue of *OZ*. After that I returned to New York and started *Other Scenes* as a tabloid paper.

JON GOODCHILD: I can hardly say we designed the early *OZ*s. They came together in a unique sort of way. I didn't know I was doing anything innovative, more like sloshing it together just to make it look interesting. But it really was innovative because we didn't have any money to do it properly, so you sort of cheat and the cheating starts to give you a different way of doing it. Then things were put together on living-room tables, and on the floor. We didn't really have any type, we didn't really have anything much. Until later on I started taking it over to my studio in Gunter Grove. That was after issue five.

KEITH MORRIS: I shared a studio with Jon Goodchild in Gunter Grove, where *OZ* was designed. And that was how I met all the *OZ* people. At that point they didn't really have a resident photographer, and I was sharing a place with Goodchild and just starting to go freelance, so I wasn't exactly over-worked, and I liked the things they liked – drugs and so on – so I just became their photographer by default. They never had any dope. I was the only person who ever had any dope around *OZ*. Richard used to tick me off for turning on the people who were laying it out. 'You can't do that, Keith, it'll stop them working!'

PHILIP HODGSON: There was some good art around: Mike McInnerney, Michael English, Haphash and the Coloured Coat, Martin Sharp – his Cream covers and his Dylan poster . . . the best of them all. The things they did with one-, two-, three-colour screening have still not been bettered. I think the production of things like *OZ* was bloody good, it's still great. They pushed litho-printing and screen-printing a long, long way. They were doing then, and much better, what newspapers like the *Independent* and *Today*, supposedly exploiting the new technology, are doing now. It was one of the great positive things to come out of the era, some great graphics. Some of the ways of doing images, and the nice freaky things of overprinting colours. Certainly on *OZ* they were prepared to run it and if you couldn't read it . . . tough. Which is a very nice way of doing it. People don't have that freedom any more.

PEARCE MARCHBANK: Martin Sharp was brilliant. As far as I knew he was a rich Australian, very urbane, very handsome, tall, wore beautiful clothes, very much the King's Road figure. He had this beautiful drawing style: very original and very clean. His vision of psychedelia was clean and pure and dayglo. Rather than that muddy, tie-dyed T-shirt, mixed-up liquid-slide look. Sharp had wit, he was visually witty. He also knew how to put a magazine together and use every possible colour on every page without it looking like, 'Oh, we've got to put some more red here, because we've got it to spend . . .'

FELIX DENNIS: There were a number of illustrators involved in *OZ* and first of all they found themselves. As soon as you put one or two issues out they would come. Martin Sharp was a seminal influence both in Australia and here. Because Martin was a madman, a genius, a savant, a whatever-you-want and he was extremely talented to boot. He would meet people and recommend them all the time. Richard of course would charm anybody but he didn't know if they were writers or illustrators or artists or whether they were just scrubbers who were going to take down their drawers to make Jimi Hendrix happy so he got his picture in the next issue . . . It didn't matter, Richard would just charm all of them and he didn't really care or know who they were, although he did have a kind of feeling for a certain sort of art. Richard had a sensitivity where he could spot it and then he would go and get them. Jon Goodchild had a whole string of contacts; Jim Anderson was so patient with young designers and illustrators and he'd sit there for fucking hours and hours going over a guy's work with him. At other places they'd be lucky if they got eight seconds. And I've always had a really good eye for art and whatever I'd see – a poster, a ticket, anything that I thought was of the slightest bit of interest – I'd be on the phone and bring them in.

DUNCAN FALLOWELL: *OZ* was an absolutely fantastic magazine. The quality of art, the quality of humour, the actual sensibility, the non-ghetto, the sheer generosity and colour of the thing was such as I've never seen anywhere else in my lifetime. This may well have been helped by the fact that essentially it was not run by English people. The English do go around with corks up their arses, that's their big problem.

DAVID WIDGERY: One interesting thing about *OZ* and all the under-ground – which is now blamed for illiteracy and general cultural depravity – is that it was a group of auto-didacts, of scholars, people who read books and cared about books and about poetry. What struck me most is

152

how many degrees the people on *OZ* had – we could have set up a small university! These were highly educated people, polymathic people in some ways. Far from being these mis-spelling louts that on occasion we did pretend to be, it was thinking people, intelligent people who were doing it.

Germaine Greer was possibly one of the best examples. An average-to-good literary critic who dealt with some very original ideas. She came from the anarchist culture in Sydney known as the Big Push. Old-fashioned anarchists who read Kropotkin. Sydney culture is bloody awful but there was this definite group of libertarians in which Germaine was involved. Her main contribution to *OZ* was just being Australian, and Australians were something radical. A kick in the behind for the English.

Martin Sharp pushed the art of psychedelia almost further than anyone else. The 'Magic Theatre' issue of *OZ* is the one thing created by the psychedelic era which might be looked at with interest in 100 years' time. He had that desire to push things to their absolute limits, which is re-volutionary in art. His posters are fantastic and he was a critical influence on *OZ*'s visual extremism.

VIRGINIA CLIVE-SMITH: By mid-1967 I had met Martin Sharp and Jenny Kee and all that lot. Richard Neville, Louise Ferrier, Michael Thomas: the Australian gang. They were very refreshing. After the slightly older lot I knew, they were younger and more boisterous, naughtier. Certainly not as spiritually orientated. Jon Goodchild started designing *OZ*. I helped him. I was very happy to be there. I could sit there very happily and watch all these mad antics going on and Jon and I had the most outrageous time in our own way. There were the wonderful panic stations like when Che Guevara was shot. We heard at about eight o'clock that night and we had to get the magazine out by 11.30 and Richard just said 'Right, poster. We'll do a centrefold poster.' So I did this Guevara poster and I spelt 'Guevara' wrong. As soon as it was out on the streets people were ringing up for blood!

KEITH MORRIS: I was very much a journeyman. If they needed a picture to illustrate something, I did it and that ranged from a photographic comic strip of the dreadful Anthony Haden-Guest to just pictures which were overlaid, of decorative ladies or girls fighting in mud or whatever. I didn't get paid, just occasional expenses cheques, but you don't do that sort of stuff for money – unless you're called Felix Dennis. A lonely man – tell me about his friends. You can't shit on people to that extent and be loved. In those days Felix was our number one street-seller. That's how he got in, because he could punt copies like nobody else.

FELIX DENNIS: How did I get involved? It was an abortion. I knocked up a young lady, an extremely nice middle-class girl from Pinner, whose father, I think, was something in show biz, or some nonsense. So it was a big deal. I had to sell my drum kit. In those days illegal abortions cost a hell of a lot of money and I discovered that the price of a second-hand Premier drum kit didn't actually meet Harley Street's needs, so I had to sell my only other prize possession: my Grundig reel-to-reel tape recorder. So just before I sold this kit I'd seen this kind of pilot issue of *OZ* and I took it back home and read this thing all the way through. And I thought, 'What a pile of rubbish! God almighty, these people are useless! I can see what they're trying to do but they're completely hopeless.' As a kind of last gamble, last use of my Grundig, I recorded a tape, sitting in my bedroom that night, and I sent this editor, whose name I saw in the magazine, the tape. It was a very amusing tape, cos it was done very late at night and I was a bit smashed. [The editor] was Richard Neville. Giving him lots of hints and tips about what was wrong with his magazine and how he ought to get his act together and what life was like living the way I was living and all that stuff. Anyway, I thought no more about it and I just put it in the mail, cos I knew that if you just get a tape with nothing else attached to it there's one thing for sure as hell you've got to do – you've got to listen to it.

I was living with these people, Fulham Road somewhere, a bunch of girls, seven of them, and all of a sudden, I was in the loo and one of them screams, 'You're on the television!' and I thought, 'Christ, that's that manager who's been ripping us off again, *Ready, Steady, Go* or something.' So I rushed in, expecting to see this film of the band. Instead of that there was this picture of this guy I didn't know. I said, 'What do you mean, I'm on the television?' and she said, 'Listen,' and bugger me – it's my voice coming out. Over the BBC on this documentary. Richard had sold them my tape as background for this documentary on hippies! So I thought, 'Fuck this, there must be some money in it.' So I called him up and said, 'I sent you this tape in confidence, you know, and I didn't send you this tape to send to the BBC. You must have got money for that – where's mine?' And he said, 'Look, I haven't got any money, as it happens, but come round to Palace Gardens Terrace and meet up.' So I went round there in high dudgeon and I met him and Louise.

RICHARD NEVILLE: Felix came along. He sent a tape in and I played the tape and there was this very emotional voice saying this was the greatest thing, the greatest magazine that I have ever read and I will give my life for this magazine . . . it was all that sort of stuff. Then this kid arrived and the only thing I could think of doing was to give him *OZ*s to sell in the street. And he did really well.

FELIX DENNIS: He said, 'The truth is we haven't got any money but I could give you some magazines ...' So I said, 'What fucking use are magazines to me?' and he said, 'No, no, you go out on the street and sell them.' I said, 'You don't seem to understand, I'm a musician, I don't go ...' and he said, 'No, no ... you go out there and sell them,' so I said, 'Well all right, give me a bundle of them, for fuck's sake, and at least it's some money.' So I took this bundle of magazines, went back to Fulham, woke the girls up, told them to put a short skirt on and I got about three of them out there on the King's Road. I was like a sort of hippie pimp. And bugger me! as soon as you'd go up to people and shove them in front of their face, they used to give you half a crown! It was amazing! Half a crown! So we sold about a hundred the first day. A hundred half crowns was a lot of money in those days, so I went back the next day and I said, 'I think you owe me a few more of those,' and he didn't say anything and let me have a few more bundles. And I sold those, and the next time I went round he said, 'We've got to do fifty-fifty, you've got to give me the money.' So then we had an operation going, in the King's Road.

About two issues afterwards – they kept on screwing up this magazine, the front covers were terrible, the whole thing was useless, and also they were also always running out of money – he came to me one day and said, 'We're in a bit of financial trouble, very serious financial trouble, cos this company called ECAL, which distributes our magazine, they owe us a lot of money, they owe us a fortune. They've been distributing the magazine and they haven't got any money. They say they've run out.' I said, 'I can't help you, I don't know anything about that stuff.' He said, 'I want you to go down and work there,' and I said, 'What do you mean, I'm a musician ...' though I wasn't actually working, just pretending and thinking I was going to at any moment.

MILES: ECAL – Effective Communications Arts Ltd – was a poster company which was formed from the profits from the 14-Hour Technicolor Dream. I think it was the name of the company when we bought it, rather than any kind of attempt to be hip.

FELIX DENNIS: Anyway, Richard convinced me in the end that what I had to do was to go to ECAL and get this job and Miles was around there, and Bill Butler (who's dead now), and it was at 22 Betterton Street, and I went round there to sort it out. I met a lot of interesting people who were working at *IT* at the time and sure enough they did owe *OZ* a fortune, thousands and thousands of pounds. Dave Robins, Su Small, Dave Hall, Joe Boyd. And there was this weird millionaire, Nigel Samuel, and I was always opening up his bank statements cos they used to come down with the rest of the post. I remember standing around looking at this bank statement in stunned disbelief that a man used to keep a thousand or two or three thousand in his current account: it was beyond our wildest dreams . . . anyway he was a very nice bloke, extremely rich and a very nice bloke. Bit of a fruitcake but very pleasant. So I set about trying to get their finances back on stream so they could repay *OZ* magazine. I wasn't interested in flogging posters, although ECAL was one of Osiris Visions' main distributors, and it was the main distributor of *IT*. What had happened was they were deeply in debt and I was brought in as a horrible tough little bastard to try and get the finances sorted out. The first thing I did was try to fire a lot of people, which was very difficult in those days, because as they hadn't joined in the first place it was very difficult to fire them. But we did manage to get it pretty much under control. We had a lot of posters that were winners: Che Guevara, the Martin Sharp exploding Hendrix, Martin Sharp's Dylan with the circles and so on, and in the end they made a lot of money and we got back on track and they did repay *OZ* and it was done.

RICHARD NEVILLE: Felix came in very slowly but came in more and more as the years went by. *OZ* was up and running by the time he turned up and for a long time his only influence was in distribution. Then he came into advertising.

JOHN LEAVER: I don't think Richard ever understood Felix, they were so different. Richard liked to play puppet-master. He used to wind up this extraordinary character called Lee Heater, who had dreadlocks. I think I was suspicious of Richard. It was weird being with him, or Felix, when their guard was down, when they weren't pretending for the punters. That was what made me cynical. One saw them treating the true believers as punters. They were the marks.

FELIX DENNIS: Lee Heater was an American lawyer who'd taken acid and completely gone over the top. By the time he got to England, and how he got here I do not know, he basically lived for marijuana. He'd been a lawyer and he also worked for the CIA. It was obvious that he wasn't a tramp but he looked like a vagrant and tramp in every single way. He stank, his hair was in dreadlocks, he very rarely washed, if ever, I never saw him change his clothes, and he lived for drugs. He only had

156

that one interest, drugs, as well as touching the breasts of young girls as often as he possibly could. Richard took a shine to Lee Heater because he was such a complete madman: he was a lunatic and an interesting lunatic.

One day the *News of the World* called up, in typical unsuspecting Fleet Street fashion, and they asked for an interview with *OZ*. So Richard said, 'Well, what story are you writing?' and they gave him this cock-and-bull story about how they were going to write about the new generation and all this kind of crap. It was so obvious that they were going to come and do this terrifying hatchet job. They just couldn't wait to find young girls with their tits hanging out and flowers in their hair and vibrators up their pussies and drugs in the attic. Richard actually set it up and everybody joined in this masquerade. He persuaded Lee Heater (which was very easy, you just gave him a joint) to come into the house and sit down. Then just before the reporters arrived, so he didn't have too much time to think about it and get worried, he explained to Lee how he had some people coming round and it was important that they didn't know who Richard was, which, being an ex-CIA operative, Lee fell in with immediately, and that Lee had to pretend to be the editor of *OZ* magazine. The man was transformed. He was picking up telephones: 'Hold the front page! I've got a hot story for page three . . . We've got those bastards from the CIA running a drug ring!' and all this stuff. He had these nubile young girls running in and fawning all over him and sitting in his lap. He was pretending to smoke dope. It was just a nightmare, like a caricature of Fat Freddy pretending to be the editor of a magazine. The *News of the World* photographer was delirious with joy; it was like he'd just arrived at a train accident where eighty people had died and he was the only photographer there. He was going mental taking pictures of Lee and they rushed back to print the story in the next Sunday's *NoW* with this big picture of Lee Heater saying 'Editor of *OZ*' and so on. Then Richard wrote them a letter and threatened to sue them! It was quickly met with a fast settlement out of court.

After a while, in '68, I finally went too far at ECAL – I think I was trying to turn it into a real business or something – and I was told to fuck off. So I went back to *OZ*. Richard said, 'I was wondering if you'd like to sell the advertising?' So I said, 'I don't know anything about selling advertising, I'm not interested in it and anyway I've got to get back with the lads and we've got to get this band on the road.' So Richard said, 'Never mind about that, would you like to just do it for a month . . .' and I thought, well, all right then. So I took their advertising list, which was a piece of garbage, and I made a telephone call and didn't get anywhere. So I thought, fuck this, and I made another one. So I made another one, and then I made another one, the first time I'd ever sold advertising, and I began to get the hang of it. You keep on banging the phone and you've got the rate card in front of you . . . and eventually I scored – the law of averages. I got a page, a record company, Island Records. So I thought, this isn't too bad, I've just earned about £20. After a few months of selling the ads . . . the magazine was in terrible trouble, it doesn't matter how much money you bring in. Richard was a bit of an idealist and he'd find a way to piss it away. There must be some hole we could pour it into, some wonderful charity . . . Anyway, in the end he said, 'Would you like to be the business manager?' I said, 'I don't know what the business manager does.' He said, 'It's very simple: you take the chequebook; you see: now you're the business manager.' So I got involved with being the business manager. Which still meant I sold the advertising . . .

IT: 'It was a piece of classic intimidation'

MICK FARREN: The first thing that happened in '67 was that they busted a whole lot of acid dealers. The next event was that the Obscene Publications Squad came down to the Indica bookshop and carted away loads of stuff.

MILES: The very first *IT* bust was an interview we did with Dick Gregory in about issue eight in which he talked about 'white motherfuckers' or something like that. Somebody complained to the DPP and we had the full-scale police raid. By this time we'd accumulated quite a bit of paper work – subscription lists and so on – and they came and they seized everything, every single piece of paper in the entire office including the phone books. Every single back issue. Staff members' personal address books. It was a piece of classic intimidation. They kept it all for about two months then returned it saying they weren't going to bring any charges. They completely disrupted our cash flow, taking uncashed cheques, we had no idea who our subscribers were, who owed us money, anything, they just wanted to close us down. The Establishment were very, very paranoid about it. That bust is what you expect in South America or some Third World country. No one did anything though. We told all the press, but the press did fuck all, didn't even write an article. But it was fluid enough so that the next issue was read aloud at UFO. It was miraculously recreated and it was on the streets only a week later. People worked enormously hard, all night for no wages, but they weren't working for wages – we weren't publishing for a profit.

MICK FARREN: I sort of wandered down to *IT* and there were a few
158

people hanging out – Michael McInnerney, Dave Housen – all bitching and complaining because basically the old guard – Haynes, McGrath and all the rest of them – had vanished into the hills. We decided that we might as well take over. So we did. I think we put out two issues: they weren't very good, but they were sort of lively and at least they came out. The government had fled but there were no invading troops in the city so we just grabbed the city.

JEFF NUTTALL: Mick Farren was a bad man – I thought he was a bad man, anyway. I somehow thought that he was a person who was a frustrated rock star who wasn't going to get there. He had all the attributes of a rock star except the talent. His appetites for fame were infinitely greater than his comparatively right-minded politics. And when he came onto the staff at *IT* and Peter Stanshill and David Mairowitz ran it, it was still a good paper. I went down to *IT* after they raided the office and Harry Fainlight was a corpse in a coffin which they paraded as 'The Death of *IT*'. He became friendly with Farren for one reason and another and I watched them being photographed and watched Farren getting to the front . . . About that time *IT* asked me to edit an issue so I edited a really dreadful issue which had a photo on the front of a woman sucking off a pig, a two-page article by George Barker, a lot of good poetry; Jim Burns from Preston sent in some scorching accounts of hippie tribes there trying to sell their children and so on. But they just didn't do it. They just didn't want it at all. I had a bit of a row with Farren about it.

PETER SHERTSER: Mick's been a great inspiration. He tried to do more for so many people than anybody else. All the time, anybody, they'd go along to Mick and he'd try and help them, try and do right by them, try and get them a break, even at his own sacrifice. He was always a better ideas man than actually participating himself. That's his forte.

The Maharishi: 'What I'm offering is a system of meditation'

NICHOLAS SAUNDERS: In the early 60s I got this thing of being very dissatisfied with life and I went looking for things. I got involved in one thing after another during this looking. The first thing I found was Maharishi meditation. Someone put me onto it. It was perhaps a year before the Beatles got involved. 1966. So it was all strange and funny when there was suddenly all this publicity.

PAUL MCCARTNEY: Maharishi is not a religion. It is merely a system for meditation. We used to talk to him about that: 'Well what about

159

God?' we'd say and he'd say, 'I'll leave that up to you. What I'm offering is a system of meditation.' And it was essential at the time, with acid posing all these questions of eternity. With acid you get like a Woody Allen film – asking all these questions: what is the meaning, why am I doing it? India was suggested by the fact that we heard the music first of all. It slotted very interestingly into our framework of music because Western music is arranged in a certain way by Bach, Beethoven – the old boys – who we are still echoing with the framework as set down by these Europeans. All based on different chords. Indian music is different: it's all on one chord and that's an essential, very interesting difference for us, because there's nothing greater than not having to bother with a bunch of bloody chords . . . 'What's this? F sharp, H flat minor . . . Oh my God!' whereas in Indian stuff there's one. And you can go 'Nyahhh' [imitates sitar] for twelve hours if you like. So that started to expand our interest, particularly George Harrison. He met Ravi Shankar through that. We got friends with some of the Asian Music Circle and the Commonwealth music and that kind of expanded into, 'Well, if you like the music and you like Ravi Shankar, they have all these great festivals and these guys run round naked with mud on them and why they do that is cos they believe in *this* religion . . .' and you started to hear of the *Bhagavad Gita* and stuff like that. And it was all a little bit hazy because it wasn't like an official religion, you were chucking in bits of Khalil Gibran and this sort of stuff, *Siddhartha*, which wasn't necessarily to do with it, but all seemed the same kind of thing. We'd all been brought up as Sunday school kids or whatever, traditional religious beliefs, and it hadn't really worked for most of us because we'd say, 'Why is there then suffering in the world?' and the vicar said, 'Just because,' and we said, 'Oh yeah . . . that's a great answer.' So none of us had been able to be totally convinced in prayer until meditation. Then you started to get the idea: one note, one concentrating, one lessening of stress, one reaching of a sort of new level did seem to get you in contact with a better part of yourself. It was a very hectic world one was living in and this inner peace seemed to be a better thing. If nothing else, what Maharishi was suggesting was a pleasant relief from all that in order to recharge your batteries – that basically was all he said.

They've expanded it now, they're interested in flying, actual levitation now. The joke was that when we were out in Rishikesh, that was one of the things we were interested in . . . we were almost throwing in the Indian rope trick too. It was all part of a new thing and we would ask him, 'Did they do that? Was that just a magic trick? Do they really levitate, Maharishi? What about levitation, is that actually possible?' and he said, 'Yes it is, there are people who do it,' but he took it as, 'Oh, you wanna see some levitation, well there's a fellow down the road, he does it. We can have him up, he'll do a little bit for us if you like,' and we said, 'Great,' but he never actually showed. I say, 'Give me one photograph and I'll have you on *News at Ten* tonight and you'll be a major source of interest to the world and your organisation will swell its ranks.'

The whole thing about love and peace was suggested by meditation: sitting in a room on your own doesn't suggest war.

The 14-Hour Technicolor Dream: 'Everybody I'd ever known swam before my eyes'

PETER BROWN: I still have a poster for the Technicolor Dream, but I can't remember what it was for. Was it a benefit? A celebration?

JIM HAYNES: We decided to have one big fund-raising event. We had a meeting at the Arts Lab: Hoppy, Miles and myself. I was in charge of publicity and trying to raise money to make the event take place. I think we ended up selling the film rights to some Italian film producer. We saw it as just an incredible event which would create publicity, which would be fun in itself, and that was an end in itself, and it would produce some cash for the underground. God knows where the money went.

JOHN HOPKINS: Almost everything that happened then was totally disorganised. For instance, the 14-Hour Technicolor Dream: we got ripped off for ten grand because none of us could keep control of the tickets. One hundred per cent of the ticket money got ripped off and it was only because Jim Haynes managed to get some money off a couple of film companies for shooting it that he paid the expenses. It was a total disaster as far as money goes. None of us understood how to handle it.

PETER SHERTSER: They said that anyone could come and get tickets and sell them and give them the money later. We got dozens of people to go down and we ended up with hundreds and hundreds of tickets. We're standing there, about thirty of the Firm on the door, all selling tickets. It was disgusting, I've got to admit, but they were ripe for it. It was done in such a ridiculous way. We did make a few donations – we did give *some* money in. But we could see that nobody was going to be harmed here: none of them knew what day it was anyway. If it wasn't us it would be someone else.

SPIKE HAWKINS: Byrne and I were rung up by Hopkins who said, 'Look . . . man . . . too much, I am getting together a, er, 14-Hour Technicolor Dream,' and my reply was, 'What are you taking?' and he said, 'No, man, no, babe, I'm getting a huge event together and I want you and Byrne to be something.' I said, 'Well, all right,' and he said, 'Name me a group,' and I said, 'Bader's Legs,' but he said, 'We can't do that, it's a bit too strong . . .' So I said, 'What about the Poison Bellows?' and he said, 'Yeah, yeah.' I had this wonderful old pianola, with beautiful songs such as 'When the Sergeant Major's on Parade', and we moved this enormous pianola to Alexandra Palace, and because nobody would take it back we had to leave it there.

I don't know how many people remember the event. The amount of drugs that were going around . . . I was quietly stoned on some grass and someone gave me something to swallow, to keep awake, and I was jabbering away ten to the dozen: 'Why doesn't somebody make a balloon that goes down instead of up?' Trocchi was there and looked at me and said, 'Aye . . . aye,' and what seemed eight years later, at the same event, he came to me and said 'What you were talking about, it's a wonderful idea.' I said, 'Can you give me the precise time?' He said, 'About the balloons,' and I said, 'Oh, I've moved on.'

SUE MILES: The great moment, I thought, was Hoppy standing on the steps in the morning shaking hands with people as if you'd gone to a dinner party. We had that film *Flaming Creatures* projected on bedsheets that were flapping in the breeze so you still couldn't see what the hell was going on. You could smoke a joint through a banana skin in an igloo if you wanted that kind of meaningful experience. There was Arthur Brown with a collander on his head. 'Fire!' There was the Social Deviants, with their astonishing light-show of three orange boxes with flashing lightbulbs in them. Micky Farren was great, cos Micky was angry. He wasn't into love and peace. He had the hair, with this headband round it, and kind of lime-yellow nylon loon pants.

MICK FARREN: I actually opened it – the Deviants were the first band on. It was damned good, the Alexandra Palace was such a beautiful place anyway. And there were mounds of speakers and lights. And everybody who had been fucking around in a small environment got to go completely nuts. The only thing was that there wasn't the power in either the lights or the sound, so it all became a blur, but there was lots of stuff happening. There were about 10,000 in the audience and a certain kind of exponential curve seemed to be setting in, which led some people to believe that we would now conquer the planet.

RUSSELL HUNTER: The 14-Hour Technicolor Dream was one of the first hippie things I went to. People have told me that I did play at it,

162

but I don't believe it. The Deviants played but I don't think I was with them.

JOHN DUNBAR: We were all down in Weybridge, at John [Lennon]'s. It was, 'No I'm not going to mend your fucking bike, Julian,' and snorting up Owsley tabs and coke out of a kitchen pestle and mortar. And we were watching the TV and suddenly saw that this thing was on. So we thought, fuck it, let's go! So we get into one of the space-age motors, Terry the faithful guy drives and we ended up at this place where everybody I'd ever known in my life swam before my eyes at one time or another. All eyes were vaguely on us because we were with John and I literally saw people I'd last seen at kindergarten and hadn't seen since.

Back in Weybridge, or wherever we went next day, reading the papers, we saw an ad for an island off Ireland, for sale for £1000. Phone up the office, arrange a plane and a limo and fly over and stay at the Gresham in Dublin and limo across to the other side of Ireland, rowed out in a boat to this green little hill the other side of this bay . . . So we wandered round Ireland, and that took about three or four days. We were tripping all the time and after about six days of acid everything starts to look very bleached.

JOHN PEEL: I spent most of my time wandering around looking for Brian Jones. Everyone said, 'Brian's here. Brian's here.' I'd met him once. And everyone was just walking around looking for Rolling Stones or Beatles or Hendrix. You heard all these stories that famous pop stars were going to turn up. I suspect I went on my own. I just remember wandering around in a kind of non-drug-induced, non-alcohol-induced daze. Just dazed by the event. What they called a 'contact high'. And obviously you spent most of your energies trying to get your end away – that's what it came down to in the end.

ROBERT WYATT: I got a short-back-and-sides haircut and a suit and tie to do that gig. That was my avant-garde gesture. The Floyd had those pyramids as far as I recall. They were doing very slow tunes.

PETER JENNER: That really *was* a psychedelic experience. That really was the most psychedelic experience that I've ever been to. At least half the audience were doing acid. I was doing acid. We'd had to take a long drive to get there, maybe from a gig in Holland, and I did the last bit of the drive in the van. We dropped in at home and did some acid before we went, and by the time I got to Alexandra Palace the old acid was beginning to go and trying to drive the van was getting quite exciting.

163

The band wanted to go on stage just as dawn was breaking, which they did and it was incredible.

JUNE BOLAN: This was the last gig Syd [Barrett] played with Floyd, Ally Pally, this massive, huge stage, this huge auditorium packed. I think they might have got a grand, they were top of the bill. First of all we couldn't find Syd, then I found him in the dressing-room and he was so ... gone. I kept saying, 'Syd, it's June, it's me, look at me ...' Roger Waters and I got him on his feet, we got him out to the stage. He had a white Stratocaster and we put it round his neck and he walked on stage and of course the audience went spare because they loved them. The band started to play and Syd stood there. He had his guitar round his neck and his arms just hanging down and I was in the wings and Peter was one side and Andrew was the other side and we're looking at each other and wondering what to do. And suddenly he put his hands on the guitar and we thought, 'Great, he's actually going to do it,' and he stood there, he just stood there, tripping out of his mind.

They did three, maybe four, numbers and we got him off. I had the money, which I always insisted on getting before we went on, and the readies were all in my bag and Peter [Jenner] came across behind the stage and said, 'Go and sit in the car.' He could see what was going to happen. Syd couldn't even stand up for a set, let alone do anything else. I went in the car. Immediately the promoter realised that they obviously weren't going to do a set, not cos the rest of the band didn't want to, but Syd was just non compos mentis, the promoter wanted the 'chick with the money' – and I was gone. Pete said, 'I'm awfully sorry, she's gone, she had to leave early' – and I was out in the car park. So they hustled everybody off, got all the instruments – cos you always took guitars with you, you never left them for the roadies – and they all ran out into the car. As we were driving out the promoter was haring after us. We all got back to Alexander Street going 'Phew!' and it was wonderful.

MILES: The Flies were at the Technicolor Dream. They were certainly Britain's first punk band and therefore the world's first. At that very concert the Flies pissed on the audience: even Johnny Rotten never managed that. They were absolutely appalling. They first drew attention to themselves at UFO by standing at the edge of the stage when the Pink Floyd were on, yelling and screaming abuse at them: 'Sell outs!!' they were yelling.

There was an igloo where people could take banana peel, which was that month's craze. And there was David Medalla and the Exploding

164

Galaxy; he was very gay, a frisky little chap, always foaming at the mouth.

DAVID JENKINS: The idea of drugs and hipness was around, and you took *OZ* from issue one. I heard about the 14-Hour Technicolor Dream and thought it was something we ought to go to. We all set off in a troupe from a friend's flat. I was very worried because it was raining and I'd just had my hair cut. We made our way to the Technicolor Dream, got there and there was the sudden realisation of the full horror of how boring it was probably going to be: the fact that the tubes stopped at midnight. Ambling around in that wonderfully formless way waiting for something to happen that never ever does. There was the exciting moment of John Lennon actually arriving and wandering around wearing his sheepskin, his Afghan coat and his granny specs and looking rather uninterested too. Then getting introduced to David Medalla of the Exploding Galaxy who then spent all the time asking me to go to the loo with him so he could look at my willy. It was this bizarrely yawn-making event, apart from the excitement of being whipped off to the lavvy by Mr Medalla.

CHRIS ROWLEY: Outside, the next day, afterwards, there was this group of about 60 young people gathered. It was the first time I'd really seen hippies play in the park. Making the giant joint out of a sheet of backing paper 60' long which was filled with flowers and stuff and then rolled and ceremonially tromped around the place and the last I saw some mods were beating it to death in a corner. It was that time: no one had done these silly things before. The rules had changed and it was all this do what you will, do what you like and do what you might be able to do.

Syd Barrett: 'A candle about to be snuffed out'

JUNE BOLAN: After the Ally Pally Syd left the Floyd and Dave Gilmour came in. I went through all Syd's acid breakdowns. He used to come round to my house at five in the morning covered in mud from Holland Park when he'd freaked out and the police chased him. I meant money, meant wages, meant security to him. He used to go to the Youth Hostel in Holland Park, climb up on the roof and get wrecked and spaced and he'd walk all the way to Shepherd's Bush where I was living.

He was extraordinary. I've only known two extraordinary people, Syd and Marc [Bolan]. They both had that . . . quality, like a candle that was about to be snuffed out any minute. Really all illumination. An extraordinary, wonderful man. He took a lot of acid. Lots of people can take some acid and cope with it in their lives, but if you take three or four trips in a

165

day, and you do that every day ... and then, because it was the done drug, you'd go round somebody's house for a cup of tea and they'd spike it. People did this to Syd.

JOHN MARSH: Syd was one of the earliest acid casualties. He lived at the time in a flat in the Cromwell Road with various characters, among whom was a psychotic kind of character called Scotty. He was one of the original acid-in-the-reservoir, change-the-face-of-the-world acid missionaries. He was also a desperately twisted freak and really malevolent crazy. Everyone knew that if you went round to see Syd never have a cup of tea, never take a glass of water unless you got it yourself from the tap and even then be desperately worried, because Scotty's thing was spiking everything. By this time, '65-'66, Syd was living on a diet that must have been comprised of 80% acid. Poor old Syd was really in the poo.

PETER JENNER: 101 Cromwell Road was the catastrophic flat where Syd got acided out. Acid in the coffee every morning, that's what we were told. He had one of our cats and they gave the cat acid. Then he got taken up by Storm and Po from Hipgnosis who put him in their flat on Brompton Road just by South Kensington tube station. They knew him very well and they suffered with him going down: they were very supportive and tried to keep him with us. We rescued him from Cromwell Road, which was run by heavy, loony messianic acid freaks.

JOHN MARSH: Of course the band, Jenner and King, me, we all knew what was happening but nobody had the courage or wished to be thought uncool enough to dig Syd out of this situation. And Syd was truly a beautiful person, a lovely guy. He had a creative brain, a way of looking at things that really was genuinely revolutionary and different. And he was going further and further down the tubes because nobody had the guts, nobody wished to be thought uncool and take him away from these circumstances. So this guy went further and further down the mine because of the inertia of those around him.

PETER JENNER: Syd was an exceptional figure. Far and away the most important in the band. He wrote the songs, he was the singer, he played most of the solos, he was the lead guitarist, it was his band. He was much the most interesting, much the most creative: the others were just students. Rick was at some college, maybe Trinity College of Music, Roger and Nick were architects, and Syd was at Camberwell Art School, doing fine arts. I always think that it's really important that Syd was an artist whereas the other two were architects, and that really showed in the

166

band. Syd was a really good artist too. I'm sure he was a star student. And it was a time when you just expressed yourself away – if you were good at painting then you could be good at writing songs. Why not? Syd was outstanding. He was a handsome boy, he was beautiful and one more part of the tragedy is that he became such a fat slob, he became ugly. He was true flower power. He came out in this outrageous gear, he had this permanent, which cost £20 at the time, and he looked like a beautiful woman, all this Thea Porter stuff. He had a lovely girlfriend, Lindsay, she was the spitting image of Syd.

We tried to stop him going crazy. I put all my textbook sociology, all the stuff I'd read about psychology into action; we took him to R. D. Laing. Laing didn't say much. We tried to take what he said literally, we tried to use the inner meaning of what he was saying, we tried to change the objective situations. We moved him out of Cromwell Road but by the time he was with Storm and Po it was too late.

JONATHAN MEADES: I had a friend called Harry Dodson who was at that time very friendly with a guy called Po, who was part of Hipgnosis. They were two guys – Po and Storm. They were friendly with the Pink Floyd cos they all came from Cambridge. In late '67 Harry, Po, Syd Barrett and other people lived in Egerton Court, a mansion block right opposite South Kensington tube station. Syd was certainly the crazy of the party and one got the impression that he was also rather disliked. I went there at the time when Syd had either just left the band or was ready for the final heave-ho and by this time he was obviously a total casualty. He was this rather weird, exotic and mildly famous creature by this time, who happened to be living in this flat with these people who were to some extent pimping off him both professionally and privately. I went there to see Harry and there was this terrible noise. It sounded like heating pipes shaking. I said, 'What's that?' and he sort of giggled and said, 'That's Syd having a bad trip. We put him in the linen cupboard.' And that seemed a terrible thing to do.

JOHN MARSH: He went in a fairly bloody kind of coup. Personality problems and differences within the band virtually meant that Syd was elbowed out. It was all very tragic: one week he was playing and the next it's Dave Gilmour. Syd started off on a long downward slide. I saw him years later, on South Kensington tube station. He looked like a picture of the middle-aged Aleister Crowley. Totally bald, about 15 stone, wearing a Hawaiian shirt and Bermuda shorts.

PETER JENNER: The acid brought out his latent madness. I'm sure it

167

was his latent madness which gave him his creativity. The acid brought out the creativity, but more important it brought out the madness. The creativity was there – smoking dope was quite enough to get it going. He wrote all his songs in about 18 months, two years, including the ones on his solo albums. He was extraordinarily creative and what happened was catastrophic: a total burnt-out case. All his talent just came out in this great flood in two years and then it was burnt out.

JOHN MARSH: On their first American tour the Floyd were being taken by some A&R man around Hollywood. They were taken for the classic tour of the stars' homes and so on. And they ended up on the corner of Hollywood and Vine. The band are looking around: 'Hey, made it, Hollywood,' and the A&R man's saying, 'Yes, here we are, the centre of it all, Hollywood and Vine,' and Syd's wandering around the place, wide-eyed, reckless and legged. 'Gee,' he says, 'it's great to be in Las Vegas.'

JENNY FABIAN: Syd was so beautiful. His violet eyes. I only sort of lay beside him, nothing more could be accomplished. Then he had a breakdown and was gone. He hardly spoke. He would just tolerate me because I was so overpowered, so in awe that I didn't really speak either. I only hung around him for two or three weeks just before he flipped and was virtually removed from the group. I knew Syd was wonderful because he wrote such wonderful songs. He didn't really have to speak because the fact that he couldn't speak made him who he was: this person who wrote these mysterious songs. I just liked looking at him: he was very pretty. A lot of the time with pop stars, when they open their mouths, it was all completely ruined anyway. So it was perfect that he was like that. My first pop star and it was just wonderful that he didn't speak.

Years later I found him again living up the road from Earls Court in a flat where he had a room. Again he didn't speak much. He was sitting in the corner on a mattress and he'd painted every other floorboard alternate colours, red and green. He boiled an egg in a kettle and ate it. And he listened over and over again to Beach Boys tapes, which I found a bit distressing. He was still exactly the same, only now he was only Syd Barrett the has-been rather than Syd Barrett the star. Years after that I was told that he lived in the Penthouse Club and was very fat and got a weekly cheque from the Floyd. Not quite to the extent that Anita gets a cheque from the Stones, but something. I prefer to remember him as this white, thin, violet-eyed nutter who didn't speak much and who wrote wonderful songs. I knew the others but they were absolutely nothing at all compared to him. His words and his music were the Pink Floyd and

168

I've never been interested in them since. Nothing ever reached the heights of that first album which was mad and mysterious – like him.

PETER JENNER: Creatively he was as dead as Jimi Hendrix. He appeared every now and then after that. Twink, from Tomorrow, tried to get him together, I tried, Dave Gilmour did sessions with him. He'd occasionally turn up to Floyd sessions and talk about them as 'my group'. He kept thinking he was still with them. He'd come in to Abbey Road studios and glimpses of tunes would come out, and we'd think, 'Record that!' and then it would disappear into incoherence again.

The Arts Lab: 'This smell of dirty feet'

JIM HAYNES: The Arts Lab was my baby. To a certain extent the Arts Lab carried on from the bookshop and the Traverse Theatre. At the bookshop we had a gallery and we had readings. The Traverse had a bar, a restaurant, a gallery, etc. I saw getting a couple of warehouses in London as a way of creating what I like to think of as an energy centre. My artistic policy was to try to never say the word no. If someone came in with the wildest idea . . . 'Great, let's do it, man. Let's do it. Yes.' I got some unbelievable suggestions and I tried to do them all. We did all the early Lindsay Kemp things, because I'd already met Lindsay in Dublin. A lot of theatre companies were born in the Arts Lab. Pip Simmons Company, the People Show immediately came and started using the space.

Jack [Henry Moore] probably thought up the name. It was meant to be a name that some grant foundation couldn't refuse to give money to. Who could refuse money to the Arts Laboratory? Everyone could. Nobody gave us any money. And we asked everybody. The only thing that was money-producing was that I wrote a duplicated letter on an old Gestetner machine to everyone I could find in *Who's Who of British Theatre*. And I got money back from Fred Zimmerman, Peter Brook, Tom Stoppard, and so on. That letter produced £3000. And Nigel [Samuel] paid the rent a couple of times. Sue Miles was doing the cooking; David Curtis, who is now quite an authority on British film, was our cinema man, Jack Moore was the technical wizard. We also started the first video research unit. Hoppy found video through the Arts Lab. Jack had been to an electronic junk shop and found an old TV set which he used to set up a video projector in the Arts Lab.

STEVE ABRAMS: One night I went to the Arts Lab with Jeff Dexter, after Middle Earth had closed at four in the morning. And Dexter, who is a tiny guy, used to carry this great big case full of records. I was carrying his case over to the Arts Lab. There was this German girl who was in the process of taking off her clothes. And somehow or other I managed to put them on. In about ten minutes they managed to dress up Jeff Dexter, me and Bill Levy in drag and took a picture of the three of us with our arms around each other. The picture was called the Spirit of the Underground.

JIM HAYNES: When I started the Arts Lab in London I went to bosses of companies and said, 'Look, I'm starting this theatre, can I have your lighting system that's gathering dust in the basement?' and people started giving me the crap that was gathering dust in the basement. There was a lot of enthusiasm and the enthusiasm was contagious. What happened was that when I came to London to open a sister theatre for the Traverse I had met Jennie Lee at a little conference on theatre in Colchester. I had been a speaker and Jennie had given a talk and there was a cocktail party afterwards and Mr Chutzpah went up to her and said, 'By any chance are you driving into London?' She said, 'Yes, do you need a ride?' She knew about the Traverse and she was proud of the Traverse and she was very very friendly. I said that I wanted to start a sister theatre in London and that it would be good for the Traverse and it would provide a London showcase for our Edinburgh productions. So she said, 'Talk to my friend Arnold Goodman who will be sympathetic and will plug you into the right places and will be of tremendous help.' So I called him up and he said, 'There's this white elephant of a theatre called the Jeanetta Cochrane which we will arrange for you to have.' So I said, 'OK, but it's not really what I had in mind, I had in mind a warehouse in Covent Garden,' and he more or less said, 'Do me a favour, take it.' At that time he was a lawyer for Harold Wilson, the Labour Party – Mr *Eminence Grise* of Britain. Nevertheless, Miles was bounced off the Arts Council and I never received any money from the Arts Council for the Arts Lab. Ken Tynan and about another dozen theatre people petitioned the Arts Council that the Arts Lab must have support. The Theatre Panel even had a cheque ready for his signature, but he never signed it. In the beginning I was Mr Sunshine: he liked me, I liked him, he liked what we were doing at the Jeanetta Cochrane, he was supportive, but when I wanted to leave and start some kind of crazy place in a warehouse in Covent Garden he thought I was mad. When the first issue of *IT* came out Mr Innocent here sent a copy off to Goodman, saying, 'This is the *Tribune* of our generation.' He didn't like that. He said, 'Come and see me immediately,' and I went to his office and he said, 'If you're going to be associated with this newspaper the Arts Council's not going to help the London Traverse.' That explicit. So I said, 'OK,' and I continued with the paper and we never got any help. I became a disappointment to him.

DUNCAN CAMPBELL: I went to the Arts Lab and fell asleep at three o'clock in the morning while *Citizen Kane* was playing. You lay on foam rubber, there were no seats or anything like that: you just lay and watched non-stop movies all night, slept there all night until transport started moving again the following morning, then stumbled home from Covent Garden. I don't remember any great orgies on the foam, people were just knackered. I think I saw *Citizen Kane* there twice and never got to see the whole thing.

JIM HAYNES: The cinema in the Arts Lab had no chairs. It was tiered and it was covered with foam rubber and carpets, so it was either the biggest bed in London, or it was the most intimate cinema. On Tuesday evenings we initiated open screenings, so we screened anything that anyone brought us, in the order it arrived. In our theatre when you bought tickets you also carried in your seat with you. We had these beer cases that were stacked outside. Thus there were never empty seats – the whole psychology of playing to a half-empty theatre never existed – everybody played to a full house, whether it was ten, fifty or whatever, every seat was full. Suddenly there were about fifty arts labs around the country. David Bowie even started one up in Beckenham, in Kent.

RICHARD TRENCH: The Arts Lab was the first thing that made Covent Garden vaguely trendy. It was the real pioneer of it all. It was supposedly very interesting but actually it was unbelievably boring. There was this fucking light-machine going on and people from Holland looking for a bed to sleep for the night and it was always a bit like that. Basically you were there for sex, but there wasn't any sex. This was a big myth. The Arts Lab used to go on all night and people used to think you might get a screw. You didn't. The agony would come at about 12.30 when it was either, do you leave now and get public transport or do you stay for a while, which meant a taxi, or do you stay until six o'clock in the morning when everything started again, and that was really very boring indeed. So the best thing to do was to leave early, before lethargy took over and it was too late to leave. And sometimes because it was so boring you got so lethargic that you couldn't leave!

JO CRUIKSHANK: The only memorable thing of all those nights I spent there stoned was this smell of dirty feet, because you had to take your shoes off. Then you lay on this filthy foam rubber in this black ghastly basement, watching these third-rate, amateurish porn films, while people were actually doing it in front of you, which I thought was really rude.

CHRIS ROWLEY: I dropped out of the LSE at the start of '68. Now I had to make a living and life was rather desperate. Worked a little bit at Jim Haynes' Arts Lab on Drury Lane, managed the little bookshop allied to the Arts Lab. I met Sue Miles who ran the Arts Lab kitchen. I first met her at the *IT* launch where she had this incredible make-up with these enormous saucer-shaped black eyes and was drifting around with a joint in the end of a long cigarette holder and the remainder of a beautiful 1920s dress and she looked like something very strange – from the Addams family perhaps – but beautiful.

Downstairs was the amazing cinema with the mattresses which became one of the great make-out centres of the Western world. Jim Haynes lived at the back and he was taking innumerable young women down there and Jack Moore lived opposite and he was taking innumerable young men. There was a very strong sexual thing going on in the Arts Lab. I would be selling books, next to me in the small theatre there would be the People Show. The People Show's first great gig was infamous. They put the audience in cages and terrified them for half an hour.

SUE MILES: I did the Arts Lab because I got appointed. Someone said, 'You can cook, you run the Arts Lab,' and I did: it was the first time I was ever a chef. It was in '67. I did it with Carol Laws and Lindsay Bareham. It was appalling. The principle was to have an arts centre, similar to the Traverse in Edinburgh, with a bookshop, a theatre, a gallery, a restaurant and a meeting place. The truth of the matter is that Jim's great friend is Jack Henry Moore who is a very weird character, and he embezzled all the money. He did absolutely do that; he had also worked for Jack Ruby in Dallas. He is now Sony's great expert, a great star. He once came up with the great line, 'I'd rather have AIDS than paranoia.'

RUSSELL HUNTER: I went into the Arts Lab one night, seeing this very intense, bossy Japanese woman tearing about, ordering people around, and Chris Rowley sitting in a corner with a teapot, a teacup, a chair, maybe a cushion and he had this cutter and he was sawing everything in half. Yoko was mounting one of her exhibitions and he had to saw all these incredibly commonplace household articles in half. Half a table with half a tea set and so on. He was sawing it up and she was being incredibly bossy. It's very difficult to saw a cushion in half and it kept fraying and she was very upset.

CHRIS ROWLEY: When I was working at the Arts Lab I got a job working for Yoko Ono cutting things in half for an exhibition she was doing. We had to cut a whole houseful of stuff in half. Paint it white. She had a few clever things: black jars in which she'd drop people's messages – 'Have a nice day', that sort of thing – and she charged £200 for the jars. She also had a glass hammer. Things like that.

The Social Deviants: 'You'd just bang them out and they'd all bellow along'

MICK FARREN: The Deviants really started in a pub called the Artesian Well off Westbourne Park Road. I knew this geezer called Pete Munro and another guy from Newcastle, Ralph, and we went in there and he played piano and I played guitar and Pete Munro played stand-up bass and basically we sang Woody Guthrie songs and Irish rebel tunes. The Irish rebel tunes were a necessary item for the audience and you got lots of Guinness. You'd just bang them out and they'd all bellow along. They used to ask for Jim Reeves songs too but we didn't know any of those. Then we wanted to get louder and Ralph got an organ and we became some kind of blues band doing Howlin' Wolf tunes. And we all moved to the East End, we got a house on Princelet Street, just by Spitalfields, just near Gilbert and George who lived on Fournier Street, and there were a few Royal College of Art types living out there, it was sort of like Soho. So we lived in one of those and we rehearsed in the basement and rented out our basement to other bands that were rehearsing and we also ran into this guy called Marvin who was with a band called the Brothers Grimm and he played with us for a while and we started to turn into the Fugs. And then we called ourselves the Social Deviants and that didn't do much good until basically we started playing UFO.

JOE BOYD: At one point Hoppy handed me this demo tape and said, 'This guy has been pestering me, he really wants to play UFO.' It was a tape of the Social Deviants. So I listened to about 30 seconds of it and said, 'This is garbage.' So Hoppy said OK. Then about a week later he'd bring it up again: 'This guy keeps calling me, he came round to see me, he says the tape isn't really a proper reflection of how good the group is . . .' So at some point, some dank January night, Hoppy and I drove to the East End, Jack the Ripper territory. There wasn't a soul on the street, there was a blizzard coming down. We finally found this place where the Social Deviants were rehearsing. We went upstairs, heard them and they sounded just as bad as they did on the demo tape. Subsequent to my refusal to book the Deviants Mick became one of the people who helped out on the door and became very helpful. And we used to have this five am slot for auditioning bands and after he'd been helping out for a few months we gave the Social Deviants a five am slot once, and that was over my dead body – the sole appearance of the Social Deviants at UFO.

RUSSELL HUNTER: The first person who ever really latched onto me, rather than me just going down to UFO as a punter, was this guy called Mike Laslett. He lived with his mother Rhaunie off Portobello: she started the Notting Hill Housing Trust and the Carnival. Through him I got to learn that the Social Deviants, i.e. Mick Farren, needed a new drummer, because they had a very odd drummer at the time. The Social Deviants at that time were Alex Stoll, the idiot Stoll, Micky's mate, a Canadian called Pete who was a frustrated jazz bassist and a bloke called Clive Muldoon on guitar. Their drummer, who they'd picked up through a *Melody Maker* ad, was what these days would be called 'born again', and he was born again long before anybody else. He used to turn up at all these gigs wearing a dinner jacket and tie, a bow tie, and in between the sets he'd be reading the Bible to all these terrible stoned-out strippers who used to prance around, trying to teach them the error of their ways. And after a while the band decided they couldn't really handle this, so they'd better have a new drummer. So I met Micky and got my drums sent up from Dorset and that's how I started with the Social Deviants. I used to go to Micky's hideous flat where he lived with Joy in Princelet Street, next door to a gang of car thieves. They'd be spraying Ford Cortinas different colours at 4.30 in the morning. They seemed to have a fairly strange relationship, Micky and Joy.

CHRIS ROWLEY: Joy was an interesting figure, a bohemian from the North, from Carlisle. She had a lot of crucifixes and was vaguely Christian, Christian and animist, mixed.

MICK FARREN: Miles turned us on to Nigel Samuel. He wanted to start a record label and we seemed ideal material. We'd go off to Wheelers and sit with him and drink whisky and Guinness and eat oysters and try to get money out of him so we could go on living and recording too. And that's how our first record got made and it got put out and it sold lots of copies and we went on the road and took methedrine and did that for the next two and a half years.

RUSSELL HUNTER: Nigel Samuel put up the money to record *Ptoof*. We did meet him occasionally, but the guy was off his trolley. He had a big minder who used to drive him round in his Lotus or Ferrari or whatever.

He used to completely crack up every so often and either want to give all his money away or else lock himself in his room and burn it. Other times he'd try and set his lawyers on a restaurant that had overcharged him tuppence for a chocolate eclair. Which was Lord Goodman, of course. He owned Portman Square and lots more and he was on an allowance, which was always being stopped, and he seemed to be imprisoned in his flat by these minders who would not let him out. Because they knew if they let him out he'd probably go and give Portman Square to the nearest hippie. I can remember him blowing up, going white-faced and shaking, over Micky asking him for something like five quid petrol money to go somewhere. Other times he'd be running down the street in his pyjamas trying to give away land to the nearest passer-by.

Acid: 'I'm sorry I'm late, but I was given some LSD'

CHRIS ROWLEY: There was definite fall-out after the 14-Hour Dream. It did two things: one, there was a big shake-out in the underground press because a lot of the more entrepreneurial types made off with the money. People had come into the underground world who were essentially dope dealers with the morals of the market-place. When confronted by large piles of cash they didn't bring them back to *International Times* afterwards. This caused the first kind of dose of hard reality that I can recall in that six months. And there were rows afterwards about the money, although we only heard about them later. There were also changes of personnel. There were various busts. There was the famous bust where the police didn't have any particular warrant or anything but just came and drove off with everything. And Jack Henry Moore chased the police truck up Southampton Row, jumped onto it, it stopped, a couple of policemen came out and threatened him, he jumped on again. This wasn't even a bust, just police action: harassment of the dirty international anarchist scum – 'We're going to put you out of business. We turn up in the truck, we take away the papers, and you can sue for them!' Very British. The nanny state. There was also a regular supply of very, very good LSD.

DAVID GOODMAN: After being a mod I went into hibernation. I was lost, really lost. I was working hard, taking a lot of black bombers, occasionally going to gigs and things like that, and trying to work girls out. I was living in a basement in 32 Goodmayes Lane, Ilford, Essex. It became quite a legendary address. The first guy to move in there besides myself was a guy called Michael Dale who I'd gone to school with.

One day we were reading the *News of the World*: 'The Heaven and Hell Drug' and we were sitting around thinking, 'Where can we get some of this heaven and hell shit?' So Micky says, 'I think I know some of these hippie sort of people in this coffee bar out in Gants Hill.' And he reconnoitres Gants Hill and comes back and says, 'Right, we can meet this guy called Jim. Let's put our best clobber on.' So I get out my kaftan — I've got this short hair because I'm still working at the supermarket, but I've got the kaftan and I've got a bell and this big overcoat. So we're sitting at this table in this coffee bar opposite these two guys who look very shifty at each other and look at Mick and say, 'He's the fuzz.' And Mick turns to me and says, 'Show 'em,' and I had to show 'em my kaftan and bell and they said, 'OK, he's OK.' Thereupon there was a surreptitious little deal done and a couple of quid passed under the table and in return we got this bit of black stuff. So we rushed home but we didn't quite know what to do with this black stuff so we lit it and sniffed it and then we rolled it into some tobacco and smoked it and we got fucking stoned out of our heads. And we said, 'This is great . . . but what about this heaven and hell shit?' So we arranged with them to include us on their regular purchase of the weekend trip for everyone. Then we were told about this hippie wedding and we went along to this beautiful house in Ilford and we all went off to the park and tripped out, man, and it was your first trip and it was fantastic. Then I basically took acid every day. After a few weeks I was buying quantities and started selling: we took over the business.

STEVE SPARKS: You couldn't touch anything in Goodman's house in Seven Kings cos you'd trip. You'd open the fridge at this house and there'd be bottles and bottles of acid. There'd be more acid in the fridge than food and Boss likes his food. You had to be really careful what you touched — you'd be sitting there and you'd touch furniture and you'd get contact.

DAVID GOODMAN: Down in the basement we've got the bottles we used to mix the crystal acid with distilled water and drip it in single trips onto sugar cubes or blotting paper. Or sometimes we used to squirt a drop straight down someone's throat. My late friend John Cox, he was a real bad acid freak. One day we gave him twenty or maybe more day-and-a-half or even two-day-old trips on blotting paper, which were still at least half strength. And we said to him, 'John, make yourself some money, go back up to town, enjoy yourself,' because he used to flit up to town and sometimes he'd come back in the most awful state and we'd just sit on him for a week, fill him full of pie and mash and let him go again. This particular day he started unwrapping all these trips and eating them and we just pushed him out. 'Go away, go fucking away!' He came back in the middle of the night with this girl from West London. She pulls out this huge piece of blotting paper and it's got burn marks on it and it's got crystal acid all over it and I can see it in his eyes he's gonna make a fucking grab for it and he does. He dives across the room, he grabs this and he's stuffing it in his mouth. At which point we go, 'John, you are banished . . . get out! We don't want to be responsible . . .' He went so wild that he went to hospital. He climbed out of the hospital window, then the police grabbed him and I think he climbed out of the police window too. Anyway, he climbed in his mum's window and I used to go round there once or twice a week and eventually he'd come down and say, 'Hi, Dave,' and sit down for about half an hour and then he'd go, 'Phewww . . . later Dave,' and back upstairs he'd go.

CHRIS ROWLEY: The thing about LSD was that you did realise that if for some reason everybody could take it together, with the proviso that some people would undoubtedly not come back, the world would undoubtedly become a much saner and safer place because people would get hold of the problem. This was very important: the powerful psychedelic belief in the goodness of people once they'd been turned on to their inner cortex.

SAM HUTT: The first acid trips were extremely serious. A day fasting before: reading *The Tibetan Book of the Dead, The Psychedelic Experience*; having Krishnamurti playing on record while you're tripping. I don't piss on that but it's not my way now. In one sense it's quite reasonable because acid's a very strong thing, it's quite reasonable to take it seriously. It's equally quite reasonable to take it completely flippantly, but you've just got to watch out for that old mother . . .

JEFF DEXTER: Every day was lived to the full, you never stopped. Apart from when you dropped acid and stayed home. At the beginning I stayed home and went through *The Psychedelic Experience* – reading the books, doing a mantra, going inside myself, dying, seeing God, nirvana, the lot. The first trip was wonderful to begin with, then it was awful. At the beginning I levitated, truly flew from one room to another, or so it seemed. I could talk to my friends without talking. Then I died, got the horrors, puked up bugs.

VIRGINIA CLIVE-SMITH: My first acid trip was in June 1967, when *Sergeant Pepper* came out. It was absolutely wonderful and that did completely change me. The next morning I literally ditched my wardrobe and went barefoot from there on. I came out of the house, which was in Chelsea, and there was a privet hedge and bits had fallen off it or been cut off and I very lovingly picked up a piece of privet and put it back in the hedge so that it should be with its own. I then really went for it: long hair, permed hair (very tight and curly) and I really was a Dylan lookalike, in fact I went through quite a serious moment of wondering whether I wasn't sort of related to Bob Dylan. On my second trip I rechristened myself Mistress Knowing-Wink.

MICK FARREN: I didn't take acid for a while, but it was all over the place. People used to go into their rooms with bowls of cold water and rice and put on Ravi Shankar records and shut themselves in and that was what taking acid was about and it seemed most unappealing. Not to say I don't believe in psychedelics – I have in my time seen God, he didn't like the look of me so I went away again – but . . .

NICOLA LANE: I went to St Martin's [School of Art] in '67. It was very trendy and the clothes were terrific, but no one was into drugs much. I was the first person in my year to take acid. It was a bit late to join the psychedelic world and everyone gave me rather a hard time about it. I was so innocent about it that I took it over a weekend and was very late in on the Monday. And I went up to the teacher and I said, 'I'm terribly sorry I'm late, but you see I was given some LSD and it was jolly powerful. Well, I couldn't help it, I'm late.' And really in my naïveté thought that this was a perfectly good excuse. And the expression on his face! He just managed to choke out, 'Do you do this sort of thing often?' and I went, 'Oh no, it was the first time.'

ALAN MARCUSON: I went down to score on a Sunday morning with this big black guy called Keith, and a friend, Sarah Davies. I was sent down to Petticoat Lane with everybody's money to get 100 trips from Thai Sam, who was the Man. We went in this black mini cab and I'd never been down to that part of town so it was a bit disorientating and I was probably already stoned. We got to Thai Sam's and I felt slightly ill at ease. He was into all those hippie-trippie mind games, which he loved, he was The Magician . . . So we arrived at Thai Sam's and there was the most LSD I've probably ever seen, then or since. There was this huge mound of crystal on a piece of silver kitchen foil. Dangerous stuff, enough to kill an army. He was mixing it with a big jar of distilled water, I think, and he was getting droppers and each drop was a trip and we scored 100 trips. We had to wait for ages, and the taxi was still outside. And Sam said, 'Are you going to get high today?' And we said, 'Yeah!'

and he took this silver foil, from which he'd removed all the crystal by now but which still had a film all over it, and tore it in half. He gave half to me and half to Sarah. I didn't think anything of it, but here was a piece of silver paper with what would be about six lines of cocaine's worth of LSD on it. So we both licked the foil clean. It normally took an hour or two at least for anything to happen, but this time within minutes I was already on the strongest LSD trip I could imagine taking.

We stumbled into Petticoat Lane. There was just a morass of people and it was weird and wonderful. Basically I wasn't upset, but I noticed in the periphery of my consciousness Sarah, who I felt somewhat responsible for, and she was beginning to look upset. We got into the cab and she started freaking out, foaming at the mouth and all the electricity in the city was going through her and there were these two people in her talking out loud to each other and I knew I had to look after her but I was finding it enormously difficult to stay in touch with her. She said, 'I'm dying, take me to a hospital,' but I knew . . . you don't go to a hospital. But I knew I needed help desperately, just to sort the situation out. And I thought, 'What the fuck – I'll go to Ronnie Laing!'

This trip was quite extraordinary. It was coursing through me. I was on another planet. I managed to get to the door and I managed somehow to knock on the door and I pointed to the car, and by this time these two black guys – Keith and the driver – were carrying Sarah out of the car and she was rigid, in a sitting position, with the most terrible look on her face and bubbles coming out of her mouth. Laing said, 'Are you all right?' And I said, 'Yes,' and he pushed me into this room with his wife Uta who I knew and their baby Adam and pushed me onto the bed and took Sarah into the front room where there was the most extraordinary pandemonium going on – screaming and crying and he was shouting, 'Die, you bitch, if that's what you want to do!' and he was into exorcism, some form of therapy, and he was very good, but it's a wonder that girl ever came back. In the meantime I was thrown into this room, but although I wasn't frightened I was uptight. All this tension had built up in my body and I didn't know what to do.

At one point – I knew people upstairs – I ran upstairs and they weren't in, and I ran downstairs, and I ran upstairs and I still had this very literal kind of anxiety. I just couldn't let go and go with this trip. Then I was on the bed and I noticed this baby who was one minute crying in a contorted upset state and then he was cooing and I thought, 'Aah! if he can change his mood so easily, I can change my mood so easily.' And I let go and as I let go I just had this great wave of nausea and I went into the lavatory and went aarrgghh! and it was this great relief of tension and I knew the vomiting was all this tension passing out of my body and when that happened I felt great all of a sudden and I didn't give a shit about Sarah any more: Ronnie was looking after her. The Man. I'd taken her to the Man. I went and lay on the bed and in the end it was the greatest trip I ever took.

I remember Uta standing looking rather concerned. They'd been in bed together on a Sunday morning with their three-month-old baby to be confronted by Marcuson and Sarah out of their total minds and there I was in their bed on a Sunday morning and I was watching Uta and just slowly her eyes separated and I entered into this crystal world – it's the only way I could describe it – and left my body, the only time, left my body, hovered above the bed, looked at myself lying there and voom! I was gone, I don't know where. It was total loss. Apparently I lay on the bed for some five hours without moving or saying a word and came round at about four o'clock that afternoon and all of a sudden I was back on an ordinary acid trip. I knew the territory.

I felt like a fucking god after going through that. The white light like you cannot imagine. He brought Sarah and I together and we were very nervous to see each other and it was all very wonderful and we felt extremely high and Sarah was all right. She'd come back – God knows how he did it. Then he put us back on the street and we went home. And I went on tripping for three days and in the end it was a real hassle, I wanted to sleep and I got jagged. And I was very very careful of LSD after that.

RICHARD NEVILLE: One day I went down to visit Martin Sharp in the Pheasantry. I'd resisted taking acid. Mainly because there was always some jerk that had to get the copy edited and take it down to the printers. And that jerk was me. So I went down to Martin's, we had a cup of tea and I began to feel strange and I said, '*Martin* . . .' but he'd done it completely as an act of friendship. I don't resent that, that was the way it happened, but he spiked my tea. I cancelled my dinner appointment and it was perfectly wonderful, perfectly terrific. I didn't take a lot. Some people took frighteningly large amounts – I took frighteningly small ones. I took acid extremely seriously, and not all that often.

JOHN PEEL: The only time I took acid voluntarily was at UFO. It was jolly nice. I've always rather flippantly said since that it was rather like going to Stratford-on-Avon: once you'd done it I didn't see any need to do it again.

STEVE SPARKS: I have to admit that I always thought that acid was pretty boring. I was essentially a speedfreak and acid was just like a different sort of speed as far as I was concerned. I never got the glorious hallucinations that I read about.

The trouble with acid is there's no work involved. You don't have to put any effort into it. It's like giving a child a gun. It expands your consciousness but because you haven't got any discipline you don't know what to do with it once you've got it. I suspect that acid was a false lead, a red herring. Never got me off anyway.

STASH DE ROLA: Psychedelic drugs were a key element in the 60s. Acid was very powerful. It led a lot of people to re-examine themselves, people who otherwise might have been doomed to be the era's yuppies. Such as the Beatles, the Rolling Stones, this circle of rich pop stars. Success on an unparalleled scale rewarded them with all the material trappings, but in a way it was all treated a bit as a joke. And there was constantly an underlying tension, a worry and a quest: everyone sought a transcendental way to some paradise of some kind, to the other side. There was this thirst of the soul.

I do remember wonderful conversations with people like George Harrison, indeed with Mick Jagger. One morning in Cheyne Walk he confessed how difficult it was to operate since he reckoned he'd lost his ego through acid. It was very hard for him to go on at that moment. For stars this loss of ego was impossible.

DEREK TAYLOR: LSD changed everything. The Beatles gave it me and Joan, my wife. I got a double dose. I enjoyed it enormously and I took an enormous amount after that. It was at Brian Epstein's house-warming: there was no danger of a bad trip, all we could see around us was nice-looking people having a wonderful time. I had no reason to doubt that anything we were doing was right. After that it was full tilt. Looking back I can see that I was probably quite a bore about it.

MALDWYN THOMAS: Paul McCartney turned up at Michael Hollingshead's World Psychedelic Centre in Pont Street one time. It was one of the first times that I ever saw him. I was surprised. John you could imagine, but Paul was one of the last people you'd have expected to turn up there.

PAUL MCCARTNEY: When I admitted I took acid I got into trouble for being honest. The option was there to say, 'LS what? Never heard of it, sorry.' Certainly no one had ever caught me at it. But the point was that we were in a sort of group, we were a generation, and really more than anything you don't want to let each other down. You don't want to be the one who says, 'I've never had acid, sorry,' and then you go, 'Fucking hell . . .' and you have the courage to say it. And I'm not ashamed of it. This is something I've done, something Aldous Huxley had done, plenty of good precedents for experimenting in these areas amongst artists. When I did take it, once or twice I did enjoy it and once or twice I didn't. It was only ever Nature and wonder and quiet when you enjoyed it, when anything else interfered it was bum. I had it one time in some flat in Eaton Square after a club. We'd all rolled back there as you would do after one of these clubs. Somebody said, 'Has anyone ever had acid?' It was a slightly upper-class crowd. (The crowd separated itself into all us working class and the Lord Londonderrys and that kind of people which Mick and the guys always were into and still are. I never disliked that crowd but I never just found myself in with them.) So that was who had it, someone slightly upper-class. And it was on blotting paper, you just cut it up into little squares and you had one each. So it was like 'Wow, right . . . who's game for a bit of a . . .' so we all had it and it was OK. I was actually conscious of having a dirty shirt on, which was weird for me.

Before this John and George had been spiked. They had a dentist friend and he spiked them one evening. I think he wanted naughty sex games, cos they had all their wives there, and he sort of said, 'Does anyone fancy a little bit . . .' and they said, 'You fuck off, mate! But we'll have a coffee . . .' They went to a club after the coffee, because they didn't really know what would happen to them. And they got to the Ad Lib Club and it appeared to be on fire, and they decided they'd get away from that, and they drove back at about twenty miles an hour, hugging the kerb, apparently, out to Esher, where they ended up at George's house, and these huge big friendly trees were waving at them . . . It was a kind of mixed experience.

What we had heard about acid was that it would change you irrevocably. You would never be the same. I remember driving round Hyde Park Corner and we were all in a taxi and we were discussing this and one of us – John or George – said, 'I hear you're never the same after it,' and that made quite a big effect on me, and I thought, 'OK, I could change and everything, but maybe I've got something going here that I need to preserve, maybe I don't need to take a leap into the dark on this one.' So I did resist quite a lot. They said to me, 'Come on . . .' but I backed off, and that was peer pressure of the highest variety . . . your fellow group members. There you really have got to do what they do, cos you're group members, it's like being members of a commune or something. But I resisted and said, 'Well, you know . . .' because I could see what it was doing to them. And what it was doing to them basically was making them sit around very dopey and making them hear noises I couldn't hear, from miles away – 'Listen to that . . .!' and I'd go, 'What?' and couldn't hear a thing.

Anyway, one night at EMI John by mistake took an LSD tablet; he had a little pill box and he thought he was taking a pep pill. But this evening John had this acid and we had to take him home from the session – 'He's not feeling too well, George' – because we didn't really want to tell George Martin that he was tripping, although he'd probably sussed it out. So I took John back to my house and I ended up having acid with him that night.

DEREK TAYLOR: John did take an awful lot of LSD. He had a lot of leisure. He had that pop-star – it wasn't rock star, then – that pop-star space which was very conducive to acid. If he was up all night he could go to sleep all day. He didn't have any of those conventional things to deal with. At Apple we were a bad influence on each other – if you regard it as bad. He would have it now and again, and I would have it now and again at work, and that can be difficult. He went to meet Brigitte Bardot on acid and a big mistake that was because that was a very straight meeting. And we freaked out, and we panicked, making all these unnecessary explanations. McCartney stopped me doing acid at work because I think Peter Asher hinted to him that it was getting a bit out of line. So I did stop taking it at work. One day a woman journalist appeared and said, 'I need to see Mary Hopkin,' and I said, 'Need? How can anyone *need* to see Mary Hopkin. You can *want* to, you can like the idea, you can't need to, it can't be a *need*. Can we examine this word? Richard, will you come here and take notes . . .'

JIM HAYNES: The only time I got really stoned in that whole time was I went to a party for John Lennon and I like punch and I like cake and I ate a vast amount of cake and drank a lot of punch and they were all spiked. It was like a pop Who's Who, in some private club in Charing Cross Road, everybody was there. And I sat down on the floor next to Sandy Lieberson and his wife and I said, 'Sandy, please, see that I get home, I can't make it.' I couldn't stand up hardly. And they took me home to the Arts Lab and put me in my bed upstairs and twelve or sixteen hours later I woke up. This one experience with acid was not a positive experience, I was very scared. After that whenever I ate cake or drank punch I was extremely leery.

JONATHAN MEADES: One day I had to go with a friend to take her sick cat to the PDSA surgery in Chelsea. And these four neanderthal foot-soldiers from the great army of hippiedom came in with a cat that they had to keep in a bag, making the most fantastic noise. We said, 'What's the matter?' and they said, 'Like we're tripping, man, and we thought we'd shave the cat and paint it different colours.' They couldn't let it out of the bag but what you could see looked like something unpleasant from a game dealer.

LOUISE BURDEN: I had an accident in 1962, horse-riding, I broke my neck and my spine got very damaged. I spent a couple of years in hospital being put back together. All I was interested in was getting my A-levels so I could have the final bit of surgery which would make me look like other people. So I did four A-levels in 1967 aged sixteen. And then I was allowed the surgery. So in the summer of love I was in the Hammersmith Hospital on a kidney machine, but wishing I could be a hippie. When I had the second bit of surgery I expired and was made to get going again and kept going on the kidney machine. I had a very interesting experience. When I was being hooked into the machine through my stomach I jumped out of my body and watched them do it. It was like coming alive. I actually didn't want to be here – it really was very boring what happened to my body. This went on for five nights. They saw it as fighting for life, but for me it was a matter of choosing to come back and serve my sentence on earth. After that I used to swallow huge quantities of acid, trying to get that feeling back, but acid never touched it. It was almost like dying only not so good. On my first trip I sat there trying to make myself have a bad time, but that didn't work. I'd heard about the horrors so I ran water and gazed at it trying to turn it into snakes, gazed into mirrors, all that. But it didn't work.

DUNCAN FALLOWELL: In 1970 I took a lot of LSD. As you get older and move closer to death you suddenly realise how thin the wall of consciousness is, how thin the dividing line between life and death, how insecure you really are, how relative all forms of security are. But when you're young you have these rigid things you've grown up with, which you have to batter out of shape and try to remove in order to experience life for yourself. So all drug-taking – in my case – was an attempt to break out of this pattern, these deeply ingrained habits of thought. One of the most useful things acid did was demonstrate that it is possible to view reality in various ways. It stops you being a bigot, it enriches the way you look at the world. I would take three or four tabs a day and drink and wander about; this went on for about six months. Eventually it stopped working.

I had a group of about a dozen people around me and we would take it regularly. This group didn't form by a process of decision, it actually formed because of an excitement that was generated by this closed group. Among them, funnily enough, were some boxers. Robert Nairac, who was later chopped up by the IRA, was part of my little group. I was in bed one day with his favourite boxing blue and we'd both taken acid, not really having sex but sort of tripping. Having sex on acid was not easy. There was a knock on the door and this guy jumped out and answered and it was Nairac, with two heavies, saying, 'Are you in there with that shit Fallowell?' Then I heard this whispering at the door but I was so at home with acid by this stage that I could actually separate the hallucinations from the facts very easily. Then I saw him at the end of the bed, twirling a swagger-stick, wearing a chocolate suit with white stripes, a flower in his buttonhole, and two heavies: it looked like the Marquess of Queensberry come to get Oscar Wilde. And with as little justification. He was furious, but he didn't beat me up in the end, he actually wanted to join the group and take acid. He was one of those good-looking, conceited men who might have liked to have been gay, but he went to a Catholic school and this makes life a problem for anybody. So he eventually joined us for some of our acid trips, and liked it very much. He was rather silent, but when pressed just said, 'The room is full of green birds.'

'EZRA PENCE': We had this idea to make funds by making drugs. We went away somewhere and I made a bunch of this drug called PMA, which at the time wasn't illegal. It was one of a bunch of compounds discovered by a guy called Schulgin, who discovered a load of synthetic mescalin analogues, about ten of them. I found the paper in the library and we went through it with a pin and chose the easiest. I made a bunch of it. It was totally disastrous because nobody liked it except us. It was sort of like psychedelic methedrine – I'm not even sure that Ecstasy isn't the same thing, rediscovered fifteen years later. Very, very speedy ... Paramethoxyamphetamine was its name. You start off with anisol, essence of aniseed. As a money-making scam it was a total waste of time, we never sold any of it at all. We took it all ourselves and got well crazy on it. It made you into a Viking berserker. We were roaming around mountains wild-eyed with sweat popping out. One of the wonderful attributes of it was that when you actually shot it up the rush made everything go black and white and the sky went like the set for a Wagner opera and you had this certainty that you were about to die but you didn't care. This didn't exactly endear it to the punters in Notting Hill Gate.

PETER ROBERTS: I was dealing dope. I needed to score a pound weight and a regular contact said, 'Oh, I know somebody who's got some.' So, I went along with this guy and another guy, the third guy just came along to walk down the road, down the Boltons. We walked down and my guy said, 'Wait here, I'll get it.' We waited on a bench in the Boltons and he took the money off me, came back, no problem. We walked down to the Fulham Road and then suddenly we realised we were being followed. We started walking faster, they started walking faster. We saw the taxis passing: if we can get there, we can jump in a taxi. It's amazing: you get this heightened sense of perception, you could hear people switching the light off in a third-floor flat down the road. But they jumped us. The other guy still had a little airline bag with the pound weight of grass in it. On me they found maybe £300. No grass or anything but a little sugar cube wrapped up in foil, which was still legal. The third guy happened, by chance, to have a little piece of hash. He didn't even know it was there. The police looked at this foil and said: 'What's this?' 'It's a sugar cube, I carry them cos I like them as sweets.' So the detective sergeant opens it up, sees the sugar cube, wraps it up and hands it back. So I get booked into Brixton, charged with joint possession of the weight.

I came before a magistrate and had to say I was of no fixed abode: I thought it was better that I didn't tell them about the place I was actually living, 101 Cromwell Road, which was a madhouse. So I had to go on remand to Brixton, which I found quite pleasant. While I was there waiting to be inducted or whatever this heavy-looking guy was sitting next to me. 'What you in for?' 'Drugs, what are you in for?' 'GBH,' and he looked it, by Christ. He holds up his coat cuff and says, 'Feel in there,' so I felt a lump and he said, 'That's hash. Maybe we can do some business.' 'Oh shit,' I thought, 'busted for drugs and the first thing that happens in jail is I get offered dope.'

So in I went, I got a little cell, I didn't have to wear uniform since I was on remand, and I had my acid with me. It was very funny: me being obviously 'a gentleman' and the class system being still in operation in the 60s, thank goodness, I was given a certain amount of leeway. In some line-up I stood forward and started protesting and the chief screw screamed, 'You get the fuck back there!' and then he called me in and his attitude completely changed: 'I can see you're a learned man and you must understand we have some very difficult characters here . . .' Towards the end of the ten days inside my screw actually was calling me 'Sir'. We were supposed to put our food trays outside the cell, but he'd come in and take it out for me. He became my batman.

So around the middle of all this I thought I'd drop my acid. I'd got a nice little room, they lock me up at eight or nine, no one's going to disturb me for the next ten hours. So they banged me up and I took my trip. It was a lovely trip; just a bare room, the bed, the pisspot, the bare essentials. One of the things about trips was you never knew when somebody might barge in, disturb you – 'Hey man, I didn't know you were tripping, have a nice trip, man ...' – and this was absolute security. When we got to court I got off on a technicality, the other two guys got six months, but I had a good barrister, supplied by Hoppy.

Elitism: 'The cutting edge of on-going bohemianism'

JOHN PEEL: The underground was terribly small, and very very localised. I could never understand, for example, why it was that that Country Joe and the Fish LP never got into the charts. I said to the record company, 'Why isn't this in the charts? Everybody I know has got a copy.' But what I didn't realise was that it was the other way around: I knew everybody who'd got a copy. So the 300 that they'd sold were all to people that I knew.

CHERYLL PARK: The underground was exactly the same as everything else: there were rich people and there were poor people and there were people in the middle. There was a kind of a decadence there and you could belong to that because you might be beautiful or you might be able to take lots of drugs or able to get lots of drugs – it was just the same as any other society, it was class-ridden. And that elitism took the whole movement over and the people who could afford to carry on living like that did and the rest dwindled away. There was no working class in the underground because nobody did any work. And the working–class people who did join the movement, if there even was a movement, found their own little slot and they found that some people were still in control because they had the money. You didn't *have* to be an intellectual and you didn't *have* to be rich, but you had to have something that you could contribute to be one of the 'beautiful people'. If you were an ordinary person who lived in some suburb, you had no chance at all.

JONATHAN PARK: I found the elitism and the callousness very difficult to get on with. The elitism meant that I was always an outsider, I had no starry nature, no wild wit or gift of the gab, lots of money or leather trousers. I was just a friend. The callousness sprang from the elitism, the exclusivity and the fact that it wasn't soundly based on any social or political ideology. It would change to suit the fashion of the time: you could be in one moment, out the next. There was this social callousness. The callousness over drugs was what I'd call the macho aspect. It was a tremendously chauvinistic society. Alan Marcuson never rolled a joint

187

himself in the entire period, Jilly always did. She cooked and rolled joints and was very lovely. I despised that macho side.

ANDREA ADAM: There was this incredible pressure to be laid back and for a lot of people like me, who were naturally more active, this was very hard. Unless you knew how to grunt and just keep saying 'Outasight!' it was hard. It was not good to communicate. And there were a lot of morons active in it. But to those of us who were looking at the phenomenon, it did seem that a lot of the hippies were plugged into some kind of exclusive godhead that they shared with some select few and that avenue just wasn't open to me. I did take acid a few times but it did not agree with me at all. I was the antithesis of laid back and I was much too uptight to enjoy acid, but I felt I had to because everybody was doing it. The prevailing memory I have of the 60s is the fear of being uncool.

MICK FARREN: Sure the underground was elitist: we were an elite. We were the cutting edge of on-going bohemianism at that point.

PETER ROBERTS: The underground was definitely hierarchical. All institutions or groups of people are inevitably hierarchical. There were stars, there were walk-ons and there were cannon-fodder. Which is much to do with what human beings are like. Also, at certain points in time somebody becomes a star because what they can express is what happens to be what needs to be expressed at that point in time. Then they cease to be a star, they drop back out. Some people become permanent because they make themselves an institution. The thing about many of those stars was that normally a star has to be a star at something: playing the guitar, painting, something that can be bought. The point of the counterculture stars is that they were stars at living. The idea of the hippie as an aristocrat.

HORACE OVE: All the 60s counterculture leaders would always have been leaders, whenever it was. They had that ability. They were bright kids. There was an elite, a hierarchy, and then there were the followers. Although they gave the impression that everybody had a say and that you could argue and discuss and talk and say what you had to say, there was still an elite. Some people got hooked on it, they had a sense of power, they were leaders. People went up and talked to them, interviewed them, there was young girls and boys waiting to meet them, they got a great sense of power, and they felt they were doing . . . something. And they had a good time. Looking back from here you might think that they were

188

very calculating, but I don't think that they were that calculating. They did believe in what they were doing at the time, I don't think they sat down and worked it all out and said this is going to build me up into a star. But they had a certain ability, they could organise, they could articulate themselves better than a lot of other people – so they came up to the front.

ANDREW BAILEY: I was slightly in awe of the underground heavies like Richard Neville and Germaine Greer. You'd meet them, you'd be in the same room at parties, but they were stars. The underground had a star system exactly as did pop music and films and everything else. The stars knew what they were doing: they were as fundamentally insincere as everybody else. They knew what people wanted them to be, to look like, and to say and they very dutifully went ahead and performed that task for the pleasure of television and the rest of the media.

TONY ELLIOTT: There was certainly a hierarchy. There were very much senior elders, in tribal terms, who ran things. The underground was a collection of units each of which operated in their own right. There were links between the Arts Lab and *IT*, because of Jim Haynes being connected to both, things like that, but essentially each group operated within their own decision-making areas. And each unit had their own decision-making individual or group at the top and the ones that didn't failed. People use 'middle-class values' as an insulting term, but everyone was becoming middle-class. Only the middle class could actually afford to rush around shouting 'Off the pig!'

JONATHAN MEADES: Most of those state-of-the-art super-hippies seemed to live in a totally different world. One was scared to go into somewhere like the Dragon Tearooms at World's End. It was a closed and not-talking world and if you were someone who talked this was all very, very peculiar. They didn't say anything, they didn't do anything – just sat there like aspirant vegetables. I put this to a friend of mine once, who was very taken with it all, and asked him how he could bear to spend time with these sort of people. 'Oh, they're the new aristocracy,' he replied. And he used that phrase without any sense of irony, and in absolute earnest. It was rather frightening. There were all these people who I'd known previously who were kind of sucked in. The most improbable people were taken in by the whole thing. One can understand how things like Hitler happened. I don't think there were conscious conmen, there weren't people deliberately out to screw people, there wasn't a deliberate wickedness as with Hitler, but it was more a weird

189

mass hysteria. It's explainable on one level through the psychology of the crowd. The interesting point is whether this thing called the *zeitgeist* is anything more than people aping each other, or their role models. I suspect not, but the process of the aping, of the parroting, works in a very very strange way. It's like this childish thing, this infantilism – people not wanting to be different and therefore joining in. People *all* getting those moustaches, and people *all* getting that haircut and people *all* getting those fucking kaftans. What it was was a fashion which was thought to be more than a fashion; it was analogous to the way in which architectural modernism was thought to be more than a style. And instead of it being restricted to sideburns and sartorial affairs, it somehow made a grab on people's minds. It sounds now as if one is assuming a terrible superiority and attributing to oneself at that age a kind of prescience, but I just knew it was absolute shit. That business one week after *Sgt. Pepper* came out that the whole world was going to change – absolute shit.

Sgt. Pepper: 'A splendid time is guaranteed for all'

GENE MAHON: I was quite heavily involved in putting together *Sgt. Pepper*. Everybody got rowed in and everybody could do anything. I did lots. I was working with Al Vandenberg at a new advertising agency, Geer Dubois. Ostensibly I was the production manager but basically I was his sidekick. So we were using the agency's telephones to phone round and collect pictures of people for the *Pepper* cover. I was at Michael Cooper's studio when the cover photograph was taken. Everybody was involved: Vandenberg took this picture of Cooper, Lennon, Ringo, Patti Harrison, a guy called Mohamad who was Robert Fraser's Moroccan sidekick, Peter Blake, a couple of people from Madame Tussaud's and myself all standing there discussing putting together the cover. I was sitting in a side-room rolling joints and causing John Lennon to cough, and making the odd suggestion while Cooper was shooting. Michael Cooper took the photograph, but it was Al Vandenberg and I who put it all together and made the decisions. Somewhere down amongst the credits is a line from the lyrics which says, 'A splendid time is guaranteed for all,' or one of those things, and that was because I said, 'Let's pull that one out and put it down there.'

MALDWYN THOMAS: The first time I heard *Sgt. Pepper* I was at a Hendrix concert. In Leicester Square. Paul was there and John was there. Hendrix got up on stage and said, 'I've just heard a record today, and it'll be out next week.' Then he played the first track on his guitar. It was a great way to hear it. Wonderful.

190

VIRGINIA CLIVE-SMITH: I really believed it all, I absolutely did. I rang up all the answerphones I knew in London – J. Walter Thompson, my doctor and all the companies I knew that had answerphones, including the one for which I was then working, and I played the entire two sides of the album to the answerphones so that the secretaries might possibly pick up on a little love and peace.

JILL MARCUSON: Virginia had a big pocket made in her dress to carry *Sgt. Pepper* around. The whole album just fitted in.

PAUL MCCARTNEY: Much much later, when I went out on tour with Wings, we got to some university somewhere, Nottingham I think, and one student said to me, 'God, you know, man, around the time of *Sgt. Pepper*, we really thought it was going to change the world. What happened?' Looking at me as if it was sort of my fault. In actual fact I don't really think that we thought that we were going to change the world as much as you thought we were going to change the world. We ourselves were just living in the world and, OK, if things changed through a bit of meditation and through a bit of vegetarianism or through a better relationship with the business thing, then great, that's what we were always up for, quite selfishly motivated, I suppose, in a way, incidentally selflessly. I mean, we wanted 'business with pleasure' for ourselves and if we could get it for everyone else, great, we'd score it for them too. But I don't think changing the world really was in our minds. I think it came as a surprise to find that people thought that we were changing the world. I'm sure we did change a lot of things but without any sort of campaign to change it; it was just as a group of people we were talking openly about new ideas and some of them then filtered into society, and some of them are still about.

SOMA and the Cannabis Ad: 'One should remember what so many right-wing Tories were doing in '67'

STEVE ABRAMS: The idea for SOMA first appeared in an article in *Cherwell*, the Oxford University paper, in February 1967. I wish I hadn't called it the 'Society of Mental Awareness' which was how it started. Someone pointed out that 'mental awareness' is absolutely meaningless, because what other kind of awareness is there?

DICK POUNTAIN: I worked for a while for Steve Abrams as his chief chemist at SOMA. Synthesising tetra-hydra-cannabinol [THC] legally, with a licence from the Home Office. I met him while living in Lonsdale

Road. Upstairs was Felix de Mendelsohn, who was then editing *IT*, and his wife Jane, and at that time everyone came through that house. Hoppy was there as often as not, and so on. And Abrams was through there, discovered I was a chemist and just popped the question. This was at the time of the Wootton Report, and everybody thought that the Wootton Report was going to legalise cannabis. Steve got a licence to handle cannabis products and we had this lab behind Chelsea football ground where I synthesised a whole bunch of THC. And we bio-assayed it, subjectively. And Steve had these incredibly high-falutin' ideas that after the Wootton Report legalised it, we were going to industrially manu-facture it and we were going to make cigarettes soaked in THC. The problem was that one of the starting ingredients was called olivetol, and it was very difficult to synthesise and Steve bought it from Koch-Light, a custom pharmaceutical firm, and Steve paid them to make a batch which I then turned into THC. But there was no money to get any more olivetol. I fell out with Steve over money – he wasn't paying me what he'd promised and he wasn't paying on time. The *New Statesman*, which was very trendy at that time, actually reported it in their gossip column. It said that the chief chemist had quit SOMA because he'd fallen out with the director – the reason was that the chemist was a Freudian and the director was a Jungian! Typical wank. What it actually was was that the director owed me £140 that I needed.

STEVE ABRAMS: In *The Marijuana Papers* Ginsberg had an article in which he suggests an ad signed by 500 people in the *New York Times* in passing – that remained in my mind. In 1966 a very serious ad appeared in [London] *The Times*, four pages long, appealing for peace in Vietnam and arranged by a Korean, Mr Matsuda. I thought if *The Times* will print that they'll print anything. I proposed the idea of an ad at a meeting in Indica the day after Hoppy was sent to prison and Miles said he thought he knew where he could get some money. It has always been assumed that it went in because of the Rolling Stones bust, but in fact it was for Hoppy. What happened was that the idea was proposed and the money became available. I was advised before the end of the day that the money would be available and that it would be coming from McCartney: he offered to guarantee the £1800 cost of the ad.

PAUL MCCARTNEY: At the time it didn't seem in the least bit radical. It seemed like a very ordinary straightforward move. But now, to imagine that Jonathan Aitken came round and enlisted my support – it's far out! Now's when it looks far out to me. Of course times were in fact very straight, but we were sort of cocooned, not like a Bloomsbury Group, not like a Montmartre set, but it was the London set and it was a crowd that accepted certain standards. I still think that the ad was a very interesting proposition, although the trouble was that everyone was then looking for some kind of SOMA society to take over, and it suggested that cannabis was going to be this tranquilliser of the future that would deaden all the people. In actual fact I warned a few police – cos you had dealings you didn't need with the police round that time ... I would say to them, 'Look, lads, you're going to drive all the kids into booze, certainly, if not heroin, if you condemn this cannabis thing and don't sort of say, "Well, it's relatively harmless but we don't think it would be a good idea to legalise it because we've got enough relatively harmless drugs already," if you'd just come out with something like that ...' But nobody did, and they still don't, which amazes me. If you get busted now for cannabis there's still no one around to say whisky's probably worse for you.

STEVE ABRAMS: The ad didn't call for the legalisation of dope, and one of the reasons it didn't was the difficulties that would make for people like [Jonathan] Aitken. Although Aitken had argued in favour of legalisation, had written in the *Standard* describing his first trip and had debated with Robert Pitman, a right-wing journalist of the day, on dope. Somebody could sign the ad without necessarily being in favour of legalisation and the basic idea was decriminalisation. The ad itself refers to penalties, fines of £25 – which is £250 today. When it talked about allowing one's premises to be used for smoking it was a reference to the absolute offence [an offence which can be committed without the knowledge of the offender] and so on: it wasn't a call for legalisation, just a call for changing that part of the law which made it an offence to allow premises to be used for cannabis smoking.

The Stones case was pending. It was the Stones case which not only made it sure that the Beatles would come up with some money but I'm sure it was the Stones case plus the attitude taken by [Sir William] Rees-Mogg which meant that *The Times* would accept the advertisement. We were prepared to go to some lengths to persuade them to take the advertisement, but no persuasion was necessary, I just rang up the advertising manager and told him what I wanted to do. They did check all the signatures. After the ad came out a friend of mine got on the commuter train and delighted at each stop in watching people opening their copy of *The Times* and their expression of disbelief. So wonderful was this that when he got to Victoria he took another train back and did it again just to watch.

HORACE OVE: I was asked to sign the pro-cannabis ad but I didn't. No, no, no, no. I had learnt very early from my own experience that you don't sign anything. That was a more white middle-class sort of approach, not a black boy's approach.

STEVE ABRAMS: Several people were particularly helpful to me: Miles and John Dunbar, Clive Goodwin. The most important man on the ad was a guy who ran the student health system at University of London: Nick Malleson. He was the most important person on the Wootton Committee in persuading them to reach their conclusions. I went to see him and said, 'I will rewrite the text of this advertisement until it reaches the point where you yourself would feel that you could sign it if you weren't a member of the committee. I want you to let me use your name in gathering signatures.' I asked Anthony Storr and David Stafford-Clark and I used their three names and other names as I came to them. Some people I just appealed to out of the blue. I thought of Francis Crick: Crick is the greatest living scientist, why don't I write to him and ask him to sign it? I got a letter back saying he was thinking of doing something like that himself. There were a lot more names I could have got, and in fact I had a lot more names than I used.

One should remember what so many right-wing Tories were doing in '67, in particular ministers in Mrs Thatcher's government. Michael Havers was defending Mick Jagger and accusing the *News of the World* of planting drugs on the Stones. There was an adjournment debate on the cannabis advertisement four days after it appeared. This was proposed by Paul Channon. I briefed him and he gave a very good speech. The first Minister of State at the Home Office under Mrs Thatcher, Timothy Raison, was a member of the Wootton Committee. St John Stevas was speaking in Parliament in favour of legalising dope.

SAM HUTT: I became involved in the Wootton Report through Steve Abrams who got in touch with me when I was a doctor and I signed the *Times* advert ... 'George Harrison, Sam Hutt' ... I liked it. I went along to Wootton as a professional person who smoked dope. I went along with Abrams. He was much better with the words. I just said that I couldn't speak for anyone else but certainly the literature was very good about it and it didn't do me any harm.

STEVE ABRAMS: It's commonly believed that the ad was inserted in *The Times* and nothing happened. There was, of course, the Wootton Report, and if you look at the actual report you find that the very first sentence says that it was the advertisement which led them to report on cannabis

194

alone, and to go beyond their brief to make legal recommendations, to examine the sociology of it. Now they reached the conclusion that 'the long-term use of cannabis in moderate doses has no harmful effects.' And in a covering letter they say that they want to create a situation in which nobody is sent to prison for cannabis. Callaghan tried to stop the report being published and then said he refused to implement the legislation. In fact all that happened was that they waited until Labour lost the election in 1970 and then Heath reintroduced the legislation. The legislation had the effect of bringing in all the recommendations in the advertisement, in their lighter forms. It changed the premises offence, it allowed research, it made distinctions between cannabis and heroin and greatly reduced the penalties for cannabis. Since 1969 nobody's really had to worry about being in possession for smoking dope. When I was on the Frost programme with Quintin Hogg he said, 'You should be arrested,' and I said, 'I can't be arrested, I've got a script for dope,' and he said, 'What is it prescribed for?' and I said, 'Paranoia.' I'm no longer afraid of the police.

I closed down SOMA in 1970. It was no longer needed and I was going to get into trouble if I carried on any further. There was no more money. The Wootton Report had been published, the legislation had been published. I announced that dope was legal and it was all over and it wasn't necessary for me to do anything more.

The Stones Bust: 'You and I understand each other, Mick'

SUE MILES: What never came out about the West Wittering bust was that Christopher Gibbs was prancing around in a frock, and Robert Fraser was rugby-tackled by a couple of WPCs in the garden. The police then threw away all the coke – they didn't know what it was – and picked up all these complimentary soaps that were lying around and were absolutely convinced that these were really good stuff.

JOHN SHEPPARD: I was the director of the Mick-Jagger-flies-in-by-helicopter-and-meets-four-senior-members-of-the-Establishment show. The night before the trial John Birt, Jeremy Wallington, who was then the joint editor of *World in Action*, and I spent the evening with Mick. We had dinner with him, and I made out this handwritten contract for the show on a single sheet of foolscap. Then we went off to Olympic Studios to listen to the recording of 'Dandelion', the B-side of 'We Love You'. Then Mick signed the contract.

The plan worked perfectly and in fact the next day a couple of Fleet Street papers kind of said 'A pat on the back for *World in Action*' and had pictures of the helicopter taking off – because this whole convoy of

195

fast Fleet Street minis failed to keep up with this Jaguar driven by a stunt driver I knew at the BBC. I drove to Sir John Ruggles-Brise's house in Essex and Mick, Marianne and John Birt arrived in the helicopter. Mick and Marianne came into the house and they went off to a room he had so he could change his shirt and they may have done all sorts of other things – who knows. Then they had some scrambled eggs that the butler laid on and we did the show. This time the helicopter took off again with just Mick in it and it comes in and lands and Mick gets out and away we go. The conversation itself achieved absolutely nothing, but of all the shows I have ever done, it is the one that was most an *event*. The simply extraordinary nature of the event is what sustains it. There were Lord Stow Hill, William Rees-Mogg, Father Thomas Corbishley and Dr Mervyn Stockwood, who made a fool of himself by trying, as it were, to mentally shift himself so as to be seen as sitting on the same side in the debate as Mick. He tried to be more with Mick than the others, when clearly far more truth was to be had by speaking against him. Stockwood was too keen on saying, 'Well, you and I understand each other, Mick . . .'

STEVE ABRAMS: The only time I was arrested was in the King's Road at a demonstration after Brian Jones was sent to prison. They arrested me and Suzy Creamcheese and Chris Jagger and about twelve of us after I kicked a policeman in the balls. We had been demonstrating for a while; we were all very stoned, only about 30 of us in all, and it was pissing with rain. I talked to the police afterwards and they told me that they were standing around, and thought we wanted to get arrested for the publicity anyway, so they just stepped in and arrested me as the leader. I had a *Times* reporter – Stephen Jessel – on one side of me and a *Guardian* reporter on the other and a barrister with me and they just came up and arrested me. I was down on the ground. And I just went whacck!!! and got this policeman in the balls and he just flew!! I was about to get the shit kicked out of me when I was nearly run over by a car. The driver jumped out and it was Jonathan Aitken. He insisted on riding in the police van to the station. Jeff Dexter was beaten up.

JEFF DEXTER: We hit the front pages. Caroline Coon was there, and Steve Abrams and I got charged with maliciously damaging a police vehicle. They beat the shit out of me, then charged me with beating the back-door panels and the tyres of the police van with my head. Five quid's worth of damage. I got off that one. The magistrate looked down his nose at the police officer and said, 'Did the defendant have his spectacles on at the time?' He could see how thick my bins were. The cop went 'Er ... yes,' and the magistrate said, 'Well, I can't begin to understand how he would beat the side of a police car with his spectacles on – not an easy thing to do ...' That was in '67 and I was still quite small.

RUFUS HARRIS: The Stones bust was the immediate trigger for the emergence of Release but there were other strands. Steve Abrams was organising the *Times* advertisement and so on. What actually happened was fairly spontaneous in response to the gaoling of the Stones and a small number of people took to the streets and demonstrated outside the *News of the World* building, and as an aftermath of that demo, some of us ended up, for some peculiar reason, at Piccadilly Circus and decided to meet again to see if we could do something positive or constructive about the fact that there was a new class of criminal, really, because of the drug laws.

RUSSELL HUNTER: At the demo I was isolated with someone else, I forget who, and we were chased down the road by two mounted policemen who were going to get us. These two police horses were bearing down on us and a sports car stopped at some traffic lights, cos they were red, and we both leapt into the back of this sports car, the lights changed and off we went. The guy was fantastic. Perfectly normal guy, maybe 30, 40, wearing a tweed jacket. He said, 'Are they after you?' 'Yeah.' 'Right,' he said and whoosh! off we went. He drove us round the corner, the length of the Strand, pulled up at Waterloo Bridge, said, 'All right for you?' and we said, 'Thanks,' and he zoomed off.

Release: 'The one concrete thing that came out of this scene'

RUFUS HARRIS: I met Caroline Coon at the *News of the World* demo and she and I decided to set up a meeting. She became involved because she had a boyfriend who'd been arrested and sent down fairly heavily for drugs. She'd been involved in organising his defence and had been horrified by the whole system. She knew various other people who knew Steve Abrams and it escalated from there. There were a number of meetings held to decide what we could do, and it was decided to set up a 24-hour emergency phone service which was originally, if only briefly, envisioned as being manned by volunteers.

STEVE ABRAMS: There was a meeting very early on at Joe Boyd's house. Release was set up with money we had from Hoppy's bust fund: Julie Felix had given some money which wasn't needed. We were spending a lot of time bailing each other out, so we decided to set up Release. Colin MacInnes came to this meeting and he was awful. He insisted that it wouldn't work and the whole idea was nonsense. He wasn't drunk but just in this little tizzy and walked out in a fury. I came to the conclusion, though this was my only contact, that he was an asshole.

I brought Caroline into Release. We were demonstrating outside the *News of the World* and I saw this girl and I thought she was somebody called Susie Teitel, who became Sid Rawle's girlfriend. It turned out she lived very close to me. She was interested because she had a black boyfriend who had gone to prison for two years for one joint. Caroline wasn't really flower power but she was very pretty and the media liked her.

JO CRUIKSHANK: Caroline Coon was at Central with me. She was a great painter apart from being a great looker. She was also a very nice girl. She had this black boyfriend, which was how Release all started. The boyfriend got done; she felt it was unjust.

RUFUS HARRIS: We got a telephone number and advertised it in *IT* and very rapidly started getting calls on a fairly large scale. Caroline and I became full time and volunteers manned the phones. The original phone was in Caroline's flat in Sinclair Road. Although Release was drugs-orientated, we got everything from housing problems to runaway kids and, until things were liberalised, abortion problems. We were operating as a referral agency really and from the beginning we had lawyers on tap. Initially there were all sorts of people involved: Joe Boyd, Steve Abrams, Michael English. It expanded very rapidly and we had to take on more full-time people, get a typist and so on. By the end of 1967 we'd moved into a one-room office in 52 Princedale Road. The National Front had been down the street but they were gone, although there was still this shuttered-up house with huge swastikas outside. We stayed in 52 for a year, moved to number 50, where we had two floors, in January '69, then went to 70.

STEVE ABRAMS: Rufus Harris came into Release a few months after Caroline. Rufus had a sister called Zoe and it was because of Zoe that Hoppy was sent to prison. Hoppy's girlfriend then was Kate Heliczer who was a schoolteacher and older than Hoppy. Zoe was then seventeen, Kate was 29 or 30 and Hoppy was about 28. Zoe was living in the flat. The prosecution insisted that Hoppy was corrupting this seventeen-year-old girl with dope and that he was living with her rather than with Kate.

JOE BOYD: Release was formed in response to Hoppy and a lot of other people being busted. It was formed as a very straightforward response to a problem – people being arrested by the police, not being told of their rights, not getting a good solicitor, not knowing what to do or how to deal with it. Kids who had never thought of themselves as being in confrontation with the law were finally in confrontation with the law. It started with passing the hat at UFO: so-and-so's been busted, they need legal costs, pass the hat. It grew into Release.

In some ways you can put aside all the crap about the philosophies of the 60s and whether it worked or it didn't work, and look at the one concrete thing that came out of this one scene in London – and that was Release. If nothing else happened it was all almost justified for that reason, because it was a very, very excellent organisation. The original directors of Release were myself, Caroline Coon and Todd Lloyd. Basically Caroline took over. She wasn't somebody who hung out at UFO, she was somebody who Michael X knew, because she had a black boyfriend who had been busted. She showed up, looking terrific, at the meeting and every time somebody said, 'Somebody ought to do this or find out about that,' she said 'I'll do that,' and she just did. The whole thing grew because of her. You can look at all the accomplishments – the people who did things, put out papers, put on gigs – the one person who really did something, day in, day out, that had nothing to do with career-building, that had nothing to do with polemics or grandstanding, but who actually just got the work done and did it and helped a lot of people, was Caroline Coon.

Caroline did a magnificent job for Release but, for reasons one can only speculate on, a lot of people in the underground, the underground almost to a man, resented her for it. There was a tremendous hostility to her, and the better she was at it, the more they didn't like her. She was surrounded by a lot of shambolic attempts at doing things, inefficient, idealistic efforts. She had no interest in hyperbole or proclamations of philosophy, all she was interested in was answering the phone and getting people a lawyer. This, and the fact that she did it so well, and the fact that she had a rather posh accent and the fact that she was a woman led to disaffection of large segments of the male underground towards her. At one point a group, led I believe by Mick Farren, organised a takeover of the Release offices, because they felt she had 'removed Release from the people'. So they had a sit-down and wouldn't leave the offices. So Caroline said, 'OK, who's in charge, who wants the keys? Here's the keys, here's the bank mandate form, I'll sign the accounts over to you. Who's going to be the signatory on the account? Here's the files, here's the lists of lawyers, here's the phone that has to be answered 24 hours a day. If you have any questions give me a call.' She was just brilliant. Within a day they called her up and said, 'Please come back.'

RUFUS HARRIS: The police have always been very ambivalent about Release. Your average serving police officer takes the view that anybody who takes the side of a defendant is on the other side. Whatever one's motives. And the average police officer in those days just did not understand the drug problem or the drug scene at all. So the police were always suspicious. We were in touch with the Home Office from the word go – they had no doubt about Release's bona fides and saw it as a useful organisation. That wasn't the part of the HO that's responsible for the police, but the Dangerous Drugs branch. The contact was informal, but it stopped some of the maverick police from doing naughty things.

DAVID OFFENBACH: I went to a conference of police officers once where I said, 'There are policemen who plant drugs.' They felt this was somewhat unseemly, so I was never invited again. If you talked to a policeman about it, his response was, 'I'm just doing my job. I'm in the Drugs Squad.' But it was the Drugs Squad who were doing it. The middle class had never experienced this. They had no conception of what being thrown in a cell was like: you can't make your phone call, the place is like a pigsty. So they were horrified to be treated in this way and they raised a considerable outcry about it.

RUFUS HARRIS: We were really the first welfare organisation in the underground. But it was a bit more than that because what we ended up doing was kind of pioneering social and community work. The things we were doing then are now common practice and policy. There were ordinary social workers about then, but that was very formal and while they would concern themselves with hippies, they weren't necessarily able to cope.

DAVID OFFENBACH: People would ring up: 'I got your number from Release.' The phone didn't tend to ring that late, usually between five and nine pm. The police don't get overtime for arresting people in the early hours – they'd tend to hold them and then you'd get the calls the next morning. There were a number of Release lawyers: Dean Sargent, Bernie Simons, Dennis Muirhead, Ian Sheratt, Howard Weston. I became a kind of spokesman, a bridgehead between the two groups, a professional person who understood both camps. I could be relied on to put the point of view they couldn't get from other members of the Establishment at the time.

RUFUS HARRIS: Release was doing something very serious, providing something which did not exist at the time. There were no referral services around. We found ourselves filling a hole which much needed filling. We were sure what we were doing – we just hadn't bargained on the demand. We were dealing with 400 new enquiries a month, not all of them drug-related. On the drug side people would phone up, either saying that someone they knew had been arrested or that they themselves were in the cells, making their one phone call. We'd take the details and get a lawyer on the job.

DAVID OFFENBACH: I was telephoned by Caroline Coon: I was a young solicitor and she asked me to do some drug cases. I hadn't done any before but I was recommended by a client of mine in the music business. Some of his musicians had been caught smoking cannabis and I'd been interested in libertarian issues from my university days. I was a member of the Labour Party and interested in civil rights and the entertainment industry. It seemed to me that in these drugs cases there were fundamental breaches of civil rights in the way the police were behaving, that people were being incarcerated for minor offences. Middle-class culture had become interested in cannabis because of the advert in *The Times*. Middle-class parents were suddenly finding their eighteen-year-olds in police stations, being treated like working-class villains. That's when people said, 'What on earth is going on?'

RUFUS HARRIS: Our policy on drugs was very simple: criminal sanctions are counter-productive, creating a black market only drives the problem underground and makes it impossible to control. There are aspects of the drug scene which contribute to the personal problems of the users, and locking anybody up never did any good. Our attitude to drugs was based on responding to the situation that one met at a given time. For instance, with cannabis there are serious side-effects: you can get locked up for it. I wouldn't advocate taking heroin either, there are other side-effects to that, though not as serious as the mythology would suggest. The kind of people who end up presenting symptoms of drug addiction or a psychosis triggered by drug use should not be viewed as simplistically as that. That was how Caroline and I looked at it at the beginning.

Most of the people who came to Release couldn't look after themselves. People who in legal terms were otherwise perfectly law-abiding with no need of a criminal lawyer, who wouldn't know where to get one from.

The things we covered were drugs, pregnancy counselling, housing, runaway kids, and psychiatric problems. We had socialising facilities, a room with no desks or typewriters, where you could just sit and have coffee and talk. We had late-evening advice sessions with a solicitor and a doctor and even ended up selling food at these.

JOE BOYD: Hoppy was a fantastic, effective person. It made me very sad that Hoppy and Caroline didn't get on. When Hoppy came out of prison I was looking forward to sitting around a dinner-table with Hoppy and Caroline because the two of them were going to get on like a house on fire. But I said something about Caroline and he looked at me and curled up his nose and basically said, 'I've talked to her and I don't want to have anything to do with her.' I don't know whether he actually ever did talk to her, but people had talked to him about her.

When Hoppy came out of gaol he went his own way, and I have seen very little of him since. We've never talked about what happened. Perhaps if he hadn't gone to gaol UFO might have survived as it had been. By the time he came out the scene had shifted and from a career point of view I had become very involved in the music business as a business, which is what it had become. And from the point of view of underground politics I was on the side of Caroline.

RUFUS HARRIS: In terms of fund-raising we saw ourselves very much as pirates, robbing the rich to give to the poor. Robbing is the wrong word, but we had donations from very unusual sources sometimes. Who knows why a stockbroker would send us a cheque? They may have had a kid who'd been in trouble. We had money from rock musicians. I don't think dope-dealers gave, not that I'm aware of. We had various fund-raising exercises which were by and large successful. The pump-priming exercise came from a levy taken at UFO and the Electric Garden, threepence or sixpence. We had various concerts and benefits organised all over the place.

JOE BOYD: From the day that we went to the Roundhouse, UFO tithed Release. Five or ten per cent of the door. One of the main hesitations I had about winding UFO down was Release. I worried about where the money would come from for Release. Caroline did the money-raising and she was very good at it. She would go to people like George Harrison and come away with cheques for £500. But the UFO tithe had paid the salaries and the electricity bill. So I arranged a meeting between Dave Housen and George Clark, the administrator of the Roundhouse, and basically matchmade and told Dave Housen to give 10% off the door to Release, and he was happy to do it.

UFO: 'I saw couples injecting reefers'

MARK BOYLE: Joe Boyd came late to UFO. When the crunch came, when Hoppy got busted, Joe started to make UFO commercial. Our manager Mike Jeffreys, who was also Hendrix's and the Soft Machine's manager, told us that he and his colleagues had had spies out on UFO and they had decided that it was an *extremely* successful operation under Joe Boyd. But Hoppy had been running it largely for love, and also to help finance the *International Times*. Joe ran it for profit. Then the protection gangs got interested and they were demanding money and UFO wasn't paying. Then black power came down and offered to protect them from the protection gangs on the condition that they used one black band every Friday. That went on for a little bit, but the atmosphere by then had got very unpleasant. We came back from the States and they had moved to the Roundhouse and they were wanting to stamp the date on your hand and all this stuff. Horrible, horrible stuff.

JOE BOYD: The period of simplicity lasted all of six months, at least as far as UFO was concerned. By May Hoppy had been busted and I had, in retrospect, gotten a bit carried away by UFO as a music venue. To me it was part of my life in the music business, it certainly was a very special part, but that was what it was. For Hoppy and a lot of other people it was something else. To me it was always most important for music, and as a kind of arts forum. I looked upon it as a venue to book. For a lot of people who came there the social and political aspects were equally important. There began to be a feeling among certain people that the music was becoming too important and that UFO was becoming commercialised. And I think that they were probably right.

MELISSA CHASSAY: Joe was the yuppie of the party, the Harvard kid who ran UFO, which I'm sure was incredibly hard. There was never any money and everyone always claimed that Joe was running off the money. But I was going out with Joe at the time and I knew he didn't have any money. He made a lot of things work. He had this breadth that a lot of people did not.

KEITH MORRIS: The thing about Joe Boyd, why he had so much credibility, was that he was actually recording and making available music that interested the people that were involved in all that counterculture bit. Like the String Band, like Fairport Convention, John Martin, Nick

203

Drake. In terms of linking the music into the underground, Joe was the king. He used to talent spot in the underground. He's a sharp cookie.

STEVE SPARKS: The Incredible String Band were crazy. Once they were about to go on at the Royal Albert Hall and they turned round and they said, 'We cannot go on, our carpet isn't here.' So I said, 'What?' The whole place was packed, floor to ceiling, they're throwing flowers and cheering. And the band say, 'We can't go on, because our carpet isn't here.' So I said, 'Explain slowly what you mean.' And they said, 'Well, we have this Persian carpet and we can't sing unless we can sit on the Persian carpet.' So I said, 'Where is the Persian carpet?' and they said, 'It's back in the office.' This is already after they were due to go on and I have to get a cab, go back to the office in Goodge Street, get the carpet, bring it back, lay it down on the stage before they'd go on. They were nutters.

JOE BOYD: In June I managed to get the Pink Floyd back – by this time they were already big – this was from a sort of deal when they left: I said, 'You gotta come back in six months and do another gig,' and they agreed and I held them to it. At the same time I booked the Move for the next week, or the week before. They'd just had a hit record. So we had two of the biggest groups in the country in a place with a capacity of about 600 people in a basement on Tottenham Court Road on successive Friday nights. You couldn't move in the club. The people that came to those two gigs were different. It was the summer, tourists had started to come, kids were getting out of university, out of school, London was filling up. There was no longer the nice community that had grown in an organic way, naturally, as more and more people got turned on and friends brought friends and that sort of thing. Suddenly people who didn't know anybody there were turning up in kaftans to see hip bands. The atmosphere changed. So in the space of two months you had a sudden explosion of the amount of people that wanted to get in, and the inevitable result of that was the forcing out of the original constituency, who didn't want to come and jostle with a bunch of tourists. You then had Hoppy going to prison, you had the famous *News of the World* story. They had a topless teenager and drugs and so on. UFO had been a financial fillip for Mr Gannon. The police didn't like it but Mr Gannon gave them a case of whiskey at Christmas time, and they were all mates. They were just up the street . . . So he had been able to hold the police at bay until the *News of the Screws* story. Immediately, that afternoon, I got a phone call from Mr Gannon, and he said, 'I'm sorry, boys, but I can't let you open on Friday.' And I found another venue ... We found the Roundhouse. We sent people down to stand outside – we were too late for the papers – and it was a disaster. People standing outside in Tottenham Court Road telling people to go to the Roundhouse – it was hardly the way to do it.

SUE MILES: UFO was eventually shut down at the Blarney Club because the *News of the World* ran an article that said, 'I saw couples injecting reefers.' And Mr Gannon, who was a nice Irishman, by Sunday afternoon, that was it. That's how powerful the *News of the World* was.

PETER SHERTSER: We knew Joe Boyd. He used to announce us on stage at these gigs he had at the Savile: 'I don't know how, but the Firm are here, and I tried to ban them from coming in.' He employed us as the bouncers at UFO, when it was at the Roundhouse. We caused so much havoc – and when we started taking acid that was it. We used to start on Jack Henry Moore, fat guy with a beard and glasses, we called him 'the gassy grobber'. We used to give him hell. We caused so much trouble that in the end Miles, Mick Farren and Joe got us together and said, 'Look, it's easier to stop you causing trouble, why don't we employ you to be bouncers on the door to stop trouble getting in. And that way you've got the best of both worlds.' It wasn't so much security, more a protection racket as far as they were concerned, but if they gave us a few bob then we couldn't get up to chicanery. So that's what we did, keep out the mods, unless they paid us enough. These mods would turn up: 'You can't come in here, your hair's too short.' 'But you're supposed to be all for freedom and things ...' 'Yeah, but we know your sort.' 'How about a fiver?' 'Right, you're in.' And when there was trouble we'd say, 'Get Mick!' and poor Mick [Farren] would come down. He was good at the verbals. We did have a go occasionally but when it got really out of hand, with the real evil characters – the skinheads – we all disappeared. There's no reasoning with those characters. So one time it got really bad and Joe Boyd said, 'You boys, you must know someone,' and we got the Nutter up from Essex: the self-professed professor of karate, kendo, ju-jitsu, judo, the lot. This was a guy who we used to go to school with. We used to take the piss out of him – bald, bowed legs, but a real hard case. And a load of karate guys came down, a load of evil mothers. They come on stage and they announce that this was to deter violence. Then they did the demonstration, smashed the bricks and things and for two weeks: nothing, no violence. But then Joe starts saying, 'Listen – these guys are costing a lot of money, can't we do something, Peter ...?' So I said, 'Well, if we get rid of them we'll have the skinheads back.' But after a couple more weeks Joe decided it wasn't paying, got rid of the karate guys and skinheads came back and really did the place over.

Shaftesbury Avenue: 'A centre of high activities'

MICK FARREN: Times changed, very rapidly. 1967–8 was a long cold winter and most prankster occupations failed with the waning weather. The hippies either died or went home. UFO closed down. Life became more wretched: gangs of skinheads started to invade, people getting busted, Hoppy had gone to jail, a lot of other people had gone to jail.

We knew this guy called Simon Barley who had this scheme to sell psychedelic posters off the back of cornflake packets or whatever, to set up the biggest psychedelic mail order firm on the planet, and later we discovered these schemes were based purely in . . . cocaine. But he said, did we want a luxury apartment and we said, yes, and he gave us the keys and we gave him some money and he left the country and we moved into this apartment, which was palatial, on top of the Shaftesbury Theatre. About a month later these horrible geezers came round who looked like they might want to murder us, but we managed to explain that he was now on the lam and probably in Rio so they went away without killing us. We stayed there for two and a half years, taking methedrine and three or four days a week getting into a large van and being taken to some factory town somewhere where we played.

CHRIS ROWLEY: This rich Californian, who had a credit card and rich parents, had this apartment on Shaftesbury Avenue above the Shaftesbury Theatre. We ended up living there and that produced a whole new ripple effect. When he left the McInnerneys moved in and they lived there for a little while and when they moved out the Farrens moved in. So this apartment knitted together a few groups. I was at this apartment when Pete Townshend, a friend of McInnerney's, had just come back from LA. He, Daltrey and Moon, but I think not Entwistle, had just done LSD or STP, they didn't know what, on the plane! The dims! Thirteen hours you're in the plane . . . Even if you're the Who and you're rich and people treat you well, thirteen hours in a plane on acid! Later on McInnerney did the cover of *Tommy*.

RUSSELL HUNTER: I never lived there, although I spent a hell of a lot of time there. Sandy lived in one room, Tony Ferguson in the back, Boss [David Goodman] lived wherever he fell. He had a disgusting little pit in Ilford that he never went to. He'd become our roadie by then, with Tony Wiggins. Nothing really awful happened there, nobody got killed. David Bowie came round a couple of times and sat on the roof with Calvin Lee,

206

his terribly gay manager. Calvin was taking pictures of Bowie and Sandy wearing little shorts and acting coy.

DAVID GOODMAN: There was a number of us living in this flat, above *Hair*, which became a centre of high activities. I was 'fortunate' to spend about nine months there. It was very eye-opening. Basically Boss had his pit at the end of Micky's bed, because there was no room for me anywhere. I'd lost my flat in Ilford cos the Deviants couldn't pay me enough money to be able to pay the rent. So I became part of the family, the Pink Fairies/Deviants family. I had to turn a completely deaf ear to Micky's nocturnal activities. And stopping Micky jumping off the balcony every now and then. Later on Jamie Mandelkau moved in there with his girlfriend who was by then Joy Farren.

There was the end room which Jamie and Joy lived in, which was about half the size of Micky's room, which was the sort of master bedroom, with Boss in there, and the other end room was a turret which Sandy lived in with Tony Ferguson, the keyboard player, who subsequently drowned swimming between the two piers in Brighton. In the main living area, a sort of open-plan big room with the TV and sofas and book shelves, it was anybody's guess who could be living in there.

STEVE SPARKS: I used to have the room with the turret. The great thing about that flat was that all the punters who came to *Hair* bought their ticket and they thought they'd bought you as well. Cos you'd come out of the door and there'd be all these people from *Hair* and there you were in your long barnet and your hippie nonsense and they thought they'd bought you as well. That flat was unbelievable. You'd come in after a hard day's laying about somewhere and there'd be people screwing in your bed, so you'd kick them out of your bed and you'd wake up in the morning – midday, at the crack of noon – open the door to your room and the floor would be solid people. There were about 200 cats who were Joy's who shat everywhere and nobody would ever clear it up and the place stank of ammonia and catshit.

RUSSELL HUNTER: We went into the Shaftesbury Theatre during a performance of *Hair*, with smokebombs, streamers, general mayhem. We slipped in through the stage doors and started throwing things and shouting and yollicking and causing confusion. So all the foyer people dashed into the auditorium to see what was going on, and Steve Mann nicked this award, smashed this glass case and nicked it from the foyer.

STEVE MANN: I was the Marcus van der Lubbe of *IT* – the firebomb expert. There was this ship's chandler in Shaftesbury Avenue, the Covent Garden end, near the *IT* office in Endell Street. Somehow I convinced them that I was a weekend sailor, so I used to go in every week and stock up on distress flares. I could think of lots of practical applications for this. The first one was when *Hair* opened. We all got very upset – we thought, 'There's these people, they're making an awful lot of money out of the hippies, and we want some.' It wasn't so much we wanted it for ourselves, but we did want to spread it around. We felt it would be very nice if they contributed 1% of their weekly take to underground groups: the Arts Lab, Release, BIT, whoever they thought deserved it. This was proposed to them but they turned it down. So to show our disapproval we started off by picketing it, but that didn't do any good. Then I had these smoke flares, so every so often I'd just burst in through an exit door, lob a smoke flare into the audience, then run out again. I did this two or three times.

At some stage they were awarded a silver disc for sales of 250,000 copies of the cast album. Julie Felix was there to present it. *IT* got an invite and I was the music editor so I went along, with Paul Lewis. So we were there and all the people were milling around and there was this silver disc on the table. We said, 'We'll have that one away,' and Paul stuffed it under his jumper and we walked out. Then we thought, 'Well, let's see what we can do about this,' and we phoned them up and said, 'We've got your silver disc and we're holding it to ransom.' They said, 'It doesn't concern us – Polydor will just give us another one. If you play it, it isn't even a copy of *Hair*. They get any old album, spray it silver and it'll cost them about 17/6 to come up with another one.' So that didn't really work. The disc ended up under Jamie Mandelkau's bed for ages.

The Dialectics of Liberation: 'The numero uno seminal event of '67'

MILES: The Dialectics of Liberation was a very 60s idea. The concept was to get together all of the different factions involved in the liberation struggle and have a good talk about it. Stokely Carmichael, Gregory Bateson (talking about whale language), Ginsberg, Emmett Grogan, Simon Vinkenoog, Julian Beck (from the Living Theatre), Michael X. There was a whole wide range of things and people and some very vicious arguments. Psychiatry and anti-psychiatry was very big on the list then so Joe Berke and Laing and a few others were there.

JO DURDEN-SMITH: I knew Laing and [David] Cooper and I'd been to Kingsley Hall in Bow. I found Bow very interesting and very scary. It was very unsettling because what was always said about it was true: that

208

there really seemed to be no distinction between those who were there to help, in some undifferentiated way, and those who were there to act out, go through, or whatever the current term was. Laing and Cooper obviously helped a number of people, but there were a number of people they did not help.

One of the bad things was that a lot of the people who preached Laing didn't understand him and there was this idolisation of a figure who might be called 'The Holy Fool', the madman made saint. That was the most absurd over-simplification. Laing was misinterpreted and misused but he became, or his attitude towards madness became, a sort of hooray attitude, with not very much thought put into it at all. But they *were* enormously interesting. One lunchtime Laing said, 'Where can you scream? It's a serious question: where can you go in society and scream?' And this concerned the case of a man whose one ambition in life was to *let go.* He lived a very conventional life and he'd essentially built himself a cork-lined room and when it was finished he went in and screamed.

SUE MILES: The Dialectics was very important, extraordinary. That was Kingsley Hall – Joe Berke, Ronnie Laing and all those people – and they were really very, very clever people. We were all making a huge noise, but Laing was actually talking about real people and real misery and had a different view of it. I went with Ginsberg. It was quite frightening. Stokely Carmichael started this tirade against whitey. Though one could see perfectly well why he had that point of view, it was completely unworkable. Then there was this meeting afterwards back at the house where he was staying and there was extreme bad feeling and a huge argument and split between them all. Allen was going, 'This is dreadful. We have not argued this long for everyone to start getting at each other's throats and getting divided. This is not going to get us anywhere.'

ALAN MARCUSON: That was the key event, the numero uno seminal event of '67. I had been reading Ronnie Laing and arguing with my shrink, who was a rather straight Freudian psychoanalyst, but I had to stay with him to stay in England and my parents weren't in the mood at all to let me go and see Ronnie Laing, not their sort of a shrink at all – the madman who took drugs and was advising people to put LSD in the water supply to change the world. The people I met at the Dialectics: Ronnie Laing, Allen Ginsberg, Stokely Carmichael, Michael X, Joe Berke, Emmett Grogan (who I was profoundly impressed with, not least for his snake tooth necklace). Herbert Marcuse was there. Leary was there – the gods of the generation – anyone who was anyone in the counterculture. But nothing came of it. We decided not to put LSD in the water supply and the whole thing was a bit of an anti-climax. We expected something to happen: we were expecting great historical events to come out of this meeting.

There was this wonderful dinner at Laing's. Laing had all the superstars there for dinner and he was very into being honest and he said to Stokely Carmichael, 'The thing is, Stokely, I like black people but I could never stand their smell,' and Stokely didn't like that and left.

ROBIN BLACKBURN: The conference was a very important event for the counterculture. Again there was an American influence. American black culture was very important in all this. It had a resonance which it would be quite unfair to expect from either an English or Australian counterculture.

RUSSELL HUNTER: The first gig I remember doing with the Social Deviants was the Dialectics of Liberation at the Roundhouse in summer '67. There was no pretence at it being a theatre of any kind whatsoever. We were just up on a load of planks and steel girders, thrashing through this appalling set. I don't recall any other bands. There was an awful lot of talking, spouting, stuff like that.

'*IT* was a great missed opportunity'

DAVID ROBINS: In '67 I started working for *IT* and I was *IT* Assistant Editor for a year. I was taking my magazine, *Circuit*, round to Indica and Miles came up to me and said, 'Would you like to work for the paper, man?' *IT* was always referred to as 'the paper'. So I said, how much? And he said £12 a week. So I went to the office of *IT* which I'd seen on the stands but hadn't actually bought, and the paper was being edited by a man who, if I hadn't been careful, could have become a formative influence on my life: William J. Levy. Bill Levy. An American by nationality, a middle-aged American, mid-thirties then, a former college lecturer and Ezra Pound fanatic. In fact he had been working on a thesis on Ezra Pound. He had been involved in a very obscure, radical avant-garde nihilist, Dada, smell-up-your-armpits magazine called *The Insect Trust Gazette*. A small, intense American with a beard. He spoke like a lot of those guys, as if every single word were being recorded for posterity. And in their solemnity, and in their certainty that they were right, these guys made Ronald Reagan and Nixon – who they were always criticising for being portentous – look lively. They came from the same culture that produced Ronald and Richard and they had a similar line in bullshit. The extent to which the Americans dominated the scene was substantial. But I liked them, cos after all that was what we all wanted: to be American, to go there and live there.

MILES: Bill Levy loved to be very very controversial and he loved to make everybody hate him. Self-hatred, really. He was the one who put in the Ezra Pound speech in issue 2. We were immediately accused of being anti-semitic and so on and I was really pissed off because Bill Levy twisted my fucking arm to put that in. And Bill Levy's Jewish. We said, 'We can't print this, copyright problems, anti-semitism, everyone'll take it the wrong way . . .' We tried to get an ad out of Faber and they said, 'Your Ezra Pound and our Ezra Pound are different people.'

DAVID ROBINS: Bill's thing was crazies. Visionary crazies. He was always looking for visionary crazies to give the paper to the earth: enter Harry Fainlight. We'd sit there. Night would turn into day and day would turn into night and people would walk into the office in various states. Miles very rarely showed up – he was too frightened. The man who did was Michael Farren, who later saved the paper at more than one point. Mick and his undesirable mates . . . Micky was already more down with the street people. And there was Joy, his wife, and one of our slogans was 'Let Joy be unconfined'. The fashionable ones stayed away.

MILES: I don't know whether I was really a trendy, but I certainly related to the American attitude: if you liked someone's work, why not get in touch with them? I wasn't really prepared to sit back. It may be a legitimate criticism but I wasn't doing it in order to impress anyone. I used that entire scene as a way of contacting the people I'd always admired the most and wanted to meet. I was not into equality and the people and the street and so on. Our meetings with people like the Beatles were purely accidental. When I first met them I didn't even know which one was which.

The point is that my generation had all been doing this stuff for a long time, we were older than the next lot. Quite a bit older. I didn't meet any hippies at all. But we encouraged all sorts of readers. In about '68 the skinheads contacted us so we said, 'Great, here's a page, two pages, every two weeks fill it with what you want.' They were terrifying, and fascinating.

But it's interesting to be called an elitist. The thing is that a lot of the money came from the connections we had with richer people. We were sweet-talking these people – not McCartney, but others – because that was the only way to finance *IT*. And if you run a bookshop you get very bored with inarticulate hippies who burst through the window and grab a bunch of books, shout, 'Books should be free!' and run off again. You get very cynical. The difference between cynicism and elitism is a slim one in that respect.

DAVID ROBINS: They used to go to all the smart parties and we'd be sitting in the office or up in Carlisle at the printers. There were no art facilities and Steele Brothers used to do all the layout; it was a TU shop, so we had to go up there. I became very committed to *IT* and very loyal to Bill Levy, who was very loyal to me. This had nothing to do with hippies. We never saw a hippie. Bill was no hippie, I wasn't a hippie.

SUE MILES: What is really puzzling about that time is what we lived on. We lived on five quid a week, is what we lived on. I can remember that there was a theory that there was only £200 and it was moving around the underground. We had no perception of unemployment. Our whole attitude was to not get a job when you left college. You put all your efforts into not being employed, not becoming an accountant.

MILES: There were times when *IT* couldn't afford to pay the staff. The day of the big world-wide transmission of 'All You Need Is Love' – the reason I was there was to get the cheque for the staff. £200 McCartney gave me – it paid the staff. He didn't even want it put around that he'd done that, it was genuine support. It was his idea that we did a set of rock interviews. I was saying, 'Oh God, how are we going to get some money?' and he said, 'You should interview me.' So the first rock interview I ever did was with McCartney. It was an amazing great success and he said, 'Well, you should do George next,' so I called up George and George came over and we did a big interview about spiritualism and the vibes and so on. I never even thought you were supposed to do these things through press offices and so on. Then the next thing Mick Jagger was on the phone saying he'd like to be interviewed.

SAM HUTT: The silliest gear was what I wore at the showing of 'All You Need Is Love'. I was bounced off the satellite with all the others. We were all furiously smoking joints which was our contribution to Britain's export drive. It was very funny. The first ever world-wide TV link-up. Every country had a piece, Japan had a piece and Finland would have a piece and so on. But every other country had their fucking fishing fleets: Japan's fishing fleet, Finland's fishing fleet, except Britain, which was this bunch of loonies and the Beatles recording 'All You Need Is Love'.

DAVID ROBINS: One time I met John Lennon: I knew Yoko through

Tony Cox, her old man, who was a good friend. He stayed with me in Doughty Street after they broke up. He was another American, except that he made people like Haynes and Levy look like rocks of stability. He was a *meshugganeh* of the highest order. A would-be promoter. He had these rather studious spectacles and he lived in Cumberland Mansions with Yoko, around 1967. We'd talk a lot about music. He wanted to put on an Ornette Coleman concert at the Albert Hall. But it all fucked up. A disaster. He was making this doll's house for Yoko, even though she'd left him, and he was wandering around the streets with this big package, the wood for it. So my girlfriend Clare and I were going for a walk in Regent's Park and there they were: John and Yoko walking down the road arm in arm. One tried to be cool about these sort of things. But we got talking to them and Clare lived on Chiltern Street and she said, 'Would you like to come and have a cup of coffee?' and they said, 'Sure.' He was very quiet. He talked about art mainly: her exhibitions, riding bicycles . . . Yoko talked mostly, she talked almost non-stop, she always did. She was little and hairy and fantastically thin.

MILES: Nigel Samuel showed up. He came wandering in one day, wearing a long green suede coat, dragging along the ground, very fashionable, and yellow crushed velvet pants. Looking, like, very wasted. You never knew in those days whether someone was tripping out or literally starving to death. He said he admired what we were doing and could he help distribute it. So we said, 'Sure.' Our main method of distribution was street-sellers. We were always looking for someone who could deliver the paper to them. We relied an enormous amount on goodwill and help from other people. He seemed the most unlikely guy to have an old banger to drive things around. Indeed he was. He had an Aston Martin or something like that. Some unbelievable car. We thought 'Oh! this is a bit odd.' He was a bit shy, very shy.

His father was Howard Samuel, the property developer. When Nigel was about thirteen he took him to Switzerland and stayed at some fancy hotel, and he was being shown how to drink wine, smoke cigars, all that stuff, and one day his father just went out and drowned himself in the lake. Leaving Nigel just sitting there, utterly fucked up. Traditionally, every year, around the anniversary of his father's death in October, he always goes a bit loopy.

DAVID ROBINS: Nigel Samuel was a very, very sad case. He used to drink an awful lot. Nigel was looking for somewhere to put his money and he put it into *IT*. He paid our wages.

SUE MILES: He appeared, just absolutely out of the blue, eighteen years old, offering to help. Would we like him to help distribute *IT*? We were still distributing it ourselves – we'd drive round and drop it off. So I was sent off to go with him and to discover that there was a sort of jet engine with wheels on it, a Maserati or something. And it suddenly became clear that he was incredibly rich. His logic was very interesting. He was going to inherit these very large sums of money, in stages: 18, 21, 25. It was controlled by Lord Goodman. He'd seen *IT* and he was absolutely and genuinely out to fuck the politicians. He was actually politically motivated.

MILES: In 1967 Nigel and I went to New York to see what *EVO* was up to. We went on Air India, which was the hip flight in those days cos you got curry and sitar music and the wallpaper on the plane looked like scenes out of the Kama Sutra. (TWA was also a hot airline because the sinks in the lavatories were vacuum-flushed so if you wanted to smoke dope you'd lean over the sink – the smoke went straight down the plughole. So rock bands always flew TWA.) We used to go to a bar on the corner of East 9th and Avenue C, a weird place, people barely spoke English. And Nigel would be very very picky about what he wanted to drink. It was a miracle he never got robbed. Then we met up with a whole bunch of Hell's Angels. One evening after a few drinks Nigel roared off into the night on the back of a chopper, wearing this long green suede coat and velvet trousers and stuff, which was almost unheard of in New York, American hippies didn't wear that sort of stuff.

PETER SHERTSER: I went round to Nigel's once and there was a hole in the middle of the room, where the floor used to be. The only thing is it was four storeys deep. I'm looking down four storeys, in Eaton Square. He said, 'Well, a joint went on the cushion, I let it burn.' It had burnt out the entire middle portion of the room, right through the floors. And he's sitting there casually, rolling another spliff, as if nothing had happened – but then in his case nothing *had* happened. But he was a nutter, no question. Nice guy, though.

CHRIS ROWLEY: By late '67 things were changing. *OZ* had started and *IT* had changed, it was getting much more like the rest of the underground press – no more letters from Ezra Pound. Pete Stanshill and Dave Hall were running it. The first thing was that the paper moved from Tom McGrath and its rather literary bent into the hands of Miles and Jack Henry Moore and Hoppy. They went for a more eclectic, give-it-to-the-kids mix. More rock, more pictures, graphics.

CHRISTOPHER LOGUE: *IT* was a great missed opportunity. I thought it was a real possibility for a strange, weird newspaper to evolve and to keep going. It could have become like the *Village Voice* but it never did. But they were true to their cause: they didn't want to make an interesting newspaper, they wanted to do what they did, and it died. But for someone like me, who rather likes things to go on, I would rather it had gone on for 25 years then run its course and been bought up by Rupert Murdoch and changed into a sex sheet or something; I'd rather that happened than it just fizzled.

JOHNNY BYRNE: I realise that it was good to speak to one's parishioners, as it were, and there was an element of that, but look how the press developed. It simply ran out of things to do, because in order for it to succeed it had to constantly renew itself and it failed to do that. It failed to move on. It blocked minds and thinking and feeling; it didn't move ahead of itself. That's why I had always believed that there was only the need to do one edition of any magazine. The culture began to perpetuate its own myths, but the main thing it didn't do and didn't affect was the thoughts and feelings of those who knew what was going on.

The underground press failed its following in allowing the readers to feel that the movement could be stolen by other forces. They would criticise and they would carp at the commercial exploitation but that wasn't the point; they should have welcomed the fact that they had originated these things, that they had opened up new areas of exploitation and commercial activity. But they should have divorced them from the basic feelings that lay behind the press. They needed to keep those feelings going, but still allow the spin-offs to continue. In the absence of meaning, the underground press was forced, to a certain extent, to fabricate it.

'So here we are in the field, and up come the UFOs'

NICHOLAS SAUNDERS: I was fascinated by what John Michell was saying about UFOs and ley-lines and so on, but felt pretty guarded about it too. I did go to a Flying Saucer conference on an island in the middle of a lake in the northwest of Ireland. There were all these people plodding around in the rain and the mud and there were very serious talks by people who either said that flying saucers had visited, that they'd been on flights themselves or that they'd seen them.

CRAIG SAMS: I didn't see a flying saucer till October 1967 when I went down to Glastonbury. One day I got a phone call from Mark Palmer

215

saying that it would be a good idea to come down, that there was a lot of UFO activity, that John Michell, who had just written *The Flying Saucer Vision*, was camping down there, and Michael Rainey. So here we are in the field, and up come the UFOs. We weren't tripping, I'd given up acid. I was completely normal, maybe I'd had a cup of tea about half an hour before. John Michell couldn't really see them very well because he's always been very short-sighted, Mark Palmer saw them – they were definitely there. They were in the classic cigar-shaped mother-ship form. Little lights emanating from them. Then at one point you saw these other lights coming up towards them and the smaller lights just shot into the cigar-shaped mother-ship, which then just disappeared at high speed. The other lights had been RAF jets. It was obvious that the RAF had scrambled some jets. Mark had described how a few days earlier there had been this cloud in the sky and this RAF jet had just been flying around it and obviously there was something in the cloud or something showing on the radar and they weren't quite sure what it was.

Mark had just gotten the caravan at that time.

MALDWYN THOMAS: I was round at Mark's flat in Radnor Walk and he said, 'I'm going to drop out, do you want to come?' He had his shop before that, and English Boy, the model agency.

It wasn't luxurious travelling in a caravan. Quite the opposite. Mark, myself and Martin Wilkinson caught the train to Didcot and we got off the train and we spent the first night out on the Downs. Mark knew or found someone who was an old dealer, and we bought a dung-cart, a sort of tipper cart. We put a tilt on it and wrapped it in canvas and it was very, very primitive. Mark bought this horse, a huge black and white mare. That was the start – and we set off. It was far from luxurious and it never actually got luxurious. But lots of glamorous people turned up: we had visits from Brian [Jones] and Suki [Poitier] in the Rolls, they'd drop in on us at Glastonbury or somewhere. People used to come for weekends. I'd dread weekends. They'd find us and come for the weekend. Some of them were really boring, and we were having to be really practical. 'Hey, man, it's really groovy down here . . .' and we'd go, 'Yes, can you chop some fucking wood for the fire?'

It was a lovely way of life, it was great. You do anything you want. You don't need much money but we could rely on a lot of people's kindness and generosity. You didn't beg but nonetheless people were pleased to entertain you. We went to Henry Bath's one day and someone said quite innocently, 'Would you like a bath?' and without thinking I said, 'It's all right: I had one about two months ago.'

Notting Hill: 'It was like some fairy tale'

DICK POUNTAIN: After South Ken we moved to Notting Hill, which we'd discovered by going there to score dope. We also knew that flats were dirt cheap there, much cheaper than South Ken, two quid a week instead of four. At that time in Notting Hill, around '67, it was all blueses, basement dances and parties and they were largely older people, West Indians in their thirties. They all worked on the buses, the underground or whatever. The music was a mix of ska, soul and organ jazz, Jimmy Smith and so on. That was the last time that you could do that kind of thing. Later it became too polarised and you couldn't do it, but in those days we used to go to blueses and you'd get your food – a huge pan of peas and rice, you'd chip in some money and get lots of beers. It was all very integrated.

NICOLA LANE: I thought Notting Hill was the centre of the world. I didn't go on the hippie trail because that's where I wanted to be. Notting Hill was wonderful: it had the Portobello Road with all the wonderful things going on; it had all the people in their flats where you'd go and hang out; it was very cheap; you had the street life; you had black people; lots of drugs and clothes and parks to go looning in, and it was all within walking distance. An earthly paradise.

CHRIS ROWLEY: The summer of '67 was when Notting Hill was really a little paradisical. It was like some fairy tale. Mike McInnerney's wedding, in Hyde Park, was almost like something out of Tolkien or a spoof thereof. Sixty or 70 fey young people, mostly in velvet, gathered around some bongo drummers and primitive guitarists. People are smoking grass, people have taken acid, there's a big cake, Pete Townshend and his lovely wife-to-be . . . this goes on for two or three hours. Curious onlookers stare, occasionally a Japanese tourist wonders to himself about the English. The long sunset came on, the trippers would nod off under the trees. The wealthy would get into their Rolls-Royces. And Michael English would go off to Portobello to put out the next poster and capture this atmosphere of trees, golden haze, an aura of decadence and mellowed out young people.

'What we wanted to do was brighten up the streets'

NIGEL WAYMOUTH: Joe Boyd had started doing UFO and was involved with *IT* and he asked me to do some graphics for the club and he introduced me to Michael English. I started to do two things at the same time: I started working on the graphics side of things for the underground and on Granny Takes a Trip. I wasn't a trained artist but I had a keen eye, I suppose, and I was keen to do it. I started working with Michael, who was a trained art student, and with him we worked out a lot of ideas and they were great fun. We were the first psychedelic poster people in England. What we wanted to do was brighten up the streets. Before that fly-posters were very dull and wordy and had very little graphics. We decided to paint pictures and use the gaudiest and the brightest colours and rainbow colours, silver, gold, and actually have them all over the streets. It was great fun and it brightened up all those tatty corrugated iron fences.

CHRIS ROWLEY: I think when I was selling posters I must have sold two or three thousand images of Bob Dylan. We were selling the whole range of early posters. American ones at first, but they dropped out and then it was primarily ones that came out of UFO: Michael English, Nigel Waymouth, *OZ* things, Martin Sharp. Other things like Micky [Farren]'s masterwork: Mean and Filthy Productions' double Dylan. That was a complete accident: it was meant to be a shot of Dylan in silhouette, very nice, very arty, and it came back beautiful because it was the double image. We sold an awful lot of pictures of Bob Dylan, then when Jagger was busted we sold a lot of pictures of Mick Jagger.

Clothes: 'You were very pleased if your man didn't wear underwear'

CHARLES SHAAR MURRAY: My school was overwhelmingly middle-class but there were a few bright working-class kids. This one guy had always been the total mod – the crop, the roll-neck sweater with the college scarf flung round his neck, all that stuff – and I saw him downtown one Saturday afternoon and he was wearing a kaftan – not floor-length, nobody in Reading wore one of them, but down to his hips – a pair of jeans and a bell round his neck. I said, 'Hey, what's going on?' He said, 'Well, I thought I'd give it a crack, like.' But the bell that he was wearing didn't make any noise. He said, 'Well, it was making such a bleeding horrible noise I took the donger out.'

VIRGINIA CLIVE-SMITH: I had a full-length patchwork dress. I had a thick green stretchy jersey belt with this huge, almost Nordic, circular buckle that clipped together. I wore these clogs which I had hand-painted. No underpants, I never wore underpants till well into the mid-'70s. No undergarments at all. Long velvet skirts, very short blouses, very short Fair Isle pullover. In 1970 I got a large Moroccan cloak.

LAURA MULVEY: I'd been living in Rome, which was very much out of the 60s atmosphere, and coming back to London was quite a cultural shock. The place looked and felt very different. I'm afraid, given that what I'm known for is my work on feminism, that my main concern when I returned to London was the length of people's skirts. This had radically changed while I was away and my first preoccupation was with turning up my hemlines before I could appear out in the streets. So I turned up my hemlines and hung out on Saturday mornings in Biba in Kensington Church Street.

MICHELENE WANDOR: We went to UFO and I thought it was amazing because you could wander round . . . it was like another world, a kind of fairy-tale world. People did look incredible and the whole Biba thing, the Biba clothes thing was very important. I dressed in incredibly short mini-skirts. I loved wearing mini-skirts, although I was never into the hippie folk stuff, the semi-peasant costume. I did have crushed velvet trousers and they were very, very tight. A beautiful pair of really tight, green crushed-velvet trousers which I wore for years and years.

NICOLA LANE: My greatest aspiration was to dress entirely from Granny Takes a Trip. But I couldn't afford it, so I had to make do with either borrowing my friends' dresses from Granny Takes a Trip or somehow lashing something together. Granny's had little crushed velvet dresses in bottle green with medieval, leg-of-mutton sleeves. But there was still a touch of naff about that and the real style was to have beautiful old clothes. Long black velvet coats were very popular and I managed to buy one for 10/6. It had a fur collar, full-length, covered buttons, leg-of-mutton sleeves; I used to wear it over purple tights with a belt. Nothing else. No bra, preferably no knickers. It was a bit naff to wear underwear. Men didn't wear it either: you were very pleased if your man didn't wear underwear.

DICK LAWSON: I wore extremely tight, light-coloured trousers with no underwear and you knew, on the tube, that somebody was always going to be offended. And I was intending to offend them.

PETER SHERTSER: We used to go to a place called The Shit Shop in the East End (anyway that's what we called it). He used to have blinding materials. Incredible. And we used to pick out ridiculous things: flowers, designs, weirdness, then we'd go to Paul's in Berwick Street, which was a renowned tailor, and because they were Jewish and we knew them and the whole Firm went in there and we took the piss out of them, they'd knock the price down and for twenty quid we'd get a hand-made suit. They used to love it: they put our pictures up on the wall. What really drew us there was they used to make suits for Sonny Boy Williamson. So we thought, if it's good enough for him it's good enough for us.

NIGEL WAYMOUTH: I don't know how the idea for Granny's arose. I was with this girl at the time and she used to collect old clothes and we used to go down to Church Street Market and Portobello Road. We thought that it might be a good idea to open a shop with all these things. Granny's and Dandie Fashions and Hung On You were the new alternative; we were definitely not Carnaby Street. I knew nothing about retailing or the clothes trade, nothing at all. In fact I was very opposed to the idea. Later on people said to me, why don't you branch out, have branches here and there, and I wasn't really interested. We really did pioneer the idea of disposable clothes that you only wore for a while. People would come back and complain sometimes, but it was all part of the ethos of the new dressing-up: not taking it quite so seriously. Of course it was terribly vain . . .

I got the name when one night I sat down and I thought well . . . Granny Takes a Trip. Granny clothes . . . acid trips . . . obvious: Granny Takes a Trip, that's funny, let's do it. So we did. We were practically on the dole at the time, we certainly didn't have any cash. That was me and a friend of mine called John Pearce who now runs a tailoring business in Soho. We put the name up when there was a football match, millions of people going by, all looking at this psychedelic lettering: Granny . . . Takes . . . A . . . Trip . . . what's that? Thousands of kids walking by, they didn't know what to make of it. We used to change the windows every three months. We had black windows, a car coming out . . . we did everything. The whole point was just to keep it change, change, change. We used to stay up all night and do it so that people would wake up the next day and it would be a different shop front.

We started off exclusively with old clothes: rather nice beaded dresses, blazers, all that sort of camp nonsense. That was fun. Then we decided that we'd design our own clothes. It seemed fairly easy to do, but of course once we did that I began to lose interest. The manufacture of clothes, the rag trade – I hated the rag trade. You had to do all that but I couldn't stand it. I lost interest in playing shops.

JONATHAN MEADES: In '66 a friend of mine called Paddy Horsley spent his first long vac marbling paper – endpapers and so on. He went into Granny Takes a Trip and they commissioned him to marble part of the shop. I went down there to see him, and this was the first time I realised

220

this extreme snobbery based on clothes. It was all extremely excluding. I dressed then very much as I do now – jeans, jackets, black suits – and I certainly didn't have the hippie gear. I remember Nigel Waymouth sneering at me – you could hardly see his face through this mass of Afro hair and this huge collar that came up to here and down to there and what the Americans call a 'Windsor scarf'. He obviously thought I was a jerk and wanted me moved out of the way, because I was an extremely bad advertisement for his shop.

JEFF DEXTER: The people around Granny's were rich kids, beautiful people, but that was no barrier for me. They were just people making things happen. Though they had the advantage that they could get a shop together and set up businesses. There was also Robert Albag, who started I Was Lord Kitchener's Valet. He had come from a very heavy, very tasty mod background, around the Lyceum in the late 50s, early 60s. That was reflected at Lord Kitchener. The first hippie clothes weren't just bells and beads, they were very smart military wear. Robert dressed Jimi Hendrix – that beautiful red Guards jacket – and that became the uniform of that period. Up till then Jimi had always worn mohair suits.

NIGEL WAYMOUTH: The heroes of the underground, these rock stars and celebrities, were in a way too successful, too remote. The people who were really involved in it were much more grubbing around.

I suppose I became a Chelsea figure. But it was only circumstances that brought me to Chelsea – certainly not like Michael Rainey or Mark Palmer whose background was much more aristocratic and who knew this area much more. Jane Rainey – Jane Ormsby-Gore – was a marvellous figure. Let us not forget that when they came back from Washington the Ormsby-Gores brought back all that glamour, the Kennedys, the whole new-age outlook. They carried a lot of the style, the dressing-up bit, a lot of it came from the Ormsby-Gores. They were quintessential to the dressing-up process.

MALDWYN THOMAS: Jane Rainey used to have a lick of acid before she went to work at *Vogue*. 'I'll just have an A-side high,' she'd say.

Middle Earth: 'This great space filled with music and incense and drugs'

JOE BOYD: Around the same time as UFO first started, the Electric Garden started in King Street, Covent Garden. I went to the opening and it was terrible. In a kind of 'hippie' environment, an attempt to be an underground place. Jay Landesman was involved. We not exactly defeated them, but we did become the place to go to. Eventually Landesman was out and the owners put in Dave Housen. And he did a good job and turned it into a place that was not bad. By which time it became Middle Earth and eventually Middle Earth took over the Roundhouse when we left in October 1967.

JOHN PEEL: I used to go to Middle Earth quite a lot, I used to play the records quite a bit. There were all sorts of little places that hardly knew they were hippie clubs. My favourite was out in Kidderminster, a place called Frank Freeman's Dancing School. People who were raised on things like the Quicksilver Messenger Service would say, 'What a groovy name,' little realising that it was a dancing school run by a bloke called Frank Freeman. I went there for an extraordinary night with Beefheart and his band. Utterly bizarre. Frank Freeman and his wife were both quite elderly, in their sixties, and they were making cups of tea and sandwiches for Beefheart and when Beefheart started playing, as was invariably the case, half the audience left within the first number.

JO CRUIKSHANK: UFO was exotic, but it wasn't nearly as memorable for me as Middle Earth. Middle Earth took your breath away. It was the whole situation of it, in the middle of Covent Garden when it *was* Covent Garden. You'd go through these desolate, wet streets into this basement in King Street, just near the Opera House. Into this great space filled with music and incense and drugs, this great huge warehouse with pineapples and bananas. Light-shows going. You'd go out on this wonderful surge. You'd rendezvous with people at midnight at Covent Garden station. We had our own little universe, you'd walk in, everyone knew you, you'd say 'Hi' to Jeff . . .

JEFF DEXTER: I could do anything I wanted, play anything. Middle Earth lacked some of UFO's charm because it was bringing the punters in now, rather than the hardcore. But you can't survive on friends and a small group of people for ever. Everyone was trying to change the world and I wanted to attract more people. We all wanted more people to be part of it.

Middle Earth closed after the horrible scenes of the police raid. We had had a private party that night and somebody had brought along their children. The police raided, found the children and told the Covent Garden porters we were crucifying children in there. So they smashed the place to pieces. That was the death of Middle Earth really. Jenny Fabian and I were locked in the box office while they wrecked the place. I had my back on the door, feet against the wall, keeping that door closed while they smashed everything around us. They were going to kill us and we were the only two people left in there. We kept phoning the police and it took them 70 minutes to come. They had been there en masse for the raid but they didn't come back. We were screaming down the phone, 'Help! Help! They've got a gun, help us!' When they did arrive they said, 'There's nobody here, what's been going on?' as if they didn't know.

'People thought everything was going to last for ever'

JIM HAYNES: I don't think money was *the* factor in the counterculture, but I think it was a factor. London was very prosperous in the 60s . . . a culmination of things made London feel an incredible sense of confidence, whether that confidence was justified or not. People thought everything was going to last for ever.

JEFF NUTTALL: There was a shift between '66 and '67 from poetry and art and jazz and anti-nuclear politics to just sex and drugs, legalise pot. It was the arrival of capitalism. The market saw that these revolutionaries could be put in a safe pen and given their consumer goods. Electronically amplified music and narcotics. You had rock'n'roll, which is the most unchanging, conservative popular music that there had ever been, and continues to be so, under the banner of perpetual revolution. I wasn't against Dylan going electric at the time. I thought we had to invade the media, but what we misjudged was the power and complexity of the media. The media dismantled the whole thing. It bought it up. And this happened in '67, just as it seemed that we'd won.

DEREK TAYLOR: We arrived back in England from LA in November 1967. It was clear that things had changed. London had become a nice friendly place. People were smiling at each other: they were all behaving like people I remember as a child, like nice family parties where you knew everyone and you felt that everyone loved you. It felt like a permanent Christmas, that December.

CHRIS ROWLEY: And as '67 went on hundreds and hundreds and hundreds of new hippies kept appearing. It was exploding through white middle-class youth. A lot of mods changed too. Mods who I had known in south-east London, where I lived, were now turning up with suits discarded and kaftans on.

MARTIN CROPPER: Martin Stone, who now works for Shakespeare and Co. in Paris, started off playing for this ultimate mod band called the

223

Action. Then they went hippie. One day, after everyone had gone hippie overnight and grown moustaches and sideburns, they went down to some gig in Bournemouth. Their van was met off the motorway by the local mods and given a presidential entry, a scootercade into Bournemouth. All the mods turned out and then they get out on stage and start playing twenty-minute brain-damage madness.

NICK LAIRD-CLOWES: From 1967, when I was ten, I would go to Carnaby Street and look at the things there. Carnaby Street had probably already sold out but that was where I bought my copy of *Sgt. Pepper*. Then I went to the Kensington Market: you went from Carnaby Street, which was hip, to Kensington Market where the alternative market was beginning to flourish. Every weekend we'd go down and look through the greatcoats and the hordes of people looking identical. You'd hang out with people and they'd turn you onto things and you'd buy records from the record stall and they'd turn you onto drugs and good music and things like that. And you'd save up your money, generally you'd use your school lunch money, and buy the records.

KEITH MORRIS: It was all grossly absurd, because the underground and its magazines did have a lot of influence on thinking. Kids did leave home, it did change their lives. There were an awful lot of people who actually believed that the world was going to change, that the love generation was going to be significant.

RICHARD ADAMS: I was at Birmingham College of Art. Living at home, so on and so forth. *IT* had started coming out: the first issue of *OZ* appeared in February 1967. The kinds of people who were teaching at Birmingham at that time were in a number of instances London-based: painters, film-makers, designers and so on, and they were making the trek up the motorway from London. So the influence was predominantly from London; what was happening down there was influencing events in Birmingham as well.

MARK WILLIAMS: I gave up my job in early '67. That winter there was a group of people on the members' committee of the Midlands Art Centre, of whom I was one, who decided to break away from the Arts Centre and form another committee to raise money for a Birmingham Arts Laboratory. I was selected as the only full-time member, responsible for fund-raising. We knew what an Arts Lab was because of the London Arts Lab. I was making what seemed to be good money selling *IT* and working as a DJ at a club and doing discos at various colleges. We played

224

early psychedelia and stuff. I moved into a bed-sitter in Moseley and I started fund-raising events at the wonderful Victorian hall in Moseley. We started getting local bands, and bands up from London like Family, Love Sculpture, people like that. We opened the Birmingham Arts Lab in 1967. By that time I'd started writing for *IT*. When we finally got the Arts Lab open I decided to take a breather. I came down to London to meet these people from *IT* whom I'd never met.

DAVID MAY: All over the country in the 60s there were these little groups of people with long hair who went to the Arts Labs and the Arts Centres and saw the movies and basically travelled to festivals and smoked dope. That's what it came down to. Plymouth was like California. All the beats used to come through there on their way to St Ives. There were no motorways – people hitched. I was fourteen years old in a place called El Sombrero and there was a guy with a hardback of Jack Kerouac's *On the Road*. It was a Navy town, a lot of Americans came through. Blues bands played there, a lot of black American acts. So from there, naturally, you had to go to London. London was always separate from what was going on in the rest of the country, yet the vast majority of people one met in London were this flow from the provinces. Things that made the most difference were things like the *Sunday Times* colour magazine which played a vital role in taking what was happening in London and solidifying what was happening there for us.

PEARCE MARCHBANK: A main source of underground design was in the colour supplements, and you can't divorce the underground from what was going on in the mainstream. Dave King, who was doing the colour supplements, was also doing all the Jimi Hendrix covers. People were bombarded with images all the time, the colour supps were something that everyone got, they're quintessential 60s and if you didn't actually cut out these images and stick them on your wall, they'd still go into your brain and come out somehow the other end.

Apple: 'It was naïve, it was idealistic, but that's how it was'

DEREK TAYLOR: Apple had been going since December 1967 when they had opened the Apple shop. I joined in April 1968. At Apple I had access to funds to shovel out to all the people that John, particularly John, approved of. There was this general disposition to be nice to anyone who seemed to be on the trip. Anyone who wanted a small amount or who could give us a service for a reasonable sum. So if someone came in off the street with an idea and they looked right and felt right and had a nice

225

manner they would get money given to them. It was naïve, it was idealistic, but that's how it was. Apple was set up as a tax arrangement, yes, but it was also to help people. The idea's really in that song 'Baby, you're a rich man too'. Which John definitely believed: that we're all beautiful people. What do we want to do? What do we want to be? We want to help save the world. And that was the message and to make sure that people knew about it John and Paul appeared on the *Johnny Carson Show* and said, 'Come to us, we'll give you a cup of tea or a drink . . .' And they did come. And to the best of my ability I did give everyone a cup of tea or a joint or a drink. If they came in and they actually wanted cash and it wasn't a lot, I'd probably give them a fiver out of my pocket and get it back from expenses. And of course if *IT* wanted anything, they could have it.

John was into all this – though he didn't get to know about all of it – and while my instincts were usually pretty good, if I did get into a quandary, I always had it in the back of my mind: John would cover this. George too, though he didn't like Apple as much as John. He didn't like what he saw as the chaos of Apple. He was very spiritual and very hooked into Krishna. He was very much into the American version of the counterculture.

GENE MAHON: I worked for Apple from the very beginning, but I was never on the staff, never actually employed. Though I probably spent more time there, in Derek Taylor's office, than anyone who was employed.

My first contact with Apple was when I was working at the agency. I got back from lunch one day and there was a message: 'Please call Neil Aspinall at Apple.' I called. 'We want you to do some work for us.' Went over there. 'We're putting this record label together, we want you to design the logo, it's going to be called "Apple".' So I went away, put it together, got it done and took it back. The person I found myself dealing with was Derek Taylor and his sidekick, Rick Tuff – Richard Dilello. That was his nickname, and I was Gene Gluv, both like in shoes. Richard was the house hippie.

Derek Taylor's office was extraordinary. He did stuff that people didn't really realise. He worked long and hard to get Lennon into the States, for instance, things like that. He answered the telephone. Mad telephone calls from everywhere. He organised the launch of the singles – 'Give Peace a Chance' at Chelsea Town Hall, a very funny occasion – things like that.

Designing the Apple label was a relatively straightforward job. What I brought to it was the idea that it can stand as a pure symbol. Let it never

226

have any type on, put all that on the other side of the record – just designer stuff, really. And the apple that had the information on it should be sliced, to give a light surface on which to put type. It was always a green apple. I said to McCartney, 'It's a green apple, a big Granny Smith,' and he said, 'Oh, good.' Didn't make any money out of it, didn't make any out of *Sgt. Pepper* – I never made any money out of my connection with the Beatles. NEMS were actually signing the cheques and they were very loath to pay, even the expenses bills. I'd be standing outside the office, talking to a secretary through the speaker-phone from the street – very low-rent stuff – trying to get payment for an invoice that was months old.

DEREK TAYLOR: After a while Allen Klein had appeared, but John and Yoko had taken over Ron Kass's office to do Bag Productions and it was still possible to do a lot of alternative things if one could get John's monogram on a piece of paper. I was never shoving four figures to anyone, but I could raise about £150, which was quite a lot of money then. Anyone who asked for too much or asked in the wrong way or who just came to test our sincerity – they were definitely shown the door.

GENE MAHON: Apple wasn't profitable – even for me – but I had a lot of fun. Smoked a lot of dope, drank a bit of champagne. By the time they moved from Wigmore Street to Savile Row, I began to spend more and more time in the press room, in Derek's office. I'd stroll round to see Derek, get ripped, then stroll back into the office. I might not get back to work till five in the afternoon.

DEREK TAYLOR: There was Magic Alex. It wasn't his fault that we called him Magic Alex. It was the time of technology, the first stage of the 'white heat'. We had to have an inventor. There's this fellow that's done these great things. What are the things that this great man does? The back of the car that will light up and say 'Keep Off' so you'll never get rear-ended by the car behind; the camera that will photograph just sufficiently through the wall of the house to see what everyone is up to inside . . . And we all believed it. Except that I had a friend called Charlie Malling and he was a bit of an inventor too – he'd invented this mechanical finger. And Alex entertained Charlie to tea and Charlie came back saying, 'I don't know. I can't get Alex to show me any of his prototypes. He doesn't seem to have any to hand.' But there's one born every minute and in that respect we were definitely daft. He wasn't sacked but one day he just . . . wasn't there. Now you see him, now you don't.

IT: 'It was like a village scandal sheet, a parish pump'

DAVID ROBINS: Phil Cohen, with whom I wrote *Knuckle Sandwich* and who became 'Dr John' later on, had this take on the scene: Miles was the suave Noël Coward figure who was swanning around being a groove. But there was a real underground, the street people on Piccadilly and round Covent Garden, and of course they started to get closer and closer to this little cosy scene. As the riffraff came in the fashionable people got scared. On Saturday night Haynes started to get very uneasy, because it was like the Piccadilly street kids hanging out, the leather boys and guys who just wanted somewhere to doss. So there was like a class system in the underground: there was a real street world, guys who'd turn up from Borstal and offer their services. There was all that which turned into squatting in Covent Garden. Then there was the more snooty scene. There were links to the avant-garde art scene; Yoko used to come in a lot with her rubbish. The office was like a cocoon. There were incredible things happening outside and we used to be there stoned out of our minds, a permanent haze. One day this guy came in, a really weird-looking bloke with a skull face, and Bill [Levy] hissed to me, 'That's William Burroughs!' I was far too shy to speak to him. He picked up the paper and on the front page there was Timothy Leary saying 'Turn On, Tune In and Drop Out.' Burroughs said, 'Hashish has been smoked for a thousand years. Don't know about LSD, though.' That was it.

JOHN HOPKINS: When I came out of jail I spent some time running around Europe and North Africa with Suzy. Some kind friends put up some money, I still don't know who they were, but someone handed me a couple of hundred notes through my accountant and we went off. But after a few months we came back; I couldn't get by running around alternative Europe, I couldn't get by without roots. And I did a couple of issues of *IT* and I immediately started to change the structure of it. When I came back I saw that the people who were working at *IT* were not the people who owned it. Instead there was this division. So I called a company meeting in the Cosmoba restaurant off Queen's Square, which was where we'd always met when we were setting up *IT* and when we started putting it out. I got everyone who was a director there and I turned round to them and I said, 'You're fired.' Miles, Henshaw, Haynes, Jack Henry Moore. I wanted to put it in the hands of the people who were actually doing the magazine. It turned out to be the single most stupid thing I ever did, because it lost me a lot of friends. I was then the sole director, and I handed it over to the people who were working on it. My proposition was simply that people doing the work should get the action. So I behaved very brutally to people who had been my friends without realising what a stupid thing I was doing.

DAVID ROBINS: When Hoppy came back from prison he said to me, 'Dave, you've got to learn to type properly, man. It's essential, an important skill.' So I did. Jack Henry Moore called me a neon Marxist. And I started to get pissed off by their right-wingness or, in Bill's case, their outright fascism. Bill was basically a Hitler-lover. Suddenly things really changed. Bill went off to Holland and when he came back there was no job for him. There was a new regime and John Hopkins took over. They said I could stay but I resigned out of loyalty to Bill.

MILES: When Knullar took over (it means 'fuck' in Swedish) I was one of the only people left from the original group. It was Graham Keen, Peter Stanshill, possibly Dave Hall; Micky Farren was on the staff but not actually administering. In theory it was a workers' co-operative based on John Lewis, which is one of the few models that exists in England for a co-operative corporate structure. I was still very much involved in *IT*'s content: I really wanted to write for it, I was very interested in what it was doing. I wasn't worried about my formal relationship to *IT*, I just wanted to write, so I just remained part of it. From then on, because I wasn't an owner, I got paid. I wrote regularly for the next few years, rock'n'roll interviews and a literary column. Very occasionally I'd guest edit an issue if someone else was away.

TONY ELLIOTT: I remember going to the office and meeting this human being called Mick Farren. He had these skin-tight satin trousers, very thin legs, and this just enormous . . . hairdo. He looked, although I don't think he probably was, but he just looked immaculate. He looked really, really good and I was terribly impressed. He was swearing a lot. I don't know just what he was doing, but he was there and I found him a bit frightening in a way. They were a different style of people, a different generation. I always felt very much the younger newcomer in that kind of environment, and different from them.

SU SMALL: The first I knew about *IT* was when one of my mates came in selling it. That would have been about June '67. There was a special half-issue or something when Hoppy went to jail. I hadn't seen anything like it before. I'd just started taking acid about that time. I tagged along with my mate when he went to collect his next supply of issues and I got talking to Dave Hall who was the business manager. I was working as switchboard operator at a fruit importers in Covent Garden, it wasn't wildly exciting. It was about five minutes' walk from Endell Street and the girl who ran the switchboard – I believe she was called Smoky, a Swedish girl married to the distribution manager Paul Weston – had been called home cos her mother was very sick. They'd got somebody in from BIT but she was obviously hopeless. So I very sweetly offered to work the switchboard for her while she typed up the What's Happening page, which was part of the job. So when Dave Hall came back I gave him half a dozen neatly written messages, time and so on, as one does, and he said, 'Hang on a minute, come outside . . . Do you want a job?' and I said, 'Yes,' and he said, 'When do you want to start?' and I said: 'I've started.' And I never went back to the fruit importers. This was an opportunity to do something so much more interesting than anything else I'd ever done in my life.

GRAHAM KEEN: Pete Stanshill and Dave Hall borrowed the money – maybe £400 – to pay the printer from the Beatles. We actually paid it back later. We formed a new company with Pete, Dave and myself as directors. Pete Stanshill and I evolved a routine which suited the way we liked to work. We'd work very hard for a week, putting the magazine together, and then I had a week off. We didn't work all night, we worked from ten in the morning till about five or six. That was a routine which worked for two years and it was a very stable period. I was only concerned with layout. Pete had this idea that it should be a forum for other people's views and that almost anything went. Mark Williams turned up from Birmingham. He talked himself into doing a music section as a separate pull-out, which we called 'Plug and Sock-IT'. Mark also introduced us to Edward Barker, another Birmingham boy. We drove up to Birmingham to persuade him and his girlfriend to come down to London, where he was feted and lionised. He was very pretty, shagging everything in sight. Su Small started on the switchboard and then she went into advertising. To sharpen up the act all round we started to bring it out on time and it stayed being brought out on time for two years. We increased the circulation and it was all running financially very well. We upped the salaries every now and then quite happily. We got about £25 a week.

SU SMALL: I spent the whole of that time wide-eyed with amazement. All the people tended to be a bit older than me: Graham Keen doing layout, Peter Stanshill was editing. I dived in there, I couldn't wait. They paid me £15, cash in hand. There was a café on the ground floor and you came up the stairs, very rickety, and there were two little offices, one with me on the switchboard and a typewriter, and Dave Hall over there, Paul Weston in distribution and a little office where Ronnie, Dave Hall's

230

wife, did the advertising. Then she decided she didn't want to do the advertising any more and I was dumped into that.

Sometime in 1970, when I'd got a bit sloppy on my timekeeping, Dave Hall threw a wobbler and fired me. I went marching off to Manchester. I was very hurt at being sacked from *IT* cos I had worked really, really hard and I was very upset. It took me years to ask Micky [Farren] why no one ever said anything about me being fired, and he said, 'Dave used to fire someone every week and they used to just come back in. You were the only person that ever took it seriously.'

MARK WILLIAMS: I wandered into the offices of *IT* and within twenty minutes was offered the job of music editor. The business management of *IT* was a joke: where was all the money going? I don't actually know where a lot of it went. The magazine was distributed in a very haphazard and piecemeal way. There were people street-selling who were basically fairly honest and bought their copies from *IT*. But that accounted for a fairly small proportion of its income. The rest of it went to underground distribution systems – one man and a J2 van near Andover, and another man and two mini-vans in Aylesbury and so on – God knows what happened to their money. How we got paid depended: sometimes we got paid in money and drugs and sometimes just in drugs. Sometimes we didn't get paid at all. But we didn't mind: it was very cheap to live, there were a lot of fringe benefits, a lot of parties, records, free concerts, movies – your entertainment, basically, was free. Transport was paid for out of petty cash. I was very excited by it all, definitely. But we started going through incredible problems with printers. We were changing printers every other issue. As one of the few people who could drive I had to drive all over the fucking country with the artwork.

It was like a village scandal sheet, a parish pump. It was very parochial. Then there was a women's lib faction developing. There was the London Street Commune. I didn't like them: they promoted this whole principle of 'property is theft so we'll come and take over your newspaper'. They took over the offices, allegedly with the help of some Hell's Angels, and occupied the building. Then there was a moral dilemma about whether to call the police or not, and they were called in the end. There was an emergency meeting at Miles' house in Lord North Street. *IT* had no political line: it had a moral and an ideological line – which was pretty muddled – but it didn't get involved in party politics.

MILES: *IT* peaked in '68 because of May '68 in Paris. We had a whole bunch of people in Paris. In fact the whole staff was in France, Hoppy was in Paris, so were Jim and Jack. And we got an interview with Dany

Cohn-Bendit, and Jean-Jacques Lebel wrote something for us. He was the guy who had liberated the Stock Exchange in Paris and ran up the Liberation Flag – an enormous white banner with a drawing of a joint on it. At this stage *IT* began to get invaded by various people of various ideologies. The London Street Commune tried to take over, there was Chris Gray of the Situationists, who'd been around for a long time and staged a happening in the Indica Gallery. I related to the politicos in a rather stupid, dazed, laid-back way – 'Hey, man . . .' The London Street Commune takeover was repelled. It had to be repelled: it was just a bunch of Hell's Angels who were destroying everything and cost *IT* £3000. It seemed like so many things were happening, just a million things. Information overload. An unimaginable number of underground papers arrived, endless phone calls, an incredible amount of letters. I actually had a full-time secretary, Sarah Pouliakakou, answering twenty to thirty letters a day.

'There were all these Indian travelling salesmen'

TONY ELLIOTT: I went to see Dave Hall in the offices when it was in Betterton Street. I'll never forget this absolutely unbelievable smell that came out. They'd allowed some of what would now be called Yellow People to squat, all sitting around in these saffron rags, all cooking: this horrible hot dirty water with a bit of spices smell. Brown rice and vegetables.

GRAHAM KEEN: The Hare Krishnas turned up. They were the first that Britain had ever seen. Two of them were Jewish. We gave them the ground floor in Betterton Street and they established their first little ashram there with their wives. They were sluts, really awful slobs.

SUE MILES: There were all these Indian travelling salesmen, all these gurus who packed their suitcases and rushed over to England. The first Hare Krishnas were sent to Miles and me. These three couples arrived. In the great Bagwash colours. Fat women, fat spotty women, the three of them arrived and they were all ex-San Francisco storefront carpenters and they were *real nice*. They had one thought every 35 minutes, maybe, and you'd say something and they'd say, 'Sure, Miles, but remember, the little stream feeds the big pond,' and I'd think, 'Oh my God, oh no.' Miles didn't know what had hit him either. He put them in touch with a load of Pakistanis in Ealing, quite sensibly. People who knew how to eat cauliflower cheese with their fingers or chopsticks – cos we didn't and we didn't want to learn.

MILES: Ginsberg told these Hare Krishnas who were coming to England that they should contact me and immediately achieve fame and fortune in Britain. So I was inundated with all these Hare Krishna types. Fortunately George Harrison was receptive to the idea and he bought them a temple near the British Museum. I went to their temple with him once. They'd pass out all this food and there's some that you're not supposed to eat and some that you do eat. I was hearing all these whispers – 'George is eating Krishna's food' – and other people were saying 'Shut up!' Then somehow, I don't know how the hell it happened, they suddenly moved into the ground floor of the *IT* building in Betterton Street.

TONY ELLIOTT: What impressed me was this complete contrast between this . . . shit downstairs and Dave Hall. He was really very, very organised. Maybe he was really a street-corner hustler, but he came over as being a very very together organiser.

Dave Hall: 'What d'you mean, "records"?'

DAVID ROBINS: *IT* had a business manager called Dave Hall. His name wasn't really Dave Hall, but that's what we knew him as. He used what might be technically described as 'street-corner' methods of business and accounting. He'd say, 'What d'you mean, "records"?' and he'd open this drawer and there'd be all sorts of bits of paper.

SU SMALL: No one ever knew if 'Dave Hall' was his real name. The things he used to do with the *IT* finances I daren't tell you about in case he still is alive and that is his real name, in which case he'd kill me. Let's say he invested them. I knew he was laundering money but, God bless him, there was always wages and smoking dope when Dave Hall ran things and that endeared him to me. Basically he was a horrible East Anglian gangster, but he was great, he was cool . . . you needed somebody like that. *IT* was immensely efficient considering what they were up against. Constant bombardment of people just in off the street, plus constant shortage of finance, and this extremely erratic business manager . . . he was up and down, Dave. Sometimes he'd just go swanning off down to Muriel's for the afternoon. I don't know at what point he got involved, but it certainly wouldn't have survived long without him.

RUSSELL HUNTER: I worked for *IT* in '68. Ostensibly I was the distribution manager, working with Dave Hall. Whatever his other connections were, he was a lovely guy and he knocked himself out for that paper. He had a lovely wife called Ronnie, who was half gypsy. My job

233

was basically to wrap up parcels, answer the phone and test all the drugs that came in.

STEVE SPARKS: *IT* survived for at least two years on the basis of profits from dope-dealing. They'd take the advertising money and they'd go out and they'd score dope and they'd sell it and then they'd pay the wages. *IT* would never have run successfully without a layer of dope-dealing.

GRAHAM KEEN: I'm sure there were lots of things going on that I wasn't really aware of. We'd have so many grand in the bank and Dave Hall would say to me, 'I want to borrow it for a week,' or whatever. 'It'll be all right.' Pete and I used to say, 'OK, sure, fine.' And sure enough it would be OK. The money would come back into the bank with a percentage interest. Five per cent or whatever. We'd all get an ounce of dope. Dave had done his deal, financed it with the money and that was that. Dave had got in a young kid, a little whizzkid with figures, who was also doing his own dope-dealing. He and a mate of his were shipping out dope to Canada in the backs of paintings, but he'd been sussed by a customs officer working in his spare time with some sort of sergeant of police. They came up one day and did him in the office.

SUE MILES: A man walks in wearing a brand new pair of jeans, not Levis, with turnups, big shoes, very short hair, Jack Kerouac plaid shirt, sunglasses and it's raining and he says, 'I'd like to score, man.' This guy Nick, who's business manager, says, 'No problem, how much do you want?' 'How much have you got?' Nick goes round, opens the filing cabinet, looks in and says, 'Three weight,' and he says, 'I'll have it.' Nick says, 'I'll wrap it up,' and he goes whap! with the warrant card.

GRAHAM KEEN: I never went short of dope all the time I worked for *IT*. Dave would sometimes stick it in my pay packet, sometimes he'd say, 'Are you short, Gray? Grab that.' He was beautiful, I loved him. He was always very entertaining. Where he came from and where he went – nobody knows.

The Firm: 'Now they were very funny lads'

CHRIS ROWLEY: The paper had moved to Betterton Street. Nigel Samuel was involved. I didn't really see very much of him but what I did see he seemed sort of young and rich and foolish. I saw his sister a bit more: she was going out with Ian Sippen of the Firm, this terrible group of sometime mods from Ilford who'd become somehow proto-hippies. They weren't a violent group. Compared to the Highbury lads or any of the other London gangs of that era the Firm were mild indeed. I never saw them kick anybody. They were more into music and drugs and posturing.

PETER SHERTSER: Our whole introduction to this underground thing was that being avaricious consumers of music and gigs and anything different, we used to scour the music press every week. Suddenly there was this thing about a new band called the Pink Floyd playing in All Saints Hall. That's it – boom! we're down there. It was weird: they were doing R&B numbers, 'Louie Louie', things like that, and they were doing this completely weird stuff: lights and things and whatever. It stimulated us. So the next time there was something of that vein, we went along. It was UFO, and somehow we met Mick Farren. He took a fancy to us, because we took the piss out of him. Told him that he was a weak impersonator of Bob Dylan and the only thing he had in common was that he was Jewish. And that he'll never be Gene Vincent unless we break his leg. From there on Mick invited me and Ian round to his house in Princelet Street in Whitechapel and we met him and Joy. When we first knew the pair of them, way out though they may have appeared, we were weirder. We were doing smoke, acid, pills, speed, mandies, uppers, downers – and they didn't touch anything.

MICK FARREN: There were a lot of ex-mods who really went into style first and being mods ingested massive amounts of drugs, dropping acid like pills and then became extremely weird, but frequently made a lot of money. The Firm – Peter Shertser and the late Ian Sippen and all the rest of the ones from Goodmayes and Ilford. That was a sort of second-wave influx, mutant mods from out in the eastern suburbs. They were the first sort of shock troops who came in and because they were mods they went to the hot new club and took the hot new drug and listened to the hot new music. And behaved much the way mods do.

PETER SHERTSER: We quite agreed with the hippie morals, but on the other hand we thought: 'Here's some guys we can have over. They've got it all wrong: what is this "give it away"? We're from the East End, be fair.' So as much as we loved the principles, we had a bit of a crack as well. We gave a lot back, in different ways, so it was all kind of justified. But if there was advantages to be taken – we took advantage. We grew up in that kind of society and suddenly to have it on a plate ... We didn't have higher moral principles in those days. But we were quite just: if we were asked to do something or sort something out we'd do it; we wouldn't let people do horrible things. For all the acid we didn't become hippies. It's that Jewish background: you're still thinking about money

235

and survival and capitalism. We hated capitalism, but we liked survival and we liked dealing. When we got the money, what did we do with it? We spent it on cars, clothes or drugs, or enjoyment. We just wanted to get the most out of life at the time.

JOHN PEEL: Very few people retained a sense of humour throughout. There were some: a bunch of lads who called themselves the Firm. Now they were very funny lads. They were people who enjoyed the rocky aspects of it, the fact that you got to take drugs and get your end away. But they did seem to have a kind of sense of humour about it. I met them at UFO. I was terribly earnest and they must have thought, 'What a dickhead!'

PETER SHERTSER: Peel was on Radio London. We used to write in to him because no one else was playing blues. When he came over from the States he knew nobody. He used to announce us on the air, one thing and another. He said, 'I'm coming to stay in London, I don't know anybody, can you take me about?' So we did. We met him and took him to UFO, introduced him to a few people, gave him some names in the BBC, people we knew from doing the music thing. One night we decided to spike him. We thought, we'll teach the balding cunt a lesson. Down UFO. When he was at his highest we threw a bucket of water over him.

The Process: 'Nick enacted death by the Process – and then he disappeared'

CHRIS ROWLEY: A lot of people died, and that began happening in '68. Simon Fairey died then of a heroin overdose. He was a noted methedrine person. He had an apartment in Covent Garden. It was painted black, the Velvet Underground records had stayed on the turntable for two months, everyone had had scabies twice and burnt all their clothing twice. Then they painted everything black. Methedrine had this effect on people. They killed themselves, they went into Scientology . . . You had a lot of religions. The Process at one end – Nazi psychiatry. What happened to the people who went into the Process? Where are they buried?

NICHOLAS SAUNDERS: After trying the Maharishi and the Sufis I got involved with a very interesting group called the Process, who were highly unpopular. At one time, in the early 60s, I used to hold an open house, maybe as many as 70 people would turn up every second Tuesday night. One of the people I met through this was an Irishman called Pete McCormick. And he disappeared. Then, very shortly after I first took acid, I met him in the street, wearing some robes, a long purple cloak. He

236

told me he was now living in a community and I should come around any time. I was pretty curious and I did go around and to my amazement I was going up the steps of a big Mayfair house and there, inside the door, was a reception desk. So I asked where I could find Pete McCormick. The guy behind the desk, who was also wearing some sort of robes, black ones, said, 'Would you like to go downstairs and have a cup of coffee? I'll find him for you.' So I went downstairs and there was this scrupulously well-organised, clean and efficient coffee bar. There was no one there except for a girl, who was wearing long robes, and I asked her for coffee. She brought it, then sat down next to me and started a fairly superficial conversation. Pete McCormick wasn't there, but by the end of my visit I'd become more and more curious as to what was actually going on. I was told that they lived in this community and they were exploring what the point of life was. That appealed to me because I felt that was what I was doing too. They believed in your own total responsibility for whatever happened to you or already had happened to you. However unfortunate you were it was your own responsibility in some way. And they had a course that people could go along to and I went along. After going for a while I realised that it was very much based on Scientology, but I liked it.

STEVE ABRAMS: I couldn't understand how so many people got sucked into Scientology. I remember having an argument with Ginsberg about it, I couldn't understand how he could take Hubbard at all seriously. Scientology was irrelevant but there was an offshoot of Scientology that was not irrelevant: the Process. They had sort of Nazi leanings: Alsatian dogs and all that. I gave two talks to the Process. I would give a talk at the Process and there would be a curtain at the back and De Grimston and the others would be sitting behind the curtain. I gave a talk on brainwashing, which I thought would be appropriate.

NICHOLAS SAUNDERS: It was extremely intense. Everything was very disciplined and punctual. You arrived there early so it could start on the dot of 7 am. Then there were three hours of pretty intense exercises done in pairs. Normally you would sit facing someone else in the group, knees touching, looking straight into their eyes. You'd do things like trying to embarrass the other person. The idea was that you should be able to feel hurt but still accept it, feel embarrassed and still accept it. You shouldn't cut yourself off from your feelings. They were very secretive: they wouldn't answer any direct questions about who started it, where the funds came from and so on. They didn't charge much for the course, but what they did charge a lot for were individual sessions in

237

which they would reveal to you what lay beneath the conscious self. This was £25 a session.

During the time I was there they began changing from a group of people trying to discover what life was about, into a rather self-righteous religious group. They started wearing crosses on chains and I found that they weren't able to take my jokes any more. So I was feeling slightly dubious about them.

One day when I turned up as usual the woman who was running the course said, 'Nicholas, there's a vacancy in our novices' class and it's been decided to offer it to you.' I made my usual comment: 'God, you won't catch me going into that place . . .' and I brushed it off. But this came after a week in which a number of strange and disturbing things had happened – I'd had a car crash, I'd found that my then partner was cheating me, and I was nearly beaten up by two men I tried to stop forcing a girl into a car – and it started going through my mind that perhaps I was being directed this way. So ten minutes later I said I'd take it and I moved into their novices' flat in Wimpole Street. But I carried on as usual – inviting lots of people round, which was frowned on, and I didn't wear the black clothes which the other novices did. One night we were asked to enact death. So my enactment was to go through, one after another, the kind of things we were taught at the Process and then I slumped to the floor and I was dead: death by the Process. After this I was asked to stay behind and was simply told that my sitting on the fence was no good. I had to make a decision. What I did was walk out and never come back. I heard later that they were telling people that 'Nick had enacted death by the Process, and then he'd disappeared!'

The Anti-University: 'Who's going to pay the fucking phone bills?'

STEVE ABRAMS: The Bertrand Russell Peace Foundation had a building in Old Street, in the East End. Joe Berke and a lot of other people used it to set up the Anti-University, which was a wonderful place. It provided a platform for people who didn't have one, to lecture and talk. Either people who didn't have a platform at all or who had perhaps an academic appointment and could only lecture on their own subject. Huxley gave a course on dragons and another on how to stay alive; Laing gave a course; there were courses on modern music from Cornelius Cardew; Yoko Ono did a course; I taught advanced techniques for turning on and all my students had prescriptions for tincture. I'd give them lessons on joint-rolling and so on. There was a chap from the Home Office, a professor, a rabbi, a very strange group of people, all my students. I loved the Anti-University. The students were almost anybody: it was £10 to register for

238

a course and it went on for a year or two. But in the second year or the second term it started getting out of hand. The idea became to charge the teachers and pay the students.

JIM HAYNES: I taught in the Anti-University, which held some of its classes in the Arts Lab. I knew Laing and [David] Cooper. They came to the Lab. I was teaching a media course which basically told people that anything they wanted to do they could do.

JEFF NUTTALL: There was one terrible moment when Berke was really thrown on his back against the wall. It was in the Anti-University. Bob Cobbing had kind of stepped in and taken over. While he had taken over there – not because of Bob, but because this would always happen to places like this – it became a dosshouse. People with bed-rolls on their backs always wanting a place to doss down. And they used the phone. Particularly the Americans. So you'd say, 'Who's going to pay the fucking phone bills?' and they'd say, 'They will be paid.' Poor old Joe Berke, who saw himself as actually having to pay, blew his top one night. He picked up one of these guys bodily and threw him out. Then he did this strange boasting thing: 'Who's the biggest guy on the block, who can throw anybody here? I can beat you! I'm the biggest guy on this block!' It was really dippy. He just regressed. Very sad.

'As far as I was concerned, we'd abolished politics'

NIGEL WAYMOUTH: I think the whole movement, the whole psychedelic era, was finished by the end of '68. Politics came into it, Dany the Rouge, Street-Fightin' Man, and everything began to get quite heavy.

PETER ROBERTS: Politics, the whole '68 thing, derailed the other stuff. It was inevitable that the drugs and so on would come into conflict with the political structure at some point. As far as I was concerned, we'd abolished politics. We already had changed the world. Our world. In so far as we came into contact with any kind of social or governmental brutality we discussed it: don't get into that game, don't get into politics, don't set up one army to fight another.

MICHAEL STOREY: The committed politicos and their world seemed terribly on the earth; and if you're taking acid and things you're looking at the whole planet. It all seemed rather desperate. You were still taking acid and you were stoned and, rather like *Easy Rider*, it wasn't verbal. You can look at it two ways: on the one hand it's awful, everyone studiedly being cool and together and, yes, understanding, understanding the flower, understanding the wall . . . but that's looking at it hard. But if I remember rightly I did sometimes feel absolute understanding, and it was beautiful and I can't run that down. We were politically very unaware, absolutely in a bubble. A friend of mine was actually performing in Czechoslovakia when the Russians arrived and he came back and told me. So you saw things, you experienced things, but . . . one was stoned and the rest of your world was stoned, so . . . 'Straight people . . . I can't handle it, man.'

Grosvenor Square: 'Then we went home – and watched it on TV'

ROBIN BLACKBURN: Just as the Dialectics of Liberation Conference was finishing I had gone with Tariq Ali to Bolivia in an attempt to get the Bolivian authorities to admit that they'd got Régis Debray and to prevent them from murdering him, and hopefully to see if he could get released. That was when I first met Tariq and although I wasn't actually involved in the Vietnam Solidarity Campaign, I knew the people who were setting it up. Also, they used the LSE, where I was teaching, as a base for the October [1968] demonstration [in Grosvenor Square]. Probably no more than 15,000 had gone on the November 1967 anti-Vietnam demonstration, but there was quite a lot of aggro. It was a different type of demonstration from what one had had before. There were battles with the police, the chance of making a breakthrough to the Embassy. It seemed like real action rather than the usual tame demonstration.

The October '68 demonstration had the most people, but because it was billed by the bourgeoisie as 'the revolution', everybody became super-restrained and of course nothing very much happened. I didn't go along with throwing ball-bearings in the March [1968] demonstration in Grosvenor Square, but we were fighting the police, trying to get through to the Embassy, and there was this sense that it was a demonstration of a different sort. What we felt was that if we were able to smash up a bit of the Embassy it would be a way of demonstrating solidarity with the Vietnamese. It would send a signal to the White House. We were partly hoping that the media might report it and generally add to the view of an American president under siege, even from loyal allies like the British with their tame Labour government. I think at the end of the day one must say that all these demonstrations, above all those inside the United States, but also those around the world, did help produce an eventual American withdrawal.

240

JOHNNY BYRNE: We were having too much of a good time to become involved overtly in politics. The politics of that time didn't really warrant involvement . . . there was grouching and bitching about the kind of problems the police might cause when they waded in here and there. There's only one thing I remember the people I knew actually going out and demonstrating against and that was when Rhodesia declared UDI in '65. But in '67, when everybody was in a fairly negative state as regards politics, a girl called Nadia, an American girl, came to live at Cranley Mansions and she radicalised everybody. She had been at Berkeley and she was the one who got them all down to Grosvenor Square during the big demonstrations in '68. I remember endless weeks and weeks of people talking about using their banners as lances, spears, unhorsing policemen and charging them – the tactics of confrontation.

MARTIN CROPPER: I was at Grosvenor Square on March 17th. Some group had decided to protest against the US use of defoliants in Vietnam by defoliating the trees in Grosvenor Square. They turned up with all the right chemicals but they found that it was too early in the year for the leaves to have sprouted. There were also a group of people who had this idea of vomiting on the steps of the Embassy, by putting a piece of bacon on a piece of string down their throats. We got into the Square when a guy had an epileptic fit in front of me, right in the middle of this fucking riot. Everyone had to make room: 'Hang on, stop rioting, you guys.' It was great, kicking policemen's helmets along Oxford Street.

NINA FISHMAN: The point about the March demonstration was of course that it was unexpected on both sides. This is where CND is left in the past, because as opposed to making token or symbolic protest in Grosvenor Square you were really having a go. That took everyone by surprise, because it wasn't good manners. Having come from America this was less of a surprise to me. I had been on a bus going from Colorado to the South and been on a big march in Birmingham, Alabama. So when I had arrived in '65 and gone to the Oxford Teach-In, I thought, 'Christ, this is tame stuff!' And it *was* tame stuff. That was the old Marxists, the old left wing of the Labour Club, and it was frightfully proper.

I was kicked by a policeman in Grosvenor Square. I still have the scar. You went and you said, 'Right, we're gonna have a go,' and the old manners didn't apply. People didn't think about what the police might do. There were discussions before Grosvenor Square about the use of aniseed balls, and the best way to deal with dogs . . . That was very much like a game: 'Escape from Colditz'. But there weren't dogs, only horses.

The October one was very much more a set piece. Because there had been all this build-up, there couldn't be that spontaneous 'Let's get them!' And that's very important: there wasn't trouble because no one was cold-blooded enough, no one was Leninist enough, to organise it. A small group of well-organised people could have done a bloody good job of mucking it up.

DICK POUNTAIN: The first one, in March, turned into a real free-for-all afterwards – running down Park Lane, trashing cars and bank windows, very very heavy. We, the Situationists, actually had a presence on the march and made this huge banner that said 'Storm the Reality Studio and Retake the Universe'. Yellow letters on blue ... it was very professionally done. We joined the march amidst all these Trots, all chanting 'Ho, Ho, Ho Chi Minh!' and we were chanting 'Hot chocolate, drinking chocolate!' and getting lots and lots of aggravation from all the Trots around us. And as we went past Hyde Park Corner this figure clad in black leather from head to foot came out of the crowd and joined us and it was Micky Farren and it was the first time I ever spoke to him.

MICK FARREN: Saturday night, we'd been playing somewhere like Mother's Club in Birmingham and we were coming back down the M1 and ran into these humungous police roadblocks and they pulled out all our equipment. We said, 'What the fuck do you want?' and they said, 'We're looking for weapons.' And we get back to London and me and Sandy plan to go to the riot the next day. So we got up about lunchtime, two o'clock as was our wont, and got our shit together. Nobody else could be bothered to go because they were still asleep. We went downstairs and there were maybe 50 motorcycle cops at the top of Endell Street and buses full of these geezers who look like they feed on vodka and raw meat and don't get let out except on riots. I thought, 'Motherfucker! what's goin on here?' There weren't exactly tanks on the boulevards but ... shit, it was like Chile or something. So we went marching up to Centrepoint where we ran into Miles and we hooked up with the march somewhere by Tottenham Court Road and Oxford Street.

We were marching along and there were reports that Mick Jagger had been seen and this was happening and that was happening and it was all very sort of aggressive. There were all sorts of Germans who were a real nuisance because they kept linking arms and getting into that run that the Japanese had invented. We didn't really want to go that fast – we'd just got up and we didn't feel too good and we didn't need a lot of mad Krauts doing the Japanese run, very disruptive, like Zulu impis getting wound up, and they kept doing these flurries of running on the spot which got people very excited to the point that somebody tried to nose his car out of somewhere like Berwick Street through the crowd and Miles kicked in his headlamps! I thought, 'Jesus!' Me and Sandy were coming down off speed and we weren't as rambunctious as a lot of people around us. We had just meandered along.

So we got to South Audley Street and started streaming down there and everything halts and nobody knows what's going on and there's all these rumours that they're tear-gassing people here and there (in fact they weren't). We hadn't seen the US Embassy yet, although there was another rumour that there were armed marines who'd kill you if you actually got inside. Then everything started to move and we went charging down Audley Street and it seemed like the police had given way, that's what everybody assumed. We arrived on the grass in Grosvenor Square, where, although I didn't know it at the time, we had immediately been surrounded. So there we have these thousands of people boxed in on the grass, though it's not that crowded, there's room to stroll around, except down the end by the Embassy where it's so crowded you can't see anything. And we just started wandering about and I remarked to Sandy, 'It's like a fucking love-in.' Then there was a thunder of hooves and there we were in the middle of the charge of the Light Brigade, which was fucking scary. What little I knew, basically from Napoleonic history, was get under a tree, because it's very hard to swing one of those truncheons when you're on a horse and the other guy is under a tree. So the first charge goes through and they're sort of whacking people and one geezer on a white horse, who became quite notorious, whacked this girl on the head – at which point everybody became exceedingly annoyed and dragged him off his horse and kicked him. He got away a couple of times but then he was surrounded and when everyone closed ranks he was just left there. And then people were hurling bits of turf and rocks and stuff and then they'd retreat and charge again and retreat and charge and people were getting hit and hurt and injured and then we went home. Just like that. And watched it on TV.

JO DURDEN-SMITH: Television was important, in a funny kind of way, because television always was important. In the absence of a real sense of what things are about it was the mirror, in the phrase of Conrad Aiken, in which our gestures became grandiose. There was a kind of two-way parasitism between the media and the young. The media played a sort of pushing, forcing role: 'Be like that only more so. Do more, be more extreme.' At the same time there was this pressure from the radical Left of exactly the same kind, towards more and more revolutionary purity, towards final exorcism of the bourgeois elements buried deep within, etc, etc, etc. There were horrific examples of that in America and Japan. A gang-bang in a church in Chicago, the taking of acid among the original Weatherpeople before the Days of Rage, group sex and so on. So one had this constant fissipation of the Left leftwards, paralleled by this thrust coming equally from the media, which was always asking for more.

JO CRUIKSHANK: I went to Grosvenor Square with Richard Trench. We'd smashed a few windows on our way and we got to the Square and we were holding hands and there we were with all these activist characters. Then all the police started to surround us and I started to lose my bottle, I started to quake. People were getting hurt everywhere around me and Richard suddenly said, 'Fuck the bastards!' and he let go of my hand and went running towards the police horses. The last thing I saw of him was being kicked in the face by a police horse and the next thing I saw of him was in Chelsea Hospital. His uncle, who was then headmaster of Eton and his guardian, disowned him in the newspapers the next day.

RICHARD TRENCH: One never expected the March 1968 Grosvenor Square to be like that. So energetic. Thousands and thousands of people. You couldn't predict how violent it was going to become because it suddenly happened. You felt yourself part of something bigger, which included the Viet Cong. I remember getting rather over-excited and something hitting me in the face and that's the last thing I remember.

JOHN HOPKINS: When the first Grosvenor Square demonstration happened I wrote an editorial in *IT* directed at Tariq Ali. What I said was, 'Who's cannon-foddering these people?' From that day I took no part in that kind of political demonstration.

HORACE OVE: Grosvenor Square was incredible. I took pictures for *IT*. Grosvenor Square was packed; it was the first time I saw young people in this country, mostly middle-class, really angry, really come out into the streets and really stand up to the police, really fighting back. Grosvenor Square was wicked: there were thousands of police, horses and things like that. I was running down trying to get there in time and I was fixing my camera and a policeman saw me and said, 'You better go back home, curly, else you'll be in a lot of trouble.' I didn't go home, I got in the middle of it and I remember there were speeches and so on and then the whole clash. There was the pushing: I push you, you push me back and suddenly the whole thing broke down. I think it was the first time a black policeman appeared on the scene, there was one black policeman there and he got a hard time from everybody, everybody.

244

When the police started to charge with their horses and really lay into people and beat the shit out of them there was one girl that was shouting and screaming back at them and about five police really laid into her and really kicked her about on the ground and then they pulled back. I have photographs, one, two, three and four pictures, where the crowd surrounds one policeman that did not get away and they really laid into him and beat him to the ground.

RUSSELL HUNTER: It was the first time that any of us had seen anything like that. The first time that the kind of non-violent thing went right out of the window and we saw that we were involved in a real confrontation: police horses charging, people dragged through hedges and beaten up . . . Nothing happened to me but I remember running alongside Hugo, who was Miles' lieutenant at Indica, and who was heavily into Zen Buddhism and the most calm, peaceful person you could ever imagine you could meet, and he was frothing at the mouth, incensed. He was rolling marbles under police horses and threatening to kill.

MILES: I went to both Grosvenor Square demonstrations but *IT* did nothing special. I thought it was always very amusing how the police were prepared to wade through about five people to bang Micky Farren on the head. There was something about him they didn't like. It was extraordinary: he'd be right in the middle of the crowd and they'd come wading through and go whappp!! He was a troublemaker as they saw it. In March I was there with Michael X and Frankie Y, Michael's lieutenant. As soon as the horses appeared Frankie just scooted off: one moment he was there, the next moment he was gone. Jagger was there, throwing rocks and having a good time, then he wrote *Street-Fightin' Man* and made a lot of money.

PEARCE MARCHBANK: Jagger was at Grosvenor Square, hiding, running away. I got extremely frightened and I think most people were extremely frightened. It was the first time they'd ever seen English police become aggressive.

JO DURDEN-SMITH: There's a moment when Mick Jagger was on a traffic island watching the demonstration: the street-fighting man. We all got home in time for the evening news. To see ourselves, essentially to gauge what sort of reaction we had got. It was the first days of instant reaction. You got to see yourself on television, perhaps. Around the time of the March 1968 demonstration there was considerable unease amongst the hierarchy at *World in Action* that nothing would happen. There was

245

talk of calling off the coverage. But there was a strong feeling among those who had set up the coverage that, yes, it was going to be all right – something *would* happen. It was not actually created by television, but it was understood that the presence of the cameras would not stand in the way of it happening. One appreciated that instinctively, without really understanding it. What happened didn't only happen because of the presence of the cameras – the parasitism between TV and the movement was much subtler than that. 'Oh look, here are the cameras, let's do something' came much later. Nobody paid the 200,000 on that march to do something.

Being on a camera crew right at the front of that line was terrifying, feeling the pressure of the people behind us. You went on a demonstration tentatively: you didn't know whether you were a radical or not – and one of the things that happened was that it radicalised you. Because it didn't matter whether or not you were actually a radical – you still got beaten up. It was a collective rite of passage: the function of demonstrations was to make your own position clear, to make you into a radical. You dared, you tried to go as far as you could go. We were, after all, the first generation not to be conscripted, not to fight wars. Maleness was becoming peripheralised, there was no real function for maleness.

LSE: 'A big intellectual party going on'

CHRIS ROWLEY: Life at LSE in '68 had become explosive in that we had an enormous series of demonstrations going on. In their wisdom, with the most leftist radical college in their system, the governors of London University decided to appoint Mr Adams, who had most recently been running the University of Rhodesia during UDI, to become the next Chancellor of the London School of Economics. This provided us with an endless series of demonstrations.

NINA FISHMAN: English academics were tremendously arid at the time. There was a basic lack of intellectual rigour. Too much sitting and enquiring about what other academics had been doing. So students were saying that we have this intellectual heritage but it doesn't mean anything any more. And that's why the New Left hit like a ton of bricks. It brought the Continent here in a way that hadn't been done before.

DAVID WIDGERY: When I came back from America I was determined to write about some of the things I had experienced there. I was blistering with anger, non-specific anger, which was made worse by the medical school which was very conservative and full of people whose main concern was that their name would be Sellotaped on every item in their

246

pencil case. I'd imagined university would be full of wonderful people spouting poetry but medical school wasn't like that at all. It's full of people who have very good science A-levels and are very very boring. So I gravitated to LSE very fast. It was just down the road and it was open house, there was a big intellectual party going on. There were always interesting things to hear or people to talk to. So the LSE bar became my second home and I would defect from the anatomy table to the LSE. There were people like Robin Blackburn, Chris Harmon, Richard Cooper who went on to found Pluto Press, Laurie Flynn (now of *World in Action*) those sort of people. They were the Socialist Society, very much left of the Labour Party, revolutionary socialists, whatever that meant. They supported the Viet Cong, and they were anti-Russian, which I thought was good because I was fed up with Russia; they were also quite critical of Cuba, which again I thought was a good idea because I'd decided that although Cuba was wonderful there were clearly big problems. The bar was a very good place, very political. Constant arguments with people always trying to convert each other. Odd Situationists knocking around being rude to everyone, a few proper Anarchists arguing with the Trotskyists, all the Trotskyists would be arguing with each other, and occasionally the Labour Party emerged and everyone howled them down.

CHRIS ROWLEY: I was at the LSE during the time of Marshall Bloom's and David Adelstein's prominence. More people were in the street or on demonstrations than were ever in classes or lectures. The Trotskyists fought each other with venom and vituperation beyond anything I could recall from school debating classes. It was hard to imagine that we were all on the same side, when someone would stand and accuse somebody of being 'a Leninist, a filthy Leninist, a splitter, an enemy of the people!' and all the rest of that stuff – grist for the movement of the proletariat bowels. They used to get intense, then they'd all be shouted down by the Socialist Society which would be 500 strong: it was like something out of Orwell. There was no right wing, and the Socialists were the centrists. There were no women, which was another reason why I didn't hang out at LSE. The first Saturday night affair I went to there had three girls and 200 young men drinking beer and staring at them. So I said, 'No more of this.'

DAVID WIDGERY: The first LSE student sit-in was in fact a very modest affair. It was about David Adelstein's right to write a letter to *The Times*, something like that. He was disciplined for writing this letter, for God's sake. Totally trivial. The students had a half-hour or maybe one-hour sit-in, which was considered to be the height of revolutionary *élan* at that time. Later on everyone under the sun was sitting in, regardless of whether they were students, workers, strippers, footballers, whatever, but at that stage it was a very exciting thing to do. And they had a march to support the sit-in with a banner that said 'Down with the Pedagogic Gerontocracy'.

DAVID ROBINS: During the occupation of the LSE the Trotskyist-led Student Union said, 'Occupy the library.' There was a lot of feeling about occupying the library because of the books, the sacred books. Before they could do anything the director, [Ralf] Dahrendorf, had these security gates built so you couldn't get into the library. They'd just been installed and the Trotskyists were talking about sitting down in front of the gates and standing in pickets and walking around saying 'No gates' and the anarchs listened to this meeting which was going on and on. Robin Blackburn of the International Millionaires Group: 'We think, comrades, that what we should do is blah, blah, blah . . .' Then Duffy Power got up, pissed out of his mind, and shouted, 'We're the International Mine's a Pint Committee and this over here is my friend from the Black Hand Gang and we think we should fuck the gates and take them away and burn them.' And they got screwdrivers and they went up and stole the gates.

ROBIN BLACKBURN: I was a lecturer at the LSE from 1967. Partly because of the occupation of the college in '67 the authorities decided that college shouldn't be used to assist things like the Vietnam Solidarity Campaign and should never again be open to things like being seized by the students. They put steel gates and grilles in strategic places throughout the corridors and staircases of the university. The Students' Union decided to ask the authorities to take them down, which of course they refused to do. Eventually the radical group in the Students' Union got a vote that the students themselves should directly tear down the gates, which they did, with the help of some building workers who were building the Barbican and with whom they had been involved. There had been a strike and people from the Socialist Society had been helping them picket and leaflet and so forth. So when the gates had to be taken down they were able to get a couple of building workers in who had the right equipment. I had actually had nothing to do with the decision to remove the gates but I did come out in public, and the papers quoted me afterwards, saying that they'd done the right thing. So the university authorities decided to give me the sack. That caused more reaction from the students and actually by this time the whole LSE had been closed down

– there was a lockout of the students and the staff. During these occupations and so on I did try to keep doing some teaching. We did courses on the sociology of revolution, that type of thing.

ALAN MARCUSON: One of the reasons I came to London was that things had just taken off at the LSE. They were all sitting on the steps, smoking joints, and it was the place to be. So I went to LSE. I met Dave Robins, I met Dick Pountain, Pete Avery, loads of people. That introduced me to the whole Situationist crowd and I had a good time. In the end I could just walk away from it so I could afford to be very very radical because I didn't have a degree on the line, and all those other revolutionary arseholes, when it really came down to it, had to finish their courses and get their jobs and secure their careers. And that's the reason, I believe, that the LSE failed – the revolutionaries wouldn't give up their goddamn careers.

It was very interesting and exciting but it was a complete fuck-around. Just a load of talk, endless, endless meetings and arguments and bad feeling and factions of the Left. I always wanted to go out and smash the doors down. There was a group of us who were basically into vandalism and were slowly dismantling all the bits of the university that we could lay our hands on and were considered very very irresponsible by the serious Left.

DICK POUNTAIN: When we met the Situationists, in '67, we realised this was what we wanted. When the LSE occupation happened it was a total free-for-all. I was very much involved in that. A bunch of us were doing posters and pamphlets and everything. They tried to set up this thing called the RSSF (Revolutionary Socialist Students' Federation) and they had this agonising conference in the occupied LSE where all these different sects just blathered their different dogmas. Towards the end of this, this white-haired guy got up on the stage and delivered this incredibly dramatic harangue denouncing them all as 'arseholes and bastards' and at the end of it he pointed up to this banner over the stage and said, 'And as for this . . . dogshit by any other name would smell as foul!' And we were so impressed by this guy that after they'd thrown him out we sought him out on the steps of the main LSE building, and it was John Gravelle. He was just meeting Chris Gray and Don Nicholson-Smith who were the British wing of the Situationists. We got chatting with them and discovered that they lived just round the corner in Notting Hill and that was it. I started going round to Chris Gray's.

There was this group came together round him and Don, who were the only officially accredited British Situationists, although they both got

249

thrown out soon afterwards. So all these people, based in Notting Hill came together and gradually formed this group called King Mob which was expelled from Situationist International for being a sect. They wouldn't tolerate any kind of tendencies or whatever and also our take was different from theirs: they were high-powered French intellectuals, we were rapidly becoming street hippies. They didn't like the street culture, they saw it even then as part of the 'Spectacle'; they didn't like drugs although they drank vast quantities of Calvados and red wine. They were undoubtedly correct – they predicted perfectly that it would all be co-opted and turned into a huge commodity, which it was. The 'Spectacle' is a very Hegelian notion. It was their idea of what the modern state uses instead of physical coercion to keep people in their place. The state still has coercion as the last resort, but by and large they don't need it. The 'Spectacle' is the mass media, very much bread and circuses brought up to date with the modern media. TV, film, stardom, the control of everyday life by work disciplines and all this kind of stuff. The Situationist revolution was to be the revolution of everyday life which involved breaking with all those things. This naturally fitted together with the hippie thing – except that they couldn't stand hippies.

ALAN MARCUSON: The Situationists were the first people ever to provide me with a rational explanation of our irresponsible behaviour and urges and to see everything, absolutely everything, in terms of political activity. They were much more fun, their writings were more fun, they were a more interesting group of people, they were doing more interesting things, their pamphlets were more interesting than the boring fucking Trots, who really were the most tiresome bunch of people I have ever come across. The kernel of what's wrong with the British Left can be found in the sort of Trot students who were around in the 60s.

ROBIN BLACKBURN: At the LSE it was quite interesting that it was American students who were very often the ones who knew how to stand up to authority, to answer back and to make demands, sometimes even slightly outrageous demands. There's a sort of arrogance and complacency about power in Britain which these Americans were beautifully able to puncture.

The management committee of the University of London Union (ULU) was dominated by the vice-chancellor. The Union was occupied by the students in support of the LSE occupation. As soon as the vice-chancellor heard about this he rushed over and called us into a meeting in the office of the administrator of the building. He proposed to negotiate with us, the idea being to get us to leave the building. Our idea had been that the building should serve as a facility for the LSE students, who had been locked out of their own college and were homeless. Some of the other Student Unions had agreed that this would be a good way of helping the LSE students. So he was sitting there negotiating with us and he'd actually put the keys of ULU on the table in front of him. We were arguing back quite strongly, then Paul Hoch, who was an American graduate student at the LSE, said, 'I don't think you understand the situation. We are occupying this building. This is a building meant for students,' and as he spoke, he made a swift gesture and scooped up the keys from the table and put them in his pocket. He said, 'We now control this institution and we intend to do with it as we like. And we intend to help the students at the LSE and we don't care about the rules and regulations you've been telling us about.' That was the end of the discussion.

DICK POUNTAIN: When King Mob was going at full blast, after the LSE sit-in there was a sit-in at the ULU and we got involved in that. It lasted several days. Everyone was sleeping on the floor and all that. The New Left crowd tried to run it. We gave Robin Blackburn a really bad time, howled him down, told him he was a wanker. They were very worried that we might damage things – don't scratch the paintwork – so a bunch of people went and bust open the swimming pool and had this huge swimming party. The whole thing was very fraught because you'd got this mass of students, the New Left people telling them to be serious and responsible, and King Mob telling them to get their rocks off, let it all hang out, etc. It was very iffy, because the great mass in the middle were swaying both ways. Only a minority supported us; the majority wanted to be quiet and respectable, but these two guys came out of the crowd and joined in with us and said, 'We're with you.' They were a couple of art students from Goldsmith's and one was called Fred Vermorel and the other was called Malcolm Edwards. They both had long, dirty khaki macs, a couple of impoverished art students. And of course Malcolm went on to finer things and became Malcolm McLaren, and in a lot of ways the whole Sex Pistols scam was the putting into practice of a lot of Situationist theories. It was a betrayal of it in the sense that it became part of the 'Spectacle', but he did really shock the bourgeoisie of the whole country, which is something that King Mob never did.

'I don't think the powers that be saw it coming'

JON GOODCHILD: Things started to get politicised. Everyone became aware that there were certain basic injustices, but nobody seemed to have any influence and even if you didn't like or approve of something like the Vietnam War your voice wasn't being heard anywhere. So we decided to voice it. And once you started you began to realise about other things, such as sexism, though it wasn't called that then. And when people like Germaine Greer turned up who were extremely articulate, the politicisation became more acute. We saw ourselves as very much a generation, very much akin to people in San Francisco, New York, Sydney . . .

There were other themes: England's fundamental racism. All through the 60s racism was a word that was never heard, and that was another issue that was being taken up. And the feeling that a general censorship existed. It was fairly obvious that certain things weren't being reported and if they were it was with an incredible slant and so there was a definite and very strong need for a free press. At *OZ* we had certain affiliations with *Black Dwarf*, which was a socialist paper, but we were never officially socialist. And the debates began to get very intense over dinner and in restaurants and everywhere. And they began to permeate the rock and roll world very rapidly – and I don't think the powers that be saw it coming. They thought it was just a few kids causing trouble until one day they turned around and it was a fully fledged movement.

MILES: In May '68 I was of course in France. Except that it was the South of France where I was enjoying a pleasant holiday in Antibes with my accountant! We didn't even know what was happening. We did vaguely notice that the garbage wasn't being collected and the phone didn't work too well but none of us could read French, so . . . In the end we managed to translate a bit and . . . 'Oh my God!' In the end Sue and Mike Henshaw and I drove back to London, which was absolutely fantastic. The auto-routes were all taken over. At the tollbooths there were just people collecting money for the strike. You'd throw some money in and they'd all cheer and sing 'God Save the Queen'.

Paris: 'You are called parasites, now be parasites'
DAVID ROBINS: There was an organisation called the Radical Student Alliance (RSA). I didn't have any political affiliations but I'd got pissed off with the non-politics of the underground, wanking on about drugs and stuff, and I was now proud to be a student, at least proud to be called a parasitical student which was one of the cries of the streets in Paris – 'You are called parasites, now be parasites.' So I went to Paris with a guy called Robert Wistrich. Also some French who'd been in London and were going back. We went to Ostend, cos you couldn't get into France. We stayed overnight at the Free University of Brussels,

252

where there was an occupation in progress. It was very much a fraternity: there were student cars leaving from Brussels to go to Paris. Indeed we heard that there were people from all over Europe heading the same way. They were expecting the police any moment and told us to stay – 'The action's here, man' – but we said sorry and left for Paris. About four or five of us crammed into one car and we went off, almost got killed on the road, driving all night.

We arrived in Paris at night. Loads of people around, flames, no cops, water everywhere and the most appalling pong of tear gas. And none of the shops had any glass in their windows. Robert said to me, 'At last, the revolution has arrived.' There were lots of foreigners, but very few Brits. Lot of Germans, Americans, Swiss, Dutch. When we got to the Sorbonne the strike was in progress, the *quartier* was full of workers, arguing . . . unbelievable. We introduced ourselves and we had names of other people to prove we weren't cops. The worst thing to be was a revolutionary tourist so you enrolled in one of two services for the revolution. The whole thing was run by the *Comités d'Action*, about 25 of them. Most of them were student-dominated but they claimed workers, intellectuals and artists as well. They had meetings all day and all night in the Odéon. So we enlisted in the *Service d'Ordre*, we had to, in the Beaux Arts in Rue Bonaparte. This was one of the places where visitors were billeted. The whole college was filled with beds: but nobody slept, everybody talked.

At this time it was very intense. The days passed just like a blur. There was a fantastic demonstration one day when the cops chased us down this street and the people dragged us in off the street and gave us shelter. This very smart gallery owner just said, 'Come in here.' The adrenalin was flowing. I'm not a hero but this was a time when you didn't actually feel fear. And as it went on things became nastier. It wasn't so much the cops, there were also these people who would emerge out of the walls, criminals, the *barbousses*, the scumbags, and there'd be these dangerous-looking guys wandering around; it was very lawless with no cops. Then came the death of Bobby Kennedy, and there was a big meeting at the Odéon and a minute's silence.

The one event that I took part in particularly was the occupation of the British Council. Opposite the Sorbonne was the British Council building which remained open throughout the May revolt. Some Brits thought that was ridiculous – we should do something. We all went over to the British Council and there was this amazing scene where we occupied them. It was a truly British occupation: 'Should we occupy the library?' 'No, no – that's stealing . . .' 'We should speak in French.' 'No, this is the *British* Council occupation,' and so on. It lasted till we lost interest and pissed off.

When the strike began to break down, we went out of the *quartier* for the first time to visit some comrades who were putting out some pamphlets. We went across the bridge into the rich area of Paris and when we came back we found there was this ring of steel. So at seven o'clock in the morning we walked back through them. There were lorries of CRS on all the bridges all along the Seine, they were massing. It was like a military exercise. Military trucks, guys with guns, tear gas and so on. Then the word went around that they were looking for the foreign students, cos they were seen as the troublemakers. We had 24 hours to get out.

This was Chris Bott's finest hour. He'd been at the British Council too. He came from Essex University where he was a 'known troublemaker'. We knew the trouble was coming, but we'd also heard that a lot of the car factories had been occupied and that a lot of them were flying black flags, which meant they were anarchists and thus non-communist dominated. There was one in Flans, the Renault works. We were all called together by the *Comité* people who said they were looking for an international brigade of students to go to relieve and fight alongside the worker-comrades at this factory as the police were planning to go in and smash them. Chris Bott volunteered. I did not. A night in *les cages* was more than I could manage. Chris and about 50 guys went off to Flans, where one of the workers was killed in the ensuing troubles, but he was picked up before he actually got there. He was deported. I also felt that our place was not really in the factories and that we would be deceiving ourselves.

What we thought would happen would be a collapse of the government and the bourgeoisie. Everyone was on strike: TV people, footballers, everyone. What we thought was that some form of democratic assembly would emerge. I went to a meeting at the Gare du Nord. What I was doing was checking whether the trains were running, because I was on my way home and it was very dangerous to hitchhike. The rightists were pretending to give lifts to students then beating the shit out of them. At the Gare du Nord there was a mass meeting taking place and they were debating ending the strike. The unions were telling them [the railway workers] to go back to work but the anarchists and people weren't. And they went back and the tannoy was saying 'Bon voyage' and the first train took off and there was applause and I was on it. You got to the ferry and there were cops on either side as you went on.

A lot of French comrades came with us, many of whom were wanted, and when we got to the other side we started singing and causing a big distraction as they tied up and meanwhile two comrades leapt off, over

254

a big gap onto the quay, over the railway sidings, with a British bobby after them. The Customs knew we'd done this and they took about thirty of us into this room. I had a small bag, packed with posters, leaflets and stuff, and they kept me for hours and hours. They kept saying I wasn't English. They gave us a very hard time and confiscated some of my stuff. I mean basically I wanted to keep my souvenirs of the trip.

Got back, Hornsey College was in revolt and I went to meetings and told them what was happening in Paris and nobody believed us.

PETER BROWN: All of a sudden the revolution breaks out in Paris and after a whole lot of nonsense there a lot of them ran away to London and other places and we get about a dozen student revolutionaries move in. I think they squatted on the first floor of this house. They were outrageous, completely unreasonable. Us druggies living in the basement were nice and quiet and discreet. These crackpots had obviously been followed by the English version of the CIA as soon as they arrived and they were so obvious. The girls used to sit on the windowsill, legs open, no drawers, waving spray painted flags with all these slogans on them.

JOHN HOPKINS: A lot of people went off to Paris in May '68, but it was my job to edit *IT* at exactly that time. There was some politicisation before that: a lot of people demonstrated in Fleet Street about the Stones bust, against the *News of the World*. I was in the Scrubs for six months in '67, the last half. I'm grateful for the support, but all I know is that although there were a lot of people running around with signs saying 'Free Hoppy' they didn't get a minute off my sentence. I don't hold that against them, but looking back and seeing what you can and can't do in the world, it may be that running around with banners isn't always the best way to solve something. I think that a lot of what we did was making gestures because we didn't really have the mechanism of how the world worked down well enough.

CHRIS ROWLEY: In Britain it was pretty quiet. It was very hard to struggle against the nanny state, and the middle-class youth who took LSD and largely made up the movement in Britain were pacific. So alienated from it all that the idea of banding together and demonstrating was beyond them. It was not easy to maintain a high profile as a radical political activist. London was a huge party and everyone was having a good time except for those poor hippies who were on the outside and dying of overdoses of heroin or sleeping on the streets.

The 'Revolution': 'We were the flowering of the victory of 1945'

DAVID WIDGERY: I knew exactly what the revolution was going to be: workers taking over, the barricades, an actual change of power. It would be like Russia in 1917 or Spain in 1936 or Hungary in 1956 or the May events in France, which had not just been a student thing but had very rapidly become a massive workers' strike with the state faced by a mass of organised workers. I had a fairly classic political conception of class struggle and that change of power would be extra-parliamentary. But I was also convinced that in the modern post-electronic cultures all our previous imagery of revolutions had been very Russian and that we needed to look around for new kinds of ways of transmitting our ideas, a new imagery and new techniques. I saw the underground press as a disseminator of subversive ideas. I hoped that when the people had got the hang of the ideas they would be encouraged to read a bit more and perhaps become more fully-fledged socialists or Marxists.

HORACE OVE: The revolution was based, as far as I'm concerned, on the idea that there was going to be change. Great change in how things were being run in the world at that time. Maybe racism would come to an end in every racist country, wars like what was taking place in Vietnam would come to an end and we would see a more loving, understanding, communicating world ... Looking back, it seems romantic. At the time you felt there was going to be a lot of change and from a black perspective this was good because before that it was cold and it was grey and people didn't relate to you and you were on the outside. Racism was suspended for a few years in the 60s. The 60s did give something. People look back and they're very critical: flower power, drugs, what did they do? They did a lot. They opened out a lot, they exposed a lot, they questioned a lot, and I think they stopped a war. And it brought people together. And for the first time you had working-class heroes.

NINA FISHMAN: My burning desire for complete change had to do with a mixture of three or four things. One of them was that for my generation, the idealism of the Second World War was contained in every single one of us. The Atlantic Charter, the egalitarianism, the commitment to democracy which had been involved in winning that war had rubbed off and been socialised into everyone I knew. If you have that kind of positive idealism socialised into you from birth it has to be an important force. Had France not happened I think that the politics would have stayed much more where it had been, and that the drug culture would have gone off and done its own thing. France pushed these things together.

256

There is ultimately no doubt in my mind that we were the flowering of the victory of '45.

ROSIE BOYCOTT: It's hard to define the 'Revolution' but there were certain specifics: there would be no taxes, there would be no Conservative Party, there would be no forcing people into doing what they didn't want to do, there would be no discrepancy between rich and poor ... What we were offering was a freedom to do what you wanted: to take drugs if you want, to stay up all night, to work your own hours, to not be regimented, not to have to prove one's success by dressing in a particular way or catching the 8:15 to Waterloo. To prove that there was a different way of running the world. And I assumed that we'd all grow up in some way running the world.

JOHN LLOYD: I don't believe the 'Revolution' ever really had any meaning to me at all. God knows if we believed that what we said we believed in would ever become the norm. Were society to be organised according to the rules that we were supposed to be mapping out, we might have been horrified. It was a conflation of half-digested political ideas, with, much more importantly, a desire for a new form of personal liberation, and I think all of us had that kind of feeling – that was what gave it energy – a desire to slough off the internal tensions and the internal inhibitions that we were experiencing. The underground, so-called, gave us a conduit for trying to do that. For me it was very much this unresolved thing about my childhood, lack of fatherhood. That did give it the energy. It gave me the energy to work through a personal psychology in a public manner (which is a pompous way of putting it). That was the most important thing at the time – this interaction between the public and the private. I don't want to say it was all baloney, because it wasn't, but did I have a serious project of trying to change the world? I can't quite grasp that I did, but what I did want to do was impress on a number of people the perception that the way they were living was wrong. That the straight way of living, the repression of personal relationships, the repression to some extent of ideas, the repressiveness of work routine, family routine, and – insofar as it was still important – religious routine, was confining and restricting on the mind and could be by human agency lifted. As you get older you realise the constraints that are put on any form of liberty or liberation, but at the time it did seem as though there was a real promise of an open-mindedness and an openness of relationship which was different to what had gone before. Only afterwards you realise how exploitative it was, how far you were following your own games, your own pursuit of your own desires; at the time it did seem as though

257

you were opening up, forcing open a whole number of closed gates. People enjoyed the era. They liked it, it was a good time in life, they were never so much alive.

JEFF NUTTALL: I had a faith that, given liberation, the human creative spirit would predominate. I imagined some kind of a Stone Age village, really. People would build their own houses imaginatively and live there sophisticatedly and in a literate way and with a total permissiveness and that they would live with their hands and with their minds and they would not be dictated to by anybody selling them anything and they would not welcome anybody preaching to them. There would be difficulties, there would be nothing to stop people stealing, there would be no police. Eventually that would dwindle away and people would actually have the opportunity of coming into their true self, which was generous and creative and permissive. We believed in politics with a small 'p'. But we didn't believe in programmes and we didn't believe in law.

JO DURDEN-SMITH: Somebody in New York told me that he was going to the racetrack and he was going to bet all his money. This money would be of no use in the new era, and the new era was due to start next Monday. The degree of self-delusion involved in that was very very great. It's absolutely ludicrous, but it was believed, and it was believed by a lot of people.

The Deviants: 'The worst record in the history of man'
MICK FARREN: Times changed, very rapidly. 1967-8 was a long cold winter and most prankster occupations failed with the waning weather. We ceased to be the Fugs and turned into this amphetamine shriek band. It all got a little out of control. People were taking drugs, really taking drugs. I took my first acid in a biker bar and became profoundly disturbed; Russell Hunter was shooting methedrine and kids were coming up wanting to sell you pills, up and down and sideways, everywhere. We had two organ players who both died: Dennis, who took STP. He was a nice guy and then he took STP and didn't come back for a week and when he came back he was like a mild-mannered Sid Vicious and made noises on his keyboard that sounded like a B-52. I thought that was quite fun but everybody else hated it. And eventually we left him behind somewhere – we couldn't handle him and he got really obnoxious about drugs too. Sandy had turned up by now. As had Boss, who was the roadie. And Tony Wiggins and all these peculiar girls. Russell was
258

drumming. Steve Sparks managed us for a while, and then nobody managed us. Our songs were not pretty and not protest – generally about massive drug hallucinations. The Deviants went through hell with a black truck, and we all thought we were going to die – all through the winter of '68 we were hungry, just barely alive. By that time it started getting kind of oppressive. We played Newcastle City Hall, us and the Pink Floyd, Tomorrow, Pretty Things. It was a great time – we all got laid and everything was wonderful, took a lot of drugs backstage – but the kids were coming in past lines of police, and you didn't want to venture beyond your no-go area – backstage and the hotel – they busted hotel rooms too, and it was just getting stupid, they were searching trucks going down the motorway, and busting John Lennon every third day and so on. Simultaneously the colleges, which were our actual financial bread and butter, started blowing up, having sit-ins, which meant that we didn't get paid any more. Which upset us.

MILES: This was the era when Peter Shertser's company Underground Impresarios was in operation. It was formed to bring out a Deviants album called *Ptoof*. It had the *IT* girl on the label. John Peel and I wrote the sleevenotes, Kipps did the cover and it was distributed through *IT*. The company later went on to become Red Lightning.

PETER SHERTSER: Micky Farren told me he was going to start an independent record label to put out the Deviants' album, *Ptoof*. He'd found an investor: Nigel Samuel. In my summer vacation from college he said, 'Why don't you come and sell it. You know all about records, you must be able to sort the record business out.' I knew nothing. Then he said, 'The commission will be 20%.' For 20% I knew! Samuel had this *potz* running it called Nick. Long blond hair, very nice accent, suitcase, dressing like a smart hippie. If ever a guy looked out of place it was him. I thought, 'I've seen some mugs in my time, but this guy takes the cake.' I could tell from the off: here is a punter, a prize A-1 punter. He's telling me they have a million quid to fuck around with: that's the *wrong* thing to start me off. An expense chitty walked in before I got the job! So there it is: boom! I've had a go and I'm selling them. I don't know what I'm doing but I'm learning, finding out, punting, one thing and another and all of a sudden I'm selling records. I'm getting 20% of the entire turnover. Real money in those days.

STEVE SPARKS: I have the honour of having produced the worst record in the history of man, which was *Ptoof*. When I was going down to UFO and working at Witchseason Micky saw me as this sort of East

259

End hustler — I can't imagine why — and decided that I could be his Andrew Loog Oldham. So he asked me if I'd manage the Deviants at a weekly salary of £7, which I never got anyway cos it was the Deviants. The band was the classical, original Deviants: Mick, Russell, Sandy, and the other idiot guitarist whose name I can never remember who did the acoustic bit on *Ptoof* to prove he could play the guitar. And he did — prove he could play the guitar — but not very well. What the Deviants did was to produce the first independent album: *Ptoof* was made entirely outside the then record-production establishment. It was financed by Nigel Samuel. He never paid us our PRS money on the album. Some time later I rang up the PRS to find out about suing him and they said, 'Certainly, we'll put you in touch with our lawyer,' who was Lord Goodman, so I said, 'Thank you very much,' and hung up the phone.

DAVID GOODMAN: By '68 the Social Deviants had been and gone and the Deviants were evolving. They were just making *Ptoof*. They were just about to get some gigs together and they needed a road crew. Mac had recommended Tony Wiggins cos he could drive and me cos I was big and could carry the gear. I thought, 'Right, that sounds like a good route into groups,' so off I went. They weren't very good musically but their hearts were definitely in the right place. Micky Farren, God bless his cotton socks, wasn't a very good singer but really had so much fucking front it was amazing. He had the balls to go out there and do what he wanted to do.

STEVE SPARKS: All the Deviants albums were recorded entirely on methedrine. What would happen was you'd break the top of the amp, drink an inch out of the top of a can of Coca-Cola and pour the amp of methedrine in the Coca-Cola, shake it up, drink some and pass it round. We had Glyn John's younger brother for our engineer and he would take his Coke and have a sip and pass the can on and we used to get four times the length of session that we'd paid for, because he didn't know what was happening. We'd be booked in for a four-hour session and twelve hours later he'd still be there.

PETER SHERTSER: *Ptoof* was successful: it was totally unique, Mick was known, the sleeve was an exemplary production, cost a fortune. We were starting to export it and this, that and the other and I'm thinking, 'What is this? I'm at college. I'm getting eighteen quid a week grant to study boring nonsense about psycho-pharmacology, and when I graduate I'll earn fifty quid a week. What kind of game's this? I'm getting two, three hundred notes here. I've got my own desk, an electric typewriter, all

260

expenses paid and I'm working with a load of *potzes* who don't know what day it is and a millionaire who looks like a beanpole.' So I said to Ian, 'Look, there's got to be a caper here.' So Ian said, 'Let's have a go. Our hero's coming over, Walter Horton, harmonica player, king of the Chicago Blues harmonica. Let's record him.' We borrow the dosh off the folks and we go down and book a studio. So there we are: what do we do? We don't know where to start. So Mick says, 'I'll help.' And he did. So we take the guy up to *IT* to rehearse and it was brilliant, but he wouldn't let us record it. The rehearsal was absolutely magic, ten times better than the session. We're waiting to go to the session and he's sitting on the bog with a bottle of whisky, wiping his arse with old *IT*s. I thought: 'Oh no.' And it started: we've got to the studio, the ceiling's collapsed. There's arguments with the musicians, water's dripping through, Mick's trying to sort it all out, and in the end we've got an album that's half real ethnic blues, and half Martin Stone, who used to be in Chilli Willi and the Action, playing Indian ragas. Complete nonsense. You can't sell a record like that.

Then a guy comes to the offices, Seymour Stein: 'I want to lease this record. *Ptoof.*' I say, 'What are you talking about?' and he names a few thousand dollars and I think, 'Twenty per cent, maybe for this I'll tell Nick 50%.' So I ask him and he says, 'Yes,' and I thought, 'You *potz*!' But there we are, I've done a deal with this incredibly sharp, agile, Jewish guy who went on to become vice-president of Warner Brothers and ran one of the most successful independent record labels in America. Then he said, 'Why don't we do a deal? Find talent for me, new English bands.' We did a deal, a few records, but what a nightmare! And we learnt about the record industry, a very quick course of knowledge: it sucked.

PETER JENNER: The Deviants were the godfathers of punk. They've got as good a claim as anybody on that. They were working-class boys who couldn't play: what more do you want? Lots of energy, lots of enthusiasm, loads of bottle, and they articulated anger very well.

ROBERT WYATT: I didn't know Mick Farren well and I don't think he particularly welcomed what he thought we [the Soft Machine] represented. But I certainly admire *him* because he was a sort of protopunk and saw elements immediately that were false. He heard the false notes being rung all around him at a time when people thought it was all in tune.

PETER JENNER: Micky's problem was that he couldn't sing. He had all the poses, all the attitude and he did do UFO at the All Saints Hall. I remember his specially getting a guitar in to smash at the end of the show, and with great effort he was smashing away and of course the bastard thing wouldn't break. It was hysterical.

PETER SHERTSER: We used to tell them, 'You sound like shit!' and they used to say, 'Can't you be more critical?'

MICK FARREN: We got signed on with Peter Jenner at Blackhill and we started getting cash-money gigs and everything was getting real good, for a while. We used to go out as a double bill with the Pretty Things almost continually, which turned into terrible mayhem whereby the Pretty Things would come out and they'd sing their new record and they'd sing their last record and then they'd start to play 'Why?' by the Byrds and we'd all pile on the stage and make this godawful noise for about half an hour. We'd play whatever records we'd done and then we'd play 'Sister Ray' by the Velvet Underground.

STEVE SPARKS: The time of the Deviants was just sheer bliss. Boss was our roadie, selling LSD from Ilford ... We burnt down a hall in Colchester by letting off outdoor fireworks on the stage. We did a free gig at Essex University and hit down the doors to the canteen and gave out all the ice cream in the place – this was our contribution to the revolution at Essex University: free ice cream. And we stole a side of bacon as well; we had bacon for an awful long time.

Time Out: 'It was time that somebody started to catalogue what was happening'

TONY ELLIOTT: *Time Out* was started [in 1968] when I decided to do it. Working with Stephanie [Hughes] and Bob Harris, who was a friend I'd met through an art student at Hornsey, *Time Out* was very much a question of listing the events that were happening under appropriate sections. I told Pete Jenner at Blackhill about it and he immediately said, 'Oh, a hip *What's On*. Great!' and that was what everyone felt. Everybody needed it and understood what I was trying to do. And Richard [Neville] said, 'Well now you can go and get yourself a Rolls-Royce,' and Jim Haynes was very helpful. He said, you need to ring so-and-so and so-and-so for poetry, and all the rest of it. *IT* did have a What's Happening page, which was national and which was suffering from the fact that the *IT* people felt it was a boring thing to do and people working on it had let the quality of it slip.

JIM HAYNES: In *IT* I also wanted to have at least one page, and sometimes we had two, of a pre-*Time Out* free listings. When Tony Elliott decided to do *Time Out* he came in and said, 'Do you think there's room for two?' and we said, sure there's room for two – do it. I always saw that there was a connection between advertising something, giving it free publicity and making it happen, creating an audience for it. A lot of things happened as a result of *IT* and *Time Out* giving them space.

COURTNEY TULLOCH: All kinds of things started happening and people were literally 'doing their own thing'. People, four, five, six of them, seven, eight, nine, whatever, felt they were able to sit down wherever they were and do what they wanted to do, what they thought was right for them. And this is where your hip capitalists, your Tony Elliotts, and your promoters are starting to germinate. *IT* had had a listings page and Tony took it over and never looked back. That was when Hoppy was in nick. If he hadn't been in the nick they wouldn't have let Tony have it, because it was his idea and he wouldn't have let it go. So they sold it, whether for money or through idiocy or through laziness, cos it was a lot of work compiling a listings all the time.

TONY ELLIOTT: Hoppy was a very interesting guy who was then doing BIT. I made contact with him because BIT was going to be a kind of information exchange. I went round to his flat and although he didn't have computers yet he was already putting together an incredibly large filing system. Filecards, boxes . . . and he had this incredibly grandiose plan to catalogue everything possible and you'd be able just to ring up and information would be provided free. So it was natural that I should come into contact with him. He wasn't particularly helpful but when we had the first copy I went up to the Roundhouse where BIT were having their opening party, and he made a remark not dissimilar to Richard's one about the Rolls-Royce. He said basically that it was absolutely fantastic and he couldn't believe that anybody hadn't done it before.

GRAHAM KEEN: Tony Elliott came in one day with Stephanie Hughes and John Leaver. They were just fresh-faced kids from college. We had a chat and he said he was starting up this magazine and we just said, fine. He could take over listings. Whether or not that undermined the *IT* circulation I'm not so sure; it was just the freemasonry of the time.

TONY ELLIOTT: It was time that somebody started to catalogue what was happening. So we just did it very simply. We just worked through areas like poetry or politics, non-West-End films and theatre and all the rest of it. After all, this whole 60s thing was very London. I started off designing *Time Out* for about the first twelve issues, then a guy called Paul White-head came in. And Pearce Marchbank started very early. In 1970. There was Verina Glaessner, who was a funny Australian lady who made contact, saying did we want some film reviews. And we thought, 'Well, why not?'

MICHELENE WANDOR: Tony Elliott was never the sort of large-scale entrepreneur that Richard Branson became. I have a real residual fondness for Tony, although we were on opposite sides of the fence very often. Tony is very recognisable to me: he's a piece of suburban cottage industry and at one level I think he could not bear it to grow. I remember endless discussions when people were talking about *Time Out* expanding into books, for example, and Tony somehow didn't want anything that was going to be unmanageably big. He's essentially a small shopkeeper and if you're a small shop with a very good turnover you can do very well. If you continue expanding and over-capitalising you then run into quite a lot of danger. He's a suburban lad, that's his ethos, that's the ideology and that's why he isn't Richard Branson or Felix Dennis. Tony also had this great enthusiasm for the listings concept. For jam-packed bits of dynamite in a short number of words.

And Pearce Marchbank gave it its design, those brilliant covers. A lot of *Time Out*'s success is to do with all the contradictions that make up Tony. It was essentially his enthusiasm and his ability in the early days to be open to freshness – a certain innocence about him, and a real conservatism as well. It's probably true to say that he's still looking for that one perfect night out – a bit of American-college-kid-ism in a way.

SUE MILES: What was important was that you had this amateur, nutty, disorganised rabble that was the original underground press, overlaid with serious business people like Tony Elliott, Richard Branson, the second generation; they could see what could be done. Elliott came into *IT* in his tennis shoes and said he wanted to do a listings magazine and they said, 'Take it.' Anyone else could have seen the potential. The new people had less confused politics, much more pragmatic, much more merchants. So you got *Time Out* which could parcel up a watered-down version of the underground press into a commercial product. Tony's really a straight-up Tory. His aim was to run a magazine that he could pick up and find every single decent place to eat in within a quarter of a mile of Primrose Hill.

PEARCE MARCHBANK: When I arrived there *Time Out* got out by the skin of its teeth every fortnight. It took a week to print – because of its small size it had to go through a book-binding machine. It was me and John Leaver who really pushed for the weekly format. Him for the advertising, me for the feeling that the information should be absolutely fresh. The lead time was three weeks by the end of the fortnight and these little fringe theatres and rock venues didn't know what the fuck they were doing that far away. I spent my first fortnight at *Time Out* interviewing everyone who was in the building, asking them what they were trying to do. Then I re-organised the entire workings of *Time Out*, and redivided the way the information came out in the magazine into different sections and invented sections like 'Fringe Theatre', which was the first time it existed as a collective description. Information about all the stuff that had come out of the late 60s – the fringe theatre, the rock clubs, the independent films – needed organisation and I was able to encompass the content of the underground and put it into a form that had nothing to do with the underground.

TONY ELLIOTT: What was important was that we weren't exclusively dedicated to the alternative society. The alternative world was obviously a stimulus for what I did, but if you look at early *Time Out*s you'll see that we were immediately listing Middle Earth next to Marquee and whatever else. We printed 5000 of the first one, we probably sold 3500. That was very good.

MICHELENE WANDOR: *Time Out* was absolutely fantastic. It was a living contradiction. I think up until the final takeover by capitalism in 1981 *Time Out* was *the* survivor of the 60s. What it did was very cleverly combine a democratic open approach to cultural happenings, cultural events with a political edge to them, and soft-edged capitalism.

TONY ELLIOTT: We did have politics. There was a section in the first issue called 'The Fuzz', subsequently changed to 'Agitrop' and then to 'Politics'. 'Marches and Demos/Meet the Fuzz'. Embarrassing now, but totally natural at the time. We put an incredible amount of effort into actually running that section and the listings were telling people what marches and demonstrations were on, where you could hear certain speakers and whatever. And that sort of thing was part of your life then. It was as natural as going to the cinema.

Marc Bolan: 'An enormous amount of canoodling in the office'

JUNE BOLAN: One night at Blackhill, where I was working, Peter and Andrew heard a very odd record on John Peel's late-night programme. They brought it into the office and I listened to it. I said, 'That sounds extraordinary. What's he called?' It was still Marc Bolan, not yet Tyrannosaurus Rex. Then the next week John played another one, Peter listened to that too and then he found out where Marc was. They said to me, 'He's playing at Ealing College' – they used to do lunchtime sessions there. So I went in the Floyd's Rolls-Royce, and there were Marc and Steve Took. I went in as the representative from Blackhill. Walked in and Marc was sitting there cross-legged with a little AC-30, a bent coat-hanger with a microphone on it as the mike stand, and a guitar. And a presence you just couldn't believe. It was stunning. He had a pair of old boots of his mother's, trousers with holes in, his old school jacket out at the elbow, straight hair (he never had curly hair then – I got him to have curly hair cos I stopped him putting grease on it, made him wash it and leave it). I watched them and I spoke to them both and then went back to the office after I'd driven them home. Marc lived in a prefab in Wimbledon, right by the dog track. Peter and Andrew said, 'What do you think?' and I said, 'They're great. Marc Bolan's amazing, extraordinary. He gave me the same feeling I had when I first saw Syd Barrett.' So Peter rang him and made an appointment for him to come into the office on the following Monday. So about midday this thing, this scruffy little urchin came in.

PETER JENNER: David Platz put us onto Marc Bolan. He published everybody at that time – the Beatles, the Stones, the Who, the Floyd . . . Platz had a record company with Denny Cordell who had as his sidekick Tony Visconti. Tony Visconti discovered Marc Bolan, or rather came across him, because he'd been John's Children before and now he was Tyrannosaurus Rex. Peel had picked him up and there he was on the Perfumed Garden, perfumed gardening away with John Peel, who would take him to all his gigs. So Platz said, 'Why don't you look after Marc Bolan?' and we met and said, 'Great, let's do it.' He comes in and he starts doing it and it's all going rather well. It's beautiful, hippie, cross-legs, buttercup sandwiches. We add to the thing, promo, professionalism . . . it all starts going terrifically well. The Floyd are going well and we're thinking, 'We've got to become like NEMS, we've got to become an empire, like Epstein . . .' and all the rest of it – megalomania. June is working for us and June and he start falling in love and this led to an enormous amount of canoodling in the office.

JUNE BOLAN: I was with Marc ten years – lived together for three and a half, married for seven. I always worked for him, I loved him. The day he came into the office he went into Peter's room, which was next door to mine, and I was typing and suddenly something hit me on the head and I stopped typing. It was like an electric shock, the most extraordinary thing. I'll never know or love anybody like that again, ever. He finished his meeting with Peter, and he went. Two hours later the phone rang and I answered it, and it said, 'June, it's Marc Bolan. Could you come and see me?' I went into Andrew and Peter's and said, 'Marc has just phoned and he wants to see me.' We all presumed he wanted to discuss his contracts or whatever. So they said, 'Yes, take the car and go over to the prefab.'

It was a beautiful hot summer's day and Marc answered the door and he said, 'Would you like some muesli? We can sit out in the garden.' And we had this bowl of muesli and sat there and he said, 'I'm in love with you. I've just written you a poem.' (I've still got it.) He was living with his mother and I was living with Mick Milligan the jeweller, who I'd lived with for four years, and that night I left home in my van and went round to Marc's house, knocked on his door. He came out, told his mother he was going to Brighton with a friend for the weekend. We lived on Wimbledon Common for four nights in my van, then we found the attic in Blenheim Crescent for two pounds eight and six a week. And it was wonderful and I never regretted a minute of it.

SUMI JENNER: Andrew King came back from his honeymoon to find June and Marc in his bed. His wife wasn't too pleased . . .

PETER JENNER: There would be June, who was meant to be answering the phones and doing all those things that women were meant to do back then, and she would be constantly canoodling, and they'd be staring into each other's eyes. She'd apparently done it with Syd too. I'd missed that, but I couldn't help noticing it with Marc. It really was very intense. Finally it got to the crunch and I said to her, 'I don't mind what you do. It's up to you. But you can either just look after Marc, or you can have nothing to do with him and just look after other things, or you can leave and be Mrs Marc and just live with Marc and be in love. I don't mind, that's up to you. But what we can't do is have you sitting round in the office with him on your lap.' (It was definitely *him* sitting on *her* lap.) Instantly they left. Kerfuffle. He sent a note to Andrew saying that he hated me and I was an offensive person. He had this precious writing, little stars on the 'i's, slightly runic lettering. Not only was I interfering in his life, but the most important thing was that I had interfered with his art by suggesting that he should go electric. This was his excuse for leaving, it wasn't actually about June. I had indeed suggested this. We were doing very well but we needed something else to get into the charts. It all seemed commercial, but it needed something extra. He then left, and within months, or even weeks, he'd gone electric and June was his manager. But I always had a soft spot for June, I think she was lovely.

Bolan himself was a complete arsehole, the way he turned over Peel, and everything else. Quite clearly he was just a very ambitious little kid who wanted to become a pop star. He was feeding all the rest of us this bullshit which we bought. He'd sussed that the way through for him was by being a little hippie. He used me and he used John Peel. Peel's investment was far deeper, a personal commitment. He waved the flag for Bolan all the way through, until Bolan became huge and then Bolan gave him the old heave-ho in such a cynical fashion.

JOHN PEEL: I was always aware, I wasn't so stupid that I didn't see that Marc had a harder side to his character than I was generally seeing. This never really came out until he became a star. He just moved on to other people, which to me was very upsetting, because I thought he was my best friend at the time. Then all of a sudden phone calls weren't returned, someone else would say, 'Marc's really busy, he'll phone you later, man,' and so on.

JUNE BOLAN: Tony Visconti, who was working for Essex Music then, saw Marc and Steve Took at Middle Earth. He went off to see Denny Cordell and said he'd found this band . . . Denny wanted to take them over, but Marc had more empathy with Tony and he got them recorded. And it all started there. So it was 'Ride a White Swan' and 'Deborah' and off it went. Success was wonderful at first. All those years of deprivation and cold-water flats, you suddenly had . . . I had five cars. I had a 4.2 Jag, a Daytona Ferrari, a very old white Roller into which I had black windows put, a Radford Mini and an AC Cobra. I love cars, they don't argue with you. They don't hurt you unless you drive them badly and then you kill yourself. And nobody else drove them. Marc never drove, which makes it especially sad that he was killed in a car crash. People used to say, 'My God, why on earth do you need five cars?' but we did need five cars. There were cars you needed to go to grand occasions in, there were cars when you wanted a fast whiz up the motorway, the Mini I used to go shopping in, the AC was totally only mine, it was hand-built, aluminium body that never rusted and it looked splendid.

KEITH MORRIS: I had a picture of Marc sitting at the wheel of a car. He never drove and the reason for this was he always believed he'd die in a car crash. He felt not driving was a way round it. We were at this film set, *Born to Boogie*, a particularly dreadful film, and he said, 'Hey man, come here. I want you to get a picture of me sitting in this car.' So he sat in the car and I took the picture and he said, 'No one has ever before nor ever will again get a picture of me sitting at the wheel of a car and you've got a very unique picture – because I will die in a car crash.'

JEFF DEXTER: I'd known Marc Bolan since 1961 at the Lyceum, when he wasn't Bolan, but Marc Feld, the face. He first came to fame about '62 when they did a feature on him in *Town* magazine. He always looked really sharp. He was one of the sharpest of that bunch at the time. In February '63 Marc and I went to see *Summer Holiday* together, and he said, 'I want to be a star like Cliff Richard, I want to be bigger than him, will you manage me?' I said, 'Marc, you can't sing.'

JUNE BOLAN: He had been a great mod. 'John Collier the window to watch', *Town* ... all the magazines. Him and Micky Sugar – they were where it was at if you were in London. Smart Yiddish boys from Stamford Hill. Not so Jewish, but very smart. Amazing clothes, extraordinary, sort of Perry Como.

PETER JENNER: Took was around, but he never counted, he was just the other one. It was always Bolan's group: he wrote the songs, he did the singing. He gave us all this buttercup sandwich bit and I bought it all. I hadn't known Marc Feld: that was a whole different thing and he'd put it behind him. You were allowed to do that back then, you could transform, you could see the light, be born again and become a hippie.

JUNE BOLAN: Steve Took was always a bit of a dipstick. Rather sad. Very kind, terribly nice, came from an awful household south of the water. Another acid casualty. Marc left him in America cos he was so tripped out. Marc never smoked, never. He'd hold a joint, because people expected him to, but he didn't like what it did.

RUSSELL HUNTER: On the day that T. Rex were supposed to go to America for the first time, Marc had gone home, done his washing, got changed, was all ready to go. Off to the airport: no Took. So Marc got on the plane and flew off. Took had been at the Speakeasy till about seven o'clock in the morning and people had to climb through this third-floor window, wake him up, put him unconscious into a taxi, take him to the airport, slap him around enough so he could write his name and put him on a plane four hours later. He did get there but he was promptly sent home again and fired.

STEVE MANN: I met Steve Took at the Festival of the Flower Children at Woburn. Even then it was obvious that he and Bolan cordially detested each other. Basically Took had a very, very small talent. He had an incredible talent for taking drugs. Later on he always used to try to get up on stage and jam with the Fairies and they'd throw him off as quickly as they could. This terrible shambling figure emerging from the wings, knocking over cymbals.

STEVE SPARKS: Witchseason turned down Tyrannosaurus Rex . . . 'Blah, blah, blah, what a load of rubbish, they'll never make it.' Good move. Not quite as good as turning the Beatles down . . . I saw Took just before he died, in Dingwalls. 'Grrrbllhh, Steve . . . terrible, man, ggrrbbllhh.' I knew Bolan from when he was a mod, when he was Mark Feld: he was a little shit, a cocky little shit.

Paladin Books: 'There were people who never read anything else'

JO DURDEN-SMITH: Paladin Books, part of Granada, was terribly important in all of this. It was set up by Reg Davis-Poynter and Sonny Mehta. Sidney Bernstein, who ran Granada, went to Reg Davis-Poynter and said, 'I want to do something in publishing that's like *World in Action*.' That was the essential brief. He hired a man called Tony Richardson, who was dying of Hodgkinson's disease, and those in the know knew this. And they put him together with this odd Indian guy called Sonny Mehta. His one great passion was books and people said he'd read more than anyone they'd ever met in their entire life. Sonny was employed when Davis-Poynter was interviewing someone called Mark Lushington, who said, 'I'd love this job, but you shouldn't employ me, you should meet this guy called Sonny Mehta.' So suddenly there was this little office in Granada where Tony Richardson and Sonny Mehta worked, with walls painted green and Jim Dine on the walls, and pinball machines and strange things like that. And an open brief. Publishing at the time was absolutely languishing. But Paladin's first list was Nik Cohn's *Pop from the Beginning*, which Sonny retitled *Awopbopaloo-bopalopbamboom*; there was Jeff Nuttall's *Bomb Culture*; Nick Cohn's father, Norman Cohen's *In Pursuit of the Millennium*; there were books on drugs . . . all of these things. Then Tony Richardson died and Sonny was made head of Paladin. There were people who never read anything else, they thought that Paladin was it. There'd never been a small non-fiction list which was *just* this type of book.

Later I remember being at lunch with Sonny Mehta and an old friend of his called Germaine Greer. She was saying, 'What am I going to do? What am I going to do?' and he was saying, 'Well, write a book.' Which was how *The Female Eunuch* came about.

JEFF NUTTALL: *Bomb Culture* was all there in my files. I didn't have to go out to see anybody. In 1966 Harry Fainlight put me in touch with Tony Richardson who was working at Penguin under Tony Godwin. Richardson worshipped Godwin, he even sounded like him. That kind of sycophancy where you actually take on the voice and the vocabulary and the intonations and the gestures. I got on very well with Godwin: he owned Better Books at the time and was putting on all these happenings. Therefore Tony Richardson decided that he would do my poems in Penguin Modern Poets along with Fainlight's and Alan Jackson's. Fainlight backed out at the last moment, characteristically, because he was paranoiac. So we found an American poet and put him in instead. So that was *Penguin Modern Poets 12*. But this was Tony Richardson's bye-bye to Penguin. He said, 'I'm going to Granada, I'm going to start this series called Paladin and I want yours to be the launching title. I want you to write a book about the scene.' And I said, 'OK. That suits me. I'm moving out of London, I think the kids are doing it and I want to get back to my easel, back to my ivory tower.' So I wrote *Bomb Culture* in a sense as a way of disassociating myself from the underground and saying, 'That's it. Goodbye and good luck.' But of course it had the effect of forever associating me *with* the underground.

The Doors at the Roundhouse: 'There was a lot of leather'

CHRIS ROWLEY: The Jefferson Airplane and the Doors came to play the Roundhouse in 1968. Chaos. Right until the very last moment it looked like there'd be no gig, all these ego-games over who was going on first and who was going on second. But that was one of those gigs like the poetry at the Albert Hall, like Dylan at the Albert Hall: it brought a lot of people together. All the Doors fans suddenly appeared and saw each other for the first time. There was a lot of leather.

STEVE SPARKS: The Doors were doing Europe and my name came up for touring the Doors so I toured the Doors. There was a famous incident in Amsterdam when I'm taking Jim Morrison round, dragging him out of those rooms with the ladies in the windows. I took him to a bar and I

271

was trying to drink my drink and half of his when he's not looking, cos the man could drink, the man could really drink. This kid comes up and says, 'You're Jim Morrison,' so Jim Morrison says, 'Yes,' and the kid puts his hand in his pocket and pulls out a lump of hashish about half the size of a matchbox. Now I knew what was going to happen, Jim Morrison knew what was going to happen, and the kid knew what was going to happen and it was like a frozen moment. This kid with his hand out, with this piece of hash. I went for it and Jim went for it and he was nearer than I was and he got there before I did, picked it up and swallowed it! So I said, 'Fine.' I walked him back to the hotel and then we went to the gig and the Jefferson Airplane were playing support for the Doors. By now he's tripping, just a little bit, and the Airplane were on and he ran onto the stage and started dancing and then he collapsed. Marty Balin of the Airplane was absolutely not pleased. He was then carted off to hospital in a portable oxygen tent. The band went on without him . . . When we reached Stockholm I took the Doors to the local first-night party for *Hair*, and they wouldn't let us in. That just about sums up *Hair* for me.

JOHN SHEPPARD: Jo Durden-Smith had been a contemporary of mine at Oxford. He had for a period a most remarkable nose for spotting what, if one was being crude, one would call 'trends'. Saying, 'If we make such and such a film now, we'll hit it right on the nose.' And Jo and Geoffrey Cannon, who was writing serious pieces on rock music for the *Guardian*, successfully sold Granada this bill of goods: Granada was at the bow wave of creativity, an innovative company and so on. 'We're telling you from the intimate knowledge we've got – and you may not have heard of them yet – but we are telling you that the Doors are where it's at.' OK. Granada buys it and I'm to direct it. I wasn't particularly aware of the Doors before then and I wasn't that certain that they were the new Messiah. But they came over, with the Jefferson Airplane, and their visit was much awaited by the cognoscenti. The problems of making the film are summed up in a picture of the band and Geoffrey Cannon that was taken at some point during the making of it. There's the Oxbridge super-brain and these four Californian characters and there is not much communication. There's Cannon wanting to get all hot and heavy and intellectual and the Doors are just 'Hey man, you know, please . . .'

JO DURDEN-SMITH: I went to Cannon's house one night and he'd got hold of this record – the first Doors album. He was very impressed with 'the presence of silence' in their music. So I thought the Doors were very

272

interesting and I went to Dennis Foreman, my boss, and said I wanted to make a film about them. He looked at me in this quizzical way that he had, as if he thought I was completely mad, but there was no reason why not to make it – he couldn't think of a reason why not to, because he didn't know who they were. We had some kind of football outside-broadcast unit, which had never done anything like this. They were used to pursuing the right wing down the touchline, not focusing on someone and looking for interesting shots. Which may explain the way the film finally turned out.

JOHN SHEPPARD: So we brought down the crew from Manchester to the Roundhouse and the first night there was a massive conflict, there were a lot of egos clashing backstage because no one had worked out who was going to play first: the Doors or the Airplane. And the Airplane won. So the Friday night was just bad vibes: the Doors were in a bad mood because they lost out in the ego battle, although we preferred them to go first – it meant Granada paid less overtime. We were only shooting their first set anyway and whether the second might have been better was simply not a question that was asked.

Morrison was in a thoroughly pissed-off mood. The rest of the band were staying at the Royal Lancaster; he and his girlfriend had their own flat in Eaton Square, and he had already missed the sound check. And for one number he insisted on complete blackness – so there we are, filming the concert, and we have three minutes of blackness. And to cap it all, round about midnight the chief engineer came to me after we'd finished and said that we had a fault on video and that the whole of Friday night was lost anyway. So we now had to get everything on the Saturday. When we arrived at the Roundhouse it was all sweetness and light. Maybe someone had had a talk with Morrison, I don't know. Anyway, come the Saturday evening I was ready to do it right, the crew were up to the mark and the Doors played a fantastic set.

JOHN PEEL: I introduced the Doors at the Roundhouse, though I remember nothing else of it. It was a big event but at the time you're not aware it's an event, it's just another concert. The only thing I can remember was something that Jim Morrison said to Clive Selwood, who was running Elektra at the time and who subsequently ran Dandelion with me. Clive said to Morrison, 'Hey, we've got you a really groovy driver to drive you around.' And Morrison said, 'Listen, I don't want a really groovy driver, I just want a bloke who can drive.' And I thought that that seemed to be a jolly useful maxim for a lot of things in life. God save me from the groovy driver, just give me somebody who can drive. I don't know if he ever said anything else wise, but that certainly was.

JOE BOYD: The Doors and the Airplane gig at the Roundhouse brings in the postscript in many ways to Hoppy and UFO. It was an ironical one and a rather sad one. During the winter of '67-'68 and into the spring of '68 things got a bit murky at the Roundhouse. Dave Housen had taken over promotions when UFO folded, but now he couldn't come up with enough gigs. He wasn't doing it every week and Blackhill started to do promotions there. At first we didn't see this as a serious problem. Blackhill's taste in who they were booking was pretty uncommercial – it was the beginning of Edgar Broughton . . . 'Out Demons Out' – so we weren't worried about them as a threat to Housen. Jenner, who was another of the Hoppy/Farren old guard, didn't like Caroline Coon. Therefore he wouldn't give any money to Release. So as long as he was putting on these dogshit gigs that weren't making any money, it wasn't a problem, but one spring day Caroline rang me up and said, 'I've got to talk to you, a terrible situation has arisen.' Jenner and the ICA had booked the Doors and Airplane for the Roundhouse. Caroline immediately saw the implications of this, as did I. A huge boost for Blackhill, huge slap in the face for Housen, huge amount of money generated, none of which going to Release, and huge amount of money in the coffers of Blackhill for them to book anybody they wanted thereafter. And Caroline said that she'd already called Jenner and had been told to fuck off. So I summoned Jenner and Michael Kustow, who was running the ICA and was sponsoring the work permits for the bands and had helped set up the deal for Jo Durden-Smith to make the film on the Doors. So Kustow and Jenner came to my office. Along with Caroline. We said, 'Whatever your personal feelings, the fact is that Release is the most important organisation in the underground, it does tremendously good things, the underground is going to pour a fantastic amount of money through your coffers and it really isn't right that you don't give some of it to Release.' I made an impassioned plea and they said they'd talk about it. The next day I had a call from one of them, basically saying, 'Sorry, no go. We're not giving any money to Release.' So Caroline and I said, 'OK, if that's the way they want it, it's war.'

I knew the Elektra people, who put me in touch with the Doors people. I knew John Morris, who was assistant manager of the Jefferson Airplane. I knew George Clark at the Roundhouse. And literally within 48 hours the Roundhouse had failed to complete its lease contract with Blackhill and had signed a new lease, for the same weekend, with Housen. The Doors and the Airplane had informed the Harold Davidson Agency that they would not come to London if Blackhill was promoting and that they had heard about an organisation called Middle Earth that they'd like to play for. I had lunch in Bianchi's with Jo Durden-Smith and explained to him that we wouldn't jeopardise his film in any way and he agreed to write the ICA out of the deal and do it directly with the Doors. I went up to get the contract and Jenner, who had been summoned for a reason he knew not what, was in the waiting-room and he was very surprised to see me and basically walked in to see Harold Davidson tearing his contract in half. Caroline and I took the contract round to Dave Housen in Princedale Road and had to wake him up. He knew *nothing* of any of this, and we shook him awake and said, 'Dave, you're promoting the Doors and the Jefferson Airplane next month at the Roundhouse. And give us an extra 5% for Release.' And that kept Release going for another few months.

PETER JENNER: The Doors at the Roundhouse was the thing at which we got beaten by Joe Boyd and we fell out with Joe Boyd about that, because we both tried to get the Doors and the Jefferson Airplane to do the Roundhouse and Joe Boyd won. I was a bit annoyed about that, but there you go. But it put me off promoting, except for promoting in the Park which didn't cost any money.

The Rock Business: 'The sharks . . . were wearing kaftans'

JOHN PEEL: The process of disillusion in the hippie thing began for me when we started off a record label called Dandelion Records on very idealistic grounds. The chap who started it and myself were taking no money out at all. We had a vegetarian reception for the music business, without any alcohol at all: people were livid! We had Mike Hart who had been with the Liverpool Scene, he made an LP called *Mike Hart Bleeds* which had two quite wonderful songs on it. Then there was Principal Edwards Magic Theatre who were a real pain in the bum, actually, when it came right down to it. I first saw them at a thing called the Dance of Words in Portsmouth. They did a lot of prancing about without very much clothing on, playing guitar rather badly and singing half-baked songs. I thought it could turn into something – I was entirely wrong . . .

STEVE SPARKS: The music business was the engine-room of the underground, the source of the finance. You didn't need a lot of money to live in those days, but you needed some. The great thing about the music business was that there was always some cash floating about. So *IT* was financed by record company advertising. UFO provided employment, not much but some employment and a little money for a lot of people, and things like Osiris Visions provided some finance for their artists and the distributors and *IT*. And all this was generated by rock'n' roll.

Money used to arrive from nebulous advances for unnamed projects. There wasn't much money but there was enough money. The secret was that there was a concentrated effort to employ people, that all of the underground impresarios, the people who ran things, who got things together, made a conscious effort to employ people who felt all right, people who they had some sense of contact with. *IT* was a good example, employing street-sellers, and those street-sellers, just by selling the paper, could make enough to get by. The thing was always ridiculously over-manned, with people lying unconscious in the corner and stuff, but there was a definite attempt to spread the money among people with whom you had some sense of fellowship.

TONY ELLIOTT: Much of our advertising came from the progressive record companies. Island were a huge patron of ours, CBS too. What were important were all those music shops: Musicland, One Stop, Town Records in the King's Road. And there was this whole kind of preci-ousness about records, especially from all these DJs. So John Leaver wrote this piece, an album review on a band called 'Heavy Jelly', and we put it in the magazine. We just wanted to take the piss out of them and it actually had the completely desired effect which was that Pete Drum-mond, maybe John Peel, Jeff Dexter, they all had runners who would rush down the record shops to get the latest records before the other people and they were all rushing off looking for this hoax album.

KEITH MORRIS: John Leaver came up with the idea of doing a spoof review for Heavy Jelly: 'originally an eight-piece soul band, now operating as an acid-rock quartet on the West Coast, appearing on the Spur label.' He gave them this brilliant review. It came out in *Time Out* and I think *OZ* as well and of course the old punters read it and immediately off they went down to One Stop and all the groovy record shops: 'I want this record!' and they didn't stock it. Of course they weren't prepared to admit it didn't exist – they'd never heard it and they didn't know whether it existed or not – so they said, 'Haven't got it in this week, we'll get it in next week. We'll get it for you, don't worry.' Then they were ringing record companies saying, 'How do we get this record? We've heard about it, we've seen the reviews . . .'

Now the record companies, being a bit sharper than the record shops, sussed that it was a spoof: there is no such label as Spur; it was fairly

276

easy to sort out really. So their reaction was for Chris Blackwell to bring out a Heavy Jelly record and for John Curd to bring out a Heavy Jelly record. John put various people into the studio to produce one and I think Blackers just re-released an old Skip Bifferty record. And we'd actually followed it up with a whole page ad which was supposed to be the band, but was actually a dope dealer, an antique dealer, an actual guitar player and a colour attacher – which I did on Wimbledon Common, looking as bizarre as I could possibly make them.

MARK WILLIAMS: The rock business was full of the same sharks as it had always been full of except they were wearing kaftans and smoking dope instead of sinking pints of beer and wearing suits. They were all very generous but then they could afford to be – they were making a ton of money.

PETER SHERTSER: After we started our own label, we got offered bootlegs, the first that had ever come into the UK: Dylan *Live at the Albert Hall* and the Stones *Get Your Ya Yas Out*. They were the original tapes and the quality was very good and so artistically there was no reason not to do it. It was totally justified in terms of musical ability. We had a go and it was crazy: grands! We're kids and suddenly we're getting these pound notes flying in every direction. It disrupts your sense of perspective. Two or three grand at a time, when that was a lot of money. It went berserk. People were selling thousands.

One day the boss of the pressing plant, who were making these bootlegs, came down to Ian's house, where we operated the company. We happened to have Snowy, the Bowlegs, with us, who used to do a bit of our accounts work – another member of the Firm. It's ten o'clock in the morning, Ian's still in his pyjamas, and there's a ring on the door. It's the owner of the pressing plant, who himself is not an unsubstantial size. And two bookends. I said to Ian, 'Oi veh, this is trouble,' and Snowy's going, 'I'm just leaving,' and I grabbed him by the collar and said, 'No you're not, you're staying here.' So he comes in with the bookends and says, 'We'd like to talk to you lads.' It's a scene out of *Performance*. He said, 'These records that you're making – that we're making – they're not strictly legal, are they?' So I said, 'Well we do try to oversee the copyright act, utilising certain *in vivo* situations, as it were . . .' trying anything. And he said, 'Look, we'll cut the crap, sonny. I want a grand. Now! Otherwise you're going in the grinding machine.' I said to Ian, 'Make some coffee,' then I said to Snowy, 'Discuss figures with him, tell him we're not making that much . . .' I asked Ian, 'What shall we do?' 'Tell him to fuck off.' '*You* go and tell him to fuck off. We've to pay them.

They'll kill us. They're about seven foot high. Are you mental? It's protection, we've got to do it. How much have we got in the case?' (because we happened to have the case there with the readies). We had about twelve hundred quid. I said, 'Give him the grand.' So they took the grand, and they were happy as sandmen, the lot of them. Ogres. And we never heard another word.

Apple: 'This is not what I had in mind at all'

DEREK TAYLOR: None of the Beatles is strictly conventional, but Paul became more conventional when he came down to looking on Apple as his house. If you look at MPL in Soho Square, that's his idea of how an office should be. He and Linda have total control. I see very much now how Paul must have recoiled from an Apple he couldn't control. Rich, talented people tend to be what is known in the world of Alcoholics Anonymous as 'manipulators and controllers'. Because that's what they get used to being able to do. Paul couldn't believe that this outfit that he'd been so keen on had turned out to be so out of control. It wasn't just a case now of him and Miles and Steve Abrams and all that kind of stuff. It was Taylor's friends from Fleet Street getting pissed as arse-holes. 'This is not what I had in mind at all. And who is he? I know he's our friend, but he's not one of the fucking Beatles and it's *our* Apple, or at least it was.' All too much for him, I can see now. He was a young man and I was ten years older than him and not as easily manipulated and controlled as perhaps I should have been since they were paying my salary. I was becoming autonomous; I was manipulating and enjoying myself. I was doing those things that I ought to have done and doing some of those things which I ought not to have done. And by 1969 it was real madness. We didn't know where we were.

PAUL MCCARTNEY: We weren't disenchanted after setting up Apple but there was more required than we could bring to it. The theory was what we could bring to it the music, the vibes, if you want to call it that, or 'goodwill' as it would be known in business – it's worth an awful lot of money; if you look at Beatle contracts 'goodwill' is worth hundreds of thousands of pounds. We could bring all that to it and on that side the company was quite successful. What happened was that it couldn't exist on that alone. It needed business expertise.

Our idea was to create an alternative: by our goodwill we would be saying to people like Donovan, the Byrds, Bob Dylan, 'Look, we've got this really great little company, you won't be hassled by any of these business heads who are always hassling you . . . all you need to do is just flourish in this garden that we're going to provide for you, and we, as artists ourselves, will sympathise with what you're going through. We will provide these things and then the businessmen will merely structure it all for us and will make sure that we don't overspend or we don't do this when things are looking dodgy.' But they actually didn't do that. We wanted to work very hard but we wanted it enjoyable: this was how we worked and we felt sorry for all the plebs who didn't have that luxury and we wanted to bring that to everyone and I still think it's a major, great idea. Why Apple failed was that it wasn't set up well enough on a business level. So we just had pleasure with pleasure. We had Number One hits, we had everything a company needs to be a successful company, but also we had this sort of riot in the press room, which Derek was in charge of. And there were other things in there, some of John and Yoko's stuff, quite a good artistic thing. But unfortunately the business people weren't us, or even of our generation – they were suits. It was the first time I'd seen 'SA' on companies – I used to think it was 'South Africa'. It implied Switzerland, it implied dodgy deals to me. Suddenly it was Apple SA. What happened was that we gave over the business side, to be relieved, we hoped, by great business people, but in actual fact – probably our fault – we didn't staff it with really great business people. Hell, if they'd been really great they might have run off with the whole shebang – who knows? I don't.

DEREK TAYLOR: I was very unhappy at Apple some nights. It was all too much and you could get so tired by the end of the day. Sometimes on the train home to Sunningdale I'd think, 'Jesus, has it been a terrible day.' Someone kicking up a rumpus, a terrible phone call from Paul: 'You know that none of you people are any good – if you amounted to a hill of beans you'd be somewhere else doing a proper job . . .' That sort of stuff. It came very hard.

SU SMALL: I was doing the advertising for *IT* and I knew how sticky our finances were. I was going round to Apple and knocking on the door and going into Derek Taylor's office and saying, 'We're skint, we can't get the next issue out unless you buy a full page or preferably a double-page spread, and give me the money now.' And very often he did.

DEREK TAYLOR: I think it was Paul came and asked, 'What are you doing with all this money?' But we weren't spending anything like the amounts that were going out on the Ron Kass/Allen Klein end of things which involved enormous amounts of international travel and hotels. What we were spending in the press office was pennies compared to that sort of thing. But Paul objected to the sloppiness of the way we ran the operation. As a press office it certainly left a lot to be desired. The pity of it was that it would have run better if I'd been more sober. Less marijuana, less alcohol. It would have been much less fun but more coherent. That's never mentioned in the dismissive reports you read about Apple: that the Apple press officer, in addition to everything else, was a practising alcoholic.

VIRGINIA CLIVE-SMITH: One day in the summer of '69 I walked into Apple in my patchwork dress and Derek Taylor said he would pay me £25 a day just to sit at his feet. Which I found delicious, though I didn't do it. I did spend a lot of time round Apple doing things like write on large pieces of white paper 'Who Killed Hanratty?' which were then pinned to Lennon's Rolls-Royce.

DEREK TAYLOR: Apple was like Toytown and Paul was Ernest the Policeman. We couldn't have gone on and on like that. We had to have a demon king. Who was Klein. And we had to have a mad inventor, and that was Alex Mardas. But there were so many people. There was Neil [Aspinall] who was the keeper of the conscience, the keeper of the files, the man who had some sort of hand on the Beatles. You had Peter Brown running his own adventure. He was their personal assistant. Peter would lunch, it was a feature of Apple. There'd be some MP and you'd have Hardy Amies coming in, perhaps, and Andy Williams – 'Perhaps George may come in today, Andy, who knows. Keep a place for George . . .' So we'd all sit down and have lunch and champagne and then in the afternoon Lauren Bacall would appear by the request of Lord Bernstein on the off-chance that she might meet all four, but with a promise of Ringo. So there was this other level of society, and sometimes one of my friends who had drunk too much would find his way down to that floor downstairs, or Dominic Behan or a Hell's Angel, and there'd be this culture collision . . .

Cranley Mansions: 'Thommy was a terrible tyrant'

JOHNNY BYRNE: When Thommy's money came the first thing he did was move into this enormous flat in Cranley Mansions on Gloucester Road. It had seven to eight big rooms and he insisted on taking all his mates with him. By this time we were moving into the hippie, glossy, glitzy world of movies and the world of big books and celebrities. [Roger] Jones came for a week and then fled in absolute terror; he couldn't stand it because Thommy was a terrible tyrant. Steve [Abrams] was there for a time; Hawkins was there all the time; I went for a time. Cranley Mansions, what can you say about it, it was insanity, beautiful insanity, soporific from morning to night. There were hand-maidens around, we'd go to endless huge parties, endless rich parties, endless 24-hour stints, people spinning out of Cranley Mansions, rainbows in their eyes, God knows at what hour, all hours of the day, extreme sex, extreme drugs, extreme living, extreme feeling. It was really the high noon of all that creative feeling that we'd just left behind.

JOHN DUNBAR: Marianne had got this gig singing at a commem. ball at Oxford. So I went along with her. And there was this guy in a suit and shades who kept coming up and said he had been organising the ball. That was when I first met Thom Keyes. I never saw him for ages after that until I was walking by St George's Hospital and this Rolls-Royce screeches to a halt and the window rolls down and 'Hey John, get in!' and it was Keyes. He had just published *All Night Stand* and bunged it all into a Roller and he was just showing off. I stayed in Cranley Mansions for a while. That was completely mad.

NICOLA LANE: I went to Cranley Mansions many times to hang out. I met Keyes through an extraordinary boy called Adam Kish. He knew everybody. He'd just come out of Borstal and I met him in the Kensington Market and he took me round to Thom's place. And after he took me round the first time I used to go there regularly. I'd ring the doorbell and someone would always let me in. Keyes seemed infinitely older than me. He was very sophisticated, he was rich – that was the odd thing about him: he was rich and he was obviously rich. Some people were rich and they pretended not to be, but he didn't seem to have any qualms about money. Having all those things, the golfball typewriter, the black bed in the middle of the room and all that sort of stuff . . . Thom was very nice to me. One was supposed to sleep with him, but I didn't.

GENE MAHON: I took my first acid trip in Cranley Mansions. It was luxurious madness: Thom with his Roller and his fancy apartment and his golfball typewriter. Thom always had a book on the go or a filmscript or some project. The girls drifted through. I took it constantly after that, every Saturday night. I sat around Cranley with Steve Abrams, who showed me this letter from Graham Greene saying, 'I once took opium with a friend in Albany when I was a lad.'

SPIKE HAWKINS: In '69 came the time when the clock had to be wound up. This was the time when we all grew up a lot and I dropped out of the drop-outs. People were getting families, houses, things like this. They were feeling very insecure within this new security and the insecurity brought on the breakdown of the entire 60s thing. It all blew over, overnight.

A lot of what was done in the 60s has gone on but without people really knowing it. That is very important. People absorbed a lot of things but without knowing it. Yet the era produced very little. There is no definitive novel of the 60s.

By 1969 it all broke apart and some went to money and others to total obscurity and insanity. I saw the end coming with overdoses. It turned very nasty. It had a meaning: people knew for once, for a small time, in which direction they were going. All aspects of creative thinking and creative work were aimed in one direction, and then the arrow bifurcated, it split and splintered and there was a very unpleasant ending. Deaths came left, right and centre. Of people and of the general impetus. The energy went. One still had a load of energy, but not for doing the same things. I couldn't live out my life with a headband – though I never actually had one. That is in the end the conclusion, the sad conclusion.

MARTIN CROPPER: I went to Thom Keyes' wedding. It went on all day, a fifteen-hour party. That was interesting because it was a gathering of the clans. Sam Hutt was there, Steve Abrams, Jenny Fabian, all sorts of people. A hippie wedding between Keyes and this German girl called Regina who came from a smart Kraut family. Half of the church was Moss Bros Krauts and the other half was stoned hippoes. The vicar started this sermon, a bit near the knuckle since it was all about sin, and the door of the church opened and I looked around and there was this figure with a ponytail, dressed in an orange brocade suit, like he'd just got a curtain and made a suit out of it, barefoot, video camera, very slowly walking towards the vicar in the pulpit: Hoppy.

STEVE ABRAMS: Johnny Byrne and Jenny Fabian did this cast list of the underground for *Queen* magazine and Johnny left his name off and Keyes' name off and Keyes was very very angry. Keyes had one of those IBM typesetting machines, so he got a copy and printed on his name . . .

Groupie: 'I used to help fix her up with various people'

JENNY FABIAN: I didn't suggest writing *Groupie*. What happened was I was sleeping with Andy Summers at the time. I'd told Johnny [Byrne] about Syd and then there was Andy, and I told him where I was going and what I was doing, and he said, 'You really should write about this.' I

282

said, 'Well, I can't write about it,' and Johnny said, 'You write it just as you want and I'll help you with it. We'll just do it as a team.' I had nothing to lose and it quite amused me. The extraordinary thing about *Groupie* was that the main character became this person called 'Grant' who was really Tony Gourvish, Family's personal manager: he managed things, he was Mr Dynamo on the scene. We lived in this cupboard together in Lots Road, literally a cupboard with enough room for a mattress and a few shelves around the walls. I thought this was wonderful – how close can you get to someone? After the book came out first of all Germaine came up and grabbed him from me and took him off and screwed him, and the next thing is Caroline Coon's got hold of him. Both really on the strength of the book. These were two fairly powerful women on the scene at that stage and he really was only a rough boy from Leicester, on the make, but not the sexual make. Germaine – that was unbelievable. The first thing she said was that she'd read that he was a wonderful screw, though I don't think I ever actually said that in the book. It was hardly a political gesture, not at all. She surely wanted him because I'd made him into a hero: and he was only another glorified road manager. Don't tell me if he hadn't been made into a hero in a book that she'd have looked twice at him. Or Caroline.

JEFF DEXTER: Jenny Fabian was a good friend of Tony Howard's. She used to be the cashier at Middle Earth. I was the only one she didn't fuck. What she wrote in her book was totally opposite to what really happened, it was semi-fictional. I was in it as 'Len'. At the time she was writing the book she had moved in with Thom Keyes. I used to end up at Cranley Mansions every night, after the Speak. You want to call someone in America? Come back to Cranley Mansions and the phone's free: just whistle down it and that was it. Jenny suggested in her book that I might have been a changeling, a sex change. That was part of her fantasy. I think I was probably the first one that freaked her out. She was really quite an inexperienced girl, in spite of what she came to. She had carnal knowledge of lots of different situations, but was rather sweet and timid. I used to help fix her up with various people, so she could get more experience and do more of the book. She was a timid groupie really, not in the least outrageous. Almost an innocent. Germaine Greer was much more outgoing, always prepared to freak anybody out. She definitely downplayed her intelligence, but she was always a brilliant person to be with, always had something to say, always very entertaining, great for a laugh. You'd meet her at four am, walking along the Bayswater Road, and she'd light up the night.

Sam Hutt: 'Doctor, doctor, doctor!'

JOHNNY BYRNE: If I did have a political thing it was to eliminate the illegality of cannabis. Around 1964 there was a man called Dr Dunbar down in Shaftesbury Avenue and we'd heard that he still had cannabis on the Pharmacopoeia. And I went down to Dunbar and said, 'I know you've still got this and I'd like to register and I'd like to have it.' And he said, 'It must be used for a medical treatment.' I said, 'Well I've got a medical complaint,' and he said, 'What's the trouble?' and I said, 'I'm paranoid.' He said, 'Why are you paranoid?' and I said, 'Every time I smoke a joint the police want to arrest me.' So he said, 'I can't think of a more serious case than that, I shall instantly give you a prescription.'

JONATHAN MEADES: My friends in Tintern Abbey got prescriptions for cannabis tincture in late '67 from a guy called Ian Dunbar who was a doctor in Barkston Gardens, Earls Court. It was very potent stuff. There were two varieties: one which you soaked tobacco in and then left it to desiccate, then rolled cigarettes out of it; the other you just drank like syrup. Once I went round to their flat in Pavilion Road and there was Stew, the bass player, an absolute drongo from somewhere like Raynes Park, a real scum-of-the-earther in one of those suede things with hair down here and fur down there and a bit of embroidery – a fake Afghan coat – and he mumbled something like, 'That's really uncool gear you've got on, man,' and stumbled off to the pub. So I thought, 'Fuck it, I'll nick his tincture.' I went up to the bathroom where I knew the lads kept all their tincture and I was swigging back this bottle. Then I heard him come back into the house and I thought, 'Oh well, better get it all down then,' and drank the lot. This was about six in the evening. I went back to Sloane Square tube to get back to Notting Hill, and ended up going round the Circle Line *twice*.

SAM HUTT: In 1969 I joined Ian Dunbar who'd started a general practice for young people in Ladbroke Grove. He was particularly interested in helping people who were coming off junk. Ian had discovered this anomaly: that you could prescribe cannabis. He prescribed it and I did too, quite genuinely. Extract of cannabis extracted alcoholically from the plant and then made into tincture, this dreadful surgical spirit with the stuff in. It was a genuinely good link with people coming off heroin, because most treatment for heroin is still very authoritarian – be a good boy and stop taking heroin or go on to safe methadone, which has always been a red heroin. We were trying to give people something to get high off, not to be authoritarian. It doesn't replace the heroin experience at all but at least it's something to get high. And at least it's a connection with a doctor. We went on prescribing it, lots and lots, to prevent our patients committing illegal acts. If I found out you were going and buying dope, of course I'd prescribe it for you, to stop you being a criminal. I didn't want my patients to be criminals, I wanted them to be within the law. That practice lasted about a year, and Bernie Greenwood came and joined us. For Bernie and I the main thing was that we could actually work in a situation and a place that we enjoyed, that wasn't white-coated.

MARTIN CROPPER: They had a surgery off Ladbroke Grove. It didn't look like a doctor's surgery. The waiting-room walls were painted white, there were soft pouffe cubes to sit on, and *Zap* comics to read. Not *Horse & Hound* or *Punch*. I went there because my wife was pregnant and the first thing Sam Hutt, who then had long blond hair down to his tits and did not look like a GP, the first thing he said when he found out she was pregnant was, 'Oh, I wonder what sign it'll be,' and pulled out his astrology book.

JOHNNY BYRNE: Sam was a person I had an enormous amount of respect for, because Sam was always canny and he always understood that it wasn't all or nothing, that life was what it is, a series of small, personal changes, and that if you commit yourself to something it has to be something fairly total that you utterly believe in, but not an excuse for taking control of your life, especially if you were cut off from your family and you were in the middle of this whole seething mass of feelings and thoughts and strands coming together – cultural change. Sam was the scene doctor who was usually involved in bringing people down off bad trips. I always remember he had this little sign that said 'No Charge'. He had this ornate bronze cash register. It was uncool to talk about money and when he did a private consultation this little cash register would come up, ping! two pounds or whatever, and it was Sam's very clever way of reminding people that they did, you know, have to pay. But Sam would never push it, he often gave his services for free. The clue to Sam is that he's always been a pop singer, that's all he's ever wanted. He was Boeing Duveen before he was ever Dr Sam Hutt.

SAM HUTT: In '68 I actually released a single, as Boeing Duveen. Boeing Duveen and the Beautiful Soup – a terrific 60s name ... you couldn't get worse if you were trying. I was playing a lot, I'd learnt the guitar in the 50s, but I couldn't write words and I was taking Lewis Carroll's words and putting them to music. I did 'Jabberwocky' as the A-side and 'Which Dreamed It', the poem at the end of *Through the Looking Glass*, as the B-side, done Indian style because I was also playing sitar.

285

JENNY FABIAN: I only went to Smutty [Sam Hutt] to get a script for tincture because Dr Dunbar was getting very nervous about it. I was told, 'Dunbar's being difficult, try this fellow here.' I'd written *Groupie* by then, so to some people I was a celebrity. I got the appointment and I went in and he was *very* accommodating. And I thought, 'I'm all right here . . . and while I'm here you couldn't possibly give me some Mandrax too . . . ?' and he was *very* accommodating. I thought, 'Well, this is good.' Sam obviously wanted something and it came out that I'd just moved into this new flat. So Smutty said he was looking for a room and I thought it would be really good to have a doctor living there with all those pills, so it suited me. I did find it a bit weird though, trying to lie around stoned listening to the sounds of vaginal inspections going on behind the curtain up the other end of the sitting-room.

SAM HUTT: I started working as a private doctor from Exhibition Road, where there was Roger Chapman of Family and Jenny [Fabian]. I didn't do too well in private practice, I was having to give people Green Shield stamps to get over the embarrassment of charging money. And through knowing people like the Who and the Stones I became a rock'n'roll doctor. The Grateful Dead would come in for their vitamin B12 shots. Nobody ever got drugs from me – I'd always refer people to Dr Roberts and the people in Wimpole Street. The guys in the three-piece suits and the straight front – they dealt with all that stuff, the mandies, the speed and so on. I never had any desire to deal with that or just to be a grocer. It wasn't a moral thing – if you want to take mandies that's fine, watch out; you want to take speed, watch out – but if you do that, you just do that all the time. Not worth it. I restricted myself to hypnosis and homeopathy and holistic medicine and, as I say, the Green Shield stamps. And I had my pendulum, though I never really got it to work, cyonic medicine, vibrations – serious mumbo jumbo.

I had very few run-ins with the police except for the classic time when they came to bust us at Exhibition Road. And I had the chain on the door and I held them there for twenty minutes while I said I was a doctor and I was in consultation with my patient and everyone rushed around and cleared up and smoked lots of Gauloises . . .

SPIKE HAWKINS: Sam was a father-like figure in many ways. You could go to him and get a straight answer if you wanted an answer about something. If you went and said, 'Sam, look, I am worried about . . .' you would get the answer spelt out without lots of giggling and too much 'Look at that rhinoceros coming out of the garden shed.' You knew where you were.

SAM HUTT: The first festival I did a bit of doctoring at was the Dylan one at the Isle of Wight in 1969, but I had a serious paranoid reaction there. I was tripping myself. I wasn't officially doctoring there, but I gave a little bit of help. Then I started hallucinating that the crowd was screaming 'Doctor, doctor, doctor!' It was at the point when Dylan was coming on and the vibe and the feeling was just incredibly intense and wound up. And they had these spotlights going around the crowd and people were fainting and the only way they could get out was for them to be handed over the heads of the crowd; plus there'd be two St John's ambulance men trying to pick their way in with the stretcher between them, and the Stalag 17 lights, and the crowd – I'll swear to this day, they were chanting, it was reverberating, 'Doctor, doctor, doctor!' and I sort of crouched down by a picket fence and thought, 'Fuckin' hell . . .'

MARTIN CROPPER: Sam was also the doctor in residence at the Electric Cinema: he was the bloke who coped with the freakouts. One night there was this classic longhair, crushed-velvet type, not very bright, and he had a job for a week packing mescalin in caps. He was doing it in a bedsit in Talbot Road. Every other room in the house was inhabited by prostitutes and they would bring their johns back late at night, open his door and point out the resident hippie as they passed. And simply from packing this wretched stuff he was out of his skull. At the end of the week he decided that he needed some light relief, so he went to the Electric to watch a film. The first image he saw on the screen was of a man having his head cut off and being sewn back on the wrong way round. And he *flipped* very very loudly. Luckily Sam Hutt was in the place – 'I'll sort you out . . .' Vitamin B shot, whatever.

The Electric Cinema: 'We are the community'

PETER BROWN: There was this cinema on Portobello Road, the Electric Cinema, and it was the oldest cinema in England, the first to show movies. It was owned by some strange old man who lived up in Edgware and was managed by a man called Paul who looked like Bill Haley and was only about 4' 3" and put margarine on his hair. It was taken over by John McWilliams. He was renting films from various places, hiring a projector and a projectionist, and showing them on Friday, Saturday and Sunday nights. So I went to work at the Electric tearing tickets, a bouncer and sort of man on stage, to announce stuff. The films were a mixture of classics like stuff by Cocteau, Buster Keaton, *Metropolis*, plus modern underground things like *Pull My Daisy*, abstract movies . . . It was packed. Huge crowds. It cost a shilling to get in, later it went up to four

287

shillings. The place used to fall to bits, it had old-fashioned steam heat and every now and then a piece of the ceiling used to fall on the seats and they'd collapse, but it was a safe haven for the hippies. The ethos of the place was supposed to be 'We are the community.'

The Electric Cinema at one time was the major fund-raising organisation in the underground. I mean everybody needed money and got it from the Electric. It was generally known that the Electric gave it away and we did have a floating fund for emergencies – we gave it all away. Anybody could walk in and say, 'I need money for this,' and if it was on the level ... Mostly it went to BIT or Release. But despite all our principles we got to the stage of bickering and arguing about the programmes and where the money should go and stuff like that. There were some who favoured giving it to the London Street Commune, and others who preferred more structured and respectable organisations, so we reached a stage when it needed seven signatures on the cheque before any decisions could be made. It's a wonder we didn't ask Eric the Tramp or the editorial board of *IT* too.

Eric the Tramp: 'I'm onto a good thing here'

ANDREW BAILEY: I felt that most people in the underground had their own self-interest at heart, but there were a few, a very few real street characters. I always felt sorry for them: not because their lives were unhappy, but because they were treated as sort of pets by the underground people, the movers and the makers. That wonderful figure – Jesus. He wore a brown robe and sandals and he loon-danced in front of every gig. No matter what gig I went to, he was there, loon-dancing, beautiful smile on his face, no shoes. And he latched onto me and became a constant visitor to the office. We tolerated it for a while but in the end we got the police, not only to remove him, but to give him an official warning. A non-molestation order. Then there was Eric the Tramp: he was for real. Eric was straight out of a Kerouac novel: who was he, where did he come from? Wonderful, wonderful guy, a very nice man.

PETER BROWN: One night [at the Electric Cinema] this old tramp turns up at the door and wants to come in and we let him in and he was treated like a folk hero. He was an authentic member of the *true* underground, a man who has abandoned all. He's called Eric. So Eric plonks in. He finds these nice sort of druggy hippies accept him and they buy him a cup of tea: they are either so embarrassed by him that if he asks to come in for a cup of tea they would never say no, or they are genuinely warm-hearted and generous, and of course they are passing a joint. He was introduced
288

to hashish, he found out about free love and I presume he got some. I don't *know* if he did, but he was certainly interested in it. One night he turned up and some skinheads had knocked him about and stolen his sleeping bag, so we gave him a fiver to buy another one, and I think this must have been the turning point in his life because something happened. He either realised, 'These people are wonderful,' or he thought, 'Oh, I'm onto a good thing here and I'll stick with this lot' – probably a bit of both.

RICHARD ADAMS: The first time I met Eric I was conned rotten. I thought that this guy was a genuine off-the-wall hippie. He came in wearing his headband, littered with *OZ* Lee Heater badges, White Panther badges, *IT*, *Friends*, all the badge paraphernalia that was in circulation at that time. Huge great duffel coat, a shiny 'third eye' stuck in the middle of his forehead, a smelly old sleeping bag trailing round behind him.

PEARCE MARCHBANK: There used to be a warning in the *Time Out* office hung up from the rather rudimentary switchboard we had, saying 'Eric the Tramp's in the building' and all the girls would go and lock themselves in the lavatories. Eric would chase them round the room forcing his tongue down their throats, wearing his silver-sprayed boots.

Rolling Stone: 'We all knew it was a rip-off'

ALAN MARCUSON: I got involved with the rock business. I was managing someone called Dennis Couldry at this time. I was quite interested in the business and I was trying to develop my entrepreneurial instincts, but I was out of my depth because I was a hippie and my hair was down to my arse and I was smoking too much dope and spending a lot of time being an arsehole. I knew Jane Nicholson vaguely, through some LSE connection.

Then I heard that *Rolling Stone* was starting in London and meantime my parents were putting enormous pressure on me to get a job, and I knew a few people by then on the fringes of rock and roll. Someone knew the Stones' office manager at the time, Jo Bergman, and I went in and saw her. I was petrified – the Rolling Stones' offices – but I had to get a job and it had to be a groovy job. So I got this job running advertising on *Rolling Stone*.

FELIX DENNIS: I remember Jann Wenner coming round and dragging me round to the Rolling Stones' offices to add a bit of street cred to his pitch to get the money. I'm sitting there thinking, 'Why am I sitting here?' There I was with Charlie Watts and Jagger ... Richard Neville wouldn't have anything to do with it, he knew that it was going to fall to pieces, so he sent me round as the muppet.

GENE MAHON: Alan Marcuson got me into London *Rolling Stone*. He knew Jane Nicholson and she had asked him to help to put the package together to show Mick Jagger. They needed some ideas for covers and Alan came to me and I put together a couple of covers. They went off somewhere and got them approved and came back and asked me to work for the magazine and I suddenly found myself having an interview with Jane in a basement flat in Hampstead and I was working for *Rolling Stone* in London. By that stage it was red velvet flares, purple velvet flares, hair down to here, a string of beads, a Zapata moustache and so on.

It was quite hard work. I was responsible for putting it all together. I was basically labouring, gathering together all the bits and pieces, negs coming in from the States, pages being done in London ... I lived a very strange life then: I'd spend a week in London, then four or five days up in Redcar, on the coast, where the thing was printed. I'd put all the material in a big bag and get on the night sleeper from King's Cross with a huge J and wipe myself out for the journey and get woken up with tea and biscuits at the station next morning.

MARK WILLIAMS: I quit *IT* after the Street Commune takeover and went initially to *Rolling Stone* UK which was still-born, virtually. It was very much more a rock'n'roll paper than *IT*. I was most interested in writing about rock'n'roll by that time, so the idea of working for *Rolling Stone*, which I already thought was a great paper after reading American copies, was very attractive. I met Wenner. Wenner was greedy and ultimately brutish and he was also a fucking groupie for Mick Jagger – always was and still is as far as I'm aware. There was me, Alan Marcuson, Jane Nicholson, Gene Mahon and Jon Goodchild, Virginia Clive-Smith, Pat Bell. I was British News Editor. It very quickly became apparent to me that it wasn't real. I was hired on the understanding that we were actually going to produce a British edition and very quickly it changed into just having eight pages in what was essentially an American edition and it went downhill very quickly.

ALAN MARCUSON: There we were for the first month or so bringing editions out of the Rolling Stones' offices. Mick Jagger and Keith Richard used to come in and I used to quake in my boots – these were the gods. I remember spending an afternoon in the offices literally days

290

before Brian Jones died. This sweating figure came in and I spent the afternoon talking to him, not knowing whether to be nice to him because he was a superstar, but he looked very ill and nobody else was talking to him.

Finally we moved into 19 Hanover Square. I had a huge office and I didn't know how to conduct myself. I had no skills at all. The problem was that we never got a clear directive. Mick Jagger wanted to start an independent magazine, but US *Rolling Stone* just wanted a subsidiary. US *Rolling Stone* was very independent of the US underground press but we in London wanted to be part of the British version. Eventually Jane Nicholson left and I became editor.

JON GOODCHILD: We all knew it was a rip-off. Here we were, supposedly working for some kind of underground press, and we were in this pretty expensive, plush place. So we tended to abuse it. Jann Wenner would send us over these directives all the time, just like the King, so our first reaction was to say, 'Who do you think you are?' And after a while we began to take it over. He would send over the negatives of his magazine and we were to take out eight pages and put ours in and we would take out sixteen instead. Then we got to the point where we changed the whole damn thing. So he fired everybody and we had to close down. But we didn't close down. We carried on publishing this thing which first of all was *Friends of Rolling Stone*, and when he sued us we called it *Friends*.

CHARLES SHAAR MURRAY: I regarded London *Rolling Stone* as a poor substitute for the American one. What I liked about *Rolling Stone* was that it *was* American. It was telling you the way things looked from the States, even if it was written by complacent hippies in San Francisco. The English version was just another rock rag. When it subdivided into American *Rolling Stone* and *Friends* I thought that was at least honest: *Friends* was coming at you from Portobello Road, *Rolling Stone* from San Francisco.

The Stones in the Park: 'Mick wants to talk to you'

JOHNNY BYRNE: The events I liked best were those concerts in the Park. These seemed to me to be by far the most interesting and genuine events. At the earlier concerts one would gather in the hollow for the day's event and they were the most wonderful events, beautiful days, and they made sense of everything that we had been doing, not in any organised way, but simply lots of people being together, relaxed – a sense of peace and knowledge and communication with people.

PETER JENNER: We put on the Stones in the Park and Blind Faith. We did the first one with the Floyd and that worked and then Clapton came along and had a look. We knew Stigwood, who was his manager. I think Stigwood realised that this was the thing to do, this was the way to promote Blind Faith. He sussed that that sort of exposure and promotion was huge. The same thing went for the Stones: it was a way to relaunch their career. In a way the Beatles and the Stones had been sidetracked by all this. Although they had had a lot to do with setting everything up, they had come to the position where they couldn't play live any more. The PAs weren't loud enough to drown the screaming girls. So they had this problem of re-entry. The Beatles never solved it, but the Stones, and Jagger in particular, sussed it out, and we were asked to do it. Granada was involved and they paid for it and again, unbelievably, we didn't make any money. Neither Granada nor the Stones ever sent us a penny, not even a free video. But everybody respected us, even the police, because they knew we weren't making any money. But it just got too heavy. The trouble was that the Stones were just far too successful and with Brian Jones dying we got the front page of every paper for about a week.

JO DURDEN-SMITH: Literally out of the blue Jo [Bergman] called up one day and said, 'Mick wants to talk to you,' and Mick said, 'Do you want to do a film? We're thinking of doing this concert. The only big expenditure is the stage – do you think you can get Granada to pay for that?' The stage cost £3000, the film was £9000 and that was seen as a very big budget indeed. Granada were worried, but they've sold more videos of that since than of anything else they've got.

So the stage was built and a deal was made between us and Blackhill, the promoters, and the Stones. Then Brian Jones died. And there was suddenly this feeling of things blowing up in our face and the Stones not going to do it. But they did finally agree to do it.

JOHN SHEPPARD: When we signed the contract Brian was still alive, but he died the week of the concert and we briefly attended the first stumbling rehearsal of the new Stones with Mick Taylor. It was in the basement of Apple in Savile Row and we left pretty quickly because it was clear that our presence was not wanted. But the concert was still going ahead, which was Granada's main concern. I imagine that Mick must have been influenced by Jo Bergman here, though one mustn't forget how astute he was himself.

I spent the day with Mick. We had six or seven directors working, covering different aspects, and I followed Mick. Some time in the late morning I went round to Mick's place and chatted with him for a while, waking him up really, gently bringing him towards the day. Then we got into the limo and drove round to my flat, where Nick Knowland (who later became John Lennon's cameraman) was waiting. He and the soundman were set up in my main room and my wife had cooked a wonderfully elegant light lunch. Mick sat in a chair and toyed with one of our exquisite little cats ... Then back into the limo, pick up Marianne and Nicholas, her son, round the corner and from now on we're filming, all the way to the suite in the Inn on the Park. Stones lounging about, Mick looks at self in mirror, Mick winks at camera in mirror and leaves shot — all nice freeform hippie stuff, 60s stuff. Down in the lift to the armoured van. The crew didn't go in the van but we were right up its arse all the way into the Park. Then the van arrives, the door opens and the Stones do a rat run into the luxury caravan ... Charlie passes an apple to the fans ... the Stones tuning up ... and away we go. And then up on stage and a good time was had by all.

TONY ELLIOTT: The Stones in the Park was just another rock'n'roll concert. Of course it has got this historical position and there were a lot of people and the atmosphere and Brian Jones had died and the Stones happened to be particularly good. There were a lot of Hell's Angels there which I found a bit upsetting. And bands of skinheads who were running around the outside.

JOHNNY BYRNE: This was when I came face to face with the new reality. I was always able to get access to backstages and such. I hated it but occasionally I would go. People never objected. This time I was backstage after Brian Jones had died, and they were going to release all these butterflies. And I was on the stage and I came face to face with this New York Jewish thug who asked me, 'What the fuck are you doing up here, you fucking ...!' and I said, 'Who are you?' and he said, 'I'm Allen Klein.' I said, 'Where have you come from?' He said, 'I'm their manager and if you don't fucking clear out of here in five minutes ...' That was the first time I felt the violence coming into the whole thing.

MICHAEL STOREY: I went to the Stones in the Park and I was tripping and it was just awful, dreadful. Clinging onto trees, a huge crowd, all the skinheads and this heavy ugly music and suddenly it was all wrong.

JEFF DEXTER: I couldn't do the Stones in the Park, they didn't give clearance in time. Ricky Farr had the Who and Chuck Berry at the Albert Hall the same night and I'd decided to do the show and when the

Stones did confirm that I could MC it was too late. I did catch the first half of the Stones, but we'd been at the Albert Hall all morning, doing runthroughs and getting the stage together. I was very disappointed when I got to the Park and found Sam Cutler in my position as MC and having all those Hell's Angels as security, which I freaked about. They were part of the old scene that we wanted to change – we didn't want people being beaten, drinking beer, puking everywhere and doing rude things. You wanted them doing beautiful things.

JO DURDEN-SMITH: I've always thought that one of the reasons why Altamont happened was because somebody had the bright idea of hiring the Hell's Angels as security for Hyde Park. And they were very sweet kids. They looked very daunting with the black leather, the skull and crossbones, swastikas and all that, and they were just daunting enough to make sure nobody did anything, but they came on their Vespas from Willesden and Kilburn and Croydon. Then Sam Cutler went off to California for Altamont and said, 'We'll hire those nice Hell's Angels again.' And *they* turned up on their Harleys and they were not the same thing at all.

Hell's Angels: 'Clump, clump, clump, clump. Phew!'

STEVE SPARKS: It was a great moment when George Harrison brought the Hell's Angels over from San Francisco and we had one of them staying with us at Shaftesbury Avenue. He had his bike with him and the Shaftesbury Avenue flat had a courtyard in the middle and one Saturday morning he got up and his bike was locked in this courtyard and he started shouting. We manhandled his bike up two flights of stairs and he rode it out through the doors and across the pavement and that was the end of the trouble we had with people from *Hair*.

DEREK TAYLOR: There was this memo from George saying, 'I met these very nice fellows the Hell's Angels when I was in America and I told them that when they come to England they can come and see us at Apple and we'd treat them well.' So the memo was copied and we said, 'When they come, look after them. And more or less what they want let them have, because these are not greedy capitalists, these are . . . our kind of guys.' And they arrive with Peter Coyote and Ken Kesey and some women. I was extremely hospitable and I was astonished. Kesey, Coyote and the women were courteous and . . . not respectable, but they responded in kind. The Hell's Angels had no idea of how to behave. It was ridiculous that we should have expected them to have. But I was amazed to find how ungrateful they were. People when we were pleasant were pleasant back: they were *not* pleasant. By Christmas they were just tear-assing around demanding this and demanding that. But why be rude about the Angels? That was their destiny – somebody has to be a Hell's Angel.

JONATHON GREEN: There was a benefit for *Nasty Tales*, the *IT* comic that was busted for obscenity, at some West End club. Everyone was there, including the British Hell's Angels. Wandering around I ran into them. Buttons, the President, is sitting there, legs spread, a dyed-blond head bobbing up and down over his cock. He sees me, grasps this hapless head and drags the girl off his cock. 'Hey man, want some of this?' Great moments in underground etiquette: do I join Buttons and this not wholly appetising Mama, or do I reveal my utter wimpishness, not to mention the fact that my girlfriend is standing ten yards away and staring? Fortunately my saviour arrives: William Bloom, the publisher, appears, says he has some cocaine and suggests we vanish into the toilets to consume it. Right. 'Catch you later, Buttons. Thanks, man . . .' Saved again.

DAVID GOODMAN: Buttons was in charge. I knew them all quite well. Crazy Charlie and me go way back. I'd been at Altamont and wrote a piece in *IT* which was reasonably derogatory of the Hell's Angels. And I was living in this flat in Maida Vale and I was in the bathroom and I heard these clumping feet coming up the stairs and knocking on Micky's door and on our door and then clumping outside, and there's a knock on the bathroom door and I say, 'Who's that?' and a voice says, 'Who's that?' 'It's Boss.' 'Hello Boss, it's Buttons, can we come in?' And I sink a little deeper into the bath and in trudge a whole gang of Hell's Angels. 'Hey Boss, d'you know who this David Goodman geezer is?' and I'm thinking, 'David Goodman, why do they want to know about me?' and I say, 'Yeah, why?' 'Who is he? Cos he ain't half gonna get a fuckin' pastin'.' 'Why would that be, then?' 'This *IT* business. Look what this fuckin' cunt's written . . .' I sink a little deeper in the bath. 'Buttons, prepare yourself for a shock: I'm David Goodman,' and very very quickly, like Harry Flashman, I talked my way out of it really fast. 'It's all a misprint, I didn't say that. That Caroline McKechnie, she was doing the typesetting. You know me, guys, would I say that . . . ?' All the time waiting for this awful pasting in the bath. 'All right then, mate, sorry to have bothered you. See you then.' 'OK mate, bye-bye, cheers . . .' Clump, clump, clump, clump. Phew!

Religion: 'A mental disease if ever there was one'

NIGEL WAYMOUTH: I had lost my belief in the whole hippie thing by '69. It became all rather cynical. Endless Scientologists and Sufis. It just got worse and worse. We were near Gandalf's Garden and I never set foot in there. I had terrible contempt for all these places.

NICHOLAS SAUNDERS: Gandalf's Garden was at the World's End near a fish-and-chip shop. And the working-class chip-shop customers obviously didn't mix very well with these rather superior middle-class enlightened people. Gandalf's Garden was a shop with two big windows and you could go down there and have some sort of herb tea and there would be a room downstairs where they would have meetings and all sorts of different people – not just one guru but all sorts of different people – would give mystical enlightenment talks, or meditation talks – anything in that area, very broad. And it was all free. The sort of people it attracted were the bare-footed, the free. People who didn't quite fit in, people who felt a little lost.

MICK FARREN: Religion. There are people who immediately they break out of some kind of paternal situation go looking for another one. It becomes like psychotropic drug use and it does this and it does that and they find somebody sufficiently charismatic to be another patriarch and off they go. Jim Jones, Charlie Manson or the fucking Pope. It don't make much odds. They're looking for another daddy.

SU SMALL: I've always suspected that people need something like a religion and in this period they renounced the accepted religions and went off and started other ones. Some of them were called political and some of them were chemically based and some of them were actually bozo religions. I get much more worried by people who get into cults than drugs. There was a time when people were dropping like flies, everyone was getting into these gonzo religions. There was one friend who joined something called the Emin and came round to tell me, 'I have to go with these people, to find out what it is they believe. Since I'm forbidden my stimulants, here's my stash.' And I said, 'Oh, if any of your friends decide to join too . . .'

JONATHAN PARK: The era was tremendously godless. And the stress and strain of life does drive you to a point where you want to seek relief. And there are two forms of relief: one is called heroin and one is called God. And a lot of people got into one or another.

DUNCAN FALLOWELL: The worst thing about the 60s was the growth of religion, a mental disease if ever there was one. I was never tempted to seek out a guru. It seemed to me that the whole object of approaching reality, which was part of taking acid, was to leave all this mumbo jumbo behind.

JEFF NUTTALL: I remember at our first meeting with Laing, everybody smoked a joint, there was a Billie Holliday record playing and Laing said: 'We can find no other way of expressing our purpose but to say we are concerned to reveal a greater glory of God.' And Trocchi immediately came in and said, 'And his betters.' The anarchist finger going up immediately. The religiosity was the stumbling block of the whole damn thing. Religious faith and the belief in human freedom just don't mix.

SAM HUTT: Bernie Greenwood and I went once to R.D. Laing's house, to see a Brazilian shaman that he's got there and he's going to remove a bit of ectoplasm from somebody's back and they're going to get better and dance for ever. And the Brazilian geezer does a terrific show. He's wearing a sky-blue acrylic cardigan, Val Doonican style, sitting in this room in NW3 surrounded by intellectuals, and he does his bit. He goes into his trance and people are brought in to heal and he actually does some psychic surgery and he cuts open somebody's back and delves about in there and you see a bit of blood, but no blood pours out, and then he sucks out the ectoplasm and then he waves his hand and there is no scar and the woman gets up and dances about.

DEREK TAYLOR: At Apple there was the I Ching. At the Wigmore Street office in the early days it was thrown every morning. I got a reading: you're biting through, keep biting through, you may get there. I was a bit annoyed: I wanted mine to say that I was all right and had arrived and safe. There was a special I Ching thrower – Caleb. He wore all white and his white-blond hair parted in the middle. He got 50 quid a week.

IT: 'This cascading crescendo of vehemence'

GRAHAM KEEN: We arrived at the office one day to find that some of the bundles of papers had been pinched. Pete Stanshill was away on holiday at the time. Dave Mairowitz or Courtney Tulloch was editing the issue. Pete came back and said, 'Let the fuckers have it. What do we care?' But the rest of us decided that no, no, we wanted it back. They had taken the equipment, typewriters, and so on too. The London Street Commune, led by Phil Cohen, had been conned into taking over. Somebody went down and said, 'Why don't you move into the *IT* building.

Nobody's going to mind: it's an anarchic act, go ahead.' It was the guy who ran the distribution. He and his girlfriend were an odd combination: she had a TB hip and couldn't walk properly and he had a great scar all the way down one side of his face. They took the mailing lists and stuff like that and made off with it. I found out where they were living and went round there. I asked for it back and said they weren't going to get very far, but it was pretty much to no avail. But after a couple of weeks we were back on the streets.

SU SMALL: They came marching into the office and I was there working late on the advertising account and they tried to persuade me to go with them. I was hysterical, I was really furious because I didn't like any of the people who were involved. Their argument was that it wasn't a people's paper and it had to be liberated and they went off and did their own thing, the *International Free Press*, for one issue. It was ludicrous. I sat on top of all the advertising account books. I knew full well that if they didn't get the advertising then they wouldn't last, cos there was no way they could do it on the income from the sales. It was my trump card and I played it. I think I tore all the accounts up, cos I wasn't going to let them go, and then had to spend the next six weeks sticking them together again.

SUE MILES: Sarah Pouliakakou (Fenwick) sympathised with the Angry Brigade. She was Miles' secretary. A very, very rich girl. She was behind the London Street Commune who took over *IT*. She let them into the building, she orchestrated it. They burned all of Hop's negatives, ten years' worth.

MICK FARREN: When I came back from America something weird had happened at *IT*. I hadn't had much to do with *IT* and it had got sort of cheesy and very self-satisfied. It was full of red-brick left sociology and John Peel was writing for it and I didn't like it much. I certainly didn't hang out there. But then there was some kind of schism or takeover. I couldn't figure it out, but I was having a fling with Su Small at the time, and she was righteously involved with it. It was all very confusing. I didn't know what the fuck was going on. Both factions seemed to be soliciting my support and I didn't want to know about that.

CHRIS ROWLEY: Micky went in there and fought Dave Hall. This was serious baboon stuff. He turns up and just starts yelling at Dave Hall that Dave had to go. He just couldn't do this, this was corruption and this was the nadir of it all. They yelled and had fights and tantrums and

298

threw things and eventually Dave got up and left: the old buck had been pushed to one side. Now Micky at this stage was right in his prime. He had a deadly rap; he'd get hold of a liberal, some hapless reporter from the *Guardian* or the *Observer*, and just start on them. Start soft and gentle then gradually build it up to this cascading crescendo of vehemence.

The Deviants: 'We were fine – just a little before our time'

STEVE SPARKS: Those were the days! The Deviants fans were all psychotic, they really were. Our groupies were the ugliest in the world and also among the most aggressive in the world. You didn't dare turn down a Deviants groupie else you'd get your legs broken. The fans were like primitive Motorhead fans. Really, really strange people, weird. Take acid and go to a room full of Deviants fans and you'd end up screaming, jumping out of the window.

RUSSELL HUNTER: It wasn't so much dresses I used to wear, I just used to wear a lot of very effeminate clothes. Lace trousers, colourful girls' velvet appliqué shirts, and an awful lot of face make-up, and eye make-up. We were really into being an outrage band. Most of us were so totally fucking out to lunch that there was no way we could have done it anyway. It was really a question of how many drugs can we take and actually stay on our feet through the set. I don't think serious musicianship crossed our minds very much. We had two bass players; various dreadful speedfreaks would come and jam on keyboards; Micky would be bellowing his vocals; Sandy would be methedrined out of his brain – he was often known to fall flat on his face and hurl his guitar through windows . . . It was a question of smashing everything: how far will we get through the set before people's brains start to come apart with the noise and the speed?

STEVE SPARKS: I can remember Russell jumping out of a Transit on a dual carriageway and running screaming in the wrong direction down the motorway. It was always Russell, it was Russell lying face downwards in a puddle nearly drowning in an inch and a half of water.

We once did an anti-censorship gig at the Royal Festival Hall, Johnny Dankworth was due to come on after us. When the band came on, Sandy was wearing a dress – it was still very early for people to be wearing dresses – and the entire Royal Festival Hall audience was split into two. One half thought the Deviants were wonderful and the other half thought they were the most appalling thing they'd ever seen in their life. And they started fighting! In the Royal Festival Hall, at an anti-censorship gig! Half were booing and throwing things at the Deviants, trying to get them offstage, and the other half were fighting with that half. Johnny Dankworth was really pissed off because we wouldn't go off, cos put that in front of the Deviants and they'll play all night – wonderful!

MICK FARREN: We were fine – just a little before our time; it was the disc jockeys that hated us.

STEVE SPARKS: The central problem for the Deviants was the fact that Micky couldn't sing. Otherwise Micky would have made the perfect pop star. Everybody was a loser in that band, it was the all-time great losers' band and that's why the fans were so weird. The only fans you could get for a band full of losers were losers. We nearly killed an entire audience by bringing a motorcyle in and taping a contact mike onto the exhaust and revving it. When you rev a Triumph 650 Twin inside a small church hall . . . they were dropping like flies. There never has been nor ever will be anybody like the Deviants.

MICK FARREN: Towards the end of the summer I was going completely insane from taking too much methedrine and having emotional problems. And the trouble with rock'n'roll is not the rock'n'roll, but having to sit in a car with the same four geezers for days on end and you all get to hate each other. And we fucked up too. We weren't doing badly, putting [Paul] Rudolph in the band had been a real turn-around and we played in Hyde Park, with the Soft Machine, the concert after the Stones in the Park and at the Fleetwood Mac one. So we had a real good summer, got another record out, but it was in the studio that things started to get weird because everybody wanted to play like Led Zeppelin.

RUSSELL HUNTER: We supported Led Zeppelin at their first ever gig. It was a tryout for their big hype launch. It was at the local Bristol boxing club and the audience hated us and despised them. Somebody threw a beer glass at the stage and Sid Bishop, our guitarist, unfortunately threw it back and cut somebody's head. When Led Zeppelin came on they got through a number and a half until fire extinguishers, buckets, bricks, everything started being thrown at them.

MICK FARREN: We opened for Led Zeppelin and there was a riot when the farm boys in brown suits and haircuts who had come into town on Saturday night looking to get laid marched in. They all stood at the front of the stage harassing girls and looking at me saying, 'What you want them poofs for when you've got manly farm boys down here?' To annoy us they all put their beer mugs on the front of the stage, which was about five feet high. So being a troublemaker I was sort of doing a mincing Mick Jagger along the front of the stage kicking off all these beer mugs. One of them hurled a beer mug at me which misses but hits Sid Bishop. So he picked it up – it was thick and didn't break – and threw it back. At which point they all started playing Kill the Hippies, us included. Boss is beating them back with a microphone stand, as indeed am I, and then we just get the fuck off the stage, taking the drums with us. [Jimmy] Page and [Robert] Plant were just cracking up in the dressing-room and telling us we were fucking awful, and they get the same treatment because it's now got completely out of hand . . . We had to huddle inside the van while the farm boys bounced up and down on it and didn't escape till about two in the morning when it was safe to go home.

RUSSELL HUNTER: Not many people did like us. We really were a band that people were disgusted by. There were a few total fucking lunatics who thought all this carnage in front of them was wonderful, but most people were open-mouthed.

MICK FARREN: Jamie Mandelkau turned up. He was an Earls Court pill dealer and he started showing up and fucking everybody's wives and as a result we made him our manager. Sid Bishop went home to his wife and baby and Jamie told me he knew this lumberjack in Canada called Paul Rudolph who played guitar just like ringing a bell so we said fair enough and Rudolph came over.

RUSSELL HUNTER: Paul Rudolph came into the band through Jamie Mandelkau. Where *he* came from is a bit of a mystery to me. He appeared. And we'd actually got a little bit fed up with being the butt of all this ridicule or whatever. We weren't actually going anywhere and after a while you get bored with making an arsehole out of yourself. And if you're going to continue in the music business then you actually have to get to grips with music eventually. None of us were the greatest musicians but we picked on Sid Bishop as a scapegoat, because we didn't like his wife. He was getting a lot of flak from her, and she was basically a nice little girl from Streatham who didn't want all this: she'd married Sid to have a nice little home and she'd watched him have methedrine put in his drinks and turning into a fucking animal. So he dumped us or we dumped him. Mandelkau had this mate, Paul Rudolph, who he wanted in, and it all seemed too good to miss.

DAVID GOODMAN: There was a bunch of Canadians, one of whom was Paul Rudolph. He was Mandelkau's mate from Gibson's Landing in Vancouver. Jamie wanted to make something out of the Deviants. He was the manager and he wanted it more musical and Sid Bishop had to go. He wanted Paul Rudolph in and he did it. Jamie had probably promised him the fucking earth, knowing Jamie, and there he was in London. He looked like Horse Cartwright, with huge green elephant-cord trousers on and this orange and black striped T-shirt, really, really long hair and a withered right arm from polio. He claimed he's never played lead, only bass, but he did it and he took off. We loved him right from the word go. He played this amazing guitar and he just got better and better. But he was also very very hung up, especially about women. Tit-and-arse humour. Things started getting a little more lively with Paul Rudolph in the group. At last someone's taking it musically seriously. Micky knew what he wanted to do, but he had to have someone take care of the music. He wrote fantastic lyrics and he's even got the occasional tune in his head but because he can't sing properly in tune he found great difficulty in expressing himself to a proper musician. But Rudolph couldn't accept Micky on a musical level. It was Rudolph's attitude that led to the eventual split. Rudolph then set about hammering them into shape.

DAVID GOODMAN: The band got tighter and tighter and made a third album, for Transatlantic Records, with Seymour Stein of Sire Records as the American end. We had a series of good shows, the last one of which was the concert in Hyde Park in 1969 which everyone would agree was the very finest Deviants gig that ever happened in this country, and it was the last one. Musically it had finally got there.

MICK FARREN: We did real good in the Park and at the Roundhouse a week later and then we were stupid and went off to North America where we all became disorientated and the money ran out and Seymour Stein wouldn't pay our hotel bills . . . I came home. They all stayed out in San Francisco for a while and basically became the Pink Fairies, and I didn't.

DAVID GOODMAN: A couple of weeks after the Hyde Park gig we all went off to Vancouver. Mandelkau knew a local promoter who brought in 'The Deviants from London'. Basically nobody showed up for the shows and he couldn't pay us and he ripped us off and we lived a life of poverty in Vancouver deciding what to do. It was the end for Micky. It had all been brewing. He'd been acting very strange and there'd been a

302

couple of gigs in Vancouver, one of which was in a recording studio in front of all the head hippies of the town, and Micky had to go out there and do his whole thing . . . and we had all taken acid, it was the first time he ever had to our knowledge (he always said he had but whatever he told you, that was his first trip) and he consequently blew a fuse mid-set . . . Then the boys all met in the local launderette and it was decided that Micky must go. We'd either stay and carry on and go to America or go home too. The first thing was to tell Micky and he could make up his mind what he was going to do. So he immediately went mad, and then went home. He collapsed when he went home and had a blood change, he was very seriously ill, mentally and physically.

RUSSELL HUNTER: In 1969, through Jamie and Paul, we arranged to do a week's gigs in Vancouver. That was to be it. We went over with this dodgy promoter on these air tickets, which it turned out he had only ever paid one way on. We were promised hotels and three or four gigs in this rather plush venue in Vancouver and then home again. It seemed fantastic. We arrived and got escorted to what can only be described as a doss-house, where I'm convinced they were running an under-age prostitution racket . . . judging by the people we had to share beds with anyway.

I don't really know the reason for it all, but everything turned a bit nasty. The gigs were all right but the money was never forthcoming and we were a little disgruntled and decided to go home – and found that no one had paid the second half of the air fares. And Micky cracked up. By then a certain amount of friction had grown up between Micky and the rest of us. The way things go in bands. And we'd started to fool ourselves that we were pretty good and that Micky was holding us back. He was in a bad state. He used to completely fall apart for no apparent reason and start screaming at people and charging about. We'd got delusions of musical grandeur and we started to think, we don't need this. With hindsight it's easy to see that with the pressure Micky was under we should have been a lot more supportive. But we weren't. Everyone was too far into their own chemical chaos. We were all spread out all over town, having a great time, sleeping somewhere different each night, catching the clap and everything. But Micky was growling and mumbling and breaking up bars and having to be led home. Eventually he got on a plane and went home and collapsed soon after. I don't quite know how he got the money because by now we had no money. We had about $50 between us.

DAVID ROBINS: Micky Farren fucked up bad. He was taken home in a plane after the band told him to piss off. I was there at the terrible performance that caused this to happen. I was in Vancouver and I got a card from Micky saying that the Deviants were coming over, needed a place to crash, etc. I wasn't particularly friendly with Micky, but I was friendly with Russ and Duncan Sanderson. The band turned up. They wanted me to introduce them to any women I knew ... 'Know any women, Dave ... ?' I didn't actually. But they did like the bars. They certainly knocked it back, though not Mick. Mick amazed me, I didn't really see him as a singer, but he was lead singer and sex symbol, he told me. So come the big night he'd asked me to get as many people as I could and I tried to and I got about ten people together. We all showed up. They were billed as 'Britain's number one underground rock band direct from England'. We couldn't get in. Because when we arrived there were people fighting to get out. The reason they were fighting to get out we discovered as soon as we got in. We were hit by these noises like a buzz saw. There on stage was Farren: he was wearing a black leotard, he looked like an Italian gigolo, wild hair, white shirt, and he looked disgusting, there's no other word for it, he was revolting. He was sweating and he was making this dreadful noise – nnnggghhh nnnggghhh – like that ... My friends were no longer my friends after seeing that. They just looked at me and said, 'See you around, Dave ...'

STEVE MANN: At Transatlantic we didn't really know what happened in Canada. I was on the other side, working for the record company, and the last thing you do is tell the record company about what's really going on in a band. You bung out an anodyne press release that says 'musical differences' or whatever and that's it.

DAVID GOODMAN: Mandelkau had secured us a two-week residency in the Trolley Club in Seattle and off we went on a Greyhound bus. And we did a concert and earned lots of money. Enough for us to say, 'If we can earn this sort of money in Seattle ... if we go to San Francisco ...'

RUSSELL HUNTER: In San Francisco we fell in with the remnants of the 1967 hippies in a real commune on Oak Street, across the road from the Airplane and down the street from Big Brother. We played at the Family Dog, supporting the Velvet Underground, played with It's a Beautiful Day ... The commune was into health food but we soon sorted that crap out. There were some great girls there and we tried them all. We stayed in San Francisco for about a month. We played at the Matrix, though it was well over the top by then, went to the Fillmore, and sat in the back room during a Crosby, Stills, Nash and Young concert with the Grateful

Dead. They introduced us to nitrous oxide. This huge canister with all these pipes. 'Hey, what's this?' 'You wanna try it?' and taking huge draughts of nitrous oxide and falling over. While we were in San Francisco someone got hold of Seymour Stein, who was releasing us in America, who came out to see us. He invited us all to dinner at this crummy roadhouse bar and we had a pretty horrible dinner of hamburgers and beer and at the end of it he put his hand in his pocket and said, 'Oh shit, boys, I don't have my cards . . .' and we had to pay.

PETER SHERTSER: I started doing deals with Seymour Stein of Sire Records. At one time we went to New York, at Sire's expense, and we ran out of money. So Ian comes up with a great idea: 'Go down and see Seymour in the office and kill him.' I said, 'Terrific, are you coming?' 'No, no, I've been possessed by black magic' – he was very worried, he thought he'd been possessed. So I go down to Seymour and he's partners with a guy called Richard Gotterer at the time. I'm in there and I've got Seymour by the throat, cos he's not going to give me the dough, and his partner Richard's about to leave. He says, 'Richard, Richard, help me! He's going to kill me, he wants money.' So Richard just says, 'Huh. See if I care, I'm going,' and he's gone. So Seymour says, 'I'm phoning your partner, you're mad!' He phoned Ian: 'Your partner's here, he's trying to kill me!' 'Good, hope he does a good job.' So I got a cheque out of him, but what a performance.

DAVID GOODMAN: We spent all our money in Seattle, thinking 'Whoopee, here we go!' and arrived in San Francisco with about a dollar between us and a carrier bag full of sandwiches. We immediately caught a bus out to Chet Helms' Family Dog ballroom and got there at about nine am and we were very lucky that it was the day of the Family Dog commune meeting. So about three o'clock there was a meeting – members of the Grateful Dead, the Jefferson Airplane and so on – it was really beautiful to see. And the Deviants. And they said, 'Are there any new people here?' and Rudolph got up and explained who we were and said we were looking to stay and maybe play. And some kid got up and said, 'Well we can look after them,' and someone else said, 'I've got a gig next week,' and so on. It ended with us being billeted with this group called the Mayflower in Oakland. Basically very nice kids but that ended when Sandy started screwing one of the geezers' wives. We ended up in this fantastic house on Oak Street right by the Panhandle, across from the Airplane's house. Incredible. It was some kind of semi-religious health food group, some mad guy and his sect. We were very hungry and pretty lonely at this point. We were getting a bit . . . lost: there wasn't any gigs, there wasn't any money and we were very reliant upon people's goodwill and there was an abundance of it. I remember our first meal: there was about 25 people round this table and all of a sudden there was this linking hands and 'Ommmmmm'. And they were all fucking Omm-ing and I thought, 'Oh my God, I can't take this seriously,' and burst into laughter and left the room. When I came back in there were a few boos and things and then I got this bowl of food and I couldn't eat it. I was starving to death but I couldn't eat this soya bean stuff. It was like my very first school dinner all over again. But next day I was forced to eat the stuff and finally got very into it and what happened to us lot was we became very, very healthy. All this organically grown food really cleans your system out, especially brown rice. So we were all coming out with boils and spots and I got this headache that went on for days and we all felt fucking rough until suddenly we all felt great and healthy. But at the same time we were eating all this organic food we were all taking lots of organic mescalin and PCP, a very mild one, which we used to snort most nights with this girl with a funny dog downstairs.

We played three gigs. At the Matrix club we got 50% of the door and the first night we got $1.50. We also played at Berkeley University, at a warm-up gig the night before their football game with Harvard. We played in this huge auditorium in the middle of which was a bonfire with an effigy representing Harvard on top. In come all these students, beered out of their heads on Budweiser, throwing empty bottles at the bonfire. They're going bananas and we're going 'Wow'. Then this great flare floats down and there's a deafening explosion and this bonfire bursts into flames and the whole place goes absolutely bananas. We're going 'Fucking Ada . . .' Then in come a 150-piece marching band and cheer-leaders and all the rest. They sing this big hymn and down comes the coach and licks the fans into a fury and off they go into some sentimental song and the girls are doing their stuff and all of a sudden – 'We have a group from England, they're called the Deviants . . .!' and it's run in, plug in and they played literally for 30 seconds then it was unplug, rush out again and we got $150.

RUSSELL HUNTER: Finally Seymour Stein put up enough money to get us back to Montreal, because he had an idea we could make a lot of money there. We left San Francisco on a bus-stop jet on December 23rd. It was ten below. We arrived there and the airport was empty. Finally this Nanook of the North character appeared, swathed in fur and sealskin boots, and led us out into the maelstrom and we went and slept in a warehouse. Then we found a wonderful chap who put us up and we played a lot of gigs at McGill University and made a lot of money, cos

306

they loved us there. So we got enough money for some of us to go home; we left Rudolph. It was January 1970 and the plane got diverted to Manchester and Boss went off to buy something and came back in high dudgeon: 'Where's my fucking ten-shilling note?' They'd given him a 50p coin and he was apoplectic.

'I think we've been spiked'

JUNE BOLAN: Around September *Rolling Stone* had a party in Hanover Square. Marc went with Jeff Dexter. I was working but I said, 'I'll join you about eight and pick you up.' Marc had never had acid in his life and with a mind like his, like Syd, it was the worst thing – unless you were in a controlled circumstance – that you could possibly take. They had this huge room full of drinks and soft drinks and food. I walked upstairs to the room where all the drinks were and Jeff and Marc were sitting on the floor and they looked odd, but I thought that maybe they'd had a joint, even though Marc didn't smoke. And they said, 'Do you want to stay? Do you want a drink?' and I said, 'No, let's go,' cos we had to take Jeff to Hampstead and then go back to Blenheim Crescent where we lived. It was about ten by the time we actually left. Because Jeff had had acid before and he knew what was beginning to happen to him. Marc had never had it. Halfway down the stairs Marc started to get funny. He started to put his hands in his mouth. I said, 'What are you doing?' and he said, 'I want to eat myself.' I looked at Jeff and Jeff looked at me and said, 'I think we've been spiked.'

JEFF DEXTER: All the drinks at that party had been spiked. I'd been spiked several times before and had no fear of it. Then my friends began to get sick, fall over, become paranoid. One of them was Marc Bolan. Marc was in a terrible state, really flipping out . . .

JUNE BOLAN: We got down the stairs, into the car, my Mini, and I said, 'Jeff, get into the back.' So they both got into the back and I'm driving, up to Haverstock Hill where Jeff lived. We get to Haverstock Hill and there's this screaming in the car. And I thought, 'Any minute now I'm going to get a pull, I'm going to get stopped.' Jeff was trying to hold him down, he's screeching his head off, he's scarlet, he's purple, he's dribbling, he's crying . . . So we turn into Jeff's street and I said to Jeff, 'You're going to have to come back to Blenheim with us, because if I let you off I can't drive the car and look after him.' He was somewhere else, he couldn't understand anything I was saying or what Jeff was saying. I drove like a maniac to Blenheim Crescent. It was the most horrendous drive of my life, with this screaming banshee that I loved in the back and I could do nothing. I don't know how much they'd had – it could have been an enormous amount. I had a very good friend called Bernie Greenwood, who was a qualified doctor. I couldn't think who to phone except Bernie. Marc was still in the car, he wouldn't get out. He wouldn't let any of us out. It was midnight by now. Bernie came round, got in the car, in the front. Then Jeff and Bernie swapped seats and started talking to him. After an hour we had to prise him out – he was braced against the car – and forcibly get him up to the top of the house, a long way up. Bernie had some largactyl and he gave him a lot. Marc slept and Bernie said, 'Any minute he wakes up you give him two more.' This went on all night and all the next day and he became *compos mentis* again the following evening. He was absolutely petrified and he made me promise that nobody would ever give him acid again.

ALAN MARCUSON: Was it the strychnine LSD or the hash cookies? That was the beginning of the end, the start of the demise of London *Rolling Stone*, when we lost all credibility with the record companies. We had this great idea, to have a party. We invited all the smart record company people and we met people like Sam Hutt and Jenny Fabian and everyone else. What I remember about the party was that everyone was throwing up and Marc Bolan was taken away in an ambulance . . .

VIRGINIA CLIVE-SMITH: I waltzed in the door and was handed the draught of orange juice that had been very heavily tampered with. The acid had been cut with strychnine and a lot of people went to hospital from the party. I spent the rest of the evening lying on the bathroom floor listening to the band downstairs and every time I thought I was able to stand up I would immediately fall down again and crash into the wash basin. I found that the safest place was literally the floor, because then I couldn't fall down and hurt myself. What was nice was lying on the bathroom floor and realising that despite everything else I was still keeping time to the music with one foot. After the party *Rolling Stone* moved out to Portobello.

PAT BELL: Jane Nicholson left and Alan Marcuson took over; it was all rather unpleasant. Jann Wenner used to come over to London and he wasn't pleased at the way *Rolling Stone* was developing. He was very efficient himself and expected things to be done in a far more efficient, professional way. After one of these visits the rights were withdrawn for us to publish in London. Then we started *Friends of Rolling Stone*. We were all determined to do something, to get something out.

Implosion: 'If you're a charity, let's see your accounts'

JEFF DEXTER: Hawkwind and the Pink Fairies appeared just after Middle Earth closed and we resurrected the shows at the Roundhouse, under the name Implosion. Caroline Coon came up with the idea that we should run a show for the community as opposed to making a profit. It was a runaway success. Everyone who played got the same money and all the profits went into rebuilding the Roundhouse and supporting the community.

DOUG SMITH: Hawkwind weren't really space rock, or science fiction. That only got in there as an excuse. The reality was that it was a good way to drop acid and play a gig. When Lemmy joined they were still dropping acid, they were still doing speed like you cannot believe. I remember Dave Brock walking across the stage, kicking Lemmy up the arse and saying, 'Fucking slow down, cunt!' Then there'd be other nights when Lemmy would be speeding out of his head and he'd think, 'Can't take this any more,' and the mandies would come out and they'd go on stage and get slower and slower . . .

PETER BROWN: Implosion was started with funding from the Electric Cinema. It had a board on which was Caroline Coon, Rufus Harris, Roger Cross and his girlfriend. It started off with principles almost identical to the Electric Cinema, only they were going to use music rather than film to bring people, to give them a good time, obviously to charge them for it, then redistribute the money within the so-called underground. They hoped to persuade bands to perform for a nominal sum, usually just expenses.

NICK LAIRD-CLOWES: I was going to the Roundhouse, as every hippie child would every Sunday, for Implosion which Jeff Dexter did. What you did was stagger around the railway hut in different degrees of drugged excess, spending what little money you had on tiny little wholemeal cookies and things. The money still came from my parents, lunch money, money I was given for fares, and so on. Finally, Jeff Dexter came up to me and he already knew me – I was always jumping up on stage and asking for all sorts of obscure records, and he said, 'You ask for all these obscure records and I love all these people too. Listen, I'm managing a group called America and I would like to take on someone else and I could train them up as my assistant. They would become a DJ and they would take over when America takes off, as I'm sure they will. Would you be that person?' So I'm fourteen now, and I'm thinking of being up on that stage. So I said yes and became great friends with him and every Sunday we'd go and I'd learn how to do it. He'd give me the first couple of hours, then I'd assist. Then we'd go off and do all the festivals and when he got blind drunk or had taken acid you'd take over yourself.

JONATHAN PARK: What I remember about Jeff Dexter. His size: small; his hair: fair; his mind: pretty absent. He was a bossy little person but I think he was probably underneath it all a very nice person. I always had a slightly soft spot for him. To me he was the DJ and he introduced me to a fair amount of music that I wouldn't otherwise have been exposed to at the time.

JEFF DEXTER: The profits from the Implosion shows at the Roundhouse – half went to the Roundhouse and the rest to whoever was in trouble. We gave *IT* money, *OZ*, *INK*. We gave a lot to BIT and the guys at the Mangrove, bailed them out several times. We even gave money to the Electric Cinema, to help them get some films and buy some new seats. At one stage there were lots of wrangles. Someone said, 'If you're a charity, let's see your accounts.' Someone else said, 'What do you want to see them for? You've had plenty.' Then they wrote a story in *IT* that we'd taken all the money. But we hadn't. All the money had gone into bricks and mortar – a new roof, the reconstruction of the dressing-rooms and other facilities at the Roundhouse. We did very well for the Roundhouse and the community. The Who were there, they played for £25, just like everyone else. The only ones who didn't were the Stones: they got everything.

Jimi Hendrix: 'I knew the guy was magic'
JOHN MARSH: The 60s ended for me in 1970 when they announced on the radio that Jimi Hendrix was dead. My first reaction was I knew the 1970s were going to fuck it all. And by God they did.

PETER SHERTSER: Hendrix was a good friend of ours. We had a very strong involvement with Hendrix. We saw him the first time he appeared in England. He was at the Scotch of St James's, then London University had a gig, the Cream were on and he came on stage and jammed. We heard he was going to be on, so we steamed down there and saw him. Never paid to get in – the normal. So he's come on, blown the place apart, Ginger Baker's done his nut, Hendrix is getting all the ovations – from then on I knew the guy was magic. We followed him around, ended up meeting him in a few clubs, got talking and he was really

310

impressed that young white kids knew so much about blues. He gave us his number, said, 'Come up and see me,' and so on. We used to meet him in different places and have a laugh; he always used to put our name on the door at gigs. He played a very early gig on Boxing Day '67, at Billy Walker's Upper Cut Club in Forest Gate. We're all down there – Mother's going, 'What about Boxing Day dinner, I cooked something nice . . .' – and we've torn the place apart. There was only 20 or 30 of us and that was it. Very few other people realised who he was, and he never forgot that.

PEARCE MARCHBANK: I went to see Hendrix at Woburn. It was the second Festival of the Flower Children. I was recruited as a litter picker-upper. After about a morning of picking up stuff they were in a terrible state backstage and I suppose I looked relatively together and intelligent and I was recruited to be an assistant stage manager, which meant knocking up Donovan and Hendrix out of their little encampments behind the stage. They were staying in these little marquees, sitting on the floor, reading books with feathers as book marks . . . Hendrix arrived with *two* Transits. Really big stuff! He went straight on stage. He had these guitars, you could hear the equipment buzzing. The roadies just touched these guitars and it was instant feedback. Hendrix appeared, really beautiful, a physically beautiful man, he picked them up and nothing happened, the guitars didn't make any noise at all, but if anyone else went near them they would start howling with feedback. He just knew exactly how to pick them up. It was amazing. He was playing the entire stage, this wall of Marshall amps, 30′ long, with roadies at the back holding them up, and he was jabbing them and hitting them with the guitar.

Friends: 'A more radical magazine'

ALAN MARCUSON: By late '69 we were increasingly coming into conflict with Jann Wenner, and we were becoming increasingly independent of American *Rolling Stone*. Wenner didn't like this but Jagger was basically on our side. Then he went off to Altamont and in the middle of Altamont Jann Wenner struck and demanded that we fall under the editorial jurisdiction of San Francisco and do only what they wanted us to do and that we were to submit our material to California and all we were to do was sell advertising. Soon afterwards we were thrown out of the office and someone from Jagger's office came along and put a padlock on the door. All of a sudden we were on our own; we ripped off as much art department stuff as we could lay our hands on and moved out.

By this time Bobby Steinbrecher was on the scene. He was a rich American kid who'd taken too much acid and also suffered from *folie de grandeur* and was on a high and had come to London to see John Lennon, as people did, to suggest he replace Allen Klein as his manager. He was going to run Apple, which was getting into a mess. What I did then was go round the London record business and tell them that *Rolling Stone* was abandoning London and everyone wanted a London music paper and I gave them the impression that we would start a London *Rolling Stone* and didn't emphasise too much the political content of what I had in mind. I wanted to make a more radical magazine than *OZ* and *IT* and do it in a way that I thought they weren't doing it. I always had an idea that you could produce a paper with the underground commitment but which was well-organised and efficient and spread the word rather than being elitist and simply preaching to the converted. *Friends* was a very early and naïve attempt to move out into that bigger market.

So I organised for the London record business to transfer all their ads into a magazine which as yet did not have a name. And they all backed me. I got the money up front and I phoned my Dad in South Africa and got £400 from him. We brought out the first edition of *Friends* at Steinbrecher's apartment.

JONATHON GREEN: It was blissfully vulgar: the bedhead was wired with dimmers, stereo, God knows what else, presumably geared up for Bobby getting laid. The sitting-room was green, but shaded so that one end was quite dark and it paled down almost to white by the time it reached the other. There were no wages, of course, but Alan and I did cash a solitary advertising cheque for sixty quid or thereabouts and pop across the road to Harrods' Food Hall to get us all supper one night. In between all this Pearce Marchbank and I laboured over the boards. Poor Pearce – two weeks before he'd been at *AD* and I'd seduced him away to super-chic *Rolling Stone*. Now he was working at a kitchen table, albeit in a smart kitchen, on something with the distinctly tacky name of *Friends*. But we did put it together – and at some stage Alan presented us with these two hustlers, Eddie and Steve, who called themselves Famepushers.

ALAN MARCUSON: We were getting a certain amount of media attention and these two hustlers got to hear of us. They called themselves Famepushers and ran various underground enterprises. Businesswise I was out of my depth with those guys, they were hustling us to death. They gave us an office at 305 Portobello Road. Eddie (the fat one) saw himself as the proprietor of the magazine but we weren't having any of

312

that. In the end they dumped us when I wouldn't let him be boss. And we met Barney Bubbles who was working for Famepushers producing record covers and freelance graphics next door.

PAT BELL: When the first issue of *Friends* came out we had to fold all the copies by hand, which we did in an office at 140 Park Lane owned by these two guys who were backing the magazine, Steve and Eddie. And there we were with Alan sitting on the floor surrounded by people rushing around and he was completely out of his mind on dope and kept saying, 'Christ, we're working hard.' We were, but he wasn't.

JONATHON GREEN: Steve and Eddie installed us in 305 Portobello Road. From what we could gather, Famepushers – which was a candid name if nothing else – had one cheque for ten grand and at least ten accounts around which it proceeded as required. 305 was known as 'Motherburger' and they had various enterprises operating out of it. There was us, on the ground floor were Bob Wilson with his sidekick Little Tony Korobin who was about fourteen and whose father was apparently West London's top fence. Anyway, when he died his family found enough valuable bits and bobs to pay for the funeral. Now we'd call him streetwise: then he was a cheeky little bastard, but gradually we incorporated him into the paper. Next door was Teenburger, which was Barney Bubbles operating a freelance design studio out of one tiny room. Every week or so he'd put on an ageing rucksack, stick his thumb out and vanish to the country, where he'd drop large amounts of acid and then wander in a few days later. We knew nothing about Barney, other than that he'd been to San Francisco and worked with Stanley Mouse, who designed the posters you couldn't read for the Fillmore.

ANDREW BAILEY: I was in awe of Barney because I recognised even in my unformed mind of the time that he was a bona fide talent, that he was seminal to a whole school of design that you can still see aspects of today. The sort of things he did in print are still around in magazines like *The Face* and god knows what. All that stuff he did for Stiff a bit later. Always a sad character but a genuine hippie.

JONATHON GREEN: Barney was an inveterate hippie. Drugs with everything. He'd made an arrangement with a caff in Golborne Road. He'd give them a lump of hash and every time we went there for lunch, which was most days, they'd crumble a little over his steak and chips.

KEITH MORRIS: Barney was great. He was probably the most original and innovative designer that's worked in London, bar none. I know that sounds very extravagant but I really believe it. Now I am very good at making people's dreams come true. If someone has a picture in their head, I'm very good at interpreting it and making the scene work. I'm not the greatest guy to make the initial picture. And one of the great things about working with Barney was that in literally 30 seconds he could just generate great visual beginnings. There are very few designers you'll ever come across who are actually going to spark like that.

At one point he gave up and we found him in a supermarket stacking shelves. He was always worried about his weight, swigging 'Wate-On'. He was a bit aware of being little and physically inconsequential and he was always trying to put weight on. Like a lot of very very bright, very talented people he did live on this edge of insanity. But people who worked with him, whether they were clients, or people like me or even straight, hard-nosed printers, they all had incredible respect. He had an enormous talent, he was a terrific visionary and his design now is ahead of its time. There's a whole cult of collecting Bubbles going on now.

JONATHON GREEN: Steve and Eddie didn't seem to take a very active part in the paper, which was fine by us. They had other things to do and in March they put together their magnum opus: the great Brinsley Schwarz hype. This involved transporting dozens of freeloading hacks to New York to witness the debut of this then totally unknown English band at the legendary Fillmore East.

DOUG SMITH: The promoters in Notting Hill, apart from us, Clearwater, were Famepushers, who worked above *Friends*. Eddie and Steve. Steve was Jewish. They were a couple of film guys; they had money out of films and they wanted to get into the music business and that's how Dave Robinson, with his Irish blarney, conned them. And they did the Brinsley Schwarz hype. There was some film they'd made money out of and they were flashing it around. They put this whole Famepushers package together. They did a beautiful con, but it was Dave who did all the conning. It was he who arranged for Aer Lingus to do the airplane, it was he that arranged for Head Limousines to meet them in New York. They couldn't get the band into America. They had to get a private plane to fly them into New York without immigration.

SAM HUTT: That was my first visit to America. A brilliant scam, one of the great scams. I'd heard that we were going to be taken from the airport to our hotel by Head Limousines Incorporated, which was run by this doper taxi driver, and their pledge to us was stereo sounds and reefers in the ashtrays. So we get there and we come rushing out ahead of all the people, including the guy from the *Jewish Chronicle*. (Poor guy. Trapped in the Fillmore East and all he wants is to visit his family. 'They call this music . . .') We come rushing out and there's this long line of limos and from numbers four to twenty are guys in uniforms, but numbers one to three – fruitcakes. And we go rushing up – 'Hey man, are you from Head Limousines?' 'Yeah, man, right . . .' So six or eight of you get in and it's like all the movies you've been watching for a million years. Then you crammed it all into 24 hours because you were off the next day . . .

The guys who ran it were also my clients, I did their doctoring. Eddie was very brash, Steve was very nervous and wound-up.

Eddie and Steve organised a bridge tournament starring Omar Sharif in the Piccadilly Hotel. And because I looked like a freak the man from the *Daily Mail* was asking me a series of questions all of which were leading up to his asking, 'Are you the doctor who gives Omar his drugs?' So I said, 'Yeah, Omar needs the heroin, so I give it to him twice a day. Usually through the eyeball with a bicycle pump. He finds he likes to get it straight through to the brain.' The guy goes running off, at which point Eddie, Steve and their PR go totally spare. And they're convinced that the *Mail* will believe it and the story will be printed next day. And I'm rubbing my eyes thinking, 'Come *on*, lads . . .'

PEARCE MARCHBANK: *Friends* was the smell of feet, the mice that used to run across my drawing board at night: I used to catch them in a little sandwich box that I kept some pens in.

JONATHON GREEN: What made *Friends* much better than any of the other papers which were about was the arrival of David May in early 1970. This red-haired, rather small, West Country person appeared and said that he wanted to do news for us. The only proviso was that he had to be kept anonymous, and his pieces were to be signed 'Hack Type-writers'. He started giving us these incredible stories which I, at any rate, was far too useless to cover: the Mangrove, the Metro, lots of police harassment, black struggle, hippie angst: the proper Notting Hill scene.

DAVID MAY: In 1970 I was working for the *Kensington News*, in Church Street, off Notting Hill. Notting Hill was a great place to be a local journalist. There were fantastic stories: all these houses collapsing, people demonstrating, and the whole scene was building up. Yet there was no one to write it. The underground papers weren't doing it. They were talking about theory, in their own pop way, but had no real news, which I wanted to write. *Time Out* didn't run stories then, so I couldn't work for them. *OZ* I never really fitted in with. So I went to *Friends*. It was all a bit dodgy for me to be working for the *Kensington News* and to be writing freelance for the underground. For a long time I was the only real journalist in the underground press. People used to point this out and I didn't understand it. To me we were all in the same business. I was incredibly envious of people writing these incredibly indulgent 5000-word pieces about a pop star for *Rolling Stone*. I felt very schizophrenic about going to *Friends*. I'd walk down Portobello and go from this very straight world up in Church Street to this complete freaks' world in North Kensington.

PAT BELL: *Friends* was basically financed by Alan's dad. He used to keep dishing it out. Considering how small the whole underground was, Alan's dad could have funded the lot!

ANDREW BAILEY: I used to go to *Friends* on Portobello Road on Saturdays. It was the highlight of my week to go up there and score off Little Tony. *Friends* was unbelievable. It was so exciting. They had these little IBM typewriters that they were actually making magazines on. People doing artwork in front of you on tables . . . nothing had prepared me for this. There was *Friends*, ripping off every image they could find, doing it all on IBM golfballs and actually making a far more vibrant product than the supposedly professional techniques we used at *Rolling Stone* managed. The north end of Portobello Road on a Saturday morning to me was absolutely magic, I loved it.

JONATHON GREEN: One March evening we were all sitting around the office and there appeared this vision of brown leather and long dark hair, a silver belt and an Australian accent. The vision announced itself as Stanislav Demidjuk, then launched almost without pause into his plans for the future. These were to go at once to Paddington Green police station and blow it up, thus striking a necessary blow for the Revolution. So entranced, or perhaps so stoned, were Alan and I that we agreed to this endeavour, not quite knowing how it was to be achieved. So we called the inevitable cab and set off. En route it transpired that the Revolution might have to wait on a slight detour. We stopped at a house in Paddington and Stan rushed in. As we followed we could hear the unmistakable sounds of a fight – crashes, bangs and lots of cursing. It seemed to be coming from upstairs so we went up and there, rolling on the floor, were Stan Demidjuk and Richard Branson.

STAN DEMIDJUK: I arrived in Europe from Australia in 1969. My idea was to settle permanently in England – it seemed very interesting: the Beatles, rock music, sex and drugs and so on. I spent a year in Italy before coming to England and during this time I became politicised. I was properly introduced to Marx at the time and during the students' revolts of '68-'69 I became a convinced Marxist. I came to England in 1970, eager to become involved. I had no money and had to find work quickly. I met some guys giving out leaflets in Oxford Street, from an organisation called Help, which Richard Branson had set up. It gave help to young down-and-outs, druggies, lost children and so on. They needed people to give out leaflets: badly paid, but a job straight away, working with people who seemed to be like myself. I got on well with Branson and he was setting up a new magazine that was to be the backbone of Help, *Student* magazine. I'd written a lot in Australia and had pretensions to becoming a journalist, and he suggested I work on the magazine. The editorial board was made up of pretty interesting people, but we soon realised that *Student* was just a vehicle for selling advertising, for bringing in money, and thus its motivation became questionable. The more we began talking about real political stuff, about the contradictions in English society, the more Branson became worried and clamped down on us writing that kind of article. In the end *Student* was just a cover-up job. It did sell, it was probably well-received at the beginning, but it was not intended as an organ of youth dissidence, it was just the usual advertising hype. We confronted Branson with our views, that we weren't willing to continue working if we weren't allowed to write what we wanted. Branson got very uptight and gave us an ultimatum: knuckle down or leave. He wanted to get rid of everybody but me. I don't know why. There were six or seven of us and we decided unanimously not to back down. He fired the others and in solidarity I left too. There was another complication with Branson: I had started chatting up his charming and beautiful sister; he wasn't keen on that. The office was in his house and I became close to one of his girlfriends too. He didn't like that at all and we had a physical fight about it.

Macrobiotics: 'Can you sell me some brown rice to take home?'

CRAIG SAMS: In 1969 my brother had set up Seed, our macrobiotic restaurant in Bishop's Bridge Road. Three big rooms in the basement of the Gloucester Hotel. We were doing about 80-90 covers a night. There was a certain amount of criticism – 'hippie capitalism' – but we defused it to a certain extent. We had 'The Free Meal' as a menu item. 'If you cannot pay, a free meal is available, comprising rice, vegetables and green tea.' We always did that. At times our patience was tried – people would come down, have the free meal, and then say, 'I'll have an apple crumble,' and we'd say that the apple crumble wasn't included in the free meal and they'd say, 'Oh that's all right,' and whip out a fiver.

In 1970 there were a lot of pop festivals: Bath, Plumpton, Phun City, Isle of Wight. We went to them all. We'd just fill up a truck with food and go down and flog it: muesli for breakfast, red bean stew and brown rice later. And we made a lot of money in the restaurant. So the restaurant became my scene and I was there every evening presiding over events. But the business started to expand and there were people coming in saying, 'Can you sell me some brown rice to take home . . . ?' and so on. So we started packing little things of food for people until we got to the point where we were selling so much value of product off the shelf in the restaurant that it was simpler to start off a shop where they could buy what they wanted. Then with the shop what happened was that other shops started coming in and they wanted to buy pre-packed products and then we began wholesaling and at that point really the restaurant became of secondary importance.

Festivals: 'I must be having fun'

JEFF DEXTER: The festivals destroyed the underground: everyone trying to make a buck out of it. After Woodstock the music industry said, 'Hey, there's a mass audience out there' – it was still wide open and everyone wanted a piece.

BYRON NEWMAN: Rock festivals were pretty horrific. Lots of dope, lots of mud, no sleep, awful food.

JOHN PEEL: The festivals were always gruelling, putting up with constant indignities at the hands of Hell's Angels, and various power-mad people of one sort or another. I said very very early on in the festival game that they reminded me of nothing so much as National Service. I seriously suggested that medals should be struck for people who had survived various festivals so that they could wear them with pride when they were stupid enough to go to other festivals.

JOHNNY BYRNE: The big pop festivals I never had any time for – I

318

could never believe in joining a mass of ant-like figures watching a stage quarter of a mile away and not even able to hear.

JOHN LEAVER: Festivals. I'm sitting in the middle of a field with 50,000 other people and the Grateful Dead are half a mile away and I'm thinking, 'I must be having fun.'

DAVID GOODMAN: The greatest festival of them all was Trentishoe, an obscure little festival on the top of an 800-foot high cliff on the coast of Devon; cloud was coming in off the sea onto the site, and we were constantly warned about falling off the edge. The Pink Fairies had a big tent and Mick Farren was with us. And we were all basically completely insane. We were taking so much acid, it was beyond all reason. I remember one evening Larry Wallis saying, 'I've got X amount left, who's going to have some?' So we all ate them, lots of them, very powerful. And I sat there thinking, 'Oh my God, it's going to be a hefty one. Do I really want to sit around with my chums?' So off I went and sat down in this field. I disappeared: left the body, if you believe all that crap . . . Don't know where I went but I wasn't around. When I did come back it was getting dusky and there was this voice going in my ear which I couldn't quite focus on but which was becoming ever clearer and it was saying, 'The submarine will be arriving shortly on the coastline and don't fall off the 800-foot cliff, hippies, the submarine will be arriving shortly . . .' I thought, 'Brilliant, brilliant . . . that's me, the submarine, yeah.' Then there was another bulletin: 'The farmer has arrived by submarine on the banks of the 800-foot high cliff, now, hippies, don't crowd around, we don't want you falling off. He'll be arriving by helicopter . . .' 'Helicopter, shit, man, that's pretty heavy.' I'm on my feet. Walking towards this voice. 'The farmer has arrived . . .' and a helicopter starts up and I'm marching towards this noise and I'm at the edge of the tents and things and there's a small crowd and a ramp at the front of the stage and there's this farmer in his tweeds, his jodhpurs. He's giving out this Woodstock rap. And all of a sudden he tears off all his tweeds, and he's got a wig on and he's got this great big quiff and all these girls come out with great big polka-dot dresses and Helen Shapiro beehives and I can't believe it. It's the Bath Arts Workshop and it all comes clear to me . . .

SAM HUTT: I did the Bath Festival at Shepton Mallett in 1970. It was brilliant. I had nine doctors eight of whom were freaks and one was straight. And one of the great images of the 60s was in the medical hut at Bath: the doctors getting down on the ground with the people having the bad trips and hugging them back into being all right again. We didn't just shoot them full of largactyl. I remember loving one guy back. He was completely out of it, completely gone. He talked in this funny high voice like a cartoon from *Film Fun*. Eventually he decided that he was . . . ready for the outside world! He said, 'Hold me from the back, hold me up.' So I was behind him and he was standing on my feet and I was walking behind him with my arms under his and we were walking along and he was saying, 'OK, I'm ready now.' And I'm saying, 'OK, all right, mate, you're ready . . .' And you get to the door of the tent and there's the whole thing milling around and we stand and this guy says, 'All right, I can go another couple of feet . . . all right . . . oh, oh, doc! We'll have to go back a bit!' and all the time holding on to him. And there's one doctor, very straight, who disrespects me to this day because of that.

In fact, a pop festival was a fucking ludicrous place to take acid: the sight of a hundred thousand faces can give you the willies, seriously. Because you see the pain in those faces. For the last six hours of the Bath Festival I signed off, said, 'OK lads, it's all fine,' signed off and dropped my trips. The very last act was Dr John. He came on fourteen hours late, I think, about 6.30 in the morning, and he was the most stoned person I have ever seen in my life. He was so massively stoned he couldn't move his eyes in his head, nor could he move his head on his shoulders and if he needed to look at you he had to move his whole body. But he was brilliant.

SU SMALL: Bath was when I worked out how not to go to a festival. Which is to bum a lift and get there without any tent, no coat, no sensible shoes.

PETER BROWN: At Bath the perimeter had this wire around it, with barbed wire on top of which had been strung multi-coloured lightbulbs: psychedelic barbed wire. I was ripped to the tits but I'll never forget what happened: at about three in the morning on come Steppenwolf singing 'Born to be Wild'. The entire encampment is pretty weird by now, bonfires flaming and so on. We're inside this wire fence topped with barbed wire, the bonfires blazing up all over the place and Steppenwolf, a most inappropriate band, singing a most inappropriate song. It sounded great though, horrific but great. Then suddenly there was this extraordinary surge of dreadful-looking people who started bashing the wire, they were going round the perimeter beating out the lightbulbs to the sound of Steppenwolf . . . 'Head out on the highway, keep your motor running . . .' and it's like popping lightbulbs and explosions and then they were busting the electric cable, which was only thin, and that drops onto the wire and electrifies it, the sparks jumping . . .

320

JONATHON GREEN: The bands were uniformly late, and for most people uniformly inaudible. The queues for everything were massive, and you disciplined yourself neither to eat, drink or shit. The field sloped down towards the stage, providing a nice natural bowl, but the promoters in their wisdom had sited a ring of portaloos around the top of the field. Thus, when they overflowed, those hippies who were good vibing away immediately next to them doubtless regretted it. There was a certain romance about all the tents, the campfires and so on – enhanced, no doubt, by the fact that one didn't have to sleep in one.

Gay Liberation: 'Nobody so straight ever joined a revolutionary movement'

ANDREW LUMSDEN: In 1970 two LSE students, Bob Mellers and Aubrey Waters, came back from the States and started Gay Liberation Front meetings. (Waters is founder of the Gay Men's Press, the biggest gay publishing house.) So I became involved – nobody so straight as I was ever joined a revolutionary movement. Some of those who started it, like Waters, were Marxists of varying hues. What struck me was that I had never seen such roomfuls of wholly different-looking people as those who met at the LSE at the time. The counterculture was there, drag queens were there, a minority of lesbians, heavy-duty political people. Various people who'd worked on the Campaign for Homosexual Law Reform in the 50s and were horrified by the blatancy, the dangers, the backlash and so on.

It's pretty obvious now that GLF came out of the ethnic melting-pot of New York and Los Angeles, where people identify themselves as Italian Americans, Chinese Americans, Jewish Americans and so on. It's not much of a jump to say, 'I'm a gay American.' Whereas in Britain we didn't and we don't think like that. We'd probably have called ourselves 'Dorothys', from Dorothy in *The Wizard of Oz*.

JIM ANDERSON: I didn't do much in terms of being a political activist. I just marched when they marched, waved a banner when there was a banner to wave, and held up a placard when there was something to demonstrate against. I went to all the meetings and wore Gay Liberation buttons. I believed that what one had to do is come out and make a noise about it and be seen and the fuss will die away. You have to disseminate the message loudly and openly and publicly, which is what I did then.

ANDREW LUMSDEN: I got to know Jim Anderson at *OZ* in late 1970. Once GLF had started in October '70 efforts were made to get the alternative press to run gay stories or columns or pages – and there was terrible resistance. I think *Seven Days* was the first. I went in there with Dennis Lemon and I think they ran a page, or at least a story, on gays. Though they may not have been the first. A lot of gays were involved in *Frendz*, as I later came to know.

The Pink Fairies: 'Go to gigs, get hideously drunk and harangue the audience'

DAVID GOODMAN: King Crimson's debut at the Speakeasy was destroyed by what was then known as the Pink Fairies Drinking Club, which was anybody and everybody out of the Shaftesbury Avenue flat, the odd Pretty Thing, Steve Took . . . Mandelkau came up with the name. He'd been writing a book with the Pink Fairies in it.

RUSSELL HUNTER: The idea of becoming the Pink Fairies had been mooted while we were away. The wires had hummed about Twink dumping the Pretty Things. He and Jamie had this concept about a band. Micky, Steve Took and Twink had tried to get a band called the Pink Fairies off the ground while we were away. But all they did was go to gigs, get hideously drunk, and harangue the audience. Everybody threw things at them. Twink decided that this wasn't actually the way to further his musical career and dumped Took and Micky and suggested he should join the Deviants and form a band. Which we did.

DAVID GOODMAN: The Fairies song that used to drive everybody mad, apart from 'The Snake', the legendary single, was 'Uncle Harry's Last Freakout'. What it actually was was the best riffs from all the Deviants' songs strung together and psychedelicised out. It went on for 45 minutes. When we went back to London we got Twink to be a second drummer, because we'd seen the Grateful Dead with two drummers and, wallop! that was the Pink Fairies. So we get home and we're all penniless right at the start of 1970. The first gig was at the Roundhouse and it was just magic right from the word go.

The Fairies were working five nights a week at their peak. And we'd built a very good grass-roots following and got a very good name for ourselves and we were packing out good-sized halls at this point all over the country. Hawkwind had come along at the same time and the Pinkwind thing started. It was an amalgamation of the two bands because we were always playing at the same venues.

So I toured for years and years and years with the Pink Fairies and Paul Rudolph quit, and he was a cunt for doing that because we were just about to crack it big, and we broke up. Hawkwind released *Silver Machine* and went big. We re-formed nine months later with a guy

322

called Mick Wayne on guitar and went on a tour that was virtually sold out but by the end of each night each hall was empty cos it was so completely and utterly and drastically totally different to what the fans wanted which was 'Uncle Harry's Last Freakout'. It was just embarrassing and very sad. And we dropped Wayne and put in Larry Wallis and started clawing back our respect and our following and we did all the right work for the right people and the right benefits but we just couldn't make the money. And finally I quit and begged H who was at Dingwalls booking the bands and went in and played them all my favourite Small Faces records and so on and became the Dingwalls DJ.

H: 'I can't really believe that he's dead'

PETER SHERTSER: H was Howard Parker. I knew him very well. I first met him when he was a DJ at the In Club, which was in Baker Street, owned by John Bloom, the guy who did the washing machines. We used to get in there through the underground car park, through the back entrance. They had a guy on the door called Carlo who eventually come after us with a cosh. H was playing R&B in amongst all the rest of the shit. We got to know him because we went up and said, 'Hey, how come you're playing all this kind of stuff?' and he said how he loved the music and one thing and another and we became friends. We knew him when he was Hendrix's roadie too.

MELISSA CHASSAY: In late '65 John Bloom had a club near the Planetarium. H was working for him as a DJ. I was astonished by him because his trousers were tied on with string and his car, which was some kind of classic like a Riley, had two doors missing, and he had very long hair. Very wonderful blond hair.

H lived in Nut Cottage, Acton, and Mr Parker worked for the Gas Board. Mrs Parker was a very strong, very funny, absolutely wonderful person. And there was a sister who was slightly upwardly mobile. It was a genteel lower-middle-class home. Mr Parker built a telescope and joined the Astronomical Society. This was a clever family. Mrs Parker was always distraught that H, who'd been a clever boy at school, got into rock'n'roll and wore these weird clothes and had these terrible people around.

In '67 into town came the legendary Jimi Hendrix, and we all went to see him at the Scotch of St James's. Chas Chandler had discovered him on one of these tours, and he was the happening thing, the new thing. H was a person with obsessions. The four obsessions in H's life were Jimi Hendrix, John Lennon, Arthur Janov and Frank Zappa: these were his four role models. He became Jimi's roadie. He loved Jimi. We all loved Jimi but H wanted to be Jimi. Jimi was the most charming, polite person in the entire world. If you went to his house he took off your coat, that kind of thing. If you went backstage there'd be a queue of girls waiting there. One by one they'd go in and Jimi would fuck them and then they'd come out and the next one would go in and after an hour he'd go on stage and tear the place apart. And every day H would drive to Nut Cottage, Acton, at 5.30 with Jimi's shirts and Mrs Parker, with a lot of complaining, would iron and starch them. Then we'd put them on a hanger and we'd drive them back to Jimi's apartment and then we'd take them to the gig. It was a shame that they didn't take H to America – it broke his heart. He was devoted to Jimi, but he was his equal, he wasn't a sucking-up type. If Jimi had had H with him for ever he probably wouldn't have got so lonely.

SUE MILES: Miles knew Zappa. I'm not sure how, and we'd gone to the Royal Garden Hotel in Kensington to meet Zappa after hearing the Cream play, the first time they'd played live. And H was there. Zappa said, 'This is my great friend,' though in fact he'd met him that day too. H just appeared and from then on would just hang out. He was Hendrix's roadie until he said to him, 'Jimi, you look like a gorilla that's lost its bananas,' one morning when Hendrix was looking a bit seedy on some runway at Stockholm Airport and this wasn't taken as the best remark at the time.

MELISSA CHASSAY: After Jimi went back to the States H then got mad about Zappa, from hearing the records, and decided that he was going to LA to be his disciple. He flew off to LA on some kind of festival project and the next thing we knew he was living with Frank . . . H came back from Frank in '69. Then he had a very bad patch when he didn't really know what to do and decided that he was going mad and sat in his room in Blenheim [Crescent] writing mad lyrics. The problem with H was that he always wanted to be a pop star. He then decided that since he was mad he should go to see Arthur Janov and we must all raise the money to send him to Janov because this was the only thing that would save him. The problem was that after nine months things had changed. There was much more efficiency, much more order in the music business. It was an industry: roadies were now people who humped gear, they weren't people who hung out with the musicians and the whole thing was much more stratified and class-ridden. So H had lost his place, really. There he was, so clever, so much energy, but he was still living in this '67 mode.

STEVE SPARKS: H was very much involved with UFO. I first came in contact with him when he was Hendrix's roadie. I used to run into him at Track. I can't really believe that he's dead. H is one of the people I expect to run into in New York. You used to run into him in strange places, and he was always in control. He got run over in Portobello by a drunk policeman, yet within 24 hours, in hospital with a broken pelvis and two broken legs, he had arranged an entire year's work as a tour manager, backdated a month, so he could sue the policeman for a fortune and he did and he got it.

Apple: 'The dream was over'

DEREK TAYLOR: By 1970 the purse-strings had been tied and Paul was not now there and the falling-out began – seriously – between them. All of them really. The Beatles had become a piece of Apple and no one really liked Apple and nobody liked the Beatles. And indeed that would be where Bag Productions came from. It was Yoko. Yoko was a bona fide avant-garde woman from New York who'd established herself in London. It suited John very well. She was an extremely congenial vehicle for his own eccentricities. She validated a lot of his mad thoughts. She was someone who was every bit as barmy as he was. Or every bit as creative as he was. Which is why the Beatles had got along: they were four people who were really made for each other. And Yoko was made for a portion of John's psychology. She was very suitable. They had a mission.

JEFF DEXTER: I used to go to Apple, to see Derek. By 1970 it wasn't so friendly any more. Everyone had their own little scene, all these different camps had built up. I ran into Allen Klein in the elevator one time. I was on acid and I gave him an ear-bashing. They were trying to run Apple, being open and free, and losing everything and he'd come in to tidy them up. I said to him, 'The only way to do it, if you're really the great hero of the business world, is to set up the musical bank.' The idea was to get everyone in the music business to bank there. Putting all the music business money into one unit that would grow, play the market and become part of the Establishment, as everyone was beginning to do. That was my big acid flash: this is the way to stop the Beatles breaking up, save the whole scene. I was prepared to front it, I was fearless in those days. But Klein thought I was a complete lunatic.

JOHN DUNBAR: Allen Klein seems unpleasant but in a way he's quite good because he's one of those guys who is openly rapacious. He doesn't pretend to be some fucking vicar at a tea party. So in a way he's easier to deal with. Yet lots of my friends did have a falling-out with him – Paul and John fell out, so did the Stones – but if they were going to let him handle stuff, they just should have taken care. He's so obviously like that, his reputation is so fucking bad. You've always got to be careful, to bring in someone else to watch the guy who's handling the money. The Beatles had this firm of posh accountants and one of the partners fucked off to the Bahamas really early on with half their loot. Some offshore number. Klein is an honest rogue. And apparently he really likes the music.

DEREK TAYLOR: I think Apple must have given out a considerable amount of money, if you add it up. But it wouldn't get to six figures in all. What John was initiating with Yoko would certainly add up. John should have recognised that when he was getting panicky and saying, 'We've been bled dry,' and all that. A lot of the bleeding was done by Bag Productions.

How long did I think it would go on? One day at a time . . . for ever, really. That was the idea. Till 1970: then I wanted it to end frequently and I started looking for other work. The thing about wanting it to end was that I thought it would break their hearts if I left. But I didn't quite know how to. Because I also felt it would be disloyal. But in fact they didn't mind at all. It was less people on the payroll, less madness. They'd had the famous falling-out between Paul and John and by 1971 John had taken against all of us and was giving grumpy interviews to *Rolling Stone*. Paul had lost patience with the whole caboodle and Ringo and George were pretty much leading their own lives. George sent me home in mid-April 1970. The dream was over, as John said.

IT: 'The fuzz came in one day'

ANDREW LUMSDEN: I thought, how do I get to know a homosexual? 'Gay' was an underground camp word, and if you didn't live in that world, you didn't know the word. So I put an ad in *IT*. They got busted on a corruption charge later but at the time they were the only people printing contact ads. I got about twelve answers, mostly from Indians or Pakistanis, trainee accountants and so on.

GRAHAM KEEN: The fuzz came in one day, showed their warrants and said they wanted to take copies away. They had a warrant under the Obscene Publications Act. It was months later that they decided they were going to prosecute. One of the cops who did us kept saying, 'Nothing personal, lads, all in the line of duty,' and later he got six months himself for taking bribes from Soho pornographers.

SUE MILES: I remember seeing this bomb-squad policeman talking to Mick Farren after *IT* was busted: 'Now then, Mick, you and I are men of the world ...' and I thought, 'Which world is this guy talking about?'

GRAHAM KEEN: When they decided to charge us they didn't arrest us but came and read the charge to us in our solicitor's office. The charges were conspiracy to corrupt public morals and conspiracy to outrage public decency. We were all arraigned at Wells Street magistrates court. There was this amazing scene: the whole of the foyer was packed with gays who had been dredged from the box numbers. It was pathetic, really. We played it all down purposely. Pete Stanshill was adamant that we should go through the trial without making a fuss. The gays would come up and say, 'Let's have a procession with banners and so on,' and Pete would say, 'No, no, no. Cool it.' So we didn't try to make an *OZ* trial out of it – which I believe was a mistake. If we'd had somebody as lively as Felix behind us, I think we could have made a real song and dance. We were guilty of not vetting the ads closely enough. A lot of things got through that might have involved people under 21, which has remained the gay age of consent. The trial really ended my involvement with *IT*. The appeal came two years later, after the *OZ* trial. It only threw out one item: the conspiracy to outrage public decency. We collected money to pay the fines: Hockney gave us a couple of hundred, Defence of Literature and the Arts gave us some, we had a benefit which lost money: Phun City. I didn't even go.

MICK FARREN: By mid-1970 *IT* was in terrible disarray. The fines after the gay ads bust had been paid, through some nefarious scheme, and Stanshill and Dave Hall were really burned out. They had to liquidate the company that had been running it during the fat days – Knullar – and that went into bankruptcy through the fines. It needed another company and nobody else was going to run it, although some of the help was still there – Hamburger Mary [the typesetter] and a few people. Even before that there'd been weird sorts of turn arounds, all sorts of ideas like not putting anybody's byline on anything ... Basically the people who'd been running it had got burned out yet again, and the help were running it. After Phun City everyone conspired and we did the issue after Phun City and we started putting in all these *New York Post* headlines and it went on from there.

STEVE MANN: By the time of Phun City I had well and truly plunged into the underground world. I had been on *IT* for eight or nine months.

I was the Music Editor. I got into it basically when Micky turned the paper into a revolutionary tract. I think I was pretty deeply into that. The party line was very very vague: we had to overthrow Western civilisation as soon as possible – before lunchtime preferably, although that wasn't too easy because we didn't get up very early. It was the Black Panthers that really got Micky into it. I think he always secretly wanted to be a Black Panther – he had the hair, but he didn't have the skin colour.

The White Panthers: 'There were only two'

MICK FARREN: We formed the White Panther Party to do something, I don't know what. Some down near Greenwich, a hotbed up in Manchester, a bunch of street kids on the Grove doing the free-food thing, little bunches, groups. People want a name, post-hippies out of money wandering round wondering what had happened to flower power and walking around in worn-out velvet pants. Furious amounts of drugs – people were shooting heroin by then. Post-hippie junkies.

JOHN PEEL: There were only two White Panthers and Mick Farren was the leader. I went round to his flat one day and Mick was always telling me about all this 'property is theft' stuff. He had some Gene Vincent LPs that I was rather keen to own, so I said, 'I don't feel as strongly about it as you do, but I'll take these Gene Vincent LPs,' but it turned out that property was theft except for Gene Vincent LPs.

STEVE MANN: It all started when John Sinclair got busted in the States. He ran the US White Panthers. I forget what Micky's title was – Grand Vizier or something – but I was Minister of Information. Everybody had to be Minister of something. It was very much based on the Black Panthers. We didn't really do an awful lot, apart from try and cause trouble.

Phun City: 'It made everything worthwhile'

MICK FARREN: Phun City developed from the idea of a benefit for *IT*. It was in June 1970, the 21st, 22nd, 23rd, a date I remember because Edward Barker forgot to put the date on the posters and we had to write it on with magic marker. It was just outside Worthing, which was where I grew up and was the horrible vengeance I took on these bumpkins. There was me and Su Small and Edward and Steve Mann all living in the same apartment and the lovely Caroline McKechnie and Ingrid and we were all conspiring. And we all went up onto the top floor of Endell Street and put up a lot of charts and flow diagrams

328

all over the wall and found that we had 2/9d or something to actually fund this enterprise.

I had got it into my head to have a grandiose event in the old style, or at least find out what the new style would be. So we tried Alexandra Palace and parks and football fields and movie studios, but lacking basic funds we never really got into any of this. And then we said, 'Why don't we have a rock festival in a field?' To do this one has to know a farmer and I knew a farmer and we said, 'Will you rent us your field?' He said, 'Sure,' and then we had a field, which was our first asset. Then we started parlaying the field into various other things and we got a caterer who gave us an advance and we got an enormously wealthy dope dealer who gave us some money and we started generating money. We started running up credit on the bill, the attractions. We were bringing the MC5 over, which was quite a radical idea, and other bands came in and then we hit the crunch: we had to set up this rock festival. We actually contacted everybody in the world who had light-shows and inflatables and odd towers that they'd stolen from a Rolling Stones concert and as much of that stuff as possible was erected but it required massive amounts of money so we eventually went to Ronan O'Rahilly, after falling out with loads of other people. And Ronan started sort of paying the bills. And brought down a huge film unit, and Friday night there was a rock festival. Strange.

It became very peculiar right from the outset. We had this guy called Pete Currie doing distribution for *IT*. He was basically a trucker from Rhodesia, I believe; he had this strange accent, and he had a big Mercedes staff car which he drove around and actually became a Hell's Angel for a short while and was also one of the Blackheath Foot and Death Men – one of the only psychedelic Morris dancing groups in the world. So I'd been driving around London in a velvet suit behaving like Phil Spector raising money. Gez and Mac and Boss had been down at the field – literally I was raising money while they were there waiting to pay off the scaffolding man. And Gez [Cox] and I had already had lengthy meetings with our hair tucked down our jackets with the chief of police and so on, and there was starting to be a whiff all round that there was no money, that the thing was half erected and there was no money.

On the Tuesday or Wednesday it came and I went down with a bag of money to meet Boss. Meanwhile, 2000 hippies had moved down to this little clump of woods that was at the side of the field and had built Narnia in there. Except that they were recalcitrant and nasty and started referring to all these people with jeeps and stuff as 'superhippies'. And there was some kind of ugly rumblings and they were going to have their own festival. Anyway in the middle of the night I turned up with Peter

Currie and Edward in the Mercedes like Rommel and we transferred into the jeep with Boss and everybody carrying axe handles saying, 'Listen, motherfuckers, this festival is going to be and I don't want no shit.' I made a long speech and they all cheered. At that point we'd decided that the bands weren't going to be paid and that the money wasn't going to be collected because what we weren't ever going to be able to do was put up security fences to get the money. After we'd filled the hippies with revolutionary spirit we went up the local pub and filled ourselves with more commercial spirit. Then I stayed awake for a week.

It was great fun at times and at one time I wanted to shoot myself, telling all these bands we weren't going to pay them. The only band who wouldn't play for nothing was Free who went home in disgust. Saturday night when the MC5 played was really quite magical. It was a nice feeling to have created all that. It definitely wasn't Woodstock, it was much more peculiar. There was William Burroughs wandering about with his tape recorder, doing instant cut-ups. It rained most of the time.

The next morning the police brutality squad came in and beat everybody up. We got the fuck out of town and never went back. It didn't seem very prudent – they wanted to put somebody in jail. And no money was made from this benefit, absolutely none. We ended up with 2/9d as well.

MARTIN CROPPER: Phun City was not fun. Very much not fun. When we got there we thought, 'Right, now we can sell all this dope,' which we had spent the night before parcelling up into Oxo-cube-sized quid deals. Every time we offered some dope we found that everyone else was selling dope. The whole fucking festival was a convention of dope dealers trying to sell each other the same stuff.

CHRIS ROWLEY: Phun City was great fun. Phun City was a festival that almost didn't happen but when it did happen it was a festival for about 4000 people, so for once the crowd matched the facilities. Phun City had a great spirit, the MC5 played a memorable set of hard American revolutionary rock. Early in the afternoon David Goodman, who was the stage manager, asked the crowd to move the stage. And 800 or so people picked the stage up and rotated it.

DAVID GOODMAN: The miracle of the moving stage is still a story told amongst the folklore of hippiedom: what happened was that I'd gone down there with my crew to build the stage. So the stage has been built willy-nilly and nobody's really thought about it. And all of a sudden I start to notice – just as the roof was about to go on – that running above

330

it is the main electricity pylon. So I asked around and took advice and yes, it would be fucking dumb to have a whopping great PA directly below the main electric cables, especially if it rained. This little guy who put the stage together couldn't believe it, the thought of dismantling it all . . . But I said, 'No, man, we'll carry it,' and he said, 'Impossible,' and I said, 'Rubbish. We'll get all the hippies out of the woods and we'll go 1-2-3 and lift and we'll carry the fucker and put it over there.' So we argued and he said, 'Go on then, fucking do it!' So I got my gang and we went into the woods where there was at least 500 hippies camped out. And I said, 'Look, I don't know whether you can bear it or not, but can you do us all a favour? The stage has been put in the wrong place, we've got to move it. They say it can't be done.' So everybody goes, 'Let's go.' And I go '1-2-3,' the fucking hippies lift the stage and we carry it 100 yards across the field.

CRAIG SAMS: There were two people doing catering at Phun City – ourselves and Red Umbrella. And the guy who ran Red Umbrella had been told that there would be 30,000 people coming. So when he realised that there would be about 3000 people, he raised his prices. He had all this food and he needed to get his money back. That's when the Hell's Angels bopped him. We were also in trouble with him because while we very piously weren't serving any sugar with the porridge we were doing for breakfast, people were getting these steaming trays of porridge and shooting over to his place where they'd sprinkle his free sugar on it. Which he didn't like.

MARTIN CROPPER: The Hell's Angels got hold of the local drug squad who thought they were in plain clothes but they weren't really. They were identified from the stage. They were then tied to a tree and humiliated. When they escaped they waited till that night and first thing next morning they came team-handed and destroyed that whole teepee culture that the hippies had set up in the woods. A friend of mine from Cambridge stayed behind and he buried his dope when he heard the law were coming. Lots of people did and there were rumours that in fact there was a king's ransom in Black Pak underneath the sod of Phun City.

JEFF DEXTER: Phun City was the only festival I got handsomely paid for, and the only one I thought I wouldn't get paid for. At the end of it I was asked by Hugh Nolan, 'Have you been paid?' and I said, 'No, I don't think anyone has.' And he said, 'If anyone gets paid it should be you. All the money's supposed to have gone, but don't worry. The notes have gone, but all the silver and copper is left.' And he gave me a sack

331

full of coins. What a great way to be paid! I don't know how much it was, but it was enough, more than enough for being there.

STEVE MANN: Phun City was magnificent: it made everything worthwhile. When the MC5 finally got on stage, Wayne Kramer machine-gunning the audience, Micky was crying, I was crying, everybody was crying. It was wonderful. There was a *News of the World* reporter who freaked out totally. He came down to do a hatchet job, got given a lot of acid, and he just freaked out and he *loved* it. He actually got to be a real pest because he was so keen. Saul on the road to Damascus, it really was. This total reversal – he left his job, God knows what became of him.

DOUG SMITH: The only reason Phun City was successful was because it was a completely haphazard mess. But it was a fun gig. It was exactly what would happen if you let Boss and Micky put on a festival.

Isle of Wight Festival '70: 'The beginning of the end of hippie'

ANDREW BAILEY: The Isle of Wight festivals were all part of that phenomenon of England wanting to have its own equivalent scene. *Rolling Stone*, being a very self-conscious publication, wanted the Isle of Wight Festival to be the English equivalent of Woodstock, which it never was in a million years.

NICK LAIRD-CLOWES: I ran away from home in August 1970 to go to the Isle of Wight Pop Festival. My sister and I hoaxed my poor father into believing that I was a friend's mother calling up to ask us to stay in some remote Sussex village. My father fell for it, put us on the train, and we got off the train at the first stop, took another train back to London and tried to hitchhike. After about two hours we decided to go to Paddington or wherever it was and get on the train with no money. After about an hour or so a couple got onto our train, and they were heavily glamorous hippies. He had apple-green satin trousers, she had a turquoise suede jacket . . . They got on the train and they were incredible, it was like fate. And they sat down and we started talking. 'Where are you going?' 'The Isle of Wight,' we said. 'We've run away from home.' Then they started talking about Neil Young and I was absolutely obsessed by Neil Young already and I started saying, 'Well that guitar solo on such and such . . . that fourth note from the right . . .' and he was going, 'That's right, that's right . . .' and he was, like, 26, twice my age. They really liked us. When we got to the Isle of Wight they paid our fares and said, 'Don't worry, stick with us, we've got a tent and you can stay with us.' So you get to the Isle of Wight and you couldn't believe that there were this many people. It looked like pieces of rags. They took us out into this incredible battlefield. It was unbelievable and could have been so awful but the next morning we woke up and there were the Pink Fairies and Hawkwind playing outside the walls and there was Jeff Dexter unpacking records because he was the DJ. So finally, with incredible difficulty, we got back to London and this thing, this festival, had completely changed my life.

DAVID GOODMAN: While the mad fuckers were talking about tearing down the walls and all that stuff, what we did was liberate the big in-flatable tent that was behind the main stage. We basically held the guy to ransom, saying, 'We could make money for you and us, we're taking over. Otherwise we're going to stop the generator.' So he let us in and we had a stage and Hawkwind and the Pink Fairies played there and we charged 50p to come in and kip there.

JEFF DEXTER: Those festivals were all chaotic. I hated Micky Farren the year he pulled the alternative festival bit. That White Panther bit was so silly. We were preaching peace and love, they were trashing the fences, saying it all should be free.

STEVE MANN: The Panthers at the Isle of Wight were very effective, but then again it wasn't really our doing: it was this huge tribe of people camped out on the hill with their sign saying 'Desolation Row'. They were well into the idea of a free festival – it only needed a couple of people to shout a bit and they were well into the idea of storming the fences. And Micky shouted. We did do a news-sheet, a White Panther call to arms: 'Come on brothers! Storm the barricades!'

DUNCAN FALLOWELL: When I left university I wanted to be a writer, but seriously underestimated the amount of self-discipline this took. I thought you took lots of drugs, you splurged, you invoked the previous examples of William Burroughs and the beats and assumed that the rest of the world would find this incredibly fascinating. At the same time I wrote to the *Spectator* and told them that they didn't have anybody under the age of 40 writing about what was happening to people under the age of 40. They wrote back and offered me a column and said, 'You're absolutely right, will you go to the Isle of Wight Festival?' Bob Dylan was there. But I was so shattered and surprised by this that I'd already made arrangements for my bank holiday and I thought, 'I'm not going to rearrange my bank holiday just for this,' so I listened to it on Radio One.

I wrote my article based on what they said. Also, the next day, I bought the *Daily Express* and wrote the opposite of their interpretation. I knew that was bound to be right. They said there were lots of Hell's Angels tearing the place apart; I said there were very few Hell's Angels and they caused no trouble. And it turned out by the end of the week that I'd guessed right, and I knew I would have. Most people knew nothing about Mick Farren and the Pink Fairies pulling down the fences. And despite being important local lads, they were rather less important than the fact that 499,000 people were actually watching Bob Dylan.

JOHN LEAVER: The Isle of Wight: inadequate toilet facilities; millions of people; being very far away from the bands; pretending to oneself that one was having a good time and occasionally having it.

JONATHAN PARK: Once upon a time a number of people went to the Isle of Wight to visit a pop festival. And when they drove off the ferry lots of people in civilian clothes swooped on them. They said, 'These cars go over this way,' and then these civilians stopped the car and got the people out of the car and flattened them against the bonnet and started to rifle in their pockets and found a variety of drugs of many and various different types – enough for the weekend. One of them, who was a black guy, a very very black Rastafarian, Alan Marcuson's friend Joe who did the cooking in the tent, got away because he simply closed his eyes and they didn't see him. Phone calls were made to London to the flat of these people who were in the car, where a certain person was living, and he was so nervous that he took the stash and distributed it the length of Belsize Park Gardens.

I was travelling with Marcuson and Joe in one car and Jon Goodchild, with a couple of German girls, was driving the other. As I'd gone over Kew Bridge Alan said, 'Watch this car here, this guy is going to drive past.' As this guy drove past the window opened and a hand came out. And I put my hand out and I received a whole handful of various forms of medicaments. Some of this was mescalin. So I dropped some of the mescalin and put the rest away. We drove on and we got down to the coast and queued up and got on the ferry, larked about a bit, got off the other side and got busted. By this time I was really flying. All I can remember is sitting in the police station at Ryde with a very large, very benign, elderly Isle of Wight constable sitting there, looking at my various degrees and things, which I'd had to put down, and saying, 'What's a young chap like you doing in a place like this?' All I was doing was sitting there singing to him 'Who do you love?' I'm absolutely streaming with this mescalin. He was huge, 6′ 6″, and he was totally calm, he wasn't

334

at all upset by this, he just looked at me kindly. All the others were really aggressive – you could see the red in their eyes.

We were in there for a couple of nights. I was put in the same cell as Alan and a young French boy who had no chance of getting out. He was in there for stealing a loaf of bread. All through the night, while they were trying to sleep and I was streaming with this mescalin, I thought, 'There are lots of people in this jail who can't get out cos they don't have English addresses.' So I called the jailer over and said, 'I demand my rights, I want my pencil and paper.' He said, 'I'm not going to give you them.' So I screamed through the door 'Off the pig!' and watched his eyes turn red. Amazingly, half an hour later he brought me a small stub of a pencil and a piece of paper. I wrote down a message which said, 'There are lots of us in here who can't get out, I think we ought to start a bust fund.' I gave it to the jailer and to his eternal credit he actually let it out. It got back to the festival site and a bust fund was arranged. They passed this big cardboard box through the audience about six times and it came back absolutely full of money. Thousands of pounds, maybe two thousand. There was more before the Hell's Angels took their cut. I spoke to Caroline Coon from Release and she paid all the fines for all the foreigners in the jail, and then divided the rest of the money equally between everyone else who had been busted, so everyone got £10-£15. And for some slightly elitist reason, much against my better nature, my whole fine – £70 – was paid off. So when I got back to London I said to Jonathon Green, 'You stupid idiot. What have you done with the dope? It's the best dope we've had for years!' And he said, 'Well, you said get rid of it, and that's exactly what I did.'

STAN DEMIDJUK: When it came to giving money for the Festival bust fund the audience gave enough money to enable at least a thousand people to pay their fines. But I was backstage looking for money from the millionaire rock stars and none of them gave anything. The only one who gave was Jim Morrison: ten American dollars. These were the rock stars who were using our slogans and using our energy. And they were using these things not because they believed in it, but because that helped create their images. At the time I was quite startled by the negative, bitter, contemptuous attitude of the stars. They were singing about it, they were writing about it, but they were not living it.

JEFF DEXTER: I went out to introduce Jimi Hendrix and he said, 'Hang on, I'm not ready.' It took him about 40 minutes to get himself together, he was in a state. He didn't want me to introduce him. I was to say, 'This is Blue Angel music' – the Blue Angel was the parachute division he was in in the US Army. He went to go on in his new gear and said, 'Hey man, I can't play my guitar . . .' The sleeves were too big and got in the way of the strings. So I put another record on, went to one side and I sewed up his sleeve. By this time the audience had been waiting 70 minutes, so I said, 'Better get on, Jimi,' and I just ran on and said, 'Here's the man with the guitar!' and he was about to come on and his trousers split. So I pinned him up – I'd trained as a tailor at school, which was why I was so into clothes. And he went on stage all pinned and stitched up.

CHARLES SHAAR MURRAY: This was when my first wave of disillusionment with hippies set in. People would be standing up to get a better view, then go down because a full can of Coke caught them in the back of the head. The vibes were so bad at the Isle of Wight that Hendrix came on stage and couldn't do anything. Pretty good by anyone else's standards, but for Hendrix it was dreadful. I got quite upset, because I was very stoned, and I went up to Richard [Neville] in tears and said, 'You realise this thing's over.' For me that was the beginning of the end of hippie. For the elite it always ends when the *schlubs* discover it. That's what the elite's for: they're supposed to get out of it when the *schlubs* arrive; that's the way they see it, anyhow. I'd been to the Woodstock movie, read all the stupid books and I thought life could be an endless free rock festival. At the Isle of Wight I realised that it couldn't be and that it was dishonest to carry on claiming that it was feasible. I had bought the whole package, as much as I could swallow.

OZ: 'The art room as theatre of experiment'

FELIX DENNIS: Neville had charisma: no one else would ever have managed to get me working for nothing. I don't think anybody else could have done it, except for Richard Neville. Street-selling wasn't major money but it was a very pleasant living. Summer of Love, out there selling *OZ* on the street . . . I wasn't the first person to do street-selling, but I used to organise teams. Richard never sold copies on the street . . . Richard Neville selling copies on the street! Forget it! He was so good with the media, he was so good with everybody. He used to charm birds off trees. Who else could get Christopher Logue, Auberon Waugh and Germaine Greer to do articles in the same issue of a magazine?

COURTNEY TULLOCH: I never saw Richard Neville as an underground person. I don't think very many people understood what he was on about. I don't think he did. He presented himself as an underground entre-

336

preneur type, a thinker. But somehow it was never really real. He was bright, and full of sparkle, but he lived more above ground than he ever lived underground.

FELIX DENNIS: There were a lot of other people involved in *OZ*, but Richard remains the prime mover, there's no question about that. Richard was the world's greatest delegator. To my certain knowledge the number of hours Richard Neville actually spent working on *OZ* magazine could be counted on the fingers of one hand. The actual work was done by other people, inspired by the man. Richard's idea of a good time was not sitting down designing a whole issue of *OZ* magazine or writing a whole issue. His idea of a good time was going round getting fantastic people to write for the magazine. That was his talent. He lived on his wits. He charmed the early printers just as easily as he charmed people to write for no money. He was an opportunist, but he also believed some of what he was preaching. He did believe it. He refused to graft. Richard was one of those people, rather like Stalin, who didn't have to be there physically at the time; it was the fact that he'd already been there sometime and everybody else went on behaving as if he was still there and did things as if he was there. He got people to do things for absolutely nothing and to do things as he would have done them and he wasn't even there! If that isn't charisma I don't know what is! He was and is a fantastic writer, a writer of incredible talent. It was Richard who spotted the rot in the woodwork and wrote 'All God's Children Got the Clap' when nobody else would even have dared to mention such a subject. It was Richard that sorted wheat from chaff. However little he wrote – and it was a little – most of it was the best of what there is.

JIM ANDERSON: When Jon Goodchild left for California, Felix and me and David Wills took over as the main designers. We just took up Goodchild's design and made it slightly more coherent, very slightly more readable, so it became slightly more conventional. We paid our contributors nothing at all, or whatever we could afford. We had no money at all, we were always scraping along. The magazine didn't make any money – it wasn't bought in quantities that would make us any money. We probably got an issue out every month or six weeks; it was very haphazard because the police harassed the printers and we often had to change them. We sold perhaps 30,000 copies an issue.

RICHARD ADAMS: At that time *OZ* was in two buildings: there was the mail order department at 52, and further up Princedale Road at number 70 they shared a studio with a couple of designers who were called Clean

Machine. It was quite a smart office: green carpets, fitted desk surfaces, venetian blinds . . . a very comfortable environment which was in stark contrast to 52. I met Jim and we talked about designing the magazine and I started to get an idea about what producing this magazine might be like. So I started going over to *OZ* in the evenings, after I'd finished at Decca. Sometimes I would work until five am. And I would show up at the office and I was completely shit-faced. And at the same time Richard Neville asked me to illustrate the front cover of the paperback edition of *Play Power*. That was another freelance commission. They were already talking about *INK* and when I did the cover of *Play Power* I'd put 'Think *INK*' on one of the badges that Richard was sporting on his schoolboy blazer or on the blackboard behind him. The main people were Richard, Jim, Felix, Marsha, David Wills and Steve Litster – and Chris Rowley was around, selling advertising. There were just a procession of people, aside from these stalwarts, who would go round, who were drawn to underground magazines like shit to a tree. There were dullniks and dopers, squatters, writers, artists, groupies, underground press luminaries.

JIM ANDERSON: We published anything we could get our hands on. We knew what we were doing, or Richard certainly did. He had an idea of what he was doing and we just followed. He was the strategist. His influences were Germaine Greer, Abbie Hoffman and Jerry Rubin and that political awareness gradually spread from hippie to hippie. Dabbling in left-wing politics was part of all of this: American politics, sexual liberation, the women's movement, gay liberation. All these things were in the air and they made their appearance in *OZ*. It was quite an explosive package though I don't think any of us realised it at the time. I was certainly very naïve and so was Richard to a certain extent. There was this explosive anti-establishment package which became very popular and we became influential, I suppose, with young people, kids that had just left school. I think that's why they decided to stop us. But *OZ* was always meant to be funny, very, very amusing. If you look through *OZ* you'll find all this sexuality but it's always amusing. It's mocking pornography or mocking conventional sexual mores, mocking convention. It's all part of its satirical origins. It became a flower-power organ but it retained the satirical edge. Richard was a satirist and I'm a satirist and if you look through all the psychedelic colours and all the beautiful pictures you'll find satire.

RICHARD ADAMS: Laying out *OZ* was, I suppose, the art room as theatre, as theatre of experiment. Work would actually be going on in the middle

338

of all the chaos and spreads would be designed and articles would come in and copy would be marked up and sent off to the typesetters and proofed and so on. The design of *OZ* was very much a collective, co-operative exercise. Different people did different spreads and then somebody else would come along and put the colour onto it. There were racks of unsolicited drawings, underground magazines from America and Europe, and this was an image bank which filled up all the very many pages of *OZ*. A lot of people didn't get credit for their work: the Underground Press Syndicate wasn't even a polite way of ripping people off. Everything was up for grabs, it was copy right and left. And at the same time there were people like Adrian George, Peter Till, Peter Brooks, Rod Beddall, William Rankin, Chris Welch – this great body of freelance illustrators and artists. *OZ* was the great visual showcase. And people came from abroad like Andrei Dudzinski who came to visit, hot from Warsaw, and stayed for the next two or three years. There were all sorts of illustrators and you just used them, and sometimes, if they'd time to spare, they just sat down and drew something right on the spot and filled whatever available space there was.

I'd never worked on a magazine before, and I think it showed . . . a lot of those issues of *OZ* bore all the trademarks of incompetence and people who were just experimenting with the medium. When some of the typesetters at that particular time – such as Geoff Marsh or Steve Mann, Caroline McKechnie, Sandy Sparrow – were let loose on an IBM typesetter with several trips of LSD inside them you never knew what you were going to get back. You might have asked for it to be set across two columns and justified but you might get back this incredible piece of choreography rather than typography, and including their comments. Typesetters weren't just content to typeset – copy would be littered with interjections from one typesetter or another. The fact that you were a typesetter or a designer or an illustrator didn't stop you from exercising some sort of influence on other parts of the magazine. That's how it was done.

The final stage was when it went off to Murray's, the platemakers. Jim and I would go up to Murray's, just off Old Street, and try to explain to these people the final effect we were looking to achieve. To them this was just amusing: everybody would fall about laughing. And of course all the staff would lap up all these spread shots and tits and arses and so on; they really did enjoy it and they were part and parcel of the whole design and production experiment.

Play Power: 'A gigantic exercise in wish fulfilment'

RICHARD NEVILLE: I thought up the name of *Play Power* very close to the book's being published. It had had several other names before then: *Power Flower, You Don't Know What's Happening, Do You, Mr Jones?*. . .

The *New Statesman* had published a particularly disgusting piece by Malcolm Muggeridge: I wrote a reply which was a delineation of what I felt was going on in London at that time. Paul Johnson phoned up and said, 'Look, this is very exciting, challenging stuff. I'll pay you for it, I'll publish it but I dare not publish this as an article – the Board won't like it, it will upset too many people – I'm going to publish it as a letter, but it's a paid letter.' I said, fine. He published it as a letter and it got such a wild response and numerous letters poured in, both pro and con. It unleashed something . . . the first public debate on the topic. So after this correspondence Ed Victor, then at Jonathan Cape, phoned up and said, 'I really think you should do a book.' So I turned the letter into a synopsis, got my £3000 advance, which seemed a fortune in those days, but it was also £3000 of guilt. *OZ* was a very social phenomenon, it wasn't just a magazine. As Jonathan Cott said recently, it was also a salon – and to write the book wasn't really possible. At the beginning my hands-on involvement with *OZ* wasn't limited, but it did [become so] later, when I got involved with the book.

JIM ANDERSON: When I came back to London from Tunisia in 1969 I was taking odd jobs and just scraping along when towards the end of the year someone said, 'Why don't you go and see Richard Neville? He's working on a book about the underground press and he's looking for some help.' So I went to see Richard who said, 'Fine, there's a couple of weeks' work, do you want to do it?' and I said 'Yes.' So I started working for Richard and gradually became very closely involved. *Play Power* is rather dated now: about the 1960s, quite amusing and very much a book of its time, very influential when it was written, very funny and amusing. Now it reads like a period piece.

So I got very involved and moved into this basement apartment Richard had with his girlfriend so we could work better together. And since Richard's life was also very tied up with *OZ* I started helping him with *OZ* too. And gradually, as there was less and less work to do on *Play Power*, I began working full-time on *OZ*.

RICHARD NEVILLE: Jim really was the editor of the book. He retyped, he edited . . . without him I couldn't have done it.

MARK WILLIAMS: I always thought that *Play Power* was Richard Neville's quite brazen attempt to become a 'leader'. I always thought that it was a very middle-class book. It was written for the middle classes, it titillated, it pandered to the straight but fascinated middle classes.

CHARLES SHAAR MURRAY: *Play Power* was a gigantic exercise in wish fulfilment. A few people in London and other big cities could get away with living like this, at a time when things were cheap, when the dole and a bit of discreet dealing would enable you to live quite comfortably. One thing Richard was right about was that full employment as our parents understood it was not going to be around for very long and that people had better start making other plans. He was dead right about that. About virtually everything else he was totally wrong. The thrust of the book was basically: if everybody listened to pop music, wore funny clothes, took drugs and screwed a lot, the millennium would come. Which devalued the serious point about the coming unemployment. But his solutions for unemployment weren't particularly valid, unless you happened to be a young media type, living in a relaxed and bohemian part of a major city. The line from hippie to yuppie is not nearly as convoluted as people like to believe and a lot of the old hippie rhetoric could well be co-opted now by the pseudo-libertarian Right – which has in fact happened. Get the government off our backs, let individuals do what they want – that translates very smoothly into *laissez-faire* yuppyism, and that's the legacy of the era.

RICHARD NEVILLE: There is some stuff in *Play Power* that today I would repudiate – such as the sexism, and in a world of AIDS you are not saying we should all sleep with each other as much as possible. Time has overtaken some of the *Play Power* ideas. On the other hand, I think the spirit of questioning and dancing on the table is something that is still pretty relevant today.

The *David Frost Show*: 'A complete misuse of the opportunity'

JIM ANDERSON: The invasion of the *David Frost Show* came in the period before the [*OZ*] trial when we were very much influenced by people like Abbie Hoffman and Jerry Rubin. Rubin was in London and he was invited onto the *Frost Show* as a hippie activist. So Rubin invited all of us to go along and disrupt the show.

DAVID GOODMAN: Prior to the invasion of the *Frost Show* there was a meeting at Richard Neville's house in Notting Hill and it was decided upon there and then who were going to be the lucky people that went with Mr Rubin in the Austin Princesses to hospitality rooms A and B at TV House or wherever it was. So me and Micky went to hospitality room A and there was this very nice man with his tray and we sank the best part of two bottles of vodka in about 45 minutes. I can remember Rubin coming over at one point and saying, 'Hey listen, don't get drunk. Stay sober, you guys.' And me and Micky went, 'What the fuck's he talking about? Leave it out, mate!'

So on we went, paralytic basically, and we all sat in one little block and Hoppy was there with his camera crew. What had been arranged was that Rubin would offer Frost the joint and then there'd be some pre-arranged signal and we'd all hit the stage. The reason you don't see me on stage is that I'm attempting to do something with this camera. I wanted to take charge of the camera and this guy wasn't going to let me. The next thing was that it was commercial-break time and all these commissionaires were ushering people out. I was out in the car park and you could hear the police sirens off in the distance. Then this very fast car suddenly drew up, with two people I'd never seen in my life before, and they said, 'Hey, Boss, get in!' so I did. Then I remember sitting in the front seat of this very fast car and tearing out of the car park just as all the police cars raced in and I looked back and there were all of these smokebombs going off and flares and all these crazies. Incredible fun.

ALAN MARCUSON: I met the Yippies – Jerry Rubin and so on – and that was wholly disillusioning. I found the *Frost Show* so embarrassing: the most absurd thing to do and a complete misuse of the opportunity. Felix playing play power on television.

Jerry Rubin was just the biggest arsehole I've ever met in my fucking life. I felt sick that I was even associated with people like that and I saw for the first time what a fraud America was, including its alternative culture.

DAVID WIDGERY: Me and Sheila [Rowbotham] were recruited by Richard to go on the *Frost Show* invasion but instead we stood outside and picketed the whole thing: 'Neither hippies nor Frost' or something like that. Rubin was one of the most self-aggrandising, unpleasant people I've ever met in my life. I found Richard's kow-towing to him very, very unpleasant. It was on the same level as setting up the White Panthers in the ICA, the underground at its worst – the first place any decent revolution would head for would be the ICA.

STEVE MANN: Two days later I got punched in the face by someone who
342

recognised me in the street and had been absolutely appalled. Late at night on Ladbroke Grove, I'd just been getting some cigarettes from the Hole in the Wall and this guy came up, whacked me in the face: 'You bastard! How dare you talk to David Frost like that!'

JEROME BURNE: When I saw it on TV some years later, what was amazing was that it looked so much more purposeful and co-ordinated than it actually was. The longueur between the time we arrived, in my memory, was vast, vague and uncomfortable. On the TV it was a scurry about, a couple of shouts, a bit of talk with the audience, and off.

Black Power: 'This man ain't preaching peace and love'

JOHN HOPKINS: I was afraid of Michael X. He represented a whole world that I didn't know how to cope with: black people, a patois that I couldn't understand, gangster friends; he used to work for Rachman. I was afraid of him though he never did anything to me that was bad in the whole time I knew him. He was really nice and charming, but I think that in parts of him he was really a bad man, but to me, he was never bad. He was an opportunist and there's nothing wrong with that, and I'm sure he was winding up the white liberal underground. His view of what was happening was probably a lot different from our view of what was happening. I was sorry when he got topped.

MILES: Michael X was a very good friend, the only friend of mine who's ever been hanged. I met him through the London Free School, in '63 or '64.

COURTNEY TULLOCH: The very first time I walked into the Rio was to see Frank Critchlow and Michael Abdul Malik in order for us to talk about setting up some kind of a group to deal with the question of the police. Other things that might have been going on, they were not my world. But one of the things Frank taught me was that if you're working with people you have to accept them the way they are: you've got to go out to the gambling club and meet them down there, you have to win people's respect at whatever level, because they are the people at the end of the day who you are actually trying to do something for. This is straightforward Malcolm X really. That was the prevailing idea of the time: you go where the people are. You accept that the system is destroying your people, that colonisation creates the kind of mentality in people where they self-destruct. You have to go there and help to rescue people. Around this time the white kids from the middle-class suburbs started seeing that these black people that they were reading about in the media were perhaps more realist people, perhaps had something to offer, perhaps were creative in ways that they had not thought of, perhaps had more knowledge of life ... and they started making real contact. The kind of white person who would have a bluebeat record at a time when the rest of the world would never have heard of bluebeat.

HORACE OVE: I was very pissed off about English racism. Going to the Continent saved me a lot of that, but I left a lot of friends who were really suffering under that. The black movement had started when Malcolm X started his movement in America around '64, and that influence started to get over here and that whole movement started. So when I came back that had just started. People here were starting to get conscious of it. In the 50s you had the Notting Hill Gate riots, and that also started something. By then people like Michael X, who was Michael de Freitas before, and who in the 50s was involved with Rachman and all that sort of thing, made a change. What people don't realise, now he's been branded as a gangster, is that in those days it was hard hustle to survive. There was no black power, there wasn't anything. I mean everybody was out there hustling. Michael was used as a sort of heavy to sort of get people to pay up. But also the government had created a huge avenue for Rachman to move into. Because nobody wanted to house all these black workers that they'd brought over from the Caribbean to do the dirty work for them; nobody wanted to put them up. So Rachman provided very cheap, dirty sort of housing in the most down-beaten areas that you can find and charged a lot of rent: he exploited the situation. The horrible part about it was people were living in shit. And I don't think anything has changed. And at the same time that Michael was getting people to pay their rent, he was part of the community, knew the community and was a spokesman for it, and was brave enough to stand up for it. So when the race riots took place and blacks were getting beaten up, Michael was the one who organised and went to the police station and said, 'Listen, if you don't stop this shit, we'll put a stop to it and we'll fight back!' Now that is where the strength in his personality started. And although he is branded for one thing – and I don't think a person just does one thing, we're too complex, we don't just do one thing but several things – he got involved in the race riots with Frank Critchlow and people like that, and they actually fought back and put a stop to the brutality that was going on there. And eventually when Malcolm X and the whole black-power movement started to build and people here got conscious of it, this influenced Michael X, and Michael started the whole black-power movement here.

344

COURTNEY TULLOCH: You can also trace the origins of what is now called community work in the same place. After Rachman you got this situation where ex-CND type of people – George Clark and people like that – were moving into the area and saying, 'What these people need is kind of Saul Alinsky organising, because if we don't do it, hell! doom is going to happen.' Fear-mongering stuff. The housing issue was very important. The whole compulsory purchase/slum clearance programme was going on. Black people had originally bought their houses – they clubbed together, put down a deposit, bought the house, and now their houses were being taken away and they were being forced into council houses. They also had needed places to rent – the ships were docking and blacks weren't buying at such a rate that everyone could be absorbed – but the prevailing psychology was that the moment you could hold a place of your own, you held a place of your own. This system now, where black people are not owner-occupiers, where they are seen as being dependent on council housing, was actually the creation of the policies of the 60s. Black people weren't doing that. They were buying houses, renting rooms to other people – they couldn't afford the mortgage otherwise – and that was how the community was developing. The inner city at that stage was actually owned by black people.

So you're starting to identify a number of issues: problems with the police, the need for greater legal representation, and the need to bring to the wider society what was actually happening in those teeming inner-city bowels. Nobody believed it. But when middle-class people started getting their heads bust, that's when people started to recognise it. When the police started getting done for corruption, when they were doing it to white people, that's when people started noticing what black people had already been saying for fifteen years. So if you ask about Hoppy and people like that – they represented to the average black person white people who were less hostile to blacks, or were willing to use their talents in such a manner that if a black person could get a squeeze, they could get a squeeze.

SUE MILES: We met Michael X, then de Freitas, through Hop. Michael de Freitas thought that he'd turn himself into an English Malcolm X. Malcolm was probably hot stuff and for real; Michael was a pretty snaky character and he liked frightening people, he specialised in it. We were all very easily frightened, because we were a pack of cowards. There was a group around Michael: Courtney Tulloch, Horace Ove, Winston Branch . . . that lot. They all went around with shaved heads. And Michael then got Nigel Samuel. Michael progressed from being de Freitas, to Michael Abdul Malik to Michael X. Then all the nice people round him started leaving. Horace Ove was the first to go, Courtney, all those quite reasonable guys. Michael wasn't trying to address himself to the race issue at all. He was trying to be a big frightening black man, which he did quite successfully. He was also a very, very wonderful cook, brilliant food – he was a real old Jewish mama . . . It was very creepy that Nigel Samuel got married the day Michael was executed.

SU SMALL: Nigel Samuel was a nice, quiet, not very bright man, and Michael X got hold of him and took all his money, he had lots of it and Michael took it. I'd rather Michael had forged cheques . . . he had this man on a lead walking him around, paying the bills, and it was really sick. And Nigel just fell for it.

PETER SHERTSER: We didn't put any of the money we earned from selling our bootlegs into the underground, but we did invest in one cause, which we didn't want to. Once we started our own company we said to Nigel Samuel, 'Right, we might as well carry on selling *Ptoof*. You're not interested, you've got enough money anyway. Why don't we take over?' We did a contract and we had to weigh him money every now and again. The first payment came due, we had to weigh him a monkey. A lot of money. So he said: 'You've got to deliver it.' I said, 'Can't we just send you a cheque?' 'No, you've got to deliver it to the Black House in Holloway Road. To Michael X.' So Ian with his normal heroics said to me, 'Right. You've got the car – you go and do it.' So I've gone up there and I'm looking round thinking, 'This is dodgy.' I know all those guys, what they're up to – machine-gunning the American Embassy and all that. You get a little worried. And I thought: 'This isn't the best of causes.'

HORACE OVE: Everyone related to each other. Black Power wasn't a separate thing on its own. Black people were relating to whites; and demonstrations came together and all that sort of thing. It was like when Mick Jagger got arrested for pot, it was Michael X that created the whole demonstration at the *News of the World* and got everybody out in the streets. I was there with him, he was enjoying that. I was in a taxi with Michael X watching all those hippies demonstrating and demanding the release of Mick Jagger and Michael enjoyed it. He said, 'Look at me, I've got all those people out there demonstrating.' I think there was both manipulation of the white middle-class kids and a feeling of togetherness with them. By the end of the 60s Michael had frightened them off, but he did have some kind of power and he was able to relate with the white middle-class youth here. What people forget is that Michael had crossed

346

the borders in England, he knew everybody. Michael X knew everybody in this country. From the chief judge's daughter to people in high places in society to gangsters in the East End, the black hoods somewhere else. He knew everybody and I don't know how he managed that. If you moved with him he'd take you to places that you wouldn't dream of going.

ALAN MARCUSON: The thing that had most meaning to me, which had the most relevance, was black power which was starting to happen at that time. I got really quite involved with black people and I met this black guy Joe, who was a kind of Jamaican guy who I understood because he wasn't a fucking intellectual, he was more like the kind of black guys I was used to relating to in the shebeens of Johannesburg where I'd spent as much time as I could during the three years of my life before coming to London. Smoking a lot of dope with black people who rolled big joints. I was pretty primitive in that sense. For me the ultimate heaven was to sit with Joe in his hot little room, which was the kind of little room I was used to in South Africa with a fancy radiogram, listening to black music and smoking dope and eating really hot food. I could relate to this far more easily than I could relate to all the intellectual bullshit and all the poseurs and all the awful pretentious people who were trying so hard to liberate themselves, which I could never take that seriously. I was always much more inclined towards violence or the acceptance of violence than the white hippies. I could never let go of the idea that there was only one way we were going to get rid of the whites in South Africa and that was by violent overthrow. I always had to square that with whatever political ideas I had and I've never felt any different.

HORACE OVE: Alan Marcuson was a very strange lad. A very interesting character to me. Alan turned up and said he wanted to be part of this movement. And he just fell into things. And it was very interesting, because he was accepted right away. And I look back and ask myself, why did Alan just fit in? It was because Alan came out of that South African background, out of a colonial background. He must have grown up with black kids, playing with them, hanging about in the street – the same thing happened in the Caribbean: the white kid came out and played with you and you went to the same school for a while then you separated and he went to the big house on the hill and you went down to the shack! It was harder for the English middle-class kid who was born and brought up here, although he wanted to fit in and he did so eventually, but it was nothing for Alan to hang out with black guys. So Alan ended up being part of the whole black movement, wearing his Chinese black tunic suit and things like that that Michael X had. And I took the photograph that went in *Life* magazine . . .

ALAN MARCUSON: I got my picture in *Life* magazine in '68. I got very involved with black power and Jill and I bought ourselves jackets like theirs – they had a kind of uniform – and I went to this trial in Reading that Michael X was involved in. I just went along, it was what was happening. *Life* magazine was there and they were interested in me because I was a white South African, and as I walked out of a house where we were staying with some black people there I noticed that someone was taking photographs and my photograph was taken. The next thing I know is my picture is in *Life* magazine as 'Brother Alan – white South African black-power leader in Great Britain'. And my father is at the time on a trip to England to see his customers and he picks up a copy and he sits on the train from Leicester and comes home totally ashen-faced. There was a lot of parental paranoia as a result of that, though I was totally delighted.

DAVID ROBINS: At this time, 1968, all these black guys had started to appear. Courtney Tulloch, Frankie Dymon (or Frankie Y), Winston Branch. I didn't have much to do with Michael X. I was frightened of him, frankly, I didn't like the look of him.

ALAN MARCUSON: I was involved in the whole black movement: Horace Ove, Darcus Howe, Roddy Kentish, Ted Joans (an American poet). All around Michael X, who ripped off the black-power movement in this country for his own ends. I always thought he was an arsehole. He never struck me as an authentic black person: I understood black people and I knew that he was a poseur.

SU SMALL: It was one of those evenings – early '68 or late '67 – just after Michael X, who had been in jail, had come out. Hoppy had promised him some money for an article he had written for *IT* and one night when we were packing papers he turned up with four of his lads, all wearing dashikis and black berets. And he had this sort of large stick, carved or painted in some way. He said he'd come for his money. Of course every spare penny had been put into the franking machine, which I was operating at the time. It was the only thing in the paper that was worth anything and it had all the money in it. Dave Hall and he had a discussion about this money and Dave rather unfortunately remarked that you couldn't get blood out of a stone. Michael said that he wanted his money and he wanted it now. And at this point he sort of waved his stick and a blade the same length came out of it! The holder of this large penknife was two foot long and the blade was the same length. We all went very quiet, but you couldn't faze Dave. He kept saying that there wasn't any money and in the end Michael picked up a typewriter and went off with that and we got on with packing the papers.

COURTNEY TULLOCH: Michael was into psychodrama. He was a poet, a very, very sensitive man. He was a dramatist. And when people were talking he'd sit there and think, 'I wonder what would freak these people out?' And he'd go and act it out. He said, 'You make everything work for you. You make your clothes work for you, your looks work for you, you think where you're going, what you're doing . . .' Mike worked up everything that he ever did, and if he's going down to *IT* and he wants something and he knows who is sitting there, he's going to go there and dramatise it. And if it takes a machete, then he'll take a machete and slap it down, because he knows that this is a frightened little hippie who's out of his depth in the first place.

MICHAEL STOREY: My memories of Michael are that he used to come roaring into breakfast, steal one of Horace's bananas and say how with six good guys he could cause panic and chaos in London within half an hour. And I sat goggle-eyed. Basically I just sat and listened to all this. Stokely Carmichael came over to meet him. He stayed at Horace's. There were all these heavy black dudes everywhere. Horace put me in touch with all these musicians and I started hanging out with them. They were glamorous. They had something that I felt I hadn't; it was going into another world. We used to go to each other's houses and dance and play music all afternoon. Then I lived in St Luke's Mews. The Mangrove was round the corner and I slipped into this whole lifestyle of not really doing anything. You had shebeens, the right music, open houses, people just came in and I allowed myself to be completely swamped by these guys, strong older guys, survivors, and I was a real fresh-faced country boy. Horace told me when I came with my pink cheeks that I wouldn't last a year: I lasted less. Within six months I was ravaged. I was into being someone else and not what I was, which was a middle-class whitey. I got completely swallowed up. Eventually I was busted outside the Mangrove, I got burgled by a junkie who I had staying in the flat, and then I left.

SU SMALL: Michael X stories are always safe to tell – cos he's well dead and I'm glad. One day Michael X and some of his chaps decided that dealing was a black man's business. So he sent some of the lads out to bust a few heads and they went into a few hippie dealers around Notting Hill, walked in, took the stash, took the money and hit them. But what they failed to realise – they were a bit shortsighted about this – was that all these people were buying their supplies from people who weren't quite so sweet. In fact they weren't sweet at all. There was one guy using *IT* as an answering machine and he had a friend there who'd pick up his messages and take them round to a caff where he'd do his dealing. The production of the magazine went on upstairs and meanwhile there's Dave Hall downstairs acting as the intermediary between the three carloads of dealers driving around the West End with shooters and Michael X and his little gang. So Dave has to go over there to Michael and say, 'If I'm not out of here in one piece in half an hour there are a lot of nasty men, much nastier than me – and I'm bad enough – that will come round and sort you out.' So he went over and they had a chat and Michael backed down.

HORACE OVE: The idea of Michael X creating a division between blacks and whites in the counterculture is nonsense. Michael didn't create any division. But things started to peter out: people were growing older, people started to travel, people started to cut off their long hair and look for a job ... But there was no change for blacks. A lot of whites had somewhere to go to: jobs to go back to, careers to pick up, because they were all ex-university, public school. But there was nothing for blacks, blacks were still on the outside. And that brings a sort of anger. Michael saw this too and the one thing that made him very angry was that there was no direction for him to go to any more. He'd written a book, then there was the Black House. People grew up: Darcus Howe grew out of Michael and then went off in his own direction, other people did things, I started to make films ... Michael was left alone, in a vacuum. He then tried to recruit younger black people and that's when the Black House [the Headquarters of Black Power] came about. So he became angry and I think that a lot of the reason for this was that he was left in this vacuum, he was left out, there was no way to go. He was a very inventive person: he had started Release, though nobody gives him the credit. But he had this split personality: it was like building sandcastles and then knocking them down after. He would create something then destroy it. And it became worse. After his arrest in Reading he started to get bitter. So that is when Michael started to 'go off'. He had great ideas, and he really put them into action. I don't think that there's anybody who'll ever replace his kind of inventiveness. At the same time (and this was at some sort of meeting and MPs and people were there) it was Michael who actually

350

said, 'If something doesn't change, the day will come when those youths out there, those little black kids that are growing up, will run into the streets and burn them and create riots and kill people and blood will be shed.' He said all this ages before anyone dreamed there would be the Brixton riots and so on. Michael warned people. And he was put down by the press and other people for creating, inciting riots.

COURTNEY TULLOCH: Michael would get dressed up in his robes and say, 'I'm an African and you must dress like this if you want to be a black person,' and he used to give his outrageous interviews to the press and then it would be 'Demon Michael X' and Mike used to frighten the life out of them. Good drama. Excellent drama. The racism was there already, he didn't create it. I don't think any black person has been under the illusion that white people are free from racism, no matter who they are.

ROSIE BOYCOTT: I thought Michael X was rather impressive, I thought he was also rather frightening. I always fell out with the black-power people, and I think so did most of the people in the underground, because there was still a great emphasis on the 'Glastonbury ethic', the pop festival ethic. It's not quite religion but it did have a level of peace and love, in that there is a peaceable way of sorting things out and that the anti-war thing was still very strong. The black-power people were very much for 'get the guns' and therefore there was always that breakdown. It was not to say that you couldn't understand what they were doing but you quarrelled with their methods.

COURTNEY TULLOCH: The black-power era began around the time that I started going down to *IT* with material that was not talking about peace and love and blow bubbles and the world will be OK, but talking about black people's oppression, about violence and the need to express ourselves much more aggressively, not just in terms of organisation but of confrontation of the violence in society against us. I started writing in that kind of vein and people started looking at you: 'This man ain't preaching peace and love.' And this is where a lot of people say that they were frightened of Mike. They had always taken Mike as, 'He doesn't really mean it. It's just his way.' But Mike was a deadly serious person. He made it plain that he took what he was saying absolutely seriously. He might have projected himself in ways that were suspect but at the end of the day Mike was a person who saw the road which he was going down. If anyone could look at themselves and see themselves walking down the road it was Mike. He knew precisely . . . I wouldn't put it past him to

351

know precisely where he was going to end, and how. He was a very, very perceptive man.

HORACE OVE: In the heyday of the whole black-power movement when people had started taking Michael serious, somebody called a meeting with Michael, some MPs, people high up in society, to discuss what they could do about the problem. And everybody had an idea and gave a speech and everything and Michael was quiet as usual and sitting at the end of the table – and people were eating and having this beautiful dinner or lunch or whatever it was – and pulling his beard, and they asked, 'Well, Michael, what do you think will solve the problem?' And he pulled his beard in his usual way – he'd look around at everybody for about ten or fifteen minutes before he'd say anything – and then he says, 'I think that the way we are going to solve this problem is that a black man fucks the Queen and they have a half-caste child,' and everybody started to choke on their brandies and the dessert came out of their mouth and the whole thing came to a close.

ROSIE BOYCOTT: It seemed to me that there was a bit of a melting-pot going on. OK, we know what became of Hakim Jamal, but at the time that he walked in he was someone who breezed in a blast of something very different which made you feel that you were part of a whole world, not just part of this strange little thing at the top of Portobello Road. That you were connected by lots of strands to California, France, Tokyo . . . There were lots of people who would come and be saying, 'I want to share my experiences with you,' but those experiences were real. And that gave the underground a sense of greater collective power. Jamal was living with this girl Gale Benson, otherwise known as Hale Kimga. She was involved in the publicity for his book *From the Dead Level* and she was touting him around, in addition to his publicist, who had done a smart up-market hardback production of the book. He was a smart black-power guy. There was a sense that Michael X's British black power was pretty shaky. Jamal wanted to set up a magazine, to run lots of stuff about black power, and he gave a sense, even though I didn't really like him, that the thing was on a network.

STEVE ABRAMS: Michael X definitely did not kill the girl, Gale Ann Benson. Hakim Jamal killed her. I didn't know her but I knew her brother Greville Plugge. He made it his business to find out what happened. He had no love for Michael but he concluded that it was not Michael but that it was Hakim Jamal. Jamal was then killed in a black-power thing in Boston.

352

COURTNEY TULLOCH: I found the Mangrove. Basically the Rio was a dirty basement that was generally crumbling, it was a disgrace really. It was becoming the kind of place, a bit seedy, that you feel ashamed of. I didn't feel I wanted to sit down there. So I said to Frank, 'It's time we get out of this place. Let's find some kind of decent environment.' Frank said, 'OK,' and we found a little place through the *Kensington Post* and moved into All Saints Road and set up the Mangrove. That was a good example of using the skills, abilities and crafts of all those people who were condemned as pimps and so on. It was the first time I saw traditional old Caribbean woodcraft and bamboo work used there. It was an experience just watching that place be carved. That principle still prevails: it was those same people, the ones who were called pimps and prostitutes and drug pushers, who created Carnival and keep creating it. We demonstrated that those people who had been condemned could come out of those basements and create their art and their music, which is what they'd always wanted to do. On that level the Establishment did not suppress the black movement. We won; we more than won. We created a community. We all learnt a lot. We have books, we have bookshops, we have theatres, we have all kinds of things, all came out of the same little movement. It's all right for communities that already had their own institutions – for them this is no big deal – but we had nothing and we were starting from scratch. We created these institutions, and we created a black perspective and the Establishment has had to recognise it. And until the 60s we never had any of those things. And it's part of the struggle, part of the fight, part of making sure your voice is heard.

Alternative London: 'Suddenly I was inundated with the media'

NICHOLAS SAUNDERS: When I decided to do *Alternative London* I was fairly convinced that I could not write and I decided, 'Well, I've got the information, I'll put it together and I'll get someone else to write it.' I was also rather influenced by the way *IT* was then: the feeling that you had to write in that sort of language to get across. So I started writing it in my own words, with a view to this being just research that someone else would make into a book, but when I gave it to someone else to read they said it was perfectly all right and it didn't need a rewrite.

The research took nine months, and I did it pretty well on my own except for the last month. I dealt with religion, which was most important to me at the time and had to be absolutely complete, and there was the whole encounter-group thing that had to go in and there was the law on squatting, I had to get that done really properly. There were political groups, the left wing, Palestinian support groups, whatever. I got in a friend who was a professional researcher for the last month and she checked the addresses and phone numbers and generally got it to the point where I could find a publisher. And I couldn't. I very quickly gave up. I went to a few people but they weren't interested. Then I found that for £1500 I could publish it myself and I hired an IBM typesetting machine and put postcards all round Earls Court asking for someone who could typeset. I found this guy called Nick Lumsden who was actually in the theatre at the time, although he was a good typist. He hadn't ever actually seen a typesetting machine when he answered the ad, but he managed to pull it off and has been typesetting ever since.

I got the wretched thing finished and the printers' rep came along and picked it up and I had another 48 hours to design the cover. So I just did it with a bit of curved plastic and joined the squares together and that was it. And the rep took that away and I thought it was all due to be printed. Two or three weeks later they rang up and said, 'I'm sorry, we are returning your artwork, our solicitor has advised us not to have anything to do with it.' So I found another printer, who had already given me a quote, and I told him what had happened and he said, 'Oh yeah, we print anything, we print all sorts of stuff, filthy stuff . . .' Sure enough, two weeks later – their solicitor had advised them not to touch it. And I said, 'What's wrong with it?' and the printer said, 'We've decided not to discuss it with you.' But eventually he did tell me that usually publishers make sure that they don't send a printer anything that's socially undesirable, and since I hadn't done that, the printer felt they had to do it themselves. The third printer I took it to, who was somehow connected with the *Daily Mirror*, was very short of work and they did it and didn't ask me to change anything. I printed 50,000; it took the whole £1500. I then had to find a distributor. Moore Harness, who distributed *IT*, said immediately that they didn't like the look of it. It wasn't the contents but they just said it wasn't going to sell, without even opening it.

I started taking it round to shops by myself and had very bad luck. Then I sent off review copies to about 97 newspapers and got one tiny piece in the *Sunday Mirror* but nothing else. I was very down. I thought, 'I've put everything into this book,' it was me, and nobody wanted it . . . But I realised that I had to get into it more seriously and I worked out which writers had something in common with what I'd been doing and I found a woman on the *Observer* who'd done a piece that I'd liked and I sent her a copy and rang up saying that I liked her piece and that it related to something in the book. And she wrote a piece about two inches deep and that had the most incredible results. Suddenly I was inundated with the media. Then bookshops which had previously said no rang up and asked for copies. And I very quickly got snotty and said, 'Well, I'm not going to come around just to deliver eight copies, you can have fifty or none at all.' And they took the 50. Quite suddenly I had the upper hand and it was a most extraordinary feeling. But it was also very lonely. I really found it very difficult to handle this new-found fame. I wasn't that famous, but being a completely introverted person, always keeping right on the fringes, it did have a great effect. The underground press raved about it, and I'd been slightly afraid that they would pooh-pooh it because it wasn't written in the right language or offering the right line.

'I did have a degree of aesthetic disdain'

JEROME BURNE: I accepted quite a lot of the underground philosophy but never actually put any of it into practice in the way that a Nick Saunders did. The underground press for me was a rather wonderful answer to a problem. I was wandering around London with some of the ideas about change, of different ways of running the world sloshing round in my head, which I felt attracted to, but no idea what the bridge between the ideas and practicality was. The underground press seemed a wonderful vehicle for being at the centre of what was going on. The important things were to do with festivals and the revolution, books and ideas. And there were the social factors: abortion, women's rights, ecology, racism, homosexuality, attitudes to the police ... they all found their first expression in the underground press. It's all old hat now, but it was pretty radical stuff then.

When I meet people who didn't go through any of that I do find that their assumptions about and approach to the world are unbelievably narrow. Especially people like me – middle-class, Oxford, etc. The mixing with a load of people you wouldn't have met otherwise, the insecurity ... We weren't really living in Edge City – we all had parents and back-up systems, which the working-class people didn't have – but at the same time we were living a more precarious and more varied existence than people who went off to be bankers and lawyers. It was a democratisation of things that had always been the preserve of the upper classes. Take the issue of sexual freedom: the upper classes had always had pornography and so on; the question was whether it should be available for ordinary people on street corners. And the same with drugs. And the feeling for style and decor began then. The one thing that didn't happen was that it produced no literature.

JONATHAN MEADES: I thought that the second half of the 60s in England was a very miserable period. And I did have a degree of aesthetic disdain. I didn't like the formlessness of the *soi-distant* art. There was

355

quite a lot of good graphics, there were some quite considerable poster designers, but it was very self-referential art. It was a very mute art. It produced no Evelyn Waugh or Scott Fitzgerald who could stand outside. Later there was Martin Amis, but he was dealing more with the early 70s. In the end it was anti-art and that made it worthless. What writing it did produce was this self-excusing, pamphleteering stuff like *Play Power* or *Bomb Culture* or cash-in books like George Melly's *Revolt into Style*. The fact maybe was that there was no one in that milieu who was capable of taking a distanced view. Yet usually any kind of sub-culture, any kind of enclosed culture, tends to attract writers. Heathcote Williams is virtually the only exception. But it is very odd that there is not a single piece of serious prose writing which gets the era.

JEROME BURNE: I went home on one occasion and had with me some copies of *Friends* and *IT*. I was sitting at home, with the fire going, the King Charles spaniel lying there, my mother listening to Moira Anderson on Radio Four, my father reading the *Telegraph*, hunting prints on the walls, a few mementos from West Africa, and I was sitting there, reading *IT*, and it was full of 'Up against the wall, motherfuckers!' 'Suck my cunt, you hot little dick!' and I suddenly thought how shocking and awful it was, how totally alien to them and their way of life. A part of me was quite proud of having come such a long way. I would look around and think, 'This is where I've come from, my background' – very bland, English calm – and in some way I didn't understand I'd charted this very erratic path, ending up where I'm part of the Smash the Pigs brigade. I was amazed that we were still able to communicate.

The Angry Brigade: 'The Special Branch were just obsessed'

NINA FISHMAN: The Angry Brigade thing happened after the gates. They were on the fringes, just one more part of the mêlée at LSE. I never approved of the bombing. I'd always been enough of a good Marxist, a good Leninist, to know that terrorism will get you nowhere. There was definitely the feeling that there was no point whatsoever to what they were doing.

RICHARD TRENCH: I went up to Essex University in 1968, thinking I was much more hip than most of the others in my year, which was true. I was reading social studies and politics. The first thing I did was get involved with the left-wingers, one of whom was Chris Bott, who had long lank yellow hair, very spotty, and always trying to go to bed with people. He was regarded as a bit of a leader because he'd been to Cuba,

356

with the *Venceremos* brigade. There were other people: a marvellous black girl called Pam who later worked at Compendium, Anna Mendelsohn, Hilary Creek. There was the coffee bar and there was the library. And the Left was divided into the ones that went to the library and the ones that went to the coffee bar. The ones that went to the coffee bar became the Angry Brigade, and the ones that went to the library became junior lecturers.

MARTIN CROPPER: We went up to the University of Essex one day to sell some acid. There was some kind of festival going on. And we got into the lift with a third person, fairly tall, curly hair. There was something sus about him, he looked very dodgy and he was very nervous of us. I at that time had short hair and had a Burton's pinstriped jacket and that sort of thing, which may have looked like some sort of disguise. Anyway, he got terribly paranoid as we went up in the lift, he was actually sweating. He thought we were the Bomb Squad who'd finally tracked him down. We got out of this place and he said, 'You're not police, are you?' and we said, 'No, no we're not. We're actually totally bent, we could go down for what we've got in our pockets.' And we got talking and that was Chris Bott.

DAVID MAY: All the Angry Brigade lived in Grosvenor Avenue in Stoke Newington. A very strange household indeed. Full of these strange women who were proto-lezzies really. I got on with them very well. But this was a *radical* circle. I was writing the story: it was a typical Hack Typewriters attitude. This was something that was taking place that was phenomenally interesting: people wanting to blow up the British government. The police arrested the real Angry Brigade: they got it right. So I went to do the story. We'd written bits of it beforehand, with the bombs and the manifestos, but the story really started after the arrests. There were all these people in the defence committee, for which read the rest of the Angry Brigade. All these amazing German people kept turning up who were very, very heavy indeed. Then people with connections with Libya and God knows who else, even the odd Russian. The Special Branch, of course, were just obsessed. It was in this very intense political period. But culturally they were people who were part of that same 60s hippie thing. They looked the same, although they weren't so colourful. They came out of Essex, Cambridge and Sussex Universities. At Essex they were known as the 'Red Engine'. What they understood was the power of publicity. And you only have to read *Spycatcher* to see how important it all was to MI5, given their obsessions. They stopped chasing Russians, who they couldn't catch anyway, and concentrated on what was going on here. The Brigade did present a real threat. They were trying to blow up cabinet ministers' houses and you can't get much more direct than that.

DICK POUNTAIN: This libertarian, post-Situationist faction had developed. They were much more activist than the Situationists, who were scornful of political activists in the traditional student sense. Activism as they saw it was just another way of wasting your energies, running around being more revolutionary than thou. At the time that all this was coming together I was drifting away, back into the influence of orthodox Marxist-Leninism. So I was moving in exactly the opposite direction to the libertarians. The other thing that separated me from the libertarians was that I still had a sense of humour. In the end I'd rather hang out with someone with a sense of humour than someone who's politically correct – for which some of them, for instance Chris Bott, never forgave me. He thought I was a subjectivist, too involved in personal salvation and liberation.

ROBIN BLACKBURN: I can't help thinking that there was a link between the Situationists and the Angry Brigade. The interesting thing about England is that we didn't have a terrorist group like the Weathermen in the United States, the Red Army Faction in Germany, the Red Brigades in Italy and so on. England is the odd one out.

DICK POUNTAIN: While I was away in America a whole load of new people had appeared, attracted by the first wave of *King Mob* Situationist literature. A lot of people from Essex and Cambridge saw *King Mob* and came to Notting Hill to seek out these people who did it. These were people like John Barker, Jim Greenfield and so on. When I came back from America they were all there. They were several years younger and they were still at university, or just out of university, and they were fresh to the scene. They were definitely a second generation and they didn't settle in Notting Hill, which they felt was too hippie and too compromised. They moved into the East End and later Stoke Newington. I sussed half way through '71 that they were actually doing it.

ROSIE BOYCOTT: Angie Weir and Hilary Creek turned up in the *Frendz* office in summer 1971 and they were much more politically orientated than me. It was my first whiff of feminism. They had various gripes about the world and one of them was specifically the lot of women. They didn't get on with Jerome [Burne] but they saw me for more of a pushover. I was deputy editor, though titles didn't mean much.

358

One of the things that *Frendz* did was pass itself over to other people to use. People could not quite take over issues but they could certainly take over sections. And they proposed that we did a woman's issue of *Frendz*. The women's movement was beginning to bubble along, but it was very non-connected to the underground. Women who worked in the underground were still getting laid on the back copies, or whatever. They were certainly not striding around. And these two were around the office from September through to the end of October.

I liked them but I was very irritated by them at the same time. I had no idea that they were actually plotting to blow up Biba's. I had no concept, none at all, of what they were up to. Had I known I wouldn't have said anything about it, but I would not have had any more to do with them. I genuinely did not have a clue that they had those sort of plans. But they did irritate me, their aggravation with everything irritated me, the fact that they didn't see any fun in anything, that there was very little joy in their lives and that they were extremely bitter about the general state of the world. There was this endless talking about the masses, the oppressed masses, without being very specific, and there was a lot to do with abortion.

One way or another we muscled together and produced an issue of the magazine. And then they scarpered. They took off almost as soon as they'd come. But they spent a long time putting this issue together and they did make a point of coming into the office quite a lot, which I can now look back and see that it was by way of creating alibis. Whether this was conscious I don't know, but I think so. They were trying to associate themselves with the underground press as a 'job'. Angie was extremely pretty in a rather cute kind of middle-class way, neatly turned out. She never looked like she'd been up all night drunk.

STEVE MANN: I got interviewed by the Bomb Squad when Robert Carr's house got blown up. They thought that possibly Micky or me or Edward Barker or somebody from *IT* might have done it, until they realised that we were much too stoned and much too untogether to even contemplate something like that.

DAVID GOODMAN: The Angry Brigade was pretty dangerous stuff – all that bombing. I didn't know them but I had an unfortunate association. I was sharing a flat with Mick Farren in Maida Vale and he was editing *IT*. And one night I got in and I told Micky I had this funny feeling, like when I had been busted in Ilford. And he said, 'Yeah, I feel a bit funny too.' So we stashed everything. Anyway, at eight o'clock in the morning all the doors cave in and it's the biggest bust I've ever been

359

involved in. It was absolutely fantastic, and it wasn't the Drug Squad. It was the Bomb Squad and they were looking for Angry Brigade shit. *IT* had been getting communiqués from the Brigade.

They took the place right to pieces. I was sitting up in bed and I've got this little chest of drawers all full of badges. This guy has these badges out and he holds up this Chairman Mao badge and he's dead serious and he says, 'OK, which one of you two is the fucking commie?' We started laughing. 'I said, which one of you two is the fucking commie!' I can't take this seriously. I said, 'Come on, mate, it's just a fucking badge.' 'Is it yours?' 'Yeah. I'm just some roadie in a rock'n'roll group, he's a fucking guitarist. The political shit, it's that geezer next door with the haircut,' meaning Micky, who had his wonderful Afro. They found some dope but they put it back in the drawer. They took Micky off to raid *IT*'s offices. And Micky said, 'What about the dope?' and they said, 'Listen, mate, we're the fucking *Bomb Squad*'.

DICK POUNTAIN: One time I went up to Liverpool to meet an outfit called Big Flame, who were another community-based libertarian group. They were having some sort of conference which I was going to write up for *Friends*. While I was there I ran into Jim Greenfield whom I knew. He was with some people and they offered me a lift home. On the way back we called in at Widnes, where his parents apparently lived and we stopped at a pub for a drink. What happened next was that the Drug Squad came in on a routine Saturday night drugs trawl and Jim started slagging them off as soon as they came through the door, saying, 'Oh my God, the fucking pigs are here!' My heart sank. At which point they grabbed us all, our arms up our backs, whipped us outside, discovered rapidly that the car was stolen, went through it, found dope, chequebooks, credit cards, hauled us all off to the cells.

When we arrived at the station I heard them all giving false names. I had a *Friends* press card, so it was obvious who I was. We were grilled by the Liverpool Special Branch all night; they kept coming in every three quarters of an hour and saying, 'Your mate . . . whatshisname?' 'Kelloway.' 'Kelloway, which one's that? Is he in that cell or that cell?'

After two days we were freed on our own bail. We all went back to London. I had to answer my bail and I got a lawyer, *King Mob*'s lawyer, and I went back. I explained that I was writing a story about Big Flame and that's why I was there and I'd met these people in a pub in Liverpool and I knew them from London cos I'd met them months before in a pub in Kilburn. They'd offered me a lift and we were having a drink and that was it. They believed me and let me go. None of the others answered bail, of course. After the police picked up [Jake] Prescott and [Ian] Purdie the Brigade all got busted and I got visited and had to go through it all again.

There was this guy called Mike the Greek. A lot of us at the time thought Mike the Greek was a grass and sure enough, just before the bust he disappeared, supposedly to Canada, and has never been seen since. But he obviously wasn't a provocateur or they'd have caught the whole lot much earlier.

The funniest thing of all those communiqués was the one they sent to *Friends*. I went into *Friends* to deliver my copy one day and Alan [Marcuson] said, 'We've had a communiqué from the Angry Brigade and I think I know someone who knows them and I want to set up a meeting here this afternoon.' And I nearly had the squitters. I spent all afternoon persuading him that this wasn't a good idea. He knew someone who was bragging about it, but this was a time when nobody knew. Micky Farren used to talk about the Brigade so much that the police began to believe he knew something about them. The problem is that in the early days they didn't have a clue where to start looking. It was a bunch of people who weren't connected with their usual sources and they had no help. So the first wave of people that they looked at were the people who were shouting loudest. Micky and people like that who were making public statements saying that they were in favour of it, in sympathy with them, they all got raided. They had no foothold into the whole scene until Prescott blew it. Without Prescott and 'Mr A' – the guy they put in the cell with him – without that break I wonder if they would ever have busted them.

ROSIE BOYCOTT: Because of the girls' involvement with *Frendz* I was called as a witness. I was there for four days altogether. I felt it was my duty to do it, but it was a duty I was not comfortable with. I didn't tell any lies but at the same time I wasn't able to tell any very substantial truths. The judge was very easily able to pick holes. They wanted me to cover time. They kept asking me specific questions: 'Can you remember what happened on . . . ? and I would say, 'No,' and the judge would say, 'Do you mean to say you don't keep a diary? You were running a newspaper and you don't keep a diary . . . what about your appointments?' And I would say, 'No, Your Honour, it didn't work like that,' and I tried to explain how a *Frendz* production cycle went and trying to explain this to an Old Bailey judge wasn't possible. So I had a rough ride, but I also had a guilty ride. I felt guilty because I was scared and I could see they were going to be in trouble. I didn't know whether they'd done it, I felt annoyed on one level at having been pulled into it, because I didn't approve of bombing, or of blowing up Biba's. I've never understood it. They became willing to take unacceptable risks with other people's safety, which was also something the black-power people did. It's perfectly all right to take risks on your own behalf, but not with other people's lives. They vanished after *Frendz* and I didn't see them again.

Frendz: 'Let's do what we're supposed to be doing'

ALAN MARCUSON: I did *Friends* for 28 issues, till the start of 1971. The thing that finished *Friends* for me was that I met Jim McCann, who was an Irish revolutionary and hustler somewhere to the left of the Provos, who'd apparently thrown him out. He dominated the course of my life for the next five or six years, one way or another. That whole story only culminated with the Howard Marks trial and it was that original introduction of Jim to Howard that set the whole story off.

The 60s really ended for me with the Angry Brigade and everything soured and we became very disillusioned. The Angry Brigade were sending us letters wanting us to be their magazine. When Jim McCann turned up I was swept away like hundreds of others by the man's lunatic charisma and organised a trip for Felix de Mendelsohn and Joe Stephens and Jilly to go to Belfast with him. This was early '71 and by this time the magazine was in the most appalling financial trouble and I was struggling and borrowing and dealing dope and taking the wages and turning over dope and rushing down to the printers with cash to get the magazine onto the press and the staff were all moaning that they weren't getting paid. And Barney Bubbles and I were laying out the magazine and we had a crushed tab of acid on the top of the art room cupboard and at three o'clock in the morning we'd just dip the finger and continue building these more and more complex pages. I think the front cover of that issue took about three days.

JEROME BURNE: The IRA was always a problematical issue. On one hand we weren't in favour of violence, but we were obviously against the British Army. We wanted to overthrow the State, but we weren't quite sure that we wanted a lot of bombers. That was a tricky one. There wasn't really a political philosophy in the underground. And there were pieces that David Widgery would write, saying the whole thing was an indulgent bourgeois wank, totally eclectic, with no coherent line or plan of action. Which, looking back, was totally true.

JILL MARCUSON: By 1971 *Friends* had become much more political and much less hippie. And James McCann coming into the office divided the office into two camps: the ones who were prepared to fight for their political beliefs and the hippies. I found I wasn't a hippie at that point. We were totally taken in by McCann. He was quite charismatic, more than most. He was very forceful and we were absolutely ripe for it, especially someone like me. He offered a chance to act – the revolution had come and we could go and do something about it; instead of pissing around being hippies we could actually go and do something important, fight the revolution in Ireland. Alan, to his credit, was much more cautious. He kept saying, 'Don't go, you're mad to go,' but I was keen to go. Felix de Mendelsohn was very perceptive and writing very politically aware essays on Belfast, but for me it was an adventure, revolutionary tourism. Although I also felt quite passionately about it. Because I always felt that the revolution was coming, but it hadn't quite hit Belsize Park so there wasn't that much one could do other than go to Grosvenor Square. And I was really ready to go and fight to change the world.

RICHARD TRENCH: I missed the *Friends* expedition to Belfast but James McCann was a conman, a dangerous person, and he was mad. I met him after he'd escaped from prison in 1971 and he was talking about fighting in the sewers, but there are no sewers in Belfast – only drains, about fourteen inches high.

ALAN MARCUSON: It all ended one day when everyone was in Belfast. I had an appointment to meet John Lennon in Apple to ask for finance for *Friends* to get us out of the shit. I went along and I passed a headline which said 'Ten in Anarchist Bomb Gang' and I thought 'Jesus, they've caught the Angry Brigade.' I bought the newspaper just outside where I was going to meet Lennon and Yoko and it wasn't the Brigade, it was Felix and Jim McCann, Jilly and Joe Stephens, and I walked into this meeting completely and utterly white as a sheet. I didn't get as far as asking him for money for the magazine, though he made vague promises the way pop stars do. But they were far more interested in knowing what these groovy events were in Ireland. They took me to an awfully smart private eating club somewhere in St James's. It was an extraordinary evening: me, Lennon, Yoko . . . Graham Hill the racing driver was at one table and Ingrid Bergman at another. I just walked away in the end.

JEROME BURNE: There were regular discussions of, what are we all doing here? Why are we doing it? None of which were ever very satisfactorily resolved. Then David Burdett turned up from America. He was English but he'd been there for some time. Marcuson was rather impressed by him. He had a bit of journalistic experience, could write, and was certainly good at laying out a package as to where we should be going, what we should be doing. He was made News Editor and within a couple of months was fomenting a revolution, which, looking back, was quite justified in many ways. He said: 'Here we are, *supposed* to be an alternative paper. We're not selling many copies, the debts are enormous, we're paying Alan so much money, we've got hire cars, seventeen people on the staff – let's try to get a set-up that reflects better what's going on here. Let's cut down on people, on expenses, let's run this thing collectively, let's do what we're supposed to be doing.' Alan was immensely hurt and upset, as a good *paterfamilias* Jewish figure. He was very much 'the Editor' and it *was* his father's money, on the backs of those poor exploited South Africans, that was paying for the whole thing. And here was this upstart to whom he'd given a job, and there were seventeen people on the staff – a good paternalistic point of view. But what we were peddling wasn't just rhetoric. I sided with Alan simply because I liked him. So Burdett gathered some people together and it got to the point where there were deputations and finally Alan sacked everybody. We all went down to the Yugoslav restaurant in Portobello and came back in paper sacks: we had been sacked, it was street theatre. Then, in a few days, maybe a week, Alan said, 'Right, this is it,' closed the whole thing down and disappeared, saying he would have nothing more to do with it.

ALAN MARCUSON: I sat down and talked to my friend Charlie Radcliffe and said, 'Charlie, is it worth it? I don't have the support of the staff any more, it's lost its flavour, and it's all bullshit anyhow.' I took the books of the company and one night I threw them in the canal, plus anything I thought relevant. And left the magazine to Jerome [Burne] and whoever was left there. I went in the next morning and said, 'You can have the magazine.' What I wasn't prepared to give up was editorial control, because I was both financially liable and I was under threat of being prosecuted under the Obscene Publications Act and unless you lot are going to be as financially liable as I am and unless you're going to stand next to me in court and be prosecuted I am the Editor of this magazine. I thought everyone was a right bunch of uncommitted arseholes.

'We had this slave who used to ring us up'
JEROME BURNE: We were left with a paper that sold perhaps 15,000 copies an issue, debts that we discovered came to £17,000 and that was it. I remember thinking that if we'd been a religious organisation what happened next would have been put down to acts of God, because people did turn up to fulfil our needs in a quite extraordinary way. We all

agreed to keep on for the sake of the community, the revolution, the counterculture and so on. But we had no resources and not very good contacts. But Marcuson helped and we got out an interim issue before the lawyers told us we had to form a new company and we started Echidna Epics (I'd been reading about this spiny anteater that was evolving at an enormous rate, developing a powerful sense of hearing: the echidna). And we started *Frendz* with a 'z'. It sort of fitted in with the spirit of the time and we just carried on. If anyone rang up and said, 'You owe me £3000 for typesetting,' we'd say, 'Terribly sorry, talk to Alan Marcuson.' And all these people turned up: John May, Kevin O'Cashflow, a girl called Jo who wanted to do the general managing job, and she brought along another girl who'd come out of mental hospital but was a lot better now, who had a certain amount of money and wanted to give us £300 to print the first issue. Rosie Boycott turned up about that time. The women's issue was coming up at that point and we were paying attention to that. Plus the idea of the community, which we wanted to address in a way that the earlier *Friends* hadn't done. The £300 donation was just enough for our first print bill.

ROSIE BOYCOTT: We had this slave who used to ring us up and then come along and clean the stairs naked. And there was Daphne, who came in on a bed of nails and gave us all that money

JEROME BURNE: For a while this mental patient girl was around. She wanted to use the dark room, write poetry and so on, which was all fine for a bit, until one night . . . We were all sitting around discussing policy when she turned up in a very hyper state saying a black guy had been trying to touch her up and there were very bad images coming from her. She suddenly fixed on some picture on the wall, someone in monk's clothing being sucked off by a nun. She got terribly upset about this. Finally we edged her out, but she came back the next day, completely naked, dragging behind her these bedsprings that she'd found on the street, and attempted to rip up all the artwork. We had a hurried confab: on the one hand we were into alternative psychotherapy, and the idea that people's mental episodes were something they needed to work through, and that shock treatment and drugs were not the thing to do, and the community ought to support and help people who were going through these episodes. On the other hand, we were trying to bring out a magazine, press day was the following day, and she was in the process of ruining the entire thing. So after a brief consultation we called the police and she was taken away in an ambulance and that was the last we saw of her.

ROSIE BOYCOTT: In some sort of odd way there was a redistribution of wealth. A few rich people did support a lot of other people, without complaining about it. It was a wonderful thing that you could live without money and it lent credence to your belief in the revolution. And when your parents said to you, 'What are you putting in its place? If people don't go to banks then society is going to fall apart,' you could say, 'We're doing fine.' And in truth, in some ways, you were doing fine. You weren't on the dole – nobody I knew went on the dole, not at that point. I had a sense of tremendous pride against the dole. I wasn't getting any other money: my salary at *Frendz* was four to five pounds a week, plus the money you made out of dealing drugs.

JEROME BURNE: Then of course there was Kevin O'Cashflow, a rogue accountant. He'd turned up out of the blue. He'd been a trained accountant and suddenly threw it all up and said, 'I want to do something with my life and join the underground press.' Doing books was anathema to us freewheeling spirits, so Kevin took over. I met Stan Demidjuk with Kevin, wearing his tight leather trousers, £400–£500 in tenners in his back pocket, long mane of lank hair, and after all the chat, Kevin turned to me and said in his rather quiet way: 'I used to know people like that when I was working before, only then we called them "salesmen".'

INK: 'There were just so many cooks . . .'

RICHARD ADAMS: In 1971 the underground press is booming, there are a lot of publications coming out. And there are more coming: *INK* is coming. *OZ* was printing and distributing 40–50,000 copies per issue. *IT* was at least 40,000, maybe even more. *Frendz* I don't know, but there were lots of people buying them all, even if it was 40,000 buying the lot, rather than a total of 200,000. Either way they were very much in demand. Wherever you went, if you went to a concert at the Roundhouse, or even the tube at Notting Hill Gate, there were people out there street-selling these damn things. Hyde Park, demonstrations, everything: the underground press was on display and it was being marketed in a very visible way. Far from having W. H. Smith distribution, it was available only in a small number of specialist bookshops and newsagents, but the fact was that it was on sale and it was being read and it was having an enormous impact.

ED VICTOR: In 1971 I was leading a very straight-up establishment life as editorial director of Jonathan Cape Ltd. During that period I got to be very friendly with Richard Neville, because I published his book *Play Power*. It was a book that a lot of people read and talked about and

366

reacted to. Richard became a great social friend and I spent a lot of time with him. I had been at Cape for three, three-and-a-half years, and at that point Cape was merging with Chatto and Windus. Tom Maschler and I were like two heroes in a Western – 'This town ain't big enough for the two of us' – and we determined that Cape wasn't big enough for the two of *us*. I was growing, it was his firm. It was determined that I was going to go over to Chatto. All this was arranged and then I had, as many people did in those days, a kind of 'What am I doing?' I'd been on this straight little path, busy achieving and doing since I was five years old. Richard was in the middle of all that *OZ* stuff, with Felix Dennis and Andrew Fisher. I had published a lot of alternative-society people here: Jerry Rubin, Abbie Hoffman, I knew all those guys. I published Eldridge Cleaver, Régis Debray . . . Insofar as there was a publisher who was publishing the revolutionary Left in the establishment press it was me. We were busy making money through our publishing houses publishing these works that said 'Blow up these publishing houses'.

I've forgotten quite how the genesis went, but I think at one point I had said to Richard – or he had said to me – wouldn't it be wonderful to have a paper in London that was a weekly newspaper, *à la Village Voice*, to perform the same kind of function that the *Village Voice* did: an alternative newspaper. It was a very good paradigm and we felt that London could use such a thing. We weren't worried about the existing underground papers because they were exactly that, underground, and part of the reason that *INK* was the screw-up that eventually it was was that Richard and I had, unbeknownst to each other, totally different ideas of what this paper would be. Richard was always going to have an underground newspaper, and I wanted to have this paper that was alternative: I wanted a paper that had writing for it the kinds of people who wrote for the *Voice*. We thought that we would pull disaffected journalists from newspapers around London in the way that *Private Eye* got a lot of people to talk to them because they couldn't talk that way in their regular jobs.

CHRIS ROWLEY: *INK* was Richard's great idea which he was nurturing, and he was wooing Ed Victor. The idea was of providing a more sensible, rational paper, aimed at people in their late twenties, early thirties, who were reacting to the firebrand that *IT* had become.

DAVID WIDGERY: *INK* to me was going to be very important. It was going to be the continuation of *OZ* in a different era. A newspaper format but with colour, visuals and so on. And it would actually become not just the internal bulletin of the underground but much more a forum for the new politics – gay, feminist, workers' insurgency and republicanism.

ED VICTOR: Because I'd got quite fed up with the career I had, bored maybe, I wanted something different. I'd always been in publishing and before that an academic. So we started talking about this paper and I was just giving him a lot of ideas and he said, 'Why don't you get involved with this?' and I thought, 'Well . . . why don't I? It would be very different; I can use a lot of the same skills, it would be a change.' I was going to leave this Chatto situation anyway, even before I went to it. My marriage broke up, a lot of dull things happened to me. In general there was a lot of wreckage around, and this seemed like a pretty interesting thing to do. So we went out and raised a lot of money and of course the people we went to to raise the money were basically people that I knew. I did most of that money-raising because I knew a lot of people who had money. Successful people in publishing, writers, journalists, all the kinds of people I would get to know. We raised £50,000, which was a lot of money then, in the form of debentures. I don't think anyone really truly expected to get it back. I mean I gave lots of money to organisations that if they'd actually had their way would probably have put me up against a wall and shot me. And we rushed that newspaper out because Tony Elliot [at *Time Out*] very cleverly decided to go weekly at that point, very much spurred on by *INK*.

JOHN LLOYD: When the original *INK* appeared I wrote to Neville and said I wanted to report politics in a new way. I wanted to do a new kind of reportage. He asked me to do a few pieces, and I did half a dozen pieces on this and that. *INK* had huge pretensions: it was supposed to be the daily paper, the daily alternative paper. It was going to go weekly, bi-weekly and then daily. It had quite a high capitalisation for the time. Ed Victor, big-time guy, already with huge ambition; Richard, big reputation from *OZ* – it couldn't fail. Ed I never quite liked, he impressed me but I always thought he was a bit of a bullshitter. Richard I liked enormously, he was so charming, you couldn't dislike him. I was always a bit overawed by him, because he always had a huge line in charm, sexiness and intelligence – it was a great honour to be allowed to talk to him.

RICHARD ADAMS: By February-March 1971 *INK* was really very much on the go. They had taken over 73 Princedale Road. Mike English was living upstairs and *INK* had the ground floor and the basement. The art room remained at 70 and shared a space with *OZ*. Black Boys model agency was on the ground floor. The *OZ* studio was in the basement, the

368

INK studio was on the first floor and Release were on the very top floor. I was the assistant designer with this chap called Mike Dowd. He had been the creative director at a big London advertising agency. And he, like a number of other people who became involved with *INK*, was coming from a completely different area from the areas from which people had been coming hitherto. Ed Victor, Mike Dowd, Alex Mitchell, Cassandra Wedd, Wynford Hicks . . . there was a very different kind of breed who started to involve themselves with *INK*. People who believed it would be the *Independent* of its time.

CASSANDRA WEDD: I was a secretary. I was twenty. I'd been a deb to a certain extent. I'd been to the sort of boarding school where the careers guidance offered the Conservative Central Office and the Women's Army. Where you were taught to be seen and not heard. To make somebody a nice wife and to ask fairly intelligent questions at dinner parties but not actually contribute much yourself. I wasn't ever very satisfied with this and I don't ever remember wanting to get married, or to do what I was expected to do. I heard that someone at *OZ* was looking for people to work there. So I went along for an interview but it was while *INK* was being set up and they said they wanted people to work at *INK*. So I started off doing typesetting – I did a course, an IBM typesetting course. *INK* was just setting up and it was in the same building as *OZ*. Then it moved to 73 Princedale Road. So I basically sat in the front room and was a receptionist and secretary for the editors.

I was very unpolitical, I'd had no political education at all. When people talked about 'wanky liberals' I thought they were talking about the Liberal Party . . . What they wanted to do was bridge the gap between the underground press and the Sunday newspapers. It was quite exciting when it was all setting up, and fairly frantic, and there were quite a lot of problems. It was a weekly, so it was quite pressurised. As a woman I was treated badly but I didn't realise at that stage – I was used to being treated badly. I'd been a secretary and I didn't expect to be treated any better.

RICHARD ADAMS: For about two months leading up to the launch I was preparing the ground, designing the logo, so on and so forth, with Mike Dowd. Mike Dowd had never done a newspaper or magazine in his life. His attitude was very much that which comes from working at a very large advertising agency: drinking gin and tonics and so on – totally unsuited for the kind of anarchy that rules in the art room of what was going to be a national newspaper, let alone an underground press national newspaper. But it wasn't just that that was going off the rails, it was also

369

the whole editorial structure. And the money and the pre-publicity and all that kind of thing. It was very different. For a start people worked during the day, you no longer slept all day and started off in the evening. I was actually feeling rather envious of the people back at *OZ* – here was I working on *INK* and really I would have liked to have carried on with *OZ* but I'd made my decision and I stuck with it. So at ten o'clock in the morning, when everyone else was doing the slow walk from Holland Park tube station to the office, Ed Victor was pitching up at the office in a maroon open-top Morgan sports car and as soon as I saw that I knew that something was wrong. And there were corporate games: Victor's people versus Richard's people. And the editors' expense account. We were going to the Prince of Wales and they were off to the Pomme d'Amour on Holland Park. They were supposed to be getting the same salary as everybody else but actually they were getting all the perks. *INK* at that time was just awash with people – there were just so many fucking cooks! You knew that this newspaper was riding for a fall.

ED VICTOR: I had always led a very sane and disciplined life and here was this hedonism, this lack of discipline . . . not that people were lazy, because they weren't: everyone was working and bubbling but in a very different way. I found it very difficult when I came to work at *INK* at the time I normally came to work – nine o'clock – and I saw everyone else drifting in at noon, two. I felt a little bit as if I had emigrated to another country, got to know the language but not perfectly; got to know the customs but not perfectly . . . a country you visit and you know people and you can speak the language but it's not really your country and it's all slightly distorted.

CASSANDRA WEDD: It was in a terrible frantic mess that first issue. They had to get David Wills in at the last minute to do the design. In the middle of the night. I think Richard Adams and Josie were pretty wild up in the art room: the art room definitely resented the editors and they were quite anarchic. Richard wasn't there a lot of the time, because of the *OZ* trial. Maybe Ed didn't know what was going on that much – he was busy writing letters to his publishing friends. Neither the first News Editor, Alex Mitchell, nor the first Art Director, Mike Dowd, ever made it beyond the first issue.

RICHARD ADAMS: In the week and a half that led up to the press deadline people were beginning to go crazy. There was a wild newspaper on the drawing board, it was just out of control. The run up to that was that

370

Mike Dowd and I and another designer called Josie Flett were far behind with producing boards: we couldn't get at the copy, we couldn't get at anything, everybody was taking longer to produce things than they'd expected. Mike was a visualiser and an art director but he couldn't handle a tin of Cow Gum and a scalpel or a ruler. He'd spend hours slaving away trying to get something straight on a board, but that wasn't the point; the point was that you had to do half a dozen bloody boards like that. Nobody's sleeping by now, everybody's been awake four days and three nights – the first issue was produced under those kind of circumstances. And on the long last night everybody's speeding out of their brains and the front page is being held over until last because Alex Mitchell, the News Editor, is sitting on the cover story. This scoop that was to stick *INK* right into the middle of Fleet Street. And the story was so hot that he couldn't tell anybody – not Victor, not Fisher, Neville, Dennis – what it was going to be. Come 2 am, finally Alex Mitchell has told Fisher, Neville, *et al* what this story is going to be. I wasn't there to witness it but there must have been one great groan that went up, but they'd committed themselves to printing it all over the front page and that was what everyone thought was the best thing to do. I was called out from the studio across the road to work in top-secret conditions, in an editorial office at no. 73 with Ed Victor across the desk peeling grapefruit to keep me awake, and me trying to stick this useless fucking article together. It was called 'The Great Uranium Robbery' and it had a map and it had plastered headlines all over the front page and only about 150 words of copy. The story was just a fart in a colander. It was no scoop: *The Times* had run the story something like two weeks before on page six.

ED VICTOR: Alex Mitchell, he worked for all kinds of papers, a big Fleet Street freelancer. We were very thrilled that he was going to write for us, because he was an important player, and he insisted that he should have the front page for his opening story. And he would deliver this great story to us. Which he did, but the story wasn't a great story. It was some kind of paranoid fantasy about some plutonium leak, and we were trusting enough to hold that for him to a point where we couldn't do anything else. We saw it and we weren't thrilled with it but it was too late. Later he said to me, in his cups, that he was engaged in some kind of double bluff, I don't know, that he believed very much in the principles of whatever party he was involved in – the Workers' Revolutionary Party – and more or less said that he sabotaged *INK. INK* was a paper that they didn't really want to exist and he did what he could to destroy it. It may have been the case that the WRP deliberately planted him. Con-

371

spiracy was very much the mode of the time. Everyone played with the revolution and probably Alex did too.

DAVID WIDGERY: Mad Alex Mitchell was hijacked by Gerry Healy of the SLL. Mitchell was a very good journalist who'd done good work for Healy and the *Sunday Times*. Mitchell wanted to inject some politics into *INK* but Healy told him, these are a bunch of bourgeois wankers, come with me to the real revolution. Presumably Mad Mitch just jumped ship. I wouldn't be surprised if he *was* a plant: that's the way Healy operates. He was very interested in the underground and he was very interested in spying and he liked to keep an eye on the underground. He was very fed up with *INK* because he'd been trying to get his paper off the ground, the *Worker's Press*, and very annoyed by the success of the underground.

RICHARD ADAMS: So here's me, banging away at this bloody front cover, Victor sitting across the table, just working in isolation – an awful experience. The next morning that was it. It went to press. There was colour on the front and maybe the centre, but however it was used it was a waste and totally unsuitable for web offset. We had been working in the wrong way for the medium. That was just another error on top of more and more errors. So it goes off to press. There was this great sigh – you could almost hear it going off on both sides of Princedale Road. And there's the wind-down. I went back across the road and the place was empty, an absolute complete fucking tip, and Mike Dowd had disappeared. I went to find him and he was on the loo, in a lotus position. He wasn't there. His body was there but his mind was out on the astral plane somewhere. This poor man was just completely knackered. He may even have nodded out the night before, I don't think he even made the course.

Richard gives me a present, which was 200 Rothmans cigarettes. It showed the attitude of the editors to my superhuman efforts. And I got on this fucking bus and I went to sleep and woke up in the bus garage at Acton at eleven o'clock that same morning. I then slept for two days. Then we had to get back in and do the next issue of *INK* . . .

When I got back in the shit had hit the fan, the newspaper was out on the streets, 50,000 copies of it. Alex Mitchell had gone, leaving behind his briefcase downstairs in the newsroom. And inside was a bottle of Johnny Walker whisky and a bag of African grass. That was his leaving card, as it were. Later it turned out that he had been deliberately planted there to fuck up the first issue of the newspaper. It all struck me as being such an incredible waste. There were some really good people, there were some top-flight professionals involved – Michael Kustow,

John du Cane, Charlie Gillett – but there wasn't the organisation to support the kind of copy that they were coming up with.

DAVID WIDGERY: I hoped for a fusion of socialist politics and the underground, who were all emotional revolutionaries but didn't have any strategy, whereas we had loads of strategy but not much style. I hoped that *INK* was going to be that. In fact *INK* was a catastrophe and a significant catastrophe.

ED VICTOR: The paper as it emerged was much more of an underground publication than it was anything else. It was a logical newspaper for the guys who started *OZ* to put on the streets as a weekly newspaper. It was an awful mess, an awful dog's dinner. There was one particular guy, who I knew very well, a very wealthy guy, though he never gave any money to it, and he looked at the second issue and he said, 'I don't know what this is. I'm looking at this thing and I have no idea what it is. What are you trying to do?' I realised that he was right. The paper had no centre to it. It didn't really know what it was doing, possibly because of the split between Richard and me, the two people who had the most input editorially. It was a disaster. It never really caught on. The underground press was just fine. They were what they were and they did the job. They reached the audience they were supposed to. Whereas *INK* was supposed to reach a much larger audience – people like me as I was, the editorial director of a big publishing house, young, interested in what was going on.

CASSANDRA WEDD: For a while they didn't know it wasn't successful. The returns take a while to come in and they probably thought it was quite successful for a bit, and then the returns came in with three-quarters of the print run.

ED VICTOR: My involvement on *INK*, this is the easiest answer, was a failure of judgement. I never thought it was going to go quite where it went. And once there it never came back. Once it went off in that particular direction there was no taking it back. In the end, however, it happened, I got it wrong and it was a failure. It ran out of steam and money, in that order, very quickly. *INK* lasted in its original version for three or four months. Then we retrenched and redesigned it, Tito Gerassi edited an issue, and it staggered on for a bit, but there was no money. The printer carried us quite a long way. Everyone had a different vision of what *INK* should be and it turned out to be a little bit of everything and not a very good paper.

I went on TV the night of the first issue. The group was me, Tony Elliot and Peregrine Worsthorne. And I was just chewed to little bits and pieces. And there was nothing I could do about it, because the product was so patently inferior. At the end I moved to Great Newport Street [from Princedale Road] and I was there for a while feeling increasingly isolated. I would just sit in this office and all these people I didn't know were coming in and I just finally left.

'Life was earnest, life was real'

CASSANDRA WEDD: I don't know why we moved from Princedale Road. Was it more space? *OZ* moved there too. Everything was falling apart. The *OZ* trial was on at the same time, so Richard was completely taken up with that, Ed and Andrew were ticking along, but it just became obvious that it wasn't selling. And probably they wanted to get out. Then John Lloyd appeared as the editor, via Andrew Fisher and Anna Coote, who got him to pull the thing together. He brought in Dave Robins, Stuart Weir, Alison Fell and those people. Dick Pountain, Mike Radford. They were all living in various communal households and were strong on running the thing collectively.

JOHN LLOYD: When *INK* folded, or was folding, I got a call one day from Ed Victor, saying, 'Could you come in and have a talk?' I hadn't known, because I was a freelance, how bad things were. I went to have lunch with him – the first literary lunch I'd ever had – and he offered me a job at £30 a week, which was quite good money at the time, and said, sorry it can't be more, and flattered me grossly – great writer and all that: really he just wanted someone to put out the paper. I hadn't realised that he'd tried twelve other people, including Anna Coote and Andrew Cockburn, both of whom had worked on it. So I ended up in Great Newport Street with the people who were left. Hardly anybody, really: Cassandra, Su Small, and Felix who was not allowed to work on *OZ*. Anna Coote had gone. I didn't really appreciate the horror I was taking on – the debts and so on – but I'd have probably still done it even if I had.

DAVE ROBINS: John Lloyd had been appointed by the smart set, they were all very smooth – Richard, Ed Victor, Andrew Fisher – smart guys who were trying to start an up-market, hip, radical revo journal reflecting the narcissisms of the underground. At this time I was basically drifting, ligging around and hanging out with libbo types. They were lefties but not involved in any party. Many were ex-Cambridge graduates, some of whom were involved in various struggles like the Claimants' Union, squatting and so on. We were all into downward social mobility. There were sub-cultures within that scene: there was Dick Pountain's scene, which was the Grove, and they didn't know what the fuck was going on outside the Grove.

JOHN LLOYD: Dave Robins came by. I don't know how he'd heard about it, and I'd never met him before. He just came by. He wandered in and stayed. He brought with him Dick Pountain, Tom Fawthrop, and others. Dick and Tom became instant contributors, particularly Dick under a whole range of pseudonyms like Laura Norder and so on.

DICK POUNTAIN: At some stage I had met Dave Robins and I heard that *INK* had been taken over by a bunch of libertarians, and I was desperate for something to do and went along there and met John Lloyd, who was still a hippie when I met him. It was rather fun. We were getting paid, only £15, but it was better than a poke in the eye. In the course of that I met Felix [Dennis] who came in once a week to paste up and design the reviews page and I was Reviews Editor. I also met Mike Radford, who was an accountant, who was a very stern Althusserian communist and he was extremely scornful of the whole libertarian outlook; he was also incredibly smart. When we were having these appalling all-afternoon meetings in order to make up our minds what our attitude to the provisional IRA was, Mike would come in and make two or three withering comments that made it perfectly obvious that none of us knew what we were talking about. He had an enormous influence on both me and John Lloyd, who were both wavering anyway about libertarianism. He punctured the balloon of believing in 'the Revolution' and so on and made it obvious that politics was something much more serious and much more difficult than the sort of facile stuff that we were playing with.

DAVID ROBINS: News came to Belsize Park via Phil Cohen's wife, Pam Brighton, who was a radical theatre director, and who was contacted by John Lloyd (who none of us had ever heard of – a new boy, Scottish) that they wanted to do an issue of *INK* called, I think, 'Alternatives': did Pam have any ideas about this issue? I contributed an article on the underground press which, needless to say, was an attack on the hippies. What it said was that the underground press was all very well but it lacked politics and it was all dreams. The next thing that happened was that all the trendies disappeared from the paper and it was wide open and there was John in a kaftan and no staff. He was a hippie then, he'd been on the hippie trail to India or wherever and he had multiple relationships of the most unbelievable kind . . . But he was a very serious guy

375

and he was looking for answers. Me and Pamela Brighton went out for a drink with him in the Belsize Tavern. And we started drinking and then we began to rant and we did his head. And he called up the next day and said, 'I want you to come in and we've got to form a collective. You're right about what you say about Ed Victor and all these people, they're not really where it's at . . .' I thought this was interesting. He was open and above all he was obviously very talented. I was very excited: I thought well, we're going to get this paper because nobody else seemed to want it. It was in a dreadful state financially, with telephone bills of £2000 and so on. So Pamela went into the office and the most incredible thing was that although the high-struttin' dudes had left the place, no sign of them, all the secretarial staff was still intact: various young women of impeccable class background. We didn't know what to do about them. John said, 'Well, we don't want to start our first revolutionary socialist newspaper by firing anybody,' and we were caught in a quandary. Here were these girls who'd joined the paper cos they thought they were going to meet a better class of person. Then all these unshaven liggers appear.

JOHN LLOYD: Dave and I became joint Editors and wrote much of the paper. Dave was responsible for much of the political stance. He'd been through Situationism. Our first issue was on Working-Class Heroes. We both had chips on our shoulders about our working-class upbringing, followed by the education system, the hippie thing and the far Left, but were still half-guilty about leaving the working class behind and full of half-resolved tensions about being where we were, coming from where we did – and all this gave an energy to the politics of the paper. So the John Lennon line was terribly important, personally rather than politically. We were also grafting onto things like the IRA. This *INK* was much harder edged. Another very important person was Alison Fell, who just turned up and started contributing, and what she introduced was feminism. Both Dave and I were deeply into being pigs. She also had this deep Scots Calvinist morality, the working-class background, a quite miserable one in her case, and a very very dour and hard attitude. A good sense of humour but by and large life was earnest, life was real. And she brought in this very hard-edged feminism which co-existed with the Fabulous Furry Freak Brothers and the IRA stuff and the rock stuff that Su Small brought in. We also introduced editorial meetings, even if a lot of it was just whoever spoke loudest dominating the meeting. What I had gathered from the Neville *INK* was that the charismatic Neville knew or was sleeping with almost everybody in the building. The girls were there very much as people for him to sleep with. Dave and I were not like that and it was a bit more democratic because there was no charismatic figure. But at the same time we still made most of the editorial decisions, although people like Su Small were very important and Colette Meissner, Stan Demidjuk's girlfriend, who did layout. It took about ten months before we had to face the real financial position, and that was put off so long by a tremendous effort by Mike Radford who fiddled the cash flow, juggling the figures and so on. We had a creditors meeting at Conway Hall in early '72 and closed it. Dave cooked up a load of fantasies about keeping going but they were never more than fantasies.

RICHARD ADAMS: The second version of *INK* hit its peak as a newspaper by late 1971. The copy and the whole editorial nature of the newspaper was sharper, just much more inspired than the original. Though it was very doctrinaire. Much more political than anything else produced by the underground. The fact that the main *OZ* people were involved in the trial freed the editorial staff to create a newspaper in a way that had been suffocated in the first four months. On August 7 *OZ* was found guilty; *INK* suspended publication till September. Richard still had this impending drug trial. On August 18 there was the repression issue of *INK* (Number 16) and that was after a collective had taken over the editorial and from there on they dropped the colour, all the old gang had gone, and they started producing black and white *INK*s. They got Gerald Scarfe, Richard Yound and a great many well-known people. They did a whole issue about pornography, obscenity and so on.

CHARLES SHAAR MURRAY: *INK* was peculiar. It was the last time that anybody tried to weld the hippies and the Left into anything coherent. And nothing with hippies in it could be coherent, so it went drastically down. John Lloyd had long hair and purple loon pants. He was an uncomfortable cross between the surrealist acid wing and the proper politicos. But that meant that when he decided to indulge himself he did so far less casually. If he wanted to get high, he'd get drastically high; if he wanted to get pissed, he'd be the most pissed person there. By the time of *INK* the feminists were getting serious. Alison Fell would give anybody hell – she was great.

Gay Liberation: 'Join the *Observer* and pee in the lift'

JIM ANDERSON: When I left school I studied Law. I went to Sydney University Law School and became a barrister and worked for the New South Wales Department of Justice. I was being groomed for success, but I was always gay and I think it's partly my homosexuality that made me dissatisfied. Being gay was very difficult, for me anyway. There was no sort of liberation movement in the late 50s/early 60s, at all, so the three years after leaving school in 1954 were wasted, black, suicidal years which I didn't get out of until I met Germaine [Greer] and the beatniks, the Sydney Push, as they were known. So I read the beatniks and the existentialists and that made an excuse for not having a life of my own. Working as a lawyer meant that my working life and my private life became more and more disparate. And it was a time when my own department was starting to investigate various elements of the Push and people who lived outrageous sexual lifestyles, and I felt it was an appropriate moment to leave. So I resigned and left Australia for England.

ANDREW LUMSDEN: When I realised that I was gay I went to a psychotherapist and had two sessions with him which were nothing but laughter, mainly from him. He specialised in Fleet Street marital bustups. I was just about to join *The Times*. He said, 'My best advice to you is join the *Observer* and pee in the lift. If you do that, they'll give you six months' sabbatical and take you back afterwards. So if you really want to sort yourself out, do that.'

I started coming out, to friends though not to family, between '69 and '70. I found it very difficult. Then in 1970 I decided to write an article on GLF [Gay Liberation Front] for *The Times*, a couple of months after it had started, saying that the serious media are not paying attention to this movement: there's lots of sniping in the popular press, but not one news-analysis piece. I'd given it to the Features Editor, and heard it was going to be run on the centre spread. Then abruptly I was told the Editor had pulled it out. I had an interview with William Rees-Mogg about it a couple of days later. I was a bit put out, but after all I was employed as a financial journalist, so I was ambivalent. But I did say, 'Well, I'd like to send it somewhere else,' and he said, 'All right, provided you don't say you work at *The Times*.' George Gale took it at the *Spectator* and that meant I had to come out to my parents. So because of that article I was 'out' everywhere – a convenient way of doing it.

DUNCAN FALLOWELL: Gay Lib started about '69. The wonderful thing about it was that it had nothing whatsoever to do with sex. Politicised gay life is not a sexual thing. Gay clubs actually came later. There were pubs from before the war, but not actual gay clubs, which took longer to develop. The first one of any size, any cohesion, was the Gigolo, in the King's Road. That was just coffee. Then there was the Catacombs in Earls Court and that just served coffee, and then the whole thing took off. But Gay Lib was nothing to do with sex, it was to do with political banners. It's even more true about the lesbian thing, which has nothing to do with the hunger of women to satisfy each other's lusts with each

378

other's bodies – much more to do with trying to live a life in which they're not going to be eaten up by men.

ANDREW LUMSDEN: GLF was very much divided between the activists and the anti-activists. There were those who said, 'We have to look into our own gender behaviour; all this going out and doing things, all that goes on in order to make you a man. Which is another way of not coping with the truth.' Words like 'sexual politics' didn't make much sense to me during the 60s. To me it meant that you could take part in a political movement and have sex as a result of that political movement. You could pick up people, be picked up, meet people through politics. That seemed wonderful to me. This was 1971 and women in the movement, the lesbians, were telling us that we're continuing to be aggressive, loud, domineering; as far as they were concerned we were just a lot of *men*, running around doing things, getting our rocks off. The lesbians walked out of GLF meetings in '71 and very clearly explained why they were going.

DAVID WIDGERY: The gay movement came quite late to the student and political worlds. It didn't really get accepted in the SWP, which was what IS [International Socialists] developed into, till the mid to late 70s. These ideas do travel quite slowly, although I think it indicates that they are changing people's lives and people are coming to terms with new ideas. I remember being absolutely horrified reading Richard Neville's book *Play Power* to see in the preface 'Thanks to Jim Anderson whose new book will be *Gay Power*.' I thought, 'Jim isn't a queer, is he?' I didn't know that Jim was gay, I didn't really know what gay was. Then I thought, 'Mmm, I suppose he is a bit funny . . .' Although there were quite a lot of gay people involved in IS, the policy was the traditional Stalinist one: after the revolution there won't be any problem because we'll all be heterosexual.

ANDREW LUMSDEN: GLF was a very working-class movement, although there were a certain number of middle-class members, quite influential ones, through either their ideas or the work they did. I was never important in GLF, it was something I found a couple of weeks after it had started and began going to. All the ideas were created elsewhere, here and in the States. The first couple of meetings at the LSE attracted 30-40 people. I went to the second or third. Soon the lecture room was crowded out with 300 or more. By the time we moved to Middle Earth, after about four months, there were probably 1000 or so. But then attendance began to dwindle. People from all over the country

379

had heard about it on the grapevine and came rushing to take part, but when they went back home they started up groups of their own.

In Britain the thinkers fed in gender politics right from the start. Most of the men who turned up for GLF meetings didn't know what the hell that was about. Sounded fine: any reasonably decent man could say, 'Yes, women shouldn't be put down,' but nothing deeper than that. It was very influential in the genesis of GLF, but a handful of people had to put it there. We had consciousness-raising exercises: coming-out experiences were common. The most gruelling thing was talking about what you personally liked to do sexually – one's fantasies.

There was this difference between those people who said, 'Let's find out what we're like,' and those who said, 'Oh, we're fine, but we're put down and oppressed, let's go out and do something.' So I organised demos outside Foyles against David Reuben's *Everything You Always Wanted To Know About Sex*. And we occupied W. H. Allen's offices. Whoever was running Allen's was most put out. I said, 'I'm a journalist on *The Times*, and all my friends here' – who were all wearing frocks – 'have come in to complain bitterly about this bloody awful paperback you're putting out.' The man was completely torn: on the one hand he was behaving as a publisher does to a journalist from *The Times*, on the other he wanted to send for the police to get rid of all these men in frocks, women in trousers. I don't think it had any effect, but demos like that were a way of getting to know each other. There was a bit of publicity, but that wasn't the main idea.

RICHARD ADAMS: In 1971 the Festival of Light [an evangelical Christian movement promoting 'traditional family values'] had a big meeting in Westminster Hall and people from the GLF dressed up as nuns and let loose mice. And the Bethnal Green gay commune, comprised almost entirely of transvestites, were conducting this really bizarre form of street theatre, especially round Speakers' Corner. Things to do with both gay and women's liberation were coming very much to the fore. *Spare Rib* was in the making. There were also plans for starting *Gay News*. Jim Anderson introduced me to the people who were putting that out and I became the token het designer. Which I did for the first nine months of *Gay News*' life.

ANDREW LUMSDEN: *Gay News* started as a newspaper in November 1971. Dennis Lemon was a prime mover. I suggested at a meeting that we have a paper that just didn't give out propaganda. I pointed out that the movement was now countrywide, but people in Dundee didn't know what was happening in Manchester and so on. So we had to have a real

380

newspaper. Dennis agreed, meetings were convened to discuss it and the paper came out in summer '72. The Campaign for Homosexual Law Reform subscription list was opened to us, so we could ask for advance subscriptions. Someone put up some money. Dennis and I went to see David Hockney. He said, 'If you want to bring out a nice magazine with lots of pictures of men, then I might be interested, but I don't want anything to *read*.' Graham Chapman did send some money; Angus McGill at the *Standard* may have put some in too. But mainly we were scratching around, no substantial amounts were put up. Many monied gay men were appalled by GLF. They saw it as a socialist revolutionary enterprise and thought a connection with GLF would ruin them.

The first few issues of the paper were hand-distributed, taken round the pubs and so on. The first issue came out for Gay Pride Week, held in Hyde Park. And very good it was, the pace and energy of it. The early issues were nearly all editorial, that's why they looked so smashing. There was spot colour and a nice big format, like *Frendz*. It started off selling about 6000 and reached a ceiling by the blasphemy trial of 20-23,000 a fortnight. It was not just a GLF paper, but rather one that came out of GLF. It dealt mainly with what was going on in the straight world: what the police were doing, or the media, what somebody had said, what the Church was up to.

The Festival of Light: 'We all filed out and did a conga'

ANDREW LUMSDEN: Dennis Lemon erupted at GLF meetings in the autumn of 1971 demanding that we do something about the Festival of Light. GLF street theatre decided that they would.

Dennis was working in a music shop. He was a startling figure: the first time I met him he was thin as a rake, very tall, wearing stars-and-stripes bell bottoms. A very beautiful man. With others he successfully organised a raid on a Festival of Light meeting at the Westminster Hall. They went as nuns . . .

SU SMALL: I was getting more interested in general politics and personal politics and I'd become involved with gay liberation. I found myself at this meeting to discuss how we could combat the Festival of Light. A guy from Monty Python, Graham Chapman, was there and he said, 'I've got a bob or two, so if anyone's got any ideas . . .' and the plan was that we were going to do a whole series of things. The first was to infiltrate the first big Festival of Light rally at Westminster Hall. The plan was that A and B were going in full drag and they'd stand up and shout, 'Say it out loud: I'm gay and I'm proud!' Then we'd leave it a few minutes and so-and-so would let out the white mice and they'd all scream and stand on the chairs . . . We had about seventeen different things planned so that if some of us couldn't get in, something would still happen. We also had someone working inside the Festival of Light office keeping us abreast of things.

The evening started. The first trick was a bunch of people who at the end of every sentence burst into rapturous applause. For the first three or four times it happened everybody picked it up, and then they started realising, 'Look, we're going to be here all night . . .' Graham Chapman had put up the money for six nun's costumes, cos when he said he had some dosh I said, 'I always wanted to dress up as a nun,' and I got Debbie and Cassandra from the *INK* office, two more girls and Russell Hunter. We all got in, but they sussed us; they sent some people to sit behind us and sussed that we might not be nuns. We thought we were doing very well . . . We waited until our turn came – I think Malcolm Muggeridge was speaking at the time – and we all filed out and did a conga down the aisle of the Westminster Central Hall.

RUSSELL HUNTER: It was a time when Cliff Richard was giving out. And Mary Whitehouse, Malcolm Muggeridge, Lord Longford and so on. They had this big rally for what they called the Festival of Light at the Central Hall, Westminster. Su Small, Rose, Sandy, Debbie Knight, and myself decided to dress up as nuns to infiltrate it. They'd certainly have never let us in dressed normally. Su Small was the Mother Superior, cos her habit was a different colour, and we passed straight through with no problems. They were vetting everybody at the door and they turned away a lot of people: obvious hippies who were there to make trouble. But we went straight through. At a certain point in the proceedings we all stood up, started heckling and throwing the cushions. Then we did a conga up the middle aisle. We all lifted our skirts and started making obscene gestures until the Christian bouncers turned up and beat us up, especially me, when they discovered I wasn't what they thought.

OZ: 'We covered up the blow-job'

JON GOODCHILD: *OZ* was a way to stick your fingers up at a few things. And we got rumblings that the local police weren't too happy about it. I don't know quite how we heard that but they picked me up once and they asked about *OZ*, so we knew that they knew and they had instructions from somewhere else to check it out. We were advocating drugs, sex and rock'n'roll. They weren't actually watching us, but they'd pick up a copy and look through it and they'd see what was pornography

382

as far as they were concerned and stuff which they saw as politically dangerous.

I was picked up about a stolen bicycle and taken into the Chelsea police station. They asked me all about *OZ*. I played completely dumb. They just wanted to know what sort of people they were, what their names were, who was associated with them, and something about communists. They were larking around and giving me cigarettes and making funny cracks – but they were serious. But I didn't think twice about it at the time, because I didn't regard *OZ* as a serious thing. I didn't take them seriously either. Richard knew it was a force to be reckoned with because he had felt this before in Australia and got himself into big trouble. He knew how to provoke the authorities, he knew how to make them react and he knew what they could do. So in a way he was ready for it and in a way he was inviting it. He was doing it deliberately and we were dupes, but we didn't know. And we certainly didn't think the English authorities would be so uptight.

GEOFFREY ROBERTSON: The trial turned out to be a much more dramatic confrontation than the authorities imagined it would be. Which is why some of them so signally failed to handle it sensibly. For the defendants, of course, their raising of the temperature was both a vindication and a snare. They'd been boasting that *OZ* undermined what they saw as the corrupt fabric of society, and now the authorities were taking them at their word! So they could not logically admit that *OZ* had no effect. Yet in order to defend themselves on the obscenity charge, they had to argue that their work really had little effect, which is not an easy thing for a writer to do.

JIM ANDERSON: People regarded us as pornographic but we were very serious about what we were doing and didn't regard ourselves as pornographic. We were into sexual freedom and sexual liberation and if we wanted to publish a picture with sexual content it would also have a point to make, and we would insist on publishing it. What the police would do was go to a printer and say, 'Look, if you print this magazine we will bust you and you'll lose your licence to print.' So we had to keep switching printers and we found ourselves more and more often going to printers who *were* printing clandestine pornography, hardcore.

FELIX DENNIS: So we're looking for printers. We finally find one in Lamb's Conduit Street: Sid Spellman. I get a telephone call at home; it's nine in the morning, I'm still fast asleep. It's Sidney who says he's got two gentlemen sitting in front of him and I'd better get down there as quickly as possible. I throw my clothes on, hurl myself into a cab, 35 minutes later I'm sitting in his office, in this old wooden cabin affair up some stairs above one of the main printing machines. He's got these two flatfeet with him from Scotland Yard. They do a sort of Tom and Jerry act, nice and nasty. And their basic trick was to try and impress upon him how surprised they were that a man of his substance – and Sidney was of no substance at all – was involved in producing filth. They kept on and on emphasising to him that it wouldn't do any good for his long-term business producing this hippie rubbish. It would do nothing but demoralise the workforce and get him into trouble.

Sidney had asked me to be present and they were very very unhappy that I was there. Anyway, I listened and I didn't say anything. Sidney's basic trick was to act the old innocent, whether he was negotiating with you on print prices, paper prices, and he continued to do this with these two coppers, who had no idea what he was really like. After a lot of talking on their side he finally said, 'Now let me try to get this straight. I've got a family business to run here, and I've got to explain to my wife why I'm turning down this job. It's worth a lot of money, but obviously I'm always interested in listening to the authorities . . .' They broke in immediately, 'This is only an unofficial visit, we don't want you to think this an official instruction, Mr Spellman.' 'But let me get this straight,' says Sidney. 'You're telling me that I shouldn't print this magazine because it's illegal.' 'No, no, not at all, not at all. It's just that it's dirty. Now isn't it, John?' 'Yes. Filth. Filth, I think, is a good description, don't you, Dave?' 'Yes indeed, John . . . we're just surprised to see a man such as yourself involved in this, Mr Spellman, and we don't really know how it's happened, but it's probably an accident and the sooner you get rid of it the better.'

So Sidney finally turns round to one of the guys, and at this point even I was bewildered, and he says, 'I've seen you before,' and the guy goes, 'I don't think so, Mr Spellman, certainly your company has never been in any trouble before.' But Sidney's a sly old bastard and he's still playing the innocent and he says, 'I'm certain I have seen you before, I could swear to God I've seen you before.' This copper is now bemused, and he suspects something, he's not an idiot but he's walking right into it. 'I'm certain we've never met, Mr Spellman. Of course, we do make mistakes, it's possible, we're all legitimate citizens, we're all likely to meet . . .' and so on. And suddenly Sidney turned and I could see that what I thought was him actually buckling under, the old trembling-lip routine, I suddenly realised, probably only five seconds before the recipients realised this wasn't fear and trembling, this was white-lipped rage. And Sidney said, 'It was in Düsseldorf, Düsseldorf,' and the copper said,

384

'No, Mr Spellman, you're completely mistaken, I've never been in Germany in my life . . .' 'Yes it was, yes it was! I was about eleven years old, and I think you had a fucking leather coat on, you bastard, and an Alsatian dog and it was my fucking father running it and you came round and said, "It would be a good idea if you did this or did that," and you fucking popped him in the end!!!' And he starts screaming, 'John, John' (that's his print minder, about 400 pounds), 'get these people out of here!' and the whole place is in a frenzy and these guys are running upstairs escorting the police officers out. They'd never met anything like it: and they left him alone, he was too much of a nutter for them.

JIM ANDERSON: Schoolkids' *OZ* was Richard Neville's idea, I think. I remember him talking about feeling old and boring at a New Year's Eve party, and from that eventually came the insertion in *OZ* 26 of an advertisement:

> Some of us at *OZ* are feeling old and boring. So we invite any of our readers who are under 18 to come and edit the April issue. Apply at the *OZ* office in Princedale Road W.11 any time from 10 am to 7 pm on Friday March 13. We will choose one person, several, or accept collective applications from a group of friends. You will receive no money except expenses and you will enjoy almost complete editorial freedom.

About thirty kids showed up and in one way or another, over several hard-working, party weekends, they all helped us put the issue together.

'You know,' said Richard after the first editorial meeting, 'they're much more intelligent and articulate than I was at that age. Come to think of it, they're much more intelligent and articulate than I am at *this* age.'

CHARLES SHAAR MURRAY: Schoolkids' *OZ* was the spring of '70. I had issue number 26 of *OZ* with the ad in it looking for schoolkids and I thought: I bet I can write as well as at least half of these people, and it's a chance to get into print and get away from Reading. So I went up there and there was a meeting. A lot were Holland Park Comprehensive people like Viv Berger – younger than me but immeasurably more urbane. I was terribly excited to be there. From my naïve and impressionable perspective it seemed terribly glamorous. Richard, Jim and Felix were all at the meeting. Jim was very louche, sardonic, quite kindly. I couldn't get over the fact that he looked exactly like Johnny Winter. Felix was in a suit, waving a briefcase about, being gruff, occasionally laughing like a maniac. Richard was very urbane. He was about 31-32 at the time. They all seemed terribly sophisticated and bohemian and I thought it must be wonderful to be like that. They wanted to know what we were interested in, and I was mainly interested in pop music at the time. It was, What do you think about your education? etc, etc – what we thought about everything. Another meeting was arranged and there were more and more trips to London, ending up by staying overnight in various places like Richard and Louise's place in Palace Gardens Terrace.

The first time I handed in a piece of copy Richard wrote 'Bold unjustified' on the side: I didn't realise that it was instructions for the typesetter – I thought he was having a go at what I'd written. We were up for four days and nights, sleeping in shifts, getting the stuff down, everyone writing their little bits. The Rupert Bear cartoon came out of a book of Robert Crumb's stuff which was all new to me – you could only get that in London. I thought it was outrageous – Viv had the idea of putting the Rupert heads on. It all seemed wonderful.

FELIX DENNIS: Basically the decision to do the Schoolkids' issue was policy. In the nicest possible way, and I mean it that way, in the nicest possible way Richard was bone idle. He was totally bone idle. His idea was a moment of glory, a flash of inspiration, everybody claps for fourteen years and he goes on vacation. This meant that it put a lot of pressure on his peers to produce a magazine. Occasionally we would get very bored and we couldn't do it or we didn't feel like doing it so we would invite nutters to produce issues. Like we did a Flying Saucer issue. We would guide them and help them to produce the magazine which they didn't know how to do but basically it was their magazine and it was shit. Then we did a women's issue and Germaine did all that and then we thought of having a schoolkids' issue. It was totally innocent. That's how it happened. The police got it completely wrong: it wasn't *for* them, it was *by* them. They understood it towards the end, just about, but they didn't believe that children could have produced it. They actually truly believed that we'd got a bunch of children and that we pretended they'd written it but that really we'd written it.

JOHN LEAVER: One evening in 1970 I went along to Jim Anderson's place and there was a bunch of kids from Holland Park putting together Schoolkids' *OZ*. They were actually doing it. There was all this shit talked later about how they had been manipulated into doing it, but as I recall it it was the other way round: they actually turned down a lot of the input from the kids, they actually censored their stuff.

CHARLES SHAAR MURRAY: I never felt I was being corrupted. I was

386

trying to find out about the world, about London, about the media, about people whose lives and work I considered interesting, something to be emulated.

JIM ANDERSON: 'Bit strong, isn't it, Jim?' Sid the printer commented when I was there checking the colours. He pointed at the blue soft-focus naked ladies that we'd put on the cover with '*OZ – SCHOOLKIDS' ISSUE*' in yellow lettering. 'We covered up the blow-job,' I said. 'We're not totally crazy.' 'Well, I hope you know what you're doing,' said Sid. 'Hate to see you get caught.'

GEOFFREY ROBERTSON: The *OZ* trial was a case which was brought predominantly as a 'conspiracy to corrupt public morals' charge. To understand it you've got to look at the indictment, which charged them with 'conspiring to corrupt the morals of liege subjects of Her Majesty the Queen by raising in their minds inordinate and lustful desires'. These charges were brought in the dying days of the Labour government, as part of a purge of the underground press. It was not, however, brought by the politicians of the day, but by bureaucrats in the DPP's department, gee-ed up by angry policemen. What is so ironical, in retrospect, is the anger that these policemen felt and expressed about 'these hippies corrupting our kids' . . . Yet some of those same police officers were sent to prison a few years later for taking bribes. The Obscene Publications Squad in those days was a vast protection racket. The people they were protecting were the hardcore pornographers of Soho. There's an extraordinary irony that some of the police who were going into battle against the underground press on the basis that it was endangering their children were those who were allowing pornography of the most ugly, desolating kind to flourish in Soho.

RICHARD NEVILLE: I was just lying in bed with Louise in my basement when Inspector Luff turned up with a lot of cops to confiscate *OZ*s. At the police station that night when he came to interview me I saw a copy of *Play Power* inside his case. Luff himself was quite courteous.

FELIX DENNIS: Luff [Detective Inspector Fred Luff of the Obscene Publications Squad] was a raving Christian and he actually believed what he was doing – they couldn't have chosen a better guy. I remember him going up to Debbie Knight, the little receptionist [at *OZ*], and he said, 'Debbie, I've come round here many times.' 'I know,' she said. 'And I've always tried to behave like a gentleman and I'd like to speak to you as a father now. I don't understand how such a nice girl could possibly work

387

in a place like this, with all this filth and corruption. You could have a very nice job working in the police force.'

After the trial, just as they were sending us to the nick, Luff came round and he said, 'I'm sorry you've been sent to the nick because I didn't think it would come to that. I think on the whole you're not actually bad young lads, but you've been led astray. And you've got to pay the price. Just keep your chin up, lads, it won't be long.' It was worse than if he'd come along and said, 'Gotcha, you fucking bastards!'

RICHARD NEVILLE: I think they genuinely didn't like Schoolkids' *OZ*. To be fair to the establishment, they were deeply morally outraged by schoolchildren talking about teachers having erections or demythologising Rupert Bear. They were absolutely freaked out by the fusion of sex, drugs, rock'n'roll and schoolkids all in dayglo.

GEOFFREY ROBERTSON: It was very much a trial of the 60s, although held in the 70s. One of the interesting things about it was that there was only one juror under 40. All the rest were in their fifties or sixties. It took place just before the property qualification for jury service was abolished and the age for jury service reduced to eighteen. We obtained the jury list the day before and went through all the names and occupations and there was one man named William Blake, a name which greatly appealed to the defendants. The next day, when the usher cried 'Call William Blake,' a stern, elderly man appeared, looking nothing at all like the poet. He was challenged. We used up 28 challenges but *still* only obtained one person under 40, and that was the juror who dissented from the majority verdict. Even given the property qualification, it was still curious that in 40 jurors they could only find one under 40.

RICHARD NEVILLE: I decided to defend myself very early on in the proceedings. I'd already been through the out-of-town performance with the Australian trial. I found that sitting in a courtroom listening to lawyers talk is stultifyingly boring and I didn't want to go through that again. I thought it would actually sharpen my mind if I did it myself, and I was influenced by other cases – the Chicago 8, although they all had lawyers. Also one of the catch-cries of the times was about taking charge of your own life, and I thought that taking charge of events in the courtroom seemed to be endemic to the philosophy of the underground. So, as always with me, there were two motives: the selfish one – not to be bored by listening to others and paying them a fortune – and a desire for self-growth, perhaps, and because it was true to the principles of the movement.

388

We had Friends of *OZ*, a front organisation run by Stan Demidjuk and Sue Miles. Photos were taken, press releases were written, energy was poured into providing information to the media. I'm sure it's quite common now for radical groups to make press kits. Then it was probably one of the first times that a busted minority outfit decided, instead of hiring a PR consultant, to invent our own. *Play Power* is full of the recognition of the power of the media. It was something I didn't need to learn from anyone else. I had seen it in action in Australia with *OZ* there. I knew that the trial would go on outside the courtroom, there would be a great big public out there and we needed to get our point of view across.

SUE MILES: I had come back from America with nothing particularly to do. Richard Neville asked me in early spring '71 if I would do the publicity for Friends of *OZ*, which was a magazine I'd never been able to read cos I can't read cerise on chartreuse. And I didn't know anything about the trial. It was one of those inspired things: it would never have occurred to me to do it, I'd never done anything like it, and I knew that Felix didn't like me, cos he didn't like Miles, so I said to Richard, 'Yes, if you clear it with everyone else.' And he'd also employed Stan Demidjuk, the Australian-Yugoslav midget. I didn't have the foggiest what to do.

STAN DEMIDJUK: At Friends of *OZ* we were obliged to be on the offensive. Sue and I organised a bust fund, which was very successful. Our talent and organising ability had something to do with it, but the public were very open to everything we were proposing and everyone came through very positively. There was a real need to defend the ideals that we had, and that we were living. The charges were absurd, an insult to all freedom of thought.

SUE MILES: Stan and I were really rather a good combination. He spent most of his time getting wrinkles out of his kaftan and combing his hair. We were in Pottery Lane up above some old stable. Ian Stocks sat me down and said, 'This is how you write advertising copy.' It was like somebody turning the light on. I thought, 'Oh, that's the system. Fine.' Jim [Anderson] was very frightened by the trial: he was a trained lawyer and he knew he was going to get roasted. Felix was right on, and Richard decided to take it on, really monumentally. They would do anything: you could dress them in gymslips, bikinis, anything. I went off to see the chief constable at Bow Street to get permission for a parade with four elephants and a camel. At the end of the negotiations we got down to three chickens and a duck! We were force-marched through the City; I

389

think we were through in six minutes. The press took it up. They loved Richard and he was a great media entrepreneur.

GEOFFREY ROBERTSON: Friends of *OZ* was the first of those defence committees. There might have been one for the Angry Brigade. There were three trials – the Mangrove trial, the Angry Brigade and the *OZ* trial – going on in the Old Bailey at the same time. I found it curious that here was *OZ*, whose editors were paper revolutionaries wanting the freedom to express ideas; whereas in the next court were real revolutionaries, with whom *OZ* had absolutely nothing to do – although the Special Branch kept trying to make the connection. The people around *OZ* would have run a mile from any suggestion they might make a bomb. Then there were the Mangrove blacks who had suffered discrimination. The *OZ* people saw themselves as poets, idealists, dreamers and visionaries.

CHARLES SHAAR MURRAY: John Lennon did this song for the *OZ* trial: 'God Save *OZ*'. I was at the recording session: we all went along in a van – Felix, Stan, possibly Richard and me. I was the only one who could actually play anything, even though it was limited to three major chords and three minor chords on the guitar. There was a black girl, Olivia, too – very good-looking and could actually play keyboards, the best musician in the crew. Lennon was there, of course, in wall-to-wall denim. We went down to Ascot and there was an immense cold buffet with lots of chicken, exquisite little vegetable messes, whatever. In the session it was Lennon, Olivia and me sitting in a circle with acoustic guitars. Ringo was on drums. Felix and Stan were co-opted into the percussion section; I think Felix played congas – nothing brilliant, but he kept time. Once I got used to it I started to get mouthy and told Lennon and Phil Spector that all these acoustic guitars weren't happening and they should have some electric guitar on it. Everybody told me to shut up. When the thing came out they'd taken off all the acoustic guitars and put electrics on. I thought, 'If they'd done it while we were there I could have been playing that.' Apple put out the record but nobody played it on the radio and two weeks later it was totally forgotten. It was one of Lennon's radical gestures of the time: we've done one for the Irish, now we'll do one for *OZ*: 'From Bill Haley to the Old Bailey / Freedom's arrow flies . . .' Some bullshit like that.

FELIX DENNIS: That picture [a nude portrait] of Richard, Jim and myself which Hockney painted for the trial caused tremendous dissension. We all went there individually, because Mr Hockney really did feel he had to see us individually. He was a very nice man and he certainly didn't mess me about. I went in there and he had an assistant and I had a nice cup of tea and was sitting around, looking around and minding my p's and q's in this guy's fabulous apartment, a lovely apartment. He went on painting, took no notice of me. I was watching him work and I knew I was in the presence of somebody very important and I wasn't going to miss the opportunity of watching him work. So I sat there about half an hour. And all of a sudden I noticed that he kept on moving his eyes to the right-hand side of the canvas. And he'd go on talking to me about this and that, politics, drugs, sex, rock'n'roll, just small talk and very pleasant. Finally, I couldn't help it, I got off my seat and walked round and the bastard had a postcard – a postcard! – taped to his canvas and he was painting the postcard! I couldn't believe this. And I said, 'Do you usually paint from postcards?' And he said, 'Well, the camera's pretty good at capturing the nonsense and I just translate it.'

But the picture he did of us caused terrible trouble. When the three pictures were completed and then put together as a triptych to be sold and raise money, Richard came up to me and said, 'Did he suck your dick or something?' I said, 'I beg your pardon, Richard. I may have a dreadful reputation but as far as I know it's always been for ladies. I don't think there's been anything the other side of the blanket.' So he said, 'Well how come you've got that fucking great dick, then?' I said, 'Well, if you want, Richard, I'll show you right here . . .' It caused a terrible amount of trouble, my goodness . . . Richard was furious.

SUE MILES: Mortimer was probably the only person who could have done the trial, although I don't think Richard knew that. Richard met him at dinner and, although you're not supposed to, Richard approached him directly and he said yes. The reason that Mortimer was so good was that he had never, ever wanted to be a judge, so the law couldn't touch him. He could represent anyone he liked. *OZ* was a good case: it had all the *esprit*, it had the fun, the lunacy, it was a good cause and everybody helped. Hockney did drawings and so on. Then it was goodbye, thank you very much, enough. It was the end, and I wanted it to be the end.

DAVID OFFENBACH: The first person we went to was Tom Williams, QC, who's now a judge. He seemed slightly frightened when he realised how the case might turn out. With about a month to go he sort of declined and we thought of John Mortimer, because he'd done a good job in other obscene publications cases. He was the obvious choice, though, and they didn't want the obvious choice. So we made enquiries and Basil Wigoder, now Lord Wigoder, was someone who certainly had libertarian credentials, was considered a good counsel and was available for the trial. We also thought of Louis Blom-Cooper, but didn't go to him in the end. Wigoder was very enthusiastic until a few days before the trial but then dropped it. He saw it could turn into a show trial and became concerned. So we called Mortimer. He couldn't be there for the first couple of days because he was doing the *Little Red Schoolbook* case. We said, 'OK, we'll take notes and brief you.' He was enthusiastic, bright and was prepared to see us at home, because of the shortage of time. So we gave him all the stuff and he did the case as though he was born to it.

RICHARD NEVILLE: I don't think I ever was frightened. I don't know why. I had always drawn my strength from friends in the schoolyard rather than from my family and there was a terrific feeling of cama-raderie. There were the three of us, and our lovers, and Geoffrey Robertson and the bulk of the community on our side. I remember that there was a Save *OZ* meeting in Hyde Park and there were thousands of people. I really had great faith in Geoffrey Robertson and in John Mortimer. I believed in the justice of our cause. I believed that the movement was vital and powerful and a good thing. I didn't respect Judge Argyle particularly. I should have been scared, I suppose, but I never was; I was more pissed off. It was also very exhausting. I used to drink cold beers on the steps of the basement at the end of the day. Then I'd go in on the tube in the morning and I'd often see one or two members of the jury, all going in on the Central Line. It was a really strange feeling. I never tried to speak to them.

GEOFFREY ROBERTSON: Richard Neville chose to defend himself. He was not terribly satisfied with the legal profession and felt that he could get the ideas across himself. Which he did. It was important on the conspiracy charge that he had that opportunity to put his ideas across. I must say that I think his final speech still reads very well. It was delivered on a Friday afternoon and on the following Monday I heard one of the police officers boasting how his friends on the press benches had made sure it wasn't reported in the Saturday papers. Which of course it wasn't, except by Nicholas de Jongh in the *Guardian*. The Old Bailey journalists in those days were very pro-police. One of the most amusing things that happened was that after Richard had been cleared of everything but this minor charge of postal indecency, he was sent back by Charles Wintour of the *Evening Standard* to cover the Old Bailey, and the journalists there refused to sit on the same bench with him. Bernard Levin wrote a very comic article about their pious distaste for a fellow journalist who had actually gone to prison for freedom of expression.

392

FELIX DENNIS: We felt that Argyle wanted to find us guilty under any circumstances. So he thought that the best way to go about this first of all was to get rid of as many of the jury as possible. Which he then proceeded to do. First of all the prosecutor ran out of objections – you were only allowed to object to so many people – and the twelfth person to walk in was this girl in a kaftan. This was a bit unfortunate for Leary [the prosecuting barrister], and of course Mortimer took one look at her and said, 'Fine, wonderful, wonderful.' Anyway, in a six-, seven- or eight-week trial or whatever, she turned up late one morning. Just one. And the judge says, 'Right, ten minutes, we've all been waiting.' She says, 'I'm terribly sorry, it won't happen again. It is a long trial and I felt a little bit sick this morning. I'm pregnant.' So he said, 'Obviously the strain of this trial is much too much for you, you're dismissed.' So that was her gone. No replacement, you just go on. And even then they only got a majority verdict.

DAVID OFFENBACH: Richard defending himself was very artificial. The whole thing was done as a plan. The self-defence idea was to get one more speech to the jury, which would give us three in all: Mortimer, Richard and Keith McHale from Platts-Mills' chambers, who represented the company. So Richard's speech didn't deal with legal issues, but was a very fine speech. It was literary, jokey, and he was able to talk about other people in a way they couldn't necessarily talk about themselves. Mortimer represented Felix and Jim, McHale did the straight stuff for the company, so there was a great diversity between the speeches and that was important – each of them able to say something none of the others could say. But it was all planned and all three spokesmen knew broadly what the others would be saying. I knew what Richard was going to say because I read it through beforehand and made some suggestions. He wrote it himself but to ensure that it didn't run counter to anything it was looked at by Geoffrey Robertson, who was Mortimer's junior, and by me. Felix was fine in the dock, very straightforward; Jim wasn't a natural at it.

FELIX DENNIS: Jim's problem was not that he was a lawyer and thus knew exactly what we were up against; his problem was that he cannot deceive. All trials are just a game of wits. As Jim said in the trial, he felt an adversarial system of justice is a totally unfair system and it's absolutely rotten and whoever's got the best barrister is the winner. And he's right. Jim can't lie. So of course Leary could lead him down all sorts of garden paths. There was a piece of tension that very few people have ever been aware of: the terror was that Jim was gay, and some members of the *OZ* defence team were interested to know how Brian Leary would handle this issue. He said to Richard and I, 'I'm not going to tell lies.' Now this was a schoolchildren's issue and while Jim wouldn't have touched a schoolchild if you put a gun to the bastard's head, that was still not what a jury would think. But he said, 'If they ask me the question I'm going to tell them I'm gay.' So what was made known to Leary beyond a shadow of a doubt was that if he raised this issue with Jim Anderson I was going to fire John Mortimer and ask him the same question. It was hardball. And I had to play hardball because no one else was doing it. Richard thought all this was going to be sorted out by upper-class wit and he was an absolute nincompoop in that direction – he was just like Oscar Wilde, who brought the very case that destroyed him himself. He really believed that his wit and charm was going to work on a jury with an average IQ of 20. And of course it wasn't going to succeed. And Jim was totally useless because he would play any kind of ball; if a guy asked him a question he was going to give the answer. The worst thing you can possibly do. I had to play hardball. It was terrifying: if they'd actually asked him, 'Are you a homosexual?' Jim was going to say, 'Yes and I'm proud of it and I've been a homosexual for many years.' And that would have sent us to prison for fifty years probably. And to watch Leary asking questions of Jim and dancing round the main question – he absolutely adored it. He walked the line, he walked round it, up to it, had a look over the edge, walked back, didn't ask it, and Jim is standing there shaking like a leaf cos he knows any minute this bomb-shell that is going to put his mates in prison for fucking years is going to be asked. And Leary walks up to it and walks back and walks round it and does everything he can except ask the question. And he never actually did it. That's the reason Jim went to pieces, because he thought if he admitted that he was a homosexual – which he was de-termined to do if he was asked the question – he'd have sent us all to prison.

JIM ANDERSON: I wasn't personally harassed for being gay. It wasn't generally admitted at the time, although I was very much involved with the gay movement and was going to all the meetings. It was decided to keep quiet about it as a tactic. In retrospect I regret that very much. Leary, the prosecutor, did raise it obliquely a couple of times but I sidestepped the issue and there was like a gentleman's agreement to stay quiet about it . . . Leary did his job, and he did it quite brilliantly, really. I didn't really play up in the trial the way I should have. I hadn't prepared very much and when I was in the dock Brian Leary was able to rip me apart. I didn't make any serious errors but I didn't go on the attack.

Because I didn't believe in censorship of any sort, but had been instructed that I wasn't to say this in the dock, I hadn't thought out what I was going to say, and I was slightly on the defensive. The other thing that hamstrung me slightly was the fear that Leary would use my connection with gay liberation: 'Well, one of the editors is homosexual and is this the sort of person we want to have influencing the children of the realm?' He didn't actually mention it, but sometimes he went close. At one point he pointed to a picture and said, 'That's a male organ, isn't it, Mr Anderson?' I said, 'Yes.' He said, 'Very attractive, male organs, are they, Mr Anderson?' And I said, 'Well, sir, I suppose it is a large, attractive penis, Mr Leary, yes.' And he sort of veered off onto the next point without going any further. He was very sleazy in his approach.

FELIX DENNIS: Caroline Coon was wonderful because she did absolutely nothing except put on the shortest mini-skirt I have ever seen in the history of the universe. You could only just see the bottom of her knickers, but you could see them. And the judge thought that she was the most wonderful witness that he'd ever interviewed. And she sat there the whole time being incredibly intelligent and very polite and she'd always answer every question and so on and so forth and her only concern was that *OZ* magazine had spent its entire career telling people not to take heroin, which was a wonderful thing. She didn't do anything else but that was all she had to do. She did a great job. She was English, she was upper class and she knew exactly what to do, she knew how to play the game. John was going to come, John Lennon, but we realised that this would have been disaster beyond belief, we would have got twenty years.

RICHARD NEVILLE: The trial was the great climax of the underground movement. It gave you a chance, in a way, to sum up the era. It was the Boston tea party of the underground.

GEOFFREY ROBERTSON: The haircutting [in prison, after conviction but before sentencing] was routine at the time. The prison officers enjoyed 'shearing the hippies' and by this stage the *OZ* trial had polarised people across the generation gap. It was said that *The Times* received more letters about the *OZ* trial than it did about the Suez Crisis. It was made into a cultural collision by aggressive and unnecessary actions, the most aggressive and unnecessary being the remanding of the defendants in custody for social enquiry reports. It brought so many liberals, who had been hesitating a bit, over to the side of the defendants. To do it to three obviously sane dissident editors smacked of the Soviet Union: this is what you do to people who are psychiatrically disturbed. They were put in prison between the verdict and the sentence: the sentence was postponed for three weeks so that they could be remanded for social enquiry reports, in custody. Wholly unnecessary, wholly wrong.

JONATHON GREEN: For the day of the sentencing there was a big demo outside the Old Bailey. Rosie Boycott and I took a large effigy of Judge Argyle – God knows who had made it – and drove it to the Bailey. We left the dummy in the car and went up to the public gallery, incidentally running the regular gauntlet of Lady Birdwood, who was picketing the queue, with some kind of anti-*OZ* sign. Apparently Felix used to delight in chatting to her, after his day in court was over, and swapping opinions on the moral degeneracy of the defendants inside. Argyle went through them one by one, sentencing Richard to fifteen months, Jim to a year – both of which were to be followed by deportation – and Felix to nine months. 'Stand up, Dennis. Since you are the least intelligent of the three I shall only sentence you to . . .' I've always liked to think that this crack spurred Felix on to the millions he has today. Then we all poured out onto the pavement and milled around and, as I recall, everyone sat down. Then the police arrived and there was something of a pitched battle for a few minutes. Smoke bombs going off, then, John Trux, who worked for *Frendz* and had incredibly long hair, was dragged off to the local police station; his picture made all the front pages. 'The Wailing Wall of Weirdies' was one of the headlines.

GEOFFREY ROBERTSON: In a sense it was over-reaction by the authorities that saved their bacon. They could very well have been dealt with far more sensibly and have ended up a lot worse off. The whole case was over-egged right at the beginning. The conspiracy charge itself was rejected by the jury. One of the interesting things about the trial is that it was a victory for the defence in that the main charge, the conspiracy to corrupt public morals charge, was rejected. That was a charge which carried life imprisonment. There was a majority verdict of guilty on the obscenity count, which the judge left so incomprehensibly to the jury that the verdict had to be quashed by the court of appeal. There was a conviction, again by a majority, on the minor charge of sending an indecent article through the post. It was upheld on appeal.

FELIX DENNIS: Then, when we had been jailed, we got dragged out of the nick – Wandsworth, I think – and we'd already gone to bed, about ten o'clock. We were still in prison clothes and they put cuffs on us. We were in the Black Marias – different Marias for each one of us. I could peep through the window and I couldn't see much, but I could see the

396

streets occasionally and finally I saw Fleet Street, so I knew where I was for a while. I knew London like the back of my hand, but then I didn't know where I was. I got out. Never seen this place before in my life; I knew I was in the centre of London but I didn't know where. Very old. Upstairs. I think I arrived first, I can't remember. Walk in, fucking guy opens the door – butler. And he opens the door, doesn't turn his nose up, just ushers us in, and there's these three warders, one for each of us, coming in behind. And there's an old geezer, with a smoking cap on (I'd never seen anyone in a smoking cap in my life), sitting there in front of this fire, writing away. I wish I could say he had a quill pen, but he didn't. Took no notice. You can tell the arrogance of the upper classes – people walk in a room and they don't look up. We're just standing there, warders standing behind us, butler's standing there, no one moves. This goes on for about five minutes. Finally he looks up and says, 'I should think our guests could probably do with a drink.' We don't know what the fuck is going on, we haven't got a clue, we've been dragged up, half asleep. And then he looks at the warders and says, 'Get those ridiculous instruments off their limbs . . .' and they do and there's all this clanking and keys and then he says, 'Now get out! I'll call you if they try to murder me.' And they all go out. So he asks what would we like to drink. It's sherry or nothing. 'Sherry'; 'Sherry'; 'Sherry'. So we walk up and it was only when I came close to him that I finally pictured him with the wig on and I finally figured it out, and I don't think Richard had even figured it out, and he said, 'I suppose you know who I am?' and I said, 'You're Widgery, aren't you, but I don't recognise you without your wig . . .' 'Yes,' he said, 'I am *Lord* Widgery to you, young man. I believe you're the only Englishman amongst us . . . Sit down, sit down.' He's the Lord Chief Justice of England.

So he says, 'Well, this is a fine mess we've managed to land ourselves in, haven't we? I've had several discussions with a person who doesn't live very far away from Downing Street, and we're in a fine pickle, aren't we? Prime Minister's Question Time, Mr Foot making a fuss, Lord Benn, or Wedgie Benn as he likes to call himself, faffing about all over the place and people stealing art out of museums and marching up and down Oxford Street . . . and what for? What for? Good God,' he says, 'I used to write better stuff than this when I was in bloody college. Look at the state of it, it's terrible, isn't it? But I've got to have something, I can't let you out, I must have something. And you know what it's got to be.'

Richard's much faster than me at this sort of stuff and he's saying, 'Well, what is it?' and I'm saying, 'You can fuck off, I'm not giving you . . .' and Richard's saying, 'Shut your mouth, you bastard.' So Widgery says, 'You're going to win the appeal. At least I can't say that you're going to win the appeal, but I am going to be the lead judge on the appeal and I do have in front of me 75 complaints against Argyle, and a fat mess he managed to make of it. If I'd been the judge you'd have gone down and never got up, sunshine. And he won't get any more of those' – and he never did. So he said, 'You can't work on the magazine.' I said, 'That's how I earn my living.' 'Can't you work on something else, write some other load of rubbish for someone else?' So of course in the end we agreed and he said, 'You'll be out tomorrow morning, and not a word about this,' meaning, because no one will ever believe you. 'Now get out, and leave those sherry glasses behind you.' And we were out the next morning.

I realised where we were later, we were in his chambers in the Law Courts, round the back in one of the Inns of Court. So it was Foot and Benn that got us out, no question. Every time Heath used to walk in to Question Time, Benn would get up and say, 'I was wondering whether the Prime Minister had incarcerated any other young persons for writing on lavatory walls.'

RICHARD NEVILLE: The trial had its negative effects on all of us. I felt very trapped by my own vocalisation of the polarisation: polarised by the judge, exaggerating one's position, justifying every act as being of the most altruistic motives, when a lot of what happens in life is kind of accidental, random, selfish, a mixture of good and evil, and it's all complicated. But somehow in packaging our defence I felt I was becoming more and more of a propagandist and less and less of Richard Neville hanging out in London, working with a group of people that I liked and respected, trying to give writers and cartoonists a platform – which was basically what *OZ* was about. I really thought Martin Sharp was a genius and I wanted to give him a magazine. Just as I did with Widgery or Quattrocchi or Robert Hughes or whoever else, even Charles Shaar Murray for God's sake. Being placed in the dock and forced to justify everything you ever did on high moral grounds made me feel a little uneasy by the time it was over.

GEOFFREY ROBERTSON: One of the interesting things about the case was that it could have been the making of the defendants as serious political figures – certainly of Richard Neville. He was a household word, he had a large following. There were dozens of photographers on hand when he emerged from Wormwood Scrubs on bail, to be driven to the BBC for a David Dimbleby interview. Richard Crossman wrote a hilarious review of it in which he said, 'This politeness, these slightly Australian vowel sounds, the self-effacing pleasantness and this public school manner ... Richard Neville seems just like Prince Charles.' Richard wasn't a politician, he was an intellectual provocateur, he didn't seek to become a Petra Kelly or a Ken Livingstone.

After the trial, *OZ* could have become a kind of *Spycatcher succès de scandale* – there's nothing like an Old Bailey obscenity trial to boost your circulation. But it petered out when they all lost interest. The defendants themselves could have become political agitators, but they didn't want that. I suspect *OZ* was finished before the trial started. The 'alternative society' had already ended and this was its dying flourish. The 60s were over, it was the middle of the Tory rule, and then suddenly this failing, fading magazine was put on centre stage, charged with corrupting a generation which was no longer bothering to read it. The defendants had started *INK* – the thinking person's *Today*. All their energies were going into an exciting new magazine, and suddenly they had to turn round and defend the work they were in the process of leaving behind.

RICHARD NEVILLE: After the trial I'd had enough of *OZ*. I was ready for it to go. I felt it had lost its innocence and daring. And all that anger generated by the trial fundamentally isn't my style. I was losing my sense of humour and the magazine was losing its sense of honour. I thought of it more as a butterfly. Obviously there have been times later in my life when I've been completely broke, standing in some dreadful bus shed in Melbourne, and said to myself, 'I should have kept *OZ* going and become Richard Branson.' I certainly think it was possible to have turned *OZ* into a hot money-making proposition, but I didn't want to do that. And I didn't want to leave it to Felix. There's a lot about Felix that I admire, but to have him as a cultural voice, the voice of *OZ*, this was not something that I desired.

FELIX DENNIS: Richard knew by now that he was going back to Australia and he didn't want anything left behind. I realised this only later, much later. He wanted it to be: he arrived, the magazine started, he left, it folded. We could have carried on but it was Richard's insistence that the magazine did not become *Punch*, that was his great fear, that it would become some dreadful boring old rag with which his name would be associated. To Richard the only important thing is him, his reputation and what he stood for, and everybody else could suck dick or die. There was no in-between. Richard's idea of hell would have been a communal magazine. He was going to leave, therefore it must all close. And I was a loyal lieutenant right to the end. Richard Neville, to my certain knowledge, didn't sit in front of the creditors – I did. Even as I was doing it I was thinking, 'Why am I sitting here?' In the end the magazine didn't close because we couldn't go on, the magazine closed because Richard insisted. It was his force of personality that closed it. I've never had any doubt about his instincts. There's no question that there were a huge number of people – Jim and myself and people under us – toiling like maniacs in a mine, driven by one man's will and charisma. And I think Richard would be quite right to say, 'But they had the best time of their life.' He changed an awful lot of people's lives and he did it without harming anybody.

DAVID OFFENBACH: The judge kept going on about how in this magazine edited by schoolkids was a piece about oral sex, and was this right in a magazine produced by fifteen-year-olds to be read by fifteen-year-olds? He spent an inordinate amount of time on this. He was tickled pink by the whole thing and dined out on it for many years afterwards. When he gets invited to the Women's Institute or wherever and asked to talk about 'Trials I Have Done' he talks of *OZ* as one of his great trials.

The Underground Press: 'A hell of a lot of people did read those papers'

RICHARD ADAMS: The underground press had started off by acting as a magnet for certain people but it ended up by repelling them – the Victors, the Kustows and so on. There was this great splintering: there was the gay press, the feminist press, and what was left of the old underground press, and it didn't really add up to anything much. Just hanging on by its bloody fingernails.

One of the reasons for the collapse was quite simply the lure of money. There was no way that people were going to be able to get the same money from the weakening underground press that they could from tit mags or writing encyclopedia entries or whatever. There was one other thing: out on the sidelines throughout all this era was one particular magazine, which was out on a limb, which was called *Time Out*. It was internal collapse rather then external pressure that finished off the underground. The other thing was that there was a division within the underground press from the earliest period. Certain people were becoming more and more political, especially at *INK*. There was a shift further to the left than the underground press could comfortably accommodate in its overall ethos, which was certainly not based on some bloody coalminer up there in Yorkshire or wherever on strike, kicking shit and cutting off the power at Christmas for three or four days a week. When they struck the whole fucking nation knew about it; if the underground press had struck at most 50,000 would have got maybe a feel of it.

400

Politics was becoming much more serious at that time, and much more seriously felt by the public at large. So there was a certain kind of impotency in wanking around trying to promote this cultural revolution, this alternative, which was just a non-bloody-starter compared with the miners.

DAVID MAY: You got a narrow view of life from the underground press, but it represented a way of thinking and I'm convinced we never appreciated how many people responded to it. You only had to look at the sales to realise that thousands of people were reading this stuff every issue. The pass-on rate was five people per copy. We also had enormous arrogance: we had something to say and, fuck it! we'd say it. We didn't know really what was going to come out the other side but there were a whole bunch of people who had fantastic talents – some of that artwork was stunning, George Snow in *Frendz* was into techniques that computer animators only caught up with a couple of years ago. Two vital things: offset litho and the IBM golfball. Without them it wouldn't have happened.

ALAN MARCUSON: Over the years it seems that a hell of a lot of people did read those papers. I've been meeting people for the last seventeen or eighteen years who say, 'God, *you're* the editor of *Friends* magazine.' People generally a bit younger than we were and they say, 'God, you changed my life.' It's a delight when that happens, a great feeling to know that we were of some relevance to some people in a very personal way. But as for being a movement, we were nothing: we petered out with consumerism and ultimately our relationship with things rather than people and ideas got the better of us.

JEROME BURNE: When the underground press is discussed historically, and doubtless there'll be museums and exhibitions and so on, there will be possibly three copies, and they'll all probably be *OZ*, and in fact there were four years of appalling messes, typographical horrors, pages that were so dense they were illegible. I think it's a miracle that people read very much of it.

JOHN WILCOCK: I went to the *Daily Mirror* in the early 60s and I met all the bigshots and I told them about the way in which the underground press was revolutionising publishing in America, not only because of the content and its radical thrust, but because of the technical means of production: web offset. I said, 'Jesus, you're using all this old equipment and we can print at a quarter the cost and ten times the speed and get better reproduction.' They all looked at me like I was crazy. It took them twenty years to catch up with ideas that the underground press first introduced to the world. There were three major developments started by the underground: the use of offset printing; the San Francisco *Oracle* realising that there was no reason to keep all the colours separate – you could put them all together and they'd give you a rainbow effect; and the use of unjustified, ragged lines. That had never been done until the underground press pioneered it out of necessity and it became a hip thing to do. On top of this was the IBM typesetting machine.

PEARCE MARCHBANK: Litho printing was just coming in. The early *IT*s were set letterpress, which means that they were actually hand-set or machine-set with slugs of metal type which were put into big metal frames and then tightened up and inked up like a linocut and printed out on an old press and the end result looks diabolical. You can't 'paint', you can't move things around as you want with bits of metal. The idea of litho printing was that any mark, black on white, could be copied and printed – be it your own fingerprint or a mistake or your handwriting or a piece of typesetting that you'd had done, anything. It was clean. You didn't have to bash it into the paper. You could have nice, solid black ink lying on beautiful white paper. And anyone, once they had worked out how it worked, could do it. If you came fresh to all that world, as I did in the early 60s, you could work out for yourself how to do things. Later on I worked out how to do a magazine in a night, which other people could only do in a month, by using printing equipment in an office.

FELIX DENNIS: *OZ* was one of the very first magazines to use web offset. People like Jon Goodchild, David Wills and myself were willing to go down to printers. Now they never had people coming down before. They had all this brand new machinery, kit worth a million quid in those days. We'd go down there and meet up with the printers. There was nobody else around, they were always putting you on the night shift, you're a shit job. You'd go in and there'd be the old printers, and you'd say, 'I wonder if . . . what would happen if we sort of put red in the top of this ink duct and yellow at the other end and it all sort of went orange in the middle?' They'd sort of say, 'I dunno if we can do that, it sounds a bit . . . but it ought to work, didn't it . . . I tell you what, there's no one around, lads, so we'll have a go. Go on, you put the ink in. Don't tell the Union, for Christ's sake!' So many of the *OZ* innovations occurred as a result of getting the printing guys, who have a hell of a lot of skill, interested in doing something that they would never be able to do again. We used colour washes, silver ink, gold ink, stuff like this. In a few

402

cases, yes, though it's overstated, it was illegible: unfortunately in one of Germaine's most important articles, a reprint from *The Female Eunuch* before it was published, we did actually manage to screw it up. But it wasn't as illegible as people remember.

Underground girls: 'It wasn't really OK to be Amazonian'

NICOLA LANE: From a girl's point of view the important thing to remember about the 60s is that it was totally male-dominated. A lot of girls just rolled joints – it was what you did while you sat quietly in the corner, nodding your head. You were not really encouraged to be a thinker. You were there really for fucks and domesticity. The 'old lady' syndrome. 'My lady'. So Guinevere-y. It was quite a difficult time for a girl.

MICHELENE WANDOR: I saw the counterculture as a very highly desirable lifestyle. I didn't see it at all as a political thing. I didn't have a whole-hearted interest in the anti-censorship, let-it-all-hang-out aspect of it. I think maybe that was because there was quite a lot of sexism in that, and even though I wasn't consciously identifying it as such in that way, I was actually slightly drawn back from it, because I couldn't identify. The sexism in the underground press was appalling. It certainly wasn't striking a blow for the revolution, putting S&M pictures in *IT*.

RICHARD ADAMS: One day in the basement of 70 Princedale Road Richard Neville came in and gave a lecture on feminism and the sort of pictures we were running in *OZ*. This was after being earholed by Marsha and Louise who were starting to go off to these meetings – Women in the Underground Press. Richard talked about all this, but it all fell on pretty stony ground. On the one hand people agreed with what he was saying, but on the other there was this whole thing about censorship. He did make a bloody good stab at changing attitudes.

SU SMALL: I never thought about my role as a woman in the underground. It wasn't until *Spare Rib* started that I thought about that at all.

JOHN WILCOCK: The people who were doing the underground press were the first generation of males to be made to feel guilty about their chauvinism. We were trying as best we could to walk this line, to give credit to women and all the rest of it. We hadn't been conditioned by twenty years of the women's movement, so we were still very chauvinistic.

403

But we were trying to understand and this was a very radical aspect of the underground press: the women starting to make the men feel guilty.

LAURA MULVEY: The 60s didn't seem to be a decade for women to do much other than shorten their skirts.

NICOLA LANE: Looks were very important. Looks were far more important in the 60s than they are now. Looks were of primary importance. I don't know about for boys, but certainly for girls. Although there were beautiful boys with looks that were equivalent to all the Guineveres: very thin, lots of hair and they sort of undulated and they had very, very, very tight trousers, and the longer the hair a man had, the better chance he had of getting laid. Short hair was anti-aphrodisiac. You'd look at someone and shudder. But what really filled me with fear and loathing were these little hippie girls in long frocks, tiny little things who were always sort of wisping around the room. I used to find them very worrying. I knew that I couldn't be like that, because I was much larger. It wasn't really OK to be Amazonian in the 60s.

MICHELENE WANDOR: The pretty underground girls with the short skirts and the long hair were a version of the emancipated girl, a slightly more advanced version of emancipated girl, which is why when feminism struck some of them were able to take it up. It wasn't all oppression by any means. It's true that they were a dolly, but they were another form of dolly. They weren't just a decorative dolly, they were a dolly who could make their own choices and not be lumbered with the consequences, not in the old-fashioned way. If you'd been at art school in the 50s and a bit careless you might have ended up as a single mum. You didn't in the 60s. That was important.

Feminism: 'A group started meeting ... and I started going'

JEFF NUTTALL: Feminism was always there: there always were strenuous old-style feminists on the Aldermaston march. I wasn't aware that it was becoming a force until after *The Female Eunuch*. I knew Germaine. She was a very very bright lady and I think her kind of feminism hadn't yet become what I consider to be extremely destructive. What it became, in many hands and many voices – a vociferous, anti-erotic, anti-male lobby – was also therefore anti-revolutionary. Feminism has a very stringent puritanism, and prudery, and it has aligned itself with Mary Whitehouse, who was an enemy of the underground if anyone was. They have been a major element in the enfeeblement of a cultural movement that might have succeeded. They were very much people who dismantled the main drive – which was erotic and creative – from within. The odd-ball crazy idea that all men are the Right and all women are the Left. A complete failure to acknowledge that they're talking about a biological category and not a socio-political one.

MICHELENE WANDOR: British feminism certainly came from American origins. Consciousness-raising certainly came from America, although that also had links from things which came from Marxism, from Maoism, the 'speaking bitterness' in China – after the revolution people spoke their bitterness against their oppressors. You spoke out, you shared. There must also be some connection with the whole American encounter/psychotherapy movement. So consciousness-raising, as it was appropriated by feminism, very much followed the American model because they're very much better at talking, or appearing to talk, about themselves than the English.

NINA FISHMAN: Feminism began to surface as an important issue when I was at the University of Sussex. I knew Juliet Mitchell very well. It hadn't been an important issue for me because I'm self-willed enough for the feminine side of me never to be a real problem. My father had given my mother a copy of de Beauvoir's *The Second Sex* just about the time I was born. I was atypical: I had been socialised into thinking of myself as a person, and I discovered the feminine side of me by accident when I reached puberty, to my great surprise. So I spent a great deal of time in the late 60s, early 70s finding out about how femininity worked. Not by reading women's movement stuff, but by reading nineteenth-century novels: George Eliot, Tolstoy. My friends at Sussex had said I should be involved in the women's movement and it was very wrong not to be, but I felt it really wasn't anything to do with me. And in a sense it wasn't – since I was an emancipated person to begin with. So I've always felt uneasy with it. I really became aware of it in that I could count the number of women who were interested in politics in the late 60s on one hand, and by the early 70s it had become normal. But my attitude was totally selfish; I wanted to be where the action was and it didn't seem to me in the late 60s that it was in the women's movement.

LAURA MULVEY: I wasn't particularly political. I had close friends who were in the New Left area, but for me, like a lot of others who were involved in the early days of the women's movement, feminism was both a revolution and a revelation. It gave a sense and purpose to doing things which hadn't been there before. Quite literally. It changed one's attitude

405

to culture and consciousness. When I left Oxford in 1963 I couldn't read, write or think and it was the women's movement that made it possible for me to find a way of doing that and to overcome this sense of culture and history as a massive, oppressive block by which one was weighed down rather than in control of. Things began to take shape in discussion groups at the end of the 60s.

MICHELENE WANDOR: Sheila Rowbotham wrote a piece called 'Women's Liberation and the New Politics' which was really a cry from the heart, at that time quite a sophisticated little piece of feminist socialist thinking from within the student movement. My feminist development in 1969 started when I met a woman called Audrey Battersby down the road and she had two little kids, twins, and they were the same age as my oldest, about six. And we started moaning in the way that women do, in the street, with their kids. She knew Juliet Mitchell, through the Anti-University, and various other women through one of the early groups that had started up. Juliet was teaching there and she had written this article in 1966 called 'Women, the Longest Revolution' in the *New Left Review*. A group started meeting at Audrey's house and I started going and Ed [Victor] used to sit here reading his manuscripts looking very tense and I'd come back grinning. What we did, classically, was talk about what we experienced as our oppression, and most of us had children so one way or another there was quite a lot to talk about. And we also talked about changing the world and how the world should be. Things should be such that children are never neglected and insecure but you still have the freedom to do the things that you want to do. We talked about changes and campaigning and things like that, and school being open during half-term and the holidays, mainly geared towards what working mothers would need.

LAURA MULVEY: It is very important that a lot of the women who were involved in the movement at the time were not just influenced by America, but by the spin-off from 1968. Paris '68 was a generating point. Whereas so many other political activities became dispersed and went into decline after '68, feminism flourished.

DAVID WIDGERY: The women's movement came out of similar things to those that the student movement came out of. Expansion, rising expectations colliding with the reality of what being a woman was like in terms of jobs, in terms of childcare, in terms of how men treated you.

The underground was a particularly male-dominated thing. There were a lot of women doing a lot of work in the production of the underground

406

press, and in the thinking of the underground press, providing ideas and round-the-clock skills, who were not just providing heaps of brown rice, but laying out the articles, subbing them, typing them, and so on. And it was the same in the student Left: men talked and women did the background work. It all came to a colossal head obviously when women said, 'This is not good enough, get rid of it.' That was startling, very disturbing and very invigorating for all the men concerned. And women's lib was also deeply involved with socialism in its early days. Something one misses too easily looking at the intellectual record of the period is that there were lots of ordinary people doing things that ordinary people didn't do. There was much more questioning, people asking what the hell was going on. And feminism was like that sort of force.

MICHELENE WANDOR: We went to the Ruskin Conference as a group. That was the first time I'd ever been to anything like this. I didn't see going to those meetings down the road as a political act, but it soon was. What we saw ourselves as doing was consciousness-raising, for which there wasn't any real blueprint. Ruskin was organised around a series of workshops and general sessions. At the time it was terrifically exciting that you could have a workshop with a whole lot of other women. The workshops were closed to men; the full sessions had some men but I don't think they spoke. That you could actually be in a room with a large number of women, all of whom would have their right to speak . . . in the event you get a small number of very vocal articulate people dominating, but the feeling was that in principle this was the most democratic thing that there had ever been. That was very exciting. There was a lot of naïveté, but there always is in political newness. You thought, 'This is the first time anybody's noticed this and, by God, it won't be there tomorrow, it's going to be different tomorrow.'

LAURA MULVEY: I missed the Oxford Conference but I heard about it very soon after. Various decisions were made at the conference: one was that the women's movement would be set up not as a unified, centralised organisation, but as a loose confederation of local groups, based on women who lived in the same kind of area getting together and organising themselves. The women's movement would co-ordinate, rather than organise.

ROSIE BOYCOTT: The women's issue of *Frendz*, done by the Angry Brigade people, started the meetings of the women in the underground that then produced *Spare Rib*, so you could actually say that the Angry Brigade were responsible for *Spare Rib*. Other people from odd bits of the underground, like Louise Ferrier and Marsha Rowe, had trotted over during the period of putting this issue together and had started to be interested. They had done their 'Cunt Power' issue but that was very different. The point about what Angie and Hilary did was that it was from the female point of view, not the male point of view, of how they'd like to see more cunt power, serving their own ends. So it was the first one of its kind.

Feminism all started then for me. I knew about it, I knew about the meeting at Oxford, about the various things that were happening, but I hadn't read any theories yet. I suppose I didn't quite take seriously the extent to which maybe feminism was a necessary thing.

SUE MILES: First there was Valerie Solanas shooting Warhol, then there were bra-burning demonstrations in America, Betty Friedan, Gloria Steinem, Grace Atkinson. Then there was the beginning of women's groups in England. I thought, 'However earnest it all is I cannot do this – I am not a joiner.' It was all about talking. The next experience was Marsha, Rosie and Louise trying to get the women on the underground press together. For Louise and Marsha to get that adamant about something . . . The response was quite odd: people like Felix and Tony got absolutely hysterical. Rosie was like Sarah Pouliakakov – upper-class guilt. I thought the rise of things like the Women's Press was more interesting. Carmen Callil at Virago. I saw feminism as all the influx of books that started to be published. I hated *Spare Rib*.

CASSANDRA WEDD: The first meeting of Women in the Underground Press was at Louise's flat. Louise, Marsha, Michelene Wandor, women from most of the underground press. One walked out, from *Time Out*, who thought the whole idea was completely shocking, that we were men-hating . . . I remember having one hesitation and telling Michelene, 'I think it's all very good as long as we don't get too aggressive about it,' to which she replied, 'Why is it women are called aggressive when they do things and men are called political?' But she had been to the earliest women's movement events, like the Oxford Conference, while I hadn't even been aware of it.

I don't think the emergence of feminism actually needed the underground. It was alongside the underground rather than springing from it. It sprang from the same sort of place as the underground did: rejection of previously held values. It was an extremely interesting period for me. I went to the underground press women's groups, then consciousness-raising meetings. We read *Women's Estate*, Juliet Mitchell's book, and Shulamith Firestone's book and had study groups. I wasn't living with

408

anyone but it affected my general relationships a lot; it made me much more confident of my own worth, and I was then able to say what I wanted or what I didn't want. So it made me able to perform on my own account, as it were. It was all very earnest but things have to go through every phase: you have to, in a way, go over the top, you have to totally reject before you can get back to what's really true.

ROSIE BOYCOTT: The first meeting of Women in the Underground was in December 1971, quite shortly after the Angry Brigade/Women's issue of *Frendz*. There were rumblings going around, general dissatisfied rumblings about why couldn't the other magazines do that, what good really was the underground for women, and slowly but surely it coalesced into a meeting.

It was a sensation: everybody was talking at once about all the things that they didn't like and it was as though all those vague feelings, right back to having tried to hack it across Middle Earth on your own at the age of seventeen, trying to look cool on drugs, trying to pretend you were part of something, wondering if in fact you were going to get picked up by someone you didn't like and feeling that actually it would be worse if you weren't picked up, because then you'd have been rejected – a whole lot of things that had been bubbling for everybody for a long time then became something that was shared and obviously very dynamic and very real. Men had probably also been suffering some of these things but in that context it didn't matter.

What was insidious about the underground was that it pretended to be alternative. But it wasn't providing an alternative for women. It was providing an alternative for men in that there were no problems about screwing around or being who you wanted. You were still able to do it on a chauvinist level and there was still a power game going on in that women were typists, men were the bosses, men were the ones who decided what wages people got, whether people had jobs. Women were dependent on men. The fact that this was happening in an alternative society gave it its punch and gave it its kick. Women came into the underground expecting to get a liberal world and became more embittered when they did not.

It made it easier to have a grievance. It was harder for women who moved in the established world, living in the established way: 'This is just how things happen, honey.' The point about the underground was that this was not the way things were supposed to happen. They were meant to be equally beneficial to everybody. But for a long time even the communes felt that it was right that Sue bakes bread and Bill brings in the cows. And you only get so much zest up when you've got so much to fight against, when you can feel righteous and you can feel secure about your complaints. The revolution we preached in the underground press had no real political theory, but the moment you started to read and to learn about feminism you found that there was this huge body of work behind it, there was a huge constituency of women who seemed to think the same way. The other great thing was that both Marsha and I had managed to learn enough skills that we could go off and do something specific about this rather than just sitting around and talking about it.

RICHARD NEVILLE: It's certainly true that Louise and Marsha didn't get their full credit on the masthead. I guess we thought we were running around doing a lot of stuff and we had girlfriends and sometimes they were there to help but they didn't seem to be the prime movers. Putting their first names on was an acknowledgement, not putting their surnames was an admission of what can only be described as our sexist attitudes. And it's absolutely true that I could not have done *OZ* without Louise. There I was in London, we shared a life together, she maintained the environmental conditions that made *OZ* possible. Hers was an ecological role. But it was a role that I took for granted: that was the culture of that time.

CHARLES SHAAR MURRAY: The way women were treated on *OZ* was very influential on *Spare Rib* and had a lot to do with the founding of post-hippie feminism. The treatment they got was so offhand and casual, verging on the contemptuous. I'm not surprised that they eventually thought, 'Fuck this shit!' It was all 'Yay! Freedom! Let everyone do what they want,' but the little woman is still over in the corner. She may be wearing a flowered dress and a headband, but she's still the one who rolls the joints, cooks up the vegetable messes that everybody used to pretend they liked, and generally does what in the introduction to one of the *Rolling Stone* collections Jann Wenner refers to with his normal exquisite tact as 'the chick work'. A lot of the girls were trying to be good hippies, doing whatever good hippies did, which meant that a lot of them would literally fuck anybody, do all the washing-up and so on. Then they suddenly realised that no matter how important it was to be a good hippie, it was more important not to take this shit. So feminism was not so much an outgrowth of the hippie movement as a reaction against it.

NICOLA LANE: The first time I began to think about feminism was in 1970 when I read *The Female Eunuch* by Germaine Greer. You'd heard of her, she was a wild figure. And she could talk to those of you who'd been through that scene in some way and you'd feel, 'She knows.'

410

MARSHA ROWE: Germaine is an individualist, an anarchist. For her the experience of something like consciousness-raising was just anathema. I admire everything that she has done, but it's always in her particular way. The only way I could get out of the rut was to do things with other women, where we could support each other, and talk through the problems. Germaine's books are riddled with intellectual and political contradictions. The media really love her. Her punchiness and her willingness to perform. So there is a political point: she epitomises the career woman, but there are institutional factors in society that are going to prevent most women doing that – including responsibility for children.

MICHELENE WANDOR: Germaine was the media face of feminism. She kept away. My report of the Ruskin Conference, which appeared in *OZ*, was headlined, 'Where Were You, Germaine?' It was a bit self-righteous but the bourgeois face of feminism was very much frowned on and it was part of the collectivist spirit of suspicion of the media which came from a very simple Left analysis. There was also this very strong reaction against leadership (and anyone who either saw themselves as a leader or who was taken to be a leader) and also against any strong individual voice. It wasn't an explicit criticism of women like that as careerist but very much more to do with not needing leaders – every woman can speak for herself. So somebody like Germaine, even though she was writing things that became very popular and got to women who the rest of us were nowhere near getting to, there was a very general sense of suspicion of her. And in the end she didn't make feminism accessible. She was neither here nor there in any genuine sense. In terms of the complexity of the politics of feminism she made no difference one way or another. She was a useful populariser, but had no political function as a figure.

ROSIE BOYCOTT: I don't agree at all with those hardcore feminists who would say that Germaine has done the movement no good at all. She did the movement enormous favours just because she was able to be public and loud and flamboyant and she made it fun and she pushed it onto a level where tons of people had to find out about it and had to think about it. And if it had been any other kind of person who had been less abrasive and less challenging, it would have been shoved under the counter. And the fact that she had wit and style and intelligence and beauty and guts made her impossible to ignore.

FELIX DENNIS: I have an awful lot of respect for Germaine and I'm sure she'll kill me for this story but it is absolutely true. We were working at *OZ* on the Women's Liberation issue and I was designing it. I was working on this issue and Germaine was giving me a lot of grief. I was still learning and I was making a lot of mistakes and Germaine was saying, 'You silly cunt, this is meant to be a Women's Liberation issue and look what you've done there . . .' and I'd be saying, 'Jesus, yes, I'd better change that then, Germaine, you're right.' And she'd be round there all hours of the day and night, working. Anyway, the phone rings and I pick it up and there's this bloke on the other end of the phone. And he says, "Ello!' I say, 'This is *OZ* magazine. Can I help you?' It's about 11.30, twelve o'clock. And he says, 'Where's that biddy then?' I said, 'I beg your pardon, I think you've got the wrong number.' He says, 'Where's that bloody biddy?' I said, 'I don't think I know what you're talking about.' He says, 'Don't come the old Arthur with me, you little bastard. Where's my fucking biddy!' I said, 'I don't know who you're talking about.' He said, 'Germaine! Where's GG?' I said, 'GG!' He said, 'You tell that fucking bitch I've just got back from the fucking Continent, I've been driving for three and a half fucking days and I want my tea!' I thought, 'This is Germaine Greer . . . ? We're doing the Women's Liberation issue . . . what's going on?' I said, 'One moment please,' and said, 'Germaine, there's a man on the phone who says he wants his tea.' And she says, 'Oh fuck me!' and she was out of there in ten seconds. But she only put up with it for a few months – I think she wanted a bit of rough at the time, that was all . . . In fact we ended up with his centrefold in *OZ*.

MICHELENE WANDOR: In the spring of '71 there was a huge march by the women's movement and after that march the number of groups in London really snowballed. There were now over 100 groups with maybe seven or eight people in each. It was a very exciting march, it was in the snow and it was just fantastic, it was almost like a hippie thing, very celebratory. The student movement had had its peak and while its participants were remaining in professional radicalism, the women's movement provided a new political upsurge. Sexual politics had begun. They were very alive, very radical in the anarchic sense and they still had within them a very very strong element of lifestyle politics which had come from the 60s – the underground, the counterculture, and the summer of '68. What I'd call 'bourgeois feminism', placing feminism on the respectable map of the British ideological landscape, didn't happen until the very very end of the 70s. That early stuff was very different.

MARSHA ROWE: I actually felt suicidal just before *Spare Rib*. We were just on the cusp of saying: let's do this magazine, but I didn't know what we were going to get into. I didn't know Rosie Boycott at all. I'd done some production work on *INK* and felt critical of *INK* for many different reasons. When Michelene suggested to Louise that there be a meeting it seemed to make sense. I'd failed to feel that I was part of this new newspaper, I'd failed to feel that I could get into journalism professionally, failed to feel I had any voice. When we had our first meeting, what women talked about wasn't really work, it was the conditions of being a woman: a lot of pain and unhappiness and fear and nerves. Louise and I were awake all night. There were so many unsaid things flying in the air that you couldn't really believe you'd heard them or that anyone had said them and we just couldn't sleep, giggling and looking at each other and, really, would anyone ever talk to us again?

MICHELENE WANDOR: The problem for the underground press women was that they began to feel they weren't getting the same benefits from the underground as the men were. I organised the first meeting of Women in the Underground. I was at *Time Out* at that point, writing news pieces and the poetry column. I was quite crusading and I'd known Louise and Marsha, Caroline McKechnie, some others. A handful came to the first meeting. Some of them really laid into me for being patronising and accusing them of being oppressed. I thought, 'Oh well, perhaps I am being patronising and they're a lot of ungrateful cows,' and then the meeting dissolved and the minute it dissolved they were getting into little huddles with someone saying, 'You know, I've spent all day at the office doing this, that and the other and I get home and he still expects me to cook his fucking dinner.'

I went to the first two or three meetings, but partly because of this attack, I stopped going and they carried on and then *Spare Rib* was born very quickly after that.

LAURA MULVEY: The women's movement discovered early on that images and representation were a political issue. There'd always been a certain amount of action of the 'This advertisement exploits women' kind, sticker campaigns, things like that. So when it came to November 1971 and the Miss World competition loomed on the horizon, it seemed a challenge that one couldn't overlook. The previous year there'd been a demonstration outside the Albert Hall, and this year women who were participating realised that it would be very difficult to make any kind of entry into the hall unless we did it very carefully and surreptitiously. The first thing was to get tickets in various different parts of the hall, then slip in unobserved. We were aware that one had not to look like 'a feminist', that one had, as it were, to mingle with the crowd. Now one problem about the demonstration was how to avoid seeming to be demonstrating against the women on the stage, rather than against the organisation. That problem was solved magically for us by Bob Hope. At that time Bob Hope ran a circus, as it were, taking entertainers out to Vietnam to entertain the troops. And he had a tradition of taking the annual victor of the Miss World competition out with him. So when Bob Hope came out onto the stage and started to address the audience about Vietnam and the commitment to Miss World, that was the moment when the hidden women who had been chosen to give the signal started waving their football rattles and we all rushed forward with flour and things and managed to pelt Bob Hope with flour and drive him from the stage. That was quite an achievement in itself, but it also blacked out the television – for probably all of about 30 seconds – which was quite something. I hadn't done any demonstrating before and I was frightened. But it was enormously exciting, the adrenalin, a feeling that it was a gesture that came out of political commitment but was very contrary to any kind of actions I might have expected of myself. So in that way there was also a personal liberation side to it.

Spare Rib: 'They didn't know, they hadn't thought – they were just *doing*'

ROSIE BOYCOTT: Marsha was 28, I was 20. And I was the person who got up and said, 'Let's do it.' I never felt at the time that Louise was such a linchpin. Marsha was very hesitant and nervous, a great deal more nervous than I was. So she needed Louise's hand-holding confidence. I personally don't think that Louise ever did that much but I can see from Marsha's emotional memory Louise was extremely supportive, because together she and Louise could take on Richard, who thought that the whole idea was a fucking joke! Tessa Topolski and Bonnie Boston did a lot more at the initial stage – actually sitting down and trying to work out a magazine, sitting down and saying, 'Where are we going to get some money?' Louise was helpful about money, she was able to sling over some of Richard's contacts, like Michael White who produced initial money, Herbert the banker who had the bank round the back of Bond Street where we had our first account.

MARSHA ROWE: The person who actually suggested the idea of *Spare Rib* was someone called Bonnie Boston. She was working for Maurice Girodias who had an Olympia Press office in London at the time. She gave me a copy of *The Story of O*. And she was an American and I was an Australian and we had very much this feeling that you could do it for yourself. The ethos in Australia is, have a go, try. One day Bonnie

414

dropped into the office and suggested the idea of the magazine. And it immediately made sense to me: we used to see all this literature coming into *OZ* from America and I'd seen three issues of *Rat* magazine which the women had taken over and called *Liberation*. It hadn't really rung any bells at the time – it was very serious and political – but later it registered. So after Bonnie had suggested the magazine I put it forward at the meeting and Rosie was the only one foolhardy enough to want to help. We were both rather foolhardy but we were a good pair. It's completely ironic that in her book she said that I was the one who knew about the law: she was the one who was good with the facts and the figures. We both knew enough about magazines to see that we had to get a distributor first, that we had to do a proper budget, get a printer and do all these very practical things. She was terrific at it. If ever I was nervous or faltered, she'd say, 'No! We'll go ...' She was terrific – absolutely grounded. She was always a bit worried that I'd had more experience and was older and I suppose that we were quite competitive but we couldn't have done it without each other.

MICHELENE WANDOR: I met Marsha outside *INK* when it was in Great Newport Street and she told me about the idea they'd had. I think I was a little snooty about it at the time, because it just sounded like A. N. Other women's magazine, which indeed it partly looked like in the early stages, but they were finding their way. From a political point of view they were absolutely doing the right thing: they were doing what they knew best, and trying to do it differently. They didn't know, they hadn't thought – they were just *doing*.

ROSIE BOYCOTT: While we were putting the magazine together we started going to Women in Media meetings and going into what effec- tively felt like the big world – a world where I certainly felt very insecure, because of my lack of experience, because of not having written a serious article in a national newspaper. I had only worked on the underground press for less than a year. We went to Women in Media in March and said, 'We're planning to do this thing and we need some help.' Some people like Jill Tweedie were sympathetic and terrific, but at the same time there was that – it seems to me – inevitable feeling of being a bit patronised, because they were very successful media women, older than Marsha. They had all done exotic and glamorous things and had earned money and were seriously respected in the world. So they wanted to know how would we do this and I certainly never stopped to think.

MARSHA ROWE: We asked everyone we could think of and there was an enormous meeting with a lot of encouragement and support, ideas of where to raise money, but in the end it was up to us. I knew all the people who'd given money to *INK* and off we went, back to them. We got all our chairs and tables from *INK*, typewriters from various people. Rosie knew Pearce Marchbank so we got that office when he left it, and Pearce's friend built a work bench for us. So it was a lot of handouts, plus people buying shares. We had a fund-raising party at Michael White's at one point. We raised £2000. I knew Tony Godwin, who was very supportive, and because of his contacts in the publishing world I was able to contact various established women writers who were also very favourable and eventually gave us short stories.

ROSIE BOYCOTT: The money came from Caroline Younger, Michael White, a bit from Christopher Logue, Clive Goodwin, Felix Topolski and later a lot from Rosie Parker. Also bank loans. Even my father put money in.

One time we went to see an Arab in Park Lane in his duplex penthouse. He was screwing a couple of upper-class friends of mine for £100 a screw, maybe worth £1000 now, to support their drug habits. So I took Marsha to see the Arab in Park Lane with no very clearcut view in mind except here was a source of money. Marsha was appalled when she realised what was going on. It was all swathed in silks and you went in through an incredible entrance, escorted by a bare-footed slave wearing Nubian silk clothes, carrying bananas on his head. It was all done up like a harem and there were Marsha and I standing there in our best frocks intent on asking this Arab to finance a feminist magazine. As a level of pure naïvety it has to beat most other things we ever did.

MARSHA ROWE: What we wanted to do was prove that we could do it in this very practical way and bring out something. I think this is what happens when someone has been held back from using their own capacities in a job: when they get involved in something they become rather pernickety and rather rigid, it takes some time for them to be flexible. So that first issue looked like a knitting book. We went for these very traditional women's-role things: we wanted a women's audience and we thought that they would like these things and that we, as women, are interested in these things. Alternative make-up, a cucumber cleanser, cheaper versions . . . We didn't want to deny these things but gradually it was denied. These things weren't the stuff of proper politics. And we did it in this rather empty way because we said we were concerned about those things but we weren't that concerned – I don't think I read many cookery books.

416

ROSIE BOYCOTT: Marsha and I, certainly me, never saw *Spare Rib* as excluding men. There were men involved, some men were working in the art department, men were around. We had Edna O'Brien, we had Fay Weldon, we had Margaret Drabble ... you name it. There was no question that those sort of people were advocating worlds without men. It was still very much connected with the underground ethic. We thought we were trying to make this very straight-looking magazine and certainly, compared with *Frendz*, it was a very straight-looking magazine: it was cleanly designed, it was cleanly printed, it looked nice. It was not seen, as far as I was concerned, as a threat to my life with men. It was not seen in any way that this should be an alternative to living with men.

KEITH MORRIS: In the very first issue of *Spare Rib* they needed a cover. They gave it to a chick, who screwed it up. Marsha Rowe in all innocence rang me up and said, 'Would you help us out? Would you do this cover?' So I obviously did. Then when it was discovered that a *man* had done the picture for the first cover it was immediately cancelled.

MARSHA ROWE: Our political position when we started *Spare Rib* was very naïve. We were learning by doing. There were six of us and we knew that we did it as a group, but we still had Rosie and me as editors. We knew that *Cosmopolitan* was starting at the same time and that would have a lot of money and it would have a traditional structure with secretaries and so on. We thought, well, we must all do our own bit of typing and have a rota for office cleaning, but we still hadn't got to the idea of a collective work structure when you all had an equal sense of responsibility for what went into the magazine. Partly, we didn't know each other that well. So Rosie and I did a lot of the editorial work on our own, or going off to see people individually, and any problems that came up we would try to take responsibility for ourselves.

ROSIE BOYCOTT: We met the readers quite considerably more than we had ever done in the underground press, but at the same time not as much as we would have liked. But at the same time the magazine was being read by maybe 50,000 women – it sold 20,000 – and from the letters we got there were a hell of a lot of ordinary people, unconnected with the media, not living in communes (very few people in communes would write to *Spare Rib*: you had to leave the commune in order to appreciate *Spare Rib*). *Spare Rib* wasn't very political then, only about abortion laws and equal pay, very safe subjects that most people agree with. It's not the same as setting yourself up as saying, 'We don't like men,' or 'We think people should be lesbians,' or 'We want sperm banks.'

At this time it was very much the kind of magazine that one's papa would like. Marsha's links with feminist meetings probably gave the magazine a kind of credibility with that end of the movement that my more hedonistic stance didn't. Sheila Rowbotham wrote for *Spare Rib*, a column about the history of women's emancipation. She's a very distinguished academic. But I get bored, I get depressed by that much depression, it brings me down. It's a lack in me, I know. I get a feeling that things aren't really that bad. Somewhere inside me I'm an individualist, I'm probably a natural Tory. I think there's a level at which you have to get on with things. I didn't just do *Spare Rib* for hedonistic, selfish reasons. I did it because I believed in it and I wanted to do it. And it did good. It clearly did good or it wouldn't still be there. It's sixteen years old.

MARSHA ROWE: After a while I went to Australia for six weeks, leaving a lot of work ready for future issues, and when I came back there had developed quite a lot of hostility between Rosie and the others. They thought that she wasn't quite carrying out the responsibility of her editorial role in such a way that they were happy with it. Everyone got very fed up and said, 'Look, Rosie, you can't do your job.' Rosie found that very hard to accept. She started to backtrack, move out and be less involved. What we all felt was that she was going off into sexual life, into relationship life, and the fierce energy she used to have for work just completely went. She stopped really wanting to talk to anyone.

ROSIE BOYCOTT: I started to argue with *Spare Rib* in the sense that we had a lot of fun in our lives and there was a failure to communicate any of this through the magazine. I always said that you can't sell unremitting gloom. Nobody wants to buy it, nobody can handle it. You can sell factual advice, and you can sell a certain level of gloom that can make you OK about your *own* level of gloom, but you also have to sell something that points out that it's still worth hacking it through till tomorrow. There was this aura about feminists then, that it was very hard to see one's way out of the pit. It seemed to me that the movement had drifted very far away from my life. I couldn't work on something that was selling unremitting gloom: life just wasn't unremitting gloom for me or Marsha or Marian or Rosie or Rose. They were also all having a fucking good time, on one level. Maybe I was having a better time but they were having a lot of laughs too. Yet there was somehow this kind of censorship against happiness that seemed to affect a lot of women. They would say that I was insufficiently serious, but I say that my point of view is

418

equally valid: you're telling just as much of a fib by the unremitting gloom.

MARSHA ROWE: So I was Editor for about three issues as we lurched from one crisis to another. The distributors had said we must print in full colour and we'd already decided that we couldn't possibly afford that, but we went against our own budget to do that and that really messed up the cash flow. I thought, 'I can't take this responsibility on my own.' I didn't like being in this position. So we decided that it had to be a collective, so we could discuss these problems and share the responsibility. Also for about a year I was the only one in a women's group, trying to learn about the world and make up for all my naïveté, and I felt for a long time that no one else was as involved in the women's movement as I was and that was quite hard. It took about three years for everyone to have a similar commitment. There were these levels of stress; the attempts to change how we lived, change the way we worked, be successful in what we were doing, with alternative values, it was all too much.

Sex: 'One communicated with so many people on this erotic level'

STEVE ABRAMS: In 1987 *The Times* published a report in which it was revealed that 60% of the British population believed that the cause of AIDS was the permissive society, not a virus that didn't exist when the permissive society was flourishing. So far as sexual permissiveness is concerned, it has a single and obvious cause: the availability in the early 60s of several reliable methods of female contraception. It was safe for everybody to fuck from about 1962 onwards.

FELIX DENNIS: I was doing *OZ* because I was thoroughly enjoying myself doing it. Even in rock'n'roll days I'd never had so many biddies. It was bonk, bonk, bonk night and day.

NICOLA LANE: You had to fill so many roles: you had to be pretty and you had to be 'a good fuck', that seemed to be very important. I think it meant mostly that (a) you would do it with a lot of people, and also (b) that you'd give people blow-jobs. I didn't really fall into that category. I wanted to but there was a part of me that always fell back. Now I'm happy to say so, but at the time I used to feel very bad about it. There was a lot of fucking going on. It was paradise for men in their late twenties: all these willing girls. But the trouble with the willing girls was that a lot of the time they were willing not because they particularly

419

fancied the people concerned but because they felt they ought to. There was a huge pressure to conform to non-conformity, which left very little room for actually finding out what your preferences were. Characters like Jim Haynes, these predatory, elderly men, salivated around the Arts Lab.

JIM HAYNES: Sex was my drug. If you look at what gets you off, what gets you excited, I love sexuality. I've always been interested in it and always participated in it in one way or another, which goes back to my upbringing in South America when I used to go to the local brothel as a social centre. At the age of four the girl next door pulled up her skirt and said, 'This is me, what have you got?' and ever since then I've been obsessed with it. I had a revelation in the early 60s that sexuality, when it was positive, was one of the greatest sources of human pleasure, ever. When it was negative, it was one of the greatest sources of human pain. I started examining it, observing it, reading about it, thinking about it, talking about it. I was obsessed. Asking people, 'Is your sex life good and, if so, why? If not, why not?'

CHERYLL PARK: Jim Haynes tried to sleep with me. I wasn't alone, there were about six other women in the bed. I said 'No'. He humiliated me. He seemed to think that it was all so easy to be so permissive and free with your body. I was only nineteen and I'd come down from the north of England and it was . . . all too much. I thought that there was something wrong with me, because I wasn't going to go along with it. I told him he was a pervert and to get out of my bed. I'd love to meet Haynes again, now that he's a shrivelled-up old man, and humiliate him in the way he humiliated me.

NICOLA LANE: There was a lot of misery. Relationship miseries: ghastly, ghastly jealousy, although there was supposed to be no jealousy, no possessiveness. What it meant was that men fucked around. You'd cry a lot, and you would scream sometimes, and the man would say, 'Don't bring me down – don't lay your bummers on me . . . don't hassle me, don't crowd my space.' There were multiple relationships but usually in a very confused way; usually the man wanted it. Hoppy was into formalised communal sex. He would do it in front of you in the living-room. There was the clap but that was rather a badge, in those happy, far-off days. There was no stigma to having the clap.

JOHN HOPKINS: The single biggest change between then and now is AIDS. I really had it away with a lot of people and caught clap a lot of

420

times, but nowadays ... And if the underground was about older guys having it off with teenagers, what about the teenagers? They wanted to have it off. It was about mixing with your peer group, and your peer group isn't necessarily all the same age. Undoubtedly there was a sexual revolution.

DAVID ROBINS: Bill Levy was incredibly sexually frustrated, about to get divorced from his wife and they were both having a miserable time and he probably never got laid throughout the whole period of *IT* when I knew him. After that he went to Amsterdam and started *Suck* with this woman called Susan Janssen who called herself Purple Susan – she was a librarian. They started *Suck* and all these 60s men and women would get together to have orgies. Bill was the Editor but he wouldn't go to these country-house experimentation centres. Eventually they said, 'Hey, Bill, you can't be the Editor of *Suck* magazine if you haven't fucked for twenty years and you won't come to our orgies.' Bill said, 'I don't see why I have to ...' but eventually they dragged him kicking and screaming to this country house, where everybody was arranged in suitable poses for the orgy. Naked women sitting on naked men's knees ... Bill made his excuses and went to bed. He's in this darkened room and he can hear people hopping around and tittering and stuff. He pulls up the blankets and he's hoping that he won't be noticed and he wants to go to sleep. Then he's woken in the middle of the night by something brushing against his thigh. Moves up his leg and he says, 'Oh ... God ...' So what does he decide to do? He decides that somebody's crawled into bed next to him, is trying to rouse him to have sex with him or her. Either way he's not interested. So he decides that the thing to do is pretend to be asleep, so he lies absolutely still with this thing leaning against him. He figures that there's a big window and when it gets light enough he can figure out who or what is lying next to him. Eventually it's just light enough so that he can see ... and it's a cat! And that was the Editor of the liberated sex magazine.

JIM HAYNES: In 1969 I started *Suck* magazine with Bill Levy after we'd both left *IT* and we decided to start a sexual freedom newspaper. *Suck* was the last thing that we did in Britain because Scotland Yard pushed us both out. They closed *Suck*'s London office. We never actually published an issue in England. The reason why Scotland Yard raided the Arts Lab after I'd gone was that they thought we had a few thousand copies of *Suck* there; and the whole *OZ* trial was really for us. They wanted us, but they didn't get us. One of the big things that upset them in *OZ* was the *Suck* ad in the children's issue.

CRAIG SAMS: The Wet Dream festival was held in Amsterdam in November 1970. I went, Anthony Haden-Guest, Andrew Fisher, Richard Neville . . . It was just three days of showing various soft-core and hard-core and old scratchy black and white 1920s and 1930s [films], Japanese and American and black and just about everything else – just about everything pornographic that had been put on film. This herd just sort of trekked from one place to another. There was a party at the Paradiso. It was a convention of the sexual revolution but it was the most sexless event imaginable.

The climax of the thing was the final evening. Otto Muhl and his AA Kommune people had the Rolling Stones on very loud and were dancing around naked on stage and cavorting lewdly and the climax of his show came when he took this goose and was stroking it and obviously had it very calmed, despite the loud music and everything else, and the plan was that he would violate the goose and then cut its head off. So when he was getting ready to do all this, suddenly there's an eruption from the audience and Heathcote Williams brought him down and grabbed the goose and passed it to someone else, and Otto and his team had a tantrum on stage, continuing to dance around shaking their fists at the audience and eventually crapped on the stage and went off.

KEITH MORRIS: I was in the Speak one evening when Germaine Greer wandered up to me – this was at the height of *Female Eunuch* – and says, 'Keith, I want you to take some pictures of me.' 'What sort of pictures?' She said, 'I want them stark naked, and I want a close-up of my cunt. Because it's got to be for *Suck* magazine. And at the same time I also want some pin-ups for my boyfriend back home.' She came round at nine in the morning. It was a pretty revolting experience, photographing someone's sweaty cunt at nine in the morning. So I did them. Bending over, lips apart, anus: the whole bit. It was a light-bulb shot. A close-up, degrees of zooming in and out, maybe move the light a fraction, then into the pin-up stuff. I do these close-ups and I do these pin-ups and then I say, 'Germaine, I've got to ask you: why me?' And she says, 'Because you're the only fucking photographer I can trust who won't sell them.' The significance of this didn't really dawn on me until the phone starts ringing. The *News of the World* has heard about it. Forget the pictures of the cunt, they weren't interested in that, they wanted the pin-up shots: 'Miss Liberation', Germaine laid out naked on her side, the knee decorously covering the pubes. Classy arse. I didn't go back on my word. I didn't sell them. I think there was some way that she was conned into it, that she had to do it or lose face.

She tried to pull me once. Her thing was to hang from my minstrel

422

gallery and swing like some great bat, while murmuring sexy things at me. This was supposed to turn me on but the effect it actually had was to make me run upstairs and lock the darkroom door. I was happy to be friends but I didn't particularly want to put my dick about. These were very big ladies. It made me feel inadequate.

MARSHA ROWE: It's amazing that one communicated with so many people on this sort of erotic level. Sometimes you slept with people and it meant nothing, sometimes it was more than that. You allowed each other to touch each other very deeply and you somehow communicated through this. There was a lot of physical contact and it was like a tribal meeting, like a big teenage gang. And it was across the sexes. The sexual side of it intensified it.

In the early 70s it felt like one big family, especially after my own particularly disastrous relationship when we started the magazine. I felt that there were a lot of conflicts with men but we carried on having what we called at the time multiple relationships, duogamy, where we weren't in couples. It didn't really work but we tried very hard. It was like a substitute family. I found that the other women involved would come round if I was ill, we'd celebrate each other's birthdays. There were immense jealousies, which we tried to ignore, and other problems, but there was also a lot of passion and love and a feeling that we were trying to make a new world. It felt as if we were trying to bring out into the world some of the ideas that had been floating around in the 60s, trying to bring our dreams into life.

PAT BELL: When I first went out with John Leaver I was going out with two other guys at the same time. I don't think the sexual revolution was a total illusion. Although when we were together we stayed together. There was a certain amount of 'free love' but some people did get hurt by it. They had to pretend that was what they wanted and in fact it wasn't.

JOHN LLOYD: In our flat, which we ran as a commune, the whole sex thing was extremely earnest. There was a lot of promiscuity, everybody had to swap partners. We didn't get into homosexuality, it was all hetero-sexuality. I'm not sure whether we really did elevate it above wife-swapping. It was quite exploitative of male and female. It was a lot of men liking to fuck a lot and saying to women, 'Why won't you fuck me?' I remember saying that quite a lot. And some women who were strong and sensible enough said, 'Because I don't want to!' but quite often it was 'Well . . . all right . . .' Contraception was generally available, and there was an ethos of doing it, and it was good and it was liberating and it was an act of friendship or love. But we weren't really liberated – all of us had a lot of hang-ups. We had been brought up traditionally, even strictly, and to try to leap out of your own habits and upbringing into this blissful state where there were no hang-ups was of course interesting psychologically but it was completely impossible. And all the jealousies and tensions just grew exponentially.

RICHARD NEVILLE: Louise Ferrier and I had a complicated, highly strung relationship and we both experimented outside that relationship. I was really very concerned with breaking down oppressive sexual attitudes to do with extreme jealousy, which seemed to make one very miserable, so one tried to get to the source of jealousy. I just thought that if people wanted to sleep together they should just be able to, and they shouldn't be prevented by Catholic morality. Part of it was battling against a joyless morality – don't fuck until you get married, and when you do you'll both be so dreadful you'll probably get divorced. I had come from a very bad marriage and I was interested in men and women working out a different sort of sexual/social behaviour. But of course there is some truth in the idea that this was institutionalising getting laid, providing a political framework for sex. I loved women and I loved making love to them. I loved fucking and there were lots of people around who felt the same. I don't think that anyone was pushed into bed by me. A lot of girls climbed through my window.

KEITH MORRIS: There was an *OZ* we did when I was going through a 'let's project images onto people' phase, which most art students do. And what Goodchild and me decided we'd like to do was to project the word '*OZ*' onto a naked girl for use as the front cover. It was number six or seven, the first photographic cover. So we had some difficulty finding a young lady who was worth photographing and actually prepared to have her boobs all over an underground magazine. Then Louise, who was Richard's girlfriend, sort of volunteered. Richard actually didn't like all this; Richard tried to stop it on the grounds of morality, i.e.: my girlfriend is not baring her tits all over this magazine. And we had to bring pressure to bear: 'Look, Richard, your credibility is at stake here . . .' before he would allow it to go on. And Louise didn't give a stuff and so the deal in the end was that it was cropped at the waist. It wasn't so much Louise's money that kept *OZ* going but the trust. I would have walked through fire for Louise. I wouldn't have done it for Richard. She was great and Richard treated her appallingly. She was a great human being. And a number of people lost their hearts. She was his credibility: if Louise rang

424

up and asked you to do something, you'd find time, she was so utterly easy to like. If Richard rang up it would depend on how you felt or if it was interesting enough. Therefore Richard, not being stupid, used to get Louise to do the dirty work.

DAVID MAY: I remember going to the cinema to see Richard Neville fuck, I couldn't get over that. Richard and Louise fucking and the cinema was full of people watching Richard's arse going up and down and these squelching noises and him licking her tits. They put on a great performance. It was a genuinely extraordinary act, wonderful, the stuff of legend – but does it count for anything now, certainly not, but in another twenty years . . . maybe.

JOHN PEEL: Obviously being a kind of minor princeling among the hippies, it did mean that women did come along and sort of throw themselves at you. There were always actresses who didn't act and models who didn't model who were prepared for the price of a meal to sleep with you for the night.

ANDREA ADAM: I did fall into bed with the most extraordinary characters, and I think my taste was extremely dubious at times. I took the opportunity to experiment. I felt I owed it to myself. It was part of my growth as a human being, as a woman and as a feminist. That's how I justified it. I didn't want a revolution, I was too keen on material things to want the political status quo overthrown, but I wanted women to become equal and I wanted permissiveness. I wanted my cake and eat it too. I wanted a licence to fuck around and I did fuck around. A lot of promiscuity, a lot of one-night stands. I don't know why but I didn't liberate myself sexually until I got married; I hadn't done it before. Why I should have done it within the confines of matrimony I don't know but that's what I did.

DAVID ROBINS: The underground was rather shy and inhibited. Later, though, when 'horizontal recruitment' became the most favoured form of propagandising on the libbo [libertarian] Left, then it really did get going. The libertarian loony Left scene of the early 70s was very strong on rogering and leg-over: it was a leg-over-based scene. The centrality of leg-over.

STEVE SPARKS: What was it all about? Sex and drugs and rock'n'roll. No AIDS, no herpes. Unfortunately there was an awful lot of amphetamine, and one of the by-products of amphetamine in large quantities is that it

425

produces an inability to consummate the sexual act. So there was an awful lot of sex not happening, then being talked about afterwards as if it did happen. I suspect that the great sexual freedom of the 60s was not as great as it would appear in retrospect. Drugs and sex don't really mix. If you use too many drugs you tend to be thinking about other things than getting laid.

MARSHA ROWE: I think we grew up with a fairly stultified, Victorian attitude to sexual relationships, and the only way we had to deal with that was to do what we did; which was to lighten sex, to make it erotic play, to say that sometimes one could have a serious relationship, and sometimes you will just want to sleep with each other. What we didn't see was that this would maybe stretch our emotional or physical resources till they would collapse. We didn't see that actually this was not something you could maintain. We don't live in that sort of culture. Western human beings are not attuned to living like that. And I remember Richard saying to me when I was involved in a multiple relationship: 'Why are you with two men? It takes so long just to get to know one person.'

DAVID WIDGERY: Everyone was into multiple relationships, non-jealous and so on. Everyone was busy in large daisy chains across north London, all being non-possessive and all spending a lot of time, after a year or two, being pretty unhappy about it, and in the end by and large settling for one partner, especially when children came on the scene, children being pretty absent from the underground. I think the sexual revolution side of it all was tremendously over-rated. I don't think there was significantly any more sex going on than ten years before or ten years afterwards. There's a lot less actual fucking goes on in the world than people would like to think.

In conclusion: 'Some kind of golden age'

ROBERT WYATT: I think in the end that by not beating the system we strengthened it. In the end the culture we were involved in was an Anglo-American cultural narcissism revamped, and if you look at it from the point of view of world culture it actually reflected the power structure, the extraordinary media power of the English-speaking West. With the best will in the world the people involved might have thought that they were providing an alternative, but they were simply making the Establishment more flexible. So I'm not at all surprised that we have proceeded to vote in lots of incredibly right-wing and chauvinistic governments. I don't see that as a reaction to the 60s, but as a direct result. What a . pathetic thing to think: that you can just blow the castles down.

426

DAVID MAY: All that stuff had an enormous effect. It changed the attitude of the police. It changed the attitude of the government and the army. All that kind of subversive, revolutionary journalism, dope, all the stuff. They took the underground press a lot more seriously than it took itself. For a time it did seem that things would really change, that people were coming together. Certain key strands came out of the 60s: one was personified in the *OZ* trial: another was the Angry Brigade, the violence; the third was the hip consumerism. The 'Revolution', as preached by the Angry Brigade, I thought sucked. The overthrow of the government, of the State, was too heavy for most people. The hip consumerism was easy, and instead of smashing the State we went into advanced consumerism. It was all an incredibly romantic era: girls were incredibly beautiful and luscious and they didn't have AIDS and didn't wear knickers. There was always enough money to be comfortable, there was good music, dope, sex, and above all there was not conforming. It was like that Chinese curse: 'You will be blessed to live in interesting times.' There was an intensity to it all that I never imagined was going to go away. Nothing shocked me more than the realisation that it was going to change. As did the realisation that money meant so much. I genuinely believed that that was one of the things that had changed. But there were rich hippies and poor hippies and there were really rich hippies and really poor hippies. The class barrier was still there. But in the end they were middle-class children playing with each other. But in the end you only have to note that Richard Branson is worth £400 million or whatever to know that some people understood it and acted on it and did very well. It will probably be seen as a cultural bubble. But we didn't die and we participated in what will stand as the finest, most brilliant Technicolor display of individuality, bohemianism and revolution that has been seen in 50 years. It was brilliant, a fantastic display, but like all displays the rain comes along, the wind blows and it dies.

DEREK TAYLOR: We all have our own 60s. We all find in these things what suits us and what we have been looking for. For some people it just came and went, people for whom 1967 was just the year after 1966 and before 1968. For some people the 60s were an apparition. For Norman Tebbit it was intolerable. For us it was love yourself and forgive yourself, don't deal with the straight world, it's OK. Dig yourself. But for Tebbit it was 'While we were out there in the trenches, you cunts were living the life of Riley!' And we were. For a time we were in the ascendancy – we were the masters and mistresses. I was well into my thirties by 1967 and it was really what I had been waiting for since I was a child. Time to make whoopee in a collective way, time for everyone to be really nice to each other. It was an easy time to be. I was a thin, frail, wiry kind of young man. You could be pasty-faced, you could be wasted, wrecked, all those things – it was perfectly all right – you didn't have to be a rugby player any more. You could be misshapen, thin, fat, you could be any fucking thing: Jewish, Catholic, anything, so long as you were groovy and wanted to be pleasant. It was undoubtedly a golden age.

CHRISTOPHER LOGUE: I take what I call the 60s to run from the first night of *Look Back in Anger* to the day Lennon and McCartney parted company. I think that within that period very important things happened in English art life – and I'm using that in the broadest sense: style, fashion, dancing, music, etc, etc – it seemed to me to be a very rich period indeed. Full of good things. And the periods that follow are dull and uninteresting in comparison. The slighting comments that are made about the 60s seem to me to stem very largely from envy and from ignorance. To criticise the 60s as being in some way immoral strikes me as crazy when compared with the modern world that is dirty and crowded and frightening and ugly.

MARK BOYLE: It was one of those extraordinary moments when the British class system faltered and everyone was mixing with everyone else. You certainly felt at the time that it was some kind of golden age.

JO DURDEN-SMITH: We could constantly push at the barriers, because there weren't any. How far could you go? Nobody knew. Steve Sparks was constantly quoting this 'When the mode of the music changes the walls of the city shake.' There was a totally naive, undifferentiated belief that somehow fashion and politics and rock'n'roll were all the same somehow. All part of this pushing at the barriers of what was possible and permissible and changing society in the process. There is not very much evidence that it did any of that, not even at the time, but it was so busy, there was so much going on, who had time to sit down and analyse it?

I wrote a piece attempting to see what had changed, and I came to the conclusion that nothing much had changed. It's hard to ascribe a particular decade to that period which started with the death of Kennedy in '63 and ended with the death of George Jackson in '71. The death of Kennedy was the first event in which the world looked at itself and saw its own face. That was the first event in which you heard electronically about an event and suddenly became aware of yourself participating in it. It was the first instantaneous event, in the McLuhanite sense, that

428

happened. It was then that we began to realise that we were part of one planet and were girdled together in some odd way and that we therefore had a responsibility not only to neighbourhood and nation but perhaps to something international.

ANDREA ADAM: There is a core of validity to the 60s. 'Philosophy' may be too high-falutin' a word but there was an urge to be less consumer-orientated, to lead a more communal life, to care. There did seem to be a genuine wish in everyone to lead that kind of life. But I see no legacy of it in England whatsoever. I never felt it had reached down to the grass roots in England and whatever pockets it had reached were, by '74-'75, pretty much dispersed. We all disappeared. Suddenly one day we weren't talking to each other on the telephone, suddenly everybody had gone their own way. Suddenly everyone was knee-deep in mortgages and scrabbling for a half-decent job. Everyone woke up one day and realised that they were nearly 30, without a job and that jobs were getting very scarce and that they were broke and there was no money coming from anywhere. Living from hand to mouth was no longer possible. And the spirit of the 60s went underground in '74/'75 to emerge in the Narcotics Anonymous and Alcoholics Anonymous meetings of the late 80s.

NINA FISHMAN: The alternative society was important. English people in the mid-60s were dead. They didn't talk about what they felt, they didn't do what they felt, everybody was compartmentalised. Coming from America, the first time I ever used the word 'class' was in England. And even though I loved the working-class kids I met in Sussex, they were ultimately resigned to their fate. I wasn't that kind of person. The idealism we inherited from the Second World War becomes very important here: that egalitarianism and idealism was put into practice. And we have a society now which is infinitely more open. The alternative wasn't just play power. It had an effect in the sense that it got assimilated somehow into popular culture. Trevor-Roper made this remark that what really ruined the established system was *That Was the Week That Was* which did it by going drip, drip, drip every week. In the 60s the Establishment did end, and the underground played its part in that drip, drip, drip. The Second World War had engendered a tremendous amount of upward mobility. Given England and the rate at which things change, the assimilation of this mobility and its impact on the Establishment were delayed. In a sense the 60s, and the Wilson governments, were the final fruition, the coming of age of this democratisation, the greater egalitarianism.

ANDREW LUMSDEN: I don't think the gay liberation movement could have happened in the form that it did without the 60s. (That is for gay men: lesbians had been identified as far back as the beginning of this century and they have a different history.) But the gay movement and the gay press would never have happened without America. And it was the blacks that really made the 60s happen there: from King onwards there was a way of seeing yourself: 'I'm black, I'm American and I'm proud' allowed for 'I'm gay, I'm American and I'm proud.'

JUNE BOLAN: The basic motivating force was anti-parental, in all its senses. That's where it all stemmed from: I don't like the way my parents live and I've seen all these other people and I'll go and join them.

The summers always seemed to be good, the winters never seemed to be bad. People genuinely cared about you. You never ever felt you were hungry or that you'd gone without. One always managed. We didn't want to change the world. We lived as we did and couldn't see why other people couldn't live like that too.

VIRGINIA CLIVE-SMITH: The hippie thing was overall to do with consciousness-raising. Amidst all the fun and games there was an effort to be not so much down in the gutter and more looking at the stars. That was certainly my aim and still is. Nothing shocks any more. You can do what you want to do now without being continually stared at or criticised.

MICK FARREN: Essentially rock'n'roll was the key factor, from an early age. There's always been an underground and there always will be. It just expands and contracts. The essential thread of bohemianism, things get left over – bookshops, bars – all from the previous incarnation. As long as I can remember there has always seemed to be this conflict between conformity and individualism. Whatever is going on there will always be a response. The way you treat that response is the measure of a society. I don't think there is an alternative world. For about three weeks there was this dumb idea that you could revolutionise the whole manifest destiny of the planet by example, but on the other hand the things that have been achieved are not to be sniffed at. You can only really pinpoint what has survived from the 60s if you can see what might have been. An awful lot of stuff has been institutionalised: rock'n'roll, gay power. Compared with the 50s there is a considerable amount of individual expression, even with the waves of reaction we are experiencing now. I think really what you had was a flurry of people realising that they had more power than they thought they had. But then you had a flurry of them thinking they had more power than they really did. Then you had a disappointment . . . it goes in cycles. I don't think they ever knew what to do with the power and I'm profoundly glad of that. There were a lot of bloody silly ideas. I don't think anything would have actually happened, there's such inertia in society. Constant free-form anarchy is about the only way you can get on – once something gets iconised, attempt to destroy it. That seems to be the process, the chicken-and-egg process. You get an egg and you got to break it, it's just too perfect.

JIM HAYNES: The legacy of the 60s is that there is much more acceptance of the other for what he or she wants to be, less critical nose-in-the-air attitudes, a much more live-and-let-live feeling. Whether this is what I want to see, or whether what it really is, I don't know. The 60s is definitely a myth that people are going to deal with for a long, long time.

JOHN HOPKINS: There's something about England that I've never fathomed, but I'm sure it's true, which is: if you've got the bottle to go out and do something, anything, it's like a magnet. In that particular milieu – the early 60s – there were all kinds of people who were doing things and I was just one of those people. There were lots and lots of people. There are so many people in England who won't get up and do something, and so if you did . . . In the 60s, if you analyse it, we did stuff that if you worked it all out formally, if you made a business plan, which we've all learnt to do since, you'd never fucking do it! It was impossible!

SAM HUTT: I suppose there was something quite wimpy about it. It was largely the middle class rebelling inside their heads and trying to take the rebellion they felt inside their heads out into the exterior world. And for a moment it seemed possible. It is hard to give articulate answers about what I thought about it all because it is confusing as to the degree of posing and the degree of reality that was going on. There was an awful lot of posing, a great deal of it.

ALAN MARCUSON: For me the great lesson of the 60s is exactly what Marcuse said: 'You can change your perception as much as you like, but until you change the content of your perception, nothing changes.' It was a kind of liberating period. The good thing was that you felt less alone at the end of the 60s than you did as a teenager emerging from the 50s. That was the terrible thing about the 50s – that one felt so alone: one had this private madness. The 50s were such a rigid decade, such a conformist decade.

Now it sickens me to go to the parties of that generation who really did open up their lives and abandoned bourgeois values; now what are they talking about? Their mortgages, their careers and their au pair girls.

ANDREW BAILEY: There was a whole load of pretending by people, whether they realised it or not, because they were actually imitating an American phenomenon that sociologically and psychologically actually had very little validity in England. I think we all wanted to be American at that time and we were playing at it. But we didn't invent anything: we didn't invent jeans, boots, long hair, tie-dyed T-shirts. What did we in London actually invent? The mini-skirt. And who invented the mini-skirt: the underground? I do think the underground changed things: but it's best to look at it in business terms. What it can be seen as is a period when entrepreneurship found its feet again in England. The era gave a lot of people the opportunity to be small businessmen, some of whom, like Branson, Felix Dennis, Tony Elliot and Jann Wenner, have continued and made a great deal of money. It was a period when the rules of business broke down, when small could be profitable. Maybe not immediately in terms of the accountant's bottom line but where – because anything went and because there was a new market that was big enough to support new ideas – you could actually be a small business.

RICHARD NEVILLE: We lived in a different cultural terrain than is available today. It affected what you said, how you ate, how you danced, the music you listened to, what you read, what you wrote, what we published in *OZ* and how we designed it. Our view of the world was altered, the way we travelled around the world was altered, the capacity for meeting with other people and making friendships which went totally across national boundaries and across cultural boundaries, the shake-up of relationships between the races, between men and women . . . I think there was a cultural explosion of some sort which of course was popularised, it was perhaps commercialised, it was marketed, it can be ridiculed, but at the same time at its core it had a genuine spirit of hope for humankind. It was predicated on the idea of making the world a better place. So if you get a lot of people gathered around a fundamental idea like that, I think you can say that that is a valid cultural nexus. That happened for a while. It was a cultural event, an authentic cultural event, but of what significance it is probably still too early to judge. The 60s and the alternative society influenced hundreds of thousands of people in different ways: fashion, ecology, art . . . a lot of the groundwork was done back then. A lot of people had ideas and impulses within them that were triggered by a fleeting identification with an idea larger than themselves. What happened after that was that the idea shrank to people's own ambition which was basically the reversion to materialism: the Porsche, the stock market and the credit cards. But there was a time, a golden time, when people's ideas were larger than themselves.

SU SMALL: It changed things for me entirely. My path diverged completely and wildly from everything I was born to: working-class life in south London. Which is where I'd have been now – possibly working in a bank or possibly bringing up a couple of kids or probably dead, because I wouldn't have been able to cut it. A few coincidences, a little serendipity here and there, brought me into that milieu and sent me on. In terms of the wider view I think it's just nudged things a bit. We used to expect everything now, but I don't believe that any more. We were the baby boom and now lots of us are in power. In ten years' time the government will be mostly made up of people born the same time as us and I think some of them will have been exposed to things we were doing in the 60s. Might have changed their ideas a bit. Loads of things which were just laughed at in those days are taken for granted now. The fact that there is such a thing as feminism – it was a very obscure religion then; gay rights; certain aspects of the arts; libertarianism; wholefoods – it's not common but it's not as hysterically funny as it was then; the acceptance of a wider range of religions. Even in establishment politics there have been changes. There was a generation that was affected by that stuff. It may well have been elitist and it may well have been statistically only a small number of people and maybe we were all really jerking off and dancing to ourselves but I think there has been a ripple effect and I think you can see it.

SUE MILES: At the beginning it was supposed to be about love and peace and social equality and friendliness, and what it was really about was ripping everybody off. In the end it was about product. It was about posters and records, and it became clear that the rock'n'roll industry was making a fortune out of the whole thing. Richard Neville had the good attitude – he was just in it for a bit of fun. The idea that we were all taken seriously was so weird. All that paranoia: 'I'm not talking in this room, there's somebody with a suit on.' 'Never trust anyone over thirty' – I remember thinking, we'll live to regret that label.

STEVE SPARKS: My productive output from the whole of the 60s is one poster, two complete albums, half a dozen tracks on other albums, a dozen photographs, and ten thousand words. Maximum. I think the underground was different to the usual phenomenon of young people growing up, rushing round and discovering the world. It was different because of the externals: we had a favourable economy, which was very

433

important; we had the break-up of the post-war situation in England, not only economically but socially as well, which allowed the mixing of the classes which previously would have been unheard of. The underground shattered class barriers. You had pirate radio, which allowed you to distribute sounds that the establishment record companies weren't interested in – the only reason that independent recording was able to happen was these radio stations . . . you had all of those things coming together. It was these externals that made the difference.

RICHARD TRENCH: I think that the underground had almost no effect at all. It made quite a difference socially to a small group; it became respectable after the hippies for middle-class people to get jobs like being a wheelwright, or a furniture restorer in Norfolk – craft jobs. That made a slight difference – small businesses, doing your own thing – which all fitted slightly with Thatcherism later. Things like gay liberation and the women's movement would have come anyway. I can't think of anything in this country that wouldn't have come anyway. Except that the English character, which is very gentle in certain respects, took to the hippie quite well. A lot of the cultural things, especially the pop music, was actually far ahead of America. The English concept of individualism helped foster it. And there was no real opposition in England, apart from policemen arresting you for drugs. England was a tolerant society, there'd always been hippies, but previously they were eccentrics who were allowed to indulge themselves.

ED VICTOR: It was a fascinating moment. It's hard to believe that twenty years ago life was the way it was. Very different. How permissive it was . . . remarkable. It's also remarkable how many people never made it out of the 60s. A lot of casualties. There are a lot of casualties in every era – people come out in their early twenties, full of promise, and then nothing – but I feel that the 60s encouraged a kind of precociousness and a confidence and a brashness and a 'We can do anything and being young is the thing to be, we don't need these old farts, they shouldn't run things, we can run things' and a lot of these people got washed up on the shore. Never went back for another wave. A lot of people were arrested in their development then. On the other hand it was such an attractive period. A lot of people never felt more alive than they did then, issues seemed to be drawn, it was a very exciting time. We went as far as we could go.

MICK FARREN: Everybody dies once . . . I felt pretty callous about it. Drugs and sports cars are much the same kind of thing. I don't drive sports cars. Drugs were the equivalent of warfare and running away to sea and everything like that. That's what drugs were. Part of the problem was that they became a rite of passage because they were proscribed. The drug panic is truly ridiculous. A lot of people get excessive and the excessive die. They die of all sorts of things. Life's like that – which do you want, drugs or the Napoleonic War? The one advantage, really, of the whole drug culture was that it didn't seem to be susceptible to a lot of other very dangerous ideas, like militarism, and it may even continue to be the downfall of militarism. And who is telling us not to take drugs? Nancy Reagan, Jack.

DICK POUNTAIN: Although I took a lot of drugs I think I survived because I never had any suicidal tendencies. I think an awful lot of people who got into heavy drugs had this self-immolatory aspect which they may or may not have been aware of. I've always been of the opinion that you get hooked on smack largely because you want to. If you want to come off it you can come off it. People who don't, don't want to. I played with it for two or three years. We took it cos we liked it, not cos we wanted to be hooked. We weren't like those people of whom you'd say immediately, he's into smack because he wants to kill himself. Most of the people we knew who died died by mistake, not because they wanted to kill themselves. We took drugs for pleasure, no other reason, or possibly as a tranquilliser. It was a huge adventure, like climbing mountains, but internally.

CHRIS ROWLEY: There was a certain callousness. Acidheads regarded those who failed the test as lame, as failures. And if they went mad in your apartment then it was a drag, but if they went mad in their own, you could always leave. Acid was full of that terrible deadpan cool, and maybe that's the way the world is too. But it was horribly heartless in many ways. The rock and roll world accurately reflected some of it, the tiny elite at the top, those who could get backstage were taking cocaine and champagne, the great packed sweating mass out the front. All the old stereotypes were revived: they all became elves but they rapidly realised that they had to become good businesslike elves if they were to survive.

DAVID WIDGERY: It was to do with cool, you saw it most around something like the Rolling Stones entourage where people could be dying and no one would stop to enquire why. It was a lot of egotistical, pretty, bright young people, mostly on the make in some form or another, and they all treated each other fairly unscrupulously. The people who suffered were not this layer but those who hung on to the myths and ended up in the squalid rat-infested squat shooting up. If people as a result of reading *OZ* decided to leave their parents, hitchhike to London and then ended up in a mess, the underground, despite its occasional pretensions, couldn't provide a welfare state. And if you're going to have a new society based on new values you need new social institutions. It was more like the sort of millennial movements that emerged in the English Civil War: somehow simply by the power of thought you can transcend material needs. But that is what comes from the rich: you ignore your own actual privileges, but you generalise from the vantage point of having them. It's totally implausible for the rank-and-file hippie. There's a great Paul McCartney line when he went to see Jerry Garcia in San Francisco and they smoked the pipe of peace and stuff and McCartney came away and said, 'I thought to myself: this won't last.'

SU SMALL: Every funeral I go to I'm inspired and amazed by how many people are still alive.

SUE MILES: I thought being able to smoke drugs, being able to fuck whoever you wanted was fine, lovely. Having food spiked with heavy-duty psychedelics, bad news, dangerous. I never consumed anything in public for years. People didn't care about themselves. I used to help with the fallouts at UFO and we tried to write above their heads what they'd taken and you'd get lists of about nine things. I used to think I wouldn't do this – I had more regard for myself. I also always thought, I'm going to live beyond my twenties. I am not about to expire here and now, thank you very much. I'd like two lungs, two arms, two legs and a brain.

MICK FARREN: There are two things: one is that the 60s were a terrible mistake and all these people died and woe, woe, woe, let's not take drugs any more and let's not have any more fun and we're all going to get AIDS and die, boo! Or there's the 60s were fucked and all we got was MTV. This is possibly true, maybe all people wanted was MTV. I don't know. I have no personal sense of compromise, except insofar as I direct my energies in a particular way. I personally started out on my particular roller-coaster ride, which I did my best to map for myself, and it went off and away we went. I don't really feel that I've come out the other end yet. I see things as cyclical. I was very encouraged in about 1977 when I saw John Lydon and people marching about the streets. And a bunch of them died – pioneers always die. Does Quentin Crisp feel responsible for Boy George?

MARK WILLIAMS: The underground movement, the 60s, liberated a lot of people, who remained liberated in their thinking if not their actual

436

deeds. It liberated thinking in this country, intellectually and even politically. Labour governments were certainly influenced by it. It opened up the arts so that there was much more experimentation, much much more diversity, and that was a legacy that still exists, that was the one thing that hasn't quite been squashed. In that sense it does have an abiding value. But because it was so irresponsible it fucked up a lot of people as well who couldn't control themselves. But without it I would be living in Solihull, with a company Cavalier, membership of the local golf club, fuck the wife twice a month, and be a very sad person. I don't regret any of it as far as I was personally concerned. I don't know anyone who does.

HORACE OVE: It was very, very exciting, colourful and creative. If you look back at posters, photography, art, poetry, psychedelic film-making ... People all talk about the 60s and put it down – just a bunch of hippies – but it created a lot. I can see youth today going back to it. The whole pop-art movement. It wasn't just that we were all young. Nothing to do with that. That excitement, you felt it as you walked out into the streets, you knew it. Every week something was happening, something was taking place, and it wasn't just a disco like we have today where you exploit youth by charging lots of money. There was free concerts, there was things taking place. There was a kind of creativity taking place here, in America and on the Continent. And the good part of the 60s was that you didn't wait, you didn't discuss it, you did it, like it said, 'Do it' and you did, you'd go out there and do it.

JOE BOYD: My view of the period, from the early 60s onwards, is not of continuity so much as of constant revolution, in a sense of paternalistic revolutionaries looking upon their progeny in horror as they go off in a completely new direction which has nothing whatsoever to do with the direction which they hoped had been established. The few people I would call similar to beatniks that I met in the early 60s looked upon the civil rights folkies etc, etc with absolute horror; and then the civil rights folkies looked upon the people who took dope and were into psychedelics in the mid-60s with absolute horror; and those people then looked upon the wider spread of psychedelics into a broader community, people who were less concerned with the aesthetics of the experience, with absolute horror. You can establish a continuity, but you can also establish this continuity of divorce, that each successive wave was anathema to the leaders of the previous one.

It still has changed a lot of landscapes. That brief period. I don't think that any Western country will seriously commit large numbers of its own white, middle-class youth to a land war very readily – certainly not a conscription army – following that period. All sorts of prevailing attitudes have been moved slightly off-centre from where they were in 1965 by what happened in the late 60s. In any movement like that there's a tremendous amount of negative fallout. Every time you hear a heavy-metal guitar solo you can curse the name of Jimi Hendrix if you want, but the fact remains that he was a great guitar player and what he did was very liberating to lots of other musicians, and it was also very liberating to a lot of people who should never pick up a guitar ever. They should have their hands cut off. And the same thing goes in a lot of other areas where things didn't work out so well. A kind of drug cornucopia, the legitimisation of the intake of large quantities of narcotics without regard to what the effects might be. As with anything, there was a kind of 'Can you top this?' syndrome. It's easy to spot the ways in which it failed, the ways in which it succeeded are very difficult to spot because they've become part of the way that we think and the way we do things.

PETER SHERTSER: The 60s is unrepeatable. No second offers. It was a time of complete cultural change, to do with freedom – not just for individuals. Teenagers for the first time started taking on an identity, something that had been building up in the late 50s/early 60s to a point where, in the 70s, they became a major force. Now for the individual of any age group suddenly freedom was available; freedom of expression in any form you desired. Clothes, hair, views – whatever. It turned the whole thing around. It changed people's images, their ideals, their language. Without a doubt it gave the greatest degree of freedom that we've known this century. And at the time we all sincerely believed in all the changes we were helping to bring about. What we were doing was not changing things on a physical level, a violent level, but on a mental and intellectual level. All we were saying was we've got a world out here, it's great, let's all enjoy it together. And these are ideals that can only work in a utopia, which is never to be.

PAUL MCCARTNEY: I feel that very slowly, some of the stuff, some of the policies we tried to work on then, did change the world, but like all changes very, very, very slowly, painfully slowly. So that pollution, stuff like Greenpeace, slowly emerged. It wasn't us, but the kind of philosophies we supported – TM's success in America was us, because the Beatles gave Maharishi his great publicity, and what you'd call the Shirley Maclaine factor is the 80s version of what we started – a lot of that alternative thinking has come in. Vegetarianism for instance. I've been a vegetarian for eighteen years – it is now wildly fashionable.

438

My image of our role is that we are seen as the figureheads for the Beatle haircut, but we weren't: there was some guy in Germany and we said 'Cut our hair like yours'. We were actually copying this guy and he happened to get it wrong. We were students, we were part of the movement, but because we were one of the most visible parts of it, certainly to Americans, certainly because of this funny hairdo, we then became the spokespeople for a generation, as did the Stones, and then once people realised that John's been to art college, or this guy's got some sort of thing in literature – they know who Chaucer was, shit! – they assumed that these are the people who can change it all. No, we were just interested in it. I still am. I feel sorry in a way for [Bob] Geldof. It's a very difficult thing to be Gandhi, Geldof, Mother Teresa. I know that kind of thing. But there's a lot changing. I don't want to take all the credit by any means for us, or even for that set of people, because a lot of the seeds we were working on had been sown by Aldous Huxley, had been sown by quite a few other people, in earlier days. We didn't organise ourselves and say, 'Let's change the world,' but we happened to be sitting around and it happened to throw up theories that, had they got into place, would have changed the world, and should they get in place will change the world, and in fact *have* changed the world to some degree. There was some form of revolution and there is some form of revolution.

SPIKE HAWKINS: I look back on the 60s as being possibly the time in the UK when we had all the equipment for total revision of society: the way I look upon it is that it was rather like a Meccano set with all the nuts but no bolts, therefore it fell and I always said at the time that after a period of permissiveness, lack of censorship – in other words total freedom to express yourself without censorship of any description – there will always be a right-wing backlash. This is to calm the right wing. But it opened people's eyes – the middle classes and the working classes to an extent. Their children were getting a better education, they were experimenting in drugs – not all of them, but they were getting an insight. Once people had taken LSD they were literally on a trip for ever. Because it did expand your consciousness. I look back on the 60s as just sitting down with a tape recorder and four or five of us having a ball with words. Those were the good times. The bad times came when we had to set it upon a commercial basis.

DAVID MAY: The fact was that one participated at the time in something that was unique in this country. It had never happened before and it has never happened since. We had learnt at a very early stage that being

439

different in this country actually did produce the most excessive reaction. But one of the great lines of the era was that 'we' were going to take over, and the fact is that 'we' didn't. The people who really took over were people like Rupert Murdoch, a far more successful Australian manipulator of the media than Richard Neville ever was.

STEVE MANN: It was Andy Warhol who said that the 60s were too full, just like the 70s were too empty. I think there's a lot of truth there.

DAVID WIDGERY: I was much too optimistic. I had this incorrigible optimism about the fact that a large number of young people would go through their radical phase onward to a more understood commitment to the revolutionary Left, but that tends not to happen. I thought people would look more and more to new issues – Ireland, sexual politics – and there would be real change. But in fact we had quite the reverse and people have settled for the devil they know. Bits of the underground were co-opted into new holiday resorts pioneered by hippies, or into new graphics skills, of which Felix Dennis is the best example, Tony Elliot, Branson. Tony tells you which record to buy, you come to Virgin to buy it, Felix produces a fan magazine about it, and so on.

The first thing is to remember what Britain was like in the early 60s: a very much more conservative society than it even is now, a very monochrome society, a very class-obedient society. The attitudes about the State, about male-female relationships, about authority, really hadn't changed since before the Second World War. There was a lot of intellectual slum-clearance to be done, a lot of stuff that needed to be booted out: a lot of deference to old ideas about history, politics and philosophy, all of which needed a massive great puke to get them out of the way. I think the underground – considering how small the number of people really was, and how terribly small the number of really original people was – was fantastically successful in putting forward new ways of looking at things, new subversions, which have had a lasting effect. And while Mrs Thatcher is fighting back against everything we achieved, she can't do it, she can't restore the idea of homosexuality being a criminal act, she can't turn the clock back, however hard they try. But, and this is speaking as an orthodox Marxist, the paradox lies in the fact that although we changed our attitudes successfully, we still failed to change material circumstances, the bottom line of how society works. Pandora's Box has been opened, people had at their disposal a very different way of looking at society than it was before we started, but their reality is not much different: it's mass unemployment, shabby schools, the video culture and so on, although I don't think it will last for ever.

440

CHRISTOPHER LOGUE: Was it a counterculture? I suppose it was. It was rather pretentious and silly in some ways. I found it rather . . . kids in the playground, 'You're not part of our gang', that sort of thing. A bit childish. They certainly weren't going to change the world, no, no, no. Never had a chance. I think they thought that the world was going to follow them. That they wouldn't have to do anything. Among all these people I never thought that any of them were that bright. That was one of the things they had in common: they were intellectually flat and un-adventurous. Intellectual endeavour had no place in their scheme of things. None. There was no intellectual input. And in so far as intellectual input is critical it's supposed to be able to make at least a semi-coherent argument, and it's supposed to describe accurately in terms of an analysis what is going on, with a degree of self-knowledge – there was no such thing. There was no 'alternative society'. It was playtime.

MARK BOYLE: For people like Christopher Logue the 60s must have been a great aggravation. As a political animal he must have resented the fact that while the politics was there it was taken in what he would undoubtedly think of as in a not very serious way. And yet that movement stopped the war in Vietnam.

MARK WILLIAMS: There was never an alternative society, was there? Because if there was there would have to be an alternative currency and alternative property laws and so on. The alternative society was a misnomer: there was an alternative culture, but there was never an alternative society. There were new ways of making a living and new ways of supporting yourself. The social equivalent of the underground press reader today is the *Face* reader. A lot of it was fashion – not strictly in the clothes sense, although that had something to do with it – in terms of commercial pressure. The fact that there was a lot of money around, that there was a lot of affluence, enabled a lot of people to drop out, or at least assume that pose. Alternatively, it gave people an opportunity to make money from enterprises that were actually not very well run and wouldn't otherwise have had a market for their products. We lived in a very charmed period, economically. Because of that, fashions had a much greater influence on a greater number of people than they would now. And the straight world – the film industry, rock industry, fashion indus-try – was watching with a lot of interest to see what would happen. And they were very quick to capitalise on it. I never thought it would end, I thought it would get better: more alternative this, more alternative that, and it would therefore get more exciting and more interesting. There seemed to be no limits on what we were doing for a while and I don't

441

think any generation in our lifetime is going to enjoy that same freedom.

SPIKE HAWKINS: I would say that there was an alternative society in
one's own head, but not in the everyday world. For a while there was this
fusion and so much could have been done and I sometimes think to
myself, 'What fools!' – and I can include myself as well – 'what fools we
made of ourselves by excluding ourselves from what else was happening.'
By being an alternative society we became rather a minority that was
very, very, very open to the hard foot, to money . . .

DUNCAN FALLOWELL: People sneer at the 6os but I think it's one of
the major watersheds in modern history, in terms of attitude. In the way
that you can say the last decade of the eighteenth century and the first
decade of the nineteenth century was too. If there's any future for mankind it will be because certain ideas became popular in the 6os. There's
no question about that. Notably an awareness of patterns larger than
oneself – the ecological idea; the idea that you can be happy without
having lots of possessions. Post-modernism is completely a result of the
6os, even though we think of it as high-rise hell. The idea that an architect
will take the whole history of architecture and produce whatever he wants
is a post-modern concept; the idea that you take all religious thought and
make your necessary adjustments is a post-modern concept. I grew up in
the 6os, I was a child of the 6os and I thank God for it.

It began here, with Swinging London. All the energy that had sustained
the British Empire was brought back home, and it was still thumping
away and it had nothing to do, so it produced this extraordinary local,
colourful explosion, this fountain of activities. Of course the prominent
personalities of the time are not the ones that achieved most in the long
run. They're to be dug out of Welsh farmhouses; whereas the ones who
have achieved most were probably hacking it at Keele University or living
in some Northern town. The 6os socialites are often simply the footnotes
of social history. The really important stuff was not being done up and
down the King's Road – those people are symptoms, not causes of anything.

This was a post-imperial phase, it had to open up or die; and there was
a general opening up of Western culture. Things like 'letting it all hang
out' were very important, especially for a repressed little island like ours.
To have lived through the 6os and not have participated in it . . . And
those who are moving into political power are the ones who lived through
it without participating in it and actually hate the people who were
liberated by it.

442

INTERVIEWEES

STEVE ABRAMS: England's Timothy Leary; American researcher into ESP and founder of SOMA (Society of Mental Awareness), spearhead of the campgaign to decriminalise cannabis and organiser of the *Times* advertisement in July 1967. He now lives in Notting Hill.

ANDREA ADAM: One of the *Time* magazine editors who put together the 'Swinging London' feature of 1966. *Time*'s main reporter on the late-60's counterculture. Has lived and worked in London since 1972.

RICHARD ADAMS: Art director variously of *OZ, INK* and other underground papers. Since 1972 has worked freelance – for Felix Dennis's Bunch Books, as well as with Heathcote Williams and John Michell. Based in Notting Hill.

JIM ANDERSON: A member of the Australian bar, designer of *OZ*, leading proselytiser of the hippie trail and the gay representative among the *OZ* trial defendants. Emigrated to America in 1974 and lives in Bolinas. He published his first novel in 1988.

ANDREW BAILEY: Former RAF officer–cadet turned *Variety* reporter, Bailey edited *Rolling Stone* UK after the original staff set up *Friends*. Currently working in advertising.

PAT BELL: House mother of *Rolling Stone, Friends* and *OZ*, and involved in setting up *Spare Rib*. Married to John Leaver.

ROBIN BLACKBURN: Pioneer member of the New Left and of the editorial board of *New Left Review*. Blackburn's firing from the LSE for his support of LSE activists in 1967 helped intensify the student struggles. Now publisher for New Left Books.

JUNE BOLAN: Secretary at Blackhill Enterprises, June (née Child) met Marc Bolan when he was signed to the company. They lived together for three years and were married for seven. Currently involved with a firm building stages for rock concerts.

443

ROSIE BOYCOTT: Co-founder of *Spare Rib* with Marsha Rowe after leaving university and working on *Frendz*. She published an autobiography – *A Nice Girl Like Me* – in 1984; her first novel appears this year.

JOE BOYD: Former UK representative of Elektra Records, Boyd founded Witchseason Productions, promoting Fairport Convention, Incredible String Band, etc. Joined John Hopkins in the Notting Hill Free School and UFO and Caroline Coon in Release. Still involved in the music business.

MARK BOYLE: Boyle and his wife Joan Hills projected their first light-show in 1963 and were the leading exponents of the genre at UFO, as well as touring America with the Soft Machine. Working with their son and daughter as 'The Boyle Family', they now are among Britain's best-known artists.

PETER BROWN: Brown moved from late-50s Soho bohemia to 60s hippiedom in Portobello Road where he managed the Electric Cinema. Now living in Florida, working as an antiquarian book-dealer.

LOUISE BURDEN: Burden was co-organiser of Greasy Truckers Promotions, a community-orientated rock promotion company, putting on concerts at the Roundhouse and under the Westway. Currently involved in Liberal politics and computer graphics.

JEROME BURNE: Burne worked on *Friends* prior to editing *Frendz* after Alan Marcuson's resignation. Subsequent journalism has included editing *Time Out* and working for the *London Daily News*.

JOHNNY BYRNE: One of Liverpool's leading beats, Byrne worked closely with Spike Hawkins during the 60s and co-wrote *Groupie* with Jenny Fabian. Now primarily a TV scriptwriter, his best-known work is probably the adaptation of James Herriot's 'vet' books for the small screen.

DUNCAN CAMPBELL: Campbell was at Edinburgh University with John Lloyd during the era of Jim Haynes' role as the city's pre-eminent bohemian. After work in advertising and a trip around the world, he joined *IT* in 1973, before moving to *Time Out* and then *City Limits*. He is currently working for the *Guardian*.

MELISSA CHASSAY: Melissa North worked for the Brian Morrison

Agency, helping run the Pink Floyd and the Pretty Things, among others. Now married to architect Tchaik Chassay, she remains a leading 'alternative' socialite.

VIRGINIA CLIVE-SMITH: After a period designing for Conran with Barney Bubbles, Clive-Smith worked with John Esam on his magazine *The Image* and with Jon Goodchild on *OZ* and *Rolling Stone*. One-time star of the best-selling *Art of Sensual Massage*, she is married to Michael Storey and lives in Suffolk.

MARTIN CROPPER: Self-proclaimed 'amoral hedonist', Cropper devoted himself to the available varieties of hippie excess. Today he is a widely published freelance journalist and lives in London.

JO CRUIKSHANK: Daughter of a left-wing journalist, Cruikshank involved herself in the Richmond rock and CND scene, graduating to UFO, Middle Earth and the Speakeasy as the decade progressed. She lives in Camberwell with her husband and daughter.

STASH DE ROLA: Son of the painter Balthus, Prince Stanislaw Klossowski de Rola was an intimate of the Beatles and Rolling Stones, working for Robert Fraser and managing to have himself busted with Brian Jones, among other adventures. He lives around the world, particularly in Switzerland.

STAN DEMIDJUK: Born in Yugoslavia, brought up in Australia, Demidjuk arrived in England, via Italy, in 1970. After working at *Friends* and for Friends of *OZ*, he founded Freedom, John Lennon's shortlived involvement with the underground. Still pursuing the revolution, he works as a furniture designer and lives in southern France.

FELIX DENNIS: The most materially successful of the *OZ* defendants, Dennis parlayed his underground press expertise into an international publishing company, specialising in martial arts, TV and film tie-ins and computers. He has a Rolls-Royce, a manor house, and other homes in New York, London and Europe.

JEFF DEXTER: The first person to dance the twist in Mecca ballrooms, Dexter made himself into the underground's leading DJ, at Tiles, Middle Earth and many rock festivals. Living in north London, he continues to promote rock'n'roll.

JOHN DUNBAR: Dunbar married Marianne Faithfull, ran the gallery side of Indica and mixed with rock's elite. After a 'good' 60s he lives in Maida Vale and keeps up his old contacts.

JO DURDEN-SMITH: One of Granada TV's graduate whizzkids, Durden-Smith specialised in filming the counterculture. His major projects included films of the Doors at the Roundhouse and the Rolling Stones in Hyde Park. After many years in America, he lives in London and continues to make films and write.

TONY ELLIOT: Tony Elliot moved from street-selling *IT* at Keele University to launching *Time Out* in 1968. As well as London's top listings magazine, Elliot also owns *ID* and a number of best-selling consumer guides.

JENNY FABIAN: Fabian's autobiographical novel *Groupie* was the *succès de scandale* of 1969, titillating an audience eager for details of drugs, sex and rock'n'roll. Married to Maldwyn Thomas, she now trains greyhounds in Kent and hopes for the Waterloo Cup.

DUNCAN FALLOWELL: Fallowell spent the late 60s at Oxford, where he explored the possibilities of LSD before starting a career in writing. He has written three novels, and his journalism appears in England and America.

MICK FARREN: Leader of the Deviants, doorman at UFO, editor of *IT*, and one of the movement's most outspoken figures, Farren was England's answer to Abbie Hoffman. He lives in New York where he writes science-fiction novels, as well as journalism and a variety of non-fiction works.

NINA FISHMAN: Daughter of a victim of McCarthyite blacklisting, Fishman left America to study at Sussex University. Here she joined the student activists, mixing campus demonstrations with her involvement with the Cambridge New Left and activities at the LSE. She has remained politically active, although less overtly doctrinaire.

KIERAN FOGARTY: 'Rusticated' from Oxford for a year in 1966 Fogarty spent the period in 'Swinging London', the climax of which was turning nature to art in Antonioni's *Blow-Up*. More recently he has toured the world for the British Council and is currently employed in publishing.

JON GOODCHILD: Goodchild graduated from the 'Swinging Lon-

446

don'/King's Road world of modelling for English Boy to designing *OZ* and *Rolling Stone*. He left England to work on US *Rolling Stone* in 1970 and still lives and works in California.

DAVID GOODMAN: 'Boss' Goodman moved from warehouse management in Essex to road management of the Deviants all round the country. After many years booking bands at Dingwalls, he is now involved in the running of the Town & Country Club in Kentish Town.

RUFUS HARRIS: Harris abandoned art school and co-founded Release, with Caroline Coon, 1967. He remained with the organisation until 1974, since when he has worked as a lawyer.

SPIKE HAWKINS: Discovered in a hedge outside Aylesbury by Johnny Byrne, Hawkins moved to Liverpool and thence to London, establishing himself as a leading poet of the era. He continues to write, and lives in Finchley.

JIM HAYNES: Posted to Edinburgh by the US Army, Haynes ran both Britain's first paperback bookshop and the Traverse Theatre, prior to moving to London to work on *IT* and setting up the Arts Lab. He left England in 1970 and co-edited *Suck* magazine in Amsterdam. He lives in Paris, teaching at the University, and maintaining his 'alternative' ideals.

PHILIP HODGSON: Hodgson was one of the earliest light-show operators, working both at British underground venues and in Europe. He is now running his own design studio.

JOHN HOPKINS: Doyen of the counterculture, co-founder of the Notting Hill Free School, *IT, UFO*, and a prime mover in every 'underground' institution. After his conviction for drug offences in 1967, he moved towards the then new video revolution and remains involved in the medium, running the Fantasy Factory in London.

MICHAEL HOROVITZ: Horovitz's launch, in 1959, of the poetry magazine *New Departures* was undoubtedly one of the key events in the development of the counterculture. He continues to work as an anti-establishmentarian anthologist, jazz troubadour artist, and promoter (with 'Live *New Departures* and *Poetry Olympics*') of a globally united front for all poets.

RUSSELL HUNTER: Hunter quit Her Majesty's Stationery Office to drum

447

for the Deviants, working with them before moving on to the Pink Fairies. Today he combines bus-conducting for London Transport with more work for the Fairies, currently enjoying a popular revival.

SAM HUTT: Hutt spent the 60s as a medical student, an occasional actor, and founder of London's first alternative practice with fellow doctors Ian Dunbar and Bernie Greenwood. The rock business's favourite doctor, he has gone over to the other side, and is best known as his alter ego, Country and Western singer Hank Wangford.

DAVID JENKINS: Jenkins abandoned the BBC for an extended journey along the hippie trail before returning to work first on *IT* and then at Granada TV. He is currently Executive Editor of the *Tatler*.

PETER JENNER: Jenner was teaching economics at LSE when he helped establish the Notting Hill Free School. After meeting 'The Pink Floyd Sound' he abandoned academe for rock management, running the Floyd and Marc Bolan, among many others. He now manages Billy Bragg.

GRAHAM KEEN: Keen met Miles at art school and John Hopkins on a student trip to Moscow. As a photographer he witnessed most of the important moments of countercultural development. He is now working at *Time Out*.

NICK LAIRD-CLOWES: Aged thirteen in 1970, Laird-Clowes should have been too young to join the party but plunged right in anyhow, involving himself with *OZ* and John Lennon's ill-fated Freedom movement. He is now lead singer in the band Dream Academy.

NICOLA LANE: Other than attending art school, Lane did little other than sit in a corner, roll joints, and nod when required – virtually all that was required of a hippie 'chick'. She is now a successful painter.

DICK LAWSON: An ex-account executive, Lawson wrote for UK *Rolling Stone* and then *Friends* before exploiting fluent Spanish and a clean passport to spend several lucrative years smuggling illicit substances. Jailed for this in 1981, he has turned to more legitimate business activities since his release.

JOHN LEAVER: Leaver ranked among the underground press's unsung heroes – running the advertising departments for *OZ* and *Time Out*, that unglamorous area of the magazines that made sure that, occasionally at least, the staff were paid. He is now doing much the same for LBC Radio.

JOHN LLOYD: Lloyd left Edinburgh University and came to London, intending to be a writer. He edited *INK* (in its political phase) and *Time Out*. He has worked subsequently for the *Financial Times*, edited the *New Statesman* and appears regularly on Channel Four.

CHRISTOPHER LOGUE: Logue was already an established figure in the British avant-garde when the 60s underground began hogging the headlines. Never an uncritical participant, he was one of that older generation whose experience added gravitas to a youthful movement. He remains a pillar of bohemia.

ANDREW LUMSDEN: A Fleet Street journalist throughout the period, Lumsden was among the earliest gay men to 'come out' and join the movement for Gay Liberation. He is still writing and maintains his involvement with gay activism.

GENE MAHON: Mahon's most enduring creation is that of the Apple record logo – a green Granny Smith – but he was also involved in the *Sgt. Pepper* cover and in UK and US *Rolling Stone*. He is currently working as a freelance designer.

STEVE MANN: 'Why is Debbie crazy? Because Steve Mann made her typeset on acid?' Thus a popular underground litany, and though Mann justifiably denies the anecdote, he was the best-known of that elite corps who, no matter what their state, drove the IBM Selectrics. He is still typesetting, now for *Private Eye*.

PEARCE MARCHBANK: Graphic designer Marchbank worked on *Rolling Stone* and *Friends* before creating the highly successful new look for the launch of weekly *Time Out* in 1971. Since then he has continued to work widely in all areas of design, up to and including the cover of this book.

ALAN MARCUSON: South African-born Marcuson dropped out of his textile course at Leeds University in 1966. After a hippie '67 he joined UK *Rolling Stone* as Advertising Manager, then Editor, before setting up *Friends*. After journalism he returned to textiles, running his own oriental-carpet shop, and now combines the two as editor of *Hali*, the world's leading rug magazine.

JILL MARCUSON: Jill Marcuson married Alan in a suitably hippie wedding in 1967. As well as fulfilling the obligatory 'chick' roles, she became increasingly politicised both by 1968 and by her involvement in the problems of Northern Ireland. She lives in Muswell Hill.

JOHN MARSH: Marsh was one of the first full-time light-show operators for the Pink Floyd. Since his days in rock'n'roll he has sold antiques and worked as a joiner. He is currently living in Holland.

DAVID MAY: May gravitated from mod life in Plymouth to writing for Notting Hill's local paper, the *Kensington News*. As 'Hack Typewriters' he wrote pseudonymously for the underground press, finally joining *Time Out* under his own name. Today he works for ITN.

PAUL MCCARTNEY: Of all the Beatles Paul was the closest to the counterculture. Through his then girlfriend Jane Asher he met her brother Peter and thus Miles, John Dunbar and others of the Indica/*IT* set. He paid some bills, painted some shelves and in return the underground offered McCartney, as it did so many others, a new cultural perspective.

JONATHAN MEADES: Meades was at RADA and kept himself around, rather than wholeheartedly *in*, the underground. A 60s Savonarola, he had little time for hippie excesses. Restaurant critic for *The Times*, former Assistant Editor of *The Tatler*, regular performer on Channel Four, he is working on a first novel.

BARRY MILES: Miles dropped his given name in 1961, about the time he embarked on his role as leading progenitor of the underground. As Britain's leading advocate of US beat culture, he helped found *IT* and initiated the Albert Hall poetry reading. He has compiled a Burroughs bibliography and written a major biography of Allen Ginsberg.

SUE MILES: Sue Miles met Miles at art college and eloped to Scotland to get married. She was involved in much of the early movement, including the Albert Hall poetry reading, *IT* and the Arts Lab. She is now a professional cook, involved with the setting up of several top London restaurants.

KEITH MORRIS: Trained as a mathematician, Morris had already dropped out, done most of the hippie trail and dropped back in again as a photographer when he met Richard Neville and started working for *OZ*. He is still taking pictures, running marathons and training deep-sea divers.

LAURA MULVEY: Mulvey's close alliance with the *New Left Review* precluded any real involvement with the underground, but she was among the first British women to start popularising feminism in the UK. Today she is among the world's leading feminist film-makers.

CHARLES SHAAR MURRAY: Murray was a Reading schoolboy, interested in rock music and writing, when he read an ad in *OZ* requesting volunteers to put together a 'Schoolkids' issue. He continued to write for *OZ* until it folded, moving on to the *NME* and thence to a continuing freelance career.

RICHARD NEVILLE: Neville had already been tried for Australian *OZ* when he arrived in England in 1966 and, *faute de mieux*, launched a UK edition. After the trial he returned to Australia. Today he works in TV and lives with his wife and daughter in a house called 'Happy Daze'.

BYRON NEWMAN: Newman was a photography student when he started taking pictures for *Friends* in 1969. After a whirl around the hippie trail, during which he nearly died, he has continued taking pictures for everyone from *Playboy* to the NUM.

JEFF NUTTALL: Nuttall's *Bomb Culture* was, with Richard Neville's *Play Power*, a seminal 60s text, but he wrote it to escape rather than to embrace the underground. A CND activist, happening artist and founder of the People Show, Nuttall never abandoned his primary career as an art teacher. He is still working with the People Show.

DAVID OFFENBACH: Offenbach was one of that group of lawyers most closely acquainted with the underground, dealing both with the plethora of drug cases, often referred by Release, and such headline-grabbing cases as the *OZ* trial. He is still a lawyer.

HORACE OVE: Ove arrived in England in 1960, followed the inevitable low-paid jobs with a period learning acting in Rome, and returned to the UK in 1964. He gravitated to Notting Hill and to the group of black activists gathered around Michael de Freitas. Since then he has developed his own career as a film director.

CHERYLL PARK: Park was an art student, supplementing her income by working at the Roundhouse, when she met Jonathan Park. She became involved in a number of underground ventures, including Moonrock and Swizzprix, and is currently a full-time artist.

JONATHAN PARK: Still a structural engineer in 1969, Park became increasingly involved in counterculture activities, notably Moonrock, an alternative Saturday-morning show for children at the Roundhouse. Today he is a designer of theatrical spectaculars for such clients as the Pink Floyd.

JOHN PEEL: John Peel's 'Perfumed Garden' – both as a radio programme and as a column in *IT* – made him into one of the most visible of underground personalities. He remains a Radio One DJ, still promoting new music and still, in many ways, a true believer.

DICK POUNTAIN: Pountain mixed politics and journalism – as a prominent UK Situationist and as a writer, first for *Friends* and then for *INK*. He worked for Felix Dennis's Bunch Books through the 70s and is now a leading computer consultant.

PETER ROBERTS: 'Pete the Rat' moved from Oxford's beatnik scene to a general involvement with the nascent underground. An early voyager along the hippie trail, he returned to London to develop an on-going entrepreneurial career.

GEOFFREY ROBERTSON: Robertson's first involvment with the counterculture came as John Mortimer's junior at the *OZ* trial. Since then he has been concerned with a number of censorship trials, and has written major books on *Media Law* and *Obscenity*. He became a Queen's Counsel in 1988.

DAVID ROBINS: As a student at London University Robins was involved in much of the activities of 1968; at the same time he played a leading role at *IT* before joining *INK* in 1971. Since then he has specialised in youth culture, on which he has written two influential books.

MARSHA ROWE: Rowe worked for Australian *OZ* and rejoined the magazine when she moved to England in 1970. As co-founder of *Spare Rib* she was intimately involved with emergent British feminism. She remains a committed feminist and works in publishing.

CHRIS ROWLEY: Rowley quit his studies at the LSE to become *IT*'s office-boy and thence a stalwart of the underground press. In the last few years he has lived in New York, where he is an award-winning science-fiction novelist.

CRAIG SAMS: An early convert to macrobiotics, Sams set up the first macrobiotic restaurant in England, following it with a successor, Seed, and spreading the health-food gospel through his shop Ceres. Today he continues to promote health foods, both through Ceres and the best-selling range of Whole Earth products.

NICHOLAS SAUNDERS: Saunders turned his own interest in alternative lifestyles into several editions of the successful paperback guide, *Alternative London*. He pioneered the complex of shops in Covent Garden's Neal's Yard and remains closely involved with countercultural projects.

JOHN SHEPPARD: As one of Granada TV's *wunderkinder* Sheppard made a number of important films for the station's *World in Action* programme. He also directed two of the era's best-known rock documentaries: *The Stones in the Park* and *The Doors at the Roundhouse*. He is still working in TV.

PETER SHERTSER: With the late Ian Sippen, Peter Shertser ran the Firm, psychedelic Jewish mods from Ilford who combined traditional hustling with a prodigious intake of LSD and a surrealist approach to life. Always a blues fanatic, Shertser now runs a record company devoted to his favourite music.

SU SMALL: Small abandoned mod life in Blackheath for the world of *IT* in 1967. She stayed until 1970, surviving coups, takeovers and a singularly unorthodox business administration. Since the 70s she has worked for CND and, currently, the National Union of Students.

DOUG SMITH: Smith's Clearwater Productions was one of the first Notting Hill-based independent rock organisations. He managed Hawkwind through their peak years and is currently linked with, among others, Motorhead.

STEVE SPARKS: Sparks followed life as Ilford's 'ace face' as a rock business executive, before joining Granada TV. After a substantial career as a British Museum photographer, he has moved to New York.

MICHAEL STOREY: Storey mixed friendships in Notting Hill's West Indian community, lotus-eating on Formentera and nurturing a musical career in London. He continues to play and compose music, creating soundtracks for film, TV and advertising.

DEREK TAYLOR: Ex-Fleet Street journalist Taylor joined the Beatles as their press officer in 1964 and, after a spell in Hollywood, ran the legendary Apple Press Office from 1968 to 1970. After various senior roles in the record business, he has chosen semi-retirement, writing his autobiography and living with his family in Suffolk.

MALDWYN THOMAS: Like many ex-mods Thomas embraced the hippie world, moving happily with the rock-star elite and joining Sir Mark Palmer on his horse-drawn perambulations through England. Married to Jenny Fabian, he is now a trainer of racing greyhounds.

RICHARD TRENCH: Still a schoolboy in 1967, Trench gradually immersed himself in the London underground scene. At Essex University he joined the activists, some of whom would become the Angry Brigade, before writing for most of the underground press. He is now a full-time writer and journalist.

COURTNEY TULLOCH: Like Horace Ove, Tulloch was closely involved with the black activists who worked with Michael de Freitas to set up a variety of black institutions, based largely around Ladbroke Grove. He is now a lecturer at Goldsmith's College.

ED VICTOR: Publishing whizzkid Victor turned from editing the counterculture's gurus at Jonathan Cape to making his own bid for alternative fame as founder, with Richard Neville, of *INK*. The paper proved a disaster and Victor returned to the world he knew. He is now one of international publishing's hottest literary agents.

MICHELENE WANDOR: As Mrs Ed Victor, Wandor played the role of a fashionable publisher's smart wife but found herself increasingly attracted by more radical lifestyles. She joined one of the earliest consciousness-raising groups, helping to pioneer British feminism. She remains a feminist, combining activism with a writing career.

NIGEL WAYMOUTH: As one half of 'Hapshash and the Coloured Coat' and co-founder of Granny Takes a Trip, Waymouth was central to the commercial side of the underground, designing posters and selling the smartest of hippie clothes. He abandoned the counterculture in 1969 and turned increasingly to portrait and still-life painting.

CASSANDRA WEDD: Wedd left the world of deb dances to join *INK* as a secretary and typesetter. When the paper went radical so did she, and her subsequent career involved the setting up of a variety of feminist collectives. She is married to the head of British Greenpeace.

DAVID WIDGERY: One of the few left-wing ideologues who also chose to embrace the more hedonistic world of the underground, Widgery offered *OZ* readers an acerbic analysis of hippie-trippery. He remains committed to the Left, while practising as a doctor in a non-yuppified area of Limehouse.

JOHN WILCOCK: Expatriate Wilcock might well claim to be 'daddy of it all'. As founder of the *Village Voice* and early contributor to *EVO*, Wilcock inspired a whole generation of alternative journalists – the quintessential peripatetic cultural gadfly. He is still keeping the faith, but print has been replaced by a cable TV show.

MARK WILLIAMS: Co-founder of the Birmingham Arts Lab and proselytiser for *IT* as its first music editor. Subsequently he worked on *Rolling Stone*, founded *Strange Days* and created *Which Bike?* at Bunch Books. He is now head of his own publishing company.

ROBERT WYATT: Wyatt was drummer for the Soft Machine, running neck and neck with the Pink Floyd as the underground's favourite band. Confined to a wheelchair after an accident in 1974, he has stayed in music, creating his own and drawing succour from Radio Moscow.

EMILY YOUNG: Young was at Holland Park Comprehensive when the Notting Hill Free School was opened, and she became a devoted attender. A lengthy journey around the hippie trail was followed by a career, still in progress, as a painter.

Index

and Doors at Roundhouse 274–5
and Middle Earth 222
Howard, Tony
    and Pink Floyd 86
    and Speakeasy 86
Howe, Darcus 98, 348
Howe, John 8, 12, 16, 53
Howl 8, 10, 17
Human Ecology Fund 30
Hunter, Russell 39, 132–3, 172, 304–5
    on the Deviants 174–5, 299, 301, 303–7
    on the Dialectics of Liberation 210
    on Festival of Light 382
    on 14-Hour Technicolor Dream 162–3
    on Grosvenor Square 244
    on *IT* 233–4
    and Jagger bust 197
    on Pink Fairies 322
    on Nigel Samuel 174–5
    on Shaftesbury Avenue flat 206–7
    on Tiles 85
    on Steve Took 269–70
Hutt, Sam 31, 42, 212
    at Bath Festival 319–20
    as 'Boeing Duveen' 285
    on cannabis tincture 194, 284–6
    on Dylan 80
    at Electric Cinema 287
    on *Friends* 315
    on Isle of Wight Festival '69 287
    and R.D. Laing 297
    on LSD 177
    on Speakeasy 88
    on UFO 139
    on Wooton Report 194
Huxley, Aldous 29, 182
Hyde Park, London W1 291–4

I Ching 297
IBM typesetting machine 282, 316, 339, 354, 369, 401–2
ICA
    see Institute of Contemporary Arts
Ilford 35, 175–6, 206–7, 234–5
Implosion 309–10
Incredible String Band 105, 204
Indica Bookshop 74–80, 123, 125, 144, 158
Indica Gallery 74–80
Ingrams, Richard 145–6
INK
    under Neville/Victor 367–74
    under Robins/Lloyd 374–77
Institute of Contemporary Arts 43–4
International Free Press 298
Isle of Wight Festival '70 332–6
IT 76, 92, 95, 102, 113–27, 145, 203, 210–15, 228–32, 262,
    275–6, 295, 297–9
    bust '67 158–9
    bust '69 327–8
    launch 119
    logo 119
    and London Street Commune 297–8
    name 118–19
I Was Lord Kitchener's Valet 221

Jacaranda, The (Liverpool) 18
Jagger, Mick 41, 62, 91, 181, 194–7, 212
    drugs arrest 195–7
    at Grosvenor Square 245
    and *Rolling Stone* 290
    at Stones in the Park 292–3
Jamal, Hakim 352
Janov, Arthur 323–4
Jazz
    see Music, Jazz modern; Music, Jazz trad
Jefferson Airplane 305
    at Roundhouse 271–5
Jenkins, David
    on 14-Hour Technicolor Dream 165
Jenner, Peter 27, 41, 48, 61, 99, 103, 131
    on Syd Barrett 166–9
    on Marc Bolan 266–9
    on Mark Boyle 138
    on Deviants 161–2
    on Doors at Roundhouse 275

    on 14-Hour Technicolor Dream 163–4
    on Notting Hill Free School 96–7, 102
    on Pink Floyd 104–6, 109–13
    on Stones in the Park 292
    on Steve Took 269
    on US influence 61
Joans, Ted 348
Johnson, Paul 5, 145, 340
Jones, Brian 4, 163, 196, 291
    death of 292
Jones, Roger 33

Kee, Jenny 153
Keen, Graham 4, 10, 26
    meets Hopkins 12
    on *IT* 230, 232, 234, 326
    on Notting Hill Free School 95, 99, 101
    on Pink Floyd 104
    on *Time Out* 263
Kemp, Lindsay 169
Kensington Antique Market 220
Kerouac, Jack 8, 9, 15
Kesey, Ken 294
Keyes, Thom 33, 93–4, 281–3
King Crimson 322
King Mob 126, 250–1, 358, 360
    see Situationists
King, Andrew 93
    and Blackhill Enterprises 93
    and Marc Bolan 266–7
    and Pink Floyd 103, 106–8, 110
Kings Road, London SW3 155
Kingsley Hall 208–9
Kish, Adam 281
Klein, Allen
    and Apple 280, 325–6
    at Stones in the Park 293
Knight, Debbie 382, 387–8
Knullar
    see IT
Korobin, 'Little' Tony 313
Kustow, Michael 58, 274

L'Auberge (coffee bar) 39–40
Lacey, Bruce 43
Ladbroke Grove 14
    see also Notting Hill
Laing, R.D. 14, 102, 297
    at Albert Hall poetry reading 72
    and Anti-University 239
    and Syd Barrett 167
    at the Dialectics of Liberation 208–10
    and John Esam 144
    and LSD 179–80
Laird-Clowes, Nick 224
    on Jeff Dexter 309–10
    on Isle of Wight Festival '70 332–3
Lambert, Kit 47
Landesman, Jay 221–2
Lane, Nicola
    on changing the world 129–30
    on clothes 219
    on Cranley Mansions 281
    on feminism 403, 410–11
    on Germaine Greer 410
    on Granny Takes a Trip 219
    on LSD 178
    on Notting Hill 217
    on sex 419–20
    on women in underground 403–4
Larcher, David 65, 143
Laslett, Mike 174
Laslett, Rhaunie 97–8, 101, 174
Latham, John
    at Albert Hall poetry reading 69–70
Laws, Carol 172
Lawson, Dick
    on clothes 219
Le Parc, Julio 78
Leary, Brian QC 393–5
Leary, Timothy 29–30, 228
    at the Dialectics of Liberation 209–10
Leaver, John
    on Felix Dennis 156

462

Sparks, Steve 35–6, 38, 40, 271–2
  on Marc Bolan 270
  on the Deviants 299–300
  on Dylan 80, 82
  and Hell's Angels 294
  on Russell Hunter 299
  on *IT* 234
  on Jim Morrison 271–2
  on LSD 176, 180–1
  on music business 204, 275–6
  on H. Parker 325
  on sex 425–6
  on Shaftesbury Avenue flat 206
  on UFO 133
Speakeasy Club 86–9
Spellman, Sidney 383–5, 387
Stacia
  see Hawkwind
Stamp, Chris 47
Stanshill, Peter 159, 214, 230, 297–8, 327
Starr, Ringo 78
  and Apple 280
Stein, Seymour 261, 302, 305
Steinbrecher, Bobby 312
Stephens, Joseph ('Captain Snaps') 362–3
Stewart, Rod 39
Stiff Records 313
sTigma, The 60
Stoll, Alex 52, 174
Stollman, Bernard 104
Stollman, Stephen 104
Stone, Martin 223–4
Stones in the Park '69 291–4
Storey, Michael
  and Horace Ove 84
  on Stones in the Park 293
  on Michael X 349
Storm (Thorgerson) 166–7
Streate's Coffee Bar (Liverpool) 20
Street-selling 155
Student
  see Branson, Richard
Suck 421
Suez 395
Sussex University 357, 405
Sutcliffe, Stuart 21
'Swinging London' 86, 91, 124, 146, 442

T. Rex
  see Bolan, Marc
T.F. Much Co.
  see Friends
Takis 76
Taylor, Derek 223, 427–8
  on Apple 225–7, 278–80, 297, 325–6
  on Hell's Angels 294–5
  on Paul McCartney 279–80
  on LSD 181
Television
  influence of at Grosvenor Square 245–6
Thai Sam 178–9
Thatcher, Margaret 58, 440
Thomas, Maldwyn 91, 190
  on LSD 181
  on Mark Palmer 216
  on Jane Rainey 221
  on UFOs 216
Tibetan Book of the Dead 177
Tiles Club 85
Time Out 262–6, 400
Times legalise cannabis advertisement
  see SOMA
Tomlin, Dave 96, 100–1
Took, Steve Peregrine 266, 268–70, 322
Topolski, Tessa 414
Townshend, Pete 23, 36, 47–8, 134, 206, 217
  see Who, The
Tramps 288–9
Traverse Theatre, Edinburgh 115–17, 169–70
Tree 16
Trench, Richard 52, 363
  on Angry Brigade 356–7
  and Arts Lab 171
  on changing the world 129, 434

Trench, Richard *contd.*
  on Grosvenor Square 244
  on Northern Ireland 363
Trentishoe Festival 319
Trepanning 67, 97
Trocchi, Alex 10, 50, 125, 297
  at Albert Hall poetry reading 67–8, 71
  at 14-Hour Technicolor Dream 162
Tulloch, Courtney 10–11, 103
  and *IT* 122
  on Colin MacInnes 51
  on Mangrove Restaurant 353
  on Richard Neville 336–7
  on Notting Hill Carnival 97
  on Notting Hill Free School 96–100, 102
  on El Rio 50–1, 353
  on *Time Out* 263
  and Michael X 343–4, 349, 351–2
Turner, Ike & Tina 53
'Twink' (John Alder)
  and Syd Barrett 169
  and Pink Fairies 322
2i's coffee bar 24, 38
Tynan, Ken 92, 170
Tyrannosaurus Rex
  see Bolan, Marc

UFO 76, 85, 95, 108, 110, 123, 131–40, 142, 174, 202, 218, 274
  at Blarney Club 131–2, 205
  at Roundhouse 202–6
UFOs 127, 215–16
Underdog 44
Underground Impresarios
  see Shertser, Peter
Underground Press 150, 339, 355–6, 366, 400–3
  see also individual titles
University of East Anglia 357
University of London Union (ULU) 250–1

Vegetarianism 438
Velvet Underground, The 66
Verushka 90
Victor, Ed 366–7
  on Alex Mitchell 371–2
  on *INK* 366–8, 370–3
  and *Play Power* 340, 366
Vietnam War 62, 65, 128, 441
  see Grosvenor Square demonstration
Village Voice 113–14, 118, 149–50, 367
Vinkenoog, Simon 66–7, 71
  at the Dialectics of Liberation 208
Visconti, Tony 266, 268
Vozhnesensky, Andrei 55, 66

Waller, Gordon 46
Wallis, Larry
  see Pink Fairies
Walsh, Chris
  see Bott, Chris
Walsh, Sam 18, 22
Wandor, Michelene 4, 60–1, 110
  on clothes 219
  on feminism 404–7, 411–13
  on Germaine Greer 411
  on Peter Jenner 110
  on *Spare Rib* 413, 415
  on *Time Out* 264–5
  on women in underground 403–4
Warhol, Andy 61, 65, 150, 408, 440
Washington, Geno 36
Waters, Roger
  see Pink Floyd
Waugh, Auberon 336
Waymouth, Nigel 64, 296
  on Granny Takes a Trip 218, 220
  on posters 218
  and UFO 131
Wedd, Cassandra
  on feminism 408–9
  at Festival of Light 382
  on *INK* 369–70, 373–4
Weir, Angie 358
Weir, Stuart 374

467